THE FALL OF NAPOLEON

THE FALL
OF
NAPOLEON
THE FINAL BETRAYAL

DAVID HAMILTON-WILLIAMS

'Put not your trust in Princes'
– Psalms, 146, 1–3

**ARMS AND
ARMOUR**

Arms and Armour Press
A Cassell Imprint
Villiers House, 41-47 Strand, London WC2N 5JE.

Distributed in the USA by Sterling Publishing Co. Inc.,
387 Park Avenue South, New York, NY 10016-8810.

Distributed in Australia by Capricorn Link (Australia) Pty. Ltd,
2/13 Carrington Road, Castle Hill, NSW 2154.

British Library Cataloguing-in-Publication Data:
a catalogue record for this book is available
from the British Library

ISBN 1-85409-201-4

Cartography by Cilla Eurich

Designed and edited by DAG Publications Ltd.
Designed by David Gibbons; edited by Michael Boxall;
**Printed and bound in Great Britain by
Hartnolls Limited, Bodmin, Cornwall**

CONTENTS

LIST OF MAPS

This book is dedicated to my wife,
Sally-Ann,
for all her love and inspiration

PREFACE

*'That war is not a mere act of policy but a true political instrument,
a continuation of political activity ... The Political object is the goal, war the
means of reaching it, and can never be considered in isolation from
that purpose.'* Carl von Clausewitz – *On War*, Book III, 1832

ON AT LEAST SIX OCCASIONS BETWEEN EARLY 1813 AND JULY 1815 Napoleon came within days or hours of inflicting a decisive defeat on the Allies – a defeat that was essential if he were to regain control of the lands of his lost Empire. Had he succeeded, alliances would have been reshuffled and once again he would have dominated Europe. His fall was not brought about by military failure, even at Waterloo, but by a series of carefully orchestrated betrayals. When Napoleon, Emperor of the French, finally abdicated after more than twenty years of unparalleled military and diplomatic successes, France fell once more into a dark age.

Liberty, Equality and Fraternity, together with all the enlightened reforms that the French people had acquired over twenty-five years were abolished. The right to obtain promotion on merit in any profession was restricted. Education for bright children of the lower classes was abolished. Hospitals and homes for invalids and orphans – founded by Napoleon – were closed and the inmates thrown on to the streets. The polytechnics and academies, formerly available to all, became the exclusive preserve of the sons of the old nobility. The *Code Napoléon* – the codification of French law still largely operative today – was replaced by antiquated feudal laws (prescribing mutilation for certain wrongdoers, and even the death sentence for sacrilege) that had been banned by the revolutionary government.

For three years France was occupied by several Allied armies, that had plundered and raped, and bled the nation of massive war indemnities. The people were living under a fanatical totalitarian regime, suggestive of a modern police state, its leaders, knowing that they were detested and unwanted, attempting to control the nation by terror.

Did the French nation, groaning under such suffering, blame Napoleon as the author of their misfortune? Did they loath the man who had been a 'Tyrant', a 'Usurper', and who had thrown away the hundreds of thousands of lives of husbands, sons and fathers? For if we are to believe all that was written about this man, we must assume that such a bloodthirsty tyrant's memory was execrated by the mass of the people. This was not the case. In 1815, on Napoleon's return, the entire nation — not just the army, but the nation in arms – put the country into a state of readiness to defend him and their rights which they had purchased at the cost of so much blood during the Revolution.

History, it has been truly said, is written by the victors. After his exile in 1815 – and subsequent murder – it was inevitable that Napoleon's colossal achievements and ultimate failure should enter the realm of mythology. The process was scarcely hindered by the Bourbon kings of France who lucratively encouraged respected 'literary' authors to perpetuate their mortal enemy by means of a 'black legend' whose constant iteration by modern writers has led to almost universal acceptance.

For instance, in 1814 Napoleon is exiled to Elba but escapes. This was not the case. One does not provide a prisoner with a frigate and a bodyguard of 1,200 armed men, plus about 200 cannon and sovereignty of an impregnable island fortress. Again, in 1814, Napoleon is beaten by the 'law of numbers'. Here the mythology advances as irrefutable fact the supposition that, facing 800,000–1,000,000 men, he must inevitably be defeated. This specious premise relies for plausibility on a single determining factor: that the Allies were working in harmony and with a single war aim. Such was not the case. Three months before Napoleon's return, England, Austria and Bourbon France had signed a secret treaty to support one another in a war against Russia. The Tsar, apprised of this in 1815, had no intention of marching to attack Napoleon, nor had his father-in-law, the Emperor of Austria; they did not move against him until *after* he had been defeated at Waterloo.

Napoleon's fate had been decided by William Pitt in 1800. A secret memorandum written by Lord Nelson warned him that Napoleon's occupation of Antwerp meant that he could cross the North Sea and effect a landing close to London at almost any time during the months of September to March; if, for example, the Royal Naval blockading ships were dispersed during a gale, the estimated time of twelve hours to re-assemble would be sufficient for a flotilla of landing-craft to get across. (This information was considered so secret that its release was not authorized until 1904.) Henceforward the British Government was determined to eliminate Napoleon at any cost and by any means. To this end a secret organization headed by the comte d'Artois, heir to the Bourbon throne, was established in the island of Jersey. Accredited to King Louis, it was funded with forged currency by the Bank of England and the British secret service, supplied with arms and equipment, and operationally controlled by a British admiral – who happened to be a sovereign prince of France. On Bourbon assurances that Paris could be rendered indefensible, unlimited funds to that end, laundered through Austria, were provided by the organization, Parliament being kept in the dark.

It is unfortunate that, in military circles at least, a tradition has been perpetuated wherein Napoleonic history is compartmentalized into tidy segments: the 1812 campaign; that of 1813; 1814; 1815. While this may be convenient for the writer or lecturer, it has the tendency to dislocate continuity. After all, throughout the period politicians did not cease to negotiate, political aims did not change, policy was not suspended. My book begins after Napoleon's return from Moscow in 1812, the military and political implications and social policies being portrayed against the historical background of his resurgence, and Britain's determination to oppose him *à outrance*, and ends with his murder in 1821. Thus the reader can compare the political and military objectives of all the participants in tandem, and re-evaluate them accordingly – and, I hope, come to realize the significance of Clausewitz's maxim quoted above.

I use the term 'murder' advisedly. Not 'natural causes', not 'assassination', not 'execution'; but cold-blooded murder out of political necessity. I cannot claim credit for this discovery which must go to Dr Sten Forshufvud and Ben Wieder, but I believe that I have uncovered conclusive proof to corroborate their findings.

At the time of completing this book (June 1994), Professor Maury of Montpellier University has announced to the world via the *Washington Post* that he is in possession of the comte de Montholon's written confession to the murder of Napoleon by arsenical poisoning. Strands of the Emperor's hair have been sent to the FBI's forensic laboratory to undergo tests identical with those already carried out in the Department of Forensic Medicine at Glasgow University. During his last days, it should be noted, Napoleon was exhibiting 31 of the 33 clinical symptoms of arsenical poisoing.

During ten years' research for my first book, I examined the original primary sources for Waterloo, including the celebrated 'letters' of Captain William Siborne. He had used this same material as a basis for his History of the campaign which became the primary source for our later histories. Profoundly shocked to find that his History had been fabricated, I extended my research to the much-neglected archive material, and spent several years examining all the Foreign Office, Colonial Office and Cabinet and State papers for the period 1812 to 1815. My discoveries changed my view of Napoleon and of the conflict in general.

In the same way that the concept of social reform reached France after the War of American Independence, so now it was crossing the Channel. The British people, having been at war for nearly a quarter of a century and isolated from France, were suddenly becoming aware of the ideas that had been current there. Napoleon, alive on St. Helena, was seen by the privilege-based governments of Europe to be as great a threat as he had been when at the height of his powers, and fears of a French-style revolution in Britain prompted the hasty passing of Draconian laws.

In all honesty, one can only describe as shameful the contemptible clique who ran the British Government of the time; ruthless nonentities, so despised that only the corrupt parliamentary system (that saw little change until 1831) enabled them to cling to office, and whose malefactions could scarce be redressed by the honourable conduct of such as Major-General Sir Robert Wilson, Sir Francis Burdett and the Lord Chief Justice, Lord Ellenborough. A corrupt government whose foreign minister 'went rogue' and nearly committed Britain to a war with Russia on his own behalf, this being averted only by a deliberate government leak to the Russian Ambassador. Bribery, corruption and terrorism, all were brought into play in the endeavour to be rid of Napoleon and enable themselves to remain in power. They deceived Parliament, suspended Habeus Corpus and, during a period of nine years, transported 78,000 Britons (a greater number than fought at Waterloo) to Australia – most of the more politically radical being convicted as felons on trumped-up charges.

Although, when considering the events of the Napoleonic, or for that matter any other, era, there is usually ample cause to apportion blame for acts of commission or omission, particular odium seems to attach to the House of Bourbon. The reign of this dynasty was founded upon an act of betrayal by Henry of Navarre who, to secure the throne, renounced for a second time the Protestant faith he had intermittently championed during the French religious wars. For two centuries before the Revolution, he and his progeny had battened parasitically on the vigorous body of France. Of the two remaining scions of the House during the period covered by this book, Louis Bourbon, comte de Provence, who twice became Louis XVIII by the will of the British Cabinet, lacked both the intelligence and the courage to be truly evil, while his brother Charles, comte d'Artois, later Charles X, possessed in full those qualities of will and turpitude that made him a mortal danger to those he decided were enemies, and a malignant blight on his subjects.

One cannot but admit to feelings of abhorrence for these men who were, during this twilight of the Age of Reason, the principal and most repugnant exponents of an atavistic tendency among those at the summit of the moribund feudal society of France to try to restrict the growth of individual freedom which their countrymen had enjoyed in greater measure under Napoleon than they had known since the time before Caesar set his defiling foot on their fertile soil.

History has yet to record her final judgement on Napoleon, and it is to be hoped that the new evidence offered here will change perspectives, and put her in a better position to do so. I make no claim to have composed a literary masterpiece, but having acquired this, in my judgement, historically important information, I have laid a historical ghost that has haunted me, and which would have continued to do so until I exorcized it by revealing it to others. In so doing I hope that I have succeeded in presenting the phenomenon that was Napoleon in such measure that the reader will understand why it was that the French people were willing to die for him in their hundreds of thousands, and continued to honour him during his years of exile, while they yet suffered at home under years of foreign occupation and a repressive domestic regime.

D. C. Hamilton-Williams, June 1994

ACKNOWLEDGEMENTS

I T IS ALWAYS DIFFICULT ADEQUATELY TO EXPRESS ONE'S gratitude to the many people who give so unstintingly of their time and patience in answering the multitude of questions that arise when writing any historical work. Answers inevitably lead to supplementary questions and further discussion. Few ideas are absolutely new; they are usually a development of or improvement on other peoples' predications. In the course of researching many hundreds of works for this book, my investigations have at times been extended by clues first found by other writers, and I must acknowledge my dept to the historical works of my antecedents.

Sadly, many great friends and authorities have died since the inception of this work: notably Brigadier Peter Young, whose generosity and knowledge he freely imparted. Likewise, Major-General B. P. Hughes on weaponry, and Michael Glover who gave me advice about Napoleon's marshals in the Peninsula.

I wish to thank: HIH the Prince Napoléon, whose recommendation to various French historians and institutes, opened many difficult doors for an Englishman wishing to write about the fall of Napoleon; the Most Hon. the Marquess of Anglesey, who kindly gave me his expert advice about cavalry, and answered myriad questions regarding theoretical situations; the Countess Elizabeth Longford, for her kindness, and authoritative explanations regarding the first Duke of Wellington; His Eminence Cardinal Basil Hume and His Excellency Archbishop Luigi Barbirito, Papal Nuncio, for arranging access to the Vatican archive material; Dr Otto von Habsburg, for information about his imperial forebears; Barone Pasquale Catenoso-Genoese, for his kind assistance and advice regarding the reign of Joachim Murat at Naples; His Excellency Signor Giacomo Attolico, the Italian Ambassador, and Signor Francesco Villari, Director of the Italian Institute, for assistance in obtaining material concerning the Kingdom of Naples and King Joachim Murat.

Dr David G. Chandler, of RMA Sandhurst, for ten years of extended kindness and correspondence. Many, many doors were opened to me through David's sponsorship, for which I thank him with all my heart; my friend Philip J. Haythornthwaite, author, historian, Napoleonic authority, and 'Good Samaritan', without whose intervention this book would not have seen the light of day; S. G. 'Peninsula' Ward, for his kindness and lengthy answers to my questions about Wellington's army and its headquarters structure; Professor Tullard; MM. Jean-Marcel Hubert and Jacques Logie, for their time and patience in answering questions about Napoleon and his army's command structure. My especial thanks to M. Logie, for supplying me with photocopies of rare extracts from French primary source material, some hitherto unknown to English historians; my old friend and mentor Dr Nico Vels Heijn, of

Zeist, The Netherlands, for his authoritative advice, material and guidance on the diplomacy and army of The Netherlands and The United Netherlands of 1815; my dear friend, Colonel Cyril Desmet, late Head of War Studies of the Ecole Royale Militaire in Brussels. Professor Franco Cortse, President of the Commissione per le Giornate Murratine, Pizzo; Miss Anne Crawford of the Public Record Office, Kew; Colonel Paul Willing of the Hôtel Nationale des Invalides for late printed works and information on Napoleon's final return to Paris; Signor Giovanni Azzimmaturo, President of the Istituto per gli Studi Storica; Colonel C. S. Giancarlo Gay, of the Stato Maggiore dell'Esercito; Lieutenant-Colonel Zwitzer of the Historical Section, Royal Netherlands Army; Dr Major Ostertag of the Military Historical Research Department of the German Army; Dr Karl Holz of the Prussian State Archives, Berlin; Dr Gundrun Fiedler of the State Archives, Hanover; Dr A. von Rohr of the Central Museum, Hanover Archives, for pre-1840 published material; Dr Christof Romer of the Brunswick State Museum; Dr P. von Groben of the State Archives, Wiesbaden (Nassau), for MS documents; War Archives, Vienna for advice and direction; Central Museum Archives, Vienna for references to diplomatic sources.

Dr Natali Bogomoloboy, of the History Museum of Borodino and The Panorama, Moscow, who kindly researched and obtained for me hitherto inaccessible Russian state archive material dealing with the wars of 1813-15 and the Vienna Congress; Christopher Russell, friend and family solicitor, for researching the quasi-criminal English and international law of the eighteenth century, and for the use of the old and extensive legal library at Judges Close; Miss Elizabeth Cuthbertson,, Chief Archivist, for her kind assistance with the Royal Archives at Windsor; Miss Jenny Wraight and Miss Liza Verity of the National Maritime Museum, Greenwich, for undertaking research germane to Nelson and St. Helena; Catherine Buddin, archivist of the Société Jersiase, for much research and material germane to Philippe d'Auvergne; C. Summer, of the Security Services, for pointing me in the right historical direction for pre-1909 security operations; Andrew Dickson of the Home Office Library; Mrs M. Beale, Chief Keeper of Papers at the Home Office; Sue de Bie, of the Sandhurst Academy Library, for obtaining literary works that other British military institution libraries could or would not.

I should like to thank the staff of the following institutions for their expert help and guidance: Les Archives Nationales; Archives de la Guerre; Archives de la Service Historique de l'Etat-major de l'Armée de France; Hôtel des Invalides; Archives départementales de la Marne; The British Museum Library, Manuscript Department and Map Library; Ministry of Defence Library; Royal United Services Library; The Royal Archives, Windsor; The Russian State Archives; Istituto del Risorgimento; Istituto per gli Studi Storici; Biblioteca Militare Centrale; Museo Nationale di San Martino; Museo di Capodimonte; Centro di Studi Napoleonici, Elba. For expert translation of foreign military and technical manuscripts I should thank: Brigadier Trofair, Military Attaché at the Austrian Embassy; Colonel L. Smit, of The Netherlands Embassy; Captain H. Stradiot of the Belgian Embassy; Captains Reinhard Ort and Mai of the German Embassy; Signor Antonio Spallone of the Italian Institute.

My thanks to my publisher, Rod Dymott, and to my friends Michael Boxall for editing the manuscript and David Gibbons for his sound counsel and moulding of the final result. Finally, my deepest gratitude to my long-suffering wife Sally-Ann, and my two sons, Oliver and Magnus, who provided the motivation for this book.

Having sought and received the expert advice of all the aforementioned distinguished persons, I should say that all conclusions and statements are mine alone, as are any errors or omissions.

D. C. H-W., July 1993

THE ROAD TO JUVISY

'Four hours too late!' – Napoleon, Juvisy, 29 March 1814;
'I can give you anything – except time.' – Napoleon, Paris, 1805.

ETWEEN 10 AND 11 P.M. ON 29 MARCH 1814, A COACH PULLED in to the courtyard of the post inn at Juvisy, ten miles from Paris. A small man descended into the lamplight and, while the horses were being changed, strode through the arch and out on to the Paris road, slapping his knee-length boot with a riding-whip. His shadow, thrown ahead of him on the road, was probably the most readily discernible in Europe – that of Napoleon Bonaparte, Emperor of the French, King of Italy, Mediator of the Swiss Confederation; king-maker, and one-time lieutenant of artillery in King Louis XVI's army. Ignoring the gathering crowd of his excited subjects, he peered into the gloom ahead where caval-rymen were dismounting. Glimpsing a general's uniform, he called out:

'Who is that?' His personal aide approached, carrying a lantern, 'General
    Belliard, Sire.'
'Ah good, Belliard. What's up? What are you doing here? Where's the
    enemy?'
'At the gates of Paris, Sire.'[1]
Visibly shaken, the Emperor inquired, 'And the Army?'
'Following me, Sire.'
'Then who is protecting Paris?'
'It has been evacuated. The enemy is to enter tomorrow at 9 o'clock. The
    National Guard is manning ... ' Napoleon agitated, interrupted him.
'And my wife? My son? Where are they? Where is Mortier? Where is Mar-
    mont?'

General Belliard told Napoleon that his Empress and son, the young King of Rome, had left Paris with the entire court the day before, making their way to Orléans via Rambouillet, he thought. Belliard quickly gave an account of the events that had taken place since 19 March, ending with the heroic battle that had been fought that morning by the 38,000-odd men of Marshals Marmont and Mortier outside the gates of Paris, against the 112,000 men of the Allied armies.[2] When Napoleon's For-eign Minister General Caulaincourt and his Chief of Staff Marshal Berthier arrived, the Emperor turned to them and shouted, 'What cowardice! ... Capitulating! ... Joseph has lost everything ... Four hours too late! ... If I had got here sooner, every-thing would have been saved.'

The Emperor started to walk towards Paris, calling 'Bring up my carriage! Bel-liard follow me with your cavalry.' Belliard told him that there were no troops left in the capital. Napoleon dismissed this, his mind racing ahead.

'The National Guard is there, your troops will join me, we will gain a delay, and the whole army will be with us in thirty-six hours! We can set things right.'

But the three Generals persuaded the Emperor that to continue his advance on Paris would be folly. He had covered 60 miles that day, outstripping his army which would take 36 hours to join him. With 112,000 Allied troops encamped outside Paris, he would be captured.

Deciding to accept his generals' advice to wait until morning, ascertain the positions of Marmont and Mortier's troops, and bring up his own army by the quickest possible routes, he returned to the inn, there to consult his maps and dispatch couriers to the troops strung out and forced-marching to join him. But General Belliard had been deceived by his commander who had betrayed Napoleon and sent his cavalry out of the city. At that moment more than 25,000 veteran French troops and 12,000 National Guardsmen were in the city with 800,000 citizens awaiting the signing of an armistice. Paris would not be evacuated for another eight hours. Napoleon had been betrayed: he did not know that not only were there no enemy troops between him and Paris, but that if he had continued his race he would have arrived with four hours to spare.

In Paris news of his approach had spread throughout the workers' suburbs and the cries had gone up, 'Close the shops! Barricade the houses and streets!' A Parisian royalist, who hated Napoleon and anxiously awaited the return of the Bourbons, wrote that had the Emperor arrived that night, before the Allies entered the following morning, 'His presence alone, without any escort, would have suspended all treaties, renewed uncertainties, revived hopes and fears, and changed the entire scene!' At that moment, in the Arsenal of Paris there were more than 20,000 muskets and 2 million cartridges; more than 600 cannon of large calibre with 200,000 rounds of ammunition.[3] Napoleon had been four hours too late to defend his capital; by morning he would have lost his Empire and France.

CHAPTER 1

THE ROAD TO SAXONY

'He seemed much greater than a private citizen while he still was a private citizen,
and had he never become Emperor everyone would have agreed that he had the
capacity to reign.' – Tacitus, AD 80.

I N MARCH 1814, NAPOLEON WAS 45 YEARS OLD AND HAD RULED his Empire for ten years. At its zenith in 1810, the Empire encompassed France, The Netherlands (created the Kingdom of Holland for his brother Louis), Belgium, and parts of Italy and Yugoslavia, these being considered as departments of France proper. He had sovereignty over the Kingdom of Italy, and Naples, the artificial German Kingdom of Westphalia (created for his brother Jérôme), the Kingdom of Spain (given to his brother Joseph), parts of Portugal and, as Mediator of the Swiss Confederation, a supply of troops from and right of passage through the Confederation. He controlled his 'vassal' Kingdoms of Saxony, Bavaria, Württemberg and the 'Grand Duchy' of Warsaw – the rump of Poland taken from Prussia and Austria. He had stripped the Austrian Emperor, Francis II, of his title of 'Holy Roman Emperor', thereby reducing title and numeral to Francis I of Austria. The hotchpotch of German micro-states of the old Holy Roman Empire, which were neither holy nor Roman, were converted to a manageable land area known as the Confederation of the Rhine, under Napoleon's direct control. His allies consisted of the dual Kingdom of Denmark-Norway, the Kingdom of Prussia, and the Empires of Russia and Austria, the latter having the double distinction of having fought France the longest, and being allied to Napoleon directly, he having married Francis I's daughter Marie-Louise in 1810.

Napoleon was a genius, gifted with massive mental faculties which enabled him to rise from being an obscure artillery captain at twenty-three to a brigadier-general at twenty-four. His rise was meteoric: major-general and army commander at twenty-six, he seized control of the government by *coup d'état* at thirty-one; Emperor at thirty-five; Master of most of Europe at forty-one. The range of his abilities was immense and not restricted to purely military matters, his skill in which being equalled by his ability in civil administration, education, law and science. Many of his far-reaching reforms have survived in Europe to this day. As a historical figure he emulated Charlemagne and the Roman Emperors, and in fact surpassed them. He gave his name to the epoch. A great Captain, who governed his Empire and army personally from wherever he happened to be, like Charlemagne his palace could be at Paris, Rome, or in a tent in Poland. With the aid of a vast amount of data kept in a special filing system that was continually updated, he was able to deal instantly with any matter, be it a new uniform button or a complicated law, without reference or dispute. But, as we shall see, this system was tailor-made by Napoleon, a genius, for himself, and was not flawless – in his absence it sometimes did not function, and then cracks appeared.

Let us reflect briefly on the events that had lost Napoleon his race for Paris and, ultimately, his Empire. Since the declaration of war with Britain in May 1803, when the 'experimental'[1] Peace of Amiens had been broken, Napoleon and Britain had imposed an economic war on each other; Britain by sea, Napoleon on land. In pursuit of this policy Napoleon was compelled to invade and conquer more and more countries to ensure that their ports ceased commerce with Britain. By these means he was hopeful that – as in 1801 – a peace party would come to power in Britain and seek an end to hostilities, if only for economic reasons. But the unique circumstances that had brought about the Peace of Amiens would not recur. Napoleon, ignorant of the factors involved, felt that 'the nation of shop-keepers' would, if excluded from all European markets, bring about its own demise.

For other political reasons which we will discuss later, Britain was determined to harness all her wealth and might as the largest commercial maritime nation to finance any allies against imperial France. These took the form of French pro-royalist groups, guerrillas in Spain, and coalitions of nations. Britain was prepared to expend years of national income, if necessary to the point of bankruptcy, to subsidize these allies provided they maintained their armies in the field against Napoleon in this fight to the finish. The British government passed several 'Orders in Council' (these instruments having the effect of an Act of Parliament without actually having been discussed in the House) giving the Admiralty comprehensive powers; in essence the seizure of all French vessels, and neutrals that had traded with France or her allies without first having purchased a British licence. The Royal Navy was empowered to search or detain neutral ships at will and forcibly impress any British seamen found aboard.[2] Napoleon retaliated with his own land blockade, passed several decrees confiscating all British goods and ships, and declared any British subject found in his Empire a prisoner of war, regardless of condition, age or sex.[3]

This situation damaged the economies of Europe grievously, many of the great trading ports fell idle, and smuggling became rife and mushroomed into a growth industry. The lack of luxuries suffered by France and her allies prompted exploration into synthetics, the French discovering how to extract sugar from beet and the use of chicory in place of coffee. Napoleon, hoping to fill the void in the market with French commodities, instituted favourable tariffs for French goods and towns within his Empire, which enhanced his image as benefactor to his own people, but alienated his enforced allies, for example, the Prussians. Further offence was given by the annexation of the great industrial province of the Ruhr and its incorporation, with other parts of Germany, into the artificial kingdom of Westphalia.

Having been repeatedly defeated by Napoleon, Russia had formed an alliance with France at Tilsit in 1807. Tsar Alexander was encouraged by Napoleon to seize Finland from Sweden to stop Britain obtaining tar and wood on which her Navy was dependent, and induce Sweden to adhere to the embargo. While this was happening Napoleon invaded Portugal via Spain in 1808, ostensibly for the purpose of closing

Portugal's ports. Having been given access by the Spanish Bourbons, he decided to keep his army in Spain, dethrone the monarch and replace him by his brother Joseph. This was counter-productive because the Spanish people rose *en masse* to protect their country, opened the hitherto closed ports to Britain and allowed her to land an expeditionary force.

In Italy, the only region of the peninsula to continue trading with Britain and allow British ships entry was the Romagna, the Papal territories which, by their very nature, were neutral. When the Pope refused to close his ports, French troops occupied the Romagna. In retaliation the Pope excommunicated Napoleon, for which act he was imprisoned and deprived of any means of communicating with the Church and the outside world. The Spanish clergy promptly declared a holy war against the French which resulted in 'the war even to the knife' that tied down huge forces that were constantly harassed and attacked. It has been estimated that the lines of communications with Paris alone required the deployment of one army corps to maintain effective maintenance. The drain on manpower to hold down such a huge area became 'the running sore' of the French army and the military graveyard of the Empire. On 21 July 1808, at Bailen on the road to Madrid, General Dupont with 23,000 troops found himself facing 30,000 Spanish soldiers, irregulars and civilians. Instead of withdrawing immediately, over the mountains, Dupont unwisely divided his command. Sending his subordinate General with 10,000 men to force open the road, he found himself surrounded and cut off. After several attempts to break out, Dupont capitulated. The surrender of this insignificant force, which included a unit of Napoleon's élite Imperial Guard, struck a blow at French military prestige that was irreparable. Since the elevation of Napoleon as head of state, first as Consul then as Emperor, the French army had defeated every European army and coalition that dared to stand against it. In 1805, Napoleon had defeated a combined Austro-Russian army at Austerlitz, inflicting a humiliating and crushing defeat on Austria. In a lightning campaign in 1806, the Prussian army had been annihilated at Jena and Prussia was occupied and dismembered. In 1807 at Friedland in Poland, Russia had been dealt a crushing defeat by the Emperor. It appeared to all Europe that the French army with its new methods of waging war was invincible. Now a rag-tag collection of Spanish troops – universally considered at that time as being of little account – had captured a French army including a unit of the Praetorians. This event sent shock waves throughout the Empire and a wave of hope through the courts of Napoleon's enemies. Immediately, it brought an enraged Napoleon and his Guard to Madrid.

In 1809, having defeated the junta forces in a whirlwind campaign and forcibly ejected Britain's expeditionary force commanded by General Sir John Moore, Napoleon had no time to deal with Spain personally because Austria had re-armed. Smarting from his humiliating defeat of 1805, and the loss of his lead in German affairs, the Austrian Emperor was encouraged by what had transpired in Spain and determined to regain his former status and possessions. Leaving the pacification of Spain nominally to his brother King Joseph, in practice to his marshals who, each having been assigned an area the size of a small kingdom, acted without cohesion and almost like independent warlords, Napoleon in the meantime attacked the Austrian armies with great ferocity in a series of lightning battles that sent them reeling back across the Danube. Having occupied Vienna, he now wished to conclude this episode quickly, fearful of a chain reaction of discontent among his other allies whom Britain was continuously attempting to entice away from him. Intelligence reached the Emperor that the main Austrian army was located near Brünn; in fact it was closer, in the Marchfelds on the other side of the Danube, near the city. Napoleon instructed his army corps to effect a river crossing in order to obtain the decisive battle, but the destruction of his sole bridge across the Danube trapped him and part of his army for a time, facing the entire Austrian army at Aspern-Essling. Holding his position until the bridge had been repaired, he withdrew from the field to allow his forces to concentrate. This enforced retreat from the field by Napoleon – albeit a strategic withdrawal in the true sense of the term – had far-reaching consequences. Following the episode at Bailen, the legend of French invincibility was shattered. Europe acknowledged Napoleon as a military genius, but given the right circumstances military thinkers believed that the master could be beaten. Napoleon later crossed the river on several bridges and defeated the Austrians at Wagram. Austria made peace and gave Napoleon a princess to bride.

Meanwhile events were taking place in the Iberian peninsula. Since 1809 Britain had maintained an expeditionary army in Spain to help the people to achieve freedom, command being given after the death of Sir John Moore to General Sir Arthur Wellesley. Napoleon had tried to control his armies as he had his Empire, personally, by written or verbal instructions. But the farther he was from the theatre of operations – as in Austria and later in Russia – the more outdated and useless his instructions became. By the time of his return from Russia, Wellesley had advanced into Spain and had defeated some of the best marshals and generals that Napoleon had sent against him. After defeating Marshal Marmont at Salamanca, Sir Arthur had been elevated to Viscount, Marquess and Field Marshal. In 1814 he would become Duke of Wellington, with an unprecedented record of continuous defeats of the French to his credit.

Tsar Alexander, having by now become fed up of playing second string in Napoleon's new world order, began to resume trade with Britain. This prompted Napoleon to assemble the largest invasion force that the world had yet seen, and in 1812 he invaded Russia. He had hoped either to bring Alexander to battle early and annihilate his army, or winter in Russia and resume the offensive in the spring.

At the débâcle that was the Battle of Borodino, the Russians, fighting what amounted almost to a 'holy war' to evict the heretics from Mother Russia, sustained a technical defeat and Napoleon a Pyrrhic victory, the losses totalling 30,000-40,000 men per side (25 per cent of those engaged). By nightfall Napoleon had gained the Russian positions, and the Russian troops were tenaciously holding their ground over the next ridge and eager to continue the fight on the morrow. Their commander-in-chief, Kutusov, making the most important decision of the campaign, decided to abandon the capital and withdraw. 'Moscow is a city, Moscow is not Russia,' he told his despairing generals.

Napoleon entered an empty city, with no one to receive him or surrender to him, the Governor, General Rostopchin, having evacuated the inhabitants. Soon the weather changed. Rostopchin sent in peasants as 'incendiaries' to set Moscow ablaze and make it untenable, while the Russian army lay in wait beyond the walls, attacking French patrols and harassing their lines of communication. Against his better judgement and historical precedent, Napoleon began his winter retreat, but, savaged by the Russian army, local partisans and Cossacks, the *Grande Armée* sank slowly to its knees in the mud and lay down to die in the snow. Of the 450,000 men mustered for the invasion, barely 20,000 returned.

On 5 December 1812, Napoleon left the remnant of his army in the charge of his brother-in-law, Joachim Murat, King of Naples – it has been said through fear, but the practical reasons are self-evident. Napoleon needed to assemble a new army before his coerced allies, Prussia and Austria, decided to chance their luck yet again. He was also disturbed by rumours of an attempted coup headed by a 'mad' General named Malet.

The Emperor reached Warsaw on the 10th, descending unexpectedly on his ambassador, Dominique de Pradt. This unfortunate was subjected to the pent-up wrath of Napoleon apropos the state of affairs in Europe, and the situation with regard to Britain in particular. With relish de Pradt later gave his confidant, Charles-Maurice de Talleyrand-Périgord, Prince of Bénévent, Arch-Chancellor of the Empire and one-time Bishop of Atun, an account of Napoleon's outburst, and how he had summed-up his situation with the cynical remark: 'There is but one step from the sublime – to the ridiculous.'[4] Talleyrand knew that Napoleon was paraphrasing from Thomas Paine's *The Age of Reason*: 'One step above the sublime, makes the ridiculous; and one step above the ridiculous, makes the sublime again.'[5] Napoleon reached the Tuileries in Paris at 11.45 p.m. on 18 December. As the bells rang in the New Year of 1813 in Britain, Russia and in many states all over Europe, their people celebrated with joy the end of Napoleon and his Empire.

The political repercussions of the débâcle in Russia were devastating. To understand the importance of Napoleon's Empire to him and to Europe, it is necessary to understand how and why it evolved. Napoleon had decided to assume the title 'Emperor of the French' rather than 'King' for two reasons. First, as he rightly maintained, the title of 'King' had been debased by the French Bourbons and he did not want it thought that he was turning back the clock to pre-revolutionary days; he wanted no association with the 'old regime'. Secondly, he was an avid reader of history. In 1804 he had told his Foreign Minister Talleyrand, 'France has had no Emperor since Charlemagne. I shall be its second!'[6] Charlemagne was the warrior Emperor of the Franks, who in AD 800 had been crowned Holy Roman Emperor by Pope Leo III.

On assuming the throne, Napoleon had begun to emulate Charlemagne's achievements, as a brief comparison will show. Charlemagne was anointed Emperor for bringing order and religious uniformity to his vast domains and for services to the Church. In the celebrated 'Concordat' Napoleon effected his religious settlement with Rome of all the territories he controlled – including parts of Italy. His civil administrative changes had brought order and control to post-revolutionary France and her satellites, creating effective departments, and re-opening primary schools and colleges of higher education. The old laws, based on French and German feudal sources together with some 14,000 revolutionary legal decrees, had been abolished, a new set of laws based on Roman equality before the law being formulated in the Code Napoléon. Charlemagne had been anointed Emperor in AD 800. Napoleon set his coronation date for December 1804. Charlemagne conquered Germany (called Saxony in his time) and brought order out of the chaos there. Napoleon had welded the hundreds of petty principalities into a single group, the Confederation of the Rhine. At the time of his coronation Napoleon's Empire encompassed almost the identical area of Charlemagne's realm. It could be argued that in his wish to add legitimacy to his throne and imperium, Napoleon was attempting to show continuity and identity with Charlemagne, thereby conveying to the French people that he was only restoring by conquest that which had been lost by weak and corrupt kings of France.

His rhetoric and letters during his reign show indisputably that he was either modelling himself on Charlemagne or intending that his subjects should accept him as his legitimate successor. In 1805, writing before Austerlitz, he had informed the Pope that having been anointed Emperor, he had assumed the throne of Charlemagne, and had inherited his Empire; that he was Emperor anointed by God, and thus feudal overlord of the Pope – Pope Leo III having held his temporal lands of the Romagna from Charlemagne and paid homage for them. Napoleon expected the same obedience from Pope Pius VII.[7] Writing to his uncle, Cardinal Fesch, his ambassador to the Vatican, he instructed him to inform the Pope: '... For the Pope's purposes I am Charlemagne. Like Charlemagne, I join the crown of France with the crown of the Lombards [Italy] ... I expect the Pope to accommodate his conduct to my requirements. If he behaves well, I shall make no outward changes; if not, I shall reduce him to the status of Bishop of Rome ...'[8] In reply, Pope Pius refuted Napoleon's assumptions. He denied that the papal lands were held in fief from Charlemagne; even if it were true it had never been acted upon. A thousand years of sovereignty, he declared, made as good a title as that of any ruler. He concluded by stating that if any one were the lawful descendant of Charlemagne it was not Napoleon, but Francis II of Austria who was 'Holy Roman Emperor'.

Having just defeated Francis II, at the decisive Battle of Austerlitz, Napoleon had made it the first condition of peace between them that Francis II abdicate and renounce for himself, his heirs and successors in perpetuity, the title, style and dignity of 'Holy Roman Emperor' – henceforth he would assume the title of 'Emperor of Austria' as Francis I.

Napoleon's increasing assumption of the role of 'Frankish Emperor' is evidenced by his decision to oust the meddlesome Pope who continued to flout his imperial policy. Just before the Battle of Wagram, the Imperial Decree of 1809 'made at our palace of Schönbrunn' declared: '... Rome has always been part of Charlemagne's Empire. The temporal power has interfered with the Pope's spiritual duties. His states are now annexed to the French Empire. The City of Rome is now and henceforth a free Imperial city of the Empire ...'[9]   Like Charlemagne, Napoleon created lesser kings owing duty to him as Emperor: his brothers were created kings of Holland, Spain and Westphalia; his brother-in-law, Joachim Murat, was made King of Naples, his son King of Rome, his stepson Eugène Viceroy of Italy, his sisters sovereign princesses. He rewarded the dukes and lesser princes of the old, comic-opera states of the defunct 'Holy Roman Empire' that had thrown in their lot with France, by creating them kings – of Saxony, Bavaria and Württemberg – with enlarged provinces at the expense of the small, unfaithful ones. He created grand-dukes, counts of the Empire and marshals. All in imitation of Charlemagne and his system of lesser kings and warlords.

It may be that Napoleon believed that he was destined to change – as Rome changed – the corrupt republic of France to an empire. His first act as head of state was to declare himself 'First Consul' – one of three – and appoint a Senate after the style of the Romans. When he became Emperor, his imperial eagle emblem and his terminology (for instance, referring to his soldiers as 'my legions') reveal his penchant for the ways of the old Roman Empire. He created his fanatically loyal Imperial Guard to serve him personally, in imitation of the Roman Emperors' Praetorian Guard. His coronation robes and the Paris fashions introduced the 'Classical' look, copied throughout Europe during the period.

Napoleon's subjects on the other hand did not see themselves as citizens of an Empire – obedient to imperial laws and decrees. Generals, such as Ney, were styled 'Marshals of the Empire', not 'of France' as they might as ex-French republican generals have preferred. Whatever their title, they still saw themselves as Frenchmen. In his concept of Empire, Napoleon overlooked the fact that it had taken more than a thousand years of Roman rule before non-Romans began to desire citizenship of Empire and its accruing benefits. Charlemagne, it could be said, had brutally suppressed marauding pagan tribes and given them a better civilization and culture. Napoleon's Empire had absorbed large territories encompassing different ethnic groups, languages and religions – but these had cultures and traditions already formed over many hundreds of years. Napoleon could not hope to graft his concepts on them in ten short years and expect them to be accepted as beneficial. Just as the tyrannical disregard of human rights by the useless Bourbon kings had unleashed in France the nationalistic feelings of Frenchmen, culminating in revolution, so was the enforced imperial system of Napoleonic France about to unleash nationalistic revolt in Germany.

The one fly in the imperial ointment was Prussia, the only German state to have been made a kingdom – by a previous 'Holy Roman Emperor'. Napoleon, who admired the late King, Frederick the Great, on visiting his tomb after his triumphal entry into Berlin in 1806, is reputed to have said to his Generals: 'Hats off gentlemen. If old Fritz were still alive we would not be here.' This warrior king had raised the small Kingdom of Prussia to become a great military power that had fought France, Russia and Austria to a standstill, and enlarged his kingdom in the process. His descendant, the present ruler, was a weak man with no military ability. In Napoleon's resurrected Charlemagnian Empire there was no room for a Prussia that could compete in either grandeur or military power. Napoleon systematically did everything possible to reduce and debase Prussia in the eyes of Europe and the German states. He elevated smaller kingdoms such as Saxony to greater distinction at his state functions, thereby humiliating the Prussian monarch who had to stand and wait his turn like a flunkey until the rulers of these erstwhile little duchies had been received. So Prussia was now an emotional powder-keg. Napoleon had deliberately betrayed, exploited, bullied and humiliated Prussia's King William III, and his consort, Queen Louise, revered as embodying the very soul of her country, had been exposed to insults so outrageous that most Prussians attributed her early death to Napoleon's treatment of her. The French retained garrisons in the fortresses of the Oder and at the seaports. The Continental System had brought about a total collapse of Prussia's maritime trade. Napoleon had exacted a thousand million francs in tribute, reduced Prussian territory and prestige to that of a third-rate power, and under the Franco-Prussian Treaty of 1808 her army was restricted to 42,000 men for ten years. Napoleon had induced the newly created King of Saxony – former ally of Prussia's and now given also the Grand-Duchy of Warsaw (former Prussian and Austrian provinces of Poland) – to confiscate all Prussian property in the Polish provinces, something that would never be forgotten or forgiven.

Prussian youth had empathized with their young Queen and formed anti-French *Tugendbunde*, societies promoting freedom and German unity. Napoleon knew that the Queen, whom he referred to as 'the only MAN in Prussia', with Baron Stein the minister appointed to help reconstruction, and von Scharnhorst and von Gneisenau of the military, had been refashioning Prussian life. Napoleon was convinced that William III was too frightened to offer national resistance: 'Besides, with what?' he asked those advisers who warned him of Prussia's rumblings. But he had instructed William to dismiss and exile Baron Stein and other Prussians whom his police considered subversive. All thinking Germans had been appalled by the apathy into which Prussia had sunk after the defeat at Jena in 1806. As garrison after scared garrison surrendered, even to a troop of French cavalry, it seemed as if the Prussian people had lost not only their military confidence, but also their national pride.

By this persistent contempt and personal abuse of their monarch – descendant of the 'Great Frederick' – Napoleon unwittingly gave the Prussians the stimulus of hatred and an ever-increasing thirst for vengeance that needed only the appropriate catalyst to trigger an intensely violent reaction. Since 1808 young Germans had been assimilating the philosophies of Kant and Fichte. They were introduced to the concepts of 'The Nation', and 'The Fatherland', to which each individual should devote his life – body and soul. These ideas permeated the young officer corps and especially influenced thinkers such as von Clausewitz. Henceforth the Prussian battle-cry *Die König!* would be replaced by *Die Vaterland!* In the meantime Generals Scharnhorst and Gneisenau had helped to refashion the army and had found a way to get round French restrictions. Their commission compared the faults of the old 'Fredrician Army' and Napoleon's new methods. With the concept of 'The Fatherland' as inspiration, they abolished corporal punishment – no longer would a Prussian soldier fear his officers more than he feared the enemy. Talent would replace nobility as a criteria in the army, justified as providing service to the state. New organization and tactics based on Napoleon's methods were defined and introduced. The mindless marching automata of Frederick the Great had received their obsequies on the field of Jena.

The commission introduced the shrinkage-system (*Krumper*) whereby recruits, after intensive training, passed into the army for a short period and were then demobilized, but recalled for short refresher periods. The army remained the same size – but by January 1813 had built up a reserve of some 80,000 men.

The triggering of the catalyst was the sight of the remnant of the indomitable *Grande Armée* staggering through East Prussia.

Ter ied of Napoleon, King William continued his obsequious compliance with his allies' wishes. In East Prussia on 30 December, Major-General Yorck von Wartenburg, commanding the Prussian auxiliary corps under Marshal Macdonald, had negotiated a Convention with the advancing Russians at Tauroggen. On 28 February at Kalisch, King William was induced to join the Tsar in war against Napoleon. The Tsar, through one of his advisers, the exiled Prussian minister Baron Stein, told William not to dither; the people of East Prussia and General Yorck were in open revolt against Napoleon. Stein suggested that if William wished to remain king he had better come to terms with the Tsar and his people's wishes. William promptly signed on condition that the Tsar help him regain his lost territory. On 27 March 1813, Prussia, dragging its timid and reluctant monarch in its train, declared war in an eruption of hatred against the French nation that a century would not erase.

Austria discreetly withdrew its auxiliary corps, lent to Napoleon for the invasion, first to Warsaw then to Bohemia, leaving a large gap for the Russians to pass through, and in the process, declaring itself neutral.

But speculations as to the demise of Napoleon's military machine were premature. Far from having been idle, the Emperor had been displaying all the abilities that had made him the most powerful emperor in history. By withdrawing cadres of trained troops from Spain, from the navy and coastal garrisons, and conscripting the drafts of 1809, 1810 and 1811, he put together a new *Grande Armée* of 400,000 men. Having had the foresight to call-up the class of 1813 before the invasion, he already had some 137,000 men who were on the point of completing their training.[10] The Confederation of the Rhine, Denmark and the occupied territories remained loyal, but Napoleon, no simpleton, knew that he could only rely on them as long as they feared him. He had no illusions about Austria, which would sit on the proverbial fence. That left Britain, Prussia and Russia. Britain would be contained in the peninsula; Prussia must be defeated and Berlin occupied; Russia isolated and

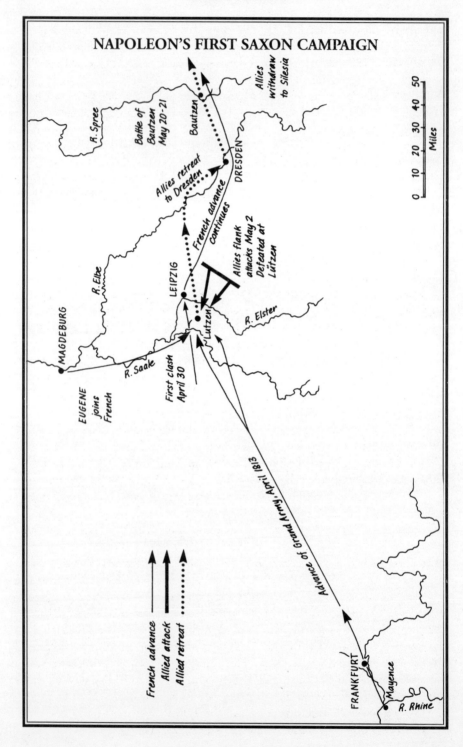

NAPOLEON'S FIRST SAXON CAMPAIGN

Allies withdraw to Silesia

R. Spree

Battle of Bautzen May 20-21

Bautzen

Miles
0 10 20 30 40 50

Allies retreat to Dresden

DRESDEN

French advance continues

Allies flank attacks May 2 Defeated at Lützen

R. Elbe

MAGDEBURG

LEIPZIG

Lützen

R. Elster

R. Saale

First clash April 30

EUGENE joins French

Advance of Grand Army, April 1813

French advance
Allied attack
Allied retreat

FRANKFURT

Mayence

R. Rhine

defeated. All then was not lost. He had chased the Russian army all the way to Moscow, expecting to deal it a decisive defeat. Now it was coming to him to receive it. The status quo would be restored, his Empire remain intact. He would then be free to oust Wellington from the peninsula.

At the beginning of the year 1813, the remnant of the *Grande Armée* that had survived 1812, together with some hastily mustered reinforcements, about 68,000 men all told, were holding the line on the right bank of the Vistula under command of Napoleon's step-son, Eugène de Beauharnais, Viceroy of Italy. Joachim Murat, King of Naples, having been entrusted with the command when Napoleon left Russia, had gone home, leaving Eugène to face some 120,000 Russian troops. By April, he had retreated, slowly giving ground until he reached the Elbe, some 8,000 troops being left intact to hold the key cities and fortresses at the strategic river ports and crossings in East Prussia. Eugène had given more ground than Napoleon would have liked – including Berlin – but there had been little choice; the rivers were frozen and no longer presented a barrier. The desertion of the Austrian and Prussian auxiliary corps had exposed his flanks, and his troops were tired. Eugène must be credited with having bought Napoleon the time he needed to assemble his new army which gathered around Erfurt and Jena in late April 1813.

The field army consisted of some 200,000 men,[11] most of whom had received weapon and tactical training. Many were very young, the 'Marie-Louises' named after the Empress who as regent in 1812 had called them up for the Emperor. They were short of equipment and of experience – which in this instance was possibly an asset; they had never faced the Russians or had their morale dinted by a harrowing fighting retreat. More importantly, Napoleon was woefully short of cavalry, a deficiency impossible to make good in the time; cavalry taking three times as long to train – impossible on the march – coupled with the fact that there was a scarcity of horses within the Empire, 160,000 of them having been lost in Russia. Napoleon had urgently recalled most of his cavalry from Spain but they would take time to arrive. The élite Imperial Guard had been expanded with choice recruits from Spain and from other formations. Given the circumstances of 1812, it is doubtful if any other nation in Europe could have produced an army of this quality in the time-scale.

In Paris Napoleon had decided upon his grand strategy for this campaign that was to secure his Empire, return his recalcitrant allies to subservience and safeguard his dynasty for his son. Briefly, his army was to hold the line of the Elbe from Hamburg to Dresden, ending near the impassable mountains of Bohemia. With his flanks secure and a diversion created around Dresden, Napoleon with his main force would cross the river high to the north near Havelberg, screened by the Harz Mountains, descend on Berlin and terrorize Prussia, relieving in the process his beleaguered garrisons as far as the Vistula. Then, by wheeling right, turning the Russians' flank and arriving in their rear, trapping them between two French forces with their backs to the Elbe, their lines of communication and supply with Russia would be cut and they would be compelled to fight the decisive battle of the campaign.[12]

Napoleon's opponents, comprising some 120,000 Russians and 80,000 Prussians, were in much the same circumstances. Tsar Alexander, the driving force, a man of many facets, and swayed by mystical philosophies, saw himself as the liberator of Germany[13] and wished to avenge the loss of Moscow by marching on Paris. Kutusov and most of his generals felt that having liberated Russia and seen the destruction of the *Grande Armée*, they had done enough. Kutusov also felt that it would be reckless now to hazard all they had won on the fields of a Germany that had taken part in the invasion of Russia. Most of his troops had marched from Moscow in the same climatical conditions as the retreating French, fighting many battles and rearguard actions on the way. Their morale was low and they were short of equipment; their lines of supply stretched hundreds of miles. Alexander instructed the wily Kutusov, whom he neither liked nor respected, to take the offensive and cross the Elbe. Prophetically as it would turn out, the General replied: 'Nothing is easier Sire, than to cross the Elbe now. But how shall we return? With a bloody nose!'[14] Prussia was in no better condition. Plundered from top to bottom, she was able – just – to equip most of the raised 80,000 men; Britain, anxious to participate in the enterprise, shipped muskets and uniforms. King William had embodied some 110,000 men of the *Landwehr* by decree, but this ragged militia, though inflamed with nationalistic enthusiasm, had little or no equipment. Armed with pikes, axes, antiquated sporting guns and farm implements, they would, even under Scharnhorst and Gneisenau's plan for integration with the main forces, need time to acquire weapons and training.

Napoleon, advancing with the main part of his army towards his objectives of the Elbe river line and Dresden, and unaware that that city was housing the headquarters of the Tsar and King William, blundered into some Russian forces on 1 May 1813 and a heavy skirmish ensued. Intelligence was scanty because of his lack of cavalry, but, alerted now to the enemy's presence, he closed up his army corps. Next day, when the Russian army of 73,000 men under General Wittgenstein, a Prussian in Russian service, attacked what he took to be an isolated French unit, he saw through the smoke a familiar figure on a white horse at the head of 110,000 men who were preparing to attack. The psychological shock of seeing a resurrected *Grande Armée* led by Napoleon bearing down on him can be imagined. Napoleon massed a battery of 70 guns facing the centre of the Allied line and these carved bloody lanes through the ranks. Then a charge by the Imperial Guard shattered the cohesion of the Russian line which disintegrated, and by evening the Russians with their 'bloodied nose' were sent reeling back towards Dresden and the Elbe, leaving 18,000 men dead or dying on the field. Only the desperate shortage of cavalry prevented Napoleon from ending the battle with 'a crash of thunder'. He had gained the initiative. The two sovereigns and their entourages quickly evacuated Dresden and crossed back over the Elbe – as predicted by Kutusov. King William was panic-stricken, stammering to the Tsar: 'This is Jena all over again. I see myself back in Memel [an isolated East Prussian stronghold].'[15] The Tsar calmed him and agreed that Berlin must be defended. Leaving von Bülow with a large force in the vicinity, he concentrated the rest of their troops – some 100,000 men – around Bautzen. Feeling somewhat humiliated, the Tsar ordered General Wittgenstein to make a stand. On 20 May, Napoleon surged forward with 115,000 men, sending Marshal Ney with a further 85,000 men in an arcing movement to fall on the flank and rear of the enemy and cut off their line of retreat. In two days' fighting, Wittgenstein lost 20,000 men, and only escaped the trap because Ney, not fully understanding his role, had failed to envelop them. The two sovereigns, defeated again, ejected from Saxony, fell back to Prussian Silesia and recriminations: the Prussians wishing to defend Berlin and Silesia, the Russian generals wanting to retreat into Poland.

On 4 June Napoleon, surprisingly, agreed to a request for an armistice. Many historians have with hindsight declared that this was the mistake that cost Napoleon his Empire. But hindsight is not history. Napoleon had marched his new army several hundred miles, had attacked with speed, won two notable victories, ever pressing onwards in the endeavour to encircle the enemy and gain the decisive battle. His new soldiers had proved their mettle, but the army had outstripped its supply line. Napoleon had but one day's artillery ammunition left, and his casualties, including men lost from the fatigue of marching, equalled those of the enemy. He had been unable to exploit his victories because of his desperate lack of cavalry. He also needed time to regroup and to figure out what his father-in-law, the Emperor of Austria, was up to; he having assembled a large army along the length of Napoleon's right flank, which bordered the Austrian Bohemian mountains.

We now enter the political realm of our story, which is important if one is to understand the reasons why Napoleon lost his Empire and ultimately France, and how and why Waterloo became the decisive battle of the Napoleonic wars. Waterloo is often portrayed as the last fling of a beaten man. The 'law of numbers' is quoted: that the Allies – yet to be formed – having three or four times Napoleon's numbers would inevitably have crushed him. This assumes that all the Allies were acting as one and with a single aim, which, as we shall see, was no more the case in June 1815 than it was in June 1813.

On 24 June 1813, at Reichenbach, Francis I's Foreign Minister Prince Metternich signed a treaty with the Tsar and King William whereby Austria agreed to act as an armed mediator between Napoleon and the sovereigns. If Napoleon failed to agree to four specific terms, Austria would declare war on him and form an alliance with the Tsar and William. The four points were: the dissolution of the Duchy of Warsaw; the enlargement of Prussia; the restitution to Austria of her Illyrian provinces; the re-establishment of the Hanseatic towns. There were three British ambassadors at Reichenbach, one to each of the courts, but they were kept in the dark about this overture from Francis. He had sent an emissary to London earlier in the year to sound out British views on peace with Napoleon, but found them intransigent: Napoleon must quit the Low Countries, give up Hanover and Spain and respect Britain's maritime rights,[16] being non-negotiable. Unless these terms were agreed Britain would not discuss the future of the captured colonies of France,

Spain, Holland, Sweden and Denmark. Prussia, which as we have seen was receiving material aid from Britain and hoping for financial assistance, leaked a copy of the treaty to its British Ambassador. It came as a profound shock to Britain's Foreign Secretary, Lord Castlereagh, that the three monarchs cared so little about Britain's point of view. Britain was viewed as unreasonable and overbearing where her maritime rights were concerned. Austria and Prussia, neither of which had a navy or colonies to speak of, considered Britain's military commitment as negligible in far-off Spain and having little bearing on the conflict in Saxony. At first glance Britain's interests seemed slight: guarantees for her navy, and her allies and the re-creation of Holland.

It will be useful here to look at the hidden agenda of each of the monarchs. (Napoleon's of course was not hidden; it was straightforward: to regain the Empire and to enlarge it.) Russian policy was twofold: to destroy Napoleon if possible and restore German liberty; to retain Poland, the whole of which was occupied by Russian soldiers. Prussia wished to regain its former pre-eminence in Germany, giving the lead to the former small German states – and all that that entailed.[17] Prussian military and popular opinion sought no less than the destruction of Saxony and confiscation of its territory, as compensation for the Prussian losses of the past seven years, and the Tsar and King William had already formed a tacit agreement to support each other in these matters. Austria was not seeking Napoleon's complete destruction. Metternich was fearful of the prospect of having Prussia on the doorstep, trying to take over Austria's role as leader in the German states of its now defunct 'Holy Roman Empire'. Fearful too of Russia's taking the whole of Poland including Austria's third. Too big and too close for comfort, it might provide a centre of disaffection for many of Austria's ethnic minorities. Austria would prefer a less powerful Napoleon, but Francis had no wish to disinherit his own grandson, the King of Rome. Then too, Metternich respected Napoleon's ability to keep order in his lands, especially after the débâcle of the revolutionary governments that had plundered their Empire, and spread dangerous heresies concerning 'human rights'. Napoleon's loss was feared as much as his presence.

One must remember that Britain had been at war with revolutionary France and then Imperial France for nearly twenty years. The Peace of Amiens had been negotiated by Lord Addington who became Prime Minister in 1801, following the resignation of William Pitt who had clashed with the King over a matter of principle concerning Catholic emancipation in Ireland. But George III and Pitt were in accord with regard to France. Addington, ill-informed, further alienated Pitt and the country by implementing reductions in the armed forces. War with France was provoked and Pitt was appointed Prime Minister again in 1804 – peace had lasted eleven months. While Napoleon controlled Belgium, England would remain at war. In fact the politico-geographic situation of Belgium was considered so critical to Britain's national security that no reference to it other than in state papers was permitted. Since the time of the Spanish Armada, Belgium had been Britain's Achilles' heel. It will be remembered that when the Armada attempted to invade England in 1588, the ships sailed up the Channel – not to land on the South Coast but to embark the Spanish Army of The Netherlands and land them on the Essex coast, which was why Elizabeth I had assembled her army at Tilbury. A flotilla of landing-craft from the Scheldt estuary and the docks at Antwerp could cross the Channel and land anywhere along the Thames in Essex or East Anglia. Britain was alarmed when revolutionary France had annexed Belgium in 1794 and declared the Belgians 'their brothers'. Austria, which had inherited Belgium from Spain by marriage, had posed no threat to Britain, having no navy or mercantile marine.

In March 1801 Napoleon, as First Consul, had put in hand the building of a fleet of small boats along the River Scheldt, at Antwerp and around Flushing and Boulogne. If Britain would not come to the peace-table he would dictate peace in London. Was not 'Antwerp a pistol aimed at the heart of England?' he asked his Generals. Britain raised more than 80,000 local militia to supplement her home defence force. The entire nation was apprehensive of imminent invasion. Nelson, who had just returned from destroying the Danish fleet at Copenhagen in pursuit of maritime rights, in a heavily underlined memorandum to Pitt and the Admiralty concerning the defence of the Thames, stated that he estimated that an invasion force of 40,000 men could cross in twelve hours. 'If a breeze springs up our ships are to deal DESTRUCTION, no delicacy can be observed ... Whatever plans we may adopt, the moment the enemy touch our coast, be it where it may, they are to be attacked by every man afloat and ashore; this must be perfectly understood. NEVER FEAR THE EVENT.'[18] In other words, the landing-craft must be destroyed without mercy before they got to shore. Nelson also pointed out that if an invasion were launched after 14 September the equinoctial gales would make it doubtful whether the Royal Navy's ships could maintain a blockade of the Scheldt. If they had to disperse to find sea room or take refuge in harbour, a crossing might be achieved during the twelve hours needed to re-assemble.

On 21 March 1801, Nelson attempted to bombard the supposed invasion port of Boulogne, but was unable to inflict any substantial damage. Eleven days later he attempted a night attack that was very costly and had no effect. The British government suppressed news of the affair lest it alarm the public.[19] Napoleon, knowing that the British government was worried about the defensive capability of Boulogne, decided to play upon their fears by using Boulogne as a feint for his invasion force of 1805. After Trafalgar, Britain carried out pre-emptive strikes against the Dutch navy in the Texel, and when Denmark refused to 'lend' Britain the remnant of her navy for the duration of the war, Copenhagen was attacked and captured by Nelson and Wellington. Denmark's overseas colonies were seized, her naval stores burned and her ships taken, merely because she wished to remain neutral – such was Britain's fear that Napoleon would obtain ships and invade.

In 1805 William Pitt decided that the best defence for Britain would be the creation of a Kingdom of Holland, with Belgium as a 'barrier'. Britain would re-fortify the great fortress towns of Oudenarde, Mons, Charleroi, Namur and Antwerp (the latter to be heavily fortified on the landward side) so that they could withstand any assembled invasion forces until such time as Britain could get an expeditionary force across. This plan was embodied in a treaty with Tsar Alexander in 1805, just before Austerlitz. It was also decided that the best solution for France would be the restoration of the Bourbons, two of the executed Louis XVI's brothers having escaped the Revolution. The treaty was considered so sensitive that only a part of it was discussed in Parliament.[20] In essence, Britain's hidden agenda comprised the removal of the French from Belgium, which was to become a satellite state, and dominance of the seas, without which her island security and colonial wealth would be threatened. These then were the political aims of the 'Allies'

Prince Metternich arrived at Dresden with his Emperor's 'armed mediation'. Already signed by the monarchs of Austria, Russia and Prussia, as being the only acceptable peace plan, it was in effect an ultimatum. Napoleon must agree to the terms or be seen as the aggressor, in which case he would have Austria's 300,000 troops against him. On 26 June he had a meeting with Napoleon that lasted for nine hours. It started badly. Napoleon was furious at the Austrian intervention and threaten armed force. He launched into a ferocious tirade: 'So you want war? Well, you shall have it. I annihilated the Prussians at Lützen; I smashed the Russians at Bautzen; now you want to have your turn. Very well – we shall meet at Vienna.' Metternich was a skilled courtier and he really did want a compromise with Napoleon. He suggested that peace lay with the Emperor. 'Well, and what is it that you want? That I should dishonour myself? Never! I know how to die, but never shall I give one inch of territory. Your sovereigns, who were born upon the throne, can allow themselves to be beaten twenty times, and always return to their capitals. I cannot do that. I am a self-made soldier.'[21]

Metternich pointed out that at Reichenbach Prussia and Russia had accepted Austria's offer of mediation and the four-point plan, and that it was for Napoleon to do likewise – Austria had 250,000 men mobilized to enforce the plan. Napoleon gave his opinion of Austrian soldiers generally, and how he had beaten them in every battle over seventeen years. Metternich retorted, 'I have seen your soldiers, they are no more than children. And when these infants have been wiped out, what will you have left?' Provoked, Napoleon flung his hat across the room and shouted, 'You are not a soldier, you know nothing of what goes on in a soldier's mind. I grew up upon the field of battle, and a man such as I am cares little for the life of a million men.' Then, more calmly, 'I may lose my throne, but I shall bury the whole world in its ruins.'[22] Napoleon often stage-managed these emotional outbursts in order to over-awe an adversary. What in fact he was implying was that young soldiers should not be discounted, as his own rise on the battlefield had shown, and that he would accept any losses to retain his throne. This sounds callous, but Napoleon knew that the Austrian army was essential to preserve the shaky integrity of the Austro-Hungarian Empire which was always simmering with revolt, particularly in Hungary, and any major military disaster could have catastrophic results. Napoleon was implying that he could afford to sustain large losses, but could Austria? He dismissed the idea, saying: 'No, you will never make war against me.' Disappointed, Metternich departed, but he had persuaded Napoleon to extend the armistice until 10 August, on which day Metternich knew the Austrian army would be fully mobilized. He had hoped to have concluded a 'Continental peace', leaving Britain to make separate terms, but in his absence the British ambassadors to Prussia and Russia indicated that Britain was no longer prepared to subsidize them with money and equipment unless Britain's interests were accepted. Further, Britain must have a leading voice in any proposals. The sum of one million pounds sterling was offered to each of the powers if they would keep a specified number of soldiers in the field in lieu of British troops, the money to be paid in instalments – to ensure compliance.

Britain also offered aid to Crown Prince Charles John of Sweden, – previously Marshal Bernadotte of France, if he and his 30,000 men would cross over to Germany. Tsar Alexander had been trying to encourage this for some time and was impressed by Britain's ability to persuade. Britain promised aid and, more importantly, the use of the Royal Navy, after hostilities had ended, in Sweden's attempt to seize Norway from Denmark in compensation for the loss of Finland which had been taken by Russia in 1809 to enforce Napoleon's land blockade.

Having been bankrupt in 1811 after persistent war with France, Austria had by every possible means conscripted 250,000 men, which number was rising rapidly to a staggering 568,000,[23] but only 300,000 of these were suitable for a field army. A British observer, General Wilson, having seen them marching in rainy weather, reported: '... drenched to the bone, most of them without shoes, many without greatcoats', and, a few weeks later: 'With the weather daily becoming worse, we shall soon have skeleton battalions, the more especially as the Austrians are ill-shod and clothed.' General Radetzky, chief of staff of the now 'Army of Bohemia', stated: '... during any army parade, artillery and infantry units appeared in linen smocks and underpants, while a third of the foot lacked cartridge pouches, so their ammunition was ruined when it rained'.[24] Austria had indeed raised its army, but for how long could it afford to keep it in the field?

While the Allies were in Prague, discussing with Napoleon's representative a formula for a peace settlement to which not one of them would consent, news arrived that on 21 June at Vitoria in Spain, Lord Wellington had defeated the armies commanded by King Joseph and captured all their equipment, 143 cannon and more than one million pounds in cash. The French had been driven back to the Pyrenees. With Wellington poised to enter France by the back door, Britain could no longer be ignored. Only with British money and equipment could the Allies remain in the field. Britain would become the paymaster; Metternich was offered half a million pounds in gold, and further subsidies – which he accepted.

The Allies, for that was what they had become, albeit uncertain partners, now had to decide upon some form of joint action. This would require a military hierarchy, and at this point it is expedient to specify the military aims of each of the Allies and the constraints placed upon them by the overriding ambitions of the respective governments. This will show too why it was that Napoleon was not only undaunted by what appeared to be overwhelming odds, but had every expectation of winning.

AUSTRIA Her 'Army of Bohemia', some 300,000 men, was the largest force in the field. The mediocre General but experienced diplomat, Prince Schwarzenberg, was given command. In Austrian military circles it had been expected that the appointment would go to Austria's best general, the Emperor's brother Archduke Charles, victor of Aspern-Essling. But Metternich did not want the 'best general' but one who would understand the army's role in political terms. Metternich would have explained to Schwarzenberg that Austria could afford no heavy losses in men; at the end of hostilities the army would be needed intact to counter Russian and Prussian territorial ambition. Let their forces bear the brunt wherever possible. Further, he was to avoid costly battles and to proceed slowly – Metternich was still hoping that Napoleon would come to terms before or after he was driven back to France; he must be given every opportunity to do so. To this end Metternich insisted to the Allies that Schwarzenberg be made supreme commander, stating: 'The power placing 300,000 men in the field is the first power, the others are auxiliaries.'[25] A state of affairs scarcely conducive to unity! Schwarzenberg was further cautioned by his Emperor who, no doubt haunted by the spectre of the 'unhappy Mack' and his fate,[26] wrote: 'We require you take care of this, our last Army.'[27] Schwarzenberg combined with his own Army of Bohemia the main Russian Army of some 130,000 men under General Barclay de Tolly who had no illusions as to which contingent would see the bulk of the fighting.

SWEDEN In the north, Crown Prince Charles John of Sweden also wished to keep his army – 30,000 men – intact so that they might challenge the Danish army for possession of Norway. Further, he did not altogether trust Russia and Prussia who saw in him an upstart French revolutionary general whose own elevation mimicked Napoleon's. His position in Sweden was delicate. If he came back a hero, and with Norway, his future would be secure, but if he suffered severe losses he would not be able to conquer Norway. Either way he would lose his right to inherit the crown. If he could be seen as having won – while preserving his Swedish forces – all would be well. He also hoped that Tsar Alexander and France might see him as a suitable replacement to Napoleon. He was given command of the Army of the North under Schwarzenberg, but had insisted that he be given one Prussian and one Russian corps totalling some 80,000 men. These two corps would do the fighting, his Swedes being held as a 'reserve'.

PRUSSIA The Army of Silesia was the only Allied formation – save Wellington's in Spain – that was imbued with the offensive spirit. It was commanded by the fiery 70-year-old Field Marshal Gebhard von Blücher, ably supported by his chief of staff General August von Gneisenau, one of the architects of Prussian reform. Their 105,000 men were organized in four corps – two Prussian, two Russian. King William of Prussia left all military matters to his generals and the Tsar whom he appeared to attend as a junior ADC. Blücher and Gneisenau's intention was to hone the army into a precision instrument and play havoc with Napoleon's forces – in short, to win. Having had seven years in which to study Napoleon's methods, they had devised corps structures and a tactical plan: rapid attack; gain the initiative; pile on the pressure at the weakest point; commit the reserves. Followed by a rapid pursuit.

RUSSIA Until now, the Russian Army under Tsar Alexander had borne the brunt of the Allied fighting, while his erstwhile allies had been mobilizing. Russian losses since May, including sickness, wounded and killed, had exceeded 50,000 men, but there were still some 100,000 men in the field, plus more than 60,000 in Poland and a like number of reinforcements coming up. Through Schwarzenberg, Metternich had cleverly dispersed the Russian troops throughout the Allied Army in such a way that the only independent force commanded solely by a Russian was Barclay de Tolly's half of the Army of Bohemia, comprising three corps, one Russian, one Prussian and the mixed Russo-Prussian Guard Corps. This mix of nationalities in each army was justified by Schwarzenberg: 'Only unity in the spirit of manoeuvre can lead to victory,'[28] he wrote to the Austrian Emperor. While this situation broke up the Tsar's power base as chief of the Allied Army, or so Metternich hoped, it caused chaotic problems in the command. Most Russians officers were illiterate and spoke little or no French or German. (Blücher himself was unable to converse in French, let alone Russian!) Russia had developed very little military strategy, either in purpose or doctrine. Since the time of Peter the Great it had been customary wherever possible to receive an attack from behind prepared fortified positions, using cannon to their best advantage, as at Poltava and Borodino. This is understandable if one remembers that Russia had been required to fight four different types of wars: against Swedes and Finns in the Baltic highland terrain among 60,000 lakes; in Siberia against the Chinese; in the Crimea against the Turk; and now in Europe they were up against modern tactics. The Tsar's closest military advisers were foreigners – and deeply resented: Generals Moreau (French), Toll (German) and Jomini (Swiss). The Tsar's military decisions depended on divine inspiration and largely on the adviser with whom he had last spoken.[29]

This then was the formidable war machine that the coalition was about to unleash against Napoleon. Understandably, he was not in awe of it. They met at Trachenberg to hammer out their grand strategy, and the unifying force on this occasion was the Crown Prince of Sweden. He was thoroughly in agreement with General Radetzky, Schwarzenberg's chief of staff, who urged that the best policy would be to wear Napoleon down by attrition. He defined it thus: 'Battle with a superior enemy main force should be avoided until the other allied armies have united with us. Avoid the ultimate confrontation until success can be assured.'[30] After grave consideration, the Crown Prince stated that: 'If Napoleon turns against the Austrians,' he, the Crown Prince, would relentlessly pursue from the rear, and 'the centre of the Austrian monarchy will become the grave of the great Napoleon,' they (the Allies) had no need of strategical considerations, 'only brave colonels at the head of their regiments with orders directing them to march straight for the enemy'. One might add, as long as the regiments were not Swedish!

The Trachenberg strategy has come down in history as a master plan whereby any army commanded by Napoleon was to be avoided; the opponent was to retreat. Any army not commanded by Napoleon was to be attacked. This sterling philosophy dictated that Napoleon's army was to be worn down by marching and counter-marching between retreating armies. This brilliant concept falls rather flat when one considers that the Allied soldier would be required to march and countermarch just as much as his French opponent. Further, as events will show, it raised the French soldiers' morale to see the retreating backs of the Allies. One can understand why the Allied soldiers considered Napoleon such a bogeyman when their own generals were prepared to run at the very sight of him. In later years Johann Strauss would compose a waltz called *The Radetzky*, which required the participants to take one step forward, two steps back and turn their partner round. It appears somewhat fitting in retrospect to state that this perfectly summed-up the Allied grand strategy. Schwarzenberg's master plan required that the two weaker armies (those of the Crown Prince and Blücher) were to 'seize the offensive, and continue it in order to give the Austrians the opportunity, once united with them, to strike the most decisive blow against the enemy'.[31]

This then was the 'Alliance'. Prussia wanted revenge, its military reputation restored, and to be given Saxony. The Tsar wanted his victory parade in Paris, and to be given the whole of Poland – his generals begged him to be content with the latter. Austria wanted a strong Napoleon out of Germany, which she wished once again to dominate, the Prussians to leave Saxony alone, and Russia to retain its one-third of Poland only. Sweden was acting in a mercenary role, but it was not intended that her 30,000 soldiers should fight; the Crown Prince hoped to get Norway and, if everyone agreed, the French throne. Britain wanted Napoleon out of Belgium and a free hand to turn it and The Netherlands into a dependent satellite. Europe must respect Britain's unilateral decisions about any settlement concerning the sea and overseas possessions. Any decisions about land settlements in central Europe must be freely discussed by the Island Kingdom —she was paying all the costs. To Commander-in-Chief Schwarzenberg we leave the last word, proclaimed to his army: 'Austria enters the war not against France, but only against French domination beyond her frontiers.'[32]

CHAPTER 2

THE ROAD TO LEIPZIG

'... behold the pale horse ...' 'Then appeared the Iron King ... and around him
and before him and behind him rode all his men, armed as they could fashion themselves; so
iron filled the fields and the ways, and the sun's rays were in every quarter reflected from iron.'
– Description of Charlemagne AD 814 in the Chronicles of Saint-Gall.

ON 16 AUGUST 1813, THE TRUCE BETWEEN NAPOLEON AND the Allies was at an end, having lasted fifty days. During that time neither side had been idle; troop movements throughout Europe had been on a scale not seen since the barbarian migrations during the latter days of the Roman Empire.

Napoleon now had some 400,000 men in Germany. Marshal Davout held the northern flank based at Hamburg, watching for dissension among King George's Germans, who for the past six years had been subjects of Napoleon's brother Jérôme in his artificially created Kingdom of Westphalia. Davout was ideally placed also to pose a threat to Berlin. Along the Elbe as far as Dresden 26,000 men were garrisoned, holding the strategical crossings. Between Magdeburg and Bautzen Marshal Oudinot commanded another 66,000 men. At Dresden, Marshal Saint-Cyr had a force of 20,000 men to watch the passes of the Erz mountains, garrison the King of Saxony's capital and hold this strategically important base of Napoleon's operations. Napoleon had written to Saint-Cyr: 'What is important to me, is not to be cut off from Dresden and the Elbe; it matters little to me to be cut off from France.'[1] Marshal Augereau had a further 19,000 men at Würzburg, 100 miles to the west of Dresden, maintaining a link with Bavaria whose army of 30,000 men were holding the River Inn against Austria. The bulk of Napoleon's 250,000 men were placed between Dresden and the River Katzbach in Silesia. Napoleon therefore was occupying the whole of Saxony. The Allies, whose total strength in Germany numbered 470,000 men, were disposed as follows. Behind the Erz and Reisen mountains that form Bohemia's boundary, running from Hof some 70 miles west of Dresden to the Katzbach, was Schwarzenberg's 245,000-strong Army of Bohemia. On the other side of the Riesen mountains, forming its right flank, was General Blücher's Army of Silesia, 105,000 men. Around Berlin Crown Prince Charles John with the 110,000 men of his Army of the North. Connecting them with the Army of Silesia – and subsequently that of Bohemia – was a 50-mile-wide corridor of Prussian Silesia that joined it to Prussia, on either side of which lay Poland to the east and Saxony to the west. Napoleon, resting his (soon to become) Army of the Bober (Bobr), some 106,000 men, behind the river and against the fortress of Glogau (which was still in French hands), had effectively cut Blücher off from the Army of the North.[2]

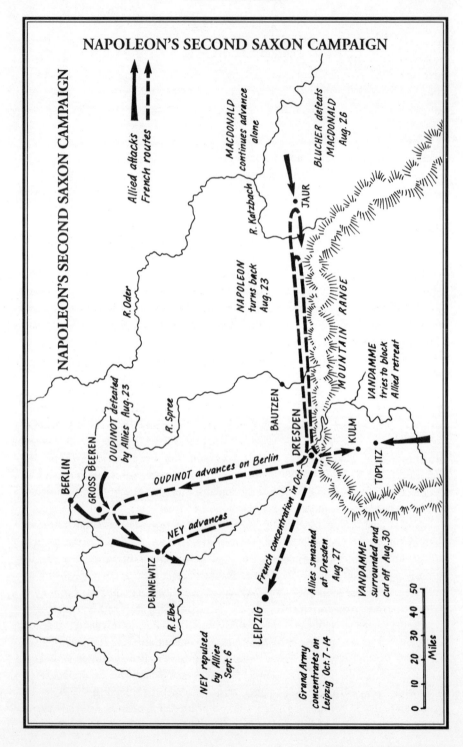

NAPOLEON'S SECOND SAXON CAMPAIGN

Schwarzenberg, having been appointed supreme commander, soon found that he had all the responsibility of the post but none of the authority. He had no official appointment except a tacit agreement and the presence at his headquarters of all three monarchs, plus their attendant advisers, ministers, and the diplomatic corps of a host of countries. These three monarchs and attendant advisers wandered in at will, interfering and changing his orders according to the interests of their own troops and personal whims.

Napoleon, by comparison, held all the reins of command and administration in his own hands. Nothing escaped him, from an error in a calculation of payment of a centime to the loss of a cannon. Wherever he arrived, his command centre was set up, and his mobile library in its partitioned boxes was installed. Twenty volumes of muster rolls were placed for easy access. From these, every unit's strength and ammunition and food supplies could be ascertained.[3] Notebooks, updated daily, gave the location of each unit, details of its training and its battle record, and detailed records of every officer and NCO. From his prodigious ability to recall these details derived incidents on parade or on the line of march when Napoleon would tweak an ear and say 'Sergeant [so-and-so], do you remember how hard we fought at Arcola?' The personal touch lent him a charisma that remained undimmed even when, in later years, his men had lost their blind faith in him. Wellington said of him: 'His hat on the field of battle was worth 40,000 men,' but this was a conservative estimate. Napoleon judged himself more accurately when he wrote to Saint-Cyr: '... I alone am worth another 100,000 men.'[4]

At his headquarters, two large tables were always set up in his study, on one of which was a huge, detailed map, lit at night by twenty candles. On it Napoleon's cartographer had clearly outlined rivers, mountains and other topographical features. Coloured pins, constantly updated, recorded the position and latest status of every formation. A pair of dividers set to the measurement of a day's march and a scaled rule were ready to hand. There are many accounts of Napoleon and his chief of topography, General Bacler d'Albe, bumping their heads while crawling about on the map on their hands and knees.[5]

At the other table Napoleon's chief of staff sorted reports and summaries: latest positions of all army units, daily reports of enemy positions, intelligence reports culled from local inhabitants, mayors, captured mail, prisoners and couriers, and status reports from each army corps at the end of each day.

Everything was scrutinized by Napoleon personally. He could calculate to within a few hours the arrival at any given place of a single unit or his entire army. His chief of staff was Louis-Alexander Berthier, Marshal of France, Prince of Wagram, and Sovereign Prince of Neuchâtel. For seventeen years he had been at Napoleon's side, directing the movements of the army. Probably the greatest administrative army chief of staff in a century, Berthier could listen to the avalanche of words fired out by Napoleon in his staccato fashion, impossible for the uninitiated to follow, unthinkable to interrupt. But Berthier could grasp the essence, fill in the gaps and correct the place names Napoleon had usually mispronounced. The clean draft copy that Berthier presented to the Emperor would be instantly recognized by Napoleon as his own, containing his expressions and ringing phrases. Berthier had developed his own system for dealing with orders and returns. All orders were numbered and sent in triplicate by three messengers, each taking a different route. They were signed out in a book recording addressee, time of departure, and by whom carried. An obligatory receipt was entered on return. Berthier therefore knew when the order was received and by whom, and if an order went astray or was captured, on what route this had occurred.

Even on the move Napoleon's command system functioned smoothly. Never the best of horsemen, Napoleon preferred to travel by coach. This had the twofold advantage of enabling him to transmit and receive messages on the move, discuss his plans with Berthier and sleep when necessary. Many historians have commented that on this or that occasion the Emperor apparently had not slept in as much as 36 hours, basing this on his nightly headquarters positions. But his coach – specially sprung, and drawn by six large grey limousine horses – contained a pull-out bed, a folding writing-top, numerous locked partitioned boxes, a hand-operated printing-press, his mobile treasury, a small armoury of weapons and a library. The coach seated two, the other occupant being invariably Berthier. During the present campaign the coach became legendary among the towns and villages of Saxony. It was painted Imperial green, had two coachman on the top and Napoleon's personal servant on the box. Four *chasseurs* of the Imperial Guard rode in pairs before the coach, and behind it rode the troop commander with 24 *chasseurs* also two abreast. Behind these rode the orderly generals, liaison and orderly officers, equerries and attendant personnel, anything from 50 to 250 men. At night the coach was illuminated by five lamps which gave it a demonic appearance as it raced through the sleepy hamlets. The drumming of so many hooves would alert the populace some 10 to 15 minutes before it burst upon them.

If Berthier wished to send or receive any communication he would beckon from the window and the troop commander would call up a rider to take the message – all at the canter; whatever Napoleon lost it would not be time. If Napoleon ordered a halt, to relieve himself or to examine the ground or a map, a set procedure ensued. The four leading *chasseurs* dismounted, fixed bayonets and stationed themselves around the Emperor, joined within minutes by the other 24 to form a square some 20 feet wide (only Berthier was permitted to pass in or out unchallenged). If required, a folding table and chair were placed within the square and sometimes a fire was lighted. Napoleon's horse was brought up and held by a page. When Napoleon ordered 'To horse!', he would either mount his horse to make a reconnaissance or get back in the coach; the entire cavalcade would be up and away within minutes. The Allies' methods of warfare, as we shall see, were locked in an eighteenth-century mode; Napoleon's were firmly of the nineteenth century.

In August 1813, Napoleon was based around Bautzen with his Guard and the reserve – ideally placed to support St-Cyr, or Macdonald who was holding the Katzbach and watching the Army of Silesia. Marshal Oudinot, with his 66,000 men, was ordered to attack the Crown Prince and capture Berlin. In this enterprise he was to be assisted by Marshal Davout who was at Hamburg with his 35,000 men. Napoleon hoped that this would goad Blücher and the Prussians into leaving the Army of Bohemia – to separate and the chance either to defeat the Army of Silesia in detail and turn Schwarzenberg's right flank and rear and defeat him against the Bohemian mountains. Or if Blücher avoided Napoleon going north, Napoleon could destroy Schwarzenberg's army and then turn north and finish both the Crown Prince and Blücher's army and the status quo would then be restored.

By 23 August Napoleon had joined Marshal Macdonald. The Emperor had received information that 40,000 Russians were moving towards Bohemia from Reichenbach. He would have liked to annihilate them en route, but found that they had passed the Reisen mountains. Changing his mind, he decided to bring Blücher to battle, but that old warrior had taken 'two steps backwards' behind the River Weistril and Napoleon, unable at this stage to fathom Allied strategy, had no time to formulate a plan. Schwarzenberg and his trio of monarchs had decided to defile through the mountain passes between Karlsbad and Komotau and then, in eighteenth-century fashion, sit astride Napoleon's communications at Leipzig. Austria hoped that this would force him to withdraw, but while they were preparing to move news was received that Napoleon was close to the Katzbach, 120 miles from Dresden. The Tsar decided that they should attack Dresden – held as we have seen by Marshal Saint-Cyr and his 20,000 men.

On learning of the advance of this huge force of 250,000 men, Saint-Cyr sent Napoleon an urgent request for aid. Leaving MacDonald to hold the line of the Katzbach and attack Blücher only 'if the opportunity presents itself of catching him in the flank',[6] otherwise to stand fast unless attacked, Napoleon ordered his Guard, and the Corps of Marshal Victor and Marmont to follow him to Dresden – rendezvous Stolpen – twelve miles west of the city. On 25 August the Allied army had started to close the city, Barclay's Russians driving the French out of the weakly held suburbs. The Tsar personally urged his men on, but his military advisers, de Toll and Jomini, agreed with Napoleon's old adversary General Moreau, now the Tsar's chief adviser, that an assault would be costly. Moreau whispered, 'Sire, you will sacrifice 20,000 men ... it is inadvisable to demoralize our troops in this manner.'[7] No more troops were committed, and a council of war convened. After wasting the daylight hours in deliberation the attack was called off. At the evening conference the Tsar again changed his mind, the King of Prussia naturally agreed, and the Emperor of Austria – studiously avoiding Schwarzenberg's eye – adjusted his uniform and decorations.

A fresh attack was scheduled for the early hours of the following morning. At dawn on the 26th, as the collection of generals, diplomats and princes were leaving Schwarzenberg's briefing for the forthcoming assault, shouting arose first from the beleaguered city then from the Allied right: 'The Emperor!, the Emperor!' Through the torrential rain could be seen the familiar figure of Napoleon, wearing his battered hat and grey riding-coat, riding his familiar pale horse, followed by the ranks of the

Imperial Guard in their famous, and now sodden, bearskins. They had marched 120 miles in four days, with full kit along atrocious roads under a continual downpour. This feat has received very little mention; the Allies might have been able to manage the same distance in 7–10 days. Close on Napoleon's heels came the corps of Victor and Marmont.

In their confidence, the Allied forces had not even bothered to encircle the city. By early morning Napoleon had 100,00 men outside the walls facing Schwarzenberg's 250,000, but the Allies were psychologically beaten before the first shot had been fired. Methodically Schwarzenberg's Austrians lined up leaving a central gap for an Austrian brigade yet to march up. Napoleon immediately launched an assault to the right of this gap, Schwarzenberg kindly obliging him, by directing the intended brigade to that point. Napoleon shifted his weight and cannon on the gap, and his brother-in-law Joachim Murat, the finest cavalry commander ever, broke the Allied left. General Moreau, watching the fiasco and hearing the garbled yelling of Russians, Germans, Hungarians and Serbo-Croats all intermingled and impossible to direct, shouted at Schwarzenberg: 'Sacrebleu, Monsieur!, I am not surprised that for seventeen years you have always been beaten!' To the Tsar he added, 'Sire, that man is going to ruin everything![8] Turning away, he was struck by a cannon-ball and later died. The Allied command, ripped by dissension and recriminations, headed for the Bohemian hills, leaving behind 40,000 men, killed, wounded or prisoners.

Napoleon, suffering from severe stomach pains and diarrhoea, had to retire to bed at Dresden, leaving the annihilation of the Allied conglomerate to his subordinates. The Allies, managing to retreat twice as fast as they had advanced, soon outstripped their pursuers. General Vandamme, sent previously by Napoleon to cut their line of retreat, had arrived above the wooded, rock-strewn defiles of Kulm, in the Bohemian hills, ideally placed for the job. But instead of waiting until the advancing corps of Marmont and Saint-Cyr with Murat's jubilant cavalry arrived to help stop the torrent of retreating men, his impetuosity prompted him to descend to the plain. The Russian advance guard of the routed Allies (previously its uncommitted rearguard), realizing that their escape route was about to be blocked, launched a ruthless all-out attack. This corps included the Imperial Russian Guards who, convinced that only their sacrifice could save the Tsar and the monarchs, charged without firing – using only the bayonet. With the traditional Russian shout of 'Hurrah!' and General Ostermann exhorting them to save the 'the little father', they tore into the French. Vandamme, recoiling from the onslaught, sought refuge by slowly returning to the high ground, but luck was not with him this day.

In support of the Army of Bohemia, and arriving in Vandamme's rear, came von Kleist's Prussian Corps. These were not the soldiers of Jena, but swarms of rifle-armed Jäger firing well-aimed bullets. Supported by battalion columns and cannon, and with carefully co-ordinated cavalry attacks, they drove into the French rear. Prussian hatred proved a match for French élan. In the rocky defiles, even the Prussian musketeers with their old smoothbore muskets slowly aimed as best they could,[9] then formed attack columns, dispersed into skirmish lines, and attacked again. Prussia was about to show Napoleon that although he held the strategical advantage, the tactical advantage was passing through neglect and necessity to Prussia. Generals Scharnhorst, Gneisenau and Yorck had vindicated their reforms and returned to the military its tarnished honour – degraded at Jena but about to be reburnished.

Sandwiched between the two forces, and trapped between the hills, Vandamme surrendered with 7,000 men. He had lost 5,000 killed and wounded in the fighting. Some 10,000, however, had been saved by General of Cavalry Corbineau who, showing the spirit that had taken France to Empire, launched a ferocious up-hill charge, determined to save his fellow countrymen. He stormed a battery of guns and sabred a way through, holding the gap by repeated controlled charges. Vandamme's survivors fell back on the advancing French vanguard who were arriving too late to avert the disaster. General Corbineau, wiping away tears of frustration, raised his sword in salute to Vandamme and withdrew the remnant of his cavalry. The dishevelled monarchs and their routed army arrived back at Toplitz, the Tsar behaving as though they had gained a great victory and won the war – instead of overwhelming 13,000 men with their nearly 200,000.

Napoleon, rising from his bed, learned that the fruits of his victory had been lost by Vandamme's impetuosity. Close on the heels of this revelation came news that Marshal Oudinot had been beaten at Grossbeeren, south of Berlin, by the Prussian von Bülow. The Crown Prince, with almost twice Oudinot's numbers, had wanted to retreat and abandon Berlin – von Bülow in no uncertain terms had indicated that the Swedes could go there or to Hell if they liked, but the Prussians would attack. Again, Prussian tactical superiority had won the day. Since 1809 Napoleon's *Grande Armée*, which had been the terror of Europe and whose tactical forte was always to take the initiative and attack, had been in decline. Its development had stagnated, more and more foreign troops were in the ranks, and since its destruction in Russia and the remaining forces being tied down in Spain, conscripts were now receiving 'on the job' training. Tactical ability in skirmishing and skilful small-unit deployment were virtually non-existent, save in the Imperial Guard, all of whom had served in the old *Grande Armee.*

If Kulm were not portent enough, Napoleon now learned that Marshal Macdonald had met with disaster. He had crossed the Katzbach with some 80,000 men in torrential rain and had advanced up a slope so precipitous that his cavalry had had to dismount. Bridges were few and far, the rain was raising the water level rapidly, and Macdonald had neglected to have temporary bridges built. General Blücher, watching from the woods, ordered a charge, but his chief of staff, Gneisenau, showing his grasp of grand tactics as well as strategy, countermanded this order. Wait, he advised his commander, until they have all crossed and have the river at their backs. Three dismounted French cavalry units had reached the summit of the slope when a brigade of Prussian Uhlans charged them with their lances, driving them pell-mell back down the slope. Thousands of Prussian infantry, preceded by swarms of light infantry, rushed from the woods. In the rain musket fire was useless, and all had to be done with sword, sabre, lance and bayonet. Soon Blücher's 20,000 cavalry were driving the French down the slippery slope to the river. Gneisenau personally directed all available artillery to pour a devastating barrage of canister into the packed ranks of Frenchmen, most of whom had not even been able to fight. As many were drowned as died under the hail of cannon-fire. Neither Blücher nor the rank and file were in a mood to take prisoners – revenge was sweet.

Not for years, not even during the appalling retreat from Moscow, had a French army been so demoralized or damaged in retreat as were Macdonald's retreating mob on this day. After Moscow, the honour of the Imperial eagles had been defended step by step by the rearguard commanded by the incomparable Marshal Ney, 'the bravest of the rave'. But Ney was not here. At the Katzbach 13,000 men were killed or drowned, 17-20,000 were taken prisoner, 150 cannon and two eagles were lost. Marshal Macdonald to his credit assembled his generals and colonels and declared: 'The loss of the battle was due to one only, myself!' But all Napoleon's careful planning and brilliant improvisation that had given him the advantage had been lost. He had beaten an army two and a half times larger than his and sent it reeling, ready for annihilation. Now three subordinates had lost three battles in as many days. Well might Napoleon have cried like the Emperor Augustus, 'Quintilius Varus give me back my legions'.

The cracks in Napoleon's command structure were beginning to show. During his rise to the imperium failure to decentralize and create a staff system that would help and encourage his field commanders to co-ordinate their activity with headquarters had left them in an unenviable situation. Most of them were unable to grasp Napoleon's grand strategy or their part in it, and at best followed his orders blindly, fearful of using their own initiative in case of failure. Those capable of independent command had been either killed – like Marshal Lannes – or were already spent. Marshal Davout, Napoleon's 'Iron' Marshal, was holding the north – no one else could be trusted. Marshal Masséna was now too old for active command. Marshal Soult had been sent post-haste to Spain to relieve Napoleon's incompetent brother Joseph after the débâcle of Vitoria, and was now holding Wellington back from France. Ney, like Blücher, was a leader of men and a superb attack commander, but since 1809 the battlefields with a frontage of a mile or two had expanded to areas of hundreds of square miles. The armies had also grown, from some 20-30,000 per side at the outset of the revolution to 200-300,000 per side. Marshals like Ney felt confident with 40-80,000 men, in units designated 'corps' (miniature armies in fact), but as these were often put together on an *ad hoc* basis and the marshals were often switched from corps to corps, they had had neither the experience nor the time to evolve an adequate staff structure to control them effectively. Unlike most of the Allies – save Wellington, who had had many years of peace between conflicts in which to analyse errors and institute reforms, France had been at war continuously for twenty-one years. Even in 1810-11, marshals such as Ney had not been given time to rest, but were sent during the lull to fight the British and Spanish in the Peninsula. They were war weary – and some were worn out. In the present situation they were hardly at their best and mistakes were bound to happen.

At the Allied command's supreme headquarters, General Schwarzenberg wrote to his Emperor – who resided in an adjacent tent.

'His Majesty the Tsar of Russia, etc. ... never leaves me alone, not in my headquarters nor on the battlefield ... he allows almost every general to give advice and suggestions ... General Barclay has absolutely neither sense of obedience nor understanding for operations and, besides, is jealous in the worst way ... I find it absolutely necessary, therefore, to request of your Imperial Majesty that either the Tsar of Russia be advised to leave the army alone, General Barclay be removed, and the corps of Kleist, Wittgenstein and Miloradovich be each advised that they are under my immediate orders, or someone else be entrusted with the Command.'[10]

This letter speaks for itself as to the shambles reigning at the Allied control centre. In addition to these personality clashes, the Austrian staff was inefficiently organized and antiquated. Further, Schwarzenberg had to formulate policy not only for his own army but for the other two as well. He was also constrained by having to implement Metternich's hidden agenda (Napoleon was not at this juncture to be destroyed, but allowed to withdraw), and had to restrain the Russians and Prussians from forcing the pace without their realizing it. It is not known how Emperor Francis replied, but Schwarzenberg was not allowed to resign, and Francis hadn't the nerve to ask the Tsar to leave or stop acting as supremo. In his spare time Schwarzenberg had also to reorganize the Army of Bohemia, re-equip the men who had thrown everything away in blind panic, and replace lost wagons, ammunition and, most of all, morale.

Napoleon now found himself having to re-evaluate his position and strategy. He could not let the Crown Prince and his Army of the North cross the Elbe behind him and encircle him. To this end Marshal Ney was allocated men, given command of the remnant of Oudinot's army and ordered to advance towards Berlin; Napoleon would join him there for the final push. He would capture Berlin, detaching the Prussians whom he felt would march at once to dislodge him, destroy them, relieve his garrisons and once again advance on the Russo-Austrian rear. Ney rushed off to comply, but Napoleon was unable to march to join him immediately; Blücher was advancing on Macdonald who was holding the river country of Silesia. Macdonald desperately called for aid – Napoleon had to secure his rear. Once again the wily Blücher evaporated on his approach and Napoleon was now summoned urgently by Saint-Cyr who was seeing shadows behind every bush. On his arrival at Dresden Napoleon received some good news: Ney had attacked the Prussians and in a skirmish had captured Blücher's son who could be traded for Vandamme.

On 8 September news came that Ney had been defeated at Dennwitz. His 50,000 men were attacked by von Bülow's 90,000, the Crown Prince commanding from the rear, husbanding his 30,000 'precious Swedes' as a reserve. At a crucial moment in the fighting, Ney's Saxon troops – until now Napoleon's most loyal Germans – had deserted, leaving a huge gap in his battle line into which rode the Prussian cavalry, splitting Ney's force in two and sending him reeling back to Torgau. Ney lost 22,000 men, 13,000 prisoners, 40 cannon and 400 wagonloads of vital stores and ammunition. Napoleon now knew that his plan could not succeed for the moment; he had three enemy armies on three fronts separated by hundreds of miles refusing to come to battle – except when he was absent. He would withdraw behind the Elbe, concentrate his army and wait for the Allies to emerge from their mountain and river enclaves and face him on the fields of Saxony near Leipzig. He would advance via Torgau and concentrate with Ney. Hearing that Blücher had left Silesia and was nearing the Crown Prince, Napoleon determined to attack him en route if possible – and annihilate him.

Blücher had performed exceedingly well thus far in the campaign, especially in view of the effects of Austria's hidden agenda. On 9 August the Russian General Barclay de Tolly had carried Schwarzenberg's orders to Blücher – to inflict as much damage on the French as possible, once the enemy had turned on either of the other Allied Armies, but to avoid battle against any superior force. Blücher had protested this order – Fabian strategy was not the Prussian way! He had insisted that Prussian tactics favoured the attack. Barclay had then agreed that if favourable conditions arose he could use his discretion. Before leaving – as a favour to Schwarzenberg – Barclay spoke to General Langeron, commander of the Russian elements of Blücher's army, and apprised him of the Trachenberg tactics, advising him to avoid superior forces whenever possible. Neither Blücher nor Langeron was aware of what the other had been told. As a consequence, on one occasion Blücher had Ney in a trap and required Langeron to cut off his retreat. Langeron refused on the grounds that his men were tired! On another occasion Blücher had ordered his army only to retreat if the French followed in close pursuit. Langeron ordered a full retreat after having made contact with a French outpost patrol, causing Blücher to abandon a key defensive position.[11] Despite these episodes, Prussian tactics were succeeding.

Blücher now decided to make contact with the Crown Prince and ask him to join forces. They would then march on Leipzig themselves, place themselves astride Napoleon's communications with the north, and threaten his rear. The Army of Bohemia would then come marching to join them and together they would crush Napoleon between a 'hammer and anvil'. The Crown Prince, hearing that Napoleon was advancing towards them with all haste, announced his plan to fall back across the River Spree to maintain his line of communication (or retreat) with Sweden. Major Ruhle von Lilienstern, Blücher's representative, stated that in that case the Army of Silesia would cross the River Salle at Halle, pass round Leipzig and join the Army of Bohemia, leaving the Crown Prince on his own in the north. '... And what will become of Berlin?' asked the Crown Prince. 'If Moscow could be burned, then Berlin can also be sacrificed,'[12] replied this disciple of Scharnhorst. The Crown Prince, not wishing to face his old Emperor alone, capitulated. Napoleon, unable to find either army and fearful that they had crossed the Elbe and were in his rear, summoned his forces to the plains of Leipzig. After much mental anguish, he decided to leave Saint-Cyr and a garrison of 30,000 men at Dresden, reasoning apparently that by concentrating at Leipzig he had gained the central position between the two armies, and confident that if he could bring either of them to battle, his 190,000 men would be more than a match. If at the onset he could smash the Army of Bohemia and send it streaming back to the Bohemian hills, Saint-Cyr would be well placed to cut off its escape route. It can also be argued that, from a psychological point of view, to surrender Dresden, the Saxon capital, would have grave consequences on his men's moral, especially among his German allies.

On 14 October, Napoleon's headquarters were at Leipzig, and he was impatiently awaiting the arrival of his outlying forces. His army numbered some 122,000 men, but by morning it had risen to 195,000 men with 700 cannon.

In 1813 Leipzig had a population of 40,000. The city is situated on a plain surrounded by waterways. The three main rivers are the Pleisse, Elster and Parthe; numerous waterways, streams and marshes connect with these rivers. Leipzig sits on the right bank of the Elster, with tributaries running between, surrounded on three sides by water, and forms a meeting place for the main highways to the whole of Saxony. To the north lies the town of Mockern, to the north-east Stötteritz, and between the two there were many hamlets. Napoleon allocated this area to the overall command of Marshal Ney. Directly south of Leipzig, astride the main highway near the right bank of the Elster, lay the village of Connewitz; stretching forward in an arc likewise were the villages of Dösen, Walchau and Leiberwolkwitz, which were held by King Murat. To the north-east of Leipzig, crossing the Elster and two other tributaries, was a mile-and-a-half causeway linked by a large, wide stone bridge.

From the north approaching fast was Blücher and his Army of Silesia, some 60,000 men, pursuing Napoleon's detachments. Behind him, travelling at a more sedate pace, was the Crown Prince and his Army of the North, some 70,000 men. From the south, Schwarzenberg's juggernaut of 210,000 men of the Army of Bohemia was advancing. Behind and to their right was General Bennigsen's Russian Army of Poland, 30,000 men. The Allies on concentration would have 365,000 men and 1,500 cannon at their disposal.

On 15 October the protagonists began squaring up for the battle on the morrow. Napoleon planned to hold the Crown Prince in check on the northern sector of the battlefield, and to this end Marshal Marmont had been placed above Leipzig opposite Mockern. To his right and stretching in a semi-circle clockwise was part of General Souham's corps. Facing south Marshal Macdonald held a line at right angles near Stötteritz and Leiberwolkwitz. On his right, Marshal Victor held the centre and General (later Marshal) Poniatowski and his brave Polish soldiers held the right flank – resting on the Pleisse and protected by the marshy ground to its front.

Napoleon intended to bring up Marmont's corps as a mass of decision in the early morning, and having pinned the Army of Bohemia frontally, send this corps round to their right flank and rear. Having broken their right flank, he would pursue and destroy the retreating Allies, relying on Saint-Cyr to close the trap; then turn on the Crown Prince and Blücher. The Empire and his dynasty, Napoleon believed, would be saved.

Schwarzenberg's forces had deployed in a semi-circle conforming approximately to Napoleon's southern arc – the northern sector being left to Blücher and the

Crown Prince. Schwarzenberg had kept most of his reserves behind the right of the Pleisse, placing the river between them and Napoleon; only one weak corps of Austrians had been placed across the Elster to block Napoleon's retreat if battle ensued. Schwarzenberg's directive of 13 October sums up his strategy – which was to avoid forcing the issue. Napoleon must be given every chance of withdrawing. That very day the Emperor of Austria had concluded a treaty with Bavaria; Austria guaranteeing its king the integrity and possession of his kingdom in return for his allying himself with the Allied (Austrian) cause and committing his 36,000-strong army. Secret talks were being held with the King of Württemberg also. This clandestine move on the part of Austria to secure her former leadership of the small German states, having been discovered by Prussian intelligence, outraged Baron Stein and the Prussians, who likewise wished to fill the power vacuum and had previously voiced their intention of reducing these secondary princes to nobodies after the conflict. So in pursuance of Austrian aims, Schwarzenberg had decreed that this was to be a reconnaissance in force only: '... we must avoid any serious action, because any large army corps which becomes prematurely engaged could force us to come to its support'.[13] The Crown Prince of Sweden immediately concurred with this point of view.

Napoleon's plan, however, had not taken the unknown factor, Blücher, into consideration. The Emperor had not yet come to terms with the fact that the Prussian army of 1813 bore little resemblance to the creaking machine of 1806. His military intelligence and secret police had been totally deceived as to its training or tactics. His knowledge to-date was based solely on his experience with the small numbers that had taken part at Dresden, and he decided that the victories of von Bülow, Kleist and Blücher had been achieved because of errors on the part of his own subordinates. That the Prussians could have watched, evaluated and improved on his own methods during the past seven years without his knowing it was inconceivable. Moreover, he did not realize that the Prussians had also shed their cumbersome supply trains and, like his own forces, were now living off the land. The Prussians could also match his marching speed, animated as they were by nationalistic pride and hatred of the French.

So Napoleon had put Blücher's army out of the reckoning. Marshal Marmont protested about his role as the mass of decision on the morrow. He pointed out that there were many bivouac fires around Mockern and thought they must be those of Blücher and his Silesian Army. Napoleon dismissed this: 'The Prussians could not move as fast as the French.' It was obviously the Crown Prince, his ex-Marshal Bernadotte – and he would not attack. The orders for the 16th would stand. From this moment Marmont, Napoleon's oldest comrade, began to lose faith in the Emperor's judgement.

At this point, after consulting his colleague Jomini, General Toll, the Tsar's military adviser, began to smell the proverbial rat and protested as to the 'unholy absurdity' of Schwarzenberg's latest plan. Schwarzenberg's reconnaissance having failed to flush Napoleon into retreat, the great man now conceived an attack on four fronts in four different directions. Squeezing Napoleon into the city – leaving him the sole

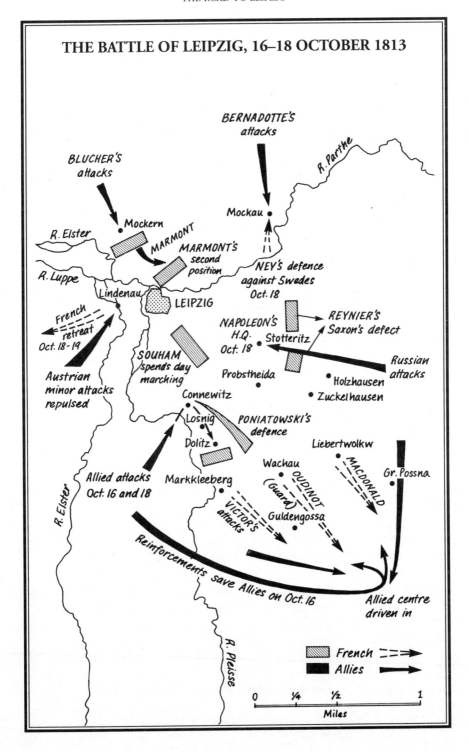

THE BATTLE OF LEIPZIG, 16–18 OCTOBER 1813

BERNADOTTE'S attacks

BLUCHER'S attacks

R. Parthe

Mockau

R. Elster

Mockern

MARMONT

MARMONT'S second position

R. Luppe

NEY'S defence against Swedes Oct. 18

Lindenau

LEIPZIG

French retreat Oct. 18-19

NAPOLEON'S H.Q. Oct. 18

Stotteritz

REYNIER'S Saxon's defect

Russian attacks

Austrian minor attacks repulsed

SOUHAM spends day marching

Probstheida

Holzhausen

Zuckelhausen

Connewitz

R. Elster

Losnig

Dolitz

PONIATOWSKI'S defence

Liebertwolkw

Allied attacks Oct. 16 and 18

Markkleeberg

Wachau

OUDINOT (Guard)

MACDONALD

Gr. Possna

VICTOR'S attacks

Guldengossa

Reinforcements save Allies on Oct. 16

Allied centre driven in

R. Pleisse

French ==⇒
Allies ⟶

0   ¼   ½   1

Miles

51

option of withdrawing with his 195,000 men by the back door, blocked by the token 19,000 Austrians who had been maintaining a masterly inactivity during the last 24 hours. It is inconceivable that any commander would not have wanted to shut this line of retreat, effectively locking Napoleon in a trap – unless it were policy not to do so – with nearly 80,000 men in reserve near the Pleisse this could be accomplished almost immediately. The Tsar then had a second confrontation with the supreme commander, Allied forces, more violent than the first. The Tsar, losing his temper and towering above Schwarzenberg, shouted: 'All right, Sir Feldmarschall, you can do what you want with your Austrian soldiers; but as far as the Russian soldiers are concerned, these will go over to the right bank of the Pleisse, where they should be, and nowhere else.'[14] So the reluctant Austrian was committed to battle.

On 16 October, Napoleon, riding with King Murat near Leiberwolkwitz, observed three Austrian canon rounds fired in rapid succession, answered by three from the north. General Barclay de Tolly, leading 78,000 Russians, attacked south of the city; Napoleon counter-attacked and threw them back. In the north Marmont was in the process of marching to assist Napoleon and become the mobile reserve when the Prussians under Blücher launched an all-out attack. Marmont appealed to Marshal Ney for help, but little was to hand and he was forced to fight the Prussians who outnumbered him 2:1. Napoleon, oblivious to this situation, watched as Prince Eugène of Württemberg, commanding a mixed Russo-Prussian corps, assailed his centre. Forty large-calibre Russian guns opened up, only to receive a nasty surprise. Napoleon's concealed battery of 100 guns manned by Imperial Guard gunners opened a furious fire. Within the space of forty minutes all but four Russian guns had been disabled and Eugène's sector was a scene of carnage and dying. Napoleon sent again for Marmont. Ney decided to go himself, but midway General Bertrand, stationed across the causeway on the other side of the Elster, called for urgent assistance, having sighted the lone corps of Austrians. Ney decided that the threat of an Austrian corps arriving in their rear was of greater priority. Meanwhile Napoleon launched Murat and the whole of his 12,000 cavalry against the Allied centre. From over a ridge, two vast masses of superb horse suddenly appeared, making for the weak point in the Allied line. Forcing the muddy slopes, they put the Allied gunners to the sabre and enveloped the Russian squares. The three monarchs only avoided capture by beating a hasty retreat. Now was the time for Marmont's corps to push through this hole punched in the Allied line 'Where is he?' the Emperor shouted. As time passed the French cavalry were becoming blown and the Russo-Prussian cavalry crossing the Pleisse, coming fresh into the fray, were able to push them back. By late afternoon the Allies, by calling up their reserves, had been able to regain all their lost ground – but their losses had been appalling.

While all this had been taking place, Ney had helped Bertrand push back the Austrian corps and had left two divisions to reinforce this vital position. Marching back through the city, Ney was making for Napoleon's position when Marmont's urgent summons arrived. Ney, reckoning that the Emperor was the better able to sustain himself, marched to Marmont's aid, and only just in time. Mockern had changed hands several times in a particularly bloody series of close-quarter fighting. Street by street, church and churchyard stormed, the Prussians had contested every house hand-to-hand. Back and forth, hour upon hour, this bloody, ritualistic dance had continued – no quarter being asked and none given. By nightfall Mockern was flying the flag of Prussia. Of General Yorck's Prussian corps, 8,000 from a total of 21,000 had been killed or wounded. The French had lost similar numbers, this battle within a battle rating as the bloodiest engagement of the Napoleonic wars, proportionate to the numbers involved. Marshal Ney had marched 15,000 men back and forth across the battlefield, denying them to either front. In his bulletin that night, Napoleon blamed Ney for this error, but in truth he had acted as the situation had dictated.

Among the prisoners taken that morning was the Austrian General Merveldt. After the Battle of Austerlitz in 1805, it was he who had brought Napoleon the request for an armistice from Emperor Francis. He was immediately summoned to the Emperor and instructed to carry an offer of an armistice leading to peace. Why had Austria deserted him? Napoleon asked. 'At Prague she might have dictated terms to Europe. But England did not want peace!' Merveldt replied that they sorely desired peace, but not a truce; a peace founded on the equilibrium of Europe. 'Well let them [England] give me back my Isles [colonies] and I will give them back Hanover. I will also re-establish the Hanse towns and the annexed departments [of North Germany].' Napoleon then began to discuss England. 'How can I treat with England, who wishes to bind me not to build more than thirty ships of the line in my ports?' He then offered to allow any member of the Confederation of the Rhine to leave who wished it. As to giving up Holland, however, he saw great difficulties because that land 'would fall under the control of England'.[15] Italy, he said, ought to be under one sovereign; that would suit the European system. He had abandoned Spain so their was no reason to discuss it.

Napoleon was offering Austria everything it wanted – except Italy. Holding this out as a carrot, he had hinted that Italy should be unified, obviously under his son – the Emperor Francis's grandson – but this seemed to leave it open for further discussion. Rightly divining England's intentions towards Holland, and her implacable resistance to him, he hoped to break the Alliance and leave England out in the cold as the only obstacle to peace. To this end he clouded the issue by introducing colonies and ships of the line as points of dispute, with which he knew Austria had little interest or sympathy. Guessing shrewdly that Austria would prefer a weak Prussia and a distant Russia, he alluded to Austria's powerful position as his benefactor, i.e., dictating peace to Europe. Napoleon had hopes that Austria would seek peace terms. If it didn't, he hoped at least to cause dissension among his enemies – and in this he was successful. Metternich noted the contents but made no reply.

By 17 October, Napoleon had lost approximately 20,000 men, the Allies nearly double that number. He had been reinforced by some 15,000 Saxons coming from Düben, but his bridging train had been left behind with other military stores. The 60,000 men of the Army of the North had at last appeared to the north of Leipzig.

General Bennigsen with a further 70,000 Russians had arrived in the south. The day was spent in preparation and reorganization. Napoleon decided to try once more to break the cohesion of the Army of Bohemia, in the hope that this would bring Austria to an armistice. Pulling back, still on an arc, using villages as strongpoints, he reduced his lateral lines of communication and shortened the area in which he could move troops from one front to the other. The Allies would be required to march four times the distances to reinforce the northern sector or vice versa. He deployed his corps as before, with the addition of General Reynier's Saxon corps holding the gap between the northern and southern sectors, centred on the village of Paunsdorf. Whatever Napoleon's plans might have been, they had little chance of coming to fruition. Marshal Marmont bore the brunt of Blücher's onslaught; outnumbered again 2:1. Ney on his right was assailed by the Prussians and Russians of the Army of the North. Attached to the Crown Prince's forces was a British rocket battery commanded by a Captain Boyd – an experimental unit under the patronage of the Prince Regent. The French had no inkling of what was to come from this unconventional-looking battery. Suddenly, out of the blue, with incredible velocity a flame appeared, followed by another and another. Within as many seconds six 32-pound rockets exploded, showering canister balls into one of Ney's divisions. Lieutenant Strangeways wrote: 'The column was blown asunder like an antheap.'[16] The Russian General Wittgenstein, aghast at the carnage inflicted, commented: 'They look as if they were made in Hell, and surely are the devil's own artillery.'[17] It was beyond reason to expect the French to advance into this unholy barrage.

The southern sector was holding well when suddenly the Saxons of Reynier's corps, some 3,000 men, went over to the enemy, taking their cannon – followed in swift succession by the Württemberg cavalry. The remaining Saxons gave way. Napoleon immediately plugged the gap with the Imperial Guard. Lacking a strike force, it was now impossible to contemplate crushing either wing; of more concern was the lack of artillery ammunition. That night Napoleon wrote, with understandable exaggeration, to General Clarke, his minister of war: 'If I had had 30,000 rounds, I should now be master of the world,' and ordered the army to retreat across the Elbe. His bridging equipment had been left at Düben; to collect timber by night and illuminate the sites would alert the enemy and perhaps precipitate an attack – and a panic rout. He would retreat slowly in the morning; by the time the enemy attacked he would have most of his army across the river whence they would could cover the rearguard. Early next morning Napoleon bade the King and Queen of Saxony farewell, advising them to make the best terms they could. When the Allies, particularly Blücher, realized what was happening they hurled themselves on the French rearguard and the city. On the previous day the Austrians, under pretext of needing reinforcements, had removed a division from the small corps guarding the opposite bank, leaving a token force of just 16,000 men – nothing was to be allowed to impede Napoleon's escape.

The one great stone bridge, its twelve arches joining the Elster causeway, had already seen some 70,000 troops to safety, when a ripple of explosions ran along its length, killing many soldiers and civilians with falling masonry. The explosion was heard by all the Allies. Napoleon's army had been cut in two. The general of engineers who had been ordered to hold the bridge until the last possible moment had crossed over to evaluate the situation; the colonel he left in charge went to arrange the removal of his unit's equipment. A solitary sergeant was left like Horatius, holding the bridge and with no idea as to how many more formations had yet to cross. He had strict orders to blow the bridge if the enemy appeared – come what may. Frustrated at losing his quarry, Blücher had ordered General Sacken's riflemen to work around the city outskirts, using the river banks; they commenced an enfilade fire and the sergeant, faithful to his charge, blew the bridge.

This single act damaged Napoleon's army more than had two days of battle. Thirty generals and two marshals were trapped on the other side with three army corps – 37,000 men and all their cannon and equipment, plus possibly 21,000 walking wounded and ancillary services. A drawn battle had become an Allied victory. The Crown Prince, deciding that now was the time to let Swedish valour shine forth, took personal command of the attack on the Grimma gate. After his Prussian and Russians troops had forced an entry, his Swedish Lifeguards and Jäger advanced to the ruins of the great bridge. Prince Metternich, taking charge of the proceedings, thought that his Imperial Highness the Tsar should review the Swedish Guards and then, perhaps, a 'Te Deum' should be sung? and prayers to God for the victory? The religious Tsar agreed. Prussia, in return for future co-operation (quid pro quo) regarding Poland, demanded the King of Saxony as a prisoner of war – the Tsar agreed. Prussia was determined that Austria was not going to come to any accommodation with him. Metternich thought the honour of arresting him should go to Blücher, who immediately agreed. Meanwhile Napoleon was allowed to march away to fight another day – or not, Metternich thought. The unhappy King of Saxony was bundled into a coach and later paraded through Berlin where the crowd, venting their spleen, stoned his coach; he was then imprisoned in one of Prussia's strongest fortresses, the Friedrichsfelde. The Tsar ordered that his kingdom be administered by the Russian General Prince Repnin. Metternich viewed this development with foreboding; first Poland and now Saxony had a Russian military governor and an occupying army.

While his monarch was at his devotions, Metternich was given a personal tour of the battlefield by Schwarzenberg, accompanied at his suggestion by the British commissioner, Lord Aberdeen, a 29-year-old philanthropist and Greek scholar. A self-opinionated young man, he had written of Napoleon in 1803 from Paris: 'I was captivated by his beauty and the winning charm of his smile.'[18] Patronage being what it was at this time, he had been chosen for this important post not because of his ability, but because he had been a ward and protégé of the Pitt family. He had immediately fallen under the spell of Metternich's charm and deference. Metternich made a point of seeking his opinion and advice on trivial matters, which made him feel important. Aberdeen had written to Castlereagh on 5 September: 'Do not think Metternich such a formidable personage. Depend upon it, I have the most substantial reasons for knowing that he is heart and soul with us; my dear Castlereagh, with all your wisdom, judgement and experience ... I think you have so much of the Englishman as not quite to be aware of the real value of modes of acting.'[19] Their tour of the battlefield covered an area of some five square miles, and Lord Aberdeen was appalled by the dead and wounded – especially the horses. The tour ended in Leipzig among the wounded in the hospitals. Aberdeen agreed with Metternich that something ought to be done to prevent a repetition of this senseless carnage.

On 9 November 1813, Napoleon arrived at his palace of Saint-Cloud in Paris, it having taken less than three weeks to cover the 200-odd miles from Leipzig. During his retreat, General Wrede, commander of the Bavarian forces and his ally of a week before, placed his army of 60,000 men across Napoleon's road with his back to the river that was spanned by a single bridge to cross by – obviously not a student of Caesar, Napoleon observed. Wrede, confident that Napoleon was being harried by the Allies, thought to gain universal fame by capturing him. The place was Hanau, the date 30 October. Wrede had compounded two grave errors by a third, placing his flank on a wood through which artillery could be driven. Napoleon brought up the Imperial Guard artillery through the wood and they began firing. Soon enlarged to 50 pieces of ordnance, the battery blew huge gaps and bloody lanes through the hitherto smartly dressed ranks of Bavarians. In desperation Wrede launched the whole of his cavalry at the battery, but they were sent reeling, suffering appalling losses from Imperial Guard cavalry emerging from the wood. Only the insufficiency of this arm saved Wrede's army from annihilation and humiliating capture. On the field lay 6,000 killed and wounded, one-tenth of his command. Wrede was fortunate to escape with his life let alone capture Napoleon.

By 6 November 70,000 French soldiers, rearmed and with new uniforms supplied by the magazine at Erfurt, had crossed the Rhine into France at Mainz. Twice in two years Napoleon had commanded an army of more than 400,000 men, only to return with fewer than 70,000, statistics that would have broken a lesser spirit. The Allies now had 345,000 men on the eastern front of Napoleon's fast dwindling Empire. Wellington commanded a further 125,000 British and Spanish troops in the south. To oppose these, Napoleon had 100,000 men of the Army of Spain, under Marshals Soult and Suchet, holding the line in the south. To face the eastern allies Napoleon had 80,000 men holding a 300-mile front. Arriving in early November at Frankfurt-on-Main, the monarchs and their entourages gave banquets and said their prayers. Even General Blücher, feeling optimistic, sent many hundreds of French prisoners home and spoke about dining at the Palais Royal. The Allies were jubilant – the war was over! But it wasn't. For many, not least Napoleon, it hadn't even begun.

CHAPTER 3

THE ROADS OF FRANCE

'Let us go to the Fight!'
'Allons, enfants de la Patrie!
Le jour de gloire est arrivé!'
– Rouget de Lisle, 'La Marseillaise', 25 April 1792

T HE ALLIED ADVANCE HALTED ABRUPTLY AT THE RHINE; Austria, having recovered all its lost provinces in Italy and Illyria, had by arms secured Napoleon's return to France. Austria had also signed a treaty with King Murat of Naples, recognizing him as *de facto* king and guaranteeing his position and the integrity of his kingdom in return for his alliance.[1] Metternich had thus secured a power base: Austria's Italian possessions protected by Murat, the kings of southern Germany – Bavaria and Württemberg – as vassals to the Austrian Emperor, the example of the King of Saxony's fate ever present as an alternative to Austrian protection. From this advantageous position, Austria wished to conclude peace with Napoleon. The Prussian generals, anxious not to lose the advantage, wanted to prosecute the war to a finish, but King William was hesitant and fearful; certainly he would not proceed without Austrian assistance. The Crown Prince of Sweden, eager to launch his army against the tiny Kingdom of Denmark and seize Norway, cautioned against crossing the Rhine.[2] Alexander of Russia wanted desperately to lead his Guards into Paris as the conquering hero – in imitation of Napoleon, but his generals felt that Russia had done enough; the heretics had been driven from Russian soil and Poland had been taken in recompense; Russian blood had been shed to free Germany – but enough was enough. The Russian generals were also fed up with the Tsar's always deferring to his 'foreign advisers' – had he not slighted the great Kutusov? Alexander had first to win over his generals, before he could continue. It was virtually a tradition in Russia that if a monarch brought his country to disaster or ill-repute, or ignored his generals, he was strangled. So it had been with his grandfather Peter III and his father Paul I. Alexander could ignore this at his peril.[3]

On the same day that Napoleon arrived at Saint-Cloud, Prince Metternich, at Frankfurt-on-Main, concluded a second interview with the comte de Saint-Aignan, brother-in-law of Napoleon's envoy and close confidant, Armand Caulaincourt, duc de Vicence. He had been the French envoy at Weimar, and had fallen into Austrian hands. Metternich told Saint-Aignan that he was now prepared to take up the overtures that Napoleon had made through General Merveldt after the first day of Leipzig. Present at this meeting were Metternich, Lord Aberdeen, British Ambassador to Austria, and Count Nesselrode, the Tsar's minister for foreign affairs – representing both the Tsar and King William of Prussia. At Aberdeen's insistence, the meeting was kept secret from his two colleagues, Lord Cathcart and Sir Charles Stewart, and from the Prussian ministers. In essence Napoleon was offered peace based on the 'natural boundaries of France'. That is to say, the left bank of the Rhine, including all of Belgium including Antwerp, and part of Savoy; in effect all the territory Napoleon had won by the Treaty of Campo Formio in 1797.[4] Everything Napoleon had asked for he was offered – except Italy, which he had known at the time would have to be forfeited. Metternich, aware that Napoleon had not only to appear to have lost no French territory by the peace, but to have gained something also – had persuaded the gullible Aberdeen to commit Britain to agreeing to the loss of Belgium and Antwerp, the *casus belli*, and to 'be reasonable' about her maritime rights – the 'sacred cow' of British policy. Saint-Aignan, not believing his luck, personally drafted the proposal, inserting the formula: 'Great Britain is ready to recognize the liberty of commerce and navigation which France has the RIGHT to claim'.[5] Aberdeen was consenting to an end to the war, and giving Napoleon everything that he had not been able to force from Britain during the last twenty years. Aberdeen had been persuaded that he would take the credit of ending the war and saving countless thousands of lives, and would be honoured by every court in Europe. Aberdeen had one stipulation, that his fellow countrymen should not be informed until Napoleon had made his decision.[6]

In a fast coach provided by Metternich, Saint-Aignan took the document post-haste to Paris where he handed it to his superior, Maret, duc de Bassano, Napoleon's foreign minister – who left it on his desk for a week. Saint-Aignan, anticipating a summons from Napoleon, waited for seven days and then consulted his brother-in-law. Caulaincourt, who was getting dressed at the time, listened in disbelief – within minutes the two men, one half-dressed, appeared at the palace. Napoleon sent for the letter. Maret was disgraced and Caulaincourt was appointed foreign minister with special powers of negotiation. He was ordered to accept the offer after having ascertained that it was genuine.[7] The delay was to prove disastrous for Napoleon. By the time that Caulaincourt had sent off a letter of unconditional acceptance (2 December) it was too late. Lord Castlereagh and Britain had intervened,[8] repudiating Britain's association with this offer and informing the trio of monarchs that 'His Royal Highness the Prince Regent would in no case ratify such an agreement.' Castlereagh arrived at Basle on 18 January 1814. He was about to cut cards with the devil; embracing the Machiavellian principle that the end justifies the means, he set about reorganizing the coalition – if the Allies were intent on putting themselves first, Britain too could play that game.

On arrival Castlereagh received a note from the Tsar asking him 'not to make his mind up on any subject until they had met'.[9] Castlereagh wrote to Lord Liverpool, the Prime Minister, that same day, amazed at the Tsar's latest idea:

'... The first and most important, and that will surprise you the most, is a disposition represented to be felt by the Emperor of Russia is to favour the Prince Royal of Sweden's views to the throne of France. I can hardly yet bring myself to give credit to this statement, but it comes to me through so many channels of authority that I cannot hesitate to believe that the project has been countenanced by his Imperial Majesty. ... The Austrian minister's confidential language is, that his court have no objection to bring forward, should the French nation think fit to restore the ancient dynasty; but that it is another question to have Madame Bernadotte [the silk merchant's daughter] substituted in the room of a princess of the House of Habsburg.'[10]

Castlereagh's first task was to change the offer on the table. Britain would not continue to fund her allies with gold, credit or *matériel* unless this were done at once. At his first meeting with the foreign ministers he diplomatically tore strips off them:

'... To suppose that the Allies could now rest satisfied with any arrangement substantially short of reducing France within her ancient limits, was to impute to them an abandonment of their most sacred duty, which, if made with a view to peace, must fail of its object, as the public mind of Europe would never remain tranquil under so improvident an arrangement.'[11]

After a little discussion the ancient limits clause was adopted unanimously.

Having received an undertaking from each of the ministers and their sovereigns on the vital British questions of Holland and the Belgian barrier, and the exclusion of all discussions on the maritime question, Castlereagh proceeded to his next objective – the prosecution of the war. Writing to the Prime Minister, he explained the crux of the matter:

'... You may estimate some of the hazards to which affairs are exposed here, when one of the leading monarchs [the Tsar], in his first interview, told me that he had no confidence in his own minister, and still less in his ally. There is much intrigue, and more fear of it. Russia distrusts Austria about Saxony; and Austria dreads Russia about Poland, especially if she is mistress of the question of peace ... Suspicion is the prevailing temper of the Emperor, and Metternich's character furnishes constant food for *intrigants* to work upon ...'[12]

To this end Castlereagh discussed the problem with Metternich and suggested that it be shelved until after the war – Britain wanted 'a just equilibrium or balance of Power in Europe',[13] indicating that he would support Austria in this matter.

To Prussia he indicated that Saxony too should be a matter for a 'congress'; however, he had stated – as would Great Britain – that Prussia should be compensated territorially for her losses and efforts.[14] Through the medium of the Hanoverian minister, Gneisenau canvassed Castlereagh's views on the idea of Prussia's taking a lead in a new confederation of smaller German states. Castlereagh replied that he did not see any objection – in principle.[15] To the Crown Prince of Sweden he offered assistance in Sweden's conquest of Norway – after France had been defeated – with the loan of a Royal Naval fleet, landing-craft and *matériel* – in return for an attack across the Rhine and help in the 'liberation of Holland and Belgium'. The Crown Prince assured Castlereagh that he would, under the circumstances, be happy to leave at once.

This left only Tsar Alexander, who wanted ex-Marshal Bernadotte to replace Napoleon on the French throne,[16] though he was unable to convey to Castlereagh

his reasons for preferring the Crown Prince rather than the Bourbons. As to Poland
– which he already possessed – he would give no answer until the end of hostilities.
Castlereagh was more interested in defeating Napoleon than answering ifs and buts.
If the Russian generals would not fight to free France, would they fight to have their
navy returned plus £1,000,000 in gold? That was a horse of a different colour. At the
beginning of the invasion of Russia, in order to safeguard the fleet, which would
inevitably have become ice-bound and vulnerable to capture by Napoleon, the Tsar
had sent it to Britain. Its upkeep and the maintenance of the crews would have to be
repaid first. Would Russia be able to pay this amount on top of her war loans,
already some £4,000,000? The Russian Navy – seventeen ships of the line, thirty-two
frigates and lesser craft[17] – would only be returned on repayment. Repayment could
take decades, but in certain circumstances Britain would accept an IOU. Alexander's
generals agreed that St. Petersburg without its navy would be a humiliation for Russia. They would fight in France – after all, Napoleon had caused this situation had
he not? If it could be said that Napoleon's hat was worth 100,000 men on the battlefield, Castlereagh's was worth 400,000 at a diplomatic conference.

Since his return to France Napoleon had not been idle. Money had been wanting – it was acquired from various sources: 55,000,000 francs from his own pocket,
a like sum seized by him from his mother's enormous savings. Forced loans and
contributions soon raised the amount needed to prosecute a new war. Napoleon
ordered the war minister to '... Procure all the cloth in France, good and bad, so as
to have 200,000 uniforms ready by the end of February.' Priority was given to the
manufacture of cannon, muskets, ammunition and equipment; work began round
the clock with very high wages as an incentive. Napoleon issued decrees that would,
given time, result in a staggering 936,000 men under arms. But time was wanting.
It is a tribute to his organizing ability that in the first three months of 1814, some
120,000 men joined the Colours.[18] The great deficiency, however, was in trained
men capable of teaching the new 'Marie-Louises' to load and fire their muskets, and
form square against cavalry. In desperation Napoleon wrote to his war minister
Clarke: 'I am told that there are between 700 and 800 individuals in the Invalides
whose disabilities are slight and who would serve again with good grace. If this is
correct, they would form an admirable source of junior officers ... I could use them
in the six regiments of the new Guard I am presently forming. I need 540 sergeants
and 1,080 corporals.'[19]

On the political front too, Napoleon had been busy. He signed a treaty with
Ferdinand VII of Spain – his prisoner since 1808 – which had it succeeded would
have released 100,000 men for his eastern army. In essence Napoleon renounced any
claim on Spain and guaranteed Ferdinand his crown; in return all French and British
troops would be required to leave Spanish soil immediately, thereby cutting the
ground from under Wellington's feet. But Napoleon's plan was too late. The Spanish Junta and Cortes rejected it out of hand. Wellington, on hearing of the treaty,
said: 'I have long suspected that Bonaparte would adopt this expedient; and if he had
had less pride and more common sense, it would have succeeded.'[20]

France in the main supported Napoleon. The national instinct was sound; the Allies had crossed the Rhine and France once more was in danger. The soldiers, peasants and middle classes were behind the Emperor. The moans about excessive taxation and conscription were forgotten – 'leave that to the rich, the *émigrés* and backsliders' – '*La patrie en danger!*' was the cry. This feeling was summed up by an old peasant: 'It's no longer a question of Bonaparte. Our soil is invaded: let us go to the fight!' To cross the Rhine was an attack, not on Napoleon but on the French Revolution. The Rhine and Belgian boundaries had been won by Generals Dumouriez, Jourdan, Pichegru and Moreau long before the name Bonaparte had been heard outside Corsica. Before crossing into France, the Allies had issued a proclamation: 'We do not make war on France, but we are casting off the yoke which your Government imposed on our countries. We had hoped to have found peace before touching your soil: we now go to find it there.'[21]

This idealistic appeal, formulated by Metternich, was not exactly what the Prussian military had in mind for France. The Army of Silesia had orders to deal mercilessly with any French inhabitants who decided to defend their homes against the marauding Prussian and Cossack troops who had been ordered to 'live off the land'. They were to be treated as insurgents and shot, their homes and adjacent villages to be burned. Smoke from the ruins of La Chaise and Morvilles, the first of many, soon blackened the sky and marked the progress of the Prussian army. General Gneisenau wrote to Baron Stein:

> 'We must take revenge for the many sorrows inflicted upon the nations, and for so much arrogance. If we do not, then we are miserable wretches indeed, and deserve to be shocked out of our lazy peace every two years and threatened with the scourge of slavery ... We must return the visits of the French to our cities, by visiting them in theirs. Until we do, our revenge and triumph will be incomplete. If the Silesian Army reaches Paris first, I shall at once have the bridges of Austerlitz and Jena blown up, as well as the Arc de Triomphe.'[22]

Hardly the sentiments of the proclamation.

Contrary to normal practice the Allies had decided to open a winter campaign because they did not want to allow Napoleon time to build up a large force. They also wanted to exploit the unrest in Belgium and Holland. They had decided on a three-pronged attack. The Crown Prince's Army of the North was split in two. One corps under General von Bülow and an expeditionary force under the British General Graham were to occupy Holland, Antwerp and the rest of Belgium, thence into northern France. The other half, under the Crown Prince, would isolate Marshal Davout in Hamburg and defeat the Danish auxiliary corps. Blücher and his 100,000-strong Army of Silesia would advance by Coblenz and Mannheim, fixing Napoleon's attention and maintaining a link between the northern forces and Schwarzenberg's 200,000-strong Army of Bohemia which would march to the plains of Langres. Having completed this stage – bypassing through neutral Switzerland and turning the flank of the French-guarded river crossings – part two of the plan envisaged Blücher frontally attacking Napoleon, while the Bohemian monolith turned his right flank, thereby saving as many Austrian lives as possible for any future conflicts.

Napoleon had hoped for at least two months' respite. His depleted forces were deployed as follows: General Maison in Belgium with 15,000 men, with orders to help Carnot hold Antwerp and its large gun-foundries at all costs. On his right, the skeletal corps of Marshal Macdonald's 13,000 men, then General Morand's 13,000, and finally Marshal Marmont's 16,000, covering an area of several hundred square miles. At Lyons, Marshal Augereau was trying to raise a new army around a core of Spanish veterans. Marshal Victor had but 10,000 men to watch Switzerland and the upper Rhine. To the rear, Marshal Mortier had the Imperial Guard and Marshal Ney was assembling two new Young Guard divisions from a mixed bag of veterans: gendarmes, foresters and naval personnel. Napoleon had hoped at least to have doubled the numbers of each corps by the time that hostilities began. A total of 30,000 National Guardsmen were assembling at Nogent and Meaux. It will be seen then that Napoleon had some 100,000 men to hold northern and eastern France against the 360,000 men of the Allies. In the south, his stepson Eugène had 50,000 men to guard northern Italy against 70,000 Austrians under General Bellegarde, and Murat's 36,000 Neapolitans. On the Franco-Spanish border Wellington had 112,000 men against Marshals Soult and Suchet who commanded 97,000 men between them. As can be seen, Wellington's force rated as large a French contingent as that facing the combined Allies with nearly four times the number. Napoleon did not underestimate Wellington's abilities.

Unable to leave Paris immediately, Napoleon instructed Caulaincourt to try to obtain peace or an armistice if possible – in the meantime he would have to leave the defence of the frontiers to his marshals. He was facing something of a crisis on the ' Home Front'. The *Corps Législatif*, having been called to vote taxes for the war, had presumed to give advice to the Emperor and, the more heinous, had proposed publishing it; their findings ending on the note that Napoleon should make peace based on the 'natural boundaries' offer (which had already been withdrawn). In the language of the barrack-room he lectured these members: 'They had done more harm to France than if he had lost two battles!' By what mandate did they dare to criticize him? They had been elected by a few hundred votes apiece! He by several millions – twice! They had thrown mud at him. He might be slain, never dishonoured. He would fight for France, hurl the enemy back and conclude an honourable peace. Then to shame them he would circulate their report! Humbled, they were dismissed to their homes.

What to do about Paris was Napoleon's greatest concern. Paris represented France in a manner entirely different from Moscow *vis-à-vis* Russia in 1812 or Berlin *vis-à-vis* Prussia in 1813. Paris was Napoleon's power base, the heart and centre, the storehouse of his military supplies, his army headquarters and administrative centre. And since the Revolution it had been the heart and conscience of the nation. It was also Napoleon's Achilles' heel.[23] He had created an emasculated administration totally subservient to his personal will; efficient and all-embracing but animated and propelled by his will alone – a bureaucratic autocracy. The obvious weakness was – remove Napoleon and it would grind to a halt like his army command structure. The machine could not run itself and there was no one he could trust to run it in his absence. Its personnel were chosen for administrative ability and obedience - not for qualities of leadership.

On two occasions during Napoleon's reign he had noticed this dangerous flaw and had failed to correct it. In 1809, taking advantage of Napoleon's absence in Austria, Castlereagh, as minister of war, had organized the largest invasion fleet ever to cross the Channel, its destination the mouth of the Scheldt. Castlereagh had planned to seize and hold Antwerp, destroy Napoleon's flotilla, blow up the great naval locks and remove all the armament production machinery from the arsenals.[24] Failures on the part of the military commander, Lord Chatham, had saved the situation for the French. At the time, Paris was paralysed by indecision. Joseph Fouché, Napoleon's minister of police and interior minister, took action. In opposition to the war minister and, more significantly, without his permission, Fouché mobilized 60,000 National Guardsmen and placed them under Marshal Bernadotte who had just returned in disgrace from the front. In the event, the troops were not needed. The British force encamped on the island of Walcheren while the army and navy commanders bickered. Although it was not realized at the time, the island was a breeding-ground for the malarial mosquito. The British lost 400 men in a skirmish, and 6,000 to 'Walcheren fever'. It has been estimated that it killed and debilitated another 23,000 men. A grateful Napoleon applauded Fouché's initiative and made him duc d'Otranto. A few months later Napoleon found out that, again on his own initiative, Fouché had made overtures to England seeking peace – without his knowledge or consent, and for this he was dismissed. But the lesson was not lost on Napoleon, one man with initiative had taken control of Paris and had raised and deployed an army of 60,000 men, without his knowledge. Fouché had appointed a commander, and issued arms and equipment, and Paris had obeyed him without question. Clearly to control Paris one only had to give orders and act like Napoleon.

The second, more important lesson was the Malet plot. General Claude de Malet was a career soldier, formerly of the late king's musketeers, who had risen to the rank of general of brigade in the republican army. Resenting the rise of the autocratic Napoleon, in 1807 he had conspired with Generals Moreau and Pichegru in an attempt to topple him. But the affair had been hushed up by Fouché, presumably because he himself had been involved. Malet was kept in a state prison until 1812 when he had been transferred to a 'private' prison cum mental asylum by Fouché's replacement, General Savary, on the petition of Malet's wife; Savary, having been told that Malet's file was 'missing', had consented. Malet was then visited by a royalist go-between, the Abbé Lafon, a member of the 'Chevaliers de la Foi', who rented a house near the prison and supplied the General with a uniform and immaculately forged documents – purporting to have been issued by the provisional government of the republic. On the night of 23 October 1812, the General merely climbed over the wall, put on the uniform and with two stooges of below average intelligence, set about taking control of Paris. He arrived at Popincourt barracks, gave the password: 'Conspiracy' and went to see the commandant. Who it was that supplied the password and documents remains a mystery – the finger tends to point at Fouché as being the only likely person to have been able to procure them. Malet informed Commandant Adjutant Major Soulier: 'The Emperor died on 7 October, under the walls of Moscow. I am the bearer of a dispatch from the Senate to you.' Malet then called on his companion, who was wearing a magisterial sash, to read the proclamation: 'The Imperial Government, having disappointed the hopes of those who believed it to be a source of peace and happiness for the French, is abolished ...'[25] A list of the new provisional government's members was followed by the next article, peace negotiations with all the belligerent powers; withdrawal from Spain, Italy and Holland; the Pope to be freed; amnesty for all political prisoners. Malet then placed the troops of the barracks under his own command. He arrested General Savary, duc de Rovigo, who was now Napoleon's chief of police and minister of the interior. The soldiers hauled Savary off to prison without any hesitation – threatening to club him if he did not shut up! Malet then ordered the Prefect of Paris to prepare the Hôtel de Ville for a meeting of the provisional government, which was done without hesitation. Malet then proceeded to release prisoners unchallenged. The coup foundered when the Governor of Paris questioned the orders and expressed his intention of having them verified. Malet shot and seriously wounded him. He compounded this mistake by attempting to take charge of No. 7 place Vendôme without the backing of the 400-odd troops he had detailed to assist him. No. 7 place Vendôme, designated the Paris Garrison, was in effect the military intelligence and counter-espionage centre of the Empire. Colonel Doucet, Adjutant-Commandant and Chief of Staff of Counter-intelligence, recognized Malet's name on the list of the 'new provisional government members' as being that of an enemy of the state and arrested him. Malet and thirteen others were shot; ten of them were soldiers merely obeying what they perceived to be genuine orders, but an example had to be made of them.[26] (See Appendix II.)

News of the attempted coup induced Napoleon to leave the army in Russia and travel back to France virtually without escort. Not only was he profoundly shocked by the near success of the coup, but he was dumbfounded that, on hearing of his supposed death, no one had thought to consult the Empress Regent and declare his son Emperor? Napoleon knew indeed how slender was the thread that bound him to his throne. Other than Fouché, the only man available with the ability to take charge in his absence, but who had not done so, was Charles-Maurice de Talleyrand-Périgord, Prince of Bénévent, one-time Bishop of Atun. An able diplomat from one of the oldest families in France, a childhood accident resulting in lameness had barred him from inheriting the family title. He was neglected by uncaring parents who decided that an ecclesiastical career would rid them of him. One wonders how much this rejection coloured his subsequent career. He deserted the Church for the Revolution, becoming ambassador to England. Highly intelligent, always adopting the role of double spy from choice, he intrigued with the royalists, but escaped execution during the Terror by seeking refuge in America. He returned to the corrupt Directory in 1797, and was offered the post of foreign minister, 'I am going to make a fortune out of it,' he gleefully told Benjamin Constant. He then intrigued to take over the state, for which he needed a general. Unable to manipulate the slow-witted Bernadotte, his first choice, he switched to Bonaparte. It was a marriage made in heaven. Talleyrand was to politics what Napoleon was to soldiering. They got on famously, until Napoleon became Emperor and had learnt all he needed to know from Talleyrand, who was now Arch-Chancellor and Imperial Grand Elector. Resentment grew between the two, Talleyrand feeling that Napoleon was ungrateful and owed everything to him. Napoleon sensitive to his new status, thought his minister too familiar and overbearing – they were on a collision course. Talleyrand used his connections as foreign minister with Russia, Austria and Britain to intrigue and pass information – for payment. This was quite acceptable in politics then, as it is today, unless of course, you get caught. Suspecting Talleyrand, Napoleon's enmity grew, and on 28 January 1809 he dismissed him as foreign minister – Napoleon, having made a quip about his tracing his Empire back to Charlemagne, was upstaged by Talleyrand who, referring to his own family, said '... and some of us go back further'. Napoleon rounded on him and all the venom and hurt of his sense of betrayal came out – in a tirade that would have made a sergeant-major blush. All those present state in their memoirs that they and Talleyrand had turned pale with shock. For twenty minutes the tirade continued unabated, finishing with the famous remark '... old family!. I'll tell you what you are – a load of shit stuffed into a silk stocking!' Talleyrand walked away with as much dignity as he could muster. Napoleon had made the worst enemy of his career, implacable, without mercy and with no intention of offering quarter.[27] But, whether through conscience or regret, Napoleon still allowed him to come to court in his position as Arch-Chancellor, perhaps because he felt deep down some gratitude for his help over the years. Fouché warned him of Talleyrand's malice, but Napoleon thought he could control it. A year later, on his own dismissal, Fouché too joined this personal vendetta against Napoleon.[28]

Napoleon was now facing his decisive campaign, but to whom could he entrust the capital? The Faubourg Saint-Germain was a hotbed of disaffection, crammed with royalists whom Napoleon, against Fouché's advice, had allowed back into France, in the hope of gaining respectability by surrounding himself with old families once he had married the Austrian arch-duchess. They however, merely schemed and intrigued with the Bourbons. Rich and idle, having had property restored or replaced, and with no stake in the France of the Revolution or Empire, they amused themselves by starting secret royalist clubs. Napoleon decided to invest the 23-year-old Empress with regency powers, knowing that she would obey all his written directives. As lieutenant of the kingdom he was entrusting to his family, he appointed his brother Joseph, the titular King of Spain, the man who had lost Spain by his disastrous Battle of Vitoria against Wellington. These then were to be the keepers of the imperial flame, entrusted to hold the capital. Fouché was not in Paris. And Tal-

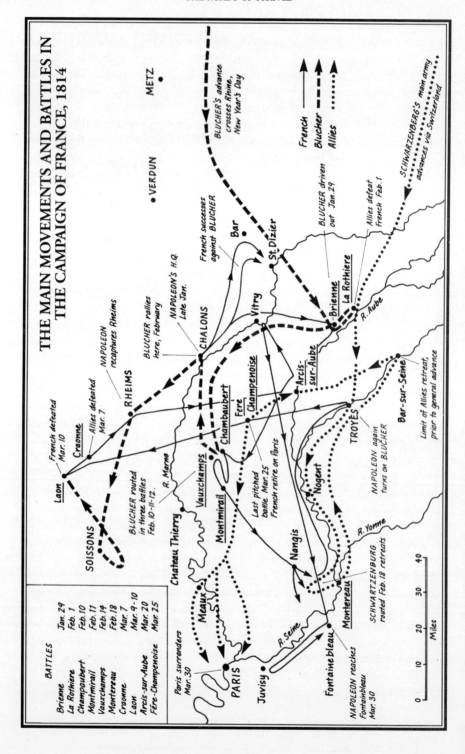

THE MAIN MOVEMENTS AND BATTLES IN
THE CAMPAIGN OF FRANCE, 1814

BATTLES

Brienne	Jan. 29
La Rothiere	Feb. 1
Champaubert	Feb. 10
Montmirail	Feb. 11
Vauxchamps	Feb. 14
Montereau	Feb. 18
Craonne	Mar. 7
Laon	Mar. 9-10
Arcis-sur-Aube	Mar. 20
Fère-Champenoise	Mar. 25

French
Blucher
Allies

BLUCHER's advance
crosses Rhine,
New Year's Day

SCHWARTZENBERG's main army
advances via Switzerland

METZ

VERDUN

BLUCHER driven
out Jan. 29

Allies defeat
French Feb. 1

French successes
against BLUCHER

Bar

St. Dizier

NAPOLEON's H.Q.
Late Jan.

Brienne

La Rothiere

R. Aube

BLUCHER rallies
here, February

CHALONS

Vitry

NAPOLEON
recaptures Rheims

Allies defeated
Mar. 7

RHEIMS

Chambaubert

Fère

Champenoise

Arcis-
sur-Aube

Bar-sur-Seine

TROYES

French defeated
Mar. 10

Craonne

Vauxchamps

Last pitched
battle, Mar. 25
French retire on Paris

Nogent

NAPOLEON again
turns on BLUCHER

Laon

Montmirail

R. Marne

BLUCHER routed
in three battles
Feb. 10-11-12.

SOISSONS

Nangis

R. Yonne

Limit of Allies retreat,
prior to general advance

Chateau Thierry

Meaux

Montereau

SCHWARTZENBURG
retreats Feb. 18

Paris surrenders
Mar. 30

PARIS

Juvisy

R. Seine

Fontainebleau

NAPOLEON reaches
Fontainebleau
Mar. 30

0   10   20   30   40
Miles

leyrand? Did Napoleon put him in the deepest dungeon of the Château de Vincennes to prevent his fomenting dissatisfaction during this national crisis? Not a bit
of it. Joseph was merely told to watch him closely; he obeyed this instruction by consulting Talleyrand on affairs of state! Joseph and the Empress liked Talleyrand's
company, he was always amusing. Caesar had given Brutus a sharpened dagger and
had obliged him by turning his back.

At midnight on 25 January 1814, Napoleon's coach clattered over the cobbles of
the frosty streets of Châlons-sur-Marne. As it halted and the familiar figure of the
Emperor alighted, rank upon rank of Imperial Guard cavalry rode by, seeking their
billets. Impatiently, Napoleon wanted an update on the situation and an intelligence
report as to the enemy's whereabouts. He was told that the Allies had been advancing on a broad front and the French, through lack of manpower, had been giving
ground. Schwarzenberg's headquarters was at Langres, his advance guard near
Bar-sur-Aube; between the two lay Chaumont where on the 28th the Allied commissioners would meet Caulaincourt to discuss a possible peace plan. Military operations
would continue, however; an armistice was refused. Blücher's Army of Silesia had
advanced 75 miles in nine days, crossing three rivers despite winter flooding and
French resistance. But the need to forage meant that it was advancing on a widely
dispersed front. General Yorck was near Verdun, Blücher and Gneisenau between
Saint-Dizier and Brienne. Blücher was only 93 miles from Paris. Gneisenau wrote to
Schwarzenberg: 'We only need a single battle to make us complete victors. For this
purpose the main army should advance as far as the middle reaches of the Seine, and
the reserves which are to cover its flank and rear should be posted not on the Rhine
but at Châlons-sur-Marne. All we have to do is press on towards Paris without
delay.'[29] Schwarzenberg ignored this sound advice, it being contrary to Metternich's
policy in which, Schwarzenberg wrote to his wife, his loathing for the Prussians is
self-evident:

'Blücher, and still more Gneisenau ... are urging the march on Paris
with such childish rage that they trample underfoot every single rule of warfare. Without placing any considerable force to guard the road from
Châlons to Nancy, they rush like mad to Brienne. Regardless of their rear
and of their flanks, they do nothing but plan fine parties at the Palais
Royal.'[30]

Napoleon, with only his 10,000 Guards and 20,000 raw recruits, advanced on
Blücher's 25,000 men at Brienne. Blücher and Gneisenau, at table in the castle, were
suddenly made aware of Napoleon's attack at about 10 o'clock on 29 January. Feeling secure, they continued their meal, but suddenly the ceiling began to collapse
about their ears. Beating a hasty retreat, the two Prussians only avoided capture by
minutes. Stubborn resistance on the part of Blücher's men turned the piecemeal battle into a stout fighting retreat. In the meantime a Prussian messenger galloped into
the Allied camp, requesting Schwarzenberg to come to Blücher's aid; Napoleon had
but 30,000-odd men, now was the chance for the Allies to encircle and trap him.
Schwarzenberg would not budge. With reluctance, and by dint of the Tsar's inter-

vention, two Russian corps were sent to help Blücher. Next day, 1 February, Blücher counter-attacked Napoleon's force which now numbered some 40,000 men. Leading 53,000 veteran Prussians and Russians, Blücher tore into the French with the cry 'Vorwarts! Vorwarts!', soon to become his nickname. Behind, coming up fast, Napoleon observed another large army – 63,000 Russians sent by the Tsar. Napoleon intended to withdraw, but the savagery of the attack pinned him down. Vicious bayonet and cavalry charges ensued, and only a severe snowstorm saved the situation. Napoleon held his ground until dusk when with great skill and imagination he disengaged from the enemy. Losses were about 6,000 per side. Napoleon could ill-afford these however. His raw conscripts had faced the Allied veterans well. At one point Marmont had asked a young recruit why he was not firing his musket? He replied 'I would sir, if I knew how!' The Marshal dismounted and showed him. The troops lacked numbers but not spirit. Napoleon, demoralized at being defeated on French soil, withdrew first to Troyes then to Nogent. The Allies were jubilant. Napoleon had been defeated! 'Blücher,' exclaimed the Tsar, 'today you have set the crown on all your victories. Mankind will bless you!'[31]

Caulaincourt, who had been waiting at Chaumont for the Allied plenipotentiaries to assemble, was summoned to the first informal meeting on 5 February, the purpose being to inform him that in no circumstances could 'maritime rights be discussed'. It appeared that the meeting was being held to allow the members to gloat at French discomfort. The Russian plenipotentiary was very insulting and tried to impress Caulaincourt with the might and majesty of the assembled coalition. Caulaincourt, with a sweeping gaze that took in the entire assembly, retorted 'I am well aware that France has the honour of being alone,' inference that not one of the four great and seven minor powers save England would dare face France alone. Caulaincourt records: 'Compared to the English, who are men of honour, frank in the defence of their own interests, but straight, the other plenipotentiaries seemed to embody passion, bitterness and resentment.'[32] The next meeting was held on the 7th when, intoxicated by the idea that they had won the war, the Allies arbitrarily informed Caulaincourt that 'France must accept her "ancient limits" of 1792.' Caulaincourt was shocked by the abrupt manner in which this declaration was made. On asking them whether, if these conditions were accepted, all present hostilities would cease, he received no reply except 'perhaps' from the Russian delegate. Austria was certainly not pleased with Russian and Prussian arrogance. Metternich confided to Schwarzenberg, 'I am rather sad, that it [Brienne] did not turn out to be a small defeat for Blücher.'[33]

On the night of 7/8 February, Napoleon received Caulaincourt's letter detailing all that had transpired. The stark reality was brought home to him. Not only was he to be humiliated, but it appeared that he would have to plead for an end to hostilities; he was to be forced to drink the cup of bitterness to the dregs. His rage was 'supernatural... his cries were those of a trapped Lion'. He shut himself up in his room and waited. Blücher was anxious to march on Paris and, surprisingly, was given permission to do so by Schwarzenberg who said that he would remain where he was until peace was concluded. He told Blücher that Napoleon was, '... to an *almost complete certainty*'[34] concentrating at Troyes for 'an attack on the main army' and could Blücher therefore sent Schwarzenberg reinforcements? Blücher obliged by detaching Kleist's corps and those of the Russian General Kapetzewitsch. Sure of victory, Blücher marched off, driving Marmont's small force out of Châlons; his cavalry pursuing Macdonald. Yorck paraded down the Marne towards Château-Thierry. Karpov formed the loose left wing at Sézanne, the other divisions were strung out still farther to the rear. Prussian and Russian depredations, looting, burning and rape, had roused the populace of Champagne. Blücher's army moved through increasingly hostile countryside; patrols disappeared, lone cavalrymen were found crucified on trees. Blücher's staff officer Henri Steffens wrote: 'We felt for the first time thrown back wholly on our own resources. I now perceive that the face of a hostile land wears a mask to the invader; every house and thicket conceals a danger; every object has an ominous meaning, and this character it never loses.'[35]

'My plans are completely changed!' exclaimed Napoleon, leaving his room with Marmont's report in his hand. 'Blücher and Schwarzenberg have separated!' Blücher was strung out on the march and – thanks to the Allied commander – ignorant of Napoleon's position. If that were not enough, he had also given away part of his army! Napoleon assembled his strike force of 30,000 men – which were all that he had to spare; the Emperor Napoleon had reverted to General Napoleon, and in so doing recaptured the genius of his youth. Having crossed the Aube on 10 February, he was about to take the Army of Silesia in the flank when suddenly he came upon the slow-moving corps of General Ossfiev. His pickets driven in, the Russian decided to stand, concentrating his 5,000 men. Napoleon poured shot and shell into the Russian lines. Ossfiev, believing that Blücher would soon come to his succour, stood firm, sustaining terrible casualties. In the afternoon, realizing that he would be overwhelmed, he attempted to withdraw only to find himself enveloped by Napoleon's cavalry. By evening the Russian force had disintegrated; Ossfiev was captured hiding in a wood. Less than 1,000 men escaped. Napoleon had suffered just 200 casualties.

Next day, the 11th, Napoleon advanced west, intending to attack General Sacken's corps of 18,000 men. With him he had his Imperial Guard and a division of conscripts under General Ricard, all told 10,500 men and 36 guns. Passing through Montmirail, he and Sacken sighted each other. The Russian launched a full corps attack which was stopped short by the Imperial Guard. Napoleon was then alerted to the advance guard of Yorck's corps, some 3,000 men, advancing from the north down the Château-Thierry road. Using Ricard's men to hold them, he sent for Marshal Mortier who forced-marched to Napoleon's right flank. Holding both forces in play until 4 o'clock when Mortier was in position, he then switched to the offensive against Sacken and by evening had routed both Sacken and Yorck's forces, sending them scurrying in different directions. Blücher's army suffered 4,000 losses and 80 guns, Napoleon 2,000, half of whom had succumbed to fatigue. Next day at Château-Thierry, where two bridges had been hastily thrown across the Marne, the Allies had to fight two terrible rearguard actions, which caused them further huge losses, in order to get the security of the Marne between them and Napoleon. Meanwhile Blücher's 15,000 men had remained stationary, awaiting news from the rest of his Army of Silesia – blissfully unaware that it had been defeated in detail.

During the evening of 12 February, he received news of Yorck's retreat. Not realizing its true import, he advanced towards Etages on the 13th. Repulsing a French division, he advanced towards Montmirail. In the interim Napoleon had called in all his available troops and stood 50,000-strong. General von Ziethen, leading the advance Prussian column, approached the town of Vauchamps and was repelled so violently that he fell back on Blücher's main force in total disorder. Next, Napoleon's cavalry swept the Prussian cavalry from the field. Only then did the awful truth dawn on Blücher; here was Napoleon, and what remained of his army was not coming to his aid – it had been destroyed. Blücher's one thought was to get away before it was too late. Pursued by cavalry, he narrowly escaped capture or death from Napoleon's élite horse grenadiers of his personal guard. Steffens says: 'I was with Blücher and his staff, who, separated from the main body and escorted by only a few troops, brought up the rear. Then we saw the enemy on the hills on both sides. Shells burst close to us; cannon-balls fell thicker into the midst of us; the musketry began to be destructive as the enemy approached; and even some single cavalry soldiers tried to hew their way into the midst of us. They were wrapped in white cloaks, and wore immense bearskins, which half-covered their faces.'[36]

The Army of Silesia had been broken and defeated in detail. Three battles in five days – 16,000 Allied losses. Schwarzenberg only avoided annihilation because – Napoleon having rejected the Allies' terms and taken the offensive – the Austrians under pressure from the Tsar and King William reluctantly allowed him to move his 170,000 men towards Paris. Metternich had reasoned privately that this move might bring Napoleon back to the peace table. In the meantime he had wrung a written statement out of Castlereagh that Britain would accept Napoleon as sovereign if he agreed to the 1792 boundaries.[37] At the same time, Castlereagh wrote to the Cabinet and the Prince Regent assuring them that he would accept nothing less than the restitution of the Bourbons, which the Prince Regent was adamant should take place.[38]

The Army of Bohemia, its commander reluctant to commit this 'last Austrian Army' to battle, had slowly been advancing on Paris since 10 February. After a brisk skirmish his leading corps had forced its way across the River Yonne and occupied Fontainebleau. By the 15th, Schwarzenberg had four army corps on a 30-mile front, eighteen miles from Paris. At Fontainebleau on the Allied left, was the Austrian Bianchi's corps. Next, at Melun, astride the road, was Eugène of Württemberg's corps. On his right, before Guignes, was Count Pahlen and to his right, forming the right flank, Wittgenstein. Schwarzenberg himself was leading from the rear with another two corps, Gyulai's at Villeneuve, Wrede's at Donnemarie. Prince Lichtenstein with the combined reserve was between Sens and Joigny.

Count Pahlen with 5,000 men of the advance guard, faced Marshals Oudinot and Macdonald at Guignes. Soon the roads would converge and Schwarzenberg's army would be forced to concentrate in front of Paris whether he liked it or not. The Tsar was already drawing up orders for the parade. Suddenly news arrived that various corps of Blücher's army were being attacked – a halt was called. The Austrians advocated retreat. General Knesebeck, King William of Prussia's adviser, whose word was always law, expressed his opinion that Blücher might have been beaten because of his march on Paris. What if the populace were aroused? The fear of the revolutionary fervour that had turned France into an armed camp of three million men haunted the coalition. What if it should spread? Prussia was already in the grip of a nationalistic euphoria that was only being contained by channelling it into the war. The Tsar's adviser, Baron Stein, was the promoter of a pan-German confederation – prudence must be applied. The Tsar was furious but in this instance Prussia agreed with Austria. The Allies remained static and waited throughout 15 to 17 February, 'in order to await the development of Napoleon's manoeuvres', Schwarzenberg declared, though in fact the Allies had a crisis of their own to resolve.

Napoleon, meanwhile, coming down from Vauchamps like an avalanche, had reached Meaux; on the 16th his army reached Guignes. On the morning of the 17th Count Pahlen was rudely awakened to find Victor's corps falling upon him; the French cavalry drove his cavalry from the field, and his infantry, throwing away their equipment, followed close on their heels – eight battalions and 24 squadrons routed. The French cavalry, advancing towards Nogent, overthrew Wrede's cavalry division en route. Fanning out, Oudinot turned to his left and drove into Wittgenstein's corps. Macdonald, behind, drove forward into Wrede. Victor, turning to the right, aimed for Montereau – if he could seize the bridge Württemberg and Bianchi's corps would be cut off. Napoleon pressed on, driving Schwarzenberg before him. He had driven into the middle of the Allied army, separated each flank and driven back the centre. Victor, who had been fighting since dawn, arrived at the heavily defended bridge at 7 o'clock – it had been dark since 4 o'clock. By morning Württemberg and Bianchi had fled in disorder, loosing guns, ammunition, equipment and transports.

In desperation, Schwarzenberg resorted to a downright lie. He sent Count Paar under truce to Napoleon with a letter to Berthier: 'Having received intelligence that preliminaries of peace were signed at Châtillon yesterday on the basis of the conditions proposed by the duc de Vicence [Caulaincourt] and accepted by the Allied sovereigns, I have countermanded all offensive movements against the French army. Your offensive operations, however, are being continued, and I suggest that they should cease equally with mine.'[39] Napoleon was not deceived. Writing to Joseph that night he said: 'An absurd proposition, which would make me lose the advantages of my manoeuvres.'[40] Keeping Paar waiting for three days at his outposts, Napoleon continued his advance, driving all the Allies before him. This was more punishment than Schwarzenberg could accept for his army, the instrument of Habsburg power. He retreated at top speed, sending all the baggage back to Bar-sur-Aube, and ordering his dispersed and routed forces to make for Troyes.

During these five hectic days Blücher rallied what was left of his army; with reinforcements it numbered some 48,000 effectives. He remained at Châlons and was deciding to effect a junction with the main army at Aube. 'We acted as if we had not been beaten,' wrote Gneisenau[41] – but they had been, and badly. Schwarzenberg had received news that Marshal Augereau was advancing from Lyons towards Geneva. Fearing for his line of communications, on 22 February he ordered a further retreat to Chaumont. The Allies agreed that a fresh request be made to Napoleon for an armistice, while their demoralized troops, half-starved and half-frozen from bivouacking in the snow, having already retreated 70 miles, continued to fall back, 'Which seems likely to come to an end only on the farther side of the Rhine,' observed a staff officer.

Prince Lichtenstein met the Emperor at Chartres. Napoleon was in no mood to be lenient: had not the Allies been insulting to him and his representative? Did not the Allies wish to replace him with a Bourbon? Prince Lichtenstein truthfully replied that as far as Austria was concerned they wished only for peace. Napoleon dismissed him with a personal letter to the Austrian Emperor. He would not grant an armistice; that would only enable the Allies to regroup, but he would send an envoy to discuss peace terms – while hostilities continued. Napoleon felt himself to be in the military ascendancy once more, having now reversed the positions since la Rothière, and soundly defeated both Allied armies, sending them scuttling back towards the border.

On 24 February Napoleon entered Troyes, the monarchs having beaten a hasty retreat. The bells were pealing, and the inhabitants cheered him for having delivered them from the depredations of the Prussians and Russians. During their occupation several royalists had come out wearing white cockades and proclaiming Louis XVIII. Among them was the Chevalier Gouault, under mandatory sentence of death by the republic; Napoleon had allowed him home under a general amnesty. He, and a few like-minded *émigrés*, had met the Tsar and asked for arms and support for the Bourbons. 'Gentlemen', he had replied, 'you are a little premature.' Alexander had other plans in mind. In his zeal Gouault had worn the hated Cross of Saint-Louis, a mark of nobility and privilege, banned by the republic. He had also trampled the tricolore in the mud. Now, to cries of '*A bas les traitres!*', the Chevalier was hauled out of his town house by the soldiers. With a placard stating '*traitre*' hung around his neck, he was taken with others to the town square. At a drum-head court-martial more than forty townsfolk testified to their treason. 'Guilty! Execute them at once,' the town major had ordered. As Napoleon rode past the square a body lay trampled in the mud, wearing the Cross of Saint-Louis.

On 26 February Napoleon was in occupation of Troyes with 74,000 men and 350 guns, concentrated between the Seine and the Aube. To his front, retreating on Chaumont and Langres, Schwarzenberg's main Allied army had been reduced to 120,000 men. On Napoleon's left was Blücher's army of 48,000, facing Marshals Marmont and Mortier's 16,000 men. General Allix was defending the line of the Yonne with 2,000 men. In the south Augereau was moving his 28,000 men against the 20,000 Austrians of Bubna. He had express orders to retake Geneva and position himself across the Basle–Langres road, cutting Schwarzenberg's communications.

Napoleon's situation was improving. Day by day recruits were arriving in Paris from all parts of France, and fitted-out companies were marching to replace the casualties of battle and fatigue.[42] Napoleon had not lost sight of the fact that he had many more troops locked up in the border garrisons; if he could release some of them to join his forces in the south what could he not accomplish?

Meanwhile the erstwhile Allies had had problems of their own on the diplomatic front. While Schwarzenberg was advancing towards Paris with all the enthusiasm of a condemned man going to the scaffold, the 'crisis of Troyes' on the 10th had come close to splitting the Alliance apart. The Tsar had arbitrarily suspended the peace negotiations at Châtillon without reference to his allies. From his headquarters at Troyes, with the support of the Prussian generals and after the victory of la Rothière, he had decided that the road to Paris was open and that it was from there that peace should be dictated. Schwarzenberg pointed out that the Allied armies were rapidly disintegrating through sickness and hunger, desertion was rife, and Napoleon was even now receiving reinforcements from the south.[43] Hardenberg, Metternich and, especially, Castlereagh all took the view that if peace on the 'ancient limits' were possible, it would be wrong to incur casualties and possible defeat by prolonging the war. At this juncture the commissioners believed that Napoleon would have to accept the offer, and by so doing would be overthrown by his own people. The Tsar replied through Nesselrode that 'a majority vote' would not be acceptable. Metternich retorted that the Russian Emperor's tyrannical approach was unacceptable; it might be in Austria's interest to withdraw the imperial army and make a separate peace with Napoleon![44] Castlereagh, desperate to hold together the coalition, then formulated an ultimatum – diplomatically called a protocol – wherein Napoleon was to be offered an immediate armistice, conditional on his surrendering the fortresses of Antwerp, Mainz, Mantua, Bergen-op-Zoom, Besançon and Hüningen; peace negotiations to be opened on the 'ancient limits'. Metternich and Castlereagh suggested that refusal by the Tsar would disrupt the coalition and Austria would withdraw its army and Britain its subsidies and *matériel* – the Russian navy was not mentioned, but hung in the balance.

Castlereagh was charged by the other delegates to deliver this protocol. His own sentiments, as has been noted, were basically in sympathy with those of the Tsar, but to coax Austria into the position he desired, it was necessary to accede to the peace proposals. If Napoleon were going to be replaced and another ambitious general prevented from taking the throne, Castlereagh needed Austrian help. He personally had added the conditions concerning the fortresses, knowing that Austria and Prussia wanted their key fortresses of Mantua and Hüningen as much as he wanted Antwerp. Castlereagh adjudged rightly that the surrender of Antwerp, his primary armaments source, would be unacceptable to Napoleon. Castlereagh was suddenly embarrassed by the Tsar who, perceiving that Castlereagh was playing a double game, rounded on him, saying that his policy was not British policy. Had not the Prince Regent and the British government stated that peace could only be achieved with the removal of Bonaparte and the return of the Bourbons? He had a letter from his ambassador Lieven in London, enclosing a letter from the British cabinet to this effect.[45] Neither was Castlereagh accurately representing British public opinion. Castlereagh extricated himself from this predicament by stating quite correctly that, as the 'man on the spot' his mandate from the government authorized him to formulate whatever policy he deemed necessary. Further, he expressed grave doubts that Lieven had reported Britain's sentiments accurately. The growing animosity engendered by this impasse, which had halted Schwarzenberg's army for three days in a vulnerable position, in which it had been attacked, now seemed set to tear the coalition apart.

News of the defeats at Champaubert, Montmirail and Vauchamps had scarcely reached the shocked Tsar and King William, when the torrent of refugees from the defeat at Montereau began to appear. This temporarily put a stop to the dangerous political wrangling at Allied headquarters. The Tsar was deflated, muttering that it was Dresden all over again. The Prussian Chancellor Hardenberg wrote in his diary: 'The Tsar has gone to pieces and the King [Frederick William] talks all the time like Cassandra [the Trojan gifted with the prophesy of doom].'[46] Tsar Alexander exclaimed to the commissioners: 'I shall never make peace so long as Napoleon is on the throne.'[47] Castlereagh suddenly understood the Tsar's dogmatic stance – he was mortally afraid of Napoleon; so long as he was in power, Alexander would not feel safe, even in Moscow.

The next diplomatic bombshell was Napoleon's letter of 21 February to the Emperor of Austria who passed it to Metternich for his comments. The letter began: 'Sir, my brother and very dear father-in-law', but then blazed with all the old authority:

'I have ... destroyed the Prussian and the Russian armies ... I urge your Imperial Majesty to make peace with me on the basis of the Frankfurt proposals ... There is not a Frenchman who would not rather die than accept conditions that would erase France from the map of Europe and render her people the slaves of England ... What interest could your Imperial Majesty have in placing the Belgians under the yoke of a Protestant Prince, one of whose sons will become the King of England?'[48]

This last alluding to the proposed engagement of the Prince of Orange with the Prince Regent's daughter, for the purpose of forming just such a union. Napoleon would not cede ground on Belgium; from Austria's point of view it was a moot point. Belgium had been a Habsburg province since 1477 when Nancy, daughter of the last Duke of Burgundy, Charles the Bold, presented it to her husband Maximilian of Austria as her dowry. Maximilian's grandson became Charles V, King of Spain. It later reverted to the Austrian branch in 1555. Its legitimate rulers had therefore been the House of Habsburg, before the French seized it during the Revolution. Three hundred years makes a very good legal title. But the Emperor of Austria, ever a stickler for protocol, had renounced this sovereignty and ceded it to France.

The Austrian Emperor asked Metternich, if Belgium were the sole sticking point to peace, why not concede it? Besides, would not his grandson inherit it in due course? Was it not their agreed policy to leave Napoleon behind a reduced frontier as support against Russian and Prussian aggrandisement in the east?[49] He went further, sending a personal instruction to Schwarzenberg, forbidding him to cross the Seine without his permission. As predicted by Napoleon, the Alliance looked as if it would break up through its own differences.

How then could Castlereagh resolve these impasses? The Tsar wanted Napoleon removed at all costs on grounds of European security, but proposed replacing him with another ambitious general who, in gratitude, would turn his back while the Tsar carved up eastern Europe and the Baltic *à la Napoléon*. Castlereagh had written to the Prime Minister that he was alarmed: '... by learning that the Prince Royal of Sweden was on the point of arriving at the Rhine, with the intention of immediately putting himself at the head of Winzingerode's corps, being the division of his army most advanced in the interior, viz., near Rheims.'[50]

At this critical juncture Napoleon needed a statesman of stature and political guile such as Talleyrand, who would have immediately seized this opportunity and exploited it. His representative Caulaincourt had been ambassador to Russia and was more a courtier than a statesman. Having won four resounding victories against such odds, Napoleon could have expected Caulaincourt to press his case for the Frankfurt terms 'while the Allies had the option'. Instead he sat meekly while they presented a new ultimatum, while their armies were retreating 70-odd miles and trying to put a major river between them and Napoleon. Personally, Caulaincourt was desperate for peace – and it showed – but he was indecisive and unable to accept responsibility. For the best part of a fortnight he had had Napoleon's *carte blanche* in his pocket to make peace on the best possible terms, but he hesitated. Now Napoleon had revoked the letter and ordered him to present the Allies with *his* ultimatum – the Frankfurt terms or no deal. He was too afraid to give it to the Allies and too scared to tell Napoleon. Never had Napoleon needed Talleyrand more than now, but it was too late. At the beginning of 1813 he had offered the foreign ministry back to Talleyrand who had refused it, saying, 'I am no longer familiar with your affairs.' Napoleon had retorted 'Then you are against me?' to which Talleyrand had offered no reply.

It was now that Castlereagh came into his own. To Metternich he said: 'I cannot express to you how much I regret the proposition of an armistice which Prince Schwarzenberg appears to have made under the sanction of the Emperor of Russia and the King of Prussia... Recollect what your military position is. You have 200,000 men in France yet unbroken ... If we act with military and political prudence, how can France resist a just peace demanded by 600,000 warriors?'[51] At this point, apparently, Castlereagh suggested that peace could not be found while Napoleon was on the throne – even as security for Austria. What would stop Napoleon building up a new army in a year or two and retaking all he had lost? What if Austria withdrew her forces and Russia, Prussia and Great Britain saw it through? What would Austria then gain with a Russian nominee on the throne of France? Poland! What of Poland and Saxony in those circumstances? Austria would be isolated and in a worse position than before. However, If a neutral Bourbon were placed on the throne, would that not secure Austria from French aggression? Further, if Austria had possession of the Empress and her son, would that not be a trump card to hold as security for French future behaviour? Could not Francis take up his grandson's inheritance whenever he needed to? Would not Italy be more secure if the King of Rome resided at Vienna? Under these circumstances Great Britain would be prepared to form an alliance to support Austria for up to twenty years after the present conflict. Metternich accepted this proposal in its entirety.

Next, Castlereagh had a meeting with the Tsar along the same lines. Peace could only be guaranteed by the removal of Napoleon. All other issues should be decided at a congress of the four superpowers after the conflict was over. Without Austria it was doubtful if they could win. Austria might not accept the replacement of its Emperor's daughter and grandson by another general and his family. But Austria might, if its ancient 'legitimate' monarch were restored. Might not Austria and the people of France wish for a regency under the Empress and her son? What then? Would Russia continue the war – possibly a civil war – on this point? Was not the greater principle the overthrow and removal of Napoleon? The Tsar agreed to a treaty on these terms – if Austria would accept them. He would not commit himself on the issue of a replacement, but he sent a curt letter to the Crown Prince of Sweden telling him that Winzingerode and Bülow's corps would be detached from his army and sent to Blücher. Which everyone thought seemed to indicate that the had made up his mind with regard to the Crown Prince's prospects of advancement.[52]

The Emperor of Austria sent an unfavourable reply to his son-in-law, expressing his disgust that Napoleon had refused an armistice; he would not have done so if he sincerely desired peace. At least this was the diplomatic reply. On 1 March 1814, Castlereagh's Treaty of Chaumont was signed, appropriately, on a card table. In essence it bound the four powers to continue the present war with armies of 150,000 men each until their objectives were attained. These were defined as: an independent Holland with Belgium as a barrier; a confederate Germany; an independent Switzerland; a free Spain under a Bourbon; restitution of the Italian states. The league was both defensive and offensive; no single power could conclude a peace without the agreement of all. It bound each power to support with at least 60,000 men any of the others in the event of any aggression against any one of them for a period of twenty years after the present conflict. Lord Castlereagh wrote jubilantly to Mr Hamilton, the permanent Under-Secretary of State:

'I send you my treaty, which I hope you will approve. We four Ministers, when signing, happened to be sitting at a Whist table. It was agreed that never were the stakes so high at any former party. My modesty prevented me offering it; but, as they chose to make us a military Power, I was determined not to play second fiddle. The fact is, that upon the face of the treaty this year, our engagement is equivalent to theirs united. We give 150,000 men and £5,000,000, equal to as many more – total 300,000. They give 450,000, of which we, however, supply 150,000, leaving their own number 300,000. The fact, however, is that, sick, lame, and lazy, they pay a great number more. On the other hand, we give to the value of 125,000 men [Wellington's] beyond the 300,000 [the £5,000,000 in lieu]. What an extraordinary display of power! This, I trust, will put an end to any doubts as to the claim we have to an opinion on continental matters.'[53]

And so it came to pass that Napoleon's overtures, and the Allied offers were both in turn rejected. Napoleon had no knowledge of the Treaty of Chaumont, and on 7 March Schwarzenberg drew up an operational memorandum stipulating that the Allied objective was Paris. To the surprise of all present, Austria's operational head-quarters seem to come alive and began to process orders and movements at an unprecedented rate.

While this diplomatic solution was formulating, military activity had continued. Napoleon had been unable to continue the rout of Schwarzenberg's army because he had no pontoon boats available, General Clarke his war minister having failed to send them from Paris. On 26 February Napoleon had written to Clarke: 'If I had had a pontoon bridge, the war would be over, and Schwarzenberg's Army would no longer exist ... For want of boats, I could not pass the Seine at the necessary points. It was not 50 boats that I needed, only 20.'[54] This failure to continue the harrying of Schwarzenberg enabled him to regroup and hold his new position in strength. Mean-while Blücher had received a letter from King William: 'The expected truce has not come to pass. Accordingly my orders to you of yesterday lose their validity. It has now been decided that Prince Schwarzenberg's army ... shall continue its retreat. Henceforth the outcome of this Campaign depends on you.'[55] He was also informed that the Tsar had ordered Winzingerode to place his Army of the North, to which had been added von Bülow's corps, under Blücher's command. They would be marching to his aid from Laon via Soissons. Blücher was then to march on Paris as and when circumstances permitted.

Napoleon was surprised to hear of Blücher's army moving from Châlons, think-ing it too weak to take the offensive again. Unable to attack the Army of Bohemia, he decided to crush Blücher. Sending Ney and Victor north to fall on his rear, and Marmont and Mortier to his front, Napoleon repaired to Arcis-sur-Aube to control the situation and smite his flank, thereby closing the trap. Blücher, advancing his 42,000 men from la Ferté-Gaucher, tried to cross the River Ourcq between Meaux and la Ferté-Milon, held by Marmont and Mortier with their 16,000 men. Hoping to gain the road to Paris and meet his reinforcements coming down from Soissons, Blücher, fearful of the prospect of having Napoleon at his heels, destroyed the bridges over the Marne behind him.

Blücher now felt rather proud of having as it were 'gained the central position' between Napoleon and Marmont, but trying to force the river in the face of Mar-mont was another matter. For all his faults, and they were many, Marmont had the courage, pride and spirit of a lion. He attacked Blücher with such vigour as to stop the Prussian cold. Blücher, wondering how many men this Frenchmen had with him, was apprised by his cavalry that Napoleon had crossed the Marne at la Ferté-sous-Jouarre and at Château-Thierry. Napoleon had with him only 26,000 men. He had left Macdonald and Oudinot 40,000 men to confront the Army of Bohemia, and told them that he would be back in three days. Blücher and Napoleon had equal numbers, but the Prussian, even with his veterans, decided not try the issue with the master, but cut and run northwards, there to join his reinforcements. Sandwiched against the River Ourcq, with Marmont on his left and Napoleon to his right and rear, his army marched at a prodigious rate! They were worn out, their clothes were in tatters and they had had little or no food for a week. The going was appalling; heavy snow had turned to slush and then to mud. Churned up by thousands of horses, wagons and cannon, the Prussians were soon knee-deep in the mire, losing boots and equipment, and constantly hard pressed by Marmont, Mortier and, finally, by Ney. Napoleon decided to crush Blücher on the morrow, 3 March, before he could cross the River Aisne, Blücher being, '... very embarrassed by the Mire'; then he would turn into Lorraine and rescue the garrisons of Verdun, Toul and Metz – some 15,000 men to augment his force. He wrote to General Durutte to break out, assemble the other garrisons and march to meet him.

The Nordic gods were with Blücher that night. A clear sky produced an excellent frost that froze the mud, enabling the weary Prussians to reach and cross the Aisne at Soissons and join von Bülow, who was besieging the garrison of some 700 loyal Poles. Its commander, however, a general named Moreau – and just about as loyal as his dead namesake – surrendered without much of a fight. Bülow, whose own men had spent the winter progressing from one warm billet to another, remarked within earshot of its men that the Army of Silesia 'led the field in shabbiness' and, writing to the king, said: 'All discipline and order are dissolved, and I confess to our shame that it looks like a band of robbers.'[56] The Russian General Winzingerode came in later with his 30,000 men from Rheims; Blücher was disgusted that he had not taken the shortest route so as to have come to his assistance the sooner. It sometimes seemed to the Prussian commanders of the Army of Silesia that they were fighting this war alone.

Blücher's army now totalled 119,000 men – on paper. His effectives numbered 80-82,000. Napoleon had some 40-42,000 men. Hearing that Napoleon had crossed the Aisne at Berry-au-Bac, Blücher guessed rightly enough that he would advance towards him along the Chemin des Dames road that formed the base line of an isosceles triangle whose apex was the natural fortress town of Laon. This road would carry Napoleon to the Laon-Paris road above Soissons and back to the Rheims-Châlons road if necessary. It ran across a natural plateau, but formed a bottle-neck at Craonne. The sides of the road were steeply wooded, and Blücher decided to await Napoleon here. Because of the limited area for deployment, he placed Woronzoff's Russian corps in front, supported behind by Sacken – in total some 30,000 men. In the wooded valley to his left, below the plateau, 10,000 cavalry were placed under Winzingerode, the hesitant Russian. Count Langeron, the *émigré* Frenchman in Russian service, had 10,000 men at Soissons; Bülow had another 20-30,000 men at Laon. Napoleon, blissfully unaware of Blücher's strength, advanced with 25,000 men; Mortier bringing up 3,500 men to the rear and Marmont, the farthest away, some ten miles off, 9,500 men. There at Craonne on 7 March was fought one of the bloodiest battles of the war. Blücher had planned to await Napoleon's attack, then launch his 10,000 cavalry and 60 guns against the French flank and rear. Winzingerode, however, perhaps adhering to the previous policy of avoiding battle, had ridden off in the wrong direction. Five times Marshal Ney lead his men up the slopes, only to be turned back. When Napoleon arrived, a sixth attack by the artillery and cavalry of the Guard battered in the defence. Blücher, unable to bring up anything on Napoleon's flank, retreated on Laon. Both sides had sustained about 7,000 casualties.

One more victory, Napoleon thought, having now been informed of the Treaty of Chaumont, would lower the Allies' terms. Meanwhile Blücher had deployed some 80,000 men around Laon, a large, hill-top town on a plateau. Napoleon intended to advance by both roads to this apex himself with 24,500 men up the Soissons road, whence he had pursued Blücher; Marmont with his belated 9,500 up the Rheims road. Napoleon still perceiving Blücher as having some 30-35,000 men. On 9 March he advanced to attack. A thick frosty fog in the early morning enabled the French to deploy unseen. Napoleon commanded the left wing with his Guard under Ney; Marmont, commanding the right wing and having the greatest distance to travel, had not yet arrived but was expected.

Three villages formed the natural bulwarks of Laon: in front of Ney, Sémilly and Ardon, in front of Marmont's route Athies. At 9 o'clock the struggle began; by mid-morning the mist had cleared to reveal Napoleon's weakness, but Blücher still stood in defence. He couldn't bring himself to believe that Napoleon would launch an all-out assault with only 20,000 men, but on the other hand he couldn't be certain. He sent in a massive reconnaissance force which drove into the middle of Napoleon's line, or so Blücher thought; it was in fact Napoleon's right. There was nothing there! Marmont had not yet come up. Again, Blücher failed to exploit this situation – the aura of apprehension that Napoleon inspired giving pause even to this old warhorse, ever wary and fearful that a hidden reserve was about to outflank him. Then Marmont appeared. Faithful to his orders, he launched his 9,500 men against Athies, forcing his way in by midday against Generals Yorck and Bülow's veteran 30,000 Prussian veterans. From one of the buildings he saw all the enemy troops in front of him. Behind them, in column upon column beyond Laon were Generals Langeron and Sacken's reserve of another 25,000 men. With only 9,000 men left, Marmont couldn't possibly turn Blücher's right so he sent messengers over to his left to apprise Napoleon, but Prussian cavalry were occupying this area and contact was impossible. Napoleon, convinced that Blücher was about to pull out of Laon – and still unaware of the Prussians' true strength – held his position until nightfall. He was deliberating his course of action for the next day when two of Marmont's dragoons were brought to him. In the darkness, while his exhausted conscripts had been foraging, collecting brushwood and preparing their bivouacs, Blücher, having determined Marmont's numbers from the heights of Laon, had launched Yorck in a night attack, hoping to destroy him, and in the morning turn Napoleon's flank. A sudden volley, and the glimmer in the fire-light of thousands of bayonets coming on in earnest had routed Marmont's exhausted men. Thousands of Prussian cavalry erupted on them with lance and sabre, hacking and killing, and panicking the French cavalry which, in the confusion of trying to mount up, had no cohesion. The virtual annihilation of Marmont's force and loss of French honour had been prevented by 125 grenadiers of Napoleon's Old Guard. Assigned to protect the wagons, they were encamped near a defile when the French cavalry and infantry, pursued by the Prussians, poured round them. Forming up three-deep across the defile, huge men in greatcoats and tall bearskins, renowned and feared throughout Europe, fire-light picking out the line of bayonets, they poured volley after volley from their muskets; fallen and flailing horses helped block the way. Fearing that they were facing Napoleon, whose presence on the battlefield was always marked by these grenadiers, the entire Prussian cavalry retreated.

Even so, Marmont had lost some 2,000 men. Napoleon, realizing that he had insufficient men to beat Blücher, decided to return to his main army. He had heard that Macdonald and Oudinot had been unable to conceal his absence and were giving ground to the Austrians. Further, that a Russian corps of the other *émigré* general, Saint-Priest, had captured Rheims. He would wipe out Saint-Priest and return via that city.

What now was there to prevent Blücher and his 80,000 men falling on the rear of Napoleon's 27,000? Nothing, except that Blücher had been taken ill with an inflammation of the eyes and ears, coupled with a soaring temperature that had brought on a rigor (with delirium). At his headquarters consternation reigned. Under Prussian regulations the next senior general should assume command. This was General Langeron but he, aware that the Prussians would not wish to serve under a French commander of Russian forces, pointed out that under Russian regulations General Gneisenau, the chief of staff should take charge. General Yorck, the hero of Tauroggen, the only general to have exercised independent Prussian command during the period 1808 to 1813, was outraged. This, coming on top of the fact that Gneisenau had been chosen instead of him to help in the army reform programme, was the last straw. He wrote a note to Blücher telling him that he was going home on 'sick' leave effective immediately, got into his coach and headed for Germany. Only a letter from Blücher, his hand held by Gneisenau, brought him back.

While this game of musical chairs was being played around the ailing Prussian commander, Napoleon had reached Rheims. On the afternoon of 13 March Saint-Priest, who had been sent there to re-establish communications with Blücher, looked out from his imposing command post in the château and suddenly saw French soldiers advancing out of the grey mist of a late winter's day. Soon the attack was on. At 10 o'clock that night the Russians tried to launch a counter-attack but it ended in their own rout. By midnight Napoleon had brought up a heavy siege battery and was pounding them. Saint-Priest was killed. The French inhabitants had illuminated every window, which 'would have allowed one to have picked up a needle anywhere'. Napoleon sent in his heavy cavalry and by half-past midnight Rheims was his again.

News of Napoleon's return soon reached Schwarzenberg, who immediately started to retreat – in what was becoming known as 'the Austrian manner'. Alone, Napoleon remained unbroken and appeared invincible. All the other Allied leaders, save Wellington, had at one time or another bent under his blows, all had bowed before him in the past. But, as in 1813, during his absence his marshals had fallen short of his high endeavour – save Davout who held Hamburg and the north for him. Suchet was locked in Catalonia. Soult he just heard had put on a bold front at Bayonne but Wellington had surprised and beaten him at Orthez. What to do? Emperor, commander-in-chief, now his own general officer commanding in the field, Napoleon decided to advance his 30,000 men against Schwarzenberg's 120,000 and try to rout him and drive him back to the Rhine.

From Rheims on 17 March he dictated his last proposal for peace. Although the Allies' time limit of 11 March had expired, an extension was granted in deference to Caulaincourt, 'in order that he might persuade his master to see reason'. Napoleon demanded that the Allies evacuate French territory. When that was done he would give up Holland, and Belgium could become an independent country under a 'French Prince' of the old order. He would also renounce any claims to Germany. All he claimed was the return of the French overseas colonies. England would not countenance this, and Austria had already made up its mind to repossess its 'borrowed' princess and her child as interest. The Tsar would not sleep soundly until the elusive grey-coated bogeyman was removed. The congress therefore broke off further discussions.

On 18 March Napoleon, assuming that Schwarzenberg was still retreating, crossed the river with his army of 25,000 men at Arcis-sur-Aube. To the north of him was Macdonald with 30,000 men. Guarding Paris were Marmont and Mortier with some 10,000 men. In front of Napoleon were General Wrede's Bavarian corps and hordes of Cossacks. Of a sudden the entire Allied cavalry appeared and drove in the Guard cavalry division and Exelmans' heavy division which retreated to the bridge. Napoleon got there first. Standing in his stirrups he shouted: 'Who will cross the bridge before me? Napoleon does not retreat before a few bandits! Would you run from Bavarians?' Shamed, the cavalry returned faster than they had come. Then calmly, as though on parade, he brought up the Imperial Guard infantry to the front of the bridge, placing each battalion personally. Ney beat off the Bavarians. The Old Guard stood impassive and immovable, withstanding countless charges by the massed Allied cavalry. A shell landed under Napoleon's horse, killing it. Napoleon calmly got up off the ground and mounted another. Next morning he sent out his cavalry to reconnoitre. Behind the ridge they found the entire Allied army in a great arc. Ranged in seemingly endless columns, all their cannon placed in the intervals, 100,000 men waited for Napoleon to attack with fewer than 30,000. On receiving this intelligence, Napoleon withdrew his army across the river. Sitting on a chair by the bridge, attended by one division of General Leval's veterans from Spain, Napoleon was his own rearguard. By the time that Schwarzenberg realized that Napoleon was withdrawing and had ordered an advance, the army was safely across.

Once again the spirit of Napoleon, his charisma, his aura, had inspired his men and frightened his enemies.

Napoleon now decided that he would advance east and, having gathered the men from the border garrisons, throw his army across Schwarzenberg's rear and force him to withdraw into Lorraine. He had strong reasons to believe that Marshal Augereau, reinforced by some of Suchet's troops, would march from the south and help to trap the Austrians. Would not then his father-in-law make peace? If not, he would have gained a breathing-space and collected a sizeable force into the bargain. Besides, the comte d'Artois, Louis's brother, was in Nancy, wearing a National Guard uniform and trying to persuade the inhabitants to rally to the Bourbon flag. Napoleon might be able to cut him off and capture him – he had a personal debt to settle with 'Monsieur'.[57]

Before departing, Napoleon took time to write a hurried letter to the Empress:
'Mon amie

I have been in the saddle all the last few days. On the 20th I took Arcis-sur-Aube. The enemy attacked me there at 6 o'clock in the evening; I beat him the same day, killing 4,000. I took 2 of his guns; he took two of mine, which leaves us quits. On the 21st, the enemy army formed up in battle array for the purpose of covering the advance of his convoys towards Brienne and Bar-sur-Aube. *I have decided to make for the Marne and his line of communications, in order to push him back further from Paris and draw nearer to his fortress. I shall be at Saint-Dizier this afternoon.* Adieu, mon amie. A kiss for my son. NAPOLEON.'[58]

Entrusting this letter to an imperial courier, Napoleon marched his army east. The courier headed west towards Paris, but he and the letter were captured by marauding Cossacks of the Army of Silesia.

Meanwhile, a Parisian had arrived at Allied headquarters, one Eugène de Vitrolles, a former *émigré* who had returned under Napoleon's amnesty. Napoleon had elevated him to a barony in 1809 and appointed him a councillor of state. An ultra-royalist, described as being 'more royal than the royals', this 'gentleman' had approached Talleyrand through the offices of Baron Dalberg, a naturalized Frenchman of German birth, on behalf of the royalist cliques in the city who supported the Bourbons' restoration. Talleyrand was quick to grasp a golden opportunity to rise once again on the world stage. After much stage-managed reflection, Talleyrand accepted and arranged for Vitrolles to carry an unsigned message to the Allies and to the comte d'Artois. The message was in two parts, the first cryptic and, to identify the sender, written in secret ink on paper bearing the Dalberg arms: 'Receive the person I send you in all confidence. Listen to him and recognize me. It is time to be clearer. You are walking on crutches use your legs and will what is in your power.'[59] The second part was verbal. The Allies would at once would 'recognize' Talleyrand and listen to him through Vitrolles. 'Walking on crutches', not only expressed the wish for the Allies to hasten, but further helped identify the lame Talleyrand. Vitrolles, under various aliases, set out on his 150-mile journey from Paris through the

French lines to the Allies' camp.

He arrived on 17 March and had several meetings with the Tsar and, more significantly, with Metternich and Castlereagh. At about the same time, Napoleon's captured letter arrived at Blücher's headquarters. Blücher and Gneisenau read it and had several copies made. Blücher sent the original on to Marie-Louise with his apologies. Then, sending a copy to Schwarzenberg, he wasted no time in setting the Army of Silesia to advance on Paris. Too ill to sit a horse, he was conveyed in a carriage, wearing a lady's green bonnet to shade his inflamed eyes.

Vitrolles, meanwhile, was informing the Tsar that 'France is ready to declare for the Bourbons'. The Tsar, incredulous as he sometimes appeared, could not accept this. Talleyrand's help he would accept – but the Bourbons! 'Do you know the Royal Princes?' he asked Vitrolles. The Baron did not. He idealized the 'concept' – which bore little semblance to the obese, middle-aged, gout-ridden claimant living at Hartwell in England – a man more deft with knife and fork than sword or pen. France and a whole generation, knew nothing of these relics from the past. Only the fanatical nobility, reminiscing about their lost feudal past, their tax-free privileges and the abject deference of the lower orders, longed for a restoration. 'If you did', continued the Tsar, 'you'd realize the burden of such a crown would be too much for them ... if the Emperor should disappear ... You say Paris will receive us with open arms, but who will prepare our reception? Not your Bourbon prince in Nancy or Louis XVIII in England. We need someone in Paris.'[60]

Vitrolles was asked to return to Paris and tell Talleyrand that the Tsar and the Allies would co-operate with him, but Vitrolles insisted on going to see the comte d'Artois first, obviously to convey Talleyrand's messages of loyalty. Twenty-five years ago, in July 1789, Talleyrand had attended the Prince at a midnight meeting and implored him to persuade his brother Louis XVI to suppress the estates – by force if necessary —before a revolution erupted. Louis had refused. But the force of Talleyrand's arguments had convinced d'Artois, who left France with his two sons next day, thereby saving all their heads. Now Talleyrand was calling in the debt.[61]

While the Tsar went forward with the army towards the Aube and Napoleon on the 23rd, the Emperor of Austria, Metternich, Castlereagh and Vitrolles announced that they would leave for the citadel at Dijon for safety. No one thought this strange, although it might have been thought more prudent to have gone back to Switzerland and the lines of communication. But the Tsar had other things on his mind – as had Metternich and Castlereagh.

Before departing for Dijon, Castlereagh sent a letter to the Prime Minister, Lord Liverpool, detailing the clandestine arrangements that he and Metternich were making with Talleyrand and the royalists in Paris, through the medium of the Comte d'Artois, known now as 'Monsieur', the old courtesy title given to the king's brother. With his letter, Castlereagh enclosed a copy of a letter from Metternich to Artois informing him that the royalists alone would never take the initiative in Paris to help the Allies, but bidding him take heart and accept unequivocally Talleyrand's guidance in all matters. The two ministers – through Vitrolles – conveyed the Allies' terms which the Bourbons should accept if they wanted assistance to bring about the restoration. These were: (1) Agreement that the king reign as a constitutional monarch. (2) That the king sanction explicitly, without exception, the validity of ownership of the '*biens nationaux*' (state lands, i.e., confiscated from the Church and the nobility and sold during the Revolution). (3) Acceptance of the public debt. (4) Maintenance of all functionaries in the public, civil and military posts – as held at the time of restoration.

To this end, Castlereagh informed the Prime Minister in a further letter from Dijon:

> '... it has been deemed expedient not to wait for an express authority [from the Austrian Emperor], but to send a confidential mission to Monsieur, to concert with His Royal Highness the course to be pursued. As it appeared to me of the highest importance to mark that the Emperor of Austria was prepared cordially to concur with his allies in the policy to be pursued towards the Bourbons, I strongly urged that an Austrian agent should be sent, the better to satisfy Monsieur and those who are disposed to support Louis XVIII – that this with His Imperial Majesty is a national and not a family question ... In this view it was the general opinion that the invitation to recur to the antient [*sic*] family ought not, in the first instance, appear in the Allied declaration, and that their disposition to support the cause should follow and not precede the proclamation of Monsieur.'[62]

For Britain and Austria's part, they agreed: (1) That the Allies would not treat with Napoleon, – but with a 'representative' of the nation and or Louis XVIII. (2) That a Bourbon be attached to the headquarters of each Allied army. (3) That the Allies should supply the comte d'Artois with funds. In return Talleyrand and the royalists would raise as much of Paris and France as they could. Vitrolles was also to convey Castlereagh and Metternich's promise to Talleyrand that if the Bourbon cause were not eventually successful, an amnesty for him would be included in the Treaty of Paris, and for Vitrolles and his accomplices should they fail.[63]

Britain was about to finance a covert operation with Austria, to overthrow the government of France and replace Napoleon by the pliable Bourbons. And if it failed they would succour their agents in Paris. If it failed, at the very least it would damage Napoleon's prestige enormously. The only political obstacle was the Tsar, whom Talleyrand was to dupe. But Castlereagh had no intention of letting the world and, more importantly, the British people know what was going on, so the provision of money to bribe royalist and bogus royalist agitators and officials had to be hidden from parliament. With Metternich's assistance he would launder the money through Austria who would receive a lesser subsidy than would appear on the books. Castlereagh wrote:

> ' ... I shall not deem it consistent, either with the good of the public service, or with the known sentiments of the Prince Regent, or his ministers, to decline charging myself with the personal responsibility of making such reasonable pecuniary advances as the exigency of the case may at the outset

appear to require, but as I know the difficulties of controlling an expenditure of this nature, more especially through *British agents* ... such aid as Great Britain can afford to grant should be appropriated to this object, under their [Austrian] application, rather than as a direct grant to be made to the *French Princes* from the British Government. I consider this course of proceeding as not only the most prudent in a financial point of view, as rendering the expense definite on our part, *but as relieving the question from much of the political difficulty, which must attend, in a Government like ours, the voting a sum of money for effectuating a change in the Government of France.*[64]

The comte d'Artois, long the driving force in the Bourbon camp, and heir apparent to the childless Louis, had since 1790 built up a network of fanatical royalists, known as 'ultras', who to protect themselves had created societies along Masonic lines. Two of the most virulent of these were the 'Chevaliers de la Foi' (Knights of the Faith) and the 'Aa' (named after the river of that name, where the Bourbons first resided in exile), whose members were mainly priests of noble descent. Through these organizations, whose function had for many years been reduced to 'talking shops', Artois had received intelligence and they had provided safe houses for his agents, notable among whom had been George Cadoudal, the man of 'the infernal machine'.

Acting for Artois, Cadoudal planned to kill Napoleon and his relatives on Christmas Eve 1800, while they were on their way to the opera. A cart carrying a huge vat, ostensibly wine but in fact packed with an explosive device, several barrels of gunpowder and several hundredweights of sharp flint stones, had been parked in the narrow rue Sainte-Niçaise. A 13-year-old girl had been paid to hold the reins until the driver returned. On the approach of Napoleon's escort cavalry, the driver lit the fuze and disappeared. Any normal driver would have had to slow down to edge past the obstructing cart, but César, Napoleon's coachman, sensing something amiss, whipped his horses through the narrow gap and into the rue de la Loi before the explosion occurred. Nine people were blown to bits, including the girl. Twenty-six others were seriously injured and many more slightly, by blown-out windows and flying stones.[65] Historically, it did little good to Pitt's government or to Great Britain that they had financed and equipped this operation, and the several other attempts on Napoleon's life. On the contrary, they led directly to his elevation as hereditary Emperor, and provoked Napoleon to retaliate by the kidnapping and execution of the Bourbon prince, the duc d'Enghien, – in lieu of Artois – an act Napoleon never regretted, even on his deathbed.

Now, in March 1814, Napoleon was heading east in the hope of leading the Allies away from Paris and in the process intending to enlarge his army and perhaps inflict a reverse on the Army of Bohemia. The Tsar, with the King of Prussia and the army, oblivious to the political undercurrent, were retracing their steps in order to join Blücher's army. Castlereagh and Metternich, in concert with Talleyrand, were resorting to subversion in order to promote the Bourbon cause in Paris. Talleyrand's price was that he retain whatever office he happened to be holding at the restoration. As incentive to others, he could offer the same plus money, lots of money. After the conflict, the comte d'Artois, in return for British and Austrian help, would commit his brother Louis to support these powers in any congress, and endorse Talleyrand and his cronies in power. To this end he would supply the 'fervour' and the political contacts of his organizations – the 'fifth column' that would attack from within.

On the surface Castlereagh and Metternich felt that they could congratulate themselves. France would not only cease to be a threat to their countries, – but overnight would become a dependant ally, its prestigious war machine aligned with them to deal with the problems of central Europe. As a pledge of this, and to ensure no Bonapartist problems, Austria planned to hold its daughter and Napoleon's son in pledge. Britain would have its maritime questions shelved and its back door shut by an artificial Kingdom of Holland, with a strongly fortified Belgium as a barrier. Artois, having attempted assassination and murder, armed insurrection and invasion to regain the throne upon which he ultimately intended to sit, was pleased to regain it at the price.

No one bothered to speculate whether this scenario was one that the people of France wanted. All these minions of the 'ruling Princes', ignored the lessons of the Revolution. So far as the average Frenchman was concerned, Napoleon may have had his faults, but he was their Emperor, no matter what fiction the Allies or royalist propagandists plastered on village walls. Most of the young soldiers had grown up during the reign of Napoleon as First Consul and then Emperor. Their fathers, grandfathers, uncles, brothers and cousins had died fighting one or all of these Allies all over Europe, and no amount of soft soap was going to erase the memory of those glorious battles fought under Napoleon. Most of the elder generation had weaned their offspring on the abuses of the detested 'aristos', and their medieval privileges that had reduced the lower classes to the status of serfs; the Revolution and the con-cept of the *Rights of Man* had erased these for ever. Many, including the town and city dwellers, had obtained their houses, land and small-holdings – previously held in tenure from some great noble – from the state (the *'biens nationaux'*). They would not surrender them to some decadent *émigré* parasite living in England, nor to some power-mad local priest. Napoleon had put the Church in its place, making it a ser-vant of the community, not a feudal overlord – as under the previous regime.

And what of Fat Louis, in England, styled XVIII? What was his attitude while his brother, as Lieutenant-General of the as yet unregained kingdom, was signing blank cheques? This factor, totally neglected by Metternich, Castlereagh, Talleyrand and Artois in their selfish quest for personal aims, held the seeds of a counter-revolu-tion that would lead to the field of Waterloo – and perhaps beyond.

CHAPTER 4

THE ROAD TO PARIS: BETRAYAL

'Yet each man kills the thing he loves,
By each let this be heard,
Some do it with a bitter look,
Some with a flattering word.
The coward does it with a kiss,
The brave man with a sword!'
– Oscar Wilde.

ON 27 FEBRUARY 1814, WELLINGTON ENGAGED MARSHAL Soult at Orthez. After an obstinate defence, Soult retired towards Mont-de-Marsan and two days later moved on Tarbes. The city of Bordeaux was uncovered, but Soult reasoned, quite rightly, that Wellington would not seize the city while Soult was on his flank. The prefect of the city, faithful to Napoleon's instructions, departed with most of the city council, leaving behind, on a pretext, M. Lynch, Count and Chevalier of the Empire and, since 14 January, mayor of Bordeaux. By any definition, however, Lynch was a traitor. Simultaneous with his swearing loyalty as mayor and receiving the Légion d'Honneur, he was admitted to the British-funded terrorist organization, the 'Chevaliers de la Foi',[1] which was clandestinely equipping the 672-strong 'Bordelais Regiment', a rag-bag of royalist and unemployed layabouts, unique in having one officer for each private.

Bordeaux was almost solidly for the Emperor in sentiment and loyalty, so Lynch reasoned that he could not declare for the Bourbons unless Wellington's troops were in occupation. Through the royalist network he heard that Artois's son, the duc d'Angoulême, had arrived at Wellington's headquarters, and the Marquis de la Rochejaquelin, intimate of the Bourbons and a fellow 'Chevalier', had arrived soon afterwards to apprise Wellington of the situation in Bordeaux. At this stage Wellington would have none of it. He wrote to the War Office to say that so long as it was government policy to deal directly with Napoleon, it would not be proper for him to be seen to be supporting the Bourbons. Whitehall replied that it would now be appropriate to support the Bourbons, as the 'legitimate' monarchy.

Still entertaining scruples, Wellington ordered Marshal Beresford to enter the city. On 12 March an English flag of truce approached the city outposts which were held by the national guard, none of whom had ammunition by order of the mayor. The Bordelais Regiment, armed and wearing the white cockade, suddenly appeared outside the town hall. Lynch announced to the populace that Wellington's entire army was approaching and that the city was to be surrendered. On the arrival of Beresford and d'Angoulême, the Bourbon flag, white with fleurs-de-lis in gold, was flown from the cathedral spire and town hall. The duc d'Angoulême was then greeted with a proclamation announcing Louis XVIII as King of France.[2]

On the morning after this stage-managed performance, the duped citizens of Bordeaux awoke to the reality of the situation. Many refused to continue service as employees of the municipality and its renegade mayor. Lynch had no police, no money – it had been removed by the prefect – and no means of ensuring law and order. Anyone seen wearing the white cockade in areas where the British were not present risked being beaten to death. The risk of d'Angoulême and Lynch being killed and a counter-revolution erupting was so great that Beresford had no alternative but to garrison the city with two-thirds of his men.[3] Bordeaux in effect had not 'gone over to the Bourbons', but was being occupied and held by force.

The damage to the image of Napoleon's imperial France was incalculable. News of this apparent disaffection lent credence to Bourbon claims in diplomatic circles throughout Europe. Castlereagh and Metternich learnt of it on 26 March. On the 28th Castlereagh gave a dinner for the diplomatic corps including members from Prussia, Russia and of course Austria, and announced a toast to 'The restoration of Louis XVIII';[4] to the amazement of those present – Paris had not yet been reached and Napoleon was not yet defeated. In England, the Prince Regent, unable to drive about in his own capital without being jeered by the mob because of his treatment of his wife, saw it as an 'act of God'. Like his insane father, George III, he was unable to comprehend that any nation would not prefer its hereditary monarch, no matter how degenerate or incompetent he might be. He saw the affair as 'divine proof' of the true feelings of the French people. To Napoleon and his armies it was a bitter, demoralizing blow. At Lyons, Marshal Augereau felt that he must now watch his back, and this gave the tired old Marshal food for thought; on which horse should he cross the political stream?[5]

On 23 March Napoleon had reached Saint-Dizier. So far, his plans appeared to be working; the Army of Bohemia was following him – away from Paris. But again, his subordinates were not running true to the imperial plan. Marmont and Mortier were supposed to delay Blücher's advance, or prevent him joining the Army of Bohemia, and then effect a junction with Napoleon. After delaying the Prussians by blowing up as many bridges as possible, Marmont had fought a tough rear-guard action, falling back on Fismes. Faced with overwhelming odds, he summoned Mortier to join him from Rheims. Mortier left General Roussel's dragoon division to hold the city as long as possible. Roussel dismounted two squadrons which held the walls against some 6,000 Russians until 7 p.m. when they too retired on Fismes. Napoleon, who was able the more clearly to perceive the enemy's intent, reckoned that Blücher would use the Rheims road to march on Châlons and effect a junction with Schwarzenberg's forces. He wrote a blistering letter berating Marmont, 'Blücher is about to join Schwarzenberg, and you are responsible!'[6] Marmont spent the next three days trying to block Blücher, only to find himself continually outflanked. Napoleon still considered Blücher too weak to take the offensive.

Events, of which Napoleon had no knowledge and which, in any case, were quite beyond his control, now began to occur. On 20-23 March, a series of documents, as momentous as they were decisive, arrived at Allied headquarters at Pougy.

First, a captured dispatch from Berthier ordering Macdonald to hurry his march to the Marne, and telling him that Napoleon was in the rear of the Army of Bohemia and about to cut its communications, and that the French cavalry were as far off as Joinville. Next, the most important, Blücher's copy of Napoleon's letter to Marie-Louise which, as we have seen, confirmed this report in detail. Last, a letter from General Savary, duc de Rovigo and, since Fouché's downfall in 1810, Napoleon's chief of police and minister of the interior, stating: The treasury, arsenals and powder stores are empty. We have no resources left. The population is discouraged and discontented. It wants peace at any price. Enemies of the imperial government are sustaining and fomenting popular agitation. Still latent, it will become impossible to suppress unless the Emperor succeeds in keeping the Allies away from Paris.'[7]

The Tsar called a council of war. Barclay de Tolly and others, including General Gneisenau, considered that as Napoleon was threatening their communications, they should fall back on Châtillon via Bar-sur-Aube. This, as Napoleon had foreseen, would be a demoralizing retreat away from Paris and Blücher, and would give him a chance to defeat them on the march. Or, by releasing his trapped garrisons, he could commence a frontier campaign. The civilian population of eastern France, having been raped, tortured, looted and pillaged for some three months, had had enough. Groups of peasants, 300–400-strong, armed with captured weapons, were hiding in the forests whence they emerged to attack Allied troops in a partisan-type campaign – familiar to veterans of Spain and Russia – around the smoking ruins of hundreds of homesteads.[8]

In light of the captured documents, however, de Toll's advice coincided with the Tsar's views: 'If you touch Paris with a finger, the colossus will be overturned,' he said. 'While he marches east, let us march west! He is two marches [days] ahead of us. March on Paris, and he will be three marches behind.' And so it was decided. General Winzingerode, with 10,000 cavalrymen, would dog Napoleon's rearguard, masking the Allies' movements and giving the impression that they were still in pursuit. The Allied march on Paris now commenced, Napoleon oblivious that his letter to Marie-Louise – not in cipher – had tipped the scales against him. Metternich immediately confirmed Schwarzenberg's authorization to march on Paris – in the name of the Emperor of Austria. Blücher, on receiving his orders to join armies near Fère-Champenoise or Meaux between 25 and 27 March, exclaimed: 'I knew well that Schwarzenberg would come round to my opinion. We are going to finish this war, for now it is not only here, but everywhere, that the word is "Forward!" Napoleon at Saint-Dizier wrote: 'Give me four days, and I have them. God delivers them into my hands.'

During the night of 24 March, Marmont's troops bivouacking around Soudé Sainte-Croix and Mortier's at Vatry – near Fère-Champenoise – saw numerous fires lighting up the eastern sky. Both Marshals, ill-informed of the events of the last few days, assumed that these were the Emperor's army on the Marne. After Fismes, Marmont had arranged to join his force with that of Mortier at Fère-Champenoise on the morrow. So they were shocked to learn from reconnaissance patrols that this was the enemy's main army, and that there was every indication that they would be attacked next day. Marmont had but 5,800 men to face nearly 80,000 of the enemy, but he decided to hold a strong position nearby instead of retreating immediately. His reasoning was sound. If he retreated before Mortier came up, the latter's force would be cut to pieces. He reckoned that he could hold the enemy's advance guard long enough for Mortier to join, and their combined forces would be strong enough – not to dispute the ground – but to withdraw before the main enemy force could make contact.

On the 25th, Marmont's troops had formed a defensive position and were waiting for Mortier to arrive. At 8 o'clock Count Pahlen and the advance guard of 7,000 cavalry and 36 guns attacked, the main body having been ordered to concentrate in their rear. Mortier arrived at last, his units having force-marched early. The Marshals had between them 12,500 infantry, 4,000 cavalry and 60 guns. Like Napoleon, Marmont was an artilleryman. He placed all his guns to his front and kept the enemy cavalry away. The action developed into an artillery duel which went in Marmont's favour. Soon the vast masses of the enemy's main body were seen in the distance. Marmont ordered a withdrawal, with his artillery covering; the guns would then withdraw covered by the cavalry. Russian hussars attacked the French cavalry in an attempt to reach the artillery which was limbering up. The French cavalry pushed them back, only to run into an entire division of Austrian heavy *cuirassiers*. Soon the French cavalry had lost all cohesion and, panic-stricken, were being routed. Marmont formed his infantry into divisional squares (rectangular formations made up of several regiments, their baggage wagons in the middle) that moved off, stopped to fire volleys and moved off again. The weather soon spoilt this text-book withdrawal. Rain and sleet blew in from the east, in the faces of the French, but behind the Allied cavalry. Unable to see, unable to load or fire because of the rainstorm, the French retreat bid fair to disintegrate. If the squares broke they would be butchered by the Allied cavalry.

In fact one square made up of a brigade of two regiments was annihilated, but Marmont reached a defile at Connantre where the squares had to form columns to pass through. He detailed General Christiani's Imperial Guard division to hold the entrance while the rest of the army passed through, but the arrival of 1,200 Cossacks on their flank caused a panic and the troops fled – carrying the Marshals with them.

Their complete annihilation was prevented by the presence of two divisions of the National Guard – the territorial army. Raw recruits, some of them still wearing wooden *sabots* and smocks, they totalled some 4,300 men. Under command of Generals Pacthod and Amey, they were part of Macdonald's corps but had been cut off and unable to reach him. They had met a large convoy of army supplies, including 100 artillery-ammunition wagons and 200,000 rations of food and brandy, whose transport officers had placed themselves under their protection. Pacthod, knowing that these supplies must not fall into the hands of the enemy, had agreed to escort them. On the 24th, learning of the presence of Mortier in the area, they had been marching to join him. Blücher's army, coming up to join Schwarzenberg, had

sighted the convoy and attacked it; Gneisenau, personally leading the 6,000 cavalrymen and horse-artillery of the Silesian Army's advance guard, had been harrying
them for some four miles. The convoy had been proceeding in six squares, with the
wagons in the middle. Time after time, the Prussian cavalry had charged to hold the
squares static, while the artillery unlimbered at less than 100 yards and poured canister into them. Still they continued, mile after mile, suffering terrible casualties. Nearing Sainte-Croix, they heard the heavy cannon duel between Marmont and Pahlen.
'It is the Emperor!' Pacthod said, and the squares advanced at an increased pace.
Coming up to the plain they saw the Tsar and the King of Prussia and their staffs.
Thinking them to be the Emperor or a Marshal under attack, this band of battered
volunteers, shouted the imperial battle-cry '*Vive l'Empereur!*' so loudly as to be heard
by the Tsar himself. The leading square formed attack column and smashed into the
Russians – and realized their error too late. The Allied cavalry pursuing Marmont
were quickly recalled, and his men reformed their squares and continued their
retreat.

Faced as he was with the combined Allied armies, Pacthod decided to abandon
the wagons, but kept the horses – they were in short supply! Soon his men, reduced
now to 3,000, were being attacked by 20,000 Allied cavalrymen. They closed ranks
and marched on towards the marshes of Saint-Gond, another four miles under continual attack by cavalry and artillery. A Russian general brought up several batteries
and the infantry of the Prussian and Russian Guards to block the road. Forty-eight
guns opened fire, blowing one square to bits; the survivors, refusing to surrender,
were sabred by the cavalry. The Tsar sent a flag of truce asking for their surrender.
Pacthod's men shot the bearer – Pacthod did not discuss terms under fire. His men
had covered sixteen miles in ten hours under constant attack and were grimly determined, but at last he felt that he could no longer permit their futile sacrifice. Called
upon again by the Tsar to surrender, he came out of his square, bleeding, his broken
right arm hanging by his side. General Delort's square, out of ammunition and fired
on by artillery canister on all four sides, also surrendered. The last square refused.
Another cannonade opened it to the Russian cavalry, but 500 men managed to
escape to the marshes. Of the 4,300 men of Pacthod's command, 500 had escaped,
1,500, most of them wounded, had surrendered, 2,300 had fallen during the last sixteen miles. The Tsar, overwhelmed by this display of courage, recalled his cavalry
from their pursuit in the marshes. He returned Pacthod's sword personally. 'Are you
Napoleon's Imperial Guard?', asked his aide. 'No sir, you were lucky, we are only the
National Guard!', he replied.[9]

In the meantime, Napoleon on the 25th had sent out cavalry under General Piré
to reconnoitre from Saint-Dizier southwards, towards Brienne, Bar-sur-Aube, and
Chaumont. He sent back reports that the Emperor of Austria had gone to Dijon, the
Allies had abandoned the country around Langres and were evacuating Troyes, and
that absolute chaos prevailed on the Allied lines of communications. Piré's men,
aided by partisans, had captured Allied reinforcements and many wagon-loads of
supplies. From Toul to Chaumont, and Saint-Mihiel to Bar-sur-Aube, every road,

track and byway was being patrolled by partisans who, from 25 to 28 March brought in more than 1,000 prisoners, 138 ammunition wagons and 24 cannon. General Piré's dispatch from Chaumont told the Emperor: 'The peasants have seen immense columns of wagons carrying loot, and they wish to recapture their cattle and goods; they wish to have their revenge for the wrongs they have suffered, and for the outrages committed on their wives and daughters. I propose to the Emperor that we should sound the alarm through all the parishes of the upper Marne. We will march on Langres and Vesoul, for the peasants know they will find there plenty of booty and little resistance. The movement, once started, will spread to all the districts pillaged by the Cossacks. We have few arms, but will capture some from the enemy. I ask for nothing but orders and cartridges.'[10]

Napoleon ordered his army forward to the south; he would soon turn west and cut the Allies off from the Langres plateau and Switzerland. The peasants had risen and only needed organizing. Soon the *levée en masse*, the Allies' nightmare, would assemble and France would wage a people's war along the frontier. General Durutte with 4,000 men had already marched out of the frontier stronghold of Metz, raising the blockade of Thionville. At Auxerre, General Allix had collected 2,000 men. General Broussier was about to leave Strasbourg with 4,000 men and 1,000 cavalry – on the Emperor's instruction. General Duvigneau was marching on Châlons from Verdun with a further 2,000 men. In four or five days Napoleon would be able to add another 25,000 men and their generals to his army, all of them veterans. Within a week he estimated that he would be able to confront the Allies with a force of 115,000 men.

Napoleon's army had reached Doulevant when news arrived that the enemy were not nearing Vitry but seemed to have withdrawn. 'But where?' Napoleon wondered. 'I shall not have a clear idea as to the enemy movements for another four or five hours ... It is necessary, therefore, that no one should move,' he instructed his corps commanders. Later, news arrived from his rearguard that 10,000 cavalrymen were advancing on the road from Vitry to Saint-Dizier and had crossed the Marne there. Napoleon wondered whether they were the Allied advance guard, or just an isolated corps operating with the main body. Here was an opportunity to find out. The enemy commander had put the river at his back. If he fell on him he would annihilate or damage him before any supports could threaten Napoleon's force. If he stood firm he was probably the advance guard – he would hold his ground until relief came up. If he was isolated he would try to escape – no supports to come up. Napoleon's patrols would then be able to follow and penetrate this screen.

On the morning of 26 March, Napoleon left Doulevant at 2.30 a.m. and reached Wassy at daybreak. He deployed all his cavalry and infantry opposite the enemy cavalry which was formed in two lines, one each side of the Vitry road. Winzingerode's cavalry was already shaken by the sudden appearance of Napoleon's army. The battle was a minor affair, the Russians being desperate to get away. In less than two hours the plain had been cleared, the enemy losing 500 casualties, 2,000 prisoners and eighteen cannon.

Napoleon was scarcely satisfied with the outcome. Where was Schwarzenberg? He had expected at least an army corps to fight. This was a smoke-screen, all shadow and no substance. Why? Prisoners had confirmed that the Allies were advancing on Paris, but was it true? Cavalry patrols brought in some escaped French prisoners who confirmed it. Napoleon went to Saint-Dizier and consulted his maps. Should he return to Paris now at the moment when his garrisons were marching to join him and the partisans were ready to be organized? The Allies had three days' march on him. A captured printed handbill announcing the Allied victory at Fère-Champenoise, showed how close they were. What of Marmont and Mortier? Paris would hold sixty hours – the largest capital in the world! He would return personally by a forced march; the army would follow. Once inside he would raise the capital and the Allies would be trapped between Paris and his army, with a hostile populace in their rear, attacking their communications, messengers, supplies and reinforcements. It would be Dresden all over again – only this time the enemy would not escape. He ordered his army to march towards Paris via Bar-sur-Aube, Troyes and Fontainebleau. This route was slightly longer but he would not have to force the river passage of the Marne at Meaux, and the Seine would protect his right flank.

On 29 March, Napoleon passed through Bar-sur-Aube. Five miles further on, at Dolancourt, he met a courier with dispatches from Paris. Several days had passed while this man, unable to get through the Allied lines, had travelled in an arc to avoid capture. The news was appalling. Marshal Augereau had surrendered Lyons – a devastating blow. From 4 to 21 March he had been handling his army in a manner unworthy of even a junior officer. He had been at Lyons for two months and had failed to bring up the 80 cannon from Avignon that would have made Lyons impregnable to the available Allied forces opposed to him. He had been ordered to move on Mâcon and destroy an advancing but not yet concentrated Austrian corps, and then assist Napoleon in threatening and perhaps entrapping the Army of Bohemia.

Augereau's forces had been reinforced by veterans from Suchet's army of Spain and morale was high. Napoleon had arranged for another 6,800 men from the army of Spain and 7,000 veterans from Tuscany to join Augereau by 25 or 27 March, to assist in his attack on the Army of Bohemia. Augereau would have had a real strength (not paper) of 36,000 men. On 20 March, without having delegated command, he had left his army in a strong position at Limonest, but with both flanks exposed, and had returned to Lyons. It was severely beaten in his absence. He had then asked the council whether he should surrender the second city of France and 'spare it the ravages that follow a useless resistance, or try to defend it?' Augereau knew the only reply that could be given.

With 21,500 men against 30,000 Austrians, an energetic defence of Lyons might have been expected from the man who at Castiglione had routed 25,000 Austrians with a division of 5,000 men. Why, if he had not felt up to the responsibility, had not Augereau resigned his vital command? The only possible explanation for this and his subsequent actions is betrayal for personal gain – which eventually followed from the Bourbons. The loss of Lyons severed Napoleon's connection with his troops in Italy, and enabled the Austrians to attack them on two fronts. Napoleon never forgave this act of treachery.[11] The dispatch also contained reports of the battle of Fère-Champenoise and announced that Meaux had fallen. The most serious news, however, was that the capital itself was under attack, not only from without but from within. Count Antoine-Marie de Lavalette, Napoleon's Post-Master General, married to a niece of the former Empress and totally loyal to him, his functions including the monitoring of information passing through the mail (Napoleon called him 'nothing less than my eyes and ears in Paris'), wrote urgently in code: '... There are men [émigrés] in league with the foreigners, encouraged by what has happened in Bordeaux, they are raising their heads, supported by secret intrigue. The Emperor's presence is vital if he wants to keep his capital from being handed over to the enemy. There is not a moment to lose.'[12]

The message was clear, concise and to the point; men were in league with foreigners ... supported by secret intrigue. Only Napoleon's presence would prevent his capital from being handed over. The race was on! Colonel Gourgaud with three squadrons of his Polish Lancers was sent to secure the bridges around Troyes, and ordered to send a messenger to the Empress and Joseph telling them to hold on at all costs – he was coming. Hardly had Gourgaud arrived at Troyes on 30 March than the familiar green coach followed by the Imperial Guard cavalry arrived, having covered 54 miles that day. Napoleon assured the alarmed colonel that he was not alone, that the remainder of the Guard was following. Resting briefly, Napoleon ordered Berthier to stay at Troyes and expedite the army behind him, then follow immediately – rendezvous Fontainebleau.

In 1814 Paris covered an area with a radius of about five miles, encircled at that time by a wall that corresponds with the modern outer boulevards. The wall, for customs collection not for defence, was called the Octroi, as was the municipal tax levied on all goods that entered for retail – the Octroi tax. There were 52 openings or barriers piercing this 20-odd-mile customs wall. (Some of them are commemorated to this day, such as the Porte Saint-Denis, with its elaborate stone archway.) The countryside began beyond the wall; Parisians could look out over green fields, at woods and windmills. The Seine, snaking behind and through Paris, protected the rear of the city. To the north the outlying suburbs of Clichy, Saint-Ouen and Saint-Denis radiated within four miles of the wall; the latter suburb was sited in front of the canal of that name, which in turn joined the Ourcq Canal. Also in the north was the dominating height of Montmartre, less than a quarter of a mile from the city, which commanded the main approaches and which, if well fortified would not be taken without heavy loss. To the right of Montmartre was a plateau which would also be costly to assault, its centre crowned by the suburban town of Romanville. To the east the military fortress château of Vincennes, with its wood and dry moat where the duc d'Enghien had been shot, guarded the approaches along the Seine–Marne. The south-east of the city was protected by the junction of the Seine with the Marne. The river snaked north-east to become the Marne and continued

94

towards Meaux where the Allies were concentrated, As the Seine dropped south-east towards Fontainebleau, the respective positions of the opposing forces were separated by fifty miles and two rivers.

Napoleon's route would lead him into the rear of the city unhindered, so long as his brother Joseph and the regency council held the line Saint-Denis to the Seine at Vincennes, some seven miles, or even the city wall on the north side of the Seine. If he arrived with his Guard, as at Dresden, would the Allies dare to attack him and his capital of 800,000 people? Within 36 hours he would have a further 60,000 men in the city. With the numbers of National Guard he planned to raise in Paris, he would have 100,000 or possibly 130,000 men. How many men had the Allies in the field? Reports put them between 120,000 and 200,000 men. Napoleon knew that a size-able force was at Dijon with the Austrian Emperor. Partisan reports had indicated Austrian cavalry outposts stretching out like the spokes of a wheel towards Lyons and round in an arc towards Auxerre and Orléans;[13] these posed no threat to the gar-risons. Napoleon assumed they were there to give early warning of his approach. He therefore estimated the Allied total at about 180,000 men. Would they fight him or, having severed their supply routes in the east, head towards Belgium or Germany? Or would they make peace? However, they were the external enemy; Lavalette's omi-nous warning about treason within was ringing in his head, as his carriage hurtled along the roads to Paris.

As we have seen, Napoleon had left the city in the stewardship of the Empress and her council, and Joseph. The 23-year-old Marie-Louise had been brought up under the rigid aristocratic system of Austria and understood obedience to authority. She was a Habsburg (Hawkscastle), descended from 'Guntram the Hawk', a robber-baron, later known as 'Guntram the Rich', who had built the first castle of Habsburg at Aargau in north-west Switzerland in 1020. No other family has left so deep a mark on European history. In 1273 Count Rudolf Habsburg became King of the Germans and Holy Roman Emperor. In 1278 Rudolf conquered Austria and the family fortune was made. In 1450, the family adopted as their motto the five vowels A. E. I. O. U. which were the first letters of the Latin words 'Austriae est imperare orbi universo' (Austria is destined to rule the world). This boast had nearly come true in 1519, when Charles V ruled most of central Europe, Italy, Spain, the Low Coun-tries and the vast empire of the New World. Since the 1700s it had been a maxim that 'Wars may be waged by others, you happy Austria, marry.'[14] Now, married to Napoleon as a political expedient, Marie-Louise found herself Empress and Regent of France, fighting her father's army. King Joseph, Napoleon's elder brother, was in charge of the security of the capital, as Napoleon's Lieutenant-General. The day-to-day business was carried on by Joseph and the council of ministers: General Clarke, duc de Feltre, Minister of War, the comte de Montalivat, Minister of the Interior, General Savary, duc de Rovigo, Minister of police.

Since Talleyrand's compact with Britain and Austria, Paris had succumbed to a creeping paralysis. Talleyrand now had control of the royalists through the Cheva-liers de la Foi, and had started to orchestrate their operations in the capital. The comte d'Artois had placed his other son, the duc de Berry, in the Chevaliers' head-quarters in Jersey to co-ordinate and implement the royalists' activities and now to assist Talleyrand in the coup.

In 1802 Napoleon had allowed 50,000 royalist *émigrés* to return under an amnesty. During the next six years a like number returned, mainly to Paris. Every night broadsheets and placards appeared in the city, imploring the people to petition the Senate for peace, begging the Bourbons to return and exhorting the people not to oppose the Allies and thereby uselessly sacrifice their loved ones. Paris was inundated with English newspapers making exaggerated claims as to the Allies' great strategy, and their promise to burn Paris if it resisted. Pro-Allied posters appeared on walls.

The royalists used their wealth to manipulate and inspire panic in the financial institutions. Since late March the stock-exchange index had begun to fall dramatically; the royalists pointed to the Allied successes as being the cause. Mass withdrawals of funds caused a run on the banks. Paper money and credit was refused by royalists and the tradesmen in their employ. Desperately needed horses for the army could not be purchased with government 'paper money'. Talleyrand's minions stopped paying their taxes and encouraged everyone else to follow suit. Displaying his letter signed by Castlereagh and Metternich, Talleyrand was able to show that he could promise money, position and honours to key civil servants under a restored regime; if the coup failed, they were promised immunity as part of an Allied peace treaty. He had only to hint as to what the victorious Allies and Bourbons might do to anyone who might have been seen as obstructing him, to receive co-operation. Look at Bordeaux and Lyons, he would say. Did they want to be on the losing side? Would he back the losers? The whole of Europe was at their door, did they want to go down with the fallen Emperor? General Clarke, the Minister of War, changed sides,[15] as did General Hulin, commander of the key First Military District. The Prefect of Police, Baron Pasquier, was also a key conspirator. Talleyrand was indeed busy during this period; to topple a regime and provide a stable replacement would take time, even for a man of his ability, and time was now of the essence.

Joseph found his desperate path littered with plausible obstructions. His common sense should have told him to incarcerate the most dangerous of the royalist agitators if only to discourage the rest, but he failed to do so, Pasquier having advised that this would cause riots and perhaps revolution; 'look at Bordeaux and Lyons'. He tried to raise 30,000 more National Guardsmen as Napoleon had ordered, but the Prefect of Police advised against it, saying that at the least alarm they would mutiny and the people would rebel. He advised Joseph not to agitate the populace because 'once stirred up they would be easily led by any faction'.[16] Joseph found that only half his present 12,000 National Guardsmen had arms. General Hulin told him that the arms that he had were reserved for the regular army. He had 20,000 weapons that were 'too old or needed repairs; why not buy some or give them pikes?'[17] Joseph, hearing that there were muskets available at Nantes, Brest and other seaports, tried to obtain them but was duped into believing that they were badly made guns destined for colonial trade and would 'blow up if fired'.[18] He tried to purchase guns in Paris, only to be told that without gold it was impossible; the government's paper money would not be accepted. There were 75,000,000 francs in gold in the palace vaults, but he was told this could not be released without written authorization from the Emperor.

Sections of the Octroi wall were in disrepair or had been removed. Joseph was told that the government could not afford to buy the wood or hire the labour needed to build ramparts and earthworks. Within two miles of the city were the forest of Vincennes and the Bois de Boulogne to provide a plentiful supply of wood at no cost, and there were 40,000 idle workmen in Paris who had had previous military service.[19] Joseph failed to utilize these assets.

The suburb of Saint-Denis, under its loyal mayor and prefect, had built extensive wood and earth fortifications, and all its able-bodied men had enrolled and drilled in its National Guard. They had moulded their own lead musket-balls, and with municipal gunpowder had made their own cartridges – all at no cost to the government. Napoleon would have expected the same from the whole of Paris, as from this little suburb in front of the city walls.

Joseph had twenty companies of artillerymen under his control, but these were not used as a cadre to expand them to forty companies as Napoleon had wished. He had 300 field cannon, but he failed to entrench them in earthworks around the approaches from Meaux, or to use some of the 600 large calibre pieces to render Montmartre's heights impregnable. He could have sited them as volley guns at the barriers or key positions near the boulevards. The cost to the Allies of trying to storm a barricaded street swept by canister or scrap metal would have been appalling. No such measures were taken.

Pasquier's secret police reports of January to March, show that the working classes of Paris were loyal to Napoleon to a man – but Joseph declined to tap this patriotic source, or to call the capital to arms to defend itself. Instead, all his correspondence, like that of the royalist conspirators, portrays the populace as a hotbed of royalist disaffection, awaiting only a spark to ignite them in the Bourbon cause. Talleyrand and his cohorts of royalists had created the 'Big Lie', and it was being believed, especially by Joseph and the middle classes. Joseph was now running scared, wishing like the ostrich to hide his head; he did so in administrative sand. Receiving nothing but obstructions and plausible excuses from the conspirators in the ministries, he replied to the loyal officers and junior officials who were concerned for the capital and badgered him to do something: 'Everything must wait until the Emperor approves the measures I have submitted to him.' All the time Talleyrand's minions were undermining the morale of the administrators, civil servants and officers of state. Talleyrand told chief of police Savary: 'France is in a deplorable state; what are we to do under the circumstances? It does not suit everyone to remain in the burning house – YOU should look after yourself.'[20] To which, Savary says, he made no reply. The point had been taken and he would not arrest Talleyrand as Napoleon had now ordered. Let Joseph do so if he wished; if things turned out in Napoleon's favour, that would let Savary out.

Joseph's letters to Napoleon of March 1814 reflect his panic-stricken state. In the selfish hope that something of the tottering Empire could be salvaged and that he could retain his exalted position, he tried to persuade Marie-Louise, who wrote daily to Napoleon, to urge the Emperor to seek peace on any terms. He kept her informed as to public opinion in the capital, or rather what Pasquier had frightened him into believing, and he also tried to charm her into giving him her support and working with him. Talleyrand, however, arrived at the palace each evening, as cool as a cucumber, to play whist with the Empress. He feigned ignorance of any of these matters – having, as he said, ' nothing to do with the government anymore'. Napoleon could not believe the letters that he was receiving from his ministers: 'Have they all gone mad? No-one obeys me anymore!' he wrote to Joseph. Then, receiving Marie-Louise's letters written at Joseph's instigation, he began to suspect Joseph of treachery. To the Empress he wrote: 'What the King says is nonsense and in any case it is not the business of the public... When the King attempts to give you advice, which it is not his business to do ... you should break off the subject and talk of something else;'[21] in his next letter: 'Everyone has betrayed me. Will it be my fate to be betrayed by the King? I should not be surprised if such was the case ... Mistrust the King; he has an evil reputation with women... show the King none of my letters, or your father's or of your own replies.[22] On the same day he wrote to Joseph, 'I shall treat as an act of rebellion the first address soliciting peace that is presented to me,' and finally, to the Empress, 'The King is intriguing; he will be the first to suffer; he is a pygmy, swelling with his own importance.'[23]

A wedge had now been effectively driven between Joseph and his imperial brother and sister-in-law. Excluded from the plans of both Napoleon and the conspirators; surrounded by unco-operative ministers; with no real authority and no access to funds; insulted and criticized at every turn, Joseph felt that enough was enough. Convinced that Napoleon's downfall was inevitable, he decided – with his wife's help – to desert.

Joseph's wife was Julie, née Clary, the daughter of a Marseilles textile merchant. Her sister, Desirée, lived in the rue d'Anjou in a house given to her by Napoleon (once her sweetheart, he had jilted her for the late Empress Josephine). Desirée had married Marshal Bernadotte, now Crown Prince of Sweden, and commander of the Allied army of the North; the man the Tsar wished to place on Napoleon's throne. Desirée hated the cold Swedish palaces and preferred to stay in Paris near her sister. Her letters, of course, were allowed through the lines thanks to Joseph and her husband, the Crown Prince. He wasted no time in enlisting Joseph's aid in his plans. If he succeeded in becoming president or dictator, Joseph would have a key position. In return, Joseph must help the Allies, clandestinely, by ensuring that Paris offer only a token resistance.[24]

The defence of Napoleon's capital was now in the hands of two self-interested groups. Talleyrand's conspirators, who had been guaranteed riches, advancement and a free hand in the restoration of the Bourbons; and King Joseph, who had abandoned his brother's sinking ship to look after his own interests. However, none of these players wished to be seen by the French public as being the betrayer of Napoleon and of France.

At this crucial point, news arrived that Marshals Marmont and Mortier, having been beaten at Fère-Champenoise, would not be able to hold the vital Meaux crossings, but they hoped to reach Paris before the Allies – who were between them and Napoleon.

Joseph confided in Clarke, telling him that the situation was critical and that he intended to evacuate the Empress and her son from Paris. To enlist Clarke's help, Joseph showed him an old letter from Napoleon dated 8 February.[25] The letter was a bombshell:

> 'I've answered you on the fate of Paris. You don't have to raise the subject again. I've given you orders regarding the Empress, the King of Rome, and our family ... If the battle is *lost* or you get news of my death ... send the Empress and the King of Rome to Rambouillet. Order the Senate, the Council of State, and all the troops to assemble on the Loire. Leave the Prefect or a mayor or an imperial commissary in Paris.'

Clarke agreed that the Emperor must be obeyed, but what had held his attention was the rest of the private letter:

> '... I tell you frankly, that if Talleyrand supports the view that the Empress should stay in Paris if our forces evacuate it, it will be because of some treachery afoot. I repeat, do not trust this man. I've known him for sixteen years. I've even felt affection for him, but he is definitely the worst enemy our house has now that fortune has abandoned it. Follow my advice. I know more about it than those other people.'[26]

Joseph told Clarke that he intended to call a meeting of the Regency council for 8.30 that evening, 28 March. Clarke went straight to Talleyrand and informed him of the contents of the letter. Talleyrand instructed his fellow conspirators on the Regency council to demand that the Empress stay in Paris. At the meeting, which was attended by the Empress and the 25 members of the council, Joseph asked Clarke to outline the position so far as the defence of the capital was concerned.

Clarke spoke factually. The Emperor was cut off from Paris on the other side of the Marne. The work of fortification had scarcely begun. The National Guard comprised 12,000 men, half of whom were armed with pikes. These added to all the available regular troops – including Marmont and Mortier's, expected hourly at the capital, might total 43,000 men who would have to face the combined Allied armies of about 200,000. Clarke gave no opinions at all. He did not point out that with 43,000 men the capital could be held for at least three days; that to attempt to seize a city the size of Paris was a commander's nightmare; that troops assaulting streets of houses soon became uncontrollable and that a resolute defence could turn them into the aggressors' graveyard; that a single gun strategically sited in a barricaded avenue would massacre advancing troops. He did not point out that the enemy might not have enough ammunition left to sustain 60 hours' of fighting. Nor the fact that as the Emperor was probably in the Allies rear, their supplies had been cut off. Food would be short for 150-200,000 men in an area already depleted by the inhabitants of the city.

Next, Talleyrand addressed the council to the effect that only the presence of the Empress in the capital would prevent rebellion. Some loyal councillors echoed this sentiment. A vote was taken, and all but Joseph and Clarke were in favour of the Empress remaining in Paris. Joseph read out the Emperor's letter that set out his instructions in the event of a lost battle – that had yet to be fought. To ensure compliance Joseph supported this letter, with an even older, out-of-date letter in which Napoleon confided that he would rather see his son drowned in the Seine than brought up as a captive. A second vote supported the demand that the Empress and her son leave the next day. Joseph also failed to implement Napoleon's instructions that the entire government leave Paris so that there would be no one left with whom the Allies could negotiate.

Later, Talleyrand, to be on the safe side, submitted to an elaborate charade with a royalist officer in the National guard who publicly prevented him from leaving the city. That night, Joseph had a proclamation posted in the city announcing the demoralizing news that Paris was about to be attacked, that the Empress and the King of Rome were leaving, but that he would be staying. Talleyrand, in light of the council's resolutions, had already arranged for the royalist presses to produce lampoons deriding Joseph and further undermining the vestiges of public morale. One handbill depicted Joseph galloping away from the city, with the caption, 'You stay, I'm only going for help.' Another bore an epigram:

'Great King Joseph, ashen pale,

Is staying here to save us all.

But rest assured, if he shall fail.

To save our heads, his own won't fall.'

In the hope of covering his treachery, Joseph asked the Empress to use her authority to override the Regency council's decision and stay. Marie-Louise was dumbfounded by this volte-face: 'Why should she reverse the decision of the council on the course he himself had advocated – and against the Emperor's instructions?' She would stay provided that he, Joseph, and the council of ministers requested it in writing. This he would not do, and next morning amidst much royalist publicity the Empress and the King of Rome left Paris, together with a vast cavalcade of coaches and wagons containing the treasury and personal wealth of the royal family. Numerous prominent officials and their families accompanied them. This sad and demoralizing spectacle lent weight to the royalists' insistence that the end was nigh.

Before departing, the Empress, feeling that 200 cavalrymen would be an adequate bodyguard, offered General Clarke 1,000 of the 1,200 Imperial Guardsmen provided by the Emperor for her protection. If the worst came to the worst, another 1,000 men would hardly suffice, but they would help to protect Paris. Clarke declined, saying that the Emperor would not approve. The last thing he or Talleyrand wanted was for the Allies to see the bearskins of these crack troops. If they thought Napoleon was in Paris it was doubtful that they would assault the city. Nor did they want these Guardsmen on the scene to inspire and raise the morale of the defenders.

No sooner had Marshals Marmont and Mortier arrived, followed by their weary troops, than the defence of Paris was handed over to Marmont by Joseph, with instructions to hold the line from the Seine near Clichy to the Seine near Vincennes. Marmont had no time to take stock of the available armaments in the capital. He was allocated the National Guard, half of whom were unarmed, and the students of the military academies and polytechnics. At first light on 30 March, the Parisians awoke to military drums sounding the alarm. Men of all classes clamoured at General Hulin's house and at the Prefecture and the police barracks, demanding to fight, the majority of them carrying their own guns and other weapons. General Hulin, Pasquier and other officials told them to disperse to their homes and leave the fighting to the military.

On the previous evening, General Hulin had ridden out to inspect the dispositions. As commander of the First Military District, he had not placed himself under Marmont's orders as he should have done, now that Marmont had been made military commander. Instead, using his authority as a member of Joseph's 'war cabinet', he inquired of the outposts why Allied officers approaching under a white flag were being driven away unheard? The picket officer replied that Marshal Marmont did not want them to gain intelligence of their dispositions under a pretext. Hulin of course knew this, but he needed to contact the Allies to let them know that the Empress was leaving next morning. To this end he commandeered the services of a civil engineer of the National Guard (*génie*), one Alexander Peyre,[27] and ordered him to make his way to the Allied lines and find out what was required. Peyre was soon captured and because he was carrying neither flag nor written instructions, the Russians officers did not at first believe his story; why had Hulin not sent one of his staff officers? But when news filtered through to Schwarzenberg, who had been briefed privately by Metternich about Talleyrand and his associates, Peyre was brought before the Commander and the Tsar. Peyre asserted later that he told the Tsar that Marie-Louise was departing and that the Tsar appeared disturbed when told that Paris would be defended. Obviously the Tsar had been informed by Joseph via the Crown Prince that Paris would offer only token resistance. The Tsar sent Peyre back with his personal aide, Count Orlov, with instructions: 'I authorize you to agree to a ceasefire when you think fit and without being responsible for the consequences. You have my authorization to suspend the most crucial attack, even one about to bring us victory, in order to spare Paris.'[28] For Joseph's benefit, the Tsar had added that once the Allies reached the enceinte and had to force it, he would not be able to stop the rape and pillage that would ensue. However, in his and Schwarzenberg's general orders for the battle he stated that he would hold any corps commander, divisional general, or brigade commander personally responsible if even one soldier under their command entered Paris without his written order.

When Peyre got back to Paris, twelve hours had elapsed since he set out on his mission. Marmont's experienced generals, aided by Marshals Mortier and Moncey, had been using every means at their disposal to put the city in some sort of defensive posture. Commandeering cab- and carthorses off the streets, Marmont had field guns dragged up to the heights of Montmartre. Two divisions had been formed out of the depots of the Old and Young Imperial Guards, Marmont fuming the while that this had not already been done. The Château de Vincennes was garrisoned with 400 men under General Dumesnil. Guns were placed on the hills of Mont Louis and on the eastern approaches. Marmont's corps was marching to Romanville; outside the walls

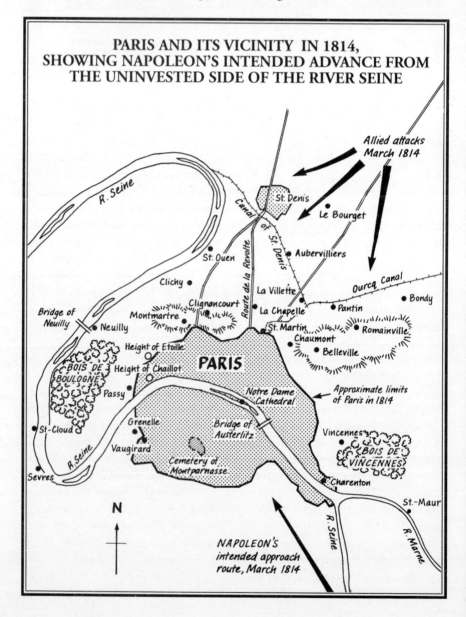

**PARIS AND ITS VICINITY IN 1814,
SHOWING NAPOLEON'S INTENDED ADVANCE FROM
THE UNINVESTED SIDE OF THE RIVER SEINE**

he was fielding some 43,000 men against 150,000 Allied troops, most of whom had yet to come up and deploy. Between 6.30 and 7 o'clock fighting broke out.

The Allies, assuming that the fall of Paris was a foregone conclusion, had sent forward their men piecemeal. The Tsar had told Schwarzenberg that, according to the Crown Prince, Joseph would not put up any strong resistance.[29] Schwarzenberg, privy to Metternich's own intrigues, had concurred, so the Allied forces advanced with their corps unconcentrated. At this critical juncture Blücher was again unwell and his orders to his army were badly transmitted.[30] Consequently each Allied attack was beaten back with some loss. By 10 o'clock Marmont had done exceedingly well and the outcome was by no means certain. The Allies hastily attempted to concentrate their forces for a more concerted attack. Peyre reached the heights of Montmartre at about 11.30 and was brought to where Joseph, Clarke and Hulin on horseback were watching through telescopes the enemy advancing across the plains. A cabal of conspirators. On the heights were sited some 30 guns which Marmont the artilleryman had hauled into position. He had 60 experienced gunners to whom he had attached 250 of the unarmed National Guard, giving each gun a crew of ten men. Marmont knew that whoever commanded the heights would command the plain and the city.

Peyre informed Joseph of everything that the Tsar had said including the hint of what might happen if the Allies breached the walls. The three traitors convened what they called the 'defence council' and without reference to or discussion with any of the Marshals, decided to capitulate. At this time all Allied attacks had been checked and repulsed, and Montmartre had yet to be tested. Joseph sent Marmont the following order:

'If Marshal Mortier and Marshal Marmont can no longer hold their positions, they are authorized to enter into negotiations with Prince Schwarzenberg and the Emperor of Russia facing them.

They will withdraw to the Loire.

Montmartre, 12:15 noon.

Joseph.'[31]

The order would leave Marmont little room to manoeuvre, referring as it did to his present situation, and not that which would obtain if he were able to hold the city. The second paragraph was explicit. Joseph delayed long enough to send notes to a few of the high dignitaries, telling them to leave the city, before galloping off to make his own exit. Before they left Montmartre, Hulin and Clarke ordered the 250 National Guardsmen to follow them back to the city, effectively reducing Marmont's *grande batterie* from 30 guns to a mere six.[32] But that was not all. Unknown to Marmont, Hulin with Clarke's approval had earlier that morning assembled (or hidden) the city's artillery garrison of 28 limbered guns into a 'reserve park', under Colonel Evain in the place du Trône. Evain had no orders, and Marmont and the other generals had not been informed of the existence of these guns.[33] After five hours the Colonel, hearing the fighting moving closer to the city, decided on his own initiative to take his 28 guns out to where they would be needed. Leaving Paris by the Vincennes gate, in the endeavour to find Marmont at Romanville, his unescorted column was spotted by Count Pahlen and part of the Russian cavalry, emerging from the Bois de Vincennes. Evain tried to fight off the cavalry with ten guns and would have been overrun, but for the arrival of the veteran dragoons of General Vincent who, galloping over ditches and garden enclosures, hit the Russians in the flank. Having lost eight guns, Evain returned to the place du Trône with the other 20 and stayed there for the rest of the day.

It was now nearly 1 o'clock. Marmont had fought prodigiously, inflicting serious losses on the Allies who had yet to fight their way up on to the plateau. Suddenly, thrust into his hand was Joseph's order to capitulate if he could not hold his position. Marmont was thunderstruck. He was intending to hold on outside the walls until at least dusk, and to hold the gates and streets next day; trusting that Napoleon would arrive by then. Marmont required further clarification before he would give up the fight. His aide, Colonel Fabvier, was sent to Montmartre to put Marmont's plans to Joseph, and to check whether Joseph's order meant that he was indeed to capitulate before an attack on the city proper began.

At the same time, Napoleon's personal aide-de-camp, General Dejean, arrived at the Palace, having been sent post-haste from Troyes. Finding the Empress gone, he tried to find Joseph and was directed to Montmartre. Borrowing a fresh horse, he arrived there to find this strategic position deserted save for 400 National Guardsmen infantry and a battery of six operational guns. Dejean, frantic, managed to catch up with Joseph at the Bois de Boulogne. Napoleon, Dejean informed Joseph, was racing to Paris with his army. The Emperor would reach Fontainebleau with part of the Guard this day, if he did not make Paris itself by nightfall. The city must hold out; Napoleon would be under its walls without fail next day.[34] Joseph would not listen – having betrayed his brother, he now wanted to distance himself. It was too late he said, Marshals Marmont and Mortier could not hold out, so he had authorized them to surrender when they could fight no more. He, Dejean must carry Napoleon's message to them. He was leaving Paris on the Emperor's instructions. Dejean raced on and found the brave old Mortier fighting between several towns in the suburbs. Dejean's message filled Mortier with hope; he was at this time totally ignorant of Joseph's order to Marmont. On his own initiative and at Dejean's suggestion, they sent a message to Schwarzenberg that Napoleon had opened peace negotiations with Emperor Francis at Dijon and had accepted terms; to avoid bloodshed would they grant 24 hours' armistice to clarify the terms? Schwarzenberg was not having any of this ruse – he had pulled the same stroke himself at Bar-sur-Aube. No, he replied, Mortier's information was untrue. The Allies had an indivisible union that forbade any one party from concluding a separate treaty. It was up to the Marshal alone to come to terms to save the city.

Fabvier returned to Marmont after nearly two hours of fruitless search for Joseph or Clarke: 'Monsieur le Maréchal, they have all flown,' he was told. Marmont had been involved in the heaviest fighting, his right arm in a sling from a previous wound, his sword in his mutilated left hand, his clothes torn and black with powder.

Forced back from the village of Belleville, his troops were attacked frontally and on both flanks simultaneously. Leading his brigade generals in person, in a furious bayonet charge they slowly drove out the enemy, house by house. His horse was shot from under him and several musket-balls ripped through his coat. Three generals fell near him, but he forced a passage for his 5,000 men out of the encirclement. Common sense told him to pull back and regroup behind the walls. All round the city the inhabitants were carrying the wounded away and bringing food and drink to the men. Many were helping to construct barricades. From the Belleville heights he watched the Allied troops preparing to assault his front at three different points. It was now half-past three. Marmont decided that he did not have the authority to fight in the streets of Paris – Joseph had denied him this. If Paris were sacked he would be blamed. Napoleon had not attacked Berlin, Vienna, Moscow or Madrid – surely if it were intended that he hold the walls Joseph would have ordered it. Marmont sent his aide to Schwarzenberg, requesting a ceasefire on two conditions: all French troops to be allowed to withdraw inside the city walls, and that they be allowed to evacuate the capital. Count Orlov, once again galloped through the lines, with the Tsar's agreement; they would meet later at an inn to discuss terms. Mortier joined Marmont and read Joseph's instructions. He did not like them, but agreed that Marmont's hands were tied; 'Why is Joseph not here?' he asked – as well he might.

At 5 o'clock the Marshals met Count Orlov and the Russian Secretary of State Count Nesselrode at the Auberge du Petit Jardinet. The Allies demanded that the city be surrendered. 'Never!' the Marshals replied to each and every argument on that point. Nesselrode returned to the Tsar for further advice. In the meantime the Allies attacked the right of the French line in direct contravention of the ceasefire. They later claimed that it had been a 'mistake', the commanders not having been notified of the armistice. However, French arms had little to be ashamed of that day. Old Marshal Moncey, the hero of the National Guard, with 400 men and six guns resisted an Allied attack by ten times that number, but the 30 guns on Montmartre fell to the Allies later that day, thanks to the treachery of Hulin who had removed the personnel of 24 of them despite Marmont's orders, and transferred the Young Guard battalion from Montmartre to Saint-Denis where they and the gallant 500 men of the town's national guard, resisted 6,000 Russians all day. When they ran out of ammunition they held on with the bayonet. The Russians decided not to waste any more lives there and bypassed them. A new expression had been coined this day: General Langeron, the *émigré* Frenchman fighting for the Allies, on being told of the ferocity of the French counter-attacks, exclaimed, 'What do you expect? They are defending their homes! It is but "the fury of the French!"

Moncey, reduced to two guns, had withdrawn step by step from Montmartre. The Marshal took himself off to the Clichy gate as the next scene of danger, and sent his aides to the nearest gates to organize their defence. At the Monceau gate, one of his aides tried to encourage the National Guard unit to advance and support two squadrons of cavalry being hotly pursued. It was a moment when their courage might have carried them forward, but one of their officers, the Duc de Fitz James, a noted royalist, ran to their front and shouted, 'The service asked of us is contrary to the constitution of the National Guard.'[35] On which note the men returned to the gate and piled arms. Artois' fifth column was working well. At the Neuilly bridge, however, fifty men of the Old Guard had held off over 600 Russians all day, and would continue to do so until the next morning.

At 7 o'clock Nesselrode returned. It was now quite dark and the fighting had ceased. The Allies, Nesselrode said, would allow the French army to leave, but only on a road stipulated by them. 'In that case, we shall defend Paris foot by foot, and when we're driven back to the Faubourg Saint-Germain we'll take the road to Fontainebleau. I cannot agree to an armistice that is incompatible with my honour and grants the Allies an advantage they would not be able to force!'[36] Orlov and Nesselrode were not authorized to accept this, but Nesselrode knew that the Tsar and Schwarzenberg were anxious to seal the fate of Paris. They knew that Napoleon was on his way and did not want him to enter the capital. More pressing was their shortage of ammunition, Napoleon in their rear having cut off their supplies. They had fought at Fère-Champenoise and at Meaux and today in Paris. They had insufficient ammunition left to both bombard and assault the city.

Mortier had heard enough. He left, saying: 'I leave further negotiations to Marshal Marmont. I must go now to take the necessary measures to assure the continual defence of the capital.' Orlov came up with a solution. It was dark now, he said, and the Allies could not stop the French from leaving by any road they chose. He, Orlov, would remain in Paris until 9 o'clock next morning as a sign of good faith, and hostilities would not commence until he returned to the Allied lines. By which time Marmont could capitulate or recommence hostilities. Nesselrode agreed and so did Marmont. Orlov was gambling on Marmont's using this respite to withdraw the French army towards Fontainebleau, and reckoned that he would not have time to organize the removal of the massive munitions stores. Marmont and Orlov went to Marmont's house in the rue de Paradis. When news of the armistice broke in the city, cries of 'Treason!' and 'Betrayal!' erupted on every hand; General Chastel echoed these sentiments in Marmont's hearing. Great crowds surrounded General Hulin's house, demanding muskets. Marmont had fought well for Paris, and it is probable that he would have held Paris until Napoleon arrived, but for the treachery of Joseph, Clarke, and Hulin. He had cost the Allies 7,000 dead and an equal number wounded.

Marmont entered his house to a tumultuous uproar. In his salon were the Postmaster Lavalette, Pasquier, Savary and Bourrienne – Napoleon's classmate and one-time secretary, whom he had sacked for fraud and theft. There were many senators and municipal councillors, the Prefect and generals, and of course Talleyrand. He immediately limped over to Count Orlov and announced for all to hear: ' My Lord, please bear your sovereign the assurance of the prince de Benevente's most profound respects toward His Majesty.' Orlov replied, 'Prince, I shall deliver this tribute to his Majesty without fail.'[37] Since Baron Vitrolles' mission, the Tsar had informed Orlov that Talleyrand was on their side, but he and his master had no idea of the compact between Castlereagh, Metternich, Artois and Talleyrand. This little demonstration of Talleyrand's standing with the Tsar impressed his minions and waverers, but someone not in on the conspiracy asked loudly, 'Has Talleyrand gone mad? What is he doing paying homage to the Tsar?'[38]

Talleyrand had not been idle during the afternoon. No sooner had Hulin and Clarke departed Montmartre, than they met him to receive his instructions. Clarke was to go to the Regency government at Blois and keep him informed. He should use his position to ensure that no men or *matériel* reached Napoleon. Hulin should leave with the army, spread despondency, and keep in touch. Talleyrand briefly outlined the course he intended to take on the Tsar's arrival. The royalist, Count Gain de Montagnac, was sent with the outline to Castlereagh and Metternich at Dijon with a request for the Allies' written approval and commitment to support him. Next morning the Baron told Castlereagh and Metternich: 'The majority of the National Guard is with us and half the Senate; Talleyrand will answer for that. The municipal council will support us by keeping order in the city, if Bonaparte is cut off from Paris. A general in the National Guard will take over the guard at the city hall. To be sure of his staff, he'll submit a list appointing new [royalist] officers to replace those he is not sure of. The municipal council will approve the list and issue a proclamation to the Parisians announcing that it is calling a senate to safeguard the security of the state. Protected by an élite of the National Guard, the Senate will meet and declare Bonaparte dethroned and Louis XVIII recalled. And I boldly predict, Messieurs, the spark will set Paris afire and sweep the country.'[39]

So Castlereagh, Metternich, Baron Hardenberg of Prussia and the Emperor of Austria knew the outcome of the 'will of the French People' a day before the Tsar, the Senate and the people of Paris themselves! Castlereagh wrote to inform the Prime Minister, Lord Liverpool:

> 'Unfortunately the messenger [Vitrolles] ... after an interview with Monsieur [Artois], was taken by peasants. However, in consequence of a letter from Castlereagh to a friend in Paris [Talleyrand] whom I knew to be with the party likely to conduct the expected movement, a new agent [de Montagnac] was sent to the Allies, from Paris. Prince Metternich, Baron Hardenberg, and myself saw him together, satisfied all his wishes and sent him back with our joint signatures to establish the fact of our full concert and trusting to his fidelity for a faithful report. His arrival, which we heard of, has no doubt had the best effects.'[40]

Castlereagh also included his intelligence from Nesselrode, that Joseph was intriguing with the Crown Prince and the Tsar. Talleyrand was now set to topple Napoleon and place Louis XVIII on the throne. It should be remembered that he had some experience of coups, having organized the one that had overthrown the Directory and replaced it with the young General Bonaparte. Meanwhile at Marmont's house, the delegation had hailed the Marshal as the hero of the hour: only he had stayed, while Joseph and the others had left them to be massacred. Talleyrand managed to ensure that he and a few important cronies remained to dine with the Marshal and Orlov. After the meal Talleyrand was closeted for a long time with Marmont, using all his wiles to win round the exhausted Marshal who had fought a record 67 engagements.

Marmont was one of Napoleon's oldest companions. The son of a royalist officer, he had been commissioned in the artillery in 1792. He made the acquaintance of Napoleon at Toulon and became his aide in 1795, accompanying him to Egypt, and being promoted General of Brigade en route. He assisted in Napoleon's *coup d'état* of 1800, and was appointed a Councillor of State by Napoleon as First Consul. At Marengo Napoleon appointed him General of Division – he was only 26 years old. To his bitter disappointment and deep resentment, he had not been made one of the original Marshals in 1804. He fought at Ulm in 1805, and in 1806 was created Governor-General of Dalmatia whence he drove out the Russians from Raguse, and earned his title – duc de Raguse. He was at Wagram in 1809, and at last gained his Marshal's baton which he felt he should have been given five years before. Napoleon had not refused it because of spite, but because of his age. After two years in Illyria, he was transferred to Spain in 1811. He fought Wellington there with great skill, until he was severely wounded in the arm at Salamanca by a cannon-shell. He saw no more action until 1813, since when he had fought without a break. Marmont was very brave, but over-sensitive. He also had an ambitious nature on which Talleyrand was now working.

CHAPTER 5

THE ROAD TO FONTAINEBLEAU

'Put not your trust in Princes.' – Machiavelli, *The Prince.*

A
T ABOUT THE TIME THAT MARMONT WAS BEING SUBORNED
by Talleyrand, Baron Pasquier had arrived at the Hôtel de Ville with officers of the National Guard and other city officials who were party to the
conspiracy. He announced that as soon as the capitulation was signed he
would go to the Tsar at his headquarters at Bondy to discuss civil matters, adding as
a rationalization for his treason that 'Marmont's authority is limited only to the military'. Pasquier now openly paraded his treason. He and the Prefect of the Seine gave
orders for bread, meat and *eau de vie* to be provided for the Allied troops, and the
requisition of billets for their officers – before any capitulation had been agreed,
drawn up or signed. As a member of the Regency Council he was in contravention of
Napoleon's order that the government should leave Paris and not assist the occupying forces. He was a collaborator.

A messenger from the Allies arrived at Marmont's house at 2 o'clock in the
morning. The Allies agreed to the French withdrawal, reserving only the right to
pursue them after Paris had been occupied. The articles were drawn up in the Marshal's salon. Colonel Fabvier, his aide, begged Marmont to reconsider; surely he
could hold Paris for one more day? Marmont declined. He would lead his troops
south to Fontainebleau. Marmont ordered Fabvier to surrender the barriers in the
morning, then join him on the River Essone. Fabvier refused, wanting no part in this
shameful capitulation.

General Flahaut, an aide-de-camp sent ahead by the Emperor, had now arrived,
covered with mud, to order Marmont to break off negotiations and defend the capital
– 'The Emperor is only ten miles from Paris!' But Talleyrand had mixed the poison
too well. No doubt he had catalogued the injustices to which Marmont had been submitted: he, the hero of Paris, had never been appreciated by Napoleon – why else had
his elevation to Marshal been so long delayed?[1] Twice recently he had been upbraided
unjustly for making unwise decisions. Yet it was left to him at a moment's notice to
defend the capital, while Napoleon's blustering brother had run away and left him to
shoulder the responsibility. He would rise under the new government if he had the
foresight to come in at the beginning – letters from Artois, Castlereagh and Metternich guaranteed it. Marmont had been convinced. Marmont now had positive news
of Napoleon's approach and intentions and, more to the point, definitive orders that
overrode Joseph's. Marmont deliberately chose to override them. The Allies could
have been delayed by him on technicalities or pretexts, from attacking before mid-
morning of the following day, by which time he and Napoleon would have been able
to defend the city. Instead he sent General Flahaut with a letter to Napoleon:

'General Flahaut asked me if I believed the Parisians were disposed to defend themselves. I tell your Majesty the complete truth. Not only have they no inclination to defend themselves, they are quite firmly resolved not to. It seems the mood changed completely when the Empress left, and the departure of King Joseph and the entire government at noon brought discontent to a head ... No effort could bring the National Guard to fight now ... We had a hot and quite glorious battle today, killed a terrific number of the enemy ... Unable to continue the fight, we concluded a convention by which we are able to have evacuated the city by 7.00 a. m., and to respect an armistice until nine. My troops will start marching at 5 a.m.'[2]

This letter was a clever stratagem. In it the Emperor is told that the people, including the National Guard, have lost the will to fight, which was patently untrue. Marmont says that he was unable to continue the fight, but in the light of Flahaut's new orders he should have been able to do so. He rightly blames all on Joseph and the Empress's departure, which Napoleon would believe; but implies that the government had also left, which he knew was a lie. On the evidence of this letter Napoleon had to gamble on entering an undefended city with a mutinous populace and no administrative structure, and defending it against the Allies. Marmont knew that Napoleon feared the mob. He reckoned that Napoleon would not enter the city before the Allies. To lend credence to this concoction of *suppressio veri* and *suggestio falsi*, Marmont was leading his troops towards Napoleon, not to Fontainebleau but stopping short at the River Essone so as to give the appearance of acting as both Napoleon's advance and rearguard. General Flahaut left with this dispatch at 4 a.m. Marmont knew that it would not arrive before 6 o'clock by which time it would be too late for Napoleon to stop his troops leaving, or to arrive before the barriers were surrendered at 7 o'clock. So, while the Tsar slept contentedly at Bondy, and the Allied troops were encamped in a semicircle between the loops of the Seine, Talleyrand worked late into the night preparing for the Allies' entry next day. Marmont's troops, meanwhile, were marching out of the rear of the city, towards the River Essone and, as they thought, their junction with the Emperor. Their commander, Marshal Marmont, duc de Raguse, however, had other ideas.

Throughout that fateful day of 30 March 1814, Napoleon had been racing for Paris. At 1 o'clock he had reached Sens where he sent for the mayor and requested him to find 50,000 rations for his army that was following in his wake. Stopping only long enough to eat, while the coach horses were changed, Napoleon and his entourage, together with the 1,000-strong escort of his élite Imperial Guard cavalry, sped on towards Paris, passing Fontainebleau without stopping. At Corbeil-Essones, just over twenty miles from Paris, he heard the grim news that there had been fighting around Paris all day. At 11 o'clock his coach clattered into the courtyard of the post inn Cour du France, at Juvisy, exactly ten miles from Paris. While the horses were being changed Napoleon strolled out to stretch his legs and came upon General Belliard and his cavalry. A brief exchange sufficed to convince him that he had lost the race.

'Who is that?'

'General Belliard, Sire.'

'Eh bien, Belliard. What's up? What are you doing here with your cavalry? Where is the enemy?'

'At the gates of Paris, Sire.'

'And the Army?'

'Following me, Sire.'

'Then who is protecting Paris?'

'It has been evacuated. The enemy is to enter tomorrow at 9 o'clock. The National Guard is manning the barriers.'

'And my wife? My son? Where are they? Where is Mortier? Where is Marmont?'

'The Empress, your son, and the entire court left for Rambouillet the day before yesterday. I think they're to go to Orléans from there. The Marshals must still be in Paris completing arrangements.'

'What arrangements?'[3]

Belliard then told him everything that had occurred since 19 March. Berthier and Caulaincourt had now joined the Emperor. 'What cowardice! ... Capitulating! ... Joseph has lost everything ... Four hours too late! ... If I'd arrived here four hours sooner, everything would be saved.' Turning to Caulaincourt and Berthier, 'Eh bien, you heard what Belliard said, Messieurs. Four hours compromised our cause. My good, loyal Parisians can still save it for a few hours of courage. Caulaincourt, my carriage! I'll put myself at the head of our National Guard and our troops. We'll save the situation yet ... General Belliard, order the troops to turn back.' Belliard tried to point out that it was doubtful if any troops were left in the capital.

Napoleon: 'The National Guard is there, your troops will join me, we'll gain a delay, and the whole army will be with us in 36 hours. We can set things right. Bring up my carriage! Follow me with your cavalry!'

Belliard: 'But Sire, Your Majesty is exposing himself to being taken ... Besides I can't go back to Paris because I left under a convention.'[4]

Napoleon: 'What convention? Who made it? Who gave the order? ... What is Joseph doing? Where is the Minister of war?' Belliard: '... I've heard the convention was made by Marshals Mortier and Marmont. As for orders, we didn't get a single order all day. I don't know where Prince Joseph and the Minister of War went. The army didn't see them all day ... And, as I've already had the honour of informing Your Majesty, the Empress, the King of Rome, and the court left for Rambouillet.'

Napoleon: 'Why were they sent out of Paris?'

Belliard: 'There I can tell Your Majesty nothing except that people say it was on Your Majesty's orders.'

Napoleon: 'We must go to Paris. When I'm not there, people bungle everything ... Paris had ten times what was needed to meet the storm if anyone had shown a little initiative, nothing was done right.'

Belliard: 'We kept hoping Your Majesty would arrive. When a rumour that you were there reached the army, cries of "Vive l'Empereur!" burst out everywhere. The men had such a surge of ardour that the enemy, already nervous about approaching such a large city, slowed down its advance ... There was one battalion of National Guardsmen on Montmartre, covering the roads to Saint-Denis and Neuilly ... As to fortifications, I didn't see any, at least not where I was.'

Napoleon's fury erupted. 'What! Montmartre wasn't fortified? Where were the heavy cannon? Where were the men?' Belliard: 'There were just a few palisades at the barriers, 1,800 horsemen in the plain, and six cannon on Montmartre, not all of which had ammunition.'

Napoleon: 'Clarke's a fool or a traitor ... Montmartre should have been fortified and equipped with big-calibre guns for a vigorous defence.'

Belliard: 'Fortunately the enemy assumed, as you do, Sire, that Montmartre would be fortified. I think they were afraid of it because they approached with great caution and not until three in the afternoon. Unfortunately no preparations had been made and there were only six 6-pounder guns.'

Napoleon: 'What happened to all my cannon then? I had at least 200 in Paris and more than 200,000 charges. Why wasn't it put in place along your front?'

Belliard: 'I don't know Sire.'

Napoleon: 'Yet everyone knew I was coming on the enemy's heels, and that was bound to influence him. With me so close, the Allies would have lost courage if you had just held out. It would have been easy to gain a day. Joseph is a *con* and Clarke's an ignoramus, a little man who should never have been pulled out of his office routine ... There is some intrigue behind this ... What a great rush everyone was in! Joseph lost me Spain, now he's losing me Paris, and that means France, Caulaincourt. Four hours too late! What a fatal blow!'[5]

Napoleon turned to Caulaincourt and continued furiously: '... If only I had my troops at hand tomorrow when the enemy's drunk with the triumph of entering Paris ... It's not over yet. If I'm supported, the retaking of Paris will launch our victory ... The enemy will pay dearly for having dared steal three marches on us. Flahaut! go see Marshal Marmont. Order him to break off the talks and resume the battle with his corps and the National Guard.'[6]

Fatally, instead of pressing on to Paris with his escort[7] where he would have been in time to prevent the capitulation, and confound the conspirators, Napoleon waited at the inn until Flahaut returned with Marmont's letter at 6 o'clock.

It was during these crucial hours that Napoleon lost Paris. The Allies, desperately short of ammunition, would have baulked at his presence and probably retreated north, fearful of his army arriving in their rear, as at Dresden. By the time

Flahaut returned with Marmont's letter, the capitulation had been signed and Marmont had sent his troops off towards him and Fontainebleau. Had Napoleon followed his natural instinct, and had not met Belliard, his arrival would have swept Paris with patriotic fervour – such as greeted Caulaincourt when he arrived a couple of hours later; the Parisians thinking that Napoleon must be close at hand. Napoleon decided to return to Fontainebleau, await his army, and plan his attack on the Allies. He had already calculated that they would have to fight outside the city walls, while keeping a large reserve within to cover their escape northwards if they should be defeated. If Schwarzenberg tried to hold the city, Napoleon would attack from the south where there were no natural defences like Montmartre. To weaken the Allies further, he planned to send a force across the Marne and Seine to approach from the north. While his army was attacking and tying down the defenders, the populace of Paris, which greatly outnumbered the Allies troops, would rise up all around them, in every street and alleyway – as at Rheims – and they would be massacred; Paris would be their graveyard.[8]

At 5 o'clock on the morning of 31 March, while Marmont's troops were marching towards the Essone, Marmont released Count Orlov. The agreement had been that he would remain with the French until 9 o'clock. Marmont, having capitulated at 2 a.m., was now allowing the Allies another four hours in which to prepare to thwart any attempt by Napoleon to recapture Paris. At Bondy the Tsar was woken at 6 o'clock by Orlov with the news of the capitulation of Paris; Baron Pasquier was awaiting outside with a delegation from the city, to greet the Tsar and co-operate in the occupation.

On 31 March 1814, at 10 o'clock, the Tsar fulfilled his dream of marching into Paris at the head of his guards, in emulation of Napoleon's triumphal entry into the capitals of Europe. The sullen crowds were silent as the Allies passed through the workers' districts. The royalists were quick to say that the white armbands worn as a recognition sign by the Allied soldiers was 'the emblem of their support' for the Bourbons. Most of the cheering along the route came from strategically sited groups of royalists or paid layabouts. Some of the royalists' antics embarrassed the Allies and showed clearly the type of supporters that the Bourbons attracted. The young noblemen of the 'Chevaliers de la Foi', such as the duc de Fitz James who had stopped his men from attacking at the barriers, Chateaubriand's nephew Sosthne de La Rochefoucauld, and the marquess de Maubreuil, who was in debt for trying to sell the army substandard military supplies, rode about dragging the insignia of the Legion of Honour through the mud. Their 'ladies', in the balconies along the Boulevard des Italiens, threw down white cockades and waved white handkerchiefs. All along the route the young royalists ran alongside Alexander cheering and shouting 'Long live the King! Long live Louis!' Tsar Alexander, unimpressed, rode straight to Talleyrand's palatial mansion. Here, he told Talleyrand, he would reside, because he had been informed that the palace had been mined with explosives. This wasn't the case, but Talleyrand had arranged for Pasquier to tell the Tsar that it was and suggest that he lodge with Talleyrand. The situation added prestige and authority to Talleyrand's claims to the royalists, and gave him direct access to the Tsar and the means of vetting his visitors.

In the presence of the King of Prussia and Prince Schwarzenburg, the Tsar began the political dialogue with Talleyrand, whom he trusted, Talleyrand having sold him information in the past when he was Napoleon's foreign secretary, and given him advice to Napoleon's detriment. But the Tsar had no knowledge of Talleyrand's secret compact with Castlereagh, Metternich and Artois. Through Nesselrode's intrigues with these ministers, Talleyrand already knew what the Tsar was about to say and had his plausible answers ready.[9] 'Monsieur Talleyrand, we now have four choices: to negotiate with the Emperor Napoleon, to establish a Regency, to make Bernadotte head of state, or to recall the Bourbons.' Talleyrand immediately replied: 'Emperor Alexander is under a slight misapprehension. There are not four choices but only one, the last his Majesty mentioned.'[10] With great verve Talleyrand rapidly eliminated the first three. Napoleon, because they had tried to negotiate – but he wouldn't. A Regency would work if Napoleon were dead, but alive Napoleon would still rule through his son. 'As for Bernadotte – a soldier again? No thank you Sire, if we wanted a soldier we would keep the one we have. He's first in the world.'

Talleyrand now played on Alexander's fears. 'To achieve something lasting, one must act on a principle. With a principle, we are strong, we meet no resistance, and any objections will be effaced in a little time. There is only one principle. Louis XVIII is a principle. He is the legitimate king of France.'[11] Alexander wasn't about to buy this idea. 'The Bourbons', he said, 'were *passés*, absolutists, inflexible and vengeful.' He Alexander 'knew this from his own dealings with them over the last decade'. France, he declared, would not accept them.

Alexander, it must be remembered, favoured a strong government, with a strong leader, preferably someone dependant on Russian support. Someone who would side with Russia after the war. Alexander, the autocrat, Tsar of all the Russias, was hampered by having been brought up by a tutor who had indoctrinated him with the idea of enlightened despotism. Like Napoleon, he believed in the dichotomy doctrine of Voltaire and others, that you could be a benevolent despot yet rule by the will of the people.

Talleyrand countered this denigration of the Bourbons by stating that they would rule constitutionally, the people of France would offer them the throne solely on that condition. This was a superb ploy. He knew what the Bourbons were like; he agreed with everything that Alexander had said. But he knew that his plan would receive absolute backing from Britain, whose system he admired. He had no faith in the Bourbons and their outdated concept of absolute monarchy; if he had, he would have backed their return in 1800 instead of helping to put Napoleon into power.

Talleyrand would back the British system for the sake of his first and foremost principle – Talleyrand. He admired it because the monarch reigned, but the power and prestige rested with the First Minister. Talleyrand was now setting wheels in motion to double-cross the Bourbons and their embarrassing 'ultra royalists' and

'Chevaliers de la Foi' terrorist organization; he despised them but he would use them. He would arrange for an emasculated Bourbon restoration, with himself as First Minister. He already had Artois's signature in his pocket and Austrian and British support – with whom else would they do business? His position after the hostilities had ended was guaranteed.

Talleyrand now drove home Castlereagh's argument against Bernadotte and the Regency. Would the Tsar impose a civil war on France? Would he use his troops to impose his faction, and for how long? 'No, not even you, who have conquered France, can impose a king on the French nation. All-powerful though you are, you are not powerful enough to choose for France. If you did, the country would rise *en masse* against the invasion, and Your Imperial Majesty is well aware of the terrible power of a nation aroused.'[12] These words were as prophetic as they were true, but Alexander was still unconvinced. Nothing he had seen supported a Bourbon restoration. He was not impressed with the behaviour of the 'ultras' – he himself was a recipient of that Legion of Honour whose insignia he had seen dragged through the mire; 'What nation degrades its own Orders of chivalry?' he had said to his aide. No, Alexander had seen the thousands of young French National Guardsmen at Fère-Champenoise preferring death to surrender, shouting '*Vive l'Empereur!*' at every step. Even yesterday, despite treachery and a weak defence, Paris had not been taken.

Talleyrand the great whist player now played his ace: let Alexander but allow the Senate to be called and he guaranteed that they would declare for the Bourbons. 'Are you sure of it?' Alexander asked in disbelief. 'I guarantee it, Sire,' Talleyrand repeated. Would not a restored Bourbon owe his throne also to the Tsar of Russia? Talleyrand hinted. The Tsar consulted the King of Prussia who, witnesses said, behaved as though he were the Tsar's junior aide, and Prince Schwarzenberg, who naturally agreed with Talleyrand's point of view. The Tsar then instructed Talleyrand to call the Senate and ask for its views. Talleyrand had learnt the lesson of the Malet conspiracy well – and was about to prove it.

No sooner had he taken his leave of the Tsar, than he instructed a royalist printer, installed in his house, to run off an invitation:

'The Prince de Benevente has been invited by His Majesty Emperor Alexander to present to the Senate the propositions of the Allied powers. He will be at the Palace of the Senate at 3.30 p.m. precisely.

Your presence is requested.'[13]

Talleyrand now moved rapidly. While Napoleon at Fontainebleau was dispatching his troops to their designated positions as unit after weary unit arrived, Talleyrand mobilized the Royalists into displays of Bourbon support. Some tried to pull Napoleon's statue down from the Vendôme Column. The Archbishop de Malines, in full clerical dress and wearing his Legion of Honour, ran about the streets shouting, '*Vive le Roi!*' which created a scandal. Chateaubriand circulated his vituperative pamphlet *De Buonaparte et des Bourbons...* accusing Napoleon of terrible war crimes. Chateaubriand, the outstanding literary genius of the early nineteenth century, had a personal grudge against Napoleon. In 1808 his cousin Armand, an agent of the

Chevaliers de la Foi, had been apprehended on his arrival from Jersey by Fouché's secret police, and executed by firing-squad. Too late to sue for a pardon, Napoleon being in Spain, Chateaubriand had found his body in a ditch being mauled by dogs.[14]

At this point, the activities of the 'ultras' were becoming an embarrassment to Talleyrand who was on the horns of a dilemma. He had to seem to be encouraging and supporting them, and their public displays were useful in that they gave the impression that the general populace was clamouring for the restoration. But at the same time, their antics were such as to remind the people just why they and their useless king had been deposed. Furthermore they were alienating the military – whom Talleyrand needed – for example, publishing Louis XVIII's Declaration of February, from Hartwell, England. In this Louis derided the Legion of Honour and other decorations instituted by Napoleon and promised any soldier who would defect 'rewards more real, distinctions more honourable than those they had received from a usurper'. This from a man who had fought nothing in his life greater than a steak-and-kidney pudding and acid-indigestion. It so angered pro-Talleyrand generals who had won these decorations on the field of battle that he deemed it expedient to have a poster put up denying its authenticity. Some 163 different anti-Napoleon posters appeared within three days of the Allied entry. But Pasquier's police reports show that some hundreds of young royalists were severely beaten up by the populace and eleven were killed. One was hanged from a lamp-post with a white cockade stuffed in his mouth – a political statement as to where the lower classes' loyalties lay.

At 3.30 on 1 April Talleyrand presided at the meeting of those senators that had decided to attend. Any senator thought likely to speak on Napoleon's behalf or against the Bourbons was prevented from entering – Cromwellian fashion – by Talleyrand's élite [royalist] National Guard. The entire proceedings were of course illegal, neither Talleyrand nor Alexander having the authority to call the Senate. As it was, only 64 of 140 senators attended – less than 50 per cent. Talleyrand proposed the formation of a provisional government, headed by himself, and the return of the Bourbons. He then coerced, bullied and bribed the senators to agree to these measures; those that wouldn't, had their signatures forged or were allowed to abstain. Talleyrand declared the result as being the unanimous decision of the whole Senate. The voice of the nation. His provisional government comprised Pasquier as Chief of Police and the Prefect, Chambrol, both retaining their former posts. Bourrienne, Napoleon's one-time secretary, who had embezzled funds, was made Post-Master General in place of Lavalette; Count Beugnot, the Chevaliers de la Foi's Prefect of Lille, was made Minister of Foreign Affairs. General Dessole replaced Marshal Moncey, who had joined Napoleon, as Commander of the National Guard. General Dupont, who had surrendered at Bailen, was made Minister of War.

Talleyrand had arranged for the Tsar to meet the senators formally after their deliberations, and to dupe him as to the extent of his support, arranged for actors and royalists to wear the impressive state robes of the missing 76 senators. The whole pantomime, dressed in gold suits and white sashes, black felt hats with white plumes, met the Tsar. He stated that he would respect their decisions, but gave no firm indication of his views as to the Bourbons. Afterwards they had a champagne supper at Talleyrand's house, to toast the restoration.

Now that Talleyrand was in possession of the official seals, he had the rump Senate rubber-stamp anything he wanted. Compromised with Napoleon, fearful of Talleyrand, the senators were promised a job and pension for life in return for compliance. Very soon the newspapers, now controlled by royalists, and their street posters, announced the will of the Senate and the people. Napoleon was deposed as an enemy of the people. The Act ending the Empire concluded by releasing the soldiers from their allegiance to Napoleon. A proclamation to the army, signed by the members of the provisional government, read: 'You have never fought for your fatherland. You can't go on fighting against her under the flag of the man who ravaged the country and delivered it, unarmed and defenceless, to the enemy … a man who isn't even French … You are no longer Napoleon's soldiers. The Senate and all France release you from your orders.'[15]

General Clarke was at Blois with the rump Regency council. Maintaining the fiction of supporting Napoleon, he was instrumental in raising local army units and making sure that they were sent anywhere other than to Napoleon. Reports of Napoleon's presence five miles from the city had sent a shiver of fear through the Allies and the conspirators. Schwarzenberg began to move his troops through the city and out of the southern gates towards the Essone. The Parisians became aware of the fact that the war was not yet over, as thousands upon thousands of Allied soldiers marched through the city heading south. Anything that Talleyrand's clique decreed was worthless so long as Napoleon sat outside with an army that already (2 April) totalled 60,000 men. Talleyrand and his fellows knew that despite any agreement they had made with the Allies, it would mean the guillotine if Napoleon caught them first.

Schwarzenberg and the Tsar now began to consider what to do in the event of an attack. Neither of them wished to lose his army in Paris. Both were conscious that none of Napoleon's garrisons, in the north – stretching to Prussia, or on the Rhine, or in Italy had surrendered or defected to the Bourbons. Nor had any army commander save Augereau at Lyons, and his had been a personal defection and had not included his men.

Schwarzenberg was for retreating north towards Meaux, putting two rivers between the Allies and Napoleon and giving a clear line of retreat. Orders were sent to corps commanders: the screen to the south would cover them. These orders were kept from the members of the provisional government in case they bolted and left the Allies facing a hostile populace.[16] Napoleon, it seemed, was about to recapture Paris. Pasquier was busy ensuring that the city ran smoothly for the Allies, but he was concerned about the military situation and said as much to Baron Dalberg. 'You are right,' said Dalberg. 'That's why we are seeking other means of security.' Dalberg enlarged on this by saying that the Chevaliers de la Foi, having risked all, had no intention of letting Napoleon succeed on the battlefield. They were planning to dress some of their fanatical young men in uniforms of Napoleon's bodyguard, the Chasseurs of the Imperial Guard, using clothing from their depot stores. Led by the marquess de Maubreuil, they would endeavour to kill Napoleon either before or during the action.[17] Within hours Lavalette, having heard of this, approached Pasquier, who had also received a report of it from one of his police inspectors. At this juncture, Napoleon had sent a messenger to Baron Pasquier with a message hidden in a knife handle, 'Can I count on you?' Pasquier immediately informed Talleyrand and they agreed that as the plot was blown it would be as well if he warned Napoleon – in case the Allies lost. Pasquier sent the report to Napoleon with a single sentence: 'Don't count on me for anything more, what I shall do should be clear from what I have done.'[18]

Napoleon had ridden out to Corbeil-Essones to inspect Marmont's troops who gave him a rapturous reception. He dined with Marmont who no doubt attempted to justify his conduct in the defence of Paris by blaming everything on Joseph and Clarke. Marmont also sowed the seeds in Napoleon's mind that Paris was rife with disaffection to his regime. But Napoleon had received intelligence that the Allied strength numbered 145,000 effectives. He also had reliable information that the Parisians, as he had predicted, would rise against the occupying forces.[19] He knew that the Allies would not risk their armies in a pitched battle around a hostile Paris, with no support. The Crown Prince's Army of the North was 115 miles away; the Austrian army corps at Lyons were 220 miles away and Wellington was at Toulouse – a staggering 380 miles by road. Napoleon had cut off the Allied supply line. His orders show that he intended to block the Allied retreat to Meaux with one corps holding the river, while he smashed the forces to the south of the city and pursued them through the city to entrap them at Meaux.

Napoleon had no idea that Marmont had turned his coat and was preparing to defect. Since the capitulation he had liaised continuously with Talleyrand. He had circulated all the subversive proclamations and letters throughout the army, and ensured that the seeds of disaffection reached the officers and generals at Fontainebleau. Not unnaturally, the urgent speculation among these gentlemen was what would happen to them and their families if they continued to support Napoleon now that he had been deposed by the Senate. Would they be declared traitors? Would their titles, pensions, lands, homes and decorations be stripped from them?

Marmont was approached by many field officers. He reassured them, saying that he believed that if they adhered to the provisional government they would retain all. But what a decision to have to make! If only Napoleon would see sense and come to terms? This was the senior officers' dilemma. To support Napoleon and be treated as traitors by those in Paris. Or support the provisional government and betray their oath to Napoleon. There was of course no dilemma for the rank-and-file or the junior officers. They were cannon-fodder for either side and had no grand titles, privileges, or wealth to worry about. For them it was either a return to an autocratic government that would allow advancement only to men of birth or wealth, who would inevitably pass the burden of taxation to their shoulders as of old. Or an autocratic Emperor who would advance anyone on merit, and had transferred their tax burden to others.

Having staked everything in forming his provisional government, it was now time for Talleyrand to play his last card. In the afternoon of 3 April he sent a messenger to Marmont. This was Charles de Montessuy, a former aide of the Marshal's. He arrived dressed as a Cossack and handed Marmont a signed copy of the Senate's resolution to call Louis XVIII to the throne, and four letters: one from Artois confirming that Marmont would not only keep his present titles, but gain others provided that he assist in bringing peace to France; one from Schwarzenberg, one from Talleyrand and one other. Talleyrand spelt out that the fate of all was in Marmont's hands and that he must once again be the man of the hour. In return he could expect the highest position in the new regime. Marmont wrote back to Schwarzenberg that not only would he defect with his corps, but would if possible help to assist in Napoleon's capture! His only stipulation being that Napoleon must not be killed. Naturally this would sully his reputation as the saviour of France.[20]

While this was taking place another drama was unfolding at Fontainebleau. Napoleon's army had now concentrated, his corps commanders Marshals Oudinot, Lefebvre and Moncey having been joined by Macdonald and Ney. The latter two were horrified that Napoleon intended to attack Paris. Neither of them was a strategist on the grand scale. They were both brave men, none could deny that, and first-class commanders, and they had been fighting without rest since 1812. But they were not politicians, being naïve and lacking the Machiavellian skills necessary for valid judgements. For them the answer was always black or white. Napoleon should accept terms and not be stubborn. They had no idea that politicians tend to change the ground rules as they go along. They had read the propaganda spewed out by the royalist press and taken part in the discussions among the commanders that Marmont had encouraged. These warlords did not want to lose everything that they had fought for, or their honours, homes, wealth and dignity. With a tacit agreement that Marshal Ney should be their spokesman, they decided to mutiny.

Ney was the hero of the army. Nicknamed '*le rougeaud*' because of his copper-coloured hair, he had a temper to match. The son of a cooper, he had started his military career under the Bourbons, and had risen to the exalted rank of sergeant-major in the Colonel-General's Hussars, which was as high as one of his lowly birth could go. During the Revolution, in rapid succession he became general of brigade in 1796 and divisional general in 1799. Napoleon created him a Marshal of the Empire in 1804. In 1808 he became duc d'Elchingen, in recognition of his role in that action. In November 1812, Ney's conduct as commander of the rear-guard of the *Grande Armée* during its parlous retreat from Moscow had saved thousands of lives and made him a living legend. Napoleon had called him the 'Bravest of the Brave' and the appellation had stuck. In 1813, in recognition of his role during the retreat he was created prince de la Moskowa. Ney's influence and opinion carried great weight, especially with the rank and file.

Napoleon was in his study discussing with Berthier, Maret and Bertrand the report of Caulaincourt's failed mission, when Ney entered unannounced. 'Is there any news from Paris, Sire?' Ney asked. 'None whatsoever,' Napoleon replied. 'Well I have heard bad news, Sire. The Senate has declared against you. It has sided with Talleyrand and announced you deposed.' Napoleon blew up at this. 'The Senate has no power to do this, since the Empire is based on the votes of the whole nation! Only the people can demand the abdication of their Emperor! and as for the Allies, I am going to crush them before Paris!'

Ney then voiced the views of the Marshals: they refused to attack Paris; they didn't want Paris destroyed like Moscow. And they didn't want to take part in a civil war. Napoleon was flabbergasted; they had been seduced by propaganda he said. Marshal Lefebvre supported Ney. 'A pity, that peace was not concluded sooner. Now the only thing left for you to do is abdicate.' 'Sire,' said Ney, 'I know that my family and myself will be only too happy to serve your son if he rules in peace.' Napoleon, however, indicated the pins on his map. 'The enemy is in a position inviting defeat. Look!' he said, indicating the north of the city, 'In a few days we will cut their communications, here! The people will rise against the Allies ...' Here Napoleon was interrupted by the entry of Macdonald and Oudinot. Gesturing at these Marshals he continued: 'You see, I have another 50,000 men, they will march with me to Paris. When we have driven the Allies from our gates, it will be time for the people to decide ...' But Ney was already speaking to Macdonald: 'Nothing short of abdication will get us out of this mess.' Macdonald spoke: 'I must declare to you that we do not mean to expose Paris to the fate of Moscow! We have reached our decision and we are resolved to make an end to all this.' Napoleon tried again to explain his plan, but the Marshals were not listening. 'But Sire,' Ney said, 'the army will not march on Paris!' Napoleon, now very angry, banged his fist on the table and shouted, 'The army will obey me!' 'Sire,' Ney retorted, 'the army will obey its commanders!' Napoleon knew that he could dismiss his Marshals; he knew that the army would follow him; and he could promote younger, ambitious divisional generals to replace the Marshals, but their dismissal would have a devastating effect on the morale of his army and provide ammunition for his enemies.

He decided to show the Marshals what he was up against on the political front. He dismissed them but recalled them in the afternoon. He handed Caulaincourt a piece of paper and indicated to him that he should show it to the Marshals:

'Since the foreign Powers have declared that the Emperor Napoleon is the only obstacle to the re-establishment of the peace in Europe, the Emperor Napoleon, faithful to his oath, declares himself ready to descend from the throne, to leave France, and even to lay down his life for the welfare of his country, which is inseparable from the rights of his son, those of the Regency of the Empress, and the maintenance of the laws of the Empire. Given at our palace of Fontainebleau: 4 April 1814.'[21]

This was a magnificent diplomatic stroke. The Allies had proclaimed and trumpeted the fact that he, Napoleon, was the sole obstacle to peace – very well, he would abdicate, and his crown would descend to his son as it would in the case of any of the Allied monarchs. It might drive a wedge between Austria and the others, naming as it did Marie-Louise as Regent, and his son, Francis's grandson, as the new Emperor of the French Empire. If accepted, it would mean that Talleyrand's clique was illegal and the imperial law valid. If, as he suspected, the Allies refused it, his Marshals would see that they were not be trusted and they would be honour-bound to fight for him against the perfidious Allies and their quisling puppet government. Besides, he had not actually abdicated but merely offered to do so in order to show his recalcitrant Marshals the facts of political life. If by mischance the Tsar accepted the offer, he would rule through his wife and son – but he knew that Alexander would not accept it.

Caulaincourt would take the offer to the Allies accompanied by Ney and Macdonald, the leaders of the mutiny, both honourable, if stubborn men. Let Marmont go too he ordered, it would perhaps help stiffen their resolve – such was the trust he reposed in his oldest colleague. However, in his gamble, he had failed to realize that his Marshals might not be subtle enough to distinguish a conditional offer to abdicate, from an abdication proper. In the meantime, however, he could get on with his plans for the forthcoming battle and talk to the other, less stubborn Marshals.

At 5 o'clock on 4 April, the Marshals arrived unexpectedly at Marmont's headquarters. He was thunderstruck at their news. If Napoleon were abdicating, Marmont's defection would be treason without the mitigating excuse that to hasten peace he was abandoning Napoleon because he would not negotiate. If the Tsar accepted Napoleon's son, his head would soon be forfeit. Treason is only rewardable if it succeeds. Marmont admitted to the Marshals that he had replied favourably to Schwarzenberg's overtures to break with Napoleon and that his letter of acceptance might be arriving at any moment. He justified himself by saying that he thought the Emperor and France lost, and hoped to save both by bringing about a prompt peace. What could he do now? The Marshals said that he had two choices: go to Napoleon and confess all, or come with them and try and undo the harm he had done. Marmont refused the first option; Napoleon, he said, would have him shot. The Marshals decided to take him along to keep an eye on him, and try to prevent his corps defecting in his absence.

The envoys were taken to Schwarzenberg's headquarters and the Austrian commander sent a messenger to Paris to ask if the Tsar would receive them. During their conversation, Marmont stayed hidden in the coach. Schwarzenberg told them that he knew that the Allies would not accept Marie-Louise as Regent. The Marshals disregarded this as being personal spite on his part; they reckoned that Francis would not abandon his daughter and his influence over the French court. Schwarzenberg left them for a while and on his return they were surprised to see him with Marmont, who now appeared to be more confident. At 10 o'clock the permission came through and they made their way to Paris.

Word of the envoy's mission reached Talleyrand from Schwarzenberg, before it had reached the Tsar. Talleyrand was with Baron Vitrolles, newly released from the

French peasants' clutches, having assumed the guise of the Austrian diplomat's servant, and had been released by Napoleon with that individual. Vitrolles was awaiting dispatches to take to Artois and Castlereagh. The Tsar decided to receive the envoys before meeting the provisional government. They assembled in 'terror', according to the Abbé de Montesquiou.

The Tsar greeted the Marshals with expressions of warm admiration for the French Army. Once again he recounted the indelible impression the boys of the National Guard had made on him at Fère-Champenoise. He said that he was no longer Napoleon's enemy, now that Napoleon's fortunes had sunk so low. He respected the Marshals for their devotion and duty, '... instead of doing as many others have done, throwing themselves into our arms and doing their best to overturn their Emperor and Empire'.[22] This statement showed the contempt he had for Talleyrand and his clique. At this point Ney nearly wrecked the mission by saying how fed up the Marshals were with Napoleon's ambition for war, but Macdonald intervened and brought the discussion back to the abdication. 'Has he abdicated?' asked the Tsar. 'On behalf of his son,' was the reply. The Tsar dwelt on this situation, and poised Castlereagh and Talleyrand's arguments against such an arrangement. The envoys were furious. 'The people didn't want the Bourbons, émigrés and royalists in power so that they could avenge themselves for a past revolution that time had forgotten! The miserable lickspittle Senate didn't represent public opinion. It had no legal right to act. It was an instrument of the Empire. If the Empire was overturned then it ceased to exist! They represented the views of the army; the army was united on this!' Macdonald then addressed the Tsar in words that were to prove as true as they were prophetic: 'Will your Majesty let us speak plainly to this miserable Senate? Every institution, everything we have today, would be threatened by a restoration ... There would be civil war. The nation has paid too high a price for the little liberty she has got, not to defend it, and the army won't let its glory be trampled on. Reduced to sad straits by the fault of its commander, it will spring from the ashes, stronger and more dedicated than ever.'[23] This argument so impressed the Tsar that he admitted that he had no liking for the Bourbons. He would, he said, put their arguments to his allies – with his support.

As soon as the Marshals had left, the frightened members of the provisional government huddled into the Tsar's presence. The Tsar, standing, summarized the Marshals' arguments with zeal. The Regency proposal, he said, would settle everything. It would assure France of a government that would respect its present customs and interests. Continuity in the government was best for the people. Austria's lively interest would be a guarantee against outside influence. Most important of all, the Regency had the support of the army, and that resolved the last remaining difficulty facing the Allies. All Talleyrand's arguments about Napoleon pulling the strings were dismissed, suitable safeguards would prevent that, he said. General Dessole spoke everyone's mind in a pathetic speech, saying that although he had always been opposed to Napoleon, he had only decided to do so publicly and accept a post in this provisional government after the Tsar had said that he would have no dealings with

Napoleon or his family. If the Allies accepted a Regency would the Tsar give him asylum in Russia? And he hoped that he would at least give all those present there a passport to go. The Tsar said he would never abandon them to revenge.

After the meeting no one was listening to Talleyrand. All the talk was about leaving for exile. The Royalist Count Rochechouart, who had been appointed commander of the city, dismissed the royalist delegation that night, saying, 'I find I have neither the time nor desire to busy myself with the restoration. For all I know, we'll have to evacuate Paris tonight.'[24] The Marshals departed for Ney's house for the night; Macdonald later wrote, 'When we reached Marshal Ney's, we learned that more than 2,000 white cockades had fallen off people's hats during the night.'[25] The Marshals were confident that by morning the Regency questioned would be settled.

Talleyrand spent the night weaving his own plans and reassuring the waverers. He knew from Castlereagh and Metternich that a Regency was out of the question. He had to ensure that the Tsar did not impose it before the Austrian Emperor could be consulted. That night, as had been arranged with him and Prince Schwarzenberg, Marmont's corps of 14,000 men marched towards Paris, thinking that they were advancing to attack the enemy. At daybreak they found themselves surrounded on four sides by 50,000 Allied troops. The men rioted and attacked their senior officers, but the situation was defused by Marmont who appeared and shouted them down. It's all over, he told them. Napoleon had abdicated. Did they want to become traitors to the new government? Marmont had finished any hope of a Regency, and saved the provisional government and with it assured the restoration of the Bourbons. For two short days he was the hero of the royalists and the provisional government. After that his title, duc de Raguse, gave rise to a new word in the French language of the time – *ragusade* (betrayer).

The Tsar, that quasi-religious mystic, spoke to his adviser, Count Pozzo di Borgo, on the morning of 5 April and told him that Marmont's corps had defected to the Bourbon cause. The army was not united, he said, it was divided against itself. 'You see, it is Providence that wills it; she manifests and declares herself. No more doubt, no more hesitation.' The envoys were instructed that the abdication must now include the whole family. If Napoleon acted quickly, the Tsar would ensure him an honourable establishment, but if he delayed, others might think him lenient. The Marshals understood the implications.

Napoleon meanwhile had received news from Marshal Mortier that Marmont's corps had been betrayed to the enemy. For him this was the end. He still had more than 50,000 men under his command, but whom could he trust? His Marshals would not fight and many senior generals were openly defiant. But the Tsar was still concerned that Napoleon could, in desperation, launch an attack that would defeat them and trigger off a civil war. Schwarzenberg admitted his concern at this possibility. At Arcis had not Napoleon faced them with fewer men against three times the number they had now? The Tsar offered Napoleon a treaty to end the war. Known as the Treaty of Fontainebleau, it would be guaranteed by the Allied powers. It offered the security of Napoleon's person and his family. The Empress and his son would be given passports to enable them to join him. He and his family could keep their titles during their respective lifetimes. France was to provide him with 2,000,000 francs per annum, his family 2,500,000 francs per annum. A suitable establishment was to be found for his adopted son, the Viceroi of Italy, Eugène, who commanded the army in Italy. Napoleon's property, movable and immovable, would be protected. He would become sovereign of the island of Elba, and could retain a bodyguard of a thousand men. He could choose a naval frigate and keep it for his own use. There were also some minor provisions. Four Allied commissioners would accompany him to ensure his personal safety during his departure and residence on the island. For his part Napoleon must abdicate for his heirs and successors.

On 6 April Napoleon tried again to rally his Marshals – but in vain. Ney was the first to send in his allegiance to the new government, even before he had left Paris. Napoleon was then deserted by Oudinot, Victor and Lefebvre. Napoleon was deeply hurt that Berthier, his right arm and constant companion, had left too, and he said so. But he was mistaken. Berthier returned on 15 April. He had only wanted to ensure a smooth hand-over of the army to the traitor Dupont. On 11 April Caulaincourt brought Napoleon the Treaty, ratified by the Allies. Napoleon still wanted to fight on but it was useless, and on 13 April he signed the document of abdication. Caulaincourt returned it and only after receiving the signed treaty did he place Napoleon's abdication into the Tsar's hands.

Whilst the Tsar and the King of Prussia were dealing with Napoleon during these eventful days, Castlereagh and Metternich remained at Dijon with the Emperor Francis, their excuse being that they could not pass through the hostile territory. Lady Burgesh gave this the lie when she left there and drove by carriage to join her husband in Paris. Castlereagh, having manipulated the restoration, wished to be seen as taking no part in the negotiations, but accepting the will of the French people and the Allies. Metternich and Francis were in like case, but their personal problem was to get to Marie-Louise and bring her back to Austria. Francis sent an agent to the Empress, telling her that the Bourbons were to be restored and that she and her son would return to Austria either in honour and splendour or, it was implied, as state prisoners if need be. Marie-Louise was an Austrian princess, her son an archduke. She was to be guided by her father and not to communicate any of this to anyone, not even to her husband.[26] She acquiesced in her father's wishes, and this was Napoleon's penultimate betrayal.

Castlereagh arrived in Paris on 10 April to find things not quite as he expected. From royalists' reports he had thought to find a Napoleon beaten and stripped even of his title, not sitting with a large army, negotiating – let alone being offered a treaty and an income. He wrote to the Prime Minister:

'The motives for accelerating the immediate conclusion of this act were the inconvenience, if not the danger, of Napoleon's remaining at Fontainebleau, surrounded by troops who still, in a considerable degree, remain faithful to him ... The Prince of Benevente on the subject of the proposed convention, to which I stated my objections, desiring at the same time, to be understood as not urging them then, at the hazard of the internal tranquillity of France, nor in impeachment of what was due, in good faith, to the assurance given under the exigency of the moment by Russia. The Prince of Benevente admitted the weight of many of the objections stated, but declared that he did consider it, on the part of the Provisional Government as an object of the first importance to avoid anything that might assume the character of a civil war ... I desired, however, to decline on the part of my Government being more than an acceding party to the Treaty, and declared that the act of accession on the part of Great Britain should not go beyond the territorial arrangements proposed in the Treaty ... At my suggestion the recognition of the Imperial Titles were limited to their respective lives ... I should have wished to substitute another position in lieu of Elba for the seat of Napoleon, but none having the quality of security, on which he insisted, seemed disposable ... I felt I own the utmost repugnance to anything like a Treaty with him after his *déchéance* had been pronounced ... I should have wished, however, if he was humble enough to accept a pension, that it had been an act of grace and not of stipulation.'[27]

There was the crux of it. Napoleon had not been beaten in the field, he had the Allies cornered in Paris, every advantage that he had strived for since 1812 to bring about a decisive battle that would have humbled the Allies and their respective nations had been achieved. Even after he had been betrayed in Paris by his ministers and his own brother he still held the advantage. Even with the loss of Marmont's men he still had adequate numbers to achieve victory. Why else were the Allies offering so much? His Marshals, men he had raised from obscure generals, to dukes and princes had betrayed him in order to keep their baubles. So be it. To Bausset, Prefect of the Palace, he said: 'I abdicate and I yield nothing.' A week later he took leave of his Old Guard, embraced the eagle, and left Fontainebleau to journey to the island of Elba. Even this journey was not without danger. The four commissioners appointed by the Allies were Sir Neil Campbell for Britain, Count Waldburg-Truchess for Prussia, General Köhler for Austria and General Schuvalov for Russia. The Tsar, perhaps weary with the provisional government and mindful that he had removed Napoleon from his throne, had ensured him a dignified position as a lesser sovereign. Having received reports of the royalists' activities and seen some of their antics, he instructed General Schuvalov to 'Safeguard the Emperor Napoleon to his destination, as you will answer to me with your head for it.' Bourrienne, the Post-Master General, knew through his office the route that Napoleon was taking and informed the royalists. Artois arranged for the Chevaliers de la Foi to try to kill him on the way, making it look like a spontaneous royalist reaction. Several score of footpads, promised a fortune, acted like a lynch mob at Organ. Only by disguising the Emperor and using bluff had General Schuvalov and the other commissioners saved his life from this serious attack.[28] The royalists used this failure to trumpet through its media that 'the people hated and wanted to kill Napoleon for his tyranny', but the common people knew the truth. On 28 April Napoleon left

France, sailing from Fréjus aboard HMS *Undaunted* to Elba. The Duke of Welling-ton, unaware of the situation in Paris, fought the bloody Battle of Toulouse on 10 April, concluding an armistice on the 17th. He later said of Napoleon's strategy in this campaign: 'Excellent – quite excellent. The study of it has given me a greater idea of his genius than any other. Had he continued that system a little longer, it is my opinion that he would have saved Paris.'[29]

Now the royalists, the far right, a minority of fanatics, financed by British money, and supported by Austrian, Russian and Prussian bayonets, had mounted a *coup d'état*, during their country's life-and-death struggle against a foreign invasion. They had emerged from 25 years of hiding and had come into their own again. France was becoming highly unstable and civil war was only just prevented by the Allies. Napoleon had sometimes been referred to as the heir of the Revolution, but his situation had been more unique than outsiders appreciated. Now all the hidden royalists were coming forth expecting rewards, especially those who had fought on in secret in the Chevaliers de la Foi since the Revolution. By contrast those dedicated Bonapartists, feeling that their country, their Emperor and indeed the revolution had been betrayed, now prudently went underground and started their own secret organizations. They, however, had a greater advantage because they had had military experience and could organize rapidly. Their greatest advantage was numbers – there were more of them. Once the occupying forces left, the resistance would rise. This part of the country's populace was already getting ready for a counter-revolution.

Napoleon's unique style of rule following the corrupt Directory, had been pre-ferred by the post-revolutionary Jacobins, to a restoration by the royalists. The royal-ists had accepted him instead of a democracy. He had been the choice of the mass of the people who hated the memory of the old aristocracy, the reign of Terror, and incessant political change under the republic. He united the various factions in that he was a better choice than each of the others' alternatives. Napoleon had been an autocrat, but an enlightened autocrat. Under his rule all citizens appeared equal and could rise on merit. He had been a ruler feared and walked with by kings, but who yet had the common touch with his subjects and his soldiers. Here perhaps was one of his secrets: a man of obscure birth, educated under strict discipline, who had passed through the lower grades of military service. A man who less than a few years before his rise to power had lived in an upstairs garret and had dined at low eating-houses. He and his 'aristocracy' belonged to the people and were of the peo-ple. Unlike the 'Old Regime', his dukes and counts owned no titles to French domains – like the Bourbons, who claimed ownership by birth to the soil of France and the people on it. Their titles were of French victories to which all Frenchmen had contributed and shared the glory. Napoleon often referred to himself as 'France', but his insight cynically told him that he in his person represented the unified fac-tions of France. The Revolution had been paid for in blood – but the price had been paid. France had since marched on. The clock would go forwards but could only be damaged by attempting to force it backwards.

CHAPTER 6

THE ROAD TO SAINT-OUEN

*'The use of force alone is but temporary. It may subdue for the moment; but it does not
remove the necessity of subduing again; and a nation is not governed which is perpetually
to be conquered.'* – Edmund Burke (Speech on conciliation with the American
colonies, Parliament, 22 March 1775)

NAPOLEON HAD BEEN OVERTHROWN AND REMOVED FROM
France. Not by a decisive battle such as those of Austerlitz, Jena or
Friedland. Nor by a brilliant and resounding defeat like Salamanca or
Vitoria. But by treason and treachery. He had stipulated the terms
whereby he would abdicate, while a cabal of traitors had foisted a quisling government on his enemy-occupied capital. Talleyrand, the arch-conspirator, had now to
reconcile the diverse political factions that had been contained under Napoleon's
imperial rule, to the restoration of an unknown and, by the majority of the populace,
unwanted Bourbon monarchy.

In his quest for personal revenge, Talleyrand had got rid of Napoleon and now
held centre stage in French politics. To achieve this position, he had betrayed his
country and had thrown in his lot with the fanatical, right-wing 'ultra-royalists'. It
was to be a bed of thorns. Talleyrand knew his countrymen well enough to understand that the only way to reconcile the republican, imperialist and royalist factions,
would be through a constitutional monarchy with a parliamentary system. The fundamental obstacle to achieving this was posed by the very people who had supported
the coup – the ultras, of whom Artois was leader. These fanatics believed in the doctrine of the divine right of kings; that the quintessence of the old monarchy was that
it was absolute and unconditional, and that its title was based not upon the will of
the people but upon hereditary right. Upon these articles of faith, any hope of creating a true constitutional monarchy could only founder.

In early April, the comte d'Artois entered Paris in the uniform of the National
Guard, his brother Louis XVIII having appointed him 'Lieutenant-General of my
Kingdom of France'. Talleyrand and the Senate refused to accept this. In the endeavour to restore Louis under constitutional restraint, and maintain the fiction that the
people had actually 'called' him back, and were now offering him the throne – not
by his right, but by their choice – Talleyrand as head of the provisional government
had humiliated Artois, the brother of the king. If that were not enough, he had the
Senate appoint Artois to the self-same position – provisional on his acceptance of a
constitutional charter in his brother's name – until Louis' return.

The charter was based on the French Constitution of 1791. It stated that Louis
was 'freely' called to the throne, and its implication was clear; the nation not the king
was to be sovereign. From this point onward, 'Monsieur' became Talleyrand's bitter

enemy. Artois had made a compact with Talleyrand to help restore the Bourbons; in return Talleyrand would retain high office under them. Artois had not expected him to attempt to shackle and impede the King politically, and humiliate himself. Artois was livid, but it was not in his nature to show it; like Talleyrand, he too could bide his time. For the moment, on the sound principle of political expediency, he co-operated with Talleyrand. During the last fourteen years all the Allied monarchs and their ministers had dealt with Talleyrand as a minister of France. His experience and position were for the moment invaluable to the Bourbons. The charter pleased Britain and the Tsar, who bade Artois accept or the Allies might seek an alternative. Artois therefore accepted with bad grace the 'broad principles' of the charter in Louis' name.

Despite Talleyrand's objections, Artois refused to retain the Tricolore as the national flag or cockade, and this was an affront to the army and the nation. For nearly a quarter of a century it had represented France. Its removal was an act of spite that served no useful purpose; Bourbon emblems could have replaced Napoleonic ones as they would on the other regalia. To the old republican and Jacobin elements in France, this immediate reversion to the old Bourbon flag boded ill.

Artois, anxious to have Talleyrand and his puppet government replaced before they could spring any more nasty surprises, wrote to Louis at Hartwell in England, telling him of Napoleon's settlement, Talleyrand's unreliability and Russia's reluctance to restore the Bourbons. He also confirmed the unflinching support of Britain and Austria. But he made clear that Louis should come to Paris as quickly as possible.

Louis had intended that his more energetic brother should establish order in the capital and prepare everything for his triumphal return. But Artois' letter changed all that. Louis' diplomatic gout improved and he hurried to Dover where he was escorted to his hotel by the Prince Regent. Both men were indolent and devout gourmets. They also liked each other. Louis, in replying to the Prince Regent's speech, said: 'It is to the counsels of Your Royal Highness, to this glorious country, and to the steadfastness of its inhabitants, that I attribute, after the will of Providence, the re-establishment of my House upon the throne of its ancestors.'[1] His remarks were recorded in *The Times*. The Russian Ambassador, feeling that his master had been slighted, sent a copy of the paper to the Tsar in Paris.

Of all the Allied monarchs, none had done more to bring about Napoleon's deposition than the Tsar. It could be argued that Britain, by her implacable stand, her command of the sea and her financial commitment, had been the instigator and driving force behind his downfall, but alone she could not have brought it about. If at any time between Napoleon's retreat from Moscow in 1812 and Marmont's defection in 1814, the Tsar had decided to cease his relentless determination not to make peace with Napoleon, or had withdrawn his army, Austria and Prussia, as we have seen, would have made peace with him, leaving him not only on his throne – but in possession of the Low Countries.

The Bourbons, therefore, owed their throne to the Tsar. If he had imposed Bernadotte or even Eugène, Napoleon's stepson and viceroi, no one would have been

Above: Prince Metternich. Contemporary engraving. (Philip Haythornthwaite collection)

Below: Emperor Francis I of Austria. Engraving by Blood after Shepperson. (Philip Haythornthwaite collection)

Above: Tsar Alexander. Contemporary engraving. (Philip Haythornthwaite collection)

Below: Admiral Lord Nelson. (Philip Haythornthwaite collection)

ove: William Pitt, British Prime Minister. (Philip Haythornthwaite collection)

ove right: Lord Castlereagh, Britain's Foreign Secretary. (Philip Haythornthwaite collection)

low: Robert Banks, second Earl of Liverpool, Prime Minister from 1812 to 1827, had held almost all the important binet posts at one time or another during the revolutionary and Napoleonic wars. As Foreign Secretary under dington, he deliberately postponed the evacuation of Malta as required under the Treaty of Amiens, thereby ovoking Napoleon into war. (Philip Haythornthwaite collection)

low: Henry Bathurst, third Earl of Bathurst and Secretary for War and the Colonies from 1809. From 1816 apoleon's Draconian detention was instigated and controlled by this mean-minded individual. (Philip aythornthwaite collection)

Above: 1812. In Russia Napoleon learns that General Malet almost succeeded in seizing Paris in a *coup d'état*.

Above right: Marshal Berthier, Napoleon's incomparable Chief of Staff. His murder by d'Artois' agents in 1815 robbed Napoleon of his 'right arm'.

Below: Marshal Soult, the 'turncoat', who was despised as a traitor by the French army in 1815. (Philip Haythornthwaite collection)

Below right: Marshal Augereau, the traitor whom Napoleon never forgave. He betrayed the city of Lyons to the enemy in 1814, and deliberately placed his men in a situation in which they could be slaughtered. Napoleon struck h name from the roll of Marshals in 1815, and again named him as one of the betrayers of France in his will. (Philip Haythornthwaite collection)

Above: King William of Prussia joins Tsar Alexander at Breslau on 15 March 1813. (Author's collection)

Right: The Prussian Army reforming committee in session: seated on the right King William, centre Oberleutnant Gneisenau, to his right Major-General von Scharnhorst; Baron Stein seated on his right and Major von Grolman standing. (Author's collection)

Lower right: Napoleon's famous green coach. A mobile command centre, an aide is seen here receiving a dispatch from Marshal Berthier at the window. The Imperial Guard cavalry escort surrounded the vehicle and the headquarters staff rode behind.

Top left: The Emperor, on his pale horse, moves forward to attack the enemy with the resurrected *Grande Armée*. (Author's collection)

Centre left: Lützen, 2 May 1813. Napoleon drives into the Allies with the Young Guard. (Author's collection)

Left: Napoleon at Lützen, rallying his new conscripts, carries the field.

Above: The Prussian Guard at Gross-Görschen (Lützen). Time and again the Prussians drove the French back with unprecedented ferocity – only to be assailed yet again. This *danse macabre* continued until nightfall. (Author's collection)

Below: Bautzen, 20-21 May 1813. Napoleon sits waiting for news of Ney's advance before springing his trap.

Left: Napoleon's meeting with Metternich on 2 June 1813. He has hurled his hat to the floor in rage at the blackmail terms sent by his father-in-law: 'armed intervention' will not be used against him if he accedes to Austria's demands. (Author's collection)

Right: Generals Vandamme and Haxo are captured after stout resistance at Kulm. (Author's collection)

Centre right: General Corbineau's cavalry force a gap through the encircling Allied troops for Vandamme's retreating men. The Prussian dragoons have been penetrated before realizing that the oncoming cavalry are French. (Author's collection)

Bottom right: A contemporary engraving depicting Blücher's reserve cavalry (all Uhlans), launched down the slope by von Gneisenau to smash into Macdonald's troops and drive them into the swollen Katzbach on 26 August 1813. (Author's collection)

Right: Napoleon arriving at the gallop in Dresden on 26 August 1813, followed by the serried ranks of the Garde Impériale. The spontaneous acclamation of the populace and his men carried across the city to the Allies.

Right: The Battle of Dresden, 27 August 1813. Murat's cavalry can be seen in the distance, about to assist Napoleon in exploiting Schwarzenberg's gap. (Author's collection)

Left: Macdonald's army is driven back towards Dresden, harried by Blücher at every turn, in a rout far worse than the Russian retreat of 1812. (Author's collection)

Right: The battlefield at Leipzig. The Allies try to regroup after Murat's cavalry charge. (Author's collection)

Left: Napoleon before Leipzig 15 October 1813, presenting an Eagle to a new infantry formation of Marshal Augereau's corps. This was on of the last to be presented before his empire was reduced to the French natural borders. (Author's collection)

Right: Von Ziethen's hussars charge at Möckern (Leipzig), 16 October 1813. (Author's collection)

Left: Dennewitz at the end of the day. Bülow is acclaimed by his soldiers. King William bestowed on him the title of Count von Bülow Graf von Dennewitz for this victory. (Author's collection)

Above: Napoleon leads forward his Guard at Leipzig to plug the gap in his perimeter left by the deserting Saxons. (Author's collection)

Left: Schwarzenberg announces to the three sovereigns that Leipzig has been won. (Author's collection)

Below left: At Leipzig, von Sacken's Prussian skirmishers work their way around the river banks to the rear and open fire on the French rearguard and the bridge. (Author's collection)

Top right: A sergeant of Engineers. 'Then out spake brave Horatius ... Hew down the bridge, Sir Consul, with all the speed you may; I with two more to help me, will hold the foe in play.' This sergeant was ordered to blow the bridge 'When the enemy is sighted or attacks the bridge.' On sighting Sacken's skirmishers – prematurely, he blew the bridge.

Below: Leipzig, Napoleon's greatest disaster. His masterful withdrawal was turned into a stunning defeat by the premature blowing of the Elster bridge which cut his army in two, one half of it being lost with all its equipment to the Allies. (Author's collection)

Above: The Allies at Leipzig: Csar Alexander greets General von Blücher as the hero of the battle. (Author's collection)

Left: Hanau. Napoleon launches his Guard cavalry against the retreating Bavarians, holding them in squares while the horse-artillery comes up to blow them away. (Author's collection)

Top: On 1 January 1814 the Allies cross the Rhine into France. (Author's collection)

Above: The Battle of Montmirail, 11 February 1814. Napoleon has launched an attack to his right along the road towards von Sacken's force, while holding Pirch II's troops in play on the right approach with cavalry of the Guard. (Author's collection)

Below: The Battle of Craonne, 7 March 1814. The plateau of the *Chemin des Dames* is seen from the direction of Craonne and along the line of the French advance. In the centre right the fight for the three farms of Heurtebise is in progress. The steep wooded sides of the plateau are clearly seen on the right. (Author's collection)

Left: The Empress Marie-Louise with Napoleon's son, the King of Rome, by Gérard. (Philip Haythornthwaite collection)

Left: Charles-Maurice de Talleyrand-Périgord, prince de Bénévent, one-time Bishop of Autun. The perfect politician, he betrayed Church, king, Revolution, Directory, Napoleon and France.

able to prevent it. Britain might not have liked it, nor Austria, but with Napoleon gone, neither would have been prepared to break with Russia on behalf of the unwanted Bourbon restoration. Yet not one word did Louis write to the Tsar in gratitude for his assistance or acknowledgement of the bloody sacrifices of Russian soldiers from Moscow to Paris. At first the Tsar did not take this as a slight, but as an omission. Hearing that Louis had arrived at Compiègne, he wrote a kind letter in which he advised him to consider the feelings of his subjects and the merits of the charter: '... There exists a national will, a few opposition parties, and some undecided opinions, over which moderation alone can triumph, if one does not wish to produce new disturbances at a time when what is needed is calm and consolation ...'[2] A more shrewd evaluation of the situation would have been hard to find in those uncertain days. Not only did Louis not bother to answer this letter, but he sent an evasive reply via a third party to the Tsar regarding acceptance of the charter.

The Tsar decided to visit him. Louis was then 60 years old and weighed nearly 310 pounds. He had spent the last 23 years in exile. In imitation of Napoleon, he had taken to wearing large gold epaulettes fitted to an ordinary coat. Louis deliberately remained seated when the Tsar entered the room – a calculated insult. The heir to Saint-Louis, puffed up with pride, beckoned him to a chair. He showed no interest in what the Tsar had to say and didn't bother to reply, merely remarking how good it was for France to have a legitimate sovereign again. The Tsar was then dismissed, on the grounds that he might like to refresh himself before dinner. He was then led through three sumptuous apartments set aside for the comte d'Artois and his sons the ducs d'Angoulême and de Berry. The Tsar of all the Russias was then taken by a maze of dark stairs and unlit corridors to the modest rooms of the former palace governor. His pent-up fury at this further premeditated insult, burst forth to his aide Czernicheff whom he instructed to take his luggage immediately back to his carriage. He would return to Paris after dinner. At that memorable meal Louis entered the dining-room before his guest and as the servants prepared to serve Alexander, Louis cried out in his high-pitched voice 'Over here if you please! Me first!'[3] Pique in a king is one thing, lack of manners another. Returning that night, the Tsar gave full rein to his anger. To his staff he said: 'Louis the Fourteenth at the height of his power, would not have received me differently at Versailles; one would have thought that it was *he* who had just put *me* back on my throne! The reception I received was the same as a bucket of ice water poured over my head! ... We of the north might be considered barbarians, but at least we have manners in our country!'[4]

This episode epitomized Bourbon stupidity and Louis' unsuitability to reign. Having been told that Alexander had been reluctant to restore him, Louis, in his pride which he should have been man enough to swallow, was trying with this display of unkingly petulance and bad manners to show Alexander that he was 'king of the castle'. Hardly a sensible way to act towards a foreign monarch who was occupying one's capital with nearly 100,000 men, especially if the man one is insulting has yet to dictate his peace terms.

Tsar Alexander's response was swift. Louis would not be permitted to enter Paris, nor would the Russians entertain any discussions about peace until Louis had signed the Charter! The Tsar now spoke openly of his regret at restoring the Bourbons; they were 'not corrected, and not correctable!' he said. A few weeks later he visited Marie-Louise at Rambouillet and asked her in front of her father if she would not like to remain Regent. Her father declined on her behalf. Later, when the ex-Empress Josephine died, Alexander sent a whole regiment of his Guards to escort the coffin and present honours. Further to drive home the lesson on one-upmanship, he demanded as part of the peace terms that Louis create Josephine's daughter ex-Queen Hortense, Duchesse of Saint-Leu.

Fouché, Napoleon's ex-minister of police, had returned to the capital. His intelligence-gathering abilities had not diminished during his absence. Having been consulted by the Tsar on several matters, for which he was well paid, he now let Alexander know the extent to which he had been manipulated by Talleyrand, Fouché's old rival. Alexander could not now disavow his actions or change his mind about the Bourbons without becoming a laughing-stock. He left Talleyrand's house without speaking one word to him. Louis, taken aback by the Tsar's display of 'absolutism' towards him, inquired whether the Tsar might consider a union between his nephew de Berry and the Tsar's sister? Alexander replied, 'Never!' Louis, deflated, made haste to declare that he would sign the Charter.

The Bourbon stubbornness that had lost Louis' brother his crown and his head was still in evidence. At Saint-Ouen on 2 May, Louis declared that he would grant his people a constitution, but he would not accept the Senate's document because he considered the Senate an unrepresentative and illegal body and the document had not been drafted adequately. A commission would be appointed to 'look again' and produce another constitutional Charter – in consultation with their monarch. This declaration was given under Louis' hand 'this nineteenth year of our reign'. With this stroke of the pen, Louis attempted to wipe out 24 years of French history. By dating his reign from the death of his nephew, he was implying that the nation had been in error and all the events of the Republic and Napoleon's rule had been a mistake and therefore illegal. No fool like an old fool. If Louis on his entry to Paris to the cheers of tens of thousands of royalists thought that the nation wanted him back he was deluding himself. Not many people in the crowd were going to object openly while Allied bayonets controlled the streets. Baron Vitrolles, whom the Tsar had asked whether he had ever seen his Bourbon prince, was profoundly shocked. Here was no warrior on a white horse, leading his famous Guards into the capital to come into his own. Down from the coach, supported by two flunkeys, tottered an obese old man, so riddled with gout from the excesses of the table, that he could neither mount a horse nor walk very far. Charlemagne, who had given France an Empire, had been replaced by Humpty Dumpty.

The Tsar, the Emperor of Austria and the King of Prussia, together with Castlereagh and their ministers, decided that they must draw up the terms of a peace with France before they resolved the fate of the rest of Napoleon's defunct empire.

The monarchs had all been invited by the Prince Regent to visit England. It was decided that France's fate should be settled now, and all other territorial considerations at a peace congress in Vienna in four months' time. Metternich arranged that he should represent Austria in England while Emperor Francis settled domestic affairs and made preparations to receive his guests in Vienna. This would give him and Castlereagh time to prepare their joint strategy, while the other monarchs amused themselves.

The terms of the Treaty of Paris, signed on 30 May 1814, were more than generous. France would keep her Bourbon borders of 1792, and would be given a token enlargement of 150 square miles, another 600,000 inhabitants, to sweeten the pill. France would also be allowed to keep all the art treasures plundered during 25 years of victory, a concession to national pride, '... as not to alienate the people against their imposed monarch'. France had to cede all claims in perpetuity to Belgium, Holland, the left bank of the Rhine, Italy, Switzerland and the German provinces. Castlereagh cleverly inserted into the proceedings the agreement to a United Netherlands of Holland and Belgium, the latter as Pitt's 'military barrier', thereby gaining everything that Britain had been fighting for since the Revolution. Britain was to return most of the captured French colonies except those of Ile de France, Santa Lucia and Tobago .

The Treaty had not been made without some difficulties, the fragile alliance of the victors soon beginning to show cracks. King William demanded war reparations, at the very least those contributions forced from Prussia since 1812. Louis refused. He would, he said, rather 'submit to be arrested and kept a prisoner in his palace' before paying a single centime. Britain and Austria, secure now that their respective backdoors of The Netherlands and Italy were shut, argued against financially crippling Louis and causing popular unrest. Prussia's king was pacified by the hint that he would be compensated at the forthcoming congress and relented. Under one of the secret articles of the treaty, Bourbon France would be allowed to attend the congress – but would have no say in territorial settlements. Within days of the monarchs departing on their state visit to Britain, their armies made preparations to depart from France.

Louis now had a rare opportunity. He had returned to France after years of exile. He was unknown to most of his subjects. Napoleon had gone, the Allies had not enforced a humiliating occupation or war reparations. Had he emulated his revered ancestor Henry IV, he might have united his country solidly behind him. Henry had ascended the throne after the massacre of his kinsmen and friends, their fate more perfidious and cruel than that meted out to Louis' kin. By his forbearance, he had united all factions – yet more grievously split by the fanaticism of a religious war. When he died he had left a France stronger and more united than before. Paris, that had been up in arms against him, had genuinely mourned his passing. Louis, on the other hand, could neither forgive nor forget – nor would his heir and brother Artois. In their train from Britain and from all over Europe came the die-hard *émigrés*. Young men grown old in exile, nurtured by ageing parents and grandparents on their families' proud histories, obsessed by thoughts of their inherited rights and privileges granted to them from the Middle Ages. They returned with a burning desire to regain all that had been theirs and to live in the style they presumed to be theirs by birthright alone.

They returned to find a country that they did not recognize. The peasants were no longer subservient, a new society had emerged, with new laws, education and administration. All that they throught splendid and that they had yearned for in their youth had passed away. Their sumptuous town houses had been converted to apartments, their great hunting parks to farm land with rural dwellings. The venerable tombs of their ancestors were in museums; châteaux had been dismantled and sold, monuments erased and cathedrals neglected. A fountain spouted on the site of the great statue of Louis XIV, and there was now an open space where the great monument to Henry IV had overlooked the Seine. At Saint-Denis the tombs of the embalmed kings were covered with a mound of turf. The old Palace of Versailles, centre of their lost world, where all the nobles had congregated, and which had been filled with light and laughter, pageantry and pleasure, had fallen sadly silent; visitors still gazed at the galleries filled with magnificent trophies and art treasures, but these had been garnered by a new dynasty. Their time had passed away.

Those adherents of Napoleon's regime that had converted or been bribed or bullied into the coup, had not envisaged that in recalling the king they would be recalling the old order. Talleyrand had convinced them that they could impose a constitutional government like Britain's, indeed that was what he himself desired. But his provisional government was a puppet government. It had not been elected, it was self-imposed, and now that the Allies were departing, like all puppets, they found that it was not themselves but others that were pulling the strings.

The aspirations of the *émigrés* were supported by those royalists who had already returned under Napoleon, and who had been awaiting the return of the king. Many of them belonged to active cells of the royalist secret society. The comte d'Artois had been their driving force for more than a quarter of a century. It was he who had waged a relentless underground war for the Bourbon inheritance, aided by his sons. King Louis, now old and crippled with gout, passed more and more executive decisions into his hands. Louis was childless; Artois and his sons would succeed to the throne, which had been Artois' great motivation. His secret society had been carefully built up and was based on Masonic lines, with secret handshakes, signs and rituals, and sinister oaths of vengeance against any member who betrayed them. It operated in cells called *bannières* under a leader called a *Sénéchal*, members progressing from a lower to a higher circle, each progression requiring re-initiation.[5] Only the inner group knew the purpose behind their directives. They were called the 'Chevaliers de la Foi', but they had changed their name several times to confuse Napoleon's secret police.

During the revolution and Consulate they had supplied information, passed counterfeit currency, kept safe houses and fomented discontent. They had attempted to assassinate Napoleon on several occasions – and nearly succeeded. They supplied officers and funds for the insurrections in the west. During the Empire, when Napoleon's power was at its peak, they had kept a low profile. Fouché's agents had penetrated some of their cells and he had forcibly 'turned' many members. Now these loyal 'soldiers of the cause' expected some reward. Artois decided to use this organization as his private intelligence and police force, and as a political party. He intended to reward these faithful by placing them in the administration, and the two Chambers. It was his intention that the 'ultras' would turn back the clock and restore absolute power to the old order.[6]

The new Charter, drawn up by a select number of 'sound' senators and deputies – aided by the king's appointed royalist commissioners, was now ready. The new two-Chamber legislative would be composed of a House of Peers, appointed only by the king and unlimited in number, deliberating in secret. It was also given the power to constitute itself a court to try cases of treason. The second Chamber was that of the people's deputies, to be composed for the present of the existing legislators. However, at the time of new elections, it would be composed only of members who paid more than 1,000 francs in taxes a year. Further, no one was now eligible to vote for a deputy unless he paid 300 francs a year in taxes. Of a nation of 30 millions in 1814, only 90,000 Frenchman were now eligible to vote. The Senators who had enacted the restoration and acted as the puppet government had done so on Talleyrand's assurance that they would be compensated – the Charter granted them a massive annual pension of 36,000 francs a year for life. The head of the government [the king] was given all the executive power – personally. The following two articles returned all power to the king: (Article 13) The King's person is inviolable and sacred ... Executive power belongs only to the King. (Article 14) The King is the supreme head of state, he   commands the armed forces on land and sea, declares war, makes peace treaties, alliances and trade agreements, nominates to all public administrative offices, and makes the rules and ordinances necessary for the execution of the laws and the safety of the state.

The right to initiate all bills and legislation was accorded to the Crown; the Chambers, however, were given the power to 'suggest the principles and details of bills'. Ministers were responsible to the king, not to the two Chambers. He was the largest element of the legislative body – since he alone could initiate laws; not even an amendment could be made without his consent. So much for any vestige of equality. The Chamber had to be renewed by one-fifth every year by rota; in five years all the present incumbents would be removed. Tens of thousands of electors, in the professional classes, shopkeepers, administrators and the civil service, had been disenfranchised at a stroke. Artois would eventually pack both assemblies with his followers. Louis and his brother were not going to have any 'tennis court' assemblies to defy them.

The King was voted a Civil List, paid annually for life. The press was accorded its freedom from censorship, but it was stated that 'laws would be enacted to chastise its abuse' – or, in lay terms, apply censorship. As a charter of a constitutional monarchy, no better example of written absolutism can be found. In his arrogance Louis

133

had ignored the lessons of history. In 1791 his brother Louis XVI, standing bare-headed before his seated subjects, had sworn to uphold the republican constitution. His schemes to break that oath and subject his people to a foreign invasion had lead the militants to have him tried and executed.

The Bourbon clan and its privileged sycophants had long memories. The old order had supported the monarchy. The middle and working classes had risen up and destroyed their power and privileges. Their residual sub-conscious fear and hatred of these classes framed their intended method of ruling. Only the wealthy and those with a property stake in the kingdom would be allowed a voice or position in the administration.

Of the Prefectural body, 28 out of 87 were immediately sacked for having been too zealous as republicans or imperialists. Thirty-six appointments went to *émigrés* and old supporters from the Chouan and Vendée. Within weeks, the number of nobles in the Prefectures doubled. The pro-royalist priests – mainly sons of the lesser nobility, the *Petite Eglise*, had also returned and were demanding the restoration of the vast manorial estates that had been their 'livings'. These, together with previously royal and noble estates, had become part of the *biens nationaux* or states lands that had been guaranteed inviolable by the 'Charter' (and by Napoleon in his coronation oath).

The peasants and the working class, 78 per cent of the population, had no rights, no vote and no constitutional role, so no attempt had been made to wean them from imperialism. During the last 24 years, Catholic and royalist support had been encouraged and financed in the departments of Brittany, the Vendée and the Chouan. During 1813–14 the prince de Condé and the royalists had proclaimed an end to the hated royal taxes of *Octroi* and *droits réunis*, but this had only been anti-Napoleon propaganda. Now the peasants demanded their removal. The King upheld the taxes. Anti-fiscal riots and rebellions occurred in the Haute-Garonne, Vendée, Gironde, Garonne, Seine-Inférieure, Pas-de-Calais, at Marseilles, Cahors, Rennes, Châlons-sur-Marne and Limoges. Officials were beaten – to death in one instance – registers burned and offices sacked.

Louis of course needed money; the treasury was depleted by war. For the first time in fourteen years France would have to raise her revenues solely from within the country. Napoleon, accused by many of bleeding his country dry of money and manpower, was in this unjustly indicted. Since 1807 his empire had provided more manpower for his army than had France. His recruitment of Dutchmen, Germans, Belgians, Spanish, Italians, Serbs, Croats, Poles, Lithuanians, and auxiliaries from Switzerland, Denmark, Prussia and Austria had obviated excessive demands on the agricultural manpower resources of France. Further, since 1796 he had developed the idea of making war pay for itself by enforced loans, plunder, requisitions, reparations and outright theft in the conquered provinces. Preferential tariffs had also given France a higher standard than that of her neighbours. Britain by contrast, had inflation and high food costs as a consequence of the £700,000,000 national debt, contracted during the last 25 years of fighting France, and now America, and subsidizing three coalitions. Pitt's 'temporary' income tax bill was enacted to help reduce this national debt.

The *émigrés* were not the only Frenchmen to return to France in 1814. From the prison hulks and the prisons at Edinburgh and on Dartmoor, in their canvas garb with the broad arrow symbol, came more than 70,000 veteran soldiers. A further 80,000 returned from Russia. Marching home in good order came the garrisons from Poland, Prussia, Germany, Holland and Antwerp. Davout, the Iron Marshal, had held Hamburg loyally with a garrison of some 37,000 men long after the abdication – until a trusted general showed him the Emperor's signature of abdication. All told, more than 200,000 veterans arrived back in France, bewildered by the turn of events and the gibes of the royalists. To the cries of '*Vive le Roi!*' they added '*de Rome!*' or '*Vive l'Empereur!*'. Some of the brave 'ultras' attempted to beat up some of the scarecrows from the Russian campaign – only to find themselves attacked by regular 'royalist' regiments, in defence of their returning comrades.

Some 12,000 officers were placed on half-pay, which was invariably delayed or not paid. These exemplary officers were also ordered out of the capital for no crime whatsoever, save that of having fought for their country. Now the Bourbons started to reduce the army. The Imperial Guard, Grenadiers and Chasseurs, the pride of France, who had inspired envy and fear in the armies of Europe during the last ten years and were to be emulated by every army for centuries to come, were humiliated. These men, individually chosen by Napoleon for bravery, campaign experience and length of service, were henceforth to be called 'The Grenadiers of France' and removed from the capital. They would remain combat troops, but not with Guards status, their pay reduced to a little over that given to the line. Their only crime had been loyalty, and a battle record second to none.[7] Artois now reconstituted the household troops of Louis XVI, beginning with the *Garde du corps du Roi*, four companies named after their commanders, all drawn from ancient noble families, young royalists and ageing *émigrés*, with a complement of artillery. Two more cavalry companies were added by Louis, one to be commanded by Marmont, duc de Raguse and the other by Marshal Berthier. These were called by the rest of the army the 'Judas' and 'Peter' companies – the one having betrayed Christ and the other having denied his Lord.[8] Their field officers were generals, their lieutenants were equal in rank to colonels in the line. They drew pay of 12–15,000 francs a year. Yet an experienced officer of the line was given 528 francs a year, half-pay. Next there was the *Maison du Roi* composed of the King's Grey and Black Mousquetaires, named after the colour of their horses. Their officers and men were nobles all. Their helmet plumes alone cost 50 francs! A musketeer's uniform cost 4,000 francs, and his general was given another 1,000 francs to buy him the finest possible horse. Even a private in the Household Guards ranked as a captain in the line. Money, equipment and privileges were lavished on the old, the infirm and the incompetent while officers and other ranks who had been awarded the Legion of Honour for valiant service were walking about in ragged uniforms, their pay in arrears.

Then too there was Artois' bodyguard, the *Gardes de Monsieur*, two companies of his loyal followers plus ancillary units, clothed in Monsieur's green livery. Altogether, 10,000 men whose upkeep and inflated salaries would have supported 60,000 combat troops. It was an insult to every half-pay officer in France. To fund this comic-opera corps of chocolate-box soldiers, massive cuts had to be made. The King's minister suggested that he shut down the Hôtel des Invalides, which had been reconstituted by Napoleon for old and disabled soldiers whose upkeep cost 700 francs a year per man. 'Let them be put out to their native parishes with a pension of 250 francs a year,' he said. There were also the orphanages for the sons and daughters of poor soldiers killed in action, maintained by the Legion of Honour: 'let them be put out as well';[9] besides, one of them occupied the confiscated estate of the King's ancient uncle, the prince de Condé, and he wanted it back.

Animosity was now burgeoning between the veterans of Napoleon's army and the administration, and friction between the peasants and the tax collectors. Former property owners of a quarter of a century earlier were now insisting on their rights; 'If the King has his legitimate rights, have not we too?' they argued – besides, they had the largest voice in the two Houses of Representatives. Trouble was also brewing among the intellectuals of the professional and artisan classes, who had been disenfranchised. The Bourbons intended also to close the doors of the military academies and polytechnics, set up by Napoleon for gifted youngsters, to all but the sons of the nobility – who could show 'unbroken' noble descent, as in Louis XVI's time. No more Marshals of France, princes or dukes would be elevated from the scum, coopers and inn-keepers' sons – nobodies from the rank and file. As in the administration, only the nobility could be trusted to lead: loyalty to the King by position and birth would guarantee the succession – or so these relics from a bygone age reasoned. Not one of them stopped to reflect that the victories won by the new men, through meritorious service and valour, had surpassed anything that had been achieved by the old nobility, or that not all the King's privileged blue-bloods had been able to stop the people rising against the previous Bourbon regime. They failed to comprehend the simple fact that noble officers would be unable to persuade common soldiers to fire upon their common kinsfolk in order to impose the will of a privileged regime.

To the younger generation of Frenchmen who, under Napoleon, had been educated and enabled to rise on merit and freely voice their opinions, the situation was unacceptable. Most of them had been brought up as Catholics, and had been taught the catechism of the Church. This had been obligatory in all educational establishments, churches, and Sunday-schools throughout France and the Empire. The catechism taught to the young Catholic included the following passages:

'Question: What are the duties of Christians towards the princes who govern them, and what, in particular, are our duties towards Napoleon I our Emperor?

Answer: Christians owe to the princes who govern them, and we, in particular, owe to Napoleon I, our Emperor, love, respect, obedience, loyalty, military service, and the taxes ordered for the preservation and defence of the Empire and his throne; we also owe him fervent prayers for his safety and for the spiritual and temporal prosperity of the state.

Question: Why are we bound in all these duties towards our Emperor?

Answer: First, because God, who creates Empires and apportions them according to His will, by heaping His gifts upon him, set him up as our sovereign and made him the agent of His power and His image on earth. Thus it is that to honour and serve our Emperor is to honour and serve God Himself. Secondly because our Saviour Jesus Christ taught us both by example and by precept what we owe our sovereign; for He was born under obedience to Caesar Augustus. He paid the prescribed taxes, and in the same breath as He said "Render to God that which belongs to God" He said "Render to Caesar that which belongs to Caesar."

Question: Are there any special reasons why we should have a particular loyalty to Napoleon I, our Emperor?

Answer: Yes there are; for God raised him up in difficult times to re-establish the public practise of the holy religion of our ancestors, and to protect it. He restored and preserved public order by his deep and active wisdom; he defends the state by the strength of his arm; he has become the Lord's anointed by the consecration he received from the Sovereign Pontiff, the head of the Church Universal.

Question: What ought one to think of those who fail in their duty towards our Emperor?

Answer: According to the Apostle Saint Paul they are resisting the order established by God Himself and making themselves worthy of eternal damnation.'[10]

This theological indoctrination had gone deep, particularly among the superstitious rural peasantry that made up 78 per cent of the population. Their attachment to Napoleon remained unbroken. He had been removed through Allied intervention and treachery, but among the majority of French youth and the Catholic congregation there was an abiding loyalty and reverence to him that had been built up over fourteen years, through the Church and their schools. Many had never travelled to a large city, few had ever read a newspaper; for them the village priest was the font of all knowledge and wisdom. He had taught them that to honour the Emperor, was to honour God and to be a good Catholic. A foreign invasion and the imposition of an unknown, uncrowned, monarch by these foreigners would scarcely suffice to break this bond. The Bourbons regarded them as the enemy – not to be trusted. They were merely the labour force, and it was left to the mayors and prefects to instruct them as to their new loyalty and obedience to the restored 'old order'.

The situation of the military worsened. Under Napoleon they had been the pride of the nation. To the new order they represented Napoleon, the Revolution and disloyalty. General Dupont had soon been replaced by Marshal Soult as Minister of War, his 'connections' having informed Artois that he was 'sound', and in fact Soult was soon to prove what a good royalist he could be. At the royal council meetings Artois was for ever interfering in military affairs, although he had never commanded troops except at the disastrous Quiberon expedition,[11] which by definition could scarcely have been called a command. His sons, especially the duc de Berry, fancied themselves as generals. Napoleon's Marshals, who had held the monetary and honorary posts of Colonel-Generals in the élite regiments, were demoted to the rank of inspectors-general, so that these useless princes could have the money, the dignity and honour of leading the men who would do the donkey-work. De Berry would ape Napoleon, chatting to the rank and file, tweaking ears, but to no avail; there was only one Napoleon, and this sort of thing was an insult to his memory. The princes constantly sought pretexts for military parades and reviews so that they could wear their uniforms – as though by parading in uniform some of Napoleon's aura would rub off.

To add to the army's humiliation, the King had made the 74-year-old duc de Havre a Marshal of France, merely because the old boy liked dressing up as a soldier. He was given to ordering reviews; bent like a hunchback, this decrepit idiot would march and counter-march the men, giggling with glee the while. At one of these reviews, de Berry remarked to a general of brigade who had an impressive war record: 'The French soldier must be happy these days. His long campaigns are over, and we have peace.' The general replied: 'Do you call a halt in the mud peace?'[12] De Berry promptly ripped the officer's epaulettes from his shoulders, stamped on them, and dismissed him.

In the cafes and barrack-rooms in 1814–15 the dejected troops recalled with dismay the glory that had departed. Less than seven months ago the French Army had been the most feared war machine in the world. Its overthrow had required the combined efforts of nine nations and several lesser states, and a *coup d'état;* 'The army has not been beaten – Never! When had it been beaten? Had Napoleon surrendered? – No! Had Davout? – No! Had Soult surrendered to Wellington? – No again! The army had been betrayed by politicians and self-serving lick-spittle officers.'[13]

Louis introduced a rigid court etiquette that set great store on precedence, and the humblest impoverished *émigré* took precedence over a Napoleonic patent which of course was of less than twenty years' creation. This was a calculated act on the part of Louis' confidant the duc de Duras, to humiliate these Napoleonic mutants imposed upon them by the Peace of Paris. The ridiculous ritual required that the ladies of 'lesser' rank wait outside the King's chamber until called, then pass through and wait outside Angoulême's chamber, and eventually that of Artois. (To secure his succession to the throne, Artois had arranged for his son to marry his niece, the daughter of his executed brother Louis XVI, now duchesse d'Angoulême[14] on her release from republican imprisonment.)

For the ladies of the Napoleonic nobility this business involved hours of waiting in draughty corridors while old nonentities from the Faubourg Saint-Germain passed in and out in front of them. The final degradation of the new protocol so far as they were concerned was that they were not allowed to retire whence they had come, but had to leave by the kitchen corridor and cross the muddy road in their court clothes and satin shoes.

Marshal Ney, the prime mover of the mutiny that had denied Napoleon his decisive battle, and who had merely wanted peace – now rued his decision. His sons would not be eligible for the new military acadamies,[15] his reputation meant little to these foreign Frenchmen. He had to humour and play lackey to the idiotic, septuagenarian Marshal and these jumped-up princes who had never heard a shot fired in anger, and had had to stand by impotently while war heroes were humiliated, old soldiers of the Legion of Honour insulted and now about to be put out to beg. The Imperial Guard had been removed and given time the Bourbons would disband it. What price a peace without honour? The last straw came in November 1814. On returning home he found his wife Aglaé in tears, she and the duchesse d'Abrantés, the widow of the late General Junot, having been insulted by the duchesse d'Angoulême. Apparently, d'Angoulême had eyed them up and down and said: 'You are, I believe, Madame Junot are you not? And you, of course, are Madame Ney.'[16] In other words, they were not a princess and a duchess in her eyes, but mere commoners. Ney rode straightaway to the palace in his ordinary uniform, his boots covered in mud. The ex-sergeant-major of hussars and commander of armies literally charged into the palace, shoving aside the chocolate-box soldiers of the *Maison du Roi* with a shout of 'Out of my way lackeys!' and felling the major-domo. He strode unannounced through the King's apartment. On seeing the King he merely lifted his hat and excused himself – Louis was absolutely frozen with fear by the look on Ney's face. The Marshal pushed open the partition doors, strode into d'Angoulême's apartment, startling her ladies, and in barrack-room language and at the top of his voice told her what he thought of her in tones that had made many a brave general quail. Only snatches of his tirade were recounted outside the palace – it was after all the Bourbons' greatest humiliation since their return – '... I and others were fighting for France while you sat sipping tea in English gardens ... 'Ney then delivered a comprehensive description of her 'noble' ancestry, her inherited blue blood and the physical appearance of all her kin including the royalist Marshal and King Louis. He ended with: '... You don't seem to know what the name Ney means, but one of these days I'll show you!' On that note he strode out and not by the back stairs. The court was shattered, as was the illusion. The Allies had gone. If the King had attempted to have Ney arrested the army would have freed him.[17] When accounts of this verbal onslaught reached the streets of Paris the people were jubilant .

What in the army had been sullen dumb insolence now erupted into open insubordination. The Bourbons had increased the size of the foreign regiments in their army, i.e., the Swiss, while reducing their own regular regiments. In the ex-Imperial Guard, no less than 700 officers, the army's élite, had been placed on half-pay, while old *émigrés*, traitors and 'ultras' who had fought in foreign armies against France were found lucrative appointments. The people were incensed; the king evidently preferred to place his safety and the national security in the hands of foreigners and traitors. Ney has shown the way, it was said; the foreigners' armies are gone, why are we putting up with it? In a cafe at Montluçon a colonel of hussars, pretending to complain about the price of his meal, shouted loudly across the room: 'It's much cheaper in Paris. There, for a 'napoleon' you get a great fat pig!' Hostility was growing. It needed only a leader or a suitable incident to spark off another revolution. .

The final error made by the Bourbons was triggered off by the Church. Louis set great store by his ancient title of 'Most Christian Majesty' and, as we have seen, many of the lesser nobles were churchmen who wanted their good livings back, i.e., the vast manorial Church estates. They also wanted to return the people to the subservience to the clergy that had existed prior to the Revolution. Napoleon as we know had created a concordat with the Church, and the role of the hierarchy had been relegated from feudal overlordship to that of being servants and supporters of the state and its citizens. Now Louis allowed these militant priests to enforce Sunday worship and to close the cafes on Sundays which was illegal even within the framework of the so-called 'Charter'. The priests also conducted religious processions with statues to various sites of 'murdered royalist martyrs', and services were held on the site of the place of execution of the late Bourbon monarchs. Those events of two decades ago were of little interest to the populace and they resented the implication that they were collectively guilty of some crime that had been committed long ago, and which to some seemed to have been just. These processions were forbidden by the criminal code which had not been repealed, and it seemed to the people that the royalists were using the law to suit themselves. Was this not exactly what parents and grandparents had always said that they did? The Revolution had taken place to remove these parasites; 'why are we now putting up with them?'[18] murmured these more enlightened citizens – who enjoyed their Sunday drink.

Pressure from the churchmen, supported by *émigrés* and 'ultras', induced the King to instruct his Minister Ferrand to introduce a bill in the Chambers to return such of the *biens nationaux* as remained to the former owners. In his speech the Minister said: 'The émigrés have followed the right line ... the King regrets that he cannot give to this measure all the latitude which in his heart of hearts he desires ...'[19] The implication of this and other phrases indicated that the King intended to do more. If the King were returning all the national lands, which included farmland, parks and public places, to the feudal owners, what next? They were already proposing to evict veterans and orphans for the same reasons; why not the present owners of *émigrés'* property? The bill caused a national uproar, the debate continuing for a record eight sittings, but the deputies had no powers to prevent it. The Charter had declared the inviolability of the land and the King had not respected it; what faith could be put in anything else he signed or promised? Two days later the King made Minister Ferrand a Count, and this indication of royal pleasure and reward further heightened the fears of the present holders of national land.

High and low – from the Napoleonic nobility such as Marmont, Ney, Clarke, Pasquier, Fouché and even Talleyrand, down to tradesmen, artisans and a high proportion of the rural population – all held national lands, town houses or estates granted to them by Napoleon. Were these now to be confiscated? The fear of dispossession was real enough to turn France into a powder-keg awaiting the spark. Louis, having learnt nothing in 24 years, by this stupid and insensitive act that would please a few thousand royalists had alienated more than 30 million Frenchmen and bid fair to set the scene for a counter-revolution.[20] The people were united in a single wish – to restore the pre-March 1814 *status quo.*

Meanwhile, on 28 June 1814, Lord Wellington, who had been created a Duke on 3 May, took his seat in the House of Lords as Viscount, Earl, Marquess and Duke. He had left England in 1809 as Sir Arthur Wellesley, the 'Sepoy' General, to reconstruct the British expeditionary force that had been chased out of Spain by Napoleon, and whose brave but outnumbered commander had died at Corunna. Wellington was the first military commander since the Duke of Marlborough to raise a British army to first-class status. Thanks to his experience in India, where he had learnt how to husband his troops and keep them well supplied, he had taken a creaky, linear army, trained along the old Prussian lines, and turned it into a military machine to rival and beat the French. Fortunately for Britain, distance and terrain had allowed him greater latitude for independent command, than would have been the case had he been operating closer to the interfering politicians and War Office officials at home. He had marched his army from Portugal, through Spain and into France, defeating and pushing back French armies commanded by some of the best of Napoleon's marshals. His tactics were unlike any that the French had come up against and he had never been defeated by them. He was lionized in England as a conquering hero and met the visiting monarchs and their generals. His meeting with Blücher was most harmonious; each was aware of the other's prowess and ruthless determination to defeat the enemy. And they liked each other.

Wellington's respite was short, however. Britain was engaged in 'assisting' the now United Netherlands government to establish itself, and had 'bought' at knock-down prices some of their overseas possessions seized from Holland during the last conflict, on condition that most of the money be spent on re-fortifying the strategic towns in Belgium – 'the military barrier'– under the supervision of British engineers. Britain was presently maintaining in Holland her military force that had assisted in the liberation of Hanover and the Low Countries.[21] Wellington was sent to France as ambassador and was asked to inspect these fortifications and the defensive capability of the barrier on the way.[22] With hindsight, his appointment can be seen as having been tactless; the French felt humiliated, the more so because Louis and his ilk, having spent so much of their lives in England, saw her as their staunchest supporter, and their obvious admiration of and respect for Wellington made matters worse.

In Vienna the Allies would soon be reaching the impasse over the division of ter-ritorial spoils that had been looming since 1813, but which had been shelved until the Congress, which was due to convene there in two months' time. Its purpose was to decide what to do with the territories that had been seized, created or altered by Napoleon and incorporated into his empire. Britain had already established the Low Countries as one unit, and her involvement now appeared to be primarily as a medi-ator, while looking after her German interests, i.e., Hanover and the ducal house of Brunswick, related by blood to the British crown. Talleyrand was to be sent to the Congress as France's representative, his position as chief minister having been deli-cately terminated. The King's favourite adviser and Chief Minister, if one could call him that, was now the comte de Blacas, who had held this post in England. Talleyrand, conscious of his need to ingratiate himself with the Bourbons whom he had attempted to restore in a constitutional role, now promised Louis that he would regain in Vienna the prestige, honour and respect due to 'legitimate' Bourbon France. Her humiliation, he said, must end with the 'usurper'. Talleyrand also advised Louis to support his Bourbon cousin, King Ferdinand of the two Sicilies, in his demand for the return of his kingdom. In this Talleyrand solicited the aid of the restored Spanish Bourbons. Napoleon's sister and brother-in-law, he said, had 'usurped this throne, and it must be returned to its 'legitimate sovereign'. Talleyrand did not add that the Murats of Naples had confiscated his own princedom of Benevente and its revenues because of his treachery, or that Ferdinand had promised to get them back for him in return for his help. Nor, for that matter, that throughout the years that he had held this sinecure from Napoleon, his conscience had never prompted him to return it to its 'legitimate' Neapolitan owners from whom it had been seized to provide him with revenues.

Meanwhile on the mountainous Mediterranean island of Elba, its sovereign Lord and Emperor, Napoleon, a small man, still cast a great shadow over Europe. Napoleon had disembarked on 3 May, to a 21-gun salute, from HMS *Undaunted*, commanded by Captain Ussher.[23] He had not been exiled, he was not a prisoner, as rumour had it, but the recognized sovereign of this island. Under the 21 articles of the Treaty of Fontainebleau he had been given the French frigate *Inconstant* as his private property and a bodyguard of 400 – later 700 men. No restrictions had been placed on him or his movements and he had not been forbidden to return to France.

Tsar Alexander, possibly on the advice of Count Pozzo di Borgo, had stipulated Elba for Napoleon's patrimony, instead of Corsica, or part of Italy, much to the annoyance of the Austrian Emperor, who laid claim to the island. Alexander had wanted to ensure Napoleon's personal safety – as he had promised Caulaincourt and the Marshals. On this point Napoleon was reassured on his arrival. The island, sixteen miles by six, derived its income from its iron mines and fishing fleet. The capital, Portoferraio, was sited on a peninsula with unscalable cliffs behind and an unbridgable moat as a killing-ground on the landward approach, protected by cannon sited in a complex system of walls, ditches, *enceintes* and forts. In the sixteenth century Philip II of Spain had given the island, long a victim of Barbary corsairs, to Don Cosimo de Medici who wished to establish there an order of knights, like those of Malta; they were to be called the Knights of Saint Stephen.

The Italian military architect Gianbattista Belluci had designed the extensive and formidable defences which embraced the whole town and port and were calculated to thwart any combined naval and land attack. The walls of the U-shaped harbour had deeply casemated gunports, two-tiered and immense. There was a fort on each of the ends of the arms of the U, and at the base of the U the fortified Water Gate provided the only access to the town.

Elba had a population of 12,000, its people and terrain were identical with those of Corsica, Napoleon's birthplace, 25 nautical miles to the west, and visible from Elba's highest point. Whether Napoleon would have been content to remain here is a matter for speculation, but several factors would soon arise that would make it impossible even if he had desired it. The Eagle might have landed, but its flight was unimpeded.

Dark clouds were now gathering on the political horizon. Louis and the Spanish and Sicilian Bourbons were determined that King Murat be removed from Naples, and Ferdinand the 'legitimate' monarch restored. Metternich had indicated to Louis, secretly, that despite her treaty with Murat, Austria might allow this if France supported Austria at the forthcoming Congress; Austria would not attack Murat, but might remain neutral while a French or Spanish force ejected him.[24] In England, Castlereagh was preparing to depart for Vienna; he wrote to Wellington in Paris, asking him to arrange a meeting with Talleyrand to find out what Louis' views were on the forthcoming Congress:

'... I have to request that you will, as early as possible after your arrival at Paris, endeavour to learn his Highness's views upon the subjects that are likely to occupy the attention of Congress, and especially upon the points of

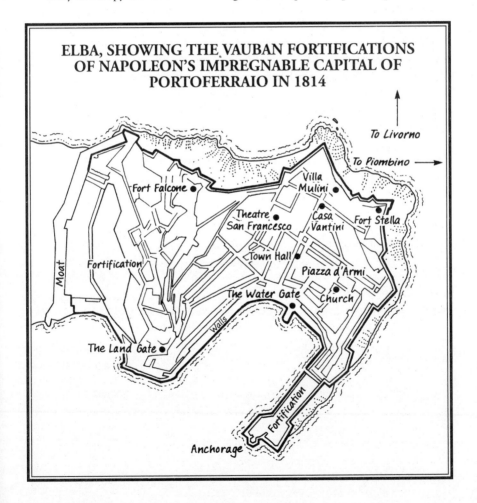

ELBA, SHOWING THE VAUBAN FORTIFICATIONS OF NAPOLEON'S IMPREGNABLE CAPITAL OF PORTOFERRAIO IN 1814

To Livorno
To Piombino

Fort Falcone
Villa Mulini
Theatre
San Francesco
Casa Vantini
Fort Stella
Town Hall
Fortification
Piazza d'Armi
Moat
The Water Gate
Church
Walls
The Land Gate
Fortification
Anchorage

Poland and Naples ... Your Grace will observe that I have explained to the Prince of Benavente the object of these preliminary conferences. So far as you can regulate the Prince's arrival, I should wish him to be there about the 25th ... It is material that your Grace should endeavour to ascertain how far France is prepared, under any and what circumstances, to support her views on these two leading questions by arms. It is particularly desirable to learn whether the French and Spanish Governments limit their hostile views against Murat to a refusal to acknowledge; or whether, in the event of other powers (Austria included) declining to give him aid, they would be disposed to employ their arms to replace the King of Sicily on the throne of Naples.'[25]

Austria had guaranteed Murat his throne and Britain had acceded to Austria's wishes, provided that Murat had deserted Napoleon and actively assisted in the expulsion of French troops from Italy. Murat had done this, even though Britain's minister in Sicily had actively tried to get this arrangement stopped. Castlereagh had overruled his objections.

On Wellington's advice, Castlereagh stopped off at Paris on his way, and had a private audience with the King and a lengthy meeting with Talleyrand. Reporting to Lord Liverpool, he confirmed that the French were in agreement with him that Poland should not be given to Russia, and that Louis had suggested that it be returned as '... an independent State in the House of Saxony'. Then, as to Naples, he reported:

> '... I took, however, advantage of the question of Naples to express that we felt no objection but the reverse to the restoration of this branch of the House of Bourbon, that we were aware that the power and influence of France must be thereby materially augmented; but that we felt no repugnance to the natural and legitimate influence of the family so long as the two principal crowns abstained from a connection which made them one State for the purpose of aggression.'[26]

So, Nine months after a war against France that had lasted nearly 25 years, Castlereagh was asking France how far she was prepared, and '... under what circumstances, to support her views on these two leading questions by arms'. First, was she prepared to use force to stop Russia, Britain's ally, acquiring Poland? Secondly, was she prepared to use force in removing Murat? – the latter having been guaranteed his possession of Naples by the Allies and Britain having acceded to this.

CHAPTER 7

THE ROAD TO VIENNA

'I am commanded by HRH to acquaint you that ... it is unnecessary for me to point out to you the impossibility of HRH consenting to involve this country in hostilities at this time for any of the objects which have been hitherto under discussion at Vienna.– 'Lord Bathurst to Lord Castlereagh, 27 November 1814.

EVEN BEFORE PEACE IN EUROPE HAD BEEN ACHIEVED, A NEW compact between Austria, Britain and France had been concluded. Lines were being drawn in the camps of the 'Allies'. Castlereagh, in ensuring the removal of Napoleon and the restoration of the Bourbons, had undertaken to assist Austria in preventing its former allies from gaining the territorial compensation they expected. Russia and Prussia had been led to believe, erroneously, by Castlereagh that the Congress would rubber-stamp their aspirations, while they in return had agreed, *carte blanche*, to refrain from any discussion of Britain's 'maritime rights' and the United Netherlands as a military barrier.

Castlereagh arrived in Vienna on 12 September 1814, and an elaborate charade was enacted by him and Metternich. The delegates arrived to find that no procedure for regulating the Congress had been formulated by Metternich. Article XXXII of the Treaty of Paris had convened the Congress, and its secret protocol stated that France could attend, but would have no say in territorial dispositions. Castlereagh suggested to the delegates that the plenipotentiaries of Austria, Russia, Prussia, Great Britain, France and Spain should 'charge themselves with this preparatory duty of forming procedure'. Prussia and Russia were against the inclusion of France who, in their eyes, was only there as a suppliant. Castlereagh and Metternich argued that Bourbon France and Spain were 'powers of the first order' and should have some role. On 20 September a compromise scheme was agreed, as summarized below:

(1) The Big Four should sign a protocol reserving to themselves the final decision in all territorial matters.

(2) This protocol would be communicated to France and Spain first, and then to the other delegates.

(3) A special committee of the five Germanic powers would draft a scheme for a Germanic federation.

(4) The future arrangements for the formal Congress would be discussed by the Big Six, i.e., Russia, Prussia, Austria, Great Britain plus France and Spain.

So it was that by seeming to reserve all the territorial decisions to the Big Four, and creating a Germanic committee – to please primarily Prussia, Metternich and Castlereagh had brought France (with Spain) into the organizing team as a sop to her national pride. The next step came on the 30th when the first meeting was scheduled to discuss procedural arrangements. Talleyrand for France and Don Pedro Labrador for Spain were invited to a 'private conference'. Talleyrand was handed a copy of the protocol summarized in (4) above. The document referred in several paragraphs to the 'Allies'. Talleyrand, with a fine display of disgust, exclaimed: 'Allies! What Allies? Are we back at Chaumont?' Allies against whom? Napoleon is at Elba. Allies against Louis XVIII? 'I do not understand. For me there are but two dates only. Between those two dates there is nothing. The first date is 30 May on which it was agreed to hold this Congress. The second date is 1 October on which it was proclaimed this Congress would open. Nothing that may have taken place in the interval exists so far as I am concerned.'[1] He argued that the quadruple alliance had ceased to have any meaning after the signing of the Peace of Paris. That all that was agreed was that a Congress would decide the apportioning of territory. The assumption of control by the Big Four, he said, was without 'legal', logical or moral justification. He demanded that the authority of the directing body be confirmed by the eight convening powers who had signed the Peace of Paris; they included Portugal and Sweden. Talleyrand then left the meeting, and went to lobby the small powers, princelings and ducal houses. The outcome was that France was admitted as an equal 'great power', thanks to Castlereagh and Metternich's support of Talleyrand's demands.

That Castlereagh and Metternich were in on this performance cannot be disputed. Without their agreement Talleyrand would not have been admitted to any of the talks. They decided that 'France and Spain should be informed of the procedure first', which gave him the opportunity to protest and be admitted before the Tsar arrived. All this had been cleverly managed so as to introduce Bourbon France into full partnership in the power-broking. Both Castlereagh and Metternich were fully aware that the interpretation of treaties was a matter for the signatories concerned and not for outside parties. It was not up to France, Bourbon or otherwise, to dispute. The Treaty of Paris was quite clear and legal. As head of the provisional government of Louis XVIII, Talleyrand knew the terms of reference which Louis had ratified.[2] In signing, France had agreed that it had no right of decision in the impending territorial questions. By these machinations Castlereagh and Metternich had aligned three 'great powers' against Russia and Prussia, thereby hoping to supply Austria with clout in the forthcoming discussions.

The Tsar arrived in Vienna on 25 September and took up residence in the imperial palace of the Hofburg where sumptuous apartments had been made available. At the first meeting he made his demands known. The defunct Duchy of Warsaw was to become his new Kingdom of Poland, with a constitutional charter. For Prussia – the whole of Saxony. These were exactly the claims that Russia and Prussia had agreed upon by their Treaty of Kalisch in 1813, before Austria came down off the fence, and when Prussia and Russia alone were fighting Napoleon in eastern Europe. Alexander justified his claims by adding: 'It is just that my subjects should be indemnified for so many sacrifices and that a military border should preserve them forever from a new invasion.'[3] This was no more than what Britain and Austria had wanted. Both Austria and Prussia, it should be remembered, had assisted Napoleon to invade

Russia through Poland in 1812. Castlereagh attempted to take the moral high ground, but Alexander would have none of it. Britain had not been invaded, her towns and cities had not been destroyed, her people had not been rendered homeless or killed. France had not paid a penny piece in reparations and, on Castlereagh's advice, their looted art treasures had not been re-possessed. Poland had not existed as an independent country since 1793; since that date it had been partitioned three times, Austria, Prussia and Russia having divided it up between them. Napoleon had formed the Duchy out of parts taken from Austria and Prussia and placed it under the nominal suzerainty of the King of Saxony. Russia would hold this bridgehead against attack and give it a constitutional monarchy. The Saxon king had supported Napoleon to the last; he had been raised from an Electoral Duke of the old Holy Roman Empire to a King by Napoleon in 1806. Prussia, as has been stated, had been degraded, looted, impoverished, humiliated and reduced to a third-rate power, while tiny Saxony had been raised high. Prussia had fought alongside Russia in most of the campaigns of 1813 and, like Russia, had expended more lives and money in bringing about Napoleon's overthrow than had his reluctant father-in-law, Francis.

Prussia had been squeezed dry by enforced contributions since 1806, its trade impoverished and its territory given to Napoleon's relatives. Castlereagh had argued against Prussia's seizing French territory, plundering Paris, recovering its lost art treasures and imposing war reparations. Its king, its people and its generals had decided that Saxony was a just recompense.

Austria was against the idea of having a Russian frontier a mere 175 miles from Vienna, and Prussia adding another 200 miles to the 250-mile border with Austria already in place. Metternich, realizing that he would have to appease one claimant, simplified his policy privately by the strategic device of accepting one claim but not both. His greatest concern was that if Russian Poland were given a constitutional charter, it might encourage Austrian Poles to seek the same. This could have a domino effect on the multi-ethnic population of Austria's empire: Germans, Italians, Hungarians, Dalmatians, Illyrians, Serbs and Croats. His second concern was that an enlarged Prussia would take the lead with the German states and supplant Austrian dominance.

The Tsar suggested for Austria, 'The north of Italy as far as the Ticino and Lake Maggiore, Venezia, the Tyrol, Salzburg, the Inn valley and Dalmatia.' All of which had been ceded by Austria to France and were now back in Austrian occupation – under the same legality by which Russia held Poland. At the meeting Alexander was annoyed to see Talleyrand whom he had not spoken to when he left Paris. Talleyrand, sheltering behind his diplomatic status, began by being insolent to him. 'Your majesty will wish to keep only what is legitimately his,' he said. 'I am in agreement with the great powers,' the Tsar declared. Talleyrand retorted that he hoped that the Tsar considered that France was one of the great powers? The Tsar said that he did, and added that if France did not like the arrangement what did she suggest? 'I put right first and what suits people afterwards,' Talleyrand replied. The Tsar cut him short: 'No! I repeat, what suits Europe is right!'[4] 'Europe! Europe! Poor Europe!'

Talleyrand mocked, pretending to knock his head against the wall. The question then turned on Saxony whose king had been a staunch friend of Talleyrand's during the years when the latter had been Napoleon's foreign minister. Talleyrand had put it to Louis and Castlereagh that if Prussia had Saxony she would become a powerful threat to France – for whom she had the greatest enmity. Alexander, who was railing against those who, like the King of Saxony, had betrayed Europe by supporting Napoleon, was interrupted by Talleyrand, who said: 'Sire, that is a question of dates and the effect of the confusion into which people may have been thrown by circumstances.' The inference being that up to 1811 Alexander had also supported Napoleon. The Tsar was referring to those who had not broken with Napoleon when the opportunity had presented itself. Moreover, Talleyrand himself had suggested several of Napoleon's diplomatic aggressions during his nine years as Napoleon's willing tool, including, it was believed, the planning of the kidnap of the duc d'Enghien. Talleyrand had persuaded the Tsar to break with Napoleon in 1810. The arch-turncoat, it should be remembered, had remained in Napoleon's employ as Arch-Chancellor of the Empire right up to the fall of Paris.

The Tsar's anger and loathing for Talleyrand was fuelled by the fact that he had trusted him and set him up as head of the provisional government. Talleyrand's reputation as a diplomat was not enhanced in this deliberate baiting of the powerful autocrat. Alexander was now fed up with Bourbon France whose king had insulted him, and more especially with Talleyrand, his abrasive mouth-piece, with his continual braying about 'legitimacy'. Normally correct and well-mannered, he now erupted in an outburst of fury that would have been a credit to Napoleon himself. He was not going to be lectured by this treacherous, jumped-up churchman who had duped him and was now deliberately insulting him. 'I thought France owed me something. You always talk about principles. Your law means nothing to me. I don't know what it is. What do you think all your parchments and treaties mean to me? The King of Prussia will be King of Prussia and Saxony, as I shall be Emperor of Russia and King of Poland ...'[5]

Castlereagh then spoke in support of Talleyrand, suggesting that 'His Imperial Majesty could not wish to rest his pretensions on a title of conquest in opposition to the general sentiments of Europe.'[6] Alexander countered Castlereagh's hypocrisy by suggesting that perhaps Britain might submit her colonial 'conquests' to the Congress to agree upon? By now he had realized what was going on. He had thought that everything had been agreed. Having allowed Castlereagh's arrangements regarding the Low Countries to be dealt with in the Paris Treaty, he now felt that was being double-crossed by Britain. He now addressed Castlereagh and the others with a clarity the more frightening because they knew that he had an army of occupation in Poland, a military governor and presence in Saxony, and another army close to the border. '*I am in occupation of Poland. I possess a large army. If England or anyone else does not like it, they can come and turn me out.*'[7] With that, the first informal meeting ended.

Castlereagh was understandably annoyed at Talleyrand's playing his, Castlereagh's, game. Having had no previous dealings with him apart from his assistance in the restoration, he had expected a grateful Bourbon France and her minister – who owed his position to Britain and Austria – merely to repay the debt by supporting them and confining himself to what Castlereagh took to be Louis' moot point – the Murats of Naples. Talleyrand had pursued his own policy independently, and his insulting attitude to the Tsar had created a dramatic splitting of the Alliance – which perhaps was Talleyrand's purpose.

Castlereagh now received a letter from Prince Hardenberg, formally asking the assent of England and Austria to the incorporation of Saxony into Prussia. Castlereagh seized this opportunity, as he explained to Lord Liverpool: '... As there seemed to be much indecision in the Austrian councils, I considered that there ought to be less hesitation on the part of the Prince Regent in marking the decided interest His Royal Highness takes in the effectual reconstruction of Prussia. I accordingly addressed to His Highness the enclosed letters.'[8] Castlereagh enclosed a copy of his letter to Hardenberg giving Britain's assent to the annexation of Saxony, contingent on Prussian co-operation in resisting Russia's claims on the Polish duchy. He later wrote to Liverpool, informing him of his dispatch to the Duke of Wellington in Paris:

> '... and shall desire the Duke of Wellington, as from himself, to insinuate through M. de Blacas, that any attempt on the part of France to make such a collateral point as that of Saxony a question of War, in subversion of the more important object of opposing a barrier to Russia, must, in all probability, not only destroy their friendly relations with England, but lead to immediate hostilities, and that its obvious and first effect must be to compel England to sign a peace with Murat, in order to place Austria in security on the side of Italy, and thus enable her to direct her efforts to her Polish frontier.'[9]

Castlereagh, through Wellington, was now dictating France's foreign policy, which bordered on outright 'blackmail'. No better example exists of the power wielded by Britain's Foreign Secretary at this point, with his roving commission from the Cabinet, than this threatening of Louis 'with hostilities'.

Castlereagh then requested and was granted an interview with the Tsar which lasted almost two hours. The Tsar opened by stating that he could not understand Britain's objections; Poland had ceased to exist two decades ago. Napoleon had created a small duchy which bordered the easiest invasion route to Russia. He and the Russian people were concerned to have this vital route in their hands. His demands were not greater than those of the other powers. He was not incorporating Poland into Russia, but keeping it as an independent entity, with a constitution drawn up by Jeremy Bentham.[10] Castlereagh, promoting Austria's point of view, suggested that Russia in juxtaposition to Austria and Prussia would pose a threat to Europe's security. Why did Britain see Russia, its ally, as a threat? Alexander asked. Who had assisted Britain more? Had he not honoured his 1805 treaty with Britain to the letter (referring to the military barrier)? Further, Russia had always had a border with both countries in Poland after the last three partitions of that country, the Tsar said, thereby exposing the weakness of Castlereagh's argument.

When the interview ended Castlereagh handed the Tsar a letter stating his views, and a memorandum on Poland.[11] His letter, dated 12 October 1814, began: 'Since Great Britain is the last Power whose interests could be endangered by any determination of HIM on the side of Poland, Castlereagh may be mistaken in his judgement, but on no question can be considered a more impartial authority.'[12] He went on to express Britain's concern that Russia, having already in the last decade acquired large possessions, might jeopardize the peace of Europe. He added that the Tsar's actions would determine whether '... the present Congress shall prove a blessing to mankind, or only exhibit a scene of discordant intrigue, and a lawless scramble for power'.[13] The memorandum, an extraordinary document, quoted sections from the Treaty of Kalisch, to which neither Britain nor Austria had been a party (nor should they have possessed copies of the treaty). Castlereagh also invoked sections of the Treaty of Reichenbach, signed by Austria, Russia and Prussia which, it will be remembered, had been kept secret from Britain. Castlereagh had tried to re-phrase these sections to show that the Tsar's treaties with Prussia over the divisions of Poland and Saxony were cancelled out by the later treaties – with Austria and then with Britain at Chaumont. His most serious charge was that Alexander was breaking the treaty of 1797, which had settled the last partition of independent Poland and wherein each of the three signatories agreed not violate the others' territories. The Tsar was doing just that by occupying parts that belonged to the other two. The document concluded: 'It is further alleged that, so long as HIM adheres to this project, it is impossible that any plan for the reconstruction of Europe can be brought forward, or that the present Congress can be assembled to discuss any such arrangement. It cannot be expected that Austria and Prussia should come forward of their own accord and propose to leave their dominions without a military frontier.'[14] The Tsar accepted the documents, and said that he would study them and give his reply in due course. He then sought the advice and assistance of his envoy, Prince Lieven, in sounding out public opinion in Britain.

The Congress had not yet formally opened, and already the Great Powers were in political disarray. Britain, supposedly with French support, was supporting Austria against the combined aspirations of Russia and Prussia. Talleyrand had irritated both the Tsar and Castlereagh with his attempt to draw attention and importance back to France. Correctly divining that the greater threat to France would come from an enlarged and vengeful Prussia, not from distant Russia, Talleyrand was opposing the annexation of Saxony; it would also be to his personal advantage to give prestige to Bourbon France by thwarting the Tsar. Austria it appeared, would have to come to an arrangement with either Russia or Prussia to thwart the pretensions of both. Castlereagh, realizing this, had accepted in principle the annexation of Saxony as the lesser of the two evils. Prussia, he thought, was a useful bulwark against France, Austria and Russia – besides, she had no navy to compete with Britain's, unlike Russia, and her territory did not stretch from Turkey and Mongolia to Norway.

On 24 October there took place a conspiratorial meeting of Metternich, Castlereagh and Prince Hardenberg of Prussia. After much persuasion from

Castlereagh, Metternich reluctantly agreed to the annexation of Saxony by Prussia – contingent on the success of the Polish negotiations.[15] Metternich indicated to Hardenberg that it was a wise decision *because the Tsar had indicated a willingness to sacrifice Prussian interests for Austrian support in Poland.* After the meeting Castlereagh wrote to the Prime Minister: '... I have throughout the last twelve months, under every change of fortune, uniformly *expressed on the part of my Court, that the fate of Saxony should be considered subordinate, after the glorious efforts of Prussia in the war, to the effectual reconstruction of that power.*'[16] During the last twelve months Castlereagh, as he explained to Wellington, had decided that if Prussia could not be weaned from Russian influence:

> '... it rendered Holland and the Low Countries dependant on France for their support, instead of having Prussia and the Northern States of Germany as their natural protectors. It presented the further inconvenience, in case of war, of exposing all the recent cessions by France to re-occupation by French Armies, as the seat of war might happen to present itself ... however pure the intentions of the King of France were, and however friendly, we ought not risk so much upon French connexion, and that it was wiser to preserve, as far as possible the goodwill of France, whilst we laboured to unite Germany.'

So Saxony was to be sacrificed to appease Prussia. To Wellington Castlereagh dismissed Talleyrand's fear that Prussia would come to dominate the German states and then France and Europe, saying:

> 'If France were a feeble and menaced Power, she might well feel jealous of such a German alliance; but, as her direct interests are out of danger, it is unreasonable that she should impede the sole means that remain to Germany of preserving its independence, in order either to indulge a sentiment towards the King of Saxony, or to create a French party amongst the minor states. France need never dread a German league: it is in its nature inoffensive, and there is no reason to fear that the union between Austria and Prussia will be such as to endanger the liberties of other states.'[17]

Having come to an agreement, Castlereagh suggested that Metternich present a joint resolution to the Tsar, as Austrian interests were principally involved. Proposing the Vistula as the Russian frontier, Metternich's presentation gave him, as he wrote later, 'more grief in three months than he had had in all his life'.[18] The Tsar fulminated against the perfidy of Austria, and Great Britain, who had not even had the courtesy to await his reply to their memorandum, and expressed total disbelief in Prussian agreement. Metternich replied to his outburst that Austria would agree to an independent Poland, but not a puppet Poland run by Russia. Austria, he said, had as much right to create a puppet government of its own in Poland as had the Tsar. This was too much; to say the least it was impolite if not downright unwise for one only recently elevated to princely status to address the ruling monarch of a 'friendly' Great Power in this fashion. The Tsar was furious. More than six feet in height, he bent to confront the smaller Metternich and said, 'You are the only man in Austria who would dare speak to me in a rebellious tone!'

The Tsar first demanded of the King of Prussia the meaning of the resolution. King William denied any personal knowledge or sanction of the document, and declared his intention to stick to their treaty.[19] The Austrian Emperor attempted to smooth things over with Alexander who tried to induce Francis to dismiss Metternich. But the Tsar had won the day. Castlereagh, who had been absent from Vienna at the time, sent a different version of the affair to Liverpool and tried to justify Metternich's undiplomatic behaviour.[20]

On 3 November the Tsar sent a formal reply to Castlereagh's memorandum. It was concise and drew attention to the fact that, 'The writer of the British Memorandum introduces his paper by the preamble of the Treaty of Kalisch. The efforts and the sacrifices of Russia are not the conclusion that he wishes to draw. He wishes to prove that the Emperor is deviating from his first principles, that he is disregarding the faith of Treaties and that he is threatening the safety of his neighbours ...' Alexander then showed that none of the latter treaties annulled the first, nor were intended to. Secondly, that Castlereagh's implied fears were imaginary; the Russian borders with Austria and Prussia had existed since 1797 and Russia had threatened neither country. Thirdly, and more to the point, he was not bound by the treaty of 1797 because the other two parties had broken it: '... *When Austria and Prussia have contributed as Allies of France* [1812] *to despoil Russia of the greater part of her Polish provinces, and when the Duchy of Warsaw is today a compensation for the enormous sacrifices of Russia, it becomes a question of a new division and the stipulations of 1797 no longer exist.*'[21] He went on to substantiate the truth of his argument. In essence, Russia had had a border with Austria and Prussia in the past without aggression. Both of those parties had ceded parts of the old partitioned Poland from which Napoleon had created the duchy which he ruled. The duchy comprised the main route of attack on Russia from the west; the other two countries had used it with Napoleon to attack Russia in 1812. Alexander was now creating his own 'military barrier' to plug the gap, for the very same reasons that Britain had not made peace with Napoleon while Belgium and Holland were in his possession. His Poland, with a constitutional monarchy, would remain separated from Russia as a buffer zone, like the United Netherlands. That as far as he was concerned was the beginning and end of the matter – and he had an army of 480,000 men to ensure that it remained so.

In London, however, news of the events in Vienna was arriving from various British and foreign sources, and the Cabinet was far from happy with Castlereagh's conduct. Embarrassing questions were being asked in the House. During his visit to Britain the public had enthusiastically welcomed the Tsar as the 'Liberator of Europe'. British public opinion was overwhelmingly in favour of a constitutional Poland under the Tsar rather than a dismembered country. It also took the view that the King of Saxony, the legitimate monarch, should not lose the whole of his kingdom, merely for doing what every other monarch in Europe had been forced to do. Nor did they like the way that defeated France was being treated by Castlereagh as the prodigal son at the expense of British allies, and that he had neither ratified a treaty with Murat nor stated his reasons for refuting the arrangement. To the people at home it seemed as if Britain were dancing at the Vienna Congress to Austria's tune. Prince Lieven, the Russian Ambassador, had wasted little time in putting the facts before Cabinet Ministers, sympathetic members of both Houses of Parliament, prominent peers and the press.

Lord Liverpool wrote to Castlereagh, enclosing a paper from Mr Vansittart, the Chancellor, that embodied, Liverpool said, the collective views of the Cabinet. Liverpool was also quite frank about the situation in Vienna and at home:

'I think his paper contains very much the impression of several of our colleagues, viz., *that we have done enough on this question of Poland ... the time is now come when, according to one of your former despatches, it would be better that we withdraw ourselves from the question altogether ... I am the more persuaded, as I have already said, that no arrangement respecting Poland can now be either creditable or satisfactory. I think it very material that we should consider that our war with America will probably now be of some duration. We owe it, therefore, to ourselves not to make enemies in other quarters if we can avoid it, for I cannot but feel apprehensive that some of our European allies will not be indisposed to favour the Americans; and if the Emperor of Russia should be desirous of taking up their cause, we are well aware ... that there is a most powerful party in Russia to support him ...*'[22]

The Chancellor's paper commenced: 'I begin to apprehend that we are making ourselves too much principals in the disputes respecting Poland ... We run the risk, therefore, of being disavowed, and represented abroad as actuated by jealousy of the greatness of Russia, and at home as the advocates and instigators of a system of Partition.' It went on to dismiss categorically all Castlereagh's objections, voicing also Britain's fear that: '*... there is even greater probability that in resentment of our interference, the Emperor of Russia may be disposed to listen to some suggestion for bringing forward questions of maritime law at the Congress.*' This, Britain's sacred cow, was to be avoided at all costs so far as he was concerned:

'... There is besides, the greatest probability that in the course of one or two generations, at the utmost, the nominal independence of Poland would become real ... In the meantime, *as far as British interests are concerned, I think the decision of the question of no great political importance to us either way* ... they lead me to the practical conclusion, that though we were bound to support to certain extent the endeavours of Austria and Prussia ... yet now we have fully performed all that could be expected from us, and that we should avoid irritating Russia by a pertinacious opposition which is so unlikely to be successful.'[23]

This letter crossed with Castlereagh's report of the Metternich affair which had so alarmed Liverpool and his government that a further letter was dispatched five days later, in which Liverpool gave this warning:

'*You will have heard from many quarters of the combustible state of the interior of France, and the expectation which exists of some explosion. If war, under such circumstances, were to be renewed, there is no saying where it would*

*end. It would very probably plunge Europe again in all the horrors from which
we have had the credit of extricating it. Between such an evil and any arrangement more or less good for Poland, Saxony or Italy, I should not hesitate.'*[24]

So the British Government's policy was quite clear. Rather than lose Russian goodwill, and stir up complications in the American war and sensitive maritime questions, which no doubt Prince Lieven had hinted at, Castlereagh should withdraw
Britain's objections. Saxony and Poland should not be Britain's concern. As a further
consideration, the Prince Regent had just elevated his father, George III, to the status
of King in his patrimony of Hanover, now that all the other Electors had kept the
crowns given to them by Napoleon. Hanover and the Low Countries should not
have a hostile Prussia on their borders. Austria was the lest important ally so far as
Britain was concerned, having no navy and no borders with Hanover and the Low
Countries to pose a land threat.

Castlereagh, having had unlimited powers in foreign affairs since 1813, chose to
'misinterpret' these instructions. In a lengthy report outlining his reasons and trying
to discredit the Chancellor's objections as being ill-informed, he re-echoed Metternich's theme: '... I deemed it of great importance to contribute as far as depended
upon me, to this concert: considering the establishment of Russia in the heart of
Germany not only as constituting a great danger in itself, but as calculated to establish a most pernicious influence both in the Austrian and Prussian Cabinets.'[25]
Meanwhile, Wellington informed him from Paris:

'... They are quite convinced, not only that M. de Talleyrand has acted
foolishly himself, but that he has led them into error by encouraging representations of your conduct and views. M. de Blacas desired me to appraise
you that you might depend upon the King's concurrence in your views, and
upon his support; and said that, if I was not satisfied with what he had said
to me, I might see the King, who would give me the same assurances himself. *Both the Palace and I are so much observed, that I thought it better to
decline this offer, with which Blacas appeared pleased; but told me that he could
let me see the King whenever I wished it, without its being known ...*'[26]

These letters from Wellington and Liverpool both refer to the explosive situation
developing in France where Wellington the Ambassador is reluctant to be seen visiting the King. After 25 years in exile the Bourbons had forgotten the mechanics of
government. Most of their experience had come from observing the British system
where the ministers of state carried on the business of running the country in the
name of the Crown. The Bourbons had taken over Napoleon's highly efficient civil
service and filled the top posts with their own creatures. But the result had been a
hotch-potch of absolutism, with a two-chamber legislature that had been emasculated to little more than a talking-shop with no real powers. The ministers of the
Crown were expected to carry on the business, as in Britain, but without any Cabinet and no collective responsibility. There was no Chief or Prime minister. Blacas
was the most influential person about the King, but he had no direct authority over
the others and merely passed on the King's views and commands. The Artois brood

usually presided over the various committees, but they merely cajoled or demanded action on a particular subject. Wellington observed that 'there was no Ministry, only Ministers'. One of the royalist Ministers, Baron Louis, commented to Pasquier on the difficulty of getting Louis to take an interest in anything related to the day-to-day government of France: 'What is the good of making reports to him? You might as well make them to a saint in a niche. I just simply give him ordinances to sign, and he signs them.'[27] Parisian wits referred to it as a government system of 'paternal anarchy'.

French public opinion had turned with a degree of sympathy towards King Joachim Murat. His wife, Queen Caroline was, after all, Napoleon's sister. Murat had made it known in Bonapartist circles that in deserting Napoleon in 1813 he had hoped to induce him to make peace. It had seemed inconceivable to him, as it had to France and many European nations at the time, that Napoleon would be ousted. Murat had also fallen foul of Britain and the other Allies for allowing French soldiers to withdraw during the late conflict, rather than attack them. French-born Murat, the son of an inn-keeper, had risen through the ranks to become one of the most famous Marshals of France, before Napoleon had elevated him to kingship. As a cavalry commander he was a living legend throughout Europe – if not the world. Austria was reluctant to attempt to remove him, or to be seen as breaking its treaty with him, for fear that he would unify the Italians against them, but they had not ratified the treaty. Having enjoyed more than fourteen years of semi-independent rule under their viceroy, the Italians were already showing signs of resentment at being placed back under German laws and control. Their old feudal dukes and princes, subservient to Austria, were filtering back, bent on arresting progress. In late 1814 Italy like France, was simmering with discontent at its alien rulers.

The people of northern Italy generally hoped that Napoleon would cross the narrow sea from Elba and take the crown that he had left to his captive son, a prospect feared by Britain, Austria, and Bourbon France. Napoleon was of Italian descent, Italian was his native tongue, and he had liberated Italy from German control and brought a sense of national identity. The naming of his only son as King of Rome had also been well received.

King Murat had a well-trained army of 85,000 men led by many French officers. If Napoleon allied himself with Murat, he would have a large army to lead into Austrian-held northern Italy where he would pose a threat to Vienna and France. Would the French army join him? The replacement of Murat by a friendly Bourbon government was seen as essential in keeping Napoleon isolated.[28] Napoleon's supporters in France included not only the greater part of the military hierarchy, but also members of the civil service. In the postal services, under Bourrienne, and in the prefectural body and police departments there were ardent imperialists. Napoleon was receiving information not only from discontented officers, of whom there were plenty, but from government sources through its servants. He was probably better informed as to the situation in France and Italy than the respective rulers.[29]

Talleyrand, with Castlereagh's assent, had asked Louis to assemble troops in the Lyons area in the hope of inducing Murat to give up his throne – with compensation of course. Failing which, they could march against him, Austria giving permission for them to pass through Austrian territory. Their presence would have the added bonus of showing a Bourbon France with a revitalized army, mobilized to back up the negotiations of Britain, France and Austria.[30]

This was a rather bad move on Louis' part, in view of the discontent seething throughout the country. A concentrated army, even a small one, might well turn on the monarchy. Napoleon, it will be remembered, had fought most of the 1814 campaign with a force no larger than the 40,000 proposed by Louis. An event now occurred that further exacerbated the tension between the nation and the Bourbons. It involved General Exelmans, one of Napoleon's cavalry commanders, now Inspector-General of Louis' cavalry and one of the leaders of the discontented imperialist officers. Exelmans, once one of Murat's aides-de-camp, and an Anglophile, had asked Lord Oxford, who was passing through Paris to Naples, to take a letter to King Joachim, to which he agreed. All ex-Napoleonic officers, even those employed, were being watched by police agents. The letter was taken from Lord Oxford. It contained an offer from Exelmans and other qualified officers to serve under Murat. France was not at war with him so there was nothing illegal in the offer. Dupont, the outgoing Minister of War, merely reprimanded the General, but Marshal Soult, having been appointed the new Minister of War and wishing to ingratiate himself, relieved Exelmans of his command, put him on half-pay and ordered him to retire to his home at Bar-sur-Ornain. Artois and his son de Berry, however, were howling for blood. Exelmans refused to leave his town house: his wife was heavily pregnant and he felt as a matter of principle that he should be allowed to chose his own abode. Soult had him arrested, in the presence of his swooning wife, and taken to Soissons. Exelmans escaped and wrote to Soult and the press demanding a court-martial, claiming that his civil liberties and the law were being abused.

No less a person than the marquis de Lafayette, hero of the War of American Independence and of the French Revolution, publicly offered Exelmans asylum and condemned the unlawful actions of the government and its ministers. The nation was outraged, and all the liberals and republicans now openly sided with the imperialists against the royalist clique who were abusing them. Exelmans was brought before a court-martial at Lille in January 1815. He was indicted on charges of 'defying the King', 'spying', 'offering his sword to the general who now ruled Naples', and 'breaking his oath of loyalty as recipient of the Order of Saint-Louis'. Finally, 'disobeying a military order', this last from Soult; namely to retire to his home town. Exelmans, conducting his own defence, stated that he had not broken his oath to the King, France was not at war with Naples, and that Soult's order was tantamount to foreign exile. He was acquitted of all charges unanimously by his fellow generals, to the chagrin of the royalists. This incident even alienated the small percentage of soldiers and civilians that had accepted with indifference the Bourbon restoration.

In Vienna, meanwhile, Hardenberg and the Prussians were now pressing for the annexation of Saxony to them as had been agreed by Castlereagh and Metternich. Castlereagh now received from Lord Bathurst his government's *first and only mandatory official instruction.*

'I am commanded by HRH to acquaint you, that whilst he deeply laments the unfortunate course which the discussions at Vienna have taken respecting Poland ... *HRH cannot contemplate the present state of Europe, and more especially the internal state of France, Italy, and the Low Countries, without entertaining the most serious apprehensions of the consequences which would result from the renewal of war on the Continent under the present circumstances ... It is unnecessary for me to point out to you the impossibility of HRH consenting to involve this country in hostilities at this time for <u>any</u> of the objects which have been hitherto under discussion at Vienna.'*[31]

There it was. Britain was not prepared to go to war on behalf of Saxony or Poland. Castlereagh was being officially informed that the Prince Regent would not ratify any act or treaty of aggression.

In London Parliament was clamouring for explanations of Castlereagh's conduct. On whose authority was he acting? On 8 November 1814, Samuel Whitbread in the House of Commons debate on Saxony voiced the Opposition views, and those of the British public, when he declared that the annexation of Saxony to Prussia would be 'as unprincipled a partition as the world ever saw!' A few days later Mr Lambton referred to 'acts of rapine and aggression of the club of confederated monarchs at Vienna ... the spoliators of Saxony'. On 28 November Whitbread read aloud the preamble to Prince Repnin's proclamation to the people, as Russian military governor of Saxony, in which he announced the handing over of authority to Prussia, as agreed by Lord Castlereagh and Prince Metternich. Whitbread then asked the Cabinet and the House whether Lord Castlereagh had agreed to such an act of brigandage? If this were the case, then surely it was 'a humiliation and degradation of this country, so low as to be beneath expression'. Contrasting Castlereagh's attempt to stop the Tsar creating a constitutional Poland, where before the country had been partitioned in three, he said:

'If the Emperor Alexander, besides the splendid triumphs he has gained, has added this fresh glory to his character, in what disadvantageous contrast must the Noble Lord appear who is resisting this plan of liberty and happiness ... The rumours are that the Emperor Alexander has strenuously contended for the independence of Poland and that he has been opposed in his benevolent views by the British Minister. We are living in an age when free nations are not to be sold and transferred like beasts of burden, and if any attempt of the kind is made the result will be a bloody and revengeful war.'[32]

Mr Horner, a government supporter, also attacked Castlereagh, accusing him of acting without authority and for not keeping his own government properly informed or consulted. 'We are not at war,' he said, 'there is surely plenty of time to consult and reflect.' Had the Foreign Secretary agreed to Austria's treaty with Murat or not? If not why not? Had Prince Repnin been correct in stating that Castlereagh had agreed to the annexation of Saxony?[33]

These embarrassing questions were followed by an attack by George Ponsonby, who accused the government of violating, in their consent to the annexation of Saxony, the preamble to the Treaty of Chaumont. 'Castlereagh', he said, 'has disgraced his title and betrayed the honour of his country.' In reply, the Chancellor, a close acquaintance of Prince Lieven's, piqued no doubt by Castlereagh's insistence that he did not fully understand the Polish question, forced his hand by stating that as Congress had yet to inaugurate itself nothing as yet was decided, and '*No British Minister would be a party to any decision involving the suppression of Saxony.*'[34] This greatly embarrassed Lord Liverpool who, as has been seen, knew that Castlereagh had already agreed to the annexation by Prussia, contingent on a satisfactory conclusion on Poland. Liverpool, yet further embarrassed by his inability to give the two Houses of Parliament adequate answers and information, wrote to Castlereagh urging him to settle the business and return quickly. He informed him privately of the mood of the public and Parliament, and asked for all relevant information so as to be able to give 'satisfactory answers' in Parliament. Liverpool ended by stating that: '... it would certainly be desirable that a *noyau* [core] of it [Saxony] at least should be preserved, even if it was under some other branch of the Saxon family'.[35]

In Vienna events were now moving apace to further the breach between the Allies. Castlereagh, in a remarkable letter to Liverpool, recounted his interview with Prince Hardenberg of Prussia, and said that much as he wanted

> '... *that Prussia should be reconstructed upon the scale to which the Treaties entitled her to lay claim; and that the only question was whether the whole of Saxony should be included in the territories assigned to her* ... I delivered to His Highness an extract of Your Lordship's private letter of the 18th ult., *as the best proof not of what those usually opposed to the King's government in Great Britain might urge in the controversy of debate upon the subject, but of the sentiments deliberately entertained by those most friendly to the interests of Prussia [Vansittart].*'[36]

He went on to explain that:

> 'It was impossible to deny that the concert on the affairs of Poland, which was the basis of the understanding, had avowedly failed through the conduct of his sovereign; that under these circumstances, neither Austria nor Great Britain could espouse his claims in the manner they might otherwise have done, and wished to do.'

Having used this escape clause to bring himself in line with his own government's policy, and wishing to appease Prussia, he added:

> '... *I represented this was not a case for war, that he was in occupation of Saxony, and that I apprehended no one would think of removing him hostilely*, from thence, but that he could not regard an acknowledged claim as constituting a good title.'[37]

He also indicated that if Prussia were to leave Saxony a tiny amount of territory, Britain would probably be quick to assent. In other words, you can see I am in sympathy with you, but the people back home don't approve of your occupation of Saxony; nothing would induce us to go to war with you in order to eject you, but I cannot officially sanction the business.

Hardenberg then asked Metternich if he would honour the undertaking if a greatly reduced Saxony, about the size of Luxembourg, were left on the map. Hardenberg felt that Prussian pride would approve of this because of the humiliation that it would give to the Saxon 'king'. Metternich, who did not have Castlereagh's problems, was less diplomatic; he not only rejected Prussia's claim on the same grounds, but stated that Austria would oppose Prussian occupation of any Saxon territory, militarily if need be. Having failed to budge the Tsar, because of lack of Prussian support, he had now decided that to thwart the Prussians would be the line of least resistance. Hardenberg, while sympathetic to Castlereagh's predicament, would not accept this insult. He went straight to the Tsar and asked him for support. He was then, according to Castlereagh, guilty of a:

> '*very incorrect act ... namely to communicate to the Emperor of Russia parts of the confidential correspondence that passed between himself and Prince Metternich with respect to Poland and their concert against the views of Russia. These secret papers were accompanied with the insinuation that Austria now broke faith with Prussia upon the point of Saxony, in consequence of Prussia refusing to enter into a hostile alliance against Russia.*'[38]

The Tsar summoned the Austrian Emperor and King William of Prussia. Francis told him that if his Minister had written such a letter, it was without his knowledge. Prince Hardenberg said that he had only agreed to the alliance against the Tsar with deepest regret, because Metternich had told him that the Tsar had approached Austria with an arrangement that would exclude Prussian rights. Metternich denied this, saying that Hardenberg, who was deaf in one ear, had 'misunderstood' him. Prince Hardenberg offered to produce all his correspondence and notes on the matter. The Tsar said that it was not necessary, he believed him. Neither he, Alexander, nor his ministers had made any contact with Metternich on this matter. Metternich, he declared, had deliberately used his position and his (the Tsar's) name to cause a breach between them; Metternich was 'a liar and not a gentleman'. He then threw his sword on the table and demanded satisfaction of Metternich. The Austrian Emperor would not hear of it. Metternich, he explained, would be instructed to show his correspondence to the Tsar. From now on Alexander would neither speak to nor acknowledge the presence of Metternich in any of his dealings. Despite King William's denials, he felt that he had been betrayed, and now decided to look after his own interests.

In return for the Austrian Emperor's swift response and frankness, Alexander said that he would cede to Austria the circle of Tarnapol with its population of 400,000 which he had received from Austria under the Peace of Vienna in 1809. This gained him the goodwill of Francis who was now looking to block Prussian expansion rather than obstruct his more powerful neighbour. Alexander had shown that he too was capable of manipulation.

Metternich, always devious, could read the signs well enough, and understood his imperial master's change of attitude to the Tsar. He now began to emphasize what the generals had been saying, that Prussia was the greater threat to Austrian security. Frederick the Great of Prussia, they remembered, had seized the wealthy Silesian lands from Austria. Now, if those were welded to Prussia and Saxony they would have an encircling border with Austria, 500 miles long. Dresden was within striking distance of Prague, Budapest and Vienna. Austrian influence would be cut off from the whole of Germany except the three southern kingdoms. This was Talleyrand's view, and now Castlereagh did a U-turn and supported it. For the best of reasons – his political life depended on it.

The Prussians felt that they had been humiliated and tricked. During the War of Liberation they had received promises of compensation, both in territory and in a confederation of the small states under Prussian leadership in the north and Austrian leadership in the south. Castlereagh had already agreed to the annexation, as had Metternich. That was the principle. Just because they had not been able to force Russia out of the Polish duchy, there was no reason to deny Prussia her rights. Russia had agreed to them at Kalisch and would honour her undertaking. Prussia now expected Britain and Austria to do the same.

Talleyrand meanwhile, with Austria and Britain's blessing, was opposing this annexation, thereby increasing his standing with his two colleagues and at home. In two notes to Hardenberg, dated 19 and 26 December 1814, he insisted that the spoliation of Saxony and the dethronement of its king was a flagrant violation of the principle of legitimacy. Further, that any cessation of Saxon territory could only be made by its legitimate monarch – after he had been reinstated. It will be remembered that at this time he was imprisoned in Prussia. Talleyrand said that he had canvassed the minor German states and that they would present a collective note to the Congress in support of this demand.[39]

This was too much for Prussian pride. During the last eight years France had caused them suffering and humiliation (especially of their late and lamented queen), and had systematically contrived to render Prussia destitute. Talleyrand had been Foreign Minister during this time and had played an active part in their degradation. Prussia had expended its national resources to remove Napoleon, and Talleyrand by trickery had turned that on its head with his 'legitimacy' principle, and had restored the Bourbons, thereby making Napoleon solely responsible and absolving the French, including himself, from any collective responsibility, or guilt, and depriving Prussia of revenge and just compensation. That the co-architect of that situation should now be bombastically dictating to Prussia about Saxony was not to be borne. At the meeting of Ministers on 29 December, Prince Hardenberg announced: '... that should Prussia continue to consider the annexation of the whole of Saxony necessary to her reconstruction, she could not, in point of expense, submit to remain in a state of provisional occupation, and that *Russia and Prussia would, in such a case, consider a refusal to acknowledge, as tantamount to a declaration of war.*'[40]

War! Prussia had laid the ultimatum on the table; Britain and Austria must honour their undertaking or settle it by war. On the same day, Castlereagh, in direct contravention of his instructions from the Cabinet and the Prince Regent, entered into a treaty with Austria and France against Russia and Prussia. In explanation to Liverpool he wrote:

> '... Under these circumstances I have felt it an act of imperative duty to concert with the French and Austrian Plenipotentiaries a Treaty of Defensive Alliance, confined within the strict necessity of this most extraordinary case ... I indulge the confident hope that my conduct on this occasion may appear to the Prince Regent and his Government to have been justified by the circumstances of the case, and the exigency of the occasion.'[41]

On 3 January 1815 Castlereagh signed the treaty. Article 1 pledged the three powers to mutual support in the event of any one of them being attacked. In Article 2 Austria and France pledged themselves to provide 150,000 men each, and Britain to furnish 'subsidies' (bankroll) or mercenary troops. Article 3 declared that an attack on Hanover or the Low Countries would be regarded as an attack on Britain. Article 4 permitted Hanover, Sardinia, Bavaria and Hesse-Darmstadt to accede to the treaty. Article 5 made provision for a command structure and joint plans in the event of a Russian advance on Vienna. A secret protocol bound the participants to absolute secrecy.[42]

So it was that on 3 January 1815 Britain and Austria had agreed to combine with their enemy of the past quarter of a century in fighting, if necessary, their two principle allies. Talleyrand joyfully wrote home to Louis: 'The Coalition is dissolved, France is no longer isolated in Europe. So great and so fortunate a change can only be attributed to that protection of Providence which has so plainly been visible in the restoration of Your Majesty.'[43]

Castlereagh had flagrantly ignored his instructions. The Government would not sanction a war against Russia in Austria's interests merely to block Russia's constitutional duchy, if only because it might inspire Austria's ethnic minorities to seek the same. Nor was it prepared to hazard its new United Netherlands and Hanover in a war with Prussia merely because Castlereagh had agreed to recognize their right to Saxony; in breach of his government's policy and then as a political expedient, Castlereagh, in the pursuit of French interests, had reneged on his undertaking. Liverpool had stated clearly enough that having gained *before* the Congress all that Britain required, he should not involve Britain in commitments, either of subsidy or armed intervention, in these particular territorial disputes that did not affect Britain's security. Alarmed at Castlereagh's belligerent stance, and fearing that Europe might erupt in war, the Cabinet had signed a hasty peace treaty with America at Ghent on Christmas Eve 1814. Its terms were more favourable to America than the Cabinet or national pride would have wished, but Britain might need to release troops and money if the crisis in Europe developed.[44]

Clearly, Castlereagh had overreached himself. Britain's Parliament would not have endorsed a commitment to endless subsidies to finance an unpopular war. Bankrupt Austria was spending nearly £1,000 a day playing host to the European dignitaries. If she declared war tomorrow, she couldn't pay a single soldier without British money. The French Minister of War in Paris could not guarantee to have 70,000 men in the field within six weeks, and if he could, would they fight? And for whom? Austria, having aggressively deployed some of her troops in her Polish provinces, was unwilling to remove any of the troops poised against Murat in northern Italy. Having stood down most of the army from a war footing, she couldn't remobilize them without funds.

Russia, on the other hand, had nearly 200,000 troops within striking distance of Austria, and could double that number within six to eight weeks. Prussia, which had deployed troops around Dresden, could field 80–100,000 men fairly quickly under its new system, and call up an equal number. Britain was not in a position to field any men except those in the Low Countries and Hanover. In the event of war they would be Prussia's obvious target. What if Prussia advanced on them? Prussia had long coveted Hanover and might seize it in compensation. Fortunately for the signatories of the treaty, the situation was diffused by Prussia and Russia continuing to negotiate, the Tsar having indicated to the Prussians via his own minister that talks should continue for the present.

The Tsar was in possession of information from London that would transform the ultimatum and the months of deadlock literally overnight. The Cabinet, harried by Parliament and its own supporters, had through the Chancellor indicated to Prince Lieven that Britain would not oppose the Tsar's Polish kingdom, and hoped that His Imperial Highness, Britain's friend and ally, would use his kind offices to modify Prussian demands on Saxony. He indicated that British public opinion and sense of justice was outraged at the proposed removal of the state of Saxony and its monarchy from the map of Europe. Saxony might be reduced, but should not disappear. Britain felt that territorial compensation could be made to Prussia in other areas, provided that goodwill existed on all sides.[45] Castlereagh's reign as independent foreign policy maker had ended. The ground had been effectively cut from beneath him by a judicious diplomatic leak from his own government.

At the beginning of January, during a meeting with the Tsar, Castlereagh was informed of the Cabinet's *rapprochement*. Castlereagh, he suggested, was not acting according to his government's instructions. Further, that Russia had no intention of being an aggressor, but that she would retain what she possessed *uti possidetis*, the same claim that Britain had maintained against America. It is probable that the Tsar indicated that he would wait until Castlereagh clarified his instructions from London if he doubted the Tsar's information. Castlereagh's bluff, and his standing, had now evaporated.

On 8 January Castlereagh was categorically questioned by Alexander about a rumour that Britain had actually signed a treaty against Russia. Castlereagh, taken aback, told Liverpool that the Tsar:

'... rather to my surprise, referred to reports that had reached him of an alliance between Austria, France, Bavaria, and Great Britain. Not feeling myself authorized to avow [reveal] the Treaty, and not choosing to hold a language of too much disguise, I assured His Imperial Majesty that acting on Pacifick [sic] principles which he had avowed in the early part of our conversation, he had nothing to fear from those powers.'[46]

In other words, Castlereagh was apparently denying the existence of such a treaty. He now proposed a plan for the reconstruction of Prussia that would give the Prussians very little of Saxony, but instead offered them parts of Hanover and United Netherlands territory. The Tsar, now having the whip hand, said that he was interested in the proposal, but asked if France would agree to it, indicating that he knew that Castlereagh dictated to Talleyrand through Louis, and pressed Castlereagh to say whether he would support his proposal if the French objected. Then, with a show of indifference, Alexander said that he would support Castlereagh's project if Prussia accepted it. Castlereagh, anxious to get off the hook at home, by achieving a settlement of Saxony that would appear to leave the king in possession of his kingdom – albeit reduced – pleaded with the Tsar. 'I asked him, in the event of being pressed for means, whether he could give something more to Prussia on the side of Poland.' Alexander, knowing that without his assistance Prussia would refuse, and that if Castlereagh's prior agreement with Prussia became known to the public in Britain it would sound his political doom, let him sweat for a few days, telling him that: '... the subject was both painful and an embarrassing one to him with the Poles, to whom he had given assurances'.[47] However, he would discuss it with his counsellors and reply shortly – sweet revenge for Castlereagh's blackmail apropos the Russian Navy during the war.

Castlereagh, despite his own views on the subject of Poland, now sent a circular to all the delegates saying that Britain accepted a Polish kingdom under the Tsar.[48] He informed Talleyrand of this, and that he had decided to change the formula on Saxony: '... *I* thought it therefore material to reduce the question to a precise issue, to make the powers, and *not* the King of Saxony, judges in the case and further, to obtain for Prussia a reasonable security for the execution of the award when made.' He and Talleyrand would complete the face-saving reversal of their policy by stating in the protocol of decision (yet to be formulated!), as Castlereagh put it, '... *We say that we will support* the King of Prussia, our Ally, in Saxony, till the suitable cessions are made to him. France says that she will *cease to support* her Ally, the King of Saxony, if he refuses to make good the cessions agreed upon.'[49] Talleyrand had little option but to agree.

Castlereagh next had a painful meeting with Metternich to whom he explained the facts of life:

'... I fully explained to Prince Metternich that, having saved the general principle, and protected his Court by a decided measure of support, when Austria was menaced by invasion, if she refused to acknowledge a new King in Saxony ... I could not suffer my Government to be involved in hostile measures upon a mere question of details, to which I now considered in fact the issue was brought.'[50]

A true politician, Castlereagh, having pledged on paper the lives of 150,000 men in defence of his principle that the Tsar should not have Poland, was not prepared risk his political life in the same battle.

The Tsar now informed Castlereagh that under the 'changed' circumstances he would give Prussia Polish territory in the east to make up Castlereagh's balance. Castlereagh was summoned to a personal meeting with the anxious Emperor of Austria, which can only be described as painful. Castlereagh had already indicated to Metternich that if Francis withheld agreement, Britain would pull out of any agreement with him, this to include any aid, material or financial, and the £500,000 subsidy yet to be paid. The Emperor of Austria tried to convince Castlereagh that Prussia, having given ground on Poland, should not have even a part of Saxony. He was unaware that Castlereagh had to concede this territory to appease Prussian pride in some measure or the Tsar would not support him. If the Tsar refused, and Prussia remained adamant and published his agreement, the British public would be howling for his blood. Castlereagh bluntly told the Emperor of Austria: '... if he looked for support from Great Britain, that the occasion of war should be either founded upon the maintenance of some principle of clear and indisputable importance, or an actual attempt by force to disturb the equilibrium of Europe'. Francis then pressed him to support him on two points only. First, that Prussia should not have the key fortress cities of Torgau and Erfurt. Secondly, that Torgau's fortifications at least should be razed. Castlereagh replied: '... For the reasons already stated, I felt myself obliged humbly, but most expressly to reply to His Majesty in the negative on both his demands.'[51]

Now had the Austrian Emperor cause to reflect on his desertion of his son-in-law. Prior to the French Revolution, Austria's bitterest enemy had been Prussia, which had risen under its warrior kings to pre-eminence in Germany. Seizing Silesia from Austria and doubling its size, Prussia under Frederick the Great had fought Austria, Russia and France, and armies from the minor states, and defeated them all. Napoleon had crushed spartan Prussia, but it had risen from the ashes with arguably the finest trained army in Europe, enlarged territory and ambitions in Germany. If that were not enough, Prussia was now hostile to Austria over the Saxon question, in which at one point both Austria and Prussia had threatened war with each other. Russia too had been alienated. In his greed to regain Austria's former Polish territory, Francis had led the opposition to the Tsar's plans. Metternich had publicly insulted him on several occasions; that would not be forgotten or easily forgiven. Now Britain, which had made great promises in return for the restoration of the Bourbons and Marie-Louis's dethronement, would not even support his demand for the destruction of a key fortress.

Castlereagh's cup of bitterness was not yet drained. Having thought up a project which, though contrary to his avowed intention of giving Saxony to Prussia as the best security for central Europe, would appease the British public, the Tsar and

Louis, now had to sell the goods to Prussia. King William, the least bellicose and most placid monarch of the Great Powers, summoned Castlereagh who: '... *had with his Majesty an audience of an hour and half, the most painful in all respects, that it has been my fate to undergo since I have been upon the Continent.*' Castlereagh's plan had envisaged giving Prussia only two-fifths of Saxony and excluding the countries two capitals, Dresden and Leipzig. Prussia at present was in occupation of the whole country. Gaining Saxony was for Prussia a matter of national pride. William had only been induced to fight so hard, and for so long, by the Tsar's and then Castlereagh's promises. Now, using Castlereagh's formula, the Tsar was still honouring his obligation to the Prussians by insisting that they be given part of Saxony and territorial compensation in other areas: close to Hanover and Denmark and in the east near Poland. He had pointed out that he had not obtained all of Poland either, and had to be content. The Prussians knew that they would not be able to hold Saxony by force if all the other powers were in opposition, but the King rightly felt cheated. Britain had agreed the deal in writing, but the new formula robbed Prussia of even half of Saxony and one of its capitals, and deprived her of Russian support.

Castlereagh who personally had wanted the King of Prussia to have Saxony, and was now reluctantly obeying his government's dictates, recounted:

'... *It is inconceivable to what degree His Majesty had been worked upon on the point of Leipsick [sic], the false importance he attached to it, and the deep disappointment, if not resentment, with which he spoke of our espousing the cause of the King of Saxony against him ... I did not escape without some severe personal reproaches for the representations I presumed to make. However, my duty was to discourage the King from any false move, which might compromise us all, and as I wished to execute this without reserve, my audience terminated as unpleasantly as it had begun .. It is certain that many of the Prussian officers, and the Friends of Liberty as they are called, who abound in the King's dominions, were indignant at losing Saxony.*'[52]

Prussia now felt thwarted by Austria, betrayed by Russia, and sold by Britain in support of her 'new' friend France. Talleyrand, it will be remembered, had been the first to oppose the annexation of Saxony. The loss of Leipzig particularly aggrieved the Prussians because a great triumphal arch had been planned for this, the site of Napoleon's first defeat – mainly it, was felt, by Prussia's exertions. The hated King of Saxony would retain his throne and both capitals.

Field Marshal Prince Blücher, now recovered from his illness, voiced the disgust of the Prussian Army when on 17 February 1815 the Berlin newspapers carried the story. Writing to Gneisenau he said: 'It honours and rejoices me to have shared in the war that is ended, but my chief satisfaction is not having shared in the peace that has been concluded ... We drove in a fine bull and have got in return a dried-up old cow.'[53] Disgusted with his old friend Prince Hardenberg, Blücher wrote to King William saying that he wished to resign from the Prussian Army.

CHAPTER 8

THE ROAD TO GRENOBLE

'Monsieur, save the King. I'll take care of saving the Monarchy.'
– Fouché to the comte d'Artois, midnight 15 March 1815.

NAPOLEON HAD BEEN LIVING ON ELBA FOR TEN MONTHS during which time he had heard very little about his wife or son. The Austrian Emperor had written to him from Rambouillet on 16 April 1814, informing him that he was taking Marie-Louise and his grandson back to Vienna for their 'health' and that: 'Once she has regained her health, my daughter will proceed to assume sovereignty of her country, and this will bring her nearer to your Majesty's place of abode.'[1] Under the Treaty of Fontainebleau the Empress had been granted the Duchies of Parma, Piancenza and Guastalla, and it had been agreed that she would be given passports for herself and her son. Francis had done nothing to ensure that his daughter received her sovereignty or her freedom. Napoleon's greatest fear for his son had also been realized – he was now a captive prince.

Under the treaty Napoleon had been granted a pension of 2,000,000 francs a year to help him maintain his court and, more importantly, his tiny army. Louis had refused to pay this, and had decreed that any military personnel that had followed Napoleon into his new kingdom must return within three years or be permanently banished. The revenues of Elba, as Louis was well informed by his civil service, were scarcely sufficient to maintain the island's administration, let alone keep an emperor, his court and a force of some 1,200 men of all arms. If, in the fullness of time, Napoleon could no longer afford to pay his soldiers or feed them, how long would they remain with him? Louis had already instructed Talleyrand to ask Castlereagh to consider moving Napoleon to 'the Azores or St. Helena', where his presence would not have an inflammatory effect on the people of France and Italy, adding that if that were arranged he would pay the usurper's pension. Louis had also failed to pay the pensions to Napoleon's family as stipulated in the treaty. Tsar Alexander was angered by this. He had signed the treaty and was not going to be dishonoured by the Bourbons. He made a point of upbraiding Talleyrand who he now despised: 'The treaty is not being carried out, and we are bound to demand its execution. It is for us an affair of honour. We cannot depart from its stipulations in any way,' said the Tsar. Talleyrand, it will be remembered, had also signed the treaty in Alexander's presence, on behalf of the Bourbons. 'Honour your treaties,' Alexander insisted. He addressed Castlereagh on the subject, who said that he would write to Louis, which he did, but Great Britain was not a party to the treaty, having merely acquiesced in the others' wishes.

Napoleon was not one with whom it was wise to break faith. He had yielded to the inevitable, because his Marshals had betrayed him. He had not surrendered, the

166

Allies had not beaten him. Now he had honoured his signature and Louis and the Allies were ignoring their obligation to him. Which in world terms was a trifle. Britain had expended seven hundred thousand times his yearly pension alone, to remove him from his throne. Now he sat brooding on his island, a Corsican, brought up on a code of honour that demanded a vendetta against any transgressor. To a Corsican the family is everything. Had not Napoleon always forgiven his wayward brothers and sisters? He could even forgive his sister Caroline and her husband Joachim Murat. He would not forgive his father-in-law for depriving him of his long-awaited son, but given the right circumstances even that could be overlooked – family matters. But Louis, Artois and the rest of the Bourbon clan were trying to destroy him. They intended to humiliate him and then kill or imprison him. That required a riposte. Artois, who had several times tried to have him murdered, once while he was on his way to Elba, had planted spies on his island. On one occasion he had had to remain in the citadel for a week when a plot against his life had been uncovered.[2] Napoleon was aware from his supporters throughout France and Italy of what was going on. He had been informed that Artois had appointed his own man to command the naval squadron at Toulon, and a new military governor for Corsica, a man who had fought against Napoleon during the revolution when the Corsican patriot Paoli had tried to betray the island to Britain. Another royalist Corsican, Mariotti, was co-ordinating espionage and conducting feasibility studies on his murder or abduction.[3]

There were even rumours that Louis and his brother were trying to bribe Barbary corsairs to kill or capture him. It was for this reason that Admiral Hallowell had adopted a policy of 'leaving a British man-of-war upon the station in case of any extraordinary circumstances'. Although many throughout Europe believed what Campbell stated: 'It is universally supposed in Italy, and publicly stated, that Great Britain is responsible to the other powers for the detention of Napoleon's person, and that I am the executive agent for this purpose,'[4] it was not the case. Campbell was to remain with Napoleon only as long as he was required to ensure his safety. This was the sole reason why Campbell alone of the Allied commissioners had not been dismissed by Napoleon when he arrived in Elba. It had been an article of faith in Great Britain for nearly a hundred years that an attack on a Royal Naval vessel was an attack on the nation. Napoleon understood this and took comfort from the presence of the warship. He put great trust in the Prince Regent's word and Britain's protection.

On 18 December 1814 Louis signed a decree authorizing the government to seize all the houses and property belonging to the Bonaparte family in France. Having broken the Treaty of Fontainebleau, Napoleon by all the laws appertaining to the conduct between nations at that time was no longer bound by its terms and had every right to assume the position of *status quo ante bellum*, which was outside Paris with his army. He began to make secret preparations for his return to France.

The question of the pension had been the acid test of whether he would be allowed to live in peaceful retirement or not. It was not just a question of money;

Napoleon had amassed sufficient funds, and could call upon more, to support him and his army until at least 1817. It was not just the principle, of having paid to him what was due under the treaty, and the honouring of all the articles. It was simply this. If Louis refused to pay and was not called to account by the other signatories, he would feel that he could do what he liked against Napoleon with impunity. Louis could certainly raise a force of several thousand loyal supporters to attack him, aided by mercenaries such as the Swiss regiments that he was expanding. Given time, Louis would feel more secure and memories of Napoleon would fade. If he was lucky Napoleon might be offered a bribe to move to some god-forsaken spot. But his intelligence from France predicted that the Bourbons would seek to have him forcibly transported or imprisoned for life in some fortress, or killed in defence of his island.

Napoleon's fears were based on his experience as the ruler of the largest European empire since the time of the Romans. He was not given to panic, as his conduct on the field of battle had testified, but as a military genius it ran against all his principles to remain cooped-up in this island fortress while all the advantages slowly passed to his opponents. He realized that if stayed where he was for even a few more months, he was a doomed man; as soon as the Congress broke up Louis and Artois would make their move. The appearance of two French frigates, *Melpomène* and *Fleur-de-Lys*, patrolling off his island were enough to indicate Louis' intentions. To the Englishman, John Macnamara, Napoleon claimed that they were there to cover an abduction or assassination attempt: ' Not by the English, they are not assassins. I am obliged to be cautious in regards to some others, especially the Corsicans, some of whom have strong feelings against me.'[5] During this conversation Macnamara discussed many topics, including Napoleon's defeat in Russia, Marmont, and the rumoured suicide attempt at Fontainebleau – which Napoleon dismissed as romantic: 'What? ?Kill myself? Had I nothing better to do than this – like a miserable bankrupt who, because he has lost his goods, determines to lose his life? Napoleon is always Napoleon, and always knows how to be content and bear any fortune. It must be confessed that I am in a better plight now than when I was a lieutenant of artillery.'[6]

He had now decided to return to France and reclaim his own. Napoleon was aware from all his secret correspondents that France was ripe to throw out the Bourbons who had alienated all but the die-hard fanatics. Even some of his old enemies such as Fouché, the best secret policeman in Europe, were unacceptable to the royalists. Fouché was considered a regicide, having been a member of the revolutionary assembly that had sentenced Louis XVI to death. Now Fouché, unacceptable but needed by the Bourbons, was conspiring with the military for a *coup d'état* to bring back Napoleon. The marquis de Lafayette, the great patriot, once Napoleon's bitterest opponent, spoke of his regret that France had lost Napoleon. Carnot, the great revolutionary architect of the army, who had come out of retirement in 1814 to fight for Napoleon and France, felt constrained to espouse his cause. Benjamin Constant and other republicans also decided that they hadn't realized when they were well off.

Napoleon had been resented for being autocratic, but at least he had retained all that had been good under the republic; he had left the people with their homes and self-respect. He had raised France from being a second-rate power, and her revolutionary mob army to the most deadly military machine the world had yet seen. His victories had allowed the nation to walk with pride.

The Legion of Honour, Napoleon's highest award for bravery, open to all ranks, had been degraded to a civil award, and Talleyrand's crony and co-conspirator the Abbé de Pradt was made its Chancellor. Louis the 'Fat', as his subjects called him, was too busy being subservient to Britain to worry about national pride. Property had dropped in value as people feared repossession. Manufacturers were being driven out of business by a recession brought on by the ending of war production and protective tariffs – putting tens of thousands out of work. The people were starving and there were food riots, especially at the ports where grain was being shipped to Britain for hard currency. Many of Napoleon's generals, some of whom had been the first to flock to the Bourbons, in the desire for peace, realized that they had made a poor bargain. Some things in life were worth fighting for, worth going the 'extra mile': dignity, self-respect and honour. General Maximilian Foy, one of Louis' Inspectors-General, and a great friend of Wellington's, summed-up the popular feeling in France at this time. In his diary in October 1814 he commented that the Bourbons were *the truly humble servants of the English*. Two days later, receiving an invitation from Wellington, he wrote: 'A famous reunion. I shall not go ... Lord Wellington and the English are held in horror by everyone. Even the Bourbonists are beginning to come out against them ... We who were lately masters of Europe, to what servitude are we reduced? Lord Wellington is Commander-in-Chief of the army of occupation in Belgium. Our telegraph is at his disposal two hours daily to send orders to his troops. He signs his letters from his headquarters in Paris; he has an air of saying to us: "If you sit on the fence it is me you will be up against." We see him coming away from the King en frac [dress-coat] and in boots. The princes go and dine with him after manoeuvres. *Oh! Napoleon where are you?*[7] Even the comte de Jarcourt, Talleyrand's deputy, wrote of his unease to his superior: 'We are really going on very badly, and we must do better if we do not wish to perish completely.'[8]

Napoleon knew the time was ripe for his return, but he needed a diversion. It was his grand strategy, his custom in battle, to fix the enemy's attention with a small diversionary attack while he moved with his main force, indirectly, to attack where he was least expected. He set about arranging his diversion.

In Italy rumours had abounded that he would place himself at the head of Murat's army and rally the whole country to his flag. Indeed this was Austria and France's fear: a swift march on Vienna to reclaim his family, then an advance into France. Austria and Britain feared that an assembled French army would then go over to Napoleon. For this reason Austria was prepared to assist France in removing Murat and neutralizing his army and putting them back under a reliable Bourbon. Napoleon had no intention of going to Italy. He would do what he always did and strike straight for the enemy's capital – Paris. Louis and Artois, Metternich and Talleyrand, for all their titles, their braid, epaulettes and noble birth, were not soldiers. Not one of them, in Napoleon's opinion, could command a 'corporal's guard' let alone predict where the thunderbolt would strike. Napoleon knew this and fed them a smoke-screen. Messages passed between him and his brother-in-law Murat. Napoleon would forgive all past sins if he supported him now. If he didn't Murat would have to face the Bourbons and Austria unaided.

Murat had no choice. Neither Austria nor Britain had ratified the treaty with him; he had served his purpose and they would either provoke him or aid his Bourbon enemies. For Murat, as for Napoleon, it was just a matter of time. But he had a chance to wipe the slate clean. Napoleon planned that he should advance his army into the Papal states and threaten Austria's Italian border, which would tie down the bulk of her army. It would also act as the smoke-screen. Napoleon knew that his correspondence with Murat would inevitably be discovered and cause his enemies to assume that he was going to land at Naples or elsewhere in Italy. Murat, however, demanded Napoleon's word in writing that all was forgiven. Knowing his family, especially his sister Caroline, Napoleon went one better: he sent a blank piece of the imperial writing-paper, with his signature on it. She could write her own terms provided that they threw in their lot with him, sink or swim. If they all succeeded, Murat could claim the whole of Italy. Napoleon, ever the realist, needed Italy as a threat to neutralize Austria: Murat had shown that he would fight to keep Naples – he would fight the harder for Italy.[9] Castlereagh, having executed a swift U-turn in his policy, was urgently required in London. Parliament was demanding answers and condemning him as irresponsible. Liverpool needed him back to get the government out of the fix of his making, and his return would provide Liverpool with an excuse to move Wellington to Vienna to replace him. In Paris Wellington's life had increasingly been put at risk by the hatred of the populace; shots had been fired at him and the duc de Berry. Writing to Wellington, Liverpool explained the need for Castlereagh to return to the front benches to defend the Government:

> 'I can assure you, that I have not known for some years such party spirit and rancour as exists at present ... if the Government in the House of Commons should lose credit, and be considered as beat in debate before Castlereagh returns, it will be no easy matter for him or any man to recover the ground which has been lost.'[10]

Having explained the facts to Castlereagh, Liverpool was relieved to hear that he would return post-haste, and instructed him to stop off in Paris on the way and inform Louis that Britain would not now assist in the removal of Murat. Liverpool did not want the government to be involved; having acceded to Austria's wish to keep Murat on the throne, an attack on him now would be opposed in Parliament. In fact he advised Castlereagh to try to dissuade Louis from attempting it either:

> 'Your audience of the King of France may be particularly useful in smoothing difficulties on the Neapolitan question. The absolute Impracticability of Great Britain engaging in war for the purpose of driving Murat from Naples. England at this moment is peace mad and thinking only of the reduction of

taxes; impossible, after so long a contest, to expect them to be favourable to a renewal of war, even in a just cause. I am fully sensible of all the inconveniences of leaving Murat on the throne of Naples, and enter into all the personal feelings of the King of France on this subject; but I think for his own interest and for that of the French nation His Majesty ought to consider well before he embarks in military operations for the purpose of expelling Murat. Any attempt of this sort might be fatal to France, if it failed of success ... is it certain that a French army could be trusted on this service? I know there are many persons attached to the Bourbons who are of the opinion that the greater part of such an army would desert if opposed to Murat, especially if there were any prospect of Murat being joined by Buonaparte ... I have no scruple in avowing that the keystone of all my external policy is the preserving of the Bourbons on the throne of France. I am satisfied that this alone can prevent the recurrence of the costs which we have suffered for the last twenty years, and all other dangers may be regarded as contemptible when compared with those which would arise out of another revolution in France.'[11]

This advice, however, was disregarded by Louis. Britain and Austria having entered into a treaty with France for mutual support, were bound to support France in the undertaking, and could not actively obstruct him.

Lord Bathurst, on behalf of the Government, had now ratified the secret treaty – after Castlereagh had carried out the government's policy regarding Poland and Saxony. The threat of war had passed, and the Cabinet could afford to ratify the treaty and save its Foreign Secretary's face. Bathurst's letter, 'commanded by the Prince Regent', approved of the treaty, and commended 'The spirit with which your Lordship resisted the menacing language of the Prussian minister.' The letter continued by stating: 'Your Lordship acts with much commendable discretion in providing that the measures taken to restrain the unjust pretensions should *not interfere* with the fair claims of the Prussian Monarchy.' Not one word, however, was said against Russia. In fact Russia was not mentioned at all. Her claims, it seems, were approved.

On 3 February 1815, Wellington took up his post in Vienna. Castlereagh returned to Parliament and refuted all the allegations made against him. He reproved the House for acting on 'information provided by foreign agents', to the detriment of the Government, and of the Foreign Secretary while engaged in crucial negotiations. He accepted the charge that he had acted without reference to his own Cabinet otherwise, 'the whole machine of Europe would have been arrested'.[12] Today, for this obvious untruth, he would be found 'guilty of misleading the House', but he did not get off entirely without censure. The House of Lords, which carried equal weight in those days, heavily criticized him, declaring that never again should a Foreign Secretary be entrusted with such 'dictatorial' powers. Lord Grey opened the debate in the Lords by saying 'Although it was the practise of Parliament during the pendency of all foreign negotiations to leave the management and direction in the hands of executive government, yet there were occasions when cases of great importance occurred, in which the justice, the good faith and the honour of the country were

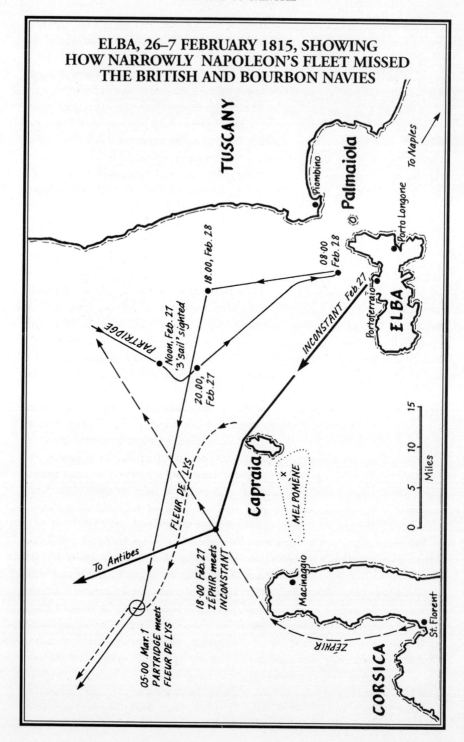

**ELBA, 26–7 FEBRUARY 1815, SHOWING
HOW NARROWLY NAPOLEON'S FLEET MISSED
THE BRITISH AND BOURBON NAVIES**

involved.'[13] Liverpool, trying to defend Castlereagh's conduct at Vienna, explained that Britain's betrayal of her promise to respect the integrity and defence of the Republic of Genoa, liberated by Britain in 1814; and her leaked agreement that it should be given to the King of Sardinia, d'Artois' brother-in-law, ostensibly as a safeguard against the use by France of the strategic Alpine passes, but in reality as a sop for Sardinian support against Murat, brought uproar in Parliament. This lame excuse to appease the French Bourbons on a *quid pro quo* basis was put down by Lord Buckingham who asked if that were the case, why had the other, more vital, passes been handed over to France instead of Austria? Liverpool could make no adequate reply. Following the government's attempts to wipe the Kingdom of Saxony and a resurrected Poland off the map, Parliament was in an aggressive mood. Buckingham described the Genoa settlement as 'foul and disgraceful!' If its policy towards Murat at this point had been made public, it is doubtful if the government would have survived.[14]

On Elba, the Bourbon agent, who it appears may have been 'uncovered', but left in place by Napoleon, was now being fed false information by officers of Napoleon's Guard. On 17 February he sent word that he thought that the English were officially helping Napoleon to leave the island. He reported, incorrectly, that Campbell had spoken at length with Napoleon before sailing to Livorno; that Captain John Ayde of the sloop *Partridge* had brought a large sum of money for the Emperor. On the 22nd he reported that a staff officer had told him that the English had agreed that Napoleon should leave Elba for France, because Louis had refused certain British demands and Napoleon had agreed to implement them.[15]

On 26 February 1815, Napoleon aboard *Inconstant*, and 1,100 men, 40 horses, two cannon and a small coach in *Saint-Esprit* and *Caroline*, set sail from Elba to retake France, in what must surely rank as the smallest invasion fleet in the history of warfare – and the most successful. In the afternoon of 1 March, after a perilous passage during which on several occasions the little flotilla narrowly avoided contact with HMS *Partridge*, and was passed on either side by ships of the French Navy, Napoleon's tiny force entered the Golfe Juan and came ashore. This was no swashbuckling adventure, but the advent of a counter-revolution.

Napoleon swiftly advanced towards Grenoble. On 5 March Monsieur Chappe, the administrator of the telegraph system invented by his brother Claude, delivered a sealed letter to Baron Vitrolles to hand to the King whose gout-ridden hands were scarcely able to open it. Louis read the letter swiftly and asked Vitrolles if he were aware of the contents. No. 'Well I will tell you. It is revolution once more! Bonaparte has landed on the coast of Provence. Have this taken to the Minister of War so that he can come and speak to me at once and decide what steps are to be taken.' The comte de Blacas, protesting at the futility of Napoleon's attempt, and the little danger that it presented to the King, was silenced by Louis, who summed-up his Chief Minister in these words: 'Blacas, my friend you are a very pleasant fellow, but that is not enough to make you sensible. You have been wrong on many occasions, and I am very much afraid you are again deluding yourself.'[16]

Marshal Soult was summoned and outlined his plans. He decided that the forces deployed in the south as a threat to Murat were more than adequate to crush 'Napoleon and his thousand men', and proposed that the comte d'Artois take command of them with Marshal Macdonald to 'advise' him. Artois's son de Berry, advised by Marshal Ney, should assemble a force in the Franche Comté area based on Besançon. D'Angoulême, based at Nimes, with Saint-Cyr to hold his hand, should command a force on the right to attack Napoleon's little column from the rear. These forces, which included the National Guard units, numbering 60,000 men, should suffice, but to be on the safe side Soult asked the king to call up a reserve of 120,000 men to be stationed at Melun south of Paris. Artois was delighted at the thought of the glory that would attach to him and his sons in 'defeating Napoleon in the field'. Soult was commended for his plan.

Napoleon meanwhile was pressing on to Grenoble. At Gap, he was ecstatically received by the populace, the 'Old Guard' joining with the people in the square who were singing the 'Marseillaise', 'Ca Ira', and 'Carmagnole', to cries of 'Down with the priests!', 'Down with the Aristos!' The spirit of the revolution, seen by the people as being personified in Napoleon, was rising again. At La Mure, 185 miles from Fréjus, came a moment of decision. General Marchand, who had enlisted in the revolutionary army and risen to his present rank, was in command of the district, his headquarters being at Grenoble. He had under command the 5th and 7th Infantry Regiments, 3rd Engineer Regiment, 4th Artillery Regiment and the 4th Hussars. After making his men re-affirm their allegiance to Louis, he sent one battalion of the 5th Regiment under Colonel Lessard to block the road and support a party of engineers who were to blow the bridge at Ponhaut. But disaffection was already rife in the ranks; the remark 'They can do what they want, but we aren't going to fight our mates,' was overheard. Lessard reached La Mure at the same time as Napoleon's advance guard, under General Cambronne, and detachments of the 'Old Guard' soon came into sight. Lessard withdrew his men to Laffrey, a defile across which his battalion could deploy. The next day the opposing forces, each of about 1,000 men, faced each other within musket range. Captain Raoul, one of Napoleon's aides, rode up under a flag of truce and asked Lessard to defect; he refused point-blank. Raoul then looked down the line, and standing in his stirrups called to the men of the 5th: 'The Emperor is about to advance towards you. If YOU fire he will fall, and you will answer for it to France!'[17]

Napoleon's force now advanced under his Elban flag, a white field with an *aurore* bend (of Cosimo de Medici) with gold Imperial Bees embroidered on it. The forty mounted Polish lancers came first; in line behind them the band of the Old Guard played its regimental march, known throughout France and Europe. The cavalry suddenly peeled away left and right to the flanks exposing the Old guard with their muskets under their left arms as a sign of peace. The sight of the men in their famous blue greatcoats with red epaulettes, and their bearskins was daunting. With precision they halted and opened square from which strode the little man in his famous hat and riding-coat. Popular legend has it that Napoleon asked: 'Soldiers of

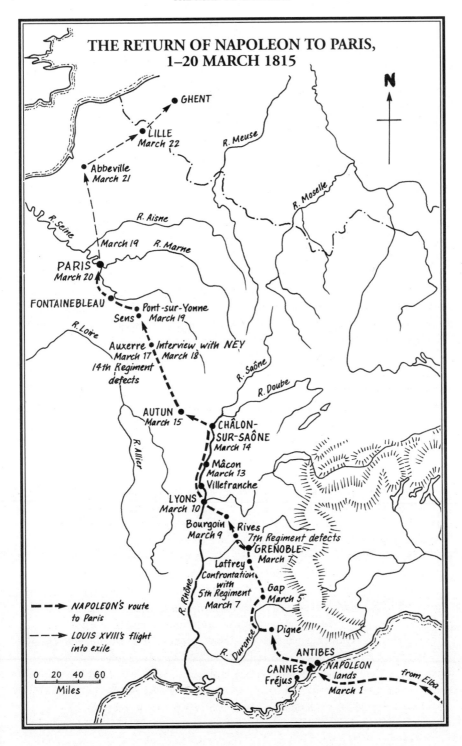

THE RETURN OF NAPOLEON TO PARIS, 1–20 MARCH 1815

N

GHENT

LILLE
March 22

R. Meuse

Abbeville
March 21

R. Moselle

R. Aisne

R. Seine

March 19 *R. Marne*

PARIS
March 20

FONTAINEBLEAU

Pont-sur-Yonne
Sens   March 19

R. Loire

Auxerre • *Interview with NEY*
March 17   March 18
14th Regiment
defects

R. Saône

R. Doube

AUTUN
March 15

CHÂLON-
SUR-SAÔNE
March 14

R. Allier

Mâcon
March 13
Villefranche

LYONS
March 10

Bourgoin   Rives
March 9   7th Regiment defects
GRENOBLE
March 7

Laffrey
Confrontation
with
5th Regiment
March 7

Gap
March 5

R. Rhône

Digne

R. Durance

ANTIBES

CANNES   NAPOLEON
Fréjus   lands   *from Elba*
March 1

- - -▶ NAPOLEON'S route
       to Paris

- - -▶ LOUIS XVIII's flight
       into exile

0   20   40   60
       Miles

175

the fifth, will you fire on your Emperor?', but in fact the men of the 5th Regiment on seeing him erupted in mass hysteria, shouting '*Vive l'Empereur!*', 'He has come back!' and weeping, and if Napoleon had spoken it is doubtful if anyone heard him. No sooner had this battalion joined Napoleon, thus doubling his numbers, than coming up the hill at an attack march were seen the battalions of the 7th Regiment, the flag at their head surmounted by an Imperial Eagle. Their commander, Colonel Charles de la Bédoyère, had recovered the Eagle and tricolore that had been hidden by the regiment at the time of the restoration. Based on the Imperial Eagle standard of the Roman legions, this symbol had been presented by Napoleon to each regiment whose men swore to defend it to the last. In the French Army it was considered that no greater disgrace could befall a regiment than to lose its Eagle, and it was defended with such tenacity that its capture represented a feat of the greatest valour. Napoleon appointed de la Bédoyère a general and one of his aides.

At Grenoble Marchand found that defence was impossible. He had closed the town gates and prepared his cannon, but his royalist artillery commander was less concerned with his honour or that of the king's. The people of Grenoble had turned ugly against the garrison, and he replied to Marchand's inquiry as to whether his men would open fire that if they did 'we should be hacked to pieces on our guns', and refused. The garrison holding the gates were too frightened to open them to Napoleon's men because of the mob which was howling at them from both sides of the wall. When several wheelwrights and blacksmiths, with a custom-made battering ram proceeded to demolish the gates, the soldiers hurriedly capitulated. During the evening the people laid the smashed gates beneath the windows of Napoleon's headquarters at the Hôtel des Trois Dauphins. Napoleon had a proclamation read to the people and the army. The poster was liberally distributed and within days was being reproduced all over France:

'Soldiers!

We were not defeated: two men [Marmont and Augereau] risen from our ranks betrayed our laurels, their country, their prince, their benefactor. Those whom we saw, for twenty-five years, scouring all Europe to raise enemies against us, who spent their lives fighting against us in the ranks of foreign armies, execrating our fair France, would they claim to command and manacle our eagles, they who could never withstand their gaze? Must we endure that they should inherit the fruits of our glorious labour, that they should seize our honours, our goods, and that they should trample on our glory? ... Soldiers! In my exile I heard your voice! ... tear off those colours which the nation proscribed, and which served for twenty-five years to rally all the enemies of France! Put up your tricolore cockade! You wore it in our great battles ... Do you think this handful of arrogant Frenchmen can withstand the sight of them? They will go back to where they come from, and there, *if they so wish, they can reign, as they claim to have reigned for nineteen years!* Your goods, your ranks, your glory, the goods, the ranks, and the glory of your children, have no greater enemies than these princes whom foreigners imposed upon us. They are the enemies of our glory ... Come and place yourself under the flags of your leader; his life is composed of yours; his rights are only those of the people and yours ... Victory will advance at the charge; the Eagle, with the national colours, will fly from steeple to steeple all the way to the towers of Notre-Dame ... In your old age, surrounded and esteemed by your fellow citizens, they will listen to you and you will say with pride: "And I too, I was part of that grand army which twice entered the walls of Vienna, of Rome, of Berlin, of Madrid, of Moscow, which delivered Paris from the stain which *treason* and the presence of the enemy imprinted there."[18]

Next day Napoleon led a force of 4,000 veteran infantrymen with 20 cannon, and a regiment of hussars on Lyons, the second city of France. His march was beginning to look more like a royal progress than a military force, with as many sightseers flocking along singing revolutionary songs. Lyons, too, was in a state of frenzy. Its importance was marked by the presence of Artois himself, with the duc d'Orléans and Marshal Macdonald. Hardly any of the 30,000 men he was expecting had arrived. The government, fearing an insurrection, had dispersed the troops in billets so widely scattered that Napoleon had been able to advance faster (as always) than they had anticipated. Even so, Artois had more than twice the number of Napoleon's men. But the mood in the streets was ominous; the people had had enough of the Bourbons. Huge mobs were on the prowl, attacking the homes and persons of known royalists. Many private scores were settled for the indignities inflicted by the *émigrés*. The chanting of '*Vive l'Empereur!*', 'Hang the Aristos!' 'Death to the priests!' and, even louder, 'Death to the Bourbons!' were unnerving not only Artois but also his reluctant force. They couldn't but remember that the men from Marseilles had come marching up to Lyons in 1793, singing like this, and bringing their revolution, their knives, ropes and axes. Artois could not bully a solitary dragoon to shout '*Vive le Roi!*'. The royalist mayor told Artois that he 'doubted that one man in Lyons would risk his life for the king'. By morning Artois and a handful of royalists were riding hard for Paris. Macdonald, deciding that his honour demand that he set an example, stood in front of the barricaded bridge, musket in hand, to fire in defence of the city. Within minutes the hussars and engineers had cleared the bridge and Macdonald, not having fired a shot, barely made his horse in time; he was chased out of the city by sabre-wielding hussars and was lucky to escape with his life.

At nine o'clock in the evening of 10 March Napoleon reached Lyons, and from there he published his first decrees as the sovereign Emperor of France. They showed that he identified his cause with that of the Revolution. He ordered that all the badges, emblems and insignia of the Bourbons be removed and replaced by those of the Revolution. Secondly, he annulled the laws that had restored the national lands. Thirdly, he abolished all the feudal titles revived by Louis. Fourthly, all *émigrés* on his proscribed list were banished. All military and naval commissions granted by the king were null and void. The hated Swiss Guard was abolished. All Bourbon honours were negated, all the changes made to the courts of justice were withdrawn. He then stated that he would call a grand council on the *Champ de Mai*[19] on his return to Paris. Napoleon now formed a provisional government, naming Marshal Davout Minister of War, Jean Cambacérès Minister of the Interior, and Fouché Minister of Police.

Fouché had been intriguing with Napoleon and all the other powers including the royalists, but with the latter he was *persona non grata*. A loner and a born spy, it was in his nature to be gratified by duplicity for its own sake. Unlike Talleyrand, who suffered from a pride and dignity that he carried as if it were so fragile that it might break, and who sought revenge for any slight, Fouché received an exhilarating lift from manipulation, intrigue and the sense of being needed. He betrayed and sold people because that was what he did best. In today's parlance he was a typical double-agent, capable of being turned again and again; in fact he was the perfect head of a secret police force.

Napoleon now had an army. His force of regular soldiers had grown to eleven infantry regiments, two cavalry regiments, a regiment of artillery with more than 50 serviceable guns; a regiment of engineers, and two *ad hoc* battalions of discharged soldiers and half-pay officers. In all, nearly 16,000 men and growing hourly. In Paris, Blacas on Louis' behalf was offering the Austrians 20,000,000 francs to undertake the invasion of Naples – ten times the sum that Louis refused to pay to Napoleon as his obligation under the Treaty of Fontainebleau. How the fat king must have rued his vindictive spite, when his brother Artois arrived on a lathered horse, covered in mud, with the news that Napoleon had reached Lyons and not one royalist shot had been fired in defence of the king.

In the north of France a curious affair now occurred. The Lallemand brothers, Generals François and Henri, together with Generals Lefebvre-Desnouettes, d'Erlon and others, unaware that Napoleon was back in France, tried to mount a coup in which Fouché was a prime, if not the main mover. It would appear that he betrayed the plot in order to ingratiate himself with the Bourbons and the Allies, while at the same time informing Napoleon of it and professing loyalty. The coup was scotched before it could get under way thanks to Fouché's treachery. But now the common people of France had heard the news from the south and imperialist agents had ensured that Napoleon's proclamation and decrees were being heard circulated throughout France. The Lallemands were taken to the staunchly imperialist town of Soissons and put in the civil gaol. A lady arrived there with her 13-year-old son who was a friend of the gaoler's boy. The son's family had fought for Napoleon, his father, a general, had died fighting for him. The boy's mother was not a strong supporter of the Emperor, but she believed in a better France than that of the Bourbons. She had given her son a brace of loaded pistols and a roll of fifty Louis and the boy, through his friend, was admitted to General Henri Lallemand's cell where he introduced himself as the son of his old friend and comrade, General Dumas. 'General,' the boy said, 'I am charged by my mother to deliver this pair of double-barrelled pistols, loaded, and a roll of fifty Louis. I have them in my pockets. Do you want them?'[20] Embracing the boy, Lallemand said: 'Are you really the son of Alexander

Dumas? You must be Alexander too? Lallemand declined to involve his friend's family, so the future literary giant of France departed. 'What did he say?' asked Madame Dumas on his return. 'He said not to worry, the Emperor will be in Paris before they tried and shot him.'

Now the people everywhere gave vent to their republican feelings, and anti-royalist and anti-clerical slogans were written up all over France. In the Puy-de-Dôme the peasants were overjoyed. 'Seigneurial pews' were taken from churches and burnt. Liberty trees, not seen since the Revolution, appeared in town squares. In Lyons the overbearing *émigré* priests were beaten and chased out of the city. Insurrections broke out at Besançon, Bar-le-Duc, Rennes, Saumur and Strasbourg. In the Isre, four châteaux were attacked by the rural national guard. At la Sône the royalist mayor, a silk merchant, was killed by the National Guard because he tried to prevent them raising the tricolore. In Brittany, Dauphin, the Lyonnais, Languedoc and elsewhere 'patriots' formed federations to protect 'Liberty and Equality' whose like had not been seen since the start of the first revolution. Students played an even greater part, having grown up under the Emperor. Independent battalions featuring a fair cross-section of the populace were formed. At one tobacco company, a state monopoly, the workers, enrolled the entire 60-man workforce in a '*fédérés*' battalion.

Napoleon himself was astonished by the extent of the revolutionary feelings that had erupted, but the fact was that the people feared and detested the rapacious nobility who seemed to be able to impose ever more Draconian laws without let or hindrance.[21]

On 12 March, a Napoleonic supporter placed a placard on the victory column in the place Vendôme: 'From Napoleon to Louis XVIII. My good brother, there is no need to send me any more soldiers. I have enough.' On the same day Louis' Minister of the Interior, the Abbé de Montesquieu, addressed a hushed chamber of deputies: 'Gentlemen, the most recent piece of news which we have to communicate to you is that Marshal Ney, who is very satisfied with the good spirits of the troops under his command, is advancing through Lons-le-Saunier.' (Not a word about the débâcle at Lyons!) Now the name of Ney is on every lip. Ney has become the great white hope of the royalists. Marshal Ney, 'the hero of the army', 'Ney of the Retreat'. No more references to the barrel-maker's son, scum, or 'Madame Ney'. If there were a single marshal in the whole of France with the courage and qualities of leadership sufficient to inspire the soldiers to attack Napoleon, Ney was that man. The King had never worked so hard or drafted so many decrees as he had during the last few days. One decree illustrates the panic of the royalists: 'The moment has come to set a great example. We are counting on the vigour of the nation free and brave; she will find us ever ready to direct her in this enterprise ... France will never be defeated in this struggle between liberty and tyranny, of loyalty against treason, of Louis XVIII against Bonaparte ...' This was followed by a decree that indicated absolute desperation: '*The law of the 4th Nivose, Year IV will continue to be applied in accordance with its form and purport and that in consequence anyone who recruits for the enemy or the rebels will be punished with death.*'[22] So it had come to that. Louis, brother of the executed Louis XVI, had in panic *invoked the law of the revolutionary convention, quoting the revolutionary calender, passed against the émigré recruiters at Coblenz,* which law he had ruled as being illegal! This document was 'given at the Château des Tuileries, March 12, 1815, in the twentieth year of our reign.'

The first that Marshal Ney knew of his mission was on 6 March when a messenger from the Minister of War had appeared at his country estate to which he had retired after having told the Duchess of Angoulême what he thought of her. He was told to report at once to Marshal Soult who ordered him to go immediately to Besançon where he would receive detailed orders from General Bourmont, a junior general and one of Artois' followers. Indignant, Ney demanded to see the king; Soult said that he was 'unwell', but Ney went anyway. Louis, lying on a couch to rest his gouty feet, appealed to Ney help put an end to this rash venture that might provoke a civil war. Ney, unaware that the agreement to pay pensions, to which he had been a signatory, was not being honoured, replied: 'You are right Sire. France must not have a civil war. Bonaparte's enterprise is madness. I am leaving at once for Besançon and if need be I will bring him back to Paris in an iron cage.'

On arriving at Besançon on 10 March, however, Ney found the situation rather different from what he had supposed. More than half the soldiers had defected and Lyons had rallied to 'The Emperor' and chased Artois and Macdonald out of the gates. Ney was now expected to face the Emperor alone, and with fewer men. This would not have deterred him, but Artois' watchdog Bourmont was disconcerting. Here was Ney, the royalists' last hope and they were still supervising him like a rehabilitated thief!

Napoleon had sent two officers of the Old Guard known personally to Ney to see him. They explained everything, including the business of the pensions. They also had two letters for him. One from Bertrand telling him that he should join the rest of the country and 'not be the cause of a civil war'. Napoleon's letter was warm but firm, ordering Ney and his troops to join him at Chalon-sur-Saône where, 'I shall receive you as I did after the battle of the Moscowa' (when Napoleon had elevated him to a princedom). For a moment Ney felt as though he were caught between a rock and a hard place. If he attacked Napoleon he would cause a civil war and in any case he doubted if his men would fight. If he didn't he would have broken his oath to Louis and be seen as the man who could have stopped the counter-revolution. But in truth it was not too difficult a decision. Napoleon had created him a marshal, a duke and a prince – which had made Aglaé a princess. Fat Louis had no time for him, the haughty Artois wouldn't even share a meal with him. They mocked him, laughed at his wife and would deprive his sons of a military career. For this they expected him to haul down his benefactor. Napoleon may have ripped strips off him in the past, or said that he had less knowledge 'than a drummer-boy'. But this was army vernacular, he understood it and, an ex-sergeant-major, he himself was no mean exponent of it. But Napoleon had always accorded him and his family respect and dignity. Ney also felt terribly guilty of having let him down at Fontainebleau. The Emperor's warnings on that occasion about the evils of the present regime had proved only too appallingly prescient.

Next day Ney told Bourmont that he was declaring for Napoleon. Bourmont reproached him. He had sworn to defend the King. What about Ney's sense of honour? Ney replied:

'Yes, I too have a sense of honour. Do you think that I can have my wife insulted by the Duchess of Angoulême and the other parasites who hang about the court? I won't accept that sort of thing any longer, for it is plain that the king does not want us. It is only by a soldier like the Emperor that the soldiers of France will ever be treated with respect. I gave Louis his chance, for I did not want France plunged into civil war and I don't want it now. The whole country is going over to the Emperor, and to fight him would be folly, even worse.'[23]

Next morning Ney entered the place d'Armes at Lons, where his soldiers had been drawn up in square facing inwards. The inhabitants had gathered to see and hear Marshal Ney. He strode to the centre and ordered the men to stand at ease. 'The cause of the Bourbons is lost forever! The legitimate dynasty chosen by France is about to re-ascend the throne. It is the Emperor Napoleon, our sovereign, who has the right to rule over our beautiful country ...' He was cut short by hysterical acclaim. The royalists' hopes had evaporated.

In Paris Artois was beginning to fight back in the way he did best – by covert action and treachery. At midnight on 15 March Monsieur went to the house of the comte d'Escars in the Faubourg Saint-Germain to meet Fouché, duc d'Otrante. Fouché, forgiven for executing two thousand royalist supporters on the plain of Brotteaux, had not been forgiven for being one of three hundred who voted for the execution of Louis XVI. But on this moonlit night a brother of that dead king had come to seek his help. When Fouché betrayed the coup in the north he had been offered his old post as Chief of Police, but had declined. Now Artois offered him the post of Chief Minister, but Fouché refused this too. It was all up with the Bourbons for the moment. He would take office under Napoleon and pretend to serve, until the Allies restored the Bourbons at which time he would set Napoleon aside. 'Monsieur, save the King,' he said, 'I'll take care of saving the Monarchy.' He and Artois then made an arrangement.[24] Next morning a charade was enacted. Fouché's coach was stopped in the street 'by order of the king', with much to-do for the benefit of the inhabitants as to why the Prefect of Police had issued a warrant for his arrest, Fouché shouting 'One does not arrest a former minister and senator of the empire in this fashion.' Conveniently, a National Guard unit of some 25 men from the rue Lepelletier arrived. The major in command was sympathetic and they repaired to Fouché's house, while someone was sent to check the validity of the warrant. The National Guard had no authority to obstruct a police warrant, indeed they were bound to assist in its execution. Fouché just happened to slip through a secret door into his garden where a ladder propped conveniently against the wall adjoining ex-Queen Hortense's garden gave access to the street where a carriage was waiting. A great hue and cry ensued. Fouché had told Hortense, Napoleon's step-daughter that he suspected that he was about to be arrested for his part in the abortive military coup in the north. He had arranged for the coach to be standing by twelve hours before Monsieur's visit which seems to indicate that their plan was well advanced. News of the affair reached Napoleon who had named Fouché his Chief of Police. Artois now had his agent in place within Napoleon's new government.

Blamed for the failure of his plan, and his loyalty suspect, Marshal Soult had been dismissed. General Clarke, duc de Feltre, regarded as being the most capable and having the most to lose, replaced him. Generals Maison and Dessolles were given command of the new army that was assembling at Melun and Essonne which they promised to defend; but they approached the comte de Blacas and pointed out that by attacking Napoleon they would be risking not only their lives but, if they lost, the well-being of their families. Blacas assured them that the king would be grateful. General Maison then turned to Dessolles and said: 'You can see he's pretending not to understand us. We must speak more clearly. Monsieur de Blacas, either you give us 200,000 francs each or you can no longer count on our services.'[25] Blacas actually ordered the Treasury to pay them immediately.

The force at Melun had been so placed as to be able to block either of the two roads on which Napoleon could approach. The deployment was a shambles from start to finish. The loyalty of many of the units was suspect and these were kept well to the rear. Those that were considered sound were untrained, over-officered and unaccustomed to taking orders; they were resentful of any form of discipline. After all, they had not obtained their commissions to obey, but to strut about telling others what to do. The duc de Berry, nominally in command of this army, sat at the front contemplating the realities of a military command. Here he was, awaiting Napoleon, the conqueror of Europe, with a large number of unreliable men behind him. He felt as though he were in a Sandwich, as they called it in England after the Earl of that name. Deciding to go for a stroll among his men as 'one of the boys', he asked to taste some of the grenadiers' soup, *à la Napoléon*. A grenadier gave him a hard look and said, 'You have come too late, Sir. You will find it cold.' The duke decided to return to Paris, his military ardour having dropped to the temperature of the soup. With his departure the force started to melt away.

Marshal Oudinot was ordered to bring the 'Old Guard' back to Paris to protect the best of sovereigns; no reference now to the 'Grenadiers of France'. Napoleon, before leaving, had commended them to the king, advised him to take these men to his heart and they would be the bulwark of his throne. Louis had despised and neglected them, envious of their legendary loyalty and frightened by their prowess. Now the sheep was summoning the wolves to the door. Oudinot kept haranguing them about loyalty to Louis, his honour and the oaths that had been sworn. This cut little ice with them. They had not sworn any oath to the fat King. When Oudinot asked them whether they would obey and follow him, they replied yes, so long as he lead them in 'the right direction'. Not since the Revolution had men in the ranks decided if and when they would obey their leaders; not during the terrible retreat from Moscow nor during the exhausting fight for France of the previous year. The army had reverted to its revolutionary roots. At Clamency General Allix, on half-pay, stood on the steps of the town hall and read Napoleon's proclamation. The mayor summoned the gendarmerie and lieutenant and a file of twelve men with muskets advanced to arrest him. Taking off his glasses, he shook the confused officer's hand and announced: 'In the name of the Emperor, I assume command of the town of Clamency! All of you present here, I call upon you to put up the national colours immediately, and to regard as enemies those who are not wearing them.' The thousands of townsfolk raised a mighty roar, and the gendarmes, in their the Bourbon colours, beat a hasty retreat to their barracks to remove them. One man had captured a town, merely by invoking the Emperor's name.

Louis had gone to the Chambers on 16 March and proclaimed that he could do nothing better at the age of sixty than die in defence of France. He and the four princes had raised and joined hands and sworn to uphold their Charter: 'Let us swear on our honour, to live and die loyal to our King and to the constitutional Charter, which ensures the well-being of the French.' This scene received good reviews in the royalist-controlled press. The sycophantic ultras actually believed the propaganda and wishful thinking printed in the papers. One report stated that General Marchand had recaptured Grenoble, Napoleon was encircled and Lyons had revolted against the usurper. Bands of thirty or more young royalists in huge white-plumed hats roamed the streets of Paris, beating up old or retired officers; one of these was killed and his body mutilated. The local gendarmes looked the other way. But retribution was fast approaching the capital.

Louis had turned back the clock 25 years only to find, as had his brother before him, the prospect of a revolution on his hands. Governments, it has been said, are instituted among men by the will of the people, not by foreign bayonets. All men were created equal according to Article 1 of *Rights of Man*, adopted by the National Assembly on 26 August 1789, and whose drafting was aided by the then American Ambassador to France, Thomas Jefferson. This fundamental truth had been incorporated into the Constitution of 1791. Napoleon had affirmed this in his articles of constitution regarding the laws of the Empire. Louis had disregarded it and would have to pay the price.

Louis and Artois went to the Chambers once more. In an attempt to retain power, Louis XVI had humiliated himself before the national convention by wearing a red cap and tricolore cockade. Louis XVIII appeared in great gold epaulettes surmounted by large crowns, and wearing the ribbon and star of the Legion of Honour. He showed this with great pride to his cousin, the republican duc d'Orléans, who said: 'I see it Sire, but would rather have seen it sooner.' Louis addressed the Chambers with appeals and promises ending with a threat, that Napoleon was bringing a foreign war and that '*We might have to be supported by the bayonets of our allies.*' Which just about summed-up the authority by which he could lay claim to his title – foreign force to subjugate his people.

In 1814, if Napoleon had reached Paris four hours before the capitulation he could have raised more than 100,000 men who would have fought and died for him. Louis XVIII, like the biblical Lot, could not even find a handful of his swaggering nobles to do the same. Now the incredible futility of the 10,000 old, lame, inadequate men of his '*Maison du Roi*' guardsmen became apparent. What chance would they have against Napoleon's élite guard? Many of them had already packed their bags. They were nobles, they had not accepted their lucrative posts and paid for expensive uniforms in order to fight in them.

On 19 March Marshal Macdonald arrived at the Tuileries, dressed in civilian clothing, as requested by the King. Louis had decided to leave Paris. He was terrified by the prospect of being taken captive by his loyal subjects as a gift for Napoleon – or worse, that he might be destined to follow his late brother to 'a certain movable framework with a sack and a knife in it, terrible in history'. The last few days had seen an exodus from the capital as countless senators, royalists and turncoats sought to escape their nemesis. Out of touch, Chateaubriand, who had delighted in his scurrilous pamphlet about Napoleon, sent a female friend to plead for a safe, remunerative position to save himself from being shot. The panic-stricken courtiers had been liquidating their assets; twenty million francs had been exchanged for foreign bills. Louis had arranged for the treasury to be liquidated for fourteen million francs in foreign bills of exchange, and had had all the state jewels removed so that he would be able to resume his exile in style. Louis was obsessed with the need of secrecy. His brother had been caught at Varennes in 1791, trying to flee the country, because the people had seen his cavalcade of coaches set off. Macdonald dismissed all the coaches and put it about that the king would review his troops on the morrow. He then arranged for the coaches to re-assemble after dark.

On Sunday 19 March, in violation of the new sabbatical laws, the cafes opened. The streets of Paris were agog with expectation. Would Napoleon arrive before or after Louis ran? Would the king fulfil his oath and remain to defend the capital? At midnight Louis XVIII shambled down the steps of the Tuileries; the candelabra were soon gutted by the wind and rain. The King of France, fearful of the mob, was leaving like a thief in the night. Later, a famous painting would show his loyal courtiers tearful at his feet. Actually they were busy shifting for themselves. Louis, took with him Artois and Marshals Marmont and Berthier. When the news of his departure filtered through on the morning of 20 March, Chateaubriand, Pasquier and the others were still in bed. Bent on saving his own neck, Louis had not informed his loyal followers, but left them to their fate for fear of a leak. All day the royalists fled the city. Many of the cocky young ultras who had been intimidating the old soldiers now found themselves on the receiving end, and again, the gendarmes looked the other way. Napoleon would later claim that he recaptured France without firing a shot, but the lampposts in the faubourgs carried more than thirty of the royalist fruits that they had borne during the first revolution.

But Paris did not sink into anarchy or riots. Louis had deserted Paris, and those in authority who had either betrayed or deserted Napoleon, or were royalist appointments, also left in a hurry. On his own initiative Lavalette took charge of the postal service and sent word to Napoleon that Louis had fled and urged him to make haste; a message reminiscent of the one sent eleven months previously. General Exelmans arrived with his cavalry hoping to capture Louis. He was wrapped in what appeared to be tricolore bunting, but which turned out to be a huge flag which he had hoisted on the palace before speeding off in hot pursuit of Louis.

Within a matter of hours all the junior officers of the civil service, mayors and imperialists in the ministries had taken control of the city. Apart from isolated attacks on the more obnoxious ultras and their homes, order had been restored to the world's largest capital. That evening Napoleon was entering his Palace of Fontainebleau which he had left eleven months ago almost to the day. The staff had prepared it for him and his Guards were on duty; his coach pulled up to their roars of '*Vive l'Empereur!*' Napoleon was back where he had started before the treaty, and in a better position than before. Lavalette's letter soon reached him and he pressed on to Paris. By nine o'clock in the evening of 20 March 1815, Napoleon I was once more the undisputed sovereign of France.

General Sébastiani, a notable *sabreur*, arrived with his regiment and informed the last royalist army at Melun that it was all over, the king had fled. The units were ordered to return to Paris. Macdonald, who had arrived there earlier, had already fled, as had Maison and Dessolles long before, taking their money with them. The only resistance to this capitulation was shown by an 18-year-old ultra, Lieutenant Negré de Massals. He tore off his epaulettes, flung them on the ground and jumped up and down on them, yelling abuse at his men. Picking them up again, he threw them and they hit an old sweat of several campaigns, who strode up and boxed the young man's ear so hard that he was knocked to the ground. And that was the end of royalist resistance at Melun. There were still one or two pockets in the South of France where the news had not yet arrived or had been suppressed, but within days all had declared for Napoleon. In twenty days Napoleon, with his army of 'a thousand men', had retaken France without incurring any casualties.

CHAPTER 9

THE ROADS TO PARIS AND GHENT

'No man can doubt that this Napoleon stands as Emperor of France
by the will of the French people. Let then the French settle their own affairs.'
– Sir Francis Burdett (Speech in Parliament, 7 April 1815).

The shifting attitudes of Parisian society towards Napoleon's progress from the coast during a period of three weeks was cleverly caught by a wit who published a broadsheet after the style of official dispatches:[1]

The Tiger has broken out of his cage.

The Ogre has been three days at sea.

The Wretch has landed at Fréjus.

The Buzzard has reached Antibes.

The Invader has arrived in Grenoble.

The General has entered Lyons.

Napoleon slept at Fontainebleau last night.

The Emperor will proceed to the Tuileries today.

His Imperial Majesty will address his loyal subjects tomorrow.

While Napoleon had been busy re-captivating his French subjects, activity on the diplomatic front had been frenetic, at Vienna and in the other major capitals of Europe. News that he had left Elba for an unknown destination had reached Vienna early on the morning of 7 March, the day after he had landed. Metternich received a dispatch marked 'Urgent' from the Imperial and Royal Austrian Consulate in Genoa: 'The English commissioner Campbell has just entered the harbour inquiring whether anyone had seen Napoleon at Genoa, in view of the fact that he had disappeared from the island of Elba. The answer being in the negative, the English frigate without further delay, put to sea.' Metternich informed his Emperor and within an hour the three monarchs and their ministers – the Duke of Wellington representing Britain – met and decided on armed intervention if Napoleon attempted to upset the equilibrium of Europe.[2] At 10 o'clock Metternich met Talleyrand who asked him if he knew where Napoleon was making for. Metternich said that he didn't. Talleyrand said: 'He will land on some part of the Italian coast and will fling himself into Switzerland.' To which Metternich is reputed to have replied 'No. He will make straight for Paris.'

No positive news arrived until Talleyrand received a communication from Blacas telling him of Napoleon's landing on 1 March, and enclosing a copy of Louis' ordinance of 6 March which enjoined all Frenchmen to:

'... fall upon Napoleon Buonaparte, declared a traitor and rebel for having introduced himself by force into the department of the Var, to apprehend him and convey him forthwith before a military tribunal.'

In other words, to be shot. On the 13th Talleyrand induced the Powers of the 'first' and 'second' rank to sign a joint declaration:

> 'The Powers who have signed the Treaty of Paris, assembled in congress at Vienna, being informed of the escape of Napoleon Buonaparte, and of his entrance into France with an armed force, owe it to their own dignity, and the interest of social order, to make a solemn declaration of the sentiments which this event has excited in them. By thus breaking the convention which established him in the Island of Elba, Buonaparte has destroyed the only legal title on which his existence depended: by appearing again in France, with projects of confusion and disorder, he has deprived himself of the protection of the Law, and has manifested to the universe that there can be neither peace nor truce with him. The powers consequently declare, that Napoleon Buonaparte has placed himself without the pale of civil and social relations; and that as an enemy and disturber of the tranquillity of the World, he has rendered himself liable to public vengeance.'[3]

Neither of these documents had any legal provenance or authority. With regard to Louis' ordinance, Napoleon was the acknowledged sovereign of Elba, so he was neither a traitor, nor a rebel, having taken no oath of allegiance to Louis, nor was he a French subject. The fantasy of having him court-martialled and shot, presumably under the fiction that he was a French general, had been dreamed up by Artois, but was ridiculous because Napoleon held no commission from Louis. Next, Louis had *deliberately* broken the Treaty of Fontainebleau, and by all the usages of law and the articles appertaining to the conduct of warfare of the period, Napoleon was entitled to return, his abdication having been given *on conditional terms*, i.e., those stipulated by the treaty which Louis had dishonoured. No sovereign had any legal right to declare the sovereign of another country a public enemy and sanction his apprehension or murder. The Bourbons hoped that, given the right incentive, someone would finish Napoleon off for them, but were anxious that it should appear to have been done legally.

On 12 March, while Napoleon was at Lyons, Castlereagh wrote to Wellington telling him that in view of the fact that Napoleon was establishing some authority back in France, the Powers: 'Should publish a joint declaration announcing their determination to maintain the inviolable Peace of Paris, and as the only security for the due observance of the same, their resolution to support the lawful sovereign of France against Buonaparte.'[4] Castlereagh at this stage envisaged a civil war in France between the two parties. He hoped that an assembly of 200,000 Allied troops on her borders, under his Treaty of Chaumont, would serve to dishearten those who would support Napoleon. This letter was based on information sent to him from Paris on the 7th, and Castlereagh had no idea that royalist France would have collapsed by the time Napoleon reached Paris. By the time it reached Wellington on the 22nd, Napoleon had already formed a government.

Castlereagh wrote a second letter to Wellington on the same day, 12 March, concerning the problem of Naples. He said that he had received proof from France, from Fouché among others, that Murat had been treacherous and should be disowned:

> '*As there will be some nicety in giving to our line on this question the form most likely to prove satisfactory to parliament,* it might be desirable that we should accede, according to our own form, to the Treaty previously agreed to by Austria and France [3 January], in which you will assist with a view of rendering the details as little objectionable as possible.'

In other words, to deceive Parliament as to British involvement in an attack on a friendly Power in order to please the Bourbons.

> 'We would appear, reluctantly to agree to accede to be bound by the terms of our secret treaty of January 3rd, i.e., not to intervene.'

Castlereagh told Wellington that Britain could only assist officially by offering the use of the navy, but that he would provide covert financial aid without going to Parliament to tell them what he was doing:

> 'I conceive this will not make any difficulty, as our military aid must be a secondary question, if we can help them a little in corn, ships, and money. In the former article we can, I have no doubt, do something, and in the latter *I have an expedient by which I hope to give them £70,000 a month, for about four months, without going to Parliament to ask for a subsidy: that is, by not deducting the value of the stores supplied to them from the Chaumont Subsidy.*'[5]

Even while Napoleon was marching on Paris, which Castlereagh was viewing as a side-show, the British Foreign Secretary, against his Cabinet's wishes, was conspiring with Austria to renege on its obligations to Murat and Naples. To please the Bourbons, he was prepared to assist in a war against Murat who represented no threat to Britain or Europe. Wellington himself gave the opinion that the so-called 'evidence' of Murat's treachery was of insufficient value to proceed upon.[6]

Twelve days later Castlereagh, somewhat subdued by the complete and utter rejection of the Bourbons by the French nation, wrote to Wellington:

> 'I am to inform you that, in the judgement of his Royal Highness's confidential servants, *the Neapolitan question has assumed a new shape under the late extraordinary events in France. Whilst Louis XVIII. was supposed to be firmly established on his throne, the difficulty was to consolidate the peace of Europe so long as a dynasty remained at Naples which neither France nor Spain would acknowledge. The case is different now ... If the Powers of Europe [Austria] should consider this overture to be bona fide on the part of Murat; if they should be of the opinion, under the actual circumstances of Europe, that it is prudent to take advantage of it;* and they find that Murat adheres to his professions notwithstanding the extent of success which has attended Buonaparte's usurpation, Your Lordship has full powers to conclude a Treaty with him ... and to leave the Austrian army free to operate on the South of France in force.'[7]

By now, however, given their condescension and contempt for him since 1814, King Joachim Murat of Naples had no faith in the Allies.

As was the case with Napoleon, the longer Murat waited the more vulnerable his position would be. Austria and Britain had refused to ratify their treaties with him, and were conspiring with Spain, France and Sicily to invade him. Napoleon, who would soon be master of his own house again, was his last hope; he at least would not abandon his brother-in-law or, like Britain and Austria, seek a legal loophole to break his treaty. On this despicable episode of bad faith on Britain's part, it was left to the distinguished Lord Grey to pass judgement in the House of Lords: 'If rumours are true we have behaved in each of these cases in a manner which exceeds everything of treachery and fraud which I have yet witnessed in the new diplomatic school of which the noble Lord Castlereagh might be considered as the founder.'[8] On 13 April 1815, the day after Castlereagh had written the first letter to Wellington, King Murat advanced his army towards northern Italy in the hope of uniting the country under one crown in its struggle for national identity, and ousting the Austrians. Then, joining with Napoleon's forces, his army would threaten Vienna, as they had done in the Italian campaigns of the Revolution, and in 1800, 1805 and 1809.

On resuming power, Napoleon sent peace overtures to the three monarchs. Metternich returned the letter addressed to his Emperor unopened, the Tsar read his without comment. The Duchess of Saint-Leu, ex-Queen Hortense, a friend of the Tsar's, wrote asking Alexander to consider giving Napoleon a chance to prove that the 'Lion had returned as a Sheep'. While appearing to make common cause with the Allies, Alexander gave this idea some thought. Napoleon had always been honest in his dealings with him. Fat Louis had insulted him, Talleyrand had duped him and arrived at the Congress unbidden and continued to insult him – in the name of Bourbon France. Thanks to Alexander, Britain had got everything she wanted at Paris and in return had not only opposed him in Poland, but had tried to bribe Prussia to turn against him. Austria too was treacherous. Having failed to support the effort against Napoleon in 1812, she had come off the fence in 1813 in self-interest. Austria had hindered the war of 1813, hoping to leave Napoleon on the throne as a buffer against Russian interests. Austria was against his Polish kingdom and had threatened him. Now he was expected to risk countless Russian lives to put the useless, ungrateful, unwanted Louis back *again* on his throne, to suit predominantly British, Austrian and Bourbon interests.

The full extent of Napoleon's counter-revolution was not yet known in Vienna, but already the Great Powers were drawing apart. In a secret dispatch from Wellington to Castlereagh, the Duke informed him of the 'Allied' military plans:

'The intention is, as soon as it shall be ascertained that he [Napoleon] can make head against the King [Louis], to assemble three large corps, one in Italy, solely Austrian, which will consist of 150,000 men. One on the upper Rhine, Austrian, Bavarian, troops of Baden and Württemberg, which will *eventually consist of 200,000 men, but will at first consist of only the troops of Bavaria, Baden, and Württemberg* [no Austrians]; the third on the lower Rhine, consisting of the Prussian corps of Kleist, the Austrian garrison of Mayence, and other troops on the Moselle, to be joined to the British and

Hannoverians in Flanders. Of this Corps they wish me to take the command. The Russian army of 200,000 men, is to be formed at Württemberg, &c., &c.; the remainder of the Prussian Army in reserve on the lower Rhine.'[9]

The Duke continued in cipher:

> '*The Emperor of Russia at first took the field [floor] with the plan of being Dictator. Razumoffski spoke to me of this notion as one of his own; and I recommended to him never to speak of it to others, among whom the Emperor of Austria, who was much alarmed by it; but supposing the idea not relished by any, and above all knowing that I should object to it, I found him very quiet and easy this day in a long conversation I had with him at my own house. He seemed* reconciled to the notion of the old system of managing the great concern in a council consisting of himself, the King of Prussia, and Schwarzenberg.'[10]

Now the mutual distrust becomes very evident. Austria will concentrate 150,000 men in Italy for fear of a Franco-Neapolitan thrust on Vienna, but offer the 11,000 men at Mayence as a token. The troops of the lesser German states will be deployed in the forefront on the upper Rhine, to ensure their loyalty and compliance while their own territories are occupied by the 200,000-strong 'reserve' army of Russia, who, on the pretext of having farther to travel, will arrive at a position which places them well back and uncommitted, unless Austria marches first. If she does not, she has 200,000 Russians in front of her borders, and another 200,000 assembling in Russia and Poland. But Austria, who cannot afford to risk her irreplaceable troops that keep her multi-ethnic empire in subservience, will not advance unless the Russians go first. A dilemma! The Tsar has no intention of allowing his troops to be used as cannon-fodder in order to preserve the Austrian army and restore the insulting Louis and Talleyrand to power, so it is up to Britain to defend its satellites of Hanover and the United Netherlands. Prussia too, with its new possessions on the Rhine and Saxony, will feel insecure. Let them bear the brunt, this time without direct Russian aid. So far as the Tsar is concerned, the Prussians have chosen to desert him for British interests; let Britain assist them then. He can afford to await the outcome, but in the meantime he will mobilize – provided that Castlereagh subsidizes him. After all, it is in the British interest to do so; it is her allies, Bourbon France and The Netherlands, that are threatened.

A fortnight later Wellington wrote again to Castlereagh:

> 'I found it much more difficult than I imagined when I wrote my despatch, No 18, to conclude a treaty with the Allies on the plan of the Treaty of Chaumont, which work I have accomplished only this night, and now enclose ... The occasion of the delay has been, first, the desire of all the powers to connect with the engagement for employing a large force, *one for the grant of a subsidy from England;* and secondly, the extreme jealousy regarding the command of the contingents of the small powers in the North of Germany. An endeavour was made to dispose of the contingents of those Powers by an entry on the protocol of the military conference held here in

presence of the Emperor of Russia; and as I refused to sign this protocol, upon finding it contained an arrangement which had not been mentioned, and to which I had not agreed, they have delayed to sign the Treaty for a week ... I likewise enclose the protocol of what passed at the conclusion of the Treaty this night, in which you will see the urgency with which they desire to be assisted by subsidies. I believe your Lordship is perfectly aware that it will be quite impossible for these powers to make an effort adequate to the occasion, unless they should obtain this aid.'[11]

His letter crossed with one from Castlereagh dated 26 March, by which time the news from France was filtering through:

'We wait with impatience for intelligence from all quarters. The great question is can the Bourbons get Frenchmen to fight *for them* against Frenchmen? If they can, Europe may soon turn the tide in their favour; and, the process of fermentation once begun, they may create *real partisans*, instead of criers of " *Vive le Roi!*' and doers of nothing. If we are to do the job, we must leave nothing to chance ... If Buonaparte could turn the tide, there is no calculating upon his plan; and we must always recollect that Poland, Saxony, and much Jacobinism [republicanism], are in our rear ... My notion is, that France must pay the price of her own deliverance; and that the King should consider the Allied troops as auxiliaries; that every corps should be accompanied by a French *ordonnateur* [commissary agent], through whom all requisitions for forage and subsistence should be made; the value to be paid in bonds, the liquidation of which should be asked upon a peace, either in whole, or in the greater proportion, at the expense of the French Government. *Unless some system of this kind is agreed upon, the war will either degenerate, as it did last year, into an indiscriminate and destructive pillage, or WE shall be bankrupts, and driven out of the field in three months. I know the difficulties of what I suggest; but the alternative in the less objectionable sense leads at once to impossibilities and ruin* ... We long to hear of you in Flanders.'[12]

Here was the rub, and Britain's dilemma. From 1812 to 1814 Britain had spent vast sums of money in subsidies, loans and *matériel* to Portugal, Spain, Russia, Prussia and Austria; then to Sweden, Sicily, Bavaria and the smaller German states, much of it as outright bribes to induce the participants to continue fighting. After the peace, Britain had also lent large sums to Austria who was spending more on entertaining the delegates to the Congress than on her military budget. France too had contracted British loans, to help stabilize the country, but now Britain herself, as indicated in the letters of Lord Liverpool and Castlereagh, was in financial straits. One third of British exports normally went to America, but that country had placed an embargo on British goods by their Embargo Act of 1807 and the Non-Intercourse Act of 1809. News of the peace had not yet reached America, and the embargo had yet to be lifted and markets re-established. Europe had been closed to all British imports, and although smuggling was rife and Holland, for example, had turned a blind eye to Napoleon's land embargo, a mere sixteenth of its normal trade had managed to filter through. While this had made little in Britain, whose industrial revolution was in full swing and who could divert her goods to markets around the world, such as South America and the Far East, it had created what we should term a cash-flow crisis.

Britain's gold reserves were at an all-time low. Foreign subsidies were required to be in gold; some countries such as Austria would accept part payment in redeemable Treasury promissory notes which were negotiable with foreign banks, such as Rothschilds, who bought them at less than their face value in gold and agreed to a delay in their redemption – at the cost of a high annual interest.

Before the war, British banknotes had been freely convertible for their gold or silver equivalent, i.e., 'Such and Such Bank promises to pay the bearer on demand One Pound Sterling' or 'Ten Gold Sovereigns'. But during the war the government passed several Orders-in-Council (i.e., that of 26 February 1797), and the Restriction Acts of 1797 and 1804, amended 1809, which stipulated that paper money could not be redeemed until one month after a peace treaty had been signed. In 1804 alone, the Bank of England had issued paper money to the value of 17.5 million pounds, and it should be remembered that there were some 800 other banks issuing notes in Britain during the period. Gold disappeared and was replaced by paper or Spanish silver dollars; in some areas workers were paid in 'company tokens'. The Bank of England's paper notes were issued in denominations as low as £2 and £1. The lowest denomination banknote issued by the Bank of France during the same period was for 500 francs (£20).[13]

In 1814 the British public were clamouring for the immediate convertibility of the notes back to gold and silver, which was not feasible. It is difficult if not impossible to equate the inflation in Britain during the period with that experienced in modern times, but masses of letters, journals and memoirs refer to the cost of living compared to that in the now accessible Europe, and show that clothing, spirits, commodities and taxes were about 106 per cent higher in Britain than in western Europe. Britain was also burdened by the 'temporary' war tax on income.[14]

So Britain was not only war weary but financially impoverished. The cost of the French wars had risen year after year. The annual budget in 1800 had been: £11,37,000 for the Army, £12,619,000 for the Navy and £3,000,000 for foreign subsidies. In 1814 this had risen to: £43,820,000 for the Army, £22,000,000 for the Navy and £18,740,000 for foreign subsidies. The National Debt had risen from £227,000,000 at 5 January 1793 to a staggering £701,437,000 by 11 February 1815. The annual interest alone on this debt amounted to one-third of the government's total revenues.[15] Now, having expended so much of her wealth, Britain was back where she was at the beginning of the wars – only this time, as Castlereagh pointed out to Wellington, '... *unless some system of this kind is agreed upon* [France footing half the bill] ... we shall be bankrupts, and driven out of the field in three months'. The Allies refused to fight without subsidies; Austria couldn't, Prussia and the lesser German states also wanted something from what they perceived as 'the gravy boat'. Under Castlereagh's Chaumont treaty, failure to field a certain number of men meant that Britain would have to pay £20–30 per man in lieu. Her only recourse would be to borrow gold from a foreign banking house and hope that Napoleon could be beaten before it ran out.

In the South of France, two pockets of resistance remained. Bordeaux, supposed to have been the first city to declare for the Bourbons, had been playing host to the Duchess of Angoulême when Napoleon landed. On 20 March, at the approach of General Clausel's troops who were marching to take possession of the city, Maria-Thérèsa Angoulême, daughter of Marie-Antoinette and grand-daughter of the great Empress whose name she bore, could muster a garrison of two regiments, Mayor Lynch's 'Bordelais' Regiment which had become the city's National Guard, and a few royalists and collaborators. The city had strong defences, and Clausel had no siege train, but the military Governor advised her and the city council to leave and 'avoid danger'. The Duchess was determined to march out with the superior forces of the city and rout Clausel's inferior force, but the Governor told her that the men would not fight. 'Then the National Guard and volunteers will be sufficient. They are eager for combat, and on their attachment and bravery I can surely rely.' The Governor pointed out that in that case the Duchess would be placing herself and her men between *two fields of fire*. The Duchess in disbelief went to the two barracks and assembled the regular soldiers, to whom she appealed: 'Will you not fight for the daughter of your King?' To which the soldiers cried 'No! No! No!' The Duchess tried a last appeal: 'Will you then remain neutral if the National Guard and volunteers attack the rebels?' Again, 'No! No! They are not rebels. *Vive l'Empereur!*'. They promised not to attack her and desired her to leave quickly.

General Clausel's men now lined the bank of the river opposite the city. The National Guard fired a volley that was not returned. The Duchess and her followers left by an English boat provided by the British Consul. Thus departed, as Napoleon said, 'the only man in the family'. Bordeaux again flew the tricolore.[16] Within days, the Duke of Angoulême, whose own force had evaporated and who was trying to raise further resistance, was captured and taken into protective custody from the populace by General Grouchy. Napoleon wrote to Grouchy:

> 'Count Grouchy. The ordinance of the king, dated 6 March, and the declaration, signed by his ministers on the 13th, at Vienna, might authorize me to treat the duc d'Angoulême as that ordinance and declaration proposed to treat me and my family [to be killed out of hand] ... it is my intention that you should give orders for conducting the duc d'Angoulême to Cette, where he shall be embarked, and that you should watch over his safety and protect him from all bad treatment.'[17]

This magnanimous gesture was not reciprocated later.

In France, Napoleon had induced his one-time opponent, the polemicist Benjamin Constant, to draft a constitution for the people. Rightly gauging the mood of the nation as being inclined to a constitutional monarchy, he produced the '*Acte Additionnel*' which amended the laws of the Empire; Napoleon regarded the Bourbons' restoration as being nullified by their breach of the Treaty of Fontainebleau.

Napoleon's Constitution repealed all the absolutist laws enshrined in 'The Charter' that had so oppressed and alienated the people. Section 1, Articles 7–16, dealt with the Chambers. Deputies were not to be excluded by reason of income, anyone could stand; they were to be subject to re-election every five years and not by rota. Article 25 stated: 'When a bill is adopted in either Chamber, it is carried to the other; and, if there approved, it is carried to the Emperor.' Section 2 dealt with taxation. No tax could continue to be imposed – except in time of war – for more than one year, unless renewed by agreement of both Chambers. Section 3, Articles 38–50, defined ministerial accountability to the two Chambers, giving them the right to accuse and try any minister for abuse, corruption or incompetence. Section 5, Article 59, stated: 'All Frenchmen are equal in the eye of the law.' Article 61, stated: 'No one can be prosecuted, arrested, detained or exiled, but in cases provided for by law, and according to the prescribed forms.' Article 62: 'Liberty of worship is guaranteed to all.' Article 63: '*All property possessed or acquired in virtue of the laws, and all debts of the state are inviolable.*'[18]

Napoleon now wrote to the Prince Regent to whom he felt indebted for his safe passage to and secure sojourn on Elba:

'The first wish of my heart is to repay so much affection by the maintenance of an honourable peace. The restoration of the imperial throne was necessary for the happiness of the French people. It is my sincerest desire to render it at the same time subservient to the maintenance of the repose of Europe. Enough of glory has shone by turns on the colours of the various nations ... After having presented to the world the spectacle of great battles,
it will now be more delightful to know no other rivalship in future ...'[19]

Given his favourable position compared to 1814, back in France and busy raising another army, this was possibly the most sincere and reasonable letter that Napoleon had ever written. Even towards the end of the late campaign his letters were still imperial in tone and unbending. Now, realizing that only England had protected him, and only England would grant him peace, he had offered this olive branch out of a sense of honourable obligation, as well as necessity. Castlereagh had it returned unopened.

In Britain the news of Napoleon's unimpeded return had now reached the public, many of whom believed that, the French nation having rejected the Bourbons in favour of Napoleon, Britain should make peace with him. Lord Byron wrote in ecstatic admiration:

'Oh, France! retaken by a single march
Whose path was through one long triumphal arch.'

Parliament decided to debate the momentous turn of events, together with the Allied Powers' declaration of 13 March of which Wellington was the eighth signatory. Castlereagh addressed the House of Commons during the evening of 7 April 1815. His theme was that Louis had been overthrown by the intrigues of '... smart army-gamesters – upon men who had shared his own excitements, spoils, and crimes – This man who impiously calls himself The Emperor of the French by the Grace of God ... I think the House will readily discern that the wise, wary trackway to be trod by our own country in this crisis, must lie between two alternatives. Of war in concert with the Continental powers, or an armed and cautionary cause.'[20] He suggested that Britain's role in the latter be an auxiliary one in support of Louis; in effect, to put down his rebellious subjects. He then moved an address by the House to the Prince Regent: '... to assure him that his faithful Commons are fully roused, to the dark hazards to which the life and equanimity of Europe are exposed by the deeds of France, in contravention of the previous pacts [i.e., Fontainebleau]. And to act in concert with those Allies in losing no time in securing a European security. So to augment by land and sea, as to empower him to set afoot the swift measures to accomplish it.'[21] But parliament was in no hurry to be pushed into another expensive war in the furtherance of Castlereagh's personal ambitions. Sir Francis Burdett:

> '... it was impossible, weighing the language of the noble lord, to catch his counsel, whether he advocates peace or war? If I translate his words to signify the expediency of watch and ward, that we may not be taken unawares, I agree; but if he is proposing to plunge this country into a sea of blood to reinstate the Bourbon line in France, I should but poorly do my duty in this House, did I not lift my voice protesting against so ruinous an enterprise! Sir, I am old enough to call to mind the first fierce frenzied speeches to the same ends. The outcome of which was to endow this man [Napoleon], the object of your present apprehensions, with such power and might as could withstand all of Europe banded against him ... Shall, then, another twenty years of sacrifice blight this land to make another Bourbon king? Wrongly has Bonaparte's excursion been called an adventure, a rude excursion into France. Who ever knew one sole and single man invade a nation of thirty million strong, and in a few days gain its full sovereignty, against that nation's will! The truth is this: the nation longed for him, and has obtained him ... No man can doubt that this Napoleon stands as Emperor of France by the will of the French people. Let then the French settle their own affairs.'[22]

George Ponsonby felt that Castlereagh's measures: '... So far from being the first step to war, appears in sense and substance to leave the House to be guided by events, on the grave question of hostilities.' He went on to say that if he understood Castlereagh correctly, we were not at war with the French people, but merely preparing to invade 'To rob the French of Bonaparte's rule and force back the Bourbon monarchy ... must war revive, let [it] be quickly waged ... though 'tis my ardent hope that peace may be preserved.' Samuel Whitbread not only denounced an expensive war, at the cost of countless lives, but the folly of putting back on the throne the Bourbons whom patently the French nation despised, and in his opinion, rightly so.

Whitbread then attacked Castlereagh and the government over the so-called declaration of 13 March. Who had authorized Wellington to sign it on Britain's behalf? By what law of England was it promulgated?

> *'The declaration signed at Vienna against Napoleon, is in my regard abhorrent, and our country's character defaced by our subscribing to its terms! If words*

have any meaning at all, it incites to assassination; it proclaims that any meeting Bonaparte may lawfully slay him. And whatever language the Allies now decide, in that outburst, at least, war was declared! The noble Lord tonight would second it. He urges that we arm, then wait for just as long as the other powers are ready, and then pounce down on France!

Castlereagh tried to deny this, but Whitbread again carried the House in indignation:

'Good God, then! What are we to understand? ... What is this new aggression urged on for now, if not to vamp [patch up] up and restore the Bourbon line? The wittiest man who ever sat in this house [Richard Sheridan] said that "half our nation's debt had been incurred in efforts to suppress the Bourbon Power, the half in efforts to restore it", and I must deprecate a further plunge for ends so futile! Why, since Ministers craved peace with Bonaparte at Châtillon, should they refuse him peace now on the same terms?'[23]

Whitbread then submitted this amendment to Castlereagh's proposed address: 'We at the same time implore that the Prince Regent graciously induce strenuous endeavours in the case of peace, so long as it be done consistently with the due honour of the British Crown.'

Ponsonby demanded of Castlereagh: '... the noble Lord, if that his meaning and pronouncement be immediate war?' Castlereagh replied, 'I have not phrased it so' to which the opposition benches cried, 'The question is un-answered!' Whitbread's amendment was rejected by 220 votes to 37, mainly on the grounds that Britain had no choice but to assist her allies according to the Treaty of Chaumont and that with Austria and France of 3 January. But, in face of such stiff opposition, the government refused to commit Britain to immediate war,[24] and Parliament dissociated itself from the incitements in the declaration of 13 March to outlaw Napoleon or deprive him of his 'legal right to exist'. Wellington was deeply mortified by this censure of his conduct by Members of Parliament, especially Whitbread, who referred to him as an 'assassin's tool'.[25] As Ambassador to France, he had been well aware of the feelings of the French majority, and had only signed the declaration supporting Louis' government and its measures at a time when he was assured that they were in control. With hindsight it is clear that he should never have signed a declaration so worded by Talleyrand.

Next day Castlereagh sent Wellington an official account of the debate and enclosed a private letter:

'Our discussion in both Houses last night was sufficiently satisfactory. Until we can open the whole extent of our confederacy, we must have a reserve; and it is better that our friends [in parliament] should be brought by degrees to look at the prospect of a renewed contest.'

He then discussed the renewed treaty of Chaumont *with an important amendment in the light of parliamentary opposition in his own ranks*:

'That which arises out of Article 8, *stands somewhat on different grounds*. In inviting the King of France, more especially when out of France, to

196

accede to the treaty, we deem it material to mark *that the object of the alliance and concert is to destroy Buonaparte's authority, and not to impose on France any particular Sovereign or form of government. We deem this declaration not less advantageous to the King's interest in France than to the maintenance of the contest in Parliament against Buonaparte.*[26]

In the official letter he added:

'*You will fully appreciate the Parliamentary importance of not having imputed to us* that Louis XVIII., by being made an Ally against Buonaparte, has been made master of the confederacy for his own restoration ... Foreign powers may justly covenant for the destruction of Buonaparte's authority as inconsistent with their own safety, but it is another question avowedly to stipulate as to his successor. *This is a Parliamentary delicacy.*[27]

So, to appease Parliament, Wellington's forces must appear to be remaining in a defensive posture as agreed by the various treaties, while actually waiting for the Allies to assemble. As a sop, Article 8 of the new treaty appeared to leave the choice of a new French government up to the French people or the Coalition partners. Castlereagh was merely playing the same game as before, but this time his inside man was not Talleyrand but, as Artois had informed him, Fouché.

To the Earl of Clancarty, who had replaced Wellington at Vienna, Castlereagh wrote:

'You will see by the papers that, *although in this country,* we are disposed rather to take our tone from the continent, we shall not fail them *in our due exertion; but the Powers of Europe must not expect us to subsidise all the world, or to go beyond certain limits in point of expense. These limits are now held by the Treasury to £5,000,000 subsidy, and 150,000 men, or their financial equivalent under the treaty. If to this you add all our extra expenditure in arms, clothing, ammunition, &c., to Holland, France, &c., you will perceive the effort is not an inconsiderable one at the close of expenditure which, for past charge, independent of this new catastrophe, has rendered it necessary to fund, in course of this year nearly £40,000,000 sterling.*'[28]

Clancarty replied that under the 'new' terms of the treaty:

'It was thought that the change of circumstances which had occurred since the publication of the declaration signed on the 13th ultimo would render it politic again to publish to the world what were the views of the coalesced Powers of Europe under the actual state of things ...'

He informed Castlereagh that the Allies had discussed the situation in France, and had arrived at the conclusion that their were three Parties. The Royalists, who were now useless, a spent force with no respectable policies. Secondly, the Jacobins (republicans), comprising men such as Fouché, La Fayette, Carnot, Benjamin Constant and a multitude of others. These were more approachable. Their demands for representation, a voice in the legislature, equality under the law and property rights accorded with the views of Russia and Britain. Thirdly, the military, some of whom might be induced to attempt a *coup d'état.* Of the three, the Jacobins seemed the best bet – according to the other delegates, most of whom, led by the Tsar, blamed Napoleon's return on the Bourbons' inability to rule, and Louis' failure to honour his treaty with him. Clancarty continued:

> '... But the project as originally framed appeared to me extremely exceptionable in as much as it pointed the whole objects of the Allies to be the removal of Bonaparte and second to have directly and immediately in view the encouragement of the Jacobin Party to raise their own on the ruin of his power and dominion. With this apparent intent all mention of the King seemed carefully excluded, and his party which we pledged by our last declaration to protect apparently deserted ... The extreme anxiety, nay even warmth, evinced upon this subject particularly by the Russians led me however ... rather than to yield my own opinion in consenting to sign an address, than hazard an interruption in the harmony so necessary to be fostered among our allies ... the declaration, a copy of which I enclose, was adopted by the Five, and was afterwards put in circulation to receive also the signatures of the several plenipotentiaries from the crowned heads of Europe. Some of these, however, Spain and Portugal, have objected to sign it in its then shape. It has not yet been published.'[29]

Clancarty also enclosed a private letter, marked 'Secret'. In it he told Castlereagh that the Tsar, Metternich and Talleyrand had each been in contact with the Jacobins, most importantly some of the Marshals and – Fouché. That Talleyrand, now that the Allies were disregarding Louis, was ingratiating himself and offering his services to various Jacobins in Napoleon's ministries. He reported an interview he had had with the Tsar during which Alexander

> '... complained to me that the British minister had impeded the issue of the declaration with a view to pledging the Sovereigns to the specific measure of forcing Louis XVIII on France.[30] Alexander said all were agreed in the necessity of bringing up the largest possible degree of force, but that it was necessary when we are going jointly into war, that we should also agree and understand each other in the particular object of that war; that he had understood that in the conferences of the Five, I had apparently endeavoured to pledge the Allies to the support of a particular dynasty [Bourbon]; this in his opinion counteracted the object which all had in view, viz.: the overthrow of Bonaparte, by leading the French nation in a thorough union against us for the purpose of defending their independence ... I here informed him that he was misinformed.'

The Tsar then talked of other matters: 'That the Jacobin party, were men of considerable talent, indefatigability, activity, extensive influence, and in some of them as Fouché in situations of trust, and in which, if they should be gained the most essential services might be rendered by them to the General cause.' Clancarty said that the Tsar was disparaging of the Bourbons and their supporters:

> '... the King's party was generally composed of *Campagnards* and men who loved the ease and quiet of their usual occupations and who it had been seen, and would continue to be seen, would not lend themselves to any

exertions for the restoration of the king ... He then said that if we were suc-cessful "I [Alexander] might consider elevating a Marshal or General to the throne, like Soult, the Prince Eugène or others"; that he did like Republi-can forms of government as, being weaker, would be less likely to disturb the peace of Europe, and if the French wished for a King, then good! if for the duc d'Orléans, as one born of the revolution, there was nothing to object – and, fixing me, as if to discover what impression his proposition was likely to make, he said, "suppose the Regency of Marie-Louise with the young Prince?"'[31]

Now that Britain had inserted a clause in Article 8 which said that the Allies were not bound to impose a Bourbon restoration, each 'Ally' was canvassing his own choice. Britain's Cabinet members were seeking clandestinely to restore the Bourbons as being weak and pro-British. As the Prime Minister Lord Liverpool had already con-fided to Wellington in February: '... *the keystone to all my policy is the preserving of the Bourbons on the throne of France.*'[32] Metternich was toying with the idea of a republic, and corresponding with Fouché, and the Tsar had sounded out Clancarty on Soult, Eugène, or the Duke of Orléans. Finally, and more ominously, he was suggesting his original 1814 choice, Napoleon's son, under the regency of his mother.

Clancarty reported to Castlereagh the wording of a new declaration that the del-egates had prepared, one more attuned to the circumstances and British parliamen-tary scruples: 'We are at war for the purpose of securing our own independence and for the reconquest of a permanent tranquillity, because France under its present chief can afford no security whatever. We do not desire to interfere with the legitimate right of the French people to choose their own government, but we consider they have a right to contend against any re-establishment of an individual whose past con-duct has demonstrated that in such a situation he will not suffer other nations to be at peace.'[33] As we have seen, Napoleon's peace overtures had been sent back unopened.

On 13 May, nearly two months after Napoleon's return, Clancarty reported that the Tsar had now taken up the cudgels for the rights of Marie-Louise and Napoleon's son under the Treaty of Fontainebleau. Count Nesselrode had requested an interview with Clancarty at which he declared: '... it to be the Emperor's opinion that the Treaty of Fontainebleau remained in full operation, as applicable to the Archduchess and her son.' Clancarty wrote:

'... I could scarcely suppress my surprise at what I heard ... I had consid-ered the matter as finally and irrevocably settled. The Duke of Wellington was present at the meeting at which the arrangement was made ... His reply was not encouraging. He said that the Emperor of Russia was decided upon this subject ... to this I peremptorily objected ... Much more passed, but before he left me he so far softened as to say that nothing short of the Arch-duchess's request could induce his Imperial Majesty to swerve from the line he had adopted in her favour, and recommended my conversing with Prince Metternich ...'[34]

This Clancarty did:

> 'Metternich admitted that the Emperor of Russia was responsible and that he had made promises to the Archduchess at variance with the arrangements of March 28th.'

Clancarty concluded this ominous report by saying that to have given in would have been to admit that the proceedings of the Congress could be altered at the wish of Russia, and that he *suspected the Emperor's motive in his interest in the Archduchess to be a desire for a political alliance with France in the event of her becoming Regent, an alliance which it would not be to the interest of Britain to further.*[35] Six days later Clancarty wrote again to Castlereagh asking for a swift reply because Nesselrode was keeping up the pressure. He told Castlereagh that: '... Nesselrode, on his part, afforded no hope that the Emperor would alter his course.' Clancarty declined to sign any treaty appertaining to Italy until the question of Parma was settled (the Treaty of Fontainebleau had given sovereignty of Parma and Placentia to Marie-Louise and her son). In an enclosed private and illuminating letter Clancarty poured out his anger, and requested instructions from Castlereagh:

> '... Upon the Parma question, I beseech you to stand our friend, and to send us your opinions without delay. I never yet was so embarrassed. Will you set a precedent of placing Buonaparte's bastard on a throne? Will you remake the treaty of Fontainebleau *quoad* this offspring of a usurper? Will you make a present *to the Emperor of Russia of the sole dictatorship of the affairs of Europe? And play into his hands, so as to further alliances for him hostile to the existence of any European balance? Will you, now the poor King of France is down, give him an additional blow, by reversing those things which, while he was in prosperity, you desired to see carried into effect? These are the questions for your decisions, which I attend with the utmost impatience.'*[36]

Clancarty's letter is very revealing of the conflicting interests and mutual mistrust of the so-called 'Allies'. Before Castlereagh's reply could arrive, however, an even more devisive breach was to materialize. Napoleon, on returning to the Tuileries, had found in a drawer of the Marquis de Jarcout, Talleyrand's deputy, the secret treaty between Austria, France, Bavaria and Britain, ratified less than three months previously. Napoleon called in Butiagin, the secretary of the Russian legation, and allowed him to make a copy – including the secret protocols dealing with operational details. This was sent to the Tsar in Vienna. Alexander had long known that there had been talk of a secret treaty; he had taxed Castlereagh outright and his denial had seemed evasive. He summoned Metternich and asked him if he knew 'this document'. Metternich stood mute with shock.[37]

Alexander then summoned King William of Prussia and asked him the same question. The King's expression changed from absolute shock, to absolute fury. Explanations, recriminations and defensive arguments were put forward by the various ministers. The Tsar cut them all short and in rage threw the document in the fireplace. The King of Bavaria attempted to apologize but was stopped abruptly by the Tsar who said. 'You were drawn into it, I no longer think about it.' Butiagin had also enclosed a letter from ex-Queen Hortense, who wrote assuring Alexander 'on my honour', that Napoleon would not interfere with the Polish settlement.

The Tsar left Vienna and went via Munich and Stuttgart to his advance head-quarters at Heilbronn. There he wrote to his brother Constantine that he could no longer trust the Austrians, or Bavarians and Britain. That he would be guided in his future actions by events. That he would *NOT* hazard his army at behest of the Aus-trians and British in order to replace their Bourbon puppet: 'It would suite Austria to weaken Russia and then turn on us in our Polish Kingdom.'[38]

Prussia's generals, especially von Gneisenau, were furious at Britain and Austria's per-fidy. Within a year of the war's end Britain had signed a secret treaty with France against Prussia, her loyal ally, in defence of France! No wonder Britain had betrayed them over Saxony! Napoleon had said that he had returned with British aid; perhaps that was true. What game was Britain up to? And what of Austria? They were two-faced. Had they not even married their daughter to Napoleon? They had reclaimed Italy, the Tyrol and more, yet out of envy they had prevented Prussia from gaining Saxony for fear of losing their predominance in Germany. Such were the views aired by the General Staff and the Berlin newspapers when the existence of the treaty was made public.[39]

War was now inevitable. Liverpool and Castlereagh's government would not countenance peace with Napoleon; to do so in their view would mean having to keep Britain on a permanent war-footing. Not only that, but a weak, subservient, even dependent, Bourbon throne would suit Britain's trading interests. Prussia feared the prospect of again being reduced by Napoleon and was out for revenge for all the wrongs suffered. The Tsar feared Napoleon's power and ambition, but had now had a taste of the bad faith of Britain, Austria and even Prussia. He was reviewing his options. Napoleon had offered him the olive branch and he was prepared to take a leaf out of the Austrian book and maintain a masterly inactivity. His so-called allies had opposed his creation of a Polish state in defence of his vulnerable border, and had agreed to declare war on him if they saw fit. They needed his manpower but did not want his leadership. Very well! He would not commit any of his troops until he saw British and Austrian troops actually engaging the French. As he said to his brother, he had little to lose and everything to gain by waiting.

The Austrian Emperor, related to Napoleon by marriage and holding his wife and son, would also wait and see. Italy and Murat were his first priority, and would be his excuse for not immediately fielding his main force against France. Let Russia expend her enormous resources of manpower in the effort, though who knew what the Tsar might require afterwards by way of compensation?

Here then were the 'Allies', after months of diplomatic squabbling, more deeply divided than before, and united only by their so-called Treaty of Chaumont, their fear of Napoleon's ability, and their greed for British subsidies.

Napoleon had hoped that with his 'bloodless' return (only to find the Crown of France 'in the gutter'), aided by virtually the entire population, his offer of constitu-tional monarchy and acceptance of the old French borders would induce the Powers to allow him to rule France in peace.

After quitting Paris, Louis and Artois with Macdonald and Berthier had headed for Lille in a huge cavalcade of carriages and wagons protected by nearly 4,000 household troops and royalist volunteers. At Lille Marshal Mortier told Louis that he had better not stay because he couldn't vouch for his safety. Louis had been deluded into thinking that he could form a provisional government here in the north – remaining on French soil, but with a secure escape route. Now he was advised to go to Dunkirk, but this would mean crossing Belgian soil, or rather that of the now United Netherlands. Once across the border, he decided not to risk his neck at Dunkirk but make for Brussels and Wellington's army. Having done their duty, Macdonald requested permission to retire to his country estate, and Berthier to his castle at Bamberg. Louis sent a request to King William of The Netherlands to be allowed the use of the Laeken palace at Brussels. Dominated by the British Cabinet, William refused this provocation of Napoleon. Offended, Louis went instead to the house of a nobleman in Ghent, d'Hane de Steenhuyse, who, being able to trace his lineage back to the 15th century, was considered 'suitable'.

Artois meanwhile was struggling along by another route with the royal household troops acting as a rearguard. These chocolate-box soldiers, noblemen all, were unable to present any semblance of being a military formation in this journey from Paris to Ghent. They were in a constant state of anxiety lest any of Napoleon's regulars were after them. Having taken to byroads to avoid detection, they found that their horses and wagons and horses were foundering in mud. Lamartine gives a vivid picture: '... the luxurious state-carriages full of the mothers, wives, and daughters of ministers, generals, and *émigrés*; the wagons and guns that mingled with these vehicles; the servants and strings of chargers and hunters belonging to the princes, interrupted and broke up and delayed the regular march of the troops at every step. The comte d'Artois, and his son the duc de Berry rode beside the troops, exposed to the inclement weather, drenched with rain and covered with mud.'[40] Some of the noble officers had served in Napoleon's army and they declared that they had suffered less on the retreat from Moscow.[41] By the time Ypres was reached, fatigue, fear and the urge for self-preservation had reduced the ranks of the 4,000 that had set out, and only a few hundred remained. When the comte d'Artois arrived at Ghent he found that only two Marshals had followed the King into exile: Marmont, duc de Raguse and Victor, duc de Bellune. Artois ranted at the folly of allowing Berthier to leave. He had been Napoleon's right arm for nearly twenty years. In every campaign he had transmitted Napoleon's orders into tangible, concise and precise forms. His system had enabled Napoleon to throw his armies at any given point with almost clockwork precision – as at Ulm in 1805 when his staffwork had brought the *Grande Armée* from Boulogne and Germany in eight corps to surround the Austrian army and trap the 'unhappy Mack' within the town. Berthier had found some favour with Louis, but his talents had not been utilized, and for the most part he had been humiliated; the Congress had been urged to strip him of his princedom of Neufchâtel and Vallengin, but he had been allowed to retain his 'battlefield' title of 'Prince of Wagram'.

The son of a minor nobleman, Berthier had been on Marshal Rochambeau's staff during the War of American Independence and had served at Yorktown. In the National Guard during the Revolution, he had assisted two of Louis XVI's sisters to escape. The revolutionary government stripped him of all his family possessions and allowed him to serve in the army as a private. In 1795 Lazare Carnot, the great organizer of the Revolutionary armies – the 'Nation in Arms' – remembered Berthier and had him appointed as a staff officer in what was to become the 'Army of Italy', which saw the beginning of his remarkable 'partnership' with Napoleon. Berthier was shown no gratitude for having risked his life for the royal family, and was despised for having fought, like Louis' cousin, Phillipe-Egalité, for the revolutionaries instead of emigrating. The Prince of Poix would deliberately insult him by addressing him by his surname only as though he were a *bourgeois*: 'It's funny, all the same Berthier, that just because of the Revolution you should be able to call yourself a prince like me.'[42]

Now that the absurd Louis had allowed the greatest staff officer of the era to leave, might he not rejoin Napoleon who had raised him so high and ensured that he married well (to a cousin of the King of Württemberg)? Napoleon urgently wanted him to return, saying to Count Rapp: 'He was the best of Staff-Generals. He had a quicker perception of every thought and plan than anyone else, and explained them better to the head of corps. I should like to see him even in his uniform as captain of the [king's] bodyguard.' In early May Berthier was attempting to rejoin his master, travelling via Basle, but had been turned back at Stockach by the Prince of Hohenzollen.[43] The comte d'Artois decided that he could not risk Berthier's joining Napoleon and arranged for his elimination. On 1 June 1815, Berthier was supposed to have been balancing on a chair by the open casemate in a turret of his castle in Bamberg, observing the Allied troops through a telescope, lost his balance or become dizzy, and fallen to his death on the flagstones below. In fact agents of Artois had thrown him from the window,[44] thereby dealing Napoleon an irreparable blow.

Peace for Napoleon was impossible. Britain feared him too much. The British people had sacrificed too much and the government had expended too much money in the effort to overthrow the 'Ogre' of British propaganda. If it could be shown that Napoleon could peacefully co-exist with Britain, it might beg the question as to why Britain's politicians had not attempted a genuine peace at Amiens and afterwards. The prospect of his remaining in power raised the frightful spectre of Voltaire's concept of an 'enlightened despot' ruling a classless society. Already this heretical doctrine had percolated into the German states and Italy to give those peoples a sense of nationhood as opposed to subservience under an autocrat. What the European monarchs, including Britain's, wanted was a return to the old order of a class-structured society in which the lower orders knew their place. Leave this *Rights of Man* nonsense to America, where it originated; it was far enough away as not to contaminate Europe. Furthermore, Napoleon was a military genius. Given time might he not regain all that he had lost?.

For these reasons, Europe would not let Napoleon rule France – even if it were the will of the French people. His peace overtures rejected, he knew now that war was imminent. He could wait to be attacked, as in 1814, but this would be demoralizing for his people and his troops. Nor was it his way of making war. A quick thrust, a decisive battle, and dictation of peace, that was his style.

Belgium! It had always been Belgium. Ever since the French Republic had incorporated Belgium, Britain had financed and waged war against them. The French people considered Belgium as an integral part of France; they shared a common language, culture and religion. Napoleon's greatest triumph as a revolutionary general had been the Treaty of Campo Formio by which Austria had ceded Belgium to France. Napoleon himself had his palace of Laeken there, purchased from Arch-Duke Charles of Austria. Louis also had taken refuge there. Napoleon had hoped that he would cross the Channel and his farcical restoration be shown up for what it was, a foreign imposition. Louis must be driven out to become once more Britain's weak, emasculated dependant. Wellington and his Netherlands army were there. So were the Prussians. If he could strike quickly and decisively defeat Britain, forcing her out of Europe, and then threaten her Kingdom of Hanover, she might think again about peace. Prussia too. If he could defeat the Prussians and send them reeling back to Prussia, weak King William would soon make peace. Then how long would his old German satellites remain loyal to their new masters and restored ducal overlords? Saxony and Poland would certainly rise. Italy was a hotbed of discontent ready to explode. In this new situation Austria would soon come to terms, or risk the loss of her army. Perhaps he might have to threaten to go to hear mass again in Vienna – as in 1805.

Russia! Napoleon doubted if the Tsar would attack him for the benefit of the Austrians or the British. How would the Russian generals react to the prospect of risking all that they had gained in order to assist those who had signed a treaty against them three months previously? What would Russia stand to gain? Napoleon could offer Alexander the whole of Poland if need be, and parts of Austria and Prussia. If he, Napoleon, could beat Wellington and Blücher in Belgium, seize Brussels and the north bank of the Rhine, all that had been lost since 1812 might be regained.

Napoleon had little to fear from Spain. Like his Bourbon cousins, King Ferdinand was having trouble turning the clock back to 1808. Having had a taste of freedom under their *juntas* and the *Cortes* and partisan groups during the six years of his exile, the people were disgruntled with their absolutist and backward-looking king. Ferdinand would not want to see another French army marching over the Pyrenees. Push the British out of The Netherlands and they would have a hard job to gain another footing in Europe. Napoleon had striven, marched and countermarched throughout 1813 and 1814 in search of the elusive decisive battle. In Belgium he would find it and, given the right circumstances, everything would be changed: his position, the Alliance, and the security of his dynasty. On this decisive battle would hang his destiny and that of Europe for years to come.

CHAPTER 10

THE ROAD TO THE NORTH

'The young men shall fight; the married men shall forge weapons and transport supplies;
the women will make tents and serve in the hospitals; the children will make up old linen into lint;
the old men will have themselves carried into the public squares to rouse the fighting men, and to
preach the hatred of kings and the unity of the republic. The public buildings shall be turned into
barracks, the public squares into munitions factories; the earthen floors of cellars shall be treated
with lye to extract saltpetre. All suitable firearms shall be turned over to the troops; the interior
shall be policed with fowling pieces and with cold steel. All saddle horses shall be seized by
the cavalry; all draft horses not employed in cultivation will draw the artillery wagons.'
– Lazare Carnot, Decree of the Committee of Public Safety, 23 August 1793.
The Nation in Arms.

NAPOLEON, ONCE AGAIN HEAD OF STATE, WAS FACED WITH a daunting situation. The Allies were united, in principle at least, against him. The Bourbons had run down the army, which was badly equipped and packed with royalist officers who neither knew nor cared anything about job. Before leaving Paris, Louis' gang had not only looted the national treasury but had stolen his personal fortune and shared most of it among themselves; it should have been handed over to the state treasury from which his pension was supposed to have been paid.[1]

Napoleon had been surprised by the revolutionary fervour displayed everywhere on his progress from the coast, and now leading Jacobins – Carnot, La Fayette and Benjamin Constant – were supporting him. Indeed it seems likely that if he had not returned, a spontaneous revolution would have erupted supported by these men. Lazare Carnot, architect of the revolutionary armies, summed-up the feelings of the nation in a memorial which he sent to King Louis six months previously. Louis, fearful of the mob, had not had him arrested. Napoleon found it among the king's papers, and authorized its publication. Needless to say it didn't appear in any foreign newspaper. Carnot upbraided Louis and his nobles for their treatment of the French people, and concluded:

'... to forgive everything that is past, to rob no one of his post nor his honours, to allow the men who are innocent of flattery to remain in the Senate, to admit to the less important offices those who have been led astray by too great a love of liberty, to honour the army without seeming to be forgiving its impious victories – that is what should be done. And what, as a matter of fact, has been done? All the men who are known to be patriots have been regarded as a hostile population surrounded by another population which has been indiscreetly treated with marked favouritism. If you wish, today, to be well received at Court, you must be careful not to say that you are one of the twenty-five million citizens who defended their country, with more or less courage, against the invasion of her enemies; for you will be told that those twenty-five millions of so-called citizens are twenty-five million rebels, and that the so-called enemies were always friends. You must say that you are fortunate enough to have been a Chouan, or a Vendéean, or a turncoat, or a Cossack, or an Englishman; or that, though you remained in France, you never asked for any office under ephemeral governments that preceded the Restoration, except with the object of being in a better position to betray them and accelerate their fall. Then, your fidelity will be lauded to the skies; you will receive tender congratulations, and decorations, and affectionate answers from all the royal family.'[2]

In an endeavour to remove political dissent, Napoleon had requested Benjamin Constant to formulate a new constitution which would reduce his status to that of a constitutional monarch. In effect, he would accept France on the terms that Louis had rejected: 'freely called to the throne by the will of the people' and approved by an overwhelming plebiscite. He reasoned that France and the security of his dynasty were worth the loss of certain prerogatives. Where before the diverse factions had united under him *faute de mieux*, the people now, having experienced the Bourbon regime, identified his cause with theirs. During the brief restoration every bumpkin, provincial squire or 'gentleman' that could lay claim to a coat of arms, no matter how spurious, had come out of the wood-work to demand compensation for supposed hardships. A title ensured employment or a military commission. The army, prefectural corps and civil service were crammed with these parvenus, many of whom had purchased their titles and posts.[3] Artois, his sons and the comte de Blacas' agents had practised a lucrative trade in these purchases which brought an added bonus of creating a lower strata of loyal nobility to keep the peasants in order. By his decree issued at Lyons, Napoleon had annulled titles and honours, but it would take time to remove this 'fifth column' from their positions, time that would allow them access to information and opportunities for sabotage.[4]

The sinews of war required money. Napoleon immediately instructed the banker Perregaux to invalidate the bills of exchange issued to the Bourbons and payable on London banks, thereby recovering 8,000,000 francs and depriving the royalists of these funds. Baron Louis, who had been making free with the national funds to speculate on the bourse, had fled without mentioning these funds to his royal master, and Napoleon recovered another 50,000,000 francs. Luckily for the Emperor, he had returned by 20 March when the three-monthly instalments of the current year's taxes fell due, and so realized a further 40,000,000 francs. Napoleon also negotiated a loan on all the state forestry lands of 150,000,000 francs, a sum that would have staggered the greedy Bourbons.

From 20 March to 1 June 1815, the energetic activity of Napoleon and his people surpassed anything manifested during the Revolution. He found the poorly equipped army standing at 200,000 men, including volunteers – on paper. Some 32,800 men were listed as being 'on leave' and 82,000 as deserters. The first figure represented men who had been sent on leave to avoid paying them. The deserters were men who didn't want to serve in anyone's army, and pro-imperialists who had simply quit when the Bourbons took charge. Napoleon's decree re-calling these men resulted by early June in 82,446 with the Colours and 23,448 on the way from the various depots to which they had reported.[5] Realizing that his navy would be of little use in the coming conflict, Napoleon ordered forty battalions to be raised from naval personnel. France was in danger, so Napoleon activated the decrees of the years 1791, 1792 and 1805 which had never been repealed. These gave him the right to mobilize the National Guard and to raise its numbers to those prescribed for time of war. There were 200,000 National Guardsmen throughout France. By mobilizing the eligible men aged between 20 and 60, Carnot informed the Chambers, France's population would yield 2,500,000 men given time – and weapons.[6] But France was an agricultural country and Napoleon had no intention of stripping the land of so many men. By 15 June, 234,720 National Guardsmen had been summoned, of whom 150,000 had already assembled at various depots. There were more half-pay officers than his field army could employ, so he used them to train and command these units. Remembering how untrained National Guardsmen had performed at Fère-Champenoise, Napoleon decided that with the right training they would become as good as line troops – differing in name only.

Napoleon knew that his previous conscriptions had alienated the people, and had surrendered this right to the new constitutional Chambers. He now asked them to call up the class of year 1815, but this they refused to do; they wanted to see whether he would ignore his charter as had the Bourbons. Napoleon would not. He consulted his War Minister, Davout, who pointed out that in 1814 Napoleon had already called up the class of 1815, but as they had been neither mobilized nor discharged, they were eligible for recall. Napoleon put this to the Chambers, stating that while respecting their prerogative, he had to point out that the country was in danger. The Council of State agreed that Napoleon had the right to recall them, that it was not a new conscription, but a valid one still in force, the ballot having been lawfully carried out.

On 11 June, one week after their recall, 46,419 men of year 1815 had been mobilized and were ready to march. 'The conscripts of 1815 have joined in three days with amazing readiness,' reported the prefect of the *département* of Seine-et-Oise. In the *département* of the Aisne, which had been heavily occupied by the Allies during the war, the prefect reported 18,200 extra volunteers! to which Napoleon commented: 'In that département will be found as many men as there are muskets to give them.'[7] These people had suffered under the Allies and wanted revenge. In less than two months Napoleon had raised the field or regular army to 284,000 men. To these he had added an auxiliary army of 220,000 National Guardsmen to give a total of 504,000 men under arms.[8] By 15 June there were a further 80,500 men in the depots. Between 15 July and 25 September a further 74,000 men of the 1815 call-up would be available, and another 84,000 men of the National Guard, plus 70,000 men in the west who would be liable for mobilization. By 1 October 1815, Napoleon would be able to field an army of 800,000 men[9] without having had to resort to any new conscription.

Having reformed his government, provided finance for the nation and raised his land forces to more than half a million men, Napoleon now applied his superlative administrative abilities to the problems of arming and equipping them. Virtually everything that the army possessed dated from the campaigns of 1814. Much *matériel* that had been accumulated had been sold off as 'army surplus' to line royalist pockets and reduce the strength of the army. The men were in want of everything. There was a scarcity of muskets, ammunition, uniforms, greatcoats and shoes; guns, gun-carriages, wagons, bayonets and flints. 'The salvation of the nation,' wrote the Emperor to Davout, 'depends on the number of muskets we can shoulder.'[10]

Under the Bourbons, unemployment had soared like a rocket. It was all one to them if the workers again had 'to eat cake' so long as they themselves had funds to squander in the pursuit of the wastrel pleasures of a bygone age.

Napoleon had mobilized the nation for war, and his and the nation's needs were great. All armourers discharged by the Bourbons and those who had been exempted from former conscription on professional grounds were recalled to employment. Imperial factories opened all over the country on Napoleon's order for 235,000 muskets with bayonets, and 15,000 pairs of pistols. The great cutlery manufacturers of Moulins and the Langres took on hundreds of employees on day and night shifts to produce bayonets and swords. In Paris and all over France, tailors, seamstresses and clothiers set up factories to produce uniforms, Paris alone turning out 1,250 uniforms a day. Tanners, leather craftsmen, cobblers and glove-makers combined to produce 195,0000 pairs of boots, leather equipment, harness and other horse equipment. Thousands were employed in the manufacture of munitions. At Vincennes, 12,000,0000 cartridges were produced by hand in two months, this involving paper manufacture, gunpowder production and the moulding of musket-balls.

Throughout the country artillery charges were likewise produced. Wheelwrights, coopers, carpenters and metal-workers combined to turn out gun-carriages, wagons, ambulances, mobile forges and bridging wagons. In all the towns, the prefects organized gunsmiths, watch-makers, cabinet-makers and brass-foundries to assist in the repair and manufacture of muskets which resulted in the production of 40,000 muskets a month. Napoleon had placards posted saying that any muskets in private possession, or retrieved from the battlefields of the previous conflict would be purchased at 12 francs each; 11,035 muskets of various calibres came in and were exchanged with the Gendarmerie muskets so that the army would have a uniform musket for ammunition purposes.

On his return, Napoleon had found that the army had only 27,864 horses; the artillery and transports a mere 7,765, the Bourbons having rented out 5,000 of the latter to save on their upkeep and to provide the new 'colonel-generals' with further income. Napoleon required every *département* to provide 8,000 suitable horses, to be paid for in cash on arrival. He also requisitioned half the Gendarmerie's horses, but each Gendarme was given 600 francs to purchase a remount; Napoleon knew that the Gendarmes would find suitable replacements more easily than could his agents.

This dodge supplied Napoleon immediately with 4,250 well-trained heavy cavalry horses, and within eight weeks he had purchased 56,500.

Invasion was certain, so fortifications were the next priority. Napoleon ordered the prefects, commanders of military districts and the mayors of towns to report the state of their defences and to commence forthwith all measures required to fortify towns, cities, strategic bridges, mountain passes and river crossings. Repairs were authorized, and stockades, earthworks and ramparts were erected. Throughout the country tens of thousands of workmen were employed continuously, building slopes, escarpments, stockades and earthworks. By these measures alone, unemployment had been removed at a stroke. The lessons of 1814 had not been lost on Napoleon or the people. Paris and Lyons were put in a state of defence and the naval arsenals were ordered to supply fortress cannon and naval guns for these defences. Mindful of the last campaign, Napoleon had 14,000 fowling pieces with ammunition issued to the peasants in the *départements* most at risk from invaders. Doubtless the Austrian and Russian forces, if they invaded, would come by the same route as before. The peasants had much to remember and avenge. This time the entire population would be behind them; the *levée en masse* would come into operation immediately. No further proof is needed to show that Napoleon's return was not just a 'rash adventure'. He had the support of the army and the nation in a counter-revolution – without the active assistance of the people none of this would have been possible.

Napoleon now had to create a new high command structure for his armies. Marshal Davout,[11] who had shown himself to be his most loyal and ardent supporter in all the marshalate, was appointed Minister of War, Governor of Paris, and commander of the National Guard. Whatever happened in the weeks to come, Paris would not be taken by intrigue, *coups d'état* or through lack of a dependable commander. Marshal Augereau, named by Napoleon as one of the two military traitors who had caused his defeat in 1814, and who had been rallying royalist supporters in the 14th Military District to remain loyal to the Bourbons, on hearing that Napoleon had reached the Tuileries had posted a placard throughout his command announcing '... The Emperor is in the capital! The name that so long was a pledge of victory has sufficed to scatter all his enemies before him ... Let us therefore wear the colours of the Nation!' This may have stopped his men lynching the traitor, but Napoleon had not forgotten his abandonment of Lyons and his men; nor his proclamation stating '... the coward didn't know how to die!'[12] He and Marmont were struck off the roll of Marshals of the Empire forthwith.

Marshal Masséna, duc de Rivoli, prince d'Essling and duc de Rivoli, was in command of the *département* of the Var when Napoleon landed and could have captured him immediately, but the Emperor had sent him a letter, which ended: '... Remember that the victor of Zurich was naturalized as a Frenchman by a Voismnil! [*sic*]'[13] (Masséna, respected by Wellington as his great adversary, had received that year a letter from the 81-year-old Joseph d'Houx, marquis de Viomésnil who, having been informed that the marshal had been born in Nice, then part of Piedmont and belonging to the King of Sardinia, stated that the great warrior was a 'foreigner'. De

Viomésnil had 'kindly' issued letters patent to Masséna naturalizing him as a 'French subject', on receipt of which Masséna had raged: 'Letters of naturalization, to me, Masséna! To me, Masséna!')[14] The great Marshal concentrated furiously on maintaining a masterful inactivity while Napoleon was advancing on Grenoble, but as soon as he had regained Paris Masséna took swift action to prevent the duc d'Angoulême from seizing Toulon and 'selling' it to the British, and effectively cut off his line of supply and reinforcement.[15] Masséna was also instrumental in the capture of Baron Vitrolles who had been sent to Toulouse to form a provisional government, aided by Marshal Pérignon; Napoleon struck the latter from the roll of marshals. Berthier had not returned so Napoleon, unaware that his faithful friend had been prevented from coming back to France, reluctantly struck him off too. Marshals Saint-Cyr, Jourdan, Kellermann and Macdonald declined to serve: Louis had accepted their oaths of allegiance and allowed them to retain the titles, wealth and estates granted by Napoleon. They decided that they would sit out the conflict without risking their lives or their liberty; whatever the outcome, they considered themselves secure. Napoleon, remembering Macdonald's loyal service *after* his abdication, sent Davout to see if he could persuade him to return. He declined, but Napoleon accepted this and did not strike him off.

When Napoleon returned to France, old Marshal Moncey had issued a proclamation against him, but in recognition of his attempted defence of Paris he was allowed to retire. Marshal Sérurier had also accepted Louis, but he was retained as governor of Les Invalides. The night before the surrender in 1814, Sérurier had ordered the old veterans of the Invalides to destroy all the trophies there to prevent their recapture by the Allies. A total of 1,417 flags were burnt, including British flags dating from the time of Charles I and the Battle of Fontenoy; Austrian, Russian and Prussian flags from the Seven Years War, the Revolution, and Napoleon's fourteen years of victories. All were consigned to the flames. Sérurier personally burned the sash, insignia and sword of Frederick the Great, Napoleon's supreme trophies, taken from the King's tomb after the defeat of Prussia in 1806. Napoleon had said his generals as they entered the tomb: 'Hats off gentlemen, if he were still alive, we would not be here!' The ashes from this pyre were shovelled into wagons and dumped in the Seine.

Marshal Lefebvre felt that he was too old to fight, but he accepted a seat in Napoleon's Senate. Masséna too was no longer very active so he was transferred from the important 9th Military District (Var) to titular command of the 4th and 5th Military Districts that encompassed the Moselle, Meurthe and Vosges where lay the key frontier fortresses of the north, which Napoleon knew Masséna would hold.

Oudinot, who had tried so hard to keep his troops loyal to Louis, begged Davout, Ney and Suchet to intercede for him; he was afraid that his children would be disinherited. Napoleon revoked his order of exile, but would not employ him again, and in fact it is doubtful whether any troops would have served under him; in their eyes he was a traitor. Napoleon was left with a much reduced Marshalate. The newly created Grouchy would command the main field army under Napoleon himself. Marshal Brune, who had rallied immediately to Napoleon on his return, had been in disgrace since 1807 for lining his pockets – in company with Bourrienne. Napoleon had it given out that it was because of Brune's wording of a treaty with Sweden. But Brune, republican and anti-Bourbon, was loyal, and Napoleon forgave him and assigned him the Army of the Var, based on that important *département*.

Marshal Suchet, who like Davout had immediately rallied to Napoleon, was given the Army of the Jura, based on Lyons, a vital command to plug access from the Swiss border to the plains of Langres.

Marshal Mortier, Napoleon's old commander of the élite Young Guard, had been honoured by Louis and made commander of the 16th Military District, based on Lille. Mortier had quashed Count d'Erlon's attempt to take the city's garrison over to Napoleon in early March, and had ignored Davout's repeated orders to arrest Louis XVIII, but helped him to escape. On his arrival at the Tuileries, Napoleon had greeted him as 'Monsieur le Blanc',[16] but had appointed him to command first the cavalry, then the newly raised Young Guard in the forthcoming campaign.

Marshal Ney was sent on a tour of inspection and kept at a distance. He had fully re-converted to the imperial fold; like the nation, he identified his future and that of his children with the restored regime. But Napoleon found it difficult to forgive Ney for forcing his abdication at Fontainebleau instead of helping him secure his decisive battle and, while undergoing a crisis of loyalties, telling Louis that he would bring Napoleon back in an iron cage. Napoleon had had genuine affection for Ney and had taken an interest in his career. He respected his courage, bravery and – up to 1814 – his loyalty. It was the feeling of personal betrayal, of hurt, which in time would have healed, that Ney did not appreciate. His point of view was that he had rallied to his chief and expected to start with a clean slate.[17] This personality/sensitivity clash did not bode well for the future.

Lastly, there was Soult. Napoleon weighed up the propaganda value of having Louis' ex-Minister of War on his side. He was not keen on being seen as having been deserted by all those that he had elevated to the highest ranks. On the other hand Soult had offended and affronted Napoleon more than any other Marshal. He had been a good field commander in Spain, and during the last campaign against Wellington had disputed every foot of soil. But he was detested by the entire army. The generals had not forgotten the Exelmans affair, or that after Napoleon had landed Soult had indicated his intention of having Generals d'Erlon, Vandamme, Reille, Dumas and the Lallemand brothers shot for the abortive coup in the north. Had Napoleon been defeated, there is little doubt that he would have carried this out. The army remembered also that he had refused General Travot, a good soldier, any employment until such time as he handed back his 'national property' estate to its rightful, pre-revolutionary, royalist owner. When Travot had purchased it for 250,000 francs, it had already had two owners since the Revolution.[18]

On 8 March, when he received the news of Napoleon's landing, Soult had alienated the rank and file by publishing a proclamation to the army:

'*Soldiers! This man who lately abdicated, under the eyes of all Europe, the usurped power, of which he made so fatal a use, this Bonaparte has returned*

211

to the soil of France, which he had no right ever to see again ... Bonaparte despises us enough to believe that we could abandon a legitimate and beloved sovereign, to share the fate of a man who is the merest adventurer ... Let us rally round the banner of the Lys, at the summons of this father of his people, this worthy heir of the great Henri's virtues.'[19]

The junior officers could not forget the ministerial order published by him on the same day: 'Many officers who ask for the royal and military Order of Saint-Louis omit to accompany their request by a declaration of religion.'[20] Royalist Soult, on his own initiative, was pushing the Artois and *émigrés'* line that nothing be given to Protestants or others who did not profess the Catholic faith.

Napoleon and the army were also aware that Soult had done everything in his power to ensure Napoleon's capture, and to carry out Louis' ordinance of 6 March by bringing the Emperor in front of a military tribunal and having him shot. The only reason that Soult was now asking for employment was because he had been dismissed at the last moment by Louis in favour of Clarke, duc de Feltre, Napoleon's ex-minister of war who had betrayed him and Paris in 1814. Under the circumstances, Clarke was unlikely to change sides. Soult, having been a professed royalist and having been dismissed by Louis, did not have the honesty, like Macdonald and Saint-Cyr, to remain in retirement, faithful to his oath to '*the worthy heir of the great Henri's virtues*'. Having seen the army and the people rallying to Napoleon, and having witnessed the débâcle of the Bourbon departure, he was worried that he might have backed the wrong side. He did not want to be stripped of his titles, his position and his income, hence his pleading for employment with the age-old excuse that 'he had only been obeying orders'. Napoleon decided under no circumstances to entrust an independent command to Soult; a man who could turn his coat so quickly might be tempted to do so again – at a critical juncture, like Marmont. On the other hand, remembering the Malet plot, Napoleon was not going to leave him behind while he went to war. Soult had long been used to an independent command, and issuing his own movement orders, and as a Minister of War, issuing orders and movements to the whole army. Napoleon decided to use him, and offered him Berthier's old post of chief of staff. Soult would continue to transmit orders to the army, but under Napoleon's direct supervision.[21]

Napoleon had no trouble finding good fighting generals, and corps commanders. A marshal, after all, was only a general who had been given a title. Since 1813, Napoleon had noticed that, loaded with honours and wealth, his marshals no longer had much incentive to risk all they had acquired on the battlefield. Grouchy had been elevated almost immediately on the Emperor's return, deliberately, as an object lesson. Napoleon, the Emperor, was the creator of marshals and reputations. The new corps commanders knew that they had the opportunity to gain a marshal's baton and be elevated to the highest ranks of the peerage; all that was required was a resounding triumph in battle. They would be eager to fight and win. Promotion was once more open to all. The Legion of Honour again meant what its title suggested and would be awarded irrespective of rank. Napoleon had also shown that what he had given, could also be taken away. Marshals had been struck from the rolls. There were now places to be filled.

The new commanders were: General d'Erlon,[22] I Corps, 20,000 men at Valenciennes; General Reille, II Corps, 25,000 men at Avesnes; General Vandamme, III Corps, 20,000 men at Rocroi; General Gérard, IV Corps, 15,000 men at Metz; General Mouton-Lobau, VI Corps, 10,000 men at Laon. The Imperial Guard, 20,000 men at Compiègne and Paris, would be under Napoleon's personal command. Marshal Grouchy was initially to command the four reserve cavalry corps of about 3,500 men each. This was Napoleon's field army, designated '*l'Armée du Nord*', totalling 124,000 men.[23]

Independent, corps-size armies were given to: General Rapp, '*Armée du Rhin*', 23,000 men; Marshal Suchet, '*l'Armée des Alpes*', 23,500 men; Marshal Brune, '*l'Armée du Var*', 5,500 men. Marshal Davout was given the Paris garrison of 20,000 men plus the city's National Guard. General Lecourbe, '*l'Armée du Jura*', 8,400 men; General Clausel, '*l'Armée des Pyrénées-Occidentales*', 6,800 men; General Decaen, '*l'Armée des Basses-Pyrénées*', 7,600 men; General Lamarque, '*l'Armée de l'Ouest*', 10,000 men. This mobile reserve, numbering 104,800 men, would guard the coastal towns, fortifications and the Mediterranean ports and borders. Another 81,000 men of the *départments*' National Guards would perform the same role in the interior. These static defences totalled 142,000 men.[24] A further 133,200 men due to report, receiving training or awaiting equipment, and destined for line regiments, the Imperial Guard and the mobilized National Guard[25] would give Napoleon 504,000 men under command.

Facing Napoleon and France were the Allied forces. In Belgium, the Duke of Wellington's Anglo-Allied army of 107,000 British, Hanoverian, Dutch, Belgian, Brunswicker and Nassau-Oranienburger troops. On the Prussian/Belgian border, Field Marshal Blücher's Army of the Lower Rhine, 128,000 troops from Prussia and Saxony. Close to him was General von Kleist with a Prussian corps of 25,000 men, converging on the French fortress of Sedan. The main Austrian Army, 210,000 men, composed mainly of Bavarians, Württembergers and other Confederation troops – fewer than half of them Austrians – would not move before the Russians arrived, but were being kept well out of range,[26] to support the 75,000 troops under Frimont who were holding the border with the Papal states and Naples. The Russian armies of Witzingerode and Barclay de Tolly, numbering 200,000 men, had begun their advance from the Vistula and Niemen on 5 April, and were still on Russian and Polish soil in late May. The Tsar was in no hurry to commit his troops; others could bear the brunt so far as he was concerned. Spain and Portugal were supposed to be sending a contingent of 80,000 troops, but this threat was not taken seriously by Napoleon; Ferdinand had enough problems without assembling a force that might well turn against him.

Napoleon's plans for the forthcoming campaign and the defence of France were brilliantly conceived. He had once said: '... the scheme of campaign often contains the plan of battle. None but superior minds can appreciate this ...'[27] He would use the same strategy as that envisaged for his 'decisive battle': in essence, detach a small part of his army to pin down part of the enemy's army; attack the rest with his main army and having defeated it bring all his forces to bear on the remainder. Napoleon had deployed his armies in three lines. The first was static, manning fortresses and fortified earthworks in strategic locations, to slow down the enemy's advance and reduce his numbers by tying them down in sieges and counter-attacks. The second line was mobile and would fight aggressively, pinning the enemy with all-out attacks when the direction of his advance was known. This would hold him long enough for the third line, the mobile field army in reserve, to turn his flank and attack indirectly as the hammer against the anvil – the mass of decision – facing its own lines of communication, and astride those of the enemy.

Napoleon had closed all his borders by land and sea. Marshal Brune's 5,500 men were holding the coastal strip between the *Alpes-maritimes* and the sea, backed by the fortified coastal towns. General Lecourbe's 8,400 men were holding the vital valley leading from Basle to the Langres plateau.[28] Marshal Brune was to hand to provide men and leadership if the Allies chose to use this route. Behind and between them were Marshal Suchet's 23,500 men as a reserve or as a strike force depending on circumstances. They were also well placed to destroy piecemeal any larger Austrian force that attempted to come through the alpine passes.

To Lecourbe's left at Strasbourg was General Rapp, one of Napoleon's trusted aides, with 23,000 men who could likewise come to his assistance. In the event of the main thrust of the Allies coming, as in 1814, through the valley between Basle and the Rhine and thence to the Langres plateau, Suchet could combine with Rapp and Lecourbe, and hold the entrance with 54,000 men. In this area, even if they had four times that number, the enemy would not be able to deploy a fighting front of more than 42,000 men.[29]

On General Rapp's left, he was in contact with the main fortresses from Strasbourg to Lille. On his immediate left was Napoleon and the main field army of 128,000 men. Behind him was Marshal Davout in Paris with 20,000 men as a reserve. In the two coastal strips guarding the Pyrenees were General Clausel's 6,800 and General Decaen's 7,600 men. Behind them were General Lamarque's 10,000 men. Lamarque's tasks were to suppress any royalist-inspired uprisings in the Vendée, prevent any amphibious landing by the British, and support Clausel and Decaen if required.

The least defendable French territory, and the flattest, was the area bordering Belgium, and it was here that the Emperor intended to assemble his main field army. While Wellington and Blücher awaited the Austrian and Russian armies' arrival on the French borders, he would attack them. He hoped to beat them both in detail, but would have to adjust to circumstances as they arose. His primary aim was to push Wellington into the sea and knock Britain out of the war. If Blücher were defeated he would pull back on his line of communications to the east. Wellington in this event would fall back on his communications and the sea to the west, and Napoleon would pursue. Having dealt with Wellington, and driven Louis out of

Ghent and King William of Holland out of Brussels – a superb propaganda victory –
he would go after Blücher and in so doing turn the right flank of the main Allied
armies which, being held by his defences, would find him advancing indirectly to roll
them up. They would then have to fall back and regroup or see their lines of communication severed. With any luck, they might find themselves between him and the
54,000 men that Marshal Suchet would bring up behind them. If not, Suchet and
the troops at present mobilizing would join him to double his forces, at which point
he was sure that the Allies would sue for peace. In Britain, he hoped that Liverpool's
government, faced with the prospect of another protracted, financially crippling war
for which it was the paymaster, would fall. Without British money the Allies could
not pursue the war. These, in essence, were the Emperor's plans; they differed little
from his overall plan of campaign in 1813–14.

Napoleon was now fielding the best army that he had commanded since 1807,
and it was totally French in composition. It had a greater proportion of veterans,

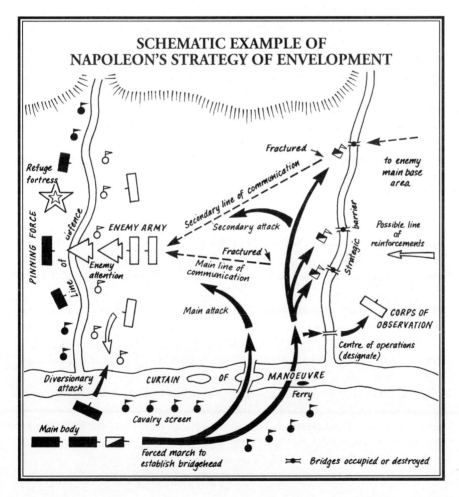

many thousands of experienced men having been returned from captivity as prisoners of war. It had few raw recruits, the conscripts of 1814 having received baptism under fire, and spent the last year being endlessly drilled and practising manoeuvres under the Bourbon regime. Morale and élan were high. The soldiers were pleased to be back under their Emperor again, and the *esprit de corps* that had been lost with the Bourbons had been regained. The army felt proud; their self-respect and honour had been restored, they knew why they were going to fight, and they felt that they had a stake in the outcome.

The corps commanders were all experienced men who had proved their subordinate leadership qualities during the Revolution and the imperial wars. In order fully to comprehend the motivation for the renowned French élan and aggressive leadership in attack, one must bear in mind that almost all the new corps commanders and divisional generals had reached their rank during the Revolution, in the early years of which a general simply had to be victorious or risk going to the guillotine. In one year alone, 668 French officers of high rank were placed under arrest. Of these, 62 were guillotined for cowardice or simply not winning the battle; 100 were imprisoned, 188 dismissed and 36 demoted to the ranks. Only 282 generals survived this ordeal and most of these were now commanding corps, divisions or brigades. Self-reliance and the will to succeed had become second nature to them, and now they had the added incentive of rapid promotion to marshal and all that went with it.

In one respect only, Napoleon's army was fragile. The troops were suspicious of their generals. The army had never forgotten how Marmont had marched a corps into the midst of the Allies, betraying them and their Emperor. They remembered that Marshal Augereau had deserted them at Lyons. They had seen some of the 'great men' like Soult, Macdonald and even Ney, debasing themselves to gain Louis' favour. The rank and file feared only treason, and betrayal by their superiors.

A disaster of the first magnitude now occurred. King Joachim Murat of Naples, Napoleon's brother-in-law, had moved on Milan, but in order to protect his base and avoid being outflanked he had split the army into two groups which advanced on either side of the Appenines. In the face of overwhelming odds, he was unable to effect a junction and fell back to regroup at Macerate, the Austrians pursuing both halves of his army. At Tolentino on 2/3 May 1815, Murat, after holding one force and defeating another Austrian force, had to withdraw because a third Austrian force, of whose presence he had been unaware, was about to come between him and his rearguard. Denied victory, he was obliged to retreat in the teeth of constant attacks, his force being continually outflanked by one of the three Austrian armies. Murat negotiated the surrender of his men and fled to Marseilles.

Napoleon was so furious that Murat had been beaten, thereby releasing more Austrian forces to move against him, that he refused to see him, and then – a grave blunder – declined Murat's offer to command his cavalry. Murat, probably the finest and most famous cavalry commander in history, was left idle at the coast.

Napoleon now decided that he must open his campaign in Belgium by 14 June. His spies[30] had informed him that as yet Wellington and Blücher's forces were widely dispersed. They were not anticipating a surprise attack, and were having to defend the border between Ghent and Liège, a distance of some 90 miles, and reaching back from the River Sambre to Brussels, some 30 miles. Napoleon calculated that it would take them six days to concentrate on either flank, or three days to converge on a central line covering Brussels.[31] Napoleon decided to concentrate his attack at the junction of the two armies.

If those armies had been concentrated, or had had a single overall commander, to attack their juncture would have been folly, but Napoleon's intelligence network had told him that neither army commander had overall control, and at the point of juncture they had no great concentration of troops to delay an advance. The bridges over the Sambre were intact and had not been mined. Charleroi, the main town, was the only one on the border lightly garrisoned and without any proper fortifications. Each of the Allied commanders had made adequate provision for any attack to his immediate front, but the area where the respective flank perimeters adjoined had, quite naturally, been overlooked. From the beginning of June until the 14th, Napoleon increased his blackout on the northern border. Patrols were increased, strangers arrested, and any unauthorized person turned back. Napoleon arranged for apparent 'deserters' to feed false information to the enemy,[32] which, with information from their own spies and those peasants who managed to cross by little known routes, would confuse them and, he hoped, gain him the three vital days. Aware that royalist supporters would transmit his whereabouts to the Allies, Napoleon delayed his departure from Paris until the last moment, which further increased the Allies' feeling of security.

Napoleon planned to concentrate his army opposite Charleroi, on a front of sixteen miles, facing the 90 miles of the enemy. He had 128,000 men with 366 guns. Wellington's forces numbered 107,000 men (including garrisons) with 216 guns. Blücher had 128,000 men (excluding those of von Kleist) and 312 guns. The combined Allied forces were almost double those of Napoleon's.

As can be seen from the last two campaigns, Napoleon was not impressed by the 'law of numbers'. His style was aggressive, even in defence. He had spent his life studying military history and had grasped the secrets of making war. He had developed a strategy to combat numerical inferiority, which he had used successfully since 1796. In essence he followed the Roman maxim of 'divide and conquer'. He had also developed what some have termed his 'secret weapon',[33] the army corps (*corps d'armée*), which was by no means his own idea, but which he had developed into a formidable instrument of war. These corps were not uniform in size. A corps could number anything from 5,000 to 40,000 men, depending on several factors, not least of which was the role it had to play, and the capability of the commander. All the corps had one thing in common – their composition. Each was a well-balanced unit comprising all arms: infantry, cavalry and artillery with attendant auxiliary trains. It had a headquarters staff, with attached engineers. To all intents and purposes it was an army in miniature, able to travel independently, living off the land, thereby reducing logistical considerations. It could attack and defend itself against a force many times its own size. Retaining its own identity and composition, it could yet act in conjunction with other corps. This 'building-block' was a miniature army that could hold or refuse the enemy, and with the arrival of other blocks grow into a huge force before the enemy's eyes. Each corps set out in full battle array, having no need to send for cavalry or artillery support. Napoleon had outlined the operational functions of the army corps to his stepson, Eugène de Beauharnais in 1809: '... a corps of 25,000–30,000 men can be left on its own. Well handled it can fight or alternatively avoid action ... an opponent cannot force it to accept an engagement, but if it chooses to do so it can fight alone for a long time.'[34]

Napoleon usually kept the Heavy Cavalry Corps of cuirassiers and dragoons, with attendant staff and mobile horse artillery, under his immediate control. He used these big men on the heaviest horses, riding boot to boot, to counter-attack the enemy's horse, or to punch a hole in the enemy line, or exploit one. Also under his immediate command was the Imperial Guard Corps, his praetorian guard and the ultimate reserve of the army. It comprised all arms, the infantry of the Grenadiers and Chasseurs of the Old Guard perhaps being the most famous. These men, his '*grognards*' (grumblers), were the cream of the army, each man chosen individually by the Emperor, on his record and number of campaigns and battles to his credit. Its traditions had grown since 1800 and its men were fearless. Their reputation alone inspired terror throughout Europe.[35] Napoleon seldom committed the Old Guard infantry unless it were vital, as in 1814. They usually spearheaded the final attack of a battle, and the sight of them advancing inspired the exhausted line infantry to a further effort. The Guard going forward became a symbol of victory in battle. The presence on the field of the Old Guard, the serried ranks in their huge bearskins silently waiting in formation, had a pyschological effect out of all proportion to the threat; the enemy being reluctant to commit his reserves while these élite troops were yet uncommitted, thereby weakening their own defences and depriving aid to threatened sectors.

The Guard Cavalry was used more frequently and it too was élite. The Young Guard division was the main fighting element, it being considered more expendable. Whenever its ranks became depleted they were made up from suitably hardened veterans from the line. The Old Guard recruited mainly from the Young Guard, so its men were case-hardened warriors. All were fanatically loyal to their Emperor, and had pay and privileges accordingly.

Napoleon used his corps to implement his system of 'inferior strategy', in this case to gain the 'central position'.[36] This was one of the methods he used to defeat the 'law of numbers' by bringing a greater local force to bear on the enemy than they could on him. In essence he would drive his army like a wedge between the enemy forces before they had time to concentrate, or combine. Using one or two corps to hold one enemy force in play, he would then attack and pin the other with his advance guard. Then he would use his reserves to extend his line and the enemy would be obliged to do likewise, to avoid being outflanked. He would then call off a corps from the force holding the other enemy army and force-march it to the other flank to turn it or exhaust the enemy's reserves, while keeping up the pressure of his attacks the while. Then, using his reserves and or the Guard and heavy cavalry he would breach the enemy line and route it, using his light cavalry to follow up. He would next quickly reverse the equation. Leaving a corps to follow up and prevent the enemy from rallying, he would force-march his other two corps, the Guard and the heavy cavalry to the other enemy army, already held in position, and repeat the process. In this fashion, 100,000 men could quite easily destroy two separate armies totalling 200,000 men or more.

This was Napoleon's intended plan of campaign for June 1815. He knew that Wellington and Blücher would require three days to get together. If he struck quickly at their centre before they could organize their own troops, let alone join with their allies, he would enjoy an advantage in numbers. The point on the map where their forces converged, and where Blücher and Wellington felt most secure, was in fact their weak spot. For not only did this dispersal suit Napoleon's method of fighting, but it featured the inherent weakness of two separate armies with separate commands. If subjected to an overwhelming attack, the outlying advance guards would fall back to their reserves. Wellington's was at Brussels, but his army was dispersed from there to the coast, so his advance guard would withdraw westwards. Blücher's was at Namur and his main force stretched back to Liège, so his advance guard at Charleroi would have to withdraw eastwards. Napoleon hoped to get between them. Then depending on circumstances he would decide his course of action. If Blücher repeated his tactics of 1814 and retreated at his approach, he would try to defeat Wellington, who appeared the more vulnerable in that his troops were dispersed over a greater area, and then turn on Blücher. If Blücher stood, he would defeat him and then attack Wellington. It all depended on what Blücher decided to do. At 3 o'clock on the morning of 12 June 1815, Napoleon's carriage with its escort and staff left Paris secretly, heading north to the army and the border.

Napoleon had offered peace on the Allies' terms, but had been rejected. He had appeased the people of France by remodelling his system of government and creating a constitutional monarchy. He had appointed Carnot, Minister of the Interior, Davout, Minister of War, Lavalette Postmaster-General, and Fouché, Minister of Police. Fouché, whom Napoleon knew had already been in touch with the Allies, and at one point had even been persuaded by Carnot not to have him shot, was now Minister of Police with no less a person than General Savary duc de Rovigo as his Chief of Gendarmerie. Savary, the man who had failed to act in 1814 to stop Paris from being betrayed, failed to arrest Talleyrand or the royalist ringleaders. Napoleon had appointed Fouché *faute de mieux*, considering him the best man to put down the royalist uprising in the Vendée and uncover any royalist plots in the capital; and his expert hand would supervise Savary whose actions – or lack of them in 1814 – Napoleon considered to be his own fault for promoting Savary to a position beyond his capabilities. Fouché he knew, would not baulk at arresting anyone.

Napoleon was now embarking on his final campaign, looking for the decisive battle that would lead to peace. He had a highly trained army with a high morale. In Paris he had left no weak regency council and a weak brother to hold the heart of the country and his main arsenal. The Chambers were with him, and Marshal Davout, his Minister of War and Governor, would hold it against all treachery, or so Napoleon believed. But against his better judgement he had also left Fouché in place. He was highly acceptable to the people and to the Chambers. He had risen high during the Revolution, had taken a personal part in royalist massacres and, as a member of the revolutionary tribunal, had voted for and urged the execution of Louis XVI. As Napoleon's Minister, he had acted with promptness against the British attempted invasion of Antwerp in 1809. As a secret policeman, and chief of anti-terrorist activities, he had unmasked hundreds of royalist agents and assassins. He had caught and executed Artois' agent Georges Cadoudal of the 'infernal machine' and had, it was alleged by most, Pichegru strangled in his cell. Fouché had infiltrated his top agent, Méhée de la Touche, into Bourbon circles in London and into the Chevaliers de la Foi, and subsequently caught or turned their agents in France. The Bourbons had refused to employ him, and appear to have tried to arrest him prior to Napoleon's return. So far as Napoleon and the republicans were concerned, therefore, he was sound.

In fact he was clandestinely working against them, in the Bourbon interest. His network of agents was still in place, because he used for the most part ordinary people. Most of them had been induced to work for him against their will. Some were royalists who had been 'turned' to betray others in exchange for their own lives or those of relatives. Some worked for money; all were frightened of death or exposure. Some he could expose for criminal offences that he could prove but had left on file: murder, sexual deviation, embezzlement, etc. As Chief of Police under the Revolution and Napoleon he had amassed a huge amount of information concerning the indiscretions of prominent and lesser people which he used to induce compliance. He had employed *agents provocateurs* to accuse falsely royalists and Bonapartists alike. He was in a position to blackmail, compromise or fabricate evidence against anyone. The threat of exposure alone, usually ensured compliance, and he would not baulk at eliminating any agent who opposed him or refused orders. Fouché was, as indeed are all heads of totalitarian secret police services, a dangerous man; dangerous to employ, dangerous to ignore. Napoleon had forgotten the lessons of 1809 and 1814 – the Judas factor. He had made Fouché a Minister of State with access to all the papers of the Council of Ministers, and a voice in the Chambers.

Napoleon had been so busy forming a government, financing the country, formulating a constitution and creating an army that he had had little time to ponder the enigma that was Fouché. Why had the Bourbons, who had decreed public mourning and attended memorial services for the dead King and Queen, and for Cadoudal and other victims of Fouché, not executed the regicide and hated secret policeman? Why had not prominent royalist fanatics, such as Chateaubriand – whose cousin Fouché had had shot like a dog outside Paris – or members of the Chevaliers, called for his death, exile, or even had him murdered? Why on Napoleon's return had he not been arrested immediately as a potential subversive? Why had his agent Méhée de la Touche been accepted into royalist society?

The truth was so obvious that it couldn't be seen. Since 1813 he had been a royalist agent. Having been disgraced by Napoleon since 1809, for communicating with enemy governments without his knowledge or approval, and isolated from government, he had placed his network of spies at the royalists' disposal. That is why the Chevaliers de la Foi, which he had thoroughly infiltrated between 1800 and 1805 and which had become a spent force by 1809, had been able to act with ruthless efficiency in 1814, transmitting information to and from the Allies. It was Fouché's ability to pass and receive information through unsuspected ineffectual or important people, that had helped the Bourbons to contact the royalists in Paris in 1814, and helped Talleyrand to stage his coup. In recognition of these services, Fouché, regicide and murderer of countless royalists, had been allowed to keep his life, his title, his wealth and his extensive ex-royalist properties.

In 1815, it was Fouché who had infiltrated the planned army uprising in the north and betrayed it. It was to Fouché as a last resort that Artois, the King's own brother, had come for help and arranged a charade to help Fouché to maintain his republican cover. Napoleon had not had time to think about these things. And now, as in 1814, he had ridden away to war leaving behind a Trojan horse within the walls of his capital, awaiting only the signal for its hidden enemies to open the gates to the Allies.

CHAPTER 11

THE ROAD TO MONT ST-JEAN

'It is even better to act quickly and err than to hesitate until the time of action is past.'
– Von Clausewitz, *On War.*

IN THE EARLY HOURS OF 5 APRIL 1815, THE DUKE OF WELLINGTON arrived at Brussels from Vienna and was appalled at what he found. The impressive military machine that he had created in Portugal, Spain and France had disappeared. Of British troops under his immediate command, he had a mere fourteen battalions and a detachment of Rifles. The King's German Legion, 7,500 men mainly from Hanover, were there but, in the expectation of disbandment, was rife with desertion.[1] Added to these were 15,000 Hanoverian militiamen. The new army of the United Netherlands, 29,500 men, was under the titular command of the Prince of Orange. They too were under Wellington's orders, but their king had insisted that they remain a separate entity.[2] The Duke of Brunswick's Black Corps of 6,700 men had been proffered – for a subsidy – and these mercenaries had been accepted. Brunswick, related to Britain by marriage, had been ousted by Napoleon; the fear of a repeat performance had been an added stimulus. The twin Duchies of Nassau also had provided 7,300 men.

The majority of Wellington's immediate army spoke German – which he did not. The Hanoverians, Brunswickers, Nassauers and Netherlanders, although obedient to his orders, had their own independent chains of command. There was no uniformity of command, supply or training within this conglomerate. At a tactical level the various forces fought differently, having differing ideas as to what constituted the best method. The Netherlanders emulated the British in fighting in line two-deep. The Nassauers preferred three deep and assault columns like the French. Commands were given variously in English, Flemish, French and three different German dialects. Wellington wrote home: 'I have got an infamous army, very weak and ill equipped, and a very inexperienced Staff.[3]

Wellington could scarcely believe that he was expected to confront Napoleon's army with this pitiful force. Since he had taken leave of the British Army in 1814, the government had removed 47,000 men from the establishment. The Royal Ordnance, which controlled the artillery, had discharged 7,000 irreplaceable men.[4] The line cavalry had also been drastically culled. Many of the best units and first battalions of infantry had been sent to America and Canada; the Peace of Ghent had been signed and the troops were expected back – but would they arrive in time?

In April 1815 Wellington's British contingent was only the size of one French army corps: six regiments of cavalry and 25 battalions of infantry, fifteen of them 'weak corps and inefficient battalions' numbering fewer than 500 men on average.[5] Even while Wellington was trying to turn this hybrid collection into an organized army, veteran troops in England and the Low Countries were taking their discharge from the last campaign – much to his chagrin.

Writing to Lord Bathurst on 6 April, Wellington's indignation was made plain:

'Your Lordship will see by my letter to Prince Schwarzenberg, in what state we stand as to numbers. I am sorry to say I have a very bad account of the Netherlands troops and the king appears unwilling to allow them to be mixed with ours ... Although I have given a favourable opinion of ours to General Schwarzenberg, I cannot help thinking, from all accounts, that they are not what they ought to be to enable us to maintain our military character in Europe. It appears to me that you have not taken in England a clear view of your situation, *that you do not think war certain ... You have not called out the militia, or announced such a measure in parliament, by which measures your troops of the line in Ireland or elsewhere might become disposable.*'[6]

The problem was this. If the militia were called out they could be used to release line troops to him from the British Isles. Further, a section of the Mutiny Act allowed for extending the service of soldiers who were being discharged. High inflation, the Corn Laws and unemployment had precipitated riots in England and Ireland. Unlike her continental neighbours, Britain had no police force during this period, law and order being in the hands of lay magistrates and private enterprise. In an emergency a magistrate could call upon the military, so not unnaturally the government was reluctant to send more troops abroad than necessary, particularly cavalry who doubled up for crowd control in the towns and customs and excise duties along the coast.[7] In the event, the only immediate reinforcements released to Wellington by the Horse Guards were a heavy cavalry brigade and four battalions of infantry from Ireland – and these in the teeth of urgent opposition from the commander there.

The whole issue turned on Samuel Whitbread's question in the House: 'Are we at peace or war?' Britain was not at war with France, but only with Napoleon. As we have seen this was unacceptable to parliament. The militia could only be called out and embodied in time of war or insurrection. Unless war were formally declared, not only could they not be called out, but the disbandment of regular troops and militia from the last campaign could not be halted. In parliament the Opposition were determined that until Castlereagh, Liverpool and the Cabinet came clean, ceased their futile efforts to prop up the Bourbons under the fiction that the British were acting as 'auxiliaries' for the French king against his rebellious subjects, and declared war on France, they would not pass the Act. In the end, too late to help Wellington, Castlereagh and the Cabinet acquiesced, and on 9 May presented a pathetic Bill authorizing *local* militia to volunteer to release the old militia. A fortnight later a second Bill was hurried through to embody the old militia itself, the preamble stating: '... There is an immediate prospect of war with France.'[8] With this 'political nicety', the Cabinet left their greatest military commander in the lurch and to his own devices.

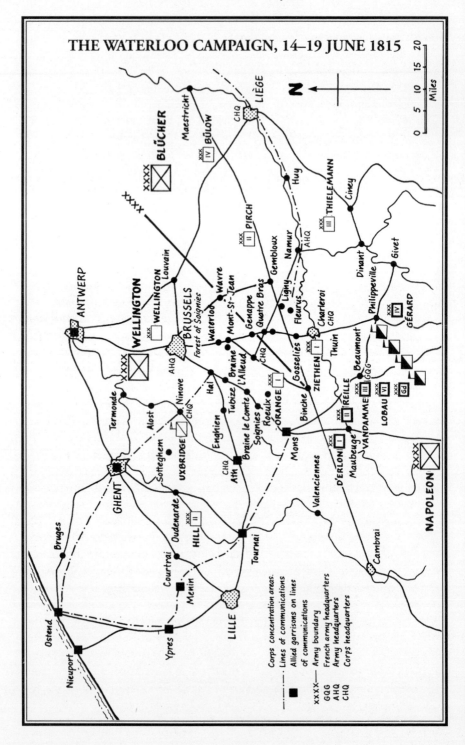

THE WATERLOO CAMPAIGN, 14–19 JUNE 1815

Like Napoleon's, Wellington's greatest asset was his administrative ability. By dint of will-power and political pressure he soon had complete command of all the men at his disposal, and by mixing experienced British troops with inexperienced foreigners and vice versa, he brought at least an element of unity to his hopelessly inadequate force. No thanks to his government which had wasted seven precious weeks in debate at his expense.[9]

By June, Wellington's strength stood at 107,000 men and 216 guns, including garrisons. For purposes of administration the army was divided into two army corps, a cavalry corps, and a reserve. Wellington's headquarters were at Brussels, with the reserve which consisted of 5th and 6th Divisions, the Nassauers under von Kruse, and the Duke of Brunswick's corps. The Prince of Orange commanded I Corps, with headquarters at Braine-le-Comte: 1st Division at Enghien, 2nd Division between Nivelles and Quatre-Bras, 3rd Division at Soignies, 4th Division (3rd Netherlands Division) at Roeulx. Lord Hill's II Corps was headquartered with its 2nd Division at Ath; 4th Division at Oudenarde. The 1st Netherlands Division and Indonesian Brigade were at Sotteghem and Alost respectively. Along the River Dendre between Ninove and Grammont was the cavalry corps under the Earl of Uxbridge. Patrols and detachments were deployed along the 60 miles of frontier.

On Wellington's left flank, covering the 30-mile stretch from Binche to Namur, with a frontage of 60 miles that included the forest of the Ardennes, was the Prussian Army of the Lower Rhine, commanded by the 72-year-old Field Marshal Prince Blücher. On arriving he had found the new Prussian Army divided up into permanent army corps. I Corps, was commanded by General Graf von Ziethen and comprised the Brigades of: von Steinmetz, von Pirch II, von Jägow and von Donnersmarck. General von Röder commanded the corps' two cavalry brigades, Colonel von Lehmann the artillery and engineers; total 32,500 men, 96 guns.

II Corps under General von Borstel (later, von Pirch II) comprising the Brigades of: von Tippelskirch, von Krafft, von Brause and von Bose; brigade cavalry under General von Wahlen-Jürgass, artillery and sappers under Colonel von Röhl; 33,000 men, 80 guns.

III Corps under General von Thielemann comprised the Brigades of: von Borcke, von Kämphen, von Luck and von Stulpnägel; cavalry under General von Hobe, artillery and engineers under Colonel von Mohnhaupt; 25,000 men, 48 guns.

IV Corps under General Graf Bülow von Dennewitz comprised the Brigades of: von Hacke, von Ryssel, von Losthin and von Hiller von Gartringen; cavalry under Prince William of Prussia, artillery and engineers under Major von Bardeleben; 32,000 men, 88 guns. Blücher's grand total amounted to 128,000 men and 312 guns, including garrisons. His Quartermaster-General and Chief of Staff, General von Gneisenau, was responsible for operational planning and control. The King of Prussia reposed great trust in Gneisenau, and had appointed him over the heads of more senior generals. His formal appointment sent via the Cabinet on 29 March had included the following directive: '... I cannot, in view of the distance from the area of operation, give you any definite orders as to how you should act in case of unforeseen events, but I must leave it to you to make such arrangements with the Duke of Wellington as suit the circumstances and to act in agreement with him in all things.'[10] This was necessary because the king was aware that Gneisenau and most of the Prussian officers had a deep mistrust of Britain and of Wellington in particular. It will be remembered that in 1813 Gneisenau had written to Castlereagh for his and Britain's help in elevating Prussia to dominance in a new German federation, to replace Napoleon's old one. Castlereagh's reply had been vaguely worded and appeared to indicate support, but later he stated that Gneisenau had mistaken his indication of 'in principle' as meaning a definite commitment which he disavowed. Gneisenau wanted nothing to do with Wellington or the British.

But King William had ordered it and Gneisenau would obey his orders to the letter. Prussia desperately needed the British subsidies, and could not afford to offend Wellington, the field commander and their paymaster. However, King William had qualified his instruction, by making it contingent to the circumstances prevailing, and Gneisenau was given unlimited discretion that could even overrule Blücher's wishes if necessary. The King's orders continued: 'While I empower you to do so and assure you of my fullest confidence in you, *I also make you responsible for acting with all prudence and the most careful consideration in every matter affecting the future of Europe.*'[11] This paragraph was open to the widest interpretation, and could have far-reaching implications. Gneisenau was also directed to take command of the army in the event of any circumstance that might incapacitate the commander, such as a recurrence of his illnesses of 1814. With such power direct from the King, Gneisenau can be seen as having greater authority than the Commander-in-Chief.

Gneisenau dutifully contacted Wellington who requested him to consolidate closer to the exposed border. The Prussians reluctantly agreed on condition that the Netherlanders supplied rations for them while they were on their territory. Gneisenau then deployed the army as follows:

II Corps' headquarters and Blücher's HQ were at Namur, held by 5 Brigade; 6 Brigade at Thorembey-les-Beguignes; 7 Brigade at Heron as a central reserve; 8 Brigade at Huy; reserve cavalry at Hannut; reserve artillery around the hamlets of Eghezee and Barriere.

I Corps was placed around Charleroi, with its headquarters in the town. Its 1 Brigade was based at Fontaine l'Evêque, keeping watch on the French border between Binche and Marchiennes, and the river crossings at Lobbes and Thuin; 2 Brigade between Marchiennes and Campinaire; 4 Brigade down-river between Campinaire and Namur; 3 Brigade in reserve at Fleurus, some seven miles behind Charleroi. Farther back at Sombreffe was the reserve corps cavalry, the artillery reserve being at Gembloux.

III Corps' headquarters was at Ciney in the Ardennes forest, with its 10 Brigade; the reserve cavalry was between Ciney and Dinant, protecting 11 Brigade which was keeping watch in front of the forest around Dinant, with sections outlying as far off as Namur; 9 Brigade was at Asserre, in front of the reserve artillery; 12 Brigade in reserve at Huy.

IV Corps' headquarters was back at Liège with 13 Brigade to its immediate front south of the River Meuse; 14 Brigade was with the reserve cavalry at Waremme in front of Tongres; 15 Brigade was behind the city on the other side of the river at Hologne; 16 Brigade was at Liers; the reserve artillery park was at Gloms.

The Allied armies were covering a front of 100 miles. Blücher met Wellington at Tierlmont on 5 May and they agreed the strategy to be adopted for each of the three obvious invasion routes. First, and that which Wellington thought most likely, was a left pincer movement: starting at Lille, driving on Ghent (removing Louis) and capturing Ostend and Antwerp, thereby severing Wellington's two lines of communication, isolating him, and seizing the vital Channel ports and Antwerp. This would allow the French to move east and turn the Allied flank. Secondly, from Mauberge around Mons and by that road straight to Brussels and Antwerp, again cutting his lines and isolating the ports, capturing Antwerp with the added bonus of gaining The Netherlands' second capital. Thirdly, Napoleon could attack away from the ports and Wellington's lines of communication, from Charleroi whose defences were inadequate. But this would place Napoleon smack in the middle of two superior forces. The only apparent advantage being that he would have a short route to Brussels. In the unlikely event of Napoleon's moving from Charleroi to attack the two Allied armies simultaneously, they would concentrate their armies side by side, Wellington's army would mass on its left at Gosselies, placing it on the Prussian right. Blücher's army would concentrate on its right flank at Fleurus, on Wellington's left. Each commander appointed a liaison officer: Gneisenau's General von Müffling was an experienced staff officer with sound battle experience; Wellington chose Lieutenant-Colonel Sir Henry Hardinge, of the 1st Foot Guards. The commanders knew that it would take three days to effect this joint concentration, but both believed in early May that Napoleon would either fight a defensive war as in 1814, or that their patrols would give them ample warning of an enemy build-up.

The arrangement was that although the armies would co-operate with each other they would act under the overall direction of Field Marshal Schwarzenberg. But his conduct would be governed by Austrian interests as dictated by Metternich. Gneisenau had been ordered to co-operate with Wellington and this he would do, but he gave Müffling explicit instructions to be wary of Wellington and to be on his guard: '... for from his relations with India, and transactions with the deceitful Nabobs, this distinguished general had accustomed himself to duplicity, that he had at last become such a master of the art, as even to outwit the Nabobs themselves'.[12]

Blücher spoke to Wellington about the necessity of advancing into France as soon as possible. Wellington agreed, but both men were tied by their respective governments' agreement to comply with the Vienna war council's decision that Schwarzenberg be supreme commander.[13] Schwarzenberg had informed Wellington that the Allies would be in position for a concerted movement towards Paris which would begin on about 20 June. It is unlikely that Wellington would have felt quite so sanguine about the outcome if he had had Blücher's experience of Austrian 'co-operation', or had known that little progress had as yet been made towards the

Rhine. At this stage he believed that the Austrians and Russians were straining every sinew to reach the start-line by the given date for invasion – 20 June 1815.

The Allies had one distinct advantage. Artois's agent Fouché had sent Wellington, via Castlereagh, the entire order of battle of Napoleon's army and all known positions as at 2 May, down to the last horse.[14] So Wellington had every reason to expect to hear from his chief of intelligence, Lieutenant-Colonel Grant, who was across the border in French territory, when and by which route Napoleon would advance. As May turned to June, Both Wellington and Blücher wrote home saying that in their opinion the danger of attack had passed .

Gneisenau too had come to believe that Napoleon's thunderbolt would fall on Schwarzenberg first, knocking him and the Austrians out of the war and back to Switzerland, as he had tried to do in 1814. They in the north would be left to reduce at will the 42 French fortresses until such time as Napoleon turned on them. Gneisenau wrote to Berlin on 9 June: 'The enemy will not attack us but will retire as far as the Aisne, Somme and Marne in order to concentrate his forces,'[15] adding, on the 12th, 'The danger of an attack has almost vanished.' But at 3 o'clock that very morning, Napoleon's much-travelled green coach, escorted by his Imperial Guard cavalry, had clattered out of Paris, heading north.

Napoleon stopped at Laon, issued instructions to his forces and arrived at Avesnes on the 13th. On the 11th Marshal Ney, hitherto left out in the cold, had received a last-minute message from Davout, enclosing a terse summons from the Emperor: 'Send for Marshal Ney and tell him that if he wishes to be present for the first battles, he ought to be at Avesnes on the fourteenth.' Ney, stopping only to pick up his aide, Colonel Heymes, had rushed by carriage to Avesnes. At their meeting Napoleon was cordial – but unforthcoming about his plans.[16] Marshal Mortier, complaining of severe sciatica, was unable to continue. Ney must surely have wondered whether this was why he had been recalled, or whether, like Soult, he was considered too dangerous to be left at home.[17] Next day Napoleon moved on to Beaumont. Ney, having dismissed his carriage and having no horses, travelled to the front in a peasant's cart, and purchased Mortier's horses. Napoleon meanwhile had begun his operations.

The Emperor had assembled d'Erlon's I Corps and Reille's II Corps on the border around Mauberge, opposite Thuin, on the road that crossed the Sambre bridge at Lobbes. In front of Beaumont, on the direct road to Charleroi and the main bridge, were placed in column, Vandamme's III Corps and Mouton-Lobau's VI Corps. Behind them were the Imperial Guard infantry corps, the Guard cavalry corps and the reserve artillery. Gérard's IV Corps was adjacent to Philippeville. Napoleon intended that d'Erlon and Reille would cross up-river and advance on Charleroi, clearing out the Prussians. D'Erlon would then advance up the main Brussels road, while a reconnaissance in force by Reille was carried out in the direction of Mons and Binche. Likewise, IV Corps, crossing down-stream at Chatelet or Farciennes, would support the main crossing at Charleroi (see campaign map).

Napoleon's entire army would converge and cross on a 5-mile frontage. His first choice of victim would depend on whether Blücher stood or not. Naturally he hoped it would be Blücher. His information lead him to believe that he would concentrate first, but previous experience had shown that the new Prussian army was unpredictable; Blücher might withdraw and make him march and counter-march looking for a battle, as in 1814, wasting his time and giving Wellington time to concentrate and come to the rescue. Napoleon issued his starting-orders for daylight (3 o'clock) on 15 June.

Wellington was quite unaware of the thunderbolt due to strike. He was confident that Grant's intelligence would advise him of any threat in good time. Unknown to him, Grant had already sent the vital news that Napoleon had concentrated and was preparing to cross the Sambre at Charleroi and its environs, but the message had been intercepted by one of Wellington's cavalry patrols and sent to the cavalry commander at Binche, Major-General Dörnberg, late of Jérôme Napoleon's bodyguard – now returned to the Hanoverian fold. He had scrutinized it, dismissed it as yet more false information put out by Napoleon's agents – and sent it back.

Soult, now Chief of Staff, transmitted Napoleon's orders, but used a single courier, whereas Berthier had invariably used three. The courier's horse falling on him, he broke his hip, and Vandamme's orders did not arrive. Consequently, when the main centre column closed on III Corps it was completely unprepared to march, which caused enormous confusion and delay. Later, there were those who reckoned that Soult had done this deliberately, and it must be said that although Soult had never commanded the *Grande Armée*, he had, during twenty years, and as ex-Minister of War, been accustomed to the practice, and had used it himself in the Peninsula.[18]

A worse disaster occurred when the commander of IV Corps' lead division, General de Bourmont, accompanied by his staff, rode over to Blücher and handed him the corps' operational orders. De Bourmont was working clandestinely for Artois, his previous job having been to keep an eye on Marshal Ney. Davout had opposed his appointment as a divisional commander, declaring him an out-and-out royalist, but Gérard had vouched for him and Napoleon had consented, perhaps in the hope of effecting a degree of reconciliation with the royalists. This act of treachery, which a measure of prudence might have prevented, not only delayed IV Corps' advance, but news of it spread throughout the army and caused great unease among the rank and file. It cannot be over stressed that Marmont's treachery of the previous year, when he marched his trusting corps into a virtual ambush in the middle of the Austrian army, had had a grievous effect on the soldiers, who now tended to equate any setback with treachery on the part of senior officers.

Charleroi was the Headquarters of von Ziethen's I Corps. His immediate brigade commander was General von Steinmetz, one of the new breed of Prussians.[19] Commanding the rearguard, his job was to hold the French as long as possible while Ziethen assembled his corps at the rendezvous designated by Gneisenau in his standing orders for this contingency – in effect to fall back in force on Sombreffe. Ziethen sent off messengers to Gneisenau and Wellington as per orders, but again, Wellington did not receive his copy until late in the evening.[20]

Steinmetz, fighting a superb rearguard action, denied for a time both the vital roads that would have placed Napoleon in his central position. During the night of June 16 the Prussian forces strained every sinew to concentrate at Sombreffe, around the villages of St-Armand and Ligny. Wellington, the curtain torn at last, issued orders at 10 p.m. for his army to concentrate towards the south and west. Still convinced that the attack at Charleroi was a feint, he was doing what Napoleon wanted, widening the gap between the armies. At the strategic crossroads of Quatre-Bras, where a lateral road linked his army with the Prussians, was positioned one Netherlands brigade under the Prince of Saxe-Weimar. Its divisional commander, General Perponcher, with the Prince of Orange's chief of staff, General Constant Rebecque, decided, in the light of the reports they had received, and in the absence of the Prince of Orange and his senior officers who were with Wellington at the Countess of Richmond's ball in Brussels, to disregard Wellington's orders. In so doing they provided the fulcrum that would decide the outcome of most of the campaign.[21]

At 2 a.m. on the 16th Wellington was awoken and apprised of the true situation.[22] He ordered his army to concentrate at Quatre-Bras. His Quartermaster, De Lancey, wrote new movement orders throughout the night, but it was 6 a.m. before they were dispatched, and not all the units received their instructions to move on Quatre-Bras. Meanwhile Napoleon, now convinced that Blücher was concentrating for battle, had issued his plan of campaign, informing Marshals Ney and Grouchy:

'I have adopted for this campaign the following *general principle*, to divide my army into two wings and a reserve ... The Guard will form the Reserve, and I shall bring it into action on either wing as the actual circumstances may dictate ... *The Major-General* [Soult] *issues the most precise orders, so that when you are detached you should not find any difficulty in obeying such orders as you receive; General officers commanding corps will take orders directly from me when I am present in person ... Also, according to circumstances, I shall draw troops from one wing to strengthen my reserve ...*[23]

The proposed *modus operandi* is significant: two wings and a reserve; corps commanders of either wing under his direct control if he were present; he would take forces from either wing if he needed to augment the reserve.

Wellington arrived at Quatre-Bras a little before 10.30 on the 16th. En route he passed Picton and the reserve halted at the edge of the forest behind Mont St-Jean as ordered.[24] At the crossroads the nature of the terrain concealed any sign of Ney's main force which was two miles farther back; all Wellington could see was a French patrol eyeing him through telescopes. Wellington's total force comprised one Netherlands infantry division – and that thanks to the foresight of the Netherlanders' chief of staff. Wellington sent a letter to Blücher:

'My dear Prince, My army is disposed as follows, The Prince of Orange's corps has a division here at Quatre-Bras, the remainder at Nivelles. The reserve is now marching to Genappe, where it will arrive at midday. At the same hour the English cavalry will have attained Nivelles. Lord Hill's corps is at Braine-le-Comte. I do not see many of the enemy in front of us, and I await the receipt of news from Your Highness, and the arrival of my troops, to decide on my operations for this day. Nothing has been seen in the direction of Binche, nor on our right. &c. &c. Wellington.'[25]

Blücher was heartened to think that by afternoon the greater part of Wellington's army, including the cavalry which he admired, would be only a few miles away; combined, he felt sure that they would crush Napoleon between them. Wellington rode over to speak to Blücher, saw the French army massing, and realized that this was no feint. He made off, saying that provided he was not attacked he would soon come to Blücher's aid.

On his return, seeing at least three French infantry divisions to his front, with several cavalry divisions in attendance, he realized that he had a battle to fight without a single British battalion at his disposal. He sent gallopers ahead to bring up his army and speed Picton on to Quatre-Bras instead of Genappe. For two and a half hours the single Netherlands division faced Ney's three infantry divisions and cavalry divisions. Ney had brought up his corps reserve artillery to supplement his three divisional batteries and their pounding reduced the effectiveness of The Netherlands' divisional artillery. By 3.30 p.m., badly mauled and low on ammunition, the Netherlanders were relieved to see Picton's reserve beginning to arrive. But 23,000 men with their equipment could not arrive by a single banked road simultaneously, and the last units were not in position until 5.30. Ney spurred on by a deceptive message from Soult telling him that: 'His Majesty desires me to tell you that you are to manoeuvre immediately in such a manner as to envelop the enemy's right and fall upon his rear; the army in our front [Prussian] is lost if you act with energy. THE FATE OF FRANCE IS IN YOUR HANDS,' launched Kellermann's heavy cavalry brigade in an attempt to capture the crossroads and prevent Wellington's concentration. Kellermann's magnificent charge gained the crossroads, captured a British Colour and cut up a square, but his cavalry in turn became a target for concentrated musketry that did terrible execution to his men and horses. Ney, unable to support him with infantry, was losing the battle. He needed to secure the crossroads in order to be able to detach part of his force to aid the Emperor – but how? His own men were tiring, but Wellington was gaining fresh strength by the hour. At 6 o'clock the British Guards Brigade, officered by a batch of 'new boys', arrived from the Nivelles road. On their way they had passed Saxe-Weimar's Nassauers, the 28th of the Dutch line, dressed in their new Netherlands blue-and-grey uniform. The Nassauers' tough, experienced Germans had fought for nearly six hours and had held, been pushed out of, and recaptured the Bossu wood – only to be repulsed again. They were now regrouping and tending to their wounded, among whom was the Prince of Saxe-Weimar. The British Guards, who did not understand German, continued for another three miles along the length of the wood and then, turning right at the crossroads, marched another mile to where the Nassauers had been positioned – five miles at right angles. Later the Guards officers would recall seeing 'hundreds of unwounded Belgics, 5 miles from the battlefield – running away'.[26]

By 8 p.m. Wellington's cavalry, which he had told Blücher was due after 'midday', had arrived, thanks to the magnificent efforts of Lord Uxbridge.[27] Now Cooke's, Clinton's, Alten's divisions and Uxbridge's cavalry, together with all the horse and foot artillery and attendant transport had to pass along a small rutted road from Enghien, converging to a bottle-neck at Braine-le-Comte and again at Nivelles where the outlying cavalry patrols were coming in. The 50,000 men were tied to the pace of the lead division. In the meantime Wellington's single British artillery battery had also arrived, having lost two pieces.

While Kellermann had been struggling for the 'fate of France', Ney had called up his II Corps which he had left farther back to concentrate and act as a reserve and corps of observation, linking his force with Napoleon's other wing.[28] Unknown to him, Napoleon, about to defeat Blücher and his Prussians at Ligny, had withdrawn this corps to augment his reserve, the mass of decision that would turn and rupture the Prussian right flank. Ney was concerned that Wellington's entire army was in front of him who had but three infantry divisions when he had thought he had eight. If Wellington had sufficient strength to push back his men who were rapidly tiring, might he not attack Napoleon's rear? Forgetting Napoleon's warning that he might withdraw troops from either wing if necessary, Ney decided, fatefully, to try to hold Wellington at Quatre-Bras to prevent his juncture with Blücher – and to this end recalled d'Erlon, thereby robbing Napoleon of this army corps which might have cut Blücher's northern line of retreat. D'Erlon, a general of vast experience, recognized Ney's dilemma and retraced his steps.[29]

Napoleon meanwhile had fought a hard battle against the Prussians. Blücher and Gneisenau, confident that d'Erlon's approaching corps was Wellington on his way, committed their reserves in an attempt to force the French out of the villages of Ligny and St-Armand. Napoleon, using his cavalry corps to hold his right wing secure, awaited d'Erlon's arrival. D'Erlon's corps, approaching from an unexpected sector along the Roman road, panicked the French troops who thought that Wellington had come across in their rear. The Prussians too, sensing the easing of pressure, as forces were diverted to thwart this supposed menace, thought this was Wellington's promised aid arriving, and launched an all-out assault to seize the important villages as a bridgehead for their counter-attack. Napoleon, having ascertained that these were d'Erlon's troops advancing by the wrong road, assumed that he had exercised his military judgement and did not waste time in sending him further orders.[30]

Napoleon now used his élite Imperial Guard to punch a hole through the Prussians who, having committed their reserves, had nothing with which to plug the gap. Blücher tried in vain to stop the disintegration of his line with an attack by his reserve cavalry. He was then rendered *hors de combat*, trapped under his fallen horse and repeatedly ridden over. Gneisenau organized the rearguard to stop the defeat turning into a rout, and decided to retreat northwards to Wavre instead of Liège. The outcome of the war was determined by this crucial decision.

Napoleon, robbed of a decisive victory by d'Erlon's withdrawal, was certain that the Prussians would fall back on their line of communications – through Gembloux,

Huy and Liège, or via Tongres. Gneisenau's map showed the same picture, but he chose Wavre in order to fool Napoleon and give himself time to regroup. The late arrival of his IV Corps meant that he could resume the offensive on equal terms, and if Napoleon had more effectives, or decided not to attack Wellington, but to pursue him, he could still withdraw in good order into Prussian territory. Gneisenau felt that Wellington had marched away to save his army at the expense of the Prussians, and wrote as much to his wife that night.[31]

Blücher, now recovered, argued the point with his chief of staff. The old Field Marshal had given his word and would continue to co-operate with Wellington; he sent a message to this effect during the early hours of the next morning. Wellington had withdrawn to the Mont St-Jean position during the 17th, leaving his cavalry under Uxbridge as a rearguard. Napoleon rode up to Ney's position next morning and told him that he had dispatched Marshal Grouchy with two infantry corps and the greater part of two cavalry corps to keep a sword in Blücher's rear, but he was to keep in touch with Napoleon via his left flank. Grouchy had nearly 33,000 men and 80 guns to keep the retreating Prussians on the run, but some 3–8,000 German troops (from Napoleon's old confederation), forcibly conscripted into the Prussian ranks, had fled in rout towards Liège, and Grouchy's cavalry mistook them for the Prussian rearguard and in pursuing them lost touch with the Prussian army.

Wellington, meanwhile, was organizing his men as they arrived at the Mont St-Jean position. Napoleon and Ney were soon in hot pursuit of the Allied rearguard which was commanded by the Earl of Uxbridge. His staff had reconnoitred Genappe and found a crossing a few hundred yards up-stream at Ways la Hutte. Uxbridge sent half his cavalry force and the infantry and all the cumbersome vehicles there while he stayed to hold the approaches to Genappe. In a number of sharp skirmishes he bloodied the French advance guard to such good effect that they remained totally unaware of the Ways la Hutte crossing. By nightfall Wellington's army had reached their positions. Müffling had contacted Blücher who gave his word that if Wellington stood his ground he would force-march at least two corps to his aid. This was an enormous commitment, and one fraught with danger. If Wellington were defeated or withdrew, or changed his mind, the Prussian army would be strung out on the march between two enemy forces, and liable to be annihilated. Gneisenau was against the plan. Blücher was determined. At this point Gneisenau could have pulled the rug from under him by citing his instructions from the king, but his distrust of Wellington was outweighed by his pathological hatred of the French and he agreed to take the risk. But he took the precaution of arranging to be kept informed of the situation by a string of relay-riders.

On the morning of 18 June, the French and Allied forces were drawn up facing one another on a front whose width was less than 2½ miles (see map). Behind Wellington's position was the vast forest of Soignes, some 10 x 10 miles in extent. Both armies were sited on a low ridge whose dips and folds gave the terrain a deceptively flat appearance. Wellington had positioned some 17,000 troops at Hal, seventeen miles away by road, to cover, he said, the exposed road to Brussels along which, for all he knew, Napoleon might have detached a corps to take him in flank or rear. In reality, If Wellington were defeated these troops at Hal would form a strong rearguard behind which he could rally his army and retreat behind the Scheldt.

Wellington had deployed his army in a line from Braine-l'Alleud along a slope behind the semi-sunken road to Ohain where a declivity concealed the farms of Papelotte, la Haye and the château of Frischermont. It was on this flank that the Prussians were expected to join. On his right, in front and below Braine-l'Alleud to its left, was the château of Hougoumont, a vast manorial *domaine* and farm complex with orchards and a copse which he had made into a veritable fortress. In his centre, where the great highway to Brussels cut through the sunken road, via the forest, lay the farmhouse of la Haye Sainte which had he thought also been fortified. His army was well placed, secure on both flanks, and his centre protected by fortified dwellings that would require a determined, sustained assault to reduce.

Napoleon, opposite, his headquarters near the inn of La Belle Alliance, had deployed his army in three echelons: the first comprised Reillle's corps to the east of the road from Braine-l'Alleud to the highway. From there, in a curved line to the western flank in the dip, was d'Erlon's corps. Behind each corps was a heavy cavalry corps. The second echelon consisted of Mouton-Lobau's corps, acting as the immediate reserve – the cutting edge that would pour through the broken line. The third echelon consisted of the Imperial Guard corps, the ultimate reserve.

Napoleon could see that Wellington had deployed more men on his right wing than on his left (Wellington was expecting the Prussians on his left by late morning). Napoleon's plan was straightforward. He would make a diversionary attack on the château of Hougoumont below Wellington's right which, he hoped, would weaken his reserves in supporting this position. If he were able to take the château wood it would enable him to place his corps within a few hundred yards of Wellington's left and lateral communications. But had no intention of sacrificing his men's lives on such a fortified position. He had defended a similar position himself at Aspen-Essling in 1809, a massive stone granary which had soaked up thousands of Austrians in their futile attempts to take it. No! So long as Wellington perceived the threat it should cause him to commit men to its defence, or further strengthen his right – away from Napoleon's true objective. While this feint was taking place he would position a grand battery of 84 guns on the high ground behind d'Erlon, then punch a hole in Wellington's weak left flank. D'Erlon's corps, fresh as it was, would advance, break through this line, wheel right, and fortify the massive farmhouse of Mont St-Jean. Then Mouton-Lobau's corps would help d'Erlon to roll up Wellington's line. Reille's corps around Hougoumont would complete the advance on Wellington's left, supported by all the cavalry. Then on to Brussels!

The ground was sodden from a heavy thunderstorm during the night. It was a hot sunny day, and Napoleon's artillery commander requested that the ground be allowed to dry out a little before being required to manoeuvre across ploughed fields. Napoleon considered this, and delayed the attack by nearly four hours. Four hours again, as in 1814, would be too late!

Behind his position, nestling in a fold, was the village of Plancenoit. Napoleon wondered why its church bell was ringing. Someone remarked that it was Sunday; the priest was probably unaware of what was about to take place. Plancenoit's church was rather unique in that it had been built on a mound some eighteen feet high that required visitors to ascend by steep steps. The mound was encircled by the cemetery wall which had a ring of trees planted along its length inside. By nightfall canister would have removed all but the tree stumps, and there would be thirty times as many bodies above ground in the churchyard as were beneath it. The road from Plancenoit led to Mousty, from where the main road led to Wavre.

At Wavre, Blücher and Gneisenau had planned their strategy. Gneisenau was worried about Wellington's reliability; he was after all unknown on the European battlefields. Thanks to Castlereagh's behaviour, the Prussian chief of staff suspected Wellington of being a devious political animal in the mould of Schwarzenberg. Gneisenau ordered von Bülow's IV Corps (which had arrived too late at Ligny) to lead the advance and old Blücher thought this was a good idea, but, last to arrive, it had to pass through two other army corps with all its wagons, guns and impedimenta, which caused a delay of several hours. If Wellington were beaten, or withdrew, Bülow's fresh corps would act as the Prussian rearguard. If he stood, he would be heavily committed by the time they arrived. He would have blunted Napoleon's attack and given the Prussians time to consolidate and launch an attack with strength. Gneisenau's scouts told him that Grouchy had been wandering about looking for the Prussians and was almost in contact. Obviously he would attack while they were advancing. Von Thielemann was given the job of holding Wavre – to the last man if necessary. If he lost the crossings or were about to be outflanked, he should withdraw slowly north-eastwards, fighting every step of the way, drawing Grouchy away from Mont St-Jean and the main Prussian Army. Blücher considered that the expenditure of Thielemann's corps would be a small price to pay for the destruction of Napoleon's forces (less Grouchy's one-third).

At about 11.30 Napoleon's divisional cannon opened fire. Prince Jérôme's division supported by that of Foy (Wellington's acquaintance of 1814) in Reille's corps advanced and began the assault of the château of Hougoumont. The battle raged for more than an hour. Wellington made no move to support the flank; indeed through the heavy smoke Napoleon had a job to discern Wellington's line at all. By 12.30 his grand battery was raining shot and shell on Wellington's left centre and doing terrible execution in the rear of the barely visible line.

But Napoleon now received appalling news. A cavalry patrol on his right flank in the woods of St-Lambert near the hamlets in the dip, had captured several Prussians. They confirmed the awful truth that Blücher's army was marching on Napoleon's right flank. He sent urgent orders for Grouchy to rejoin the main body. He then deployed his second echelon, Mouton-Lobau's corps, at right angles to his right flank, along the routes that Blücher's army would use. He now had to beat the 'Sepoy' General before Blücher arrived – then Mouton-Lobau's corps could attack Blücher's troops while they were strung out along line of march and cut them to pieces as they fell back to regroup. He would then advance the few miles to Brussels, which would constitute a resounding political victory, and if necessary move along the Louvain road to help finish off Blücher – or move left and chase Wellington to the coast, depending on the circumstances.

It was now about 1 30 p.m. D'Erlon's corps advanced in echelon, his 1st Division split into two brigades, one to assault the farmhouse and Wellington's centre beyond, supported by a brigade of cuirassiers on its left, the other to maintain contact with it on the other side of the road. Next came Donzelot and Marcognet's divisions, in massive columns, supported in the intervals by horse artillery; then Durutte's division, split so that one brigade could support the main body on the edge of the dip, the other to assault and carry the hamlets and château in the dip. Both these divisions were supported by light cavalry. Mouton-Lobau had been removed, so the breach would now be exploited by the heavy cavalry.

D'Erlon's entire corps, almost 16,000 men, now surged forward supported by about 1,000 cavalrymen, and for part of its way it had the additional support of about 100 cannon pounding the line of attack. General Picton's division was the prime objective; he had some 6,000 men deployed in two echelons, behind whom were the Union Brigade of cavalry, comprising some 1,200 men. Across the adjacent Highway was the British 1st Cavalry Brigade comprising the Household Cavalry and the Dragoon Guards, another 1,300-odd men. D'Erlon's skirmishers, greatly outnumbering Picton's troops, swept the ground clean; their strength was such that many of their opponents thought that this was the main attack. The great mass of French infantry reached the sunken road, their firepower sweeping the Allied first line back, crossed the road and started to ascend the rise. Napoleon, viewing through his telescope, was jubilant. His plan was succeeding. He ordered his heavy cavalry on his left flank to advance closer to the grand battery.

Wellington, always at the point of greatest danger, was supervising the support of Hougoumont and had ordered a troop of howitzers to come up to the ground above the château and lob shells into the woods beyond to drive back the French. The Earl of Uxbridge, whose troop this had nominally been, had just ridden back to his central position when, from the high ground behind the ridge, he observed d'Erlon's attack and the punitive assault with cuirassiers on la Haye Sainte. He ordered the Union Brigade to advance in conjunction with the Household Brigade – having already arranged that one regiment ride in a second line to act as a reserve on which the first could rally. However, the shot and shell raining down on the 2nd Dragoons, the Scots Greys, had caused their Colonel to bring them forward into the first line to avoid further casualties.

The Earl of Uxbridge gave the signal and his cavalry struck like a thunderbolt, straight into the infantry, capturing two Eagles and routing the entire corps. On the other side of the Highway the Household Cavalry had mauled the cuirassiers, hamstrung the infantry attack, and withdrawn in good order, supported by its second line. The Union Brigade was not so fortunate. Napoleon had already brought up the cavalry to assail the broken Allied infantry, and they were launched at the spent

Union Brigade which, having no support, was soon reduced to a couple of squadrons. Uxbridge blamed himself, unnecessarily; his action had smashed Napoleon's plan of attack, and routed an entire army corps. Accounts vary, but if one takes a conservative estimate of killed, captured and missing, d'Erlon was left with 11,000 effectives; but a routed corps of 20-odd battalions would take time to re-form.

Napoleon now had only two infantry divisions and the Imperial Guard at his immediate disposal. It would not be prudent or feasible to halt the attack on Hougoumont; after this reversal on his left, it would seem to Wellington that he was retreating. Knowing that Blücher was on his way, Wellington might decide to counter-attack. He could not withdraw Mouton-Lobau's corps and risk being taken by the advancing Prussians in rear and flank. To expose the Guard at this stage would be to commit his only reserve in the face of solid infantry. What to do? He needed time for d'Erlon's troops to reform. Napoleon was not a novice, nor was he given to panic. He had been in this position at Eylau in 1807; he would redress the situation in the same way. He would order a massive barrage by the more than 200 cannon available along the line, the like of which would never have been seen before. Under cover of this literal smoke-screen Ney would have to emulate Murat at Eylau and smash the Allied infantry with cavalry. Napoleon now rued his decision to leave Murat behind. (The tactic would not have been new to Murat. He had broken the Russians at Eylau, and his cavalry had ridden over the great artillery and infantry earthworks at Borodino in 1812.) It took about thirty minutes to amass the thousands of heavy cavalry from around the field in the attack position between Hougoumont and la Haye Sainte. The going was better on the ploughed fields than up the slope, which was littered with dead men and horses in front of d'Erlon's corps.

The Allied squares were easy targets for the tremendous cannonade, but they did not break. Ney, bravest of the brave, had horse after horse shot under him each time he plunged back to regroup while the rain of shell resumed between charges, but to no avail. In desperation Napoleon threw in his Guard cavalry; if he could break just one square, perhaps panic – always infectious – might spread to adjacent squares and rout Wellington's army. They did not break. Ney was a brilliant infantry commander, but had never commanded a cavalry attack, certainly not one on this scale. If he had had a single horse battery with him (Napoleon had removed them earlier) they would have been able to reduce the squares to a bloody rubble, unable to move for fear of the cavalry. Murat would have done this, indeed had done so in the past. Behind the Allied squares the Netherlands squadrons of heavy cavalry awaited the French cavalry, whose tight formations broke on the approach, and swept them back over the lip.

By now d'Erlon's corps had regrouped. Durutte's division, mauled but still intact, had begun an all-out attack to capture the hamlets in the dip, but this battle within a battle could not be seen from the main line. Mouton-Lobau now reported that the Prussians were massing for an attack. Napoleon ordered Ney to take the farmhouse of la Haye Sainte which would form a bridge-head from which Welling-ton's line might be broken. Assaulting the length of the main battle, by 6 o'clock Ney had taken the farmhouse and brought a battery up to within 150 yards of Wellington's centre. Sweeping it with canister, he now had the opportunity of break-ing through. He sent a message to Napoleon asking for more troops. Napoleon, who to stop Blücher severing his flank and his line of communications via Genappe, was having to support Mouton-Lobau in Plancenoit with all the Young Guard and an élite battalion of his Old Guard. During this operation Ney's request came through, and Napoleon snapped 'What does he expect me to do – make them?' By the time that he had stabilized the Plancenoit situation, Ney's moment had passed. Napoleon's Guards had made a fortress of Plancenoit with the church and its wall on the mound as the citadel. Wellington, apprised that the Prussians had joined, consol-idated his centre right position by abandoning most of his left.

Napoleon, now had to decide whether to retreat, or take a chance with the 4,000-odd élite troops of his Imperial Guard – his sole reserve. Wellington and his heterogeneous force must surely be finished. If the Guard went forward the army would sense victory, their morale would be heightened. One last effort would break Wellington, Blücher would then be pushed back and would have to withdraw. Besides, Grouchy's 33,000 men would surely turn the tide; he had sent a message to him apprising him of the situation. At this point General Durutte via Mouton-Lobau had informed Napoleon that the Dutch behind Smohain had come under attack, he believed from Grouchy. On this information Napoleon decided to attack. He had already boosted morale by telling his men that the cannon-fire that could be heard in rear around Papelotte was Grouchy attacking on the left.

Marshal Ney led out the Old Guard, the line cheered and joined it in an all-out attack. The Guard's leading echelon pushed back the Hanoverian and British regi-ments in the centre, but this potential rout was stabilized by the timely arrival of a horse battery and a fresh Netherlands brigade which pushed the French back in dis-order. The British Guards, farther on the right, poured a volley into one column – or rather hollow square – and pushed it back with the bayonet. Another was enfiladed by flanking fire from a crack British light infantry regiment – the 52nd. But now, from the dip at Papelotte and Smohain, streaming across the field straight through the French line towards La Belle Alliance, behind d'Erlon's flank and rear, came the masses of Ziethen's cavalry, followed by his infantry and cannon. The French infantry disintegrated in a rout. Fleeing pell-mell to avoid being surrounded, the cry went up along the whole line that the Prussians were in their rear. Later many stated that, having expected Grouchy, only to find Prussians, they suspected treachery and had fled in despair. Wellington stood in the stirrups and waved his troops forward, and the French army, the Old Guard and Napoleon were swept backwards.

The effect of this rupture was disastrous. Napoleon, who thought that he was holding the Prussian main advance at Plancenoit, had not expected that Blücher would hazard the integrity of his formations strung out along tiny cart tracks as well as the Wavre road. In effect, Blücher had used Napoleon's own tactics of the past against him, and his fresh troops had effected a rupture at the angle of his line where it turned right to defend Plancenoit. Thanks to the dip the Prussians had been able to advance to within striking distance without being observed and pierce the French centre. Having used the last of his reserves, Napoleon now had only two Old Guard battalions for a rearguard behind which to rally his broken men who were being pursued everywhere, many throwing away their weapons and equipment as they fled. Never in memory, not even at Marengo in 1800, had Napoleon been in the position of being routed with no reserve to stem the enemy and allow his force to be rallied. Loyal to the end, the two Old Guard battalions held the road – and the entire Allied army – long enough for the Emperor to escape. Napoleon reached Genappe only to find chaos; all the wagons and supplies had been sent back here in case of a retreat, when the Prussians were known to be advancing. Now the narrow main street and bridge had become a bottle-neck, adding to the panic and disorder. This might have been averted if, like Uxbridge, they had known of the other bridge at Ways la Hutte a few hundred yards down-stream, where the baggage might have been diverted.

Napoleon had sought his decisive battle in Belgium. He had waited two years for the opportunity to change the course of his destiny with a 'crash of thunder'. Now the thunderbolt had turned and struck him. He had broken his own golden rule of committing his last reserves before the enemy had expended his. His record in battle during more than twenty years shows that, even at Borodino, he had never violated this principle. Desperately needing this victory and the capture of Brussels to turn the political tide, Napoleon the political leader had overruled Napoleon the military commander. In the pursuit of the political he had lost sight of his military aims.

From his position on the field, Napoleon had not appreciated the importance of the hamlets in the declivity on his vulnerable right. Durutte, who had spent all day trying to capture the area with little success, had been unable with the remnant of his division to prevent any Prussian advance in force. Napoleon had sent Grouchy off with one- third of his army to stop Blücher intervening. Grouchy had failed. Napoleon had then committed Mouton-Lobau's corps to block the Prussians' arrival – that too had been insufficient, and required the further support of half his Guard corps, the Young Guard division, to hold the position. Napoleon had held a 2½-mile front against Wellington; by mid-afternoon he had another 2½ miles along his right flank to hold as well – to prevent his encirclement. A 5-mile front turning at the dip at right angles. But still he would not concede and withdraw his army as he would have done in 1814. When another Prussian corps appeared and pierced the right angle his line collapsed. Facing Wellington, and certain that he would now punch through his line, Napoleon did not appreciate what had happened.

Written at Laon on 20 June, Napoleon's 'Official Bulletin' played down this massive reversal to the Parisians and in particular to the two Chambers. Two days after the event, his utter disbelief at the rout comes through even this carefully worded propaganda:

'In a moment the army became a panic-stricken rabble, the different arms were even intermingled, and it was utterly impossible to rally a single corps. Noticing this astonishing disorganization, the enemy immediately attacked with their cavalry and increased the disorder, and owing to night coming on, such was the confusion that it was impossible to rally the troops and point out their error to them ... yet all was thrown away by a moment of mad terror.'[32]

Napoleon had experienced reversals before: the retreat from Moscow, the Battle of Leipzig, and many reverses during 1814. Always, however, he had managed to withdraw his army in good order. But here at Mont St-Jean his army, which had fought valiantly for three days, had evaporated into a panic-stricken mob, all guns and equipment lost. Not since Jena in 1806, when Napoleon had visited a similar defeat on the antiquated Prussian army, had such a rout been inflicted. The truth is that Napoleon had lost touch with his soldiers. He had failed to realize the depths of their apprehension with regard to senior generals who were apt to change sides if it suited their ambitions. He had inadvertently betrayed their trust in announcing that Grouchy was arriving; when they realized that the Prussians were through their flank they ran in panic, convinced that their fears of betrayal had been realized.

In Napoleon's opinion, however, all was not lost. If Grouchy could withdraw his troops in good order they could be used as a core on which to rally his dispersed army, and with the troops in the depots and at Paris, he could take the field again. The battle had been lost but not necessarily the war. Blücher and Wellington's troops had sustained heavy losses. They had marched and counter-marched for three days, their ammunition would need replenishing, and they would dissipate a great deal of their strength in investing his static defence line of the massive frontier fortresses, which they could only leave intact at peril of their lines of communication. Leaving instructions for the commanders of all the frontier fortresses to hold out as long as possible, and for Soult and Grouchy to concentrate the troops at Philippeville, Napoleon repaired to that town and held a council of war. Most of his Generals were of the opinion that he should stay with the army and send for all available reinforcements. But Napoleon, mindful of 1814, and the new constitutional Chambers, decided to return to Paris, his power-base. Sending messages to General Rapp and Marshal Suchet that he intended to create a new field army around their corps, and for them to withdraw closer to Paris, he left his army to regroup, stopped at Laon long enough to write his Bulletin and formulate defence plans, and then set off for Paris.

Meanwhile, at a small inn in the forest of Soignies, The Duke of Wellington, tired and devastated by the deaths of so many of his friends and soldiers, having greeted Blücher at La Belle Alliance and ridden back over the field covered with the dead and dying, started his dispatch to Lord Liverpool:

'... The enemy collected his army, with the exception of the 3rd corps, which had been sent to observe Marshal Blücher at Wavre, on a range of heights in our front ... at about ten o'clock he commenced a furious attack upon our post at Hougoumont ... This attack on our right centre was accompanied by a very heavy cannonade upon our whole line ... The enemy repeatedly charged our infantry with his cavalry, but these attacks were uniformly unsuccessful ... These attacks were repeated till about seven in the evening, when the enemy made a desperate effort with cavalry and infantry, supported by the fire of artillery to force our left centre ... which after a severe contest, was defeated; and having observed that the troops retired from this attack in great confusion, and *that the march of General Bülow's corps, by Frischermont, upon Planchenois* [sic] *and La Belle Alliance, had begun to take effect, and as I could perceive the fire of his cannon, and as Marshal Prince Blücher had joined in person with a corps of his army to the left of our line by Ohain, I determined to attack the enemy,* and immediately advanced the whole line of infantry, supported by cavalry and artillery. The attack succeeded in every point: the enemy was forced from his positions on the heights and *fled in the utmost confusion,* leaving behind, as far as I could judge, 150 pieces of cannon, with their ammunition, which fell into our hands.'[33]

Wellington sent this dispatch to London, dated 19 June 1815, from his headquarters at WATERLOO.

CHAPTER 12

THE ROAD TO ST. HELENA

*'Tell me O Muse, of the man of many tricks, who wandered far and wide
after he had sacked Troy's sacred city, and saw the towns of many men and
knew their minds.'* – Homer, *c.* 900 BC.
'I met Murder in the way – He had a mask like Castlereagh.' – Percy Bysshe Shelley,
The Mask of Anarchy, Act II.

AVING ORDERED THE REMNANT OF HIS ARMY, AND
Grouchy's corps to rally at Laon, Napoleon arrived at Paris on 21 June.
News of his defeat, sent by him the day before, had been acted upon by
Fouché who had already been in touch with Metternich and
Castlereagh before Napoleon had left for the campaign. Napoleon had become aware
of his intriguing before he left for the front and had wanted to have him arrested and
brought before a military tribunal. Carnot, the great republican, beguiled by Fouché,
had warned Napoleon that if he did this he would alienate the republican element
which dominated the Chambers.[1] Convinced that Fouché was a patriot, Carnot
insisted that if Napoleon had any evidence against him he should proceed through
the courts. Napoleon had tried to do this but had been thwarted. Knowing this,
Fouché had it put about by his agents that he had merely received informal inquiries
from Metternich and had rejected them; indeed, he passed Napoleon a letter
received from Metternich. This surprised Napoleon who did not know that Fouché
knew of the 'discreet' inquires he was making concerning Fouché's activities.[2] To
appease the republicans and against his better judgement Napoleon left Fouché in
place. Fouché had supplied Wellington and the Allies with Napoleon's order of battle, 'the secret of which was communicated to me by Davoust [*sic*]'.[3] and clearly he
intended to send Wellington and Schwarzenberg as much of Napoleon's plan of
campaign as he could get from Davoust, but fearing that Napoleon might be victorious, delayed transmission of it at the border until after Waterloo. If Napoleon failed
the Allies would be reassured as to Fouché's good faith.[4]

Fouché arrived at the Elysée on the morning of Napoleon's arrival. Exhausted by
the strain of the last six days, and understandably dispirited and bewildered by the
total collapse of his field army, Napoleon decided – fatally – not to go straightaway,
in his riding clothes and boots, to address the Chambers as he was urged to do.
Instead, he waited until later in the day, after he had rested and decided what he
should say. Fouché, having already amplified details of the defeat before Napoleon
had officially reported them, deceived him into thinking that the mood of the
Deputies was not hostile. Davout and Napoleon's brother Lucien, advised him to
prorogue the Chambers, as was his prerogative under the constitution, and to rule by
decree until the present emergency was passed.

Not wishing to be seen by the people as a dictator, Napoleon accepted Fouché's advice. It was to prove his downfall. As Fouché explains: 'I set in motion all my friends, all my adherents, and all my agents, whom I provided with the watch-word. As to myself, I communicated, in full council with the élite of all the parties in the state. To the unquiet, mistrustful, and obnoxious members of the Chambers, I said: "It is necessary to act; to say little; and resort to force; he is becoming perfectly insane; he is decided upon dissolving the Chambers and seizing dictatorship. I trust we shall not suffer such a tyranny as this."⁵ Fouché had already prepared the ground the night before with a whispering campaign on the grand scale, hence 'watch-word'. He goes on: 'I said to the partisans of Napoleon: "Are you not aware that the ferment against the Emperor has reached the highest pitch among the majority of the Deputies. His fall is desired; his abdication is demanded. If you are bent on serving him, you must make head vigorously against them, to show what power you still retain, and to affirm that his single word will be sufficient to dissolve the Chambers" I also entered into their language and views; they then disclosed their secret inclinations, and I was able to say to the heads of the patriots, who rallied round me: "You perceive that his best friends make no mystery of it; the danger is pressing; in a few hours the Chambers will exist no longer."'⁶

These sentiments were bruited by Fouché's agents all over Paris that morning. In the salons, drawing-rooms and cafés the imperialists and republicans railed at one another. While Napoleon slept the Allies were advancing, and France was under threat; Fouché was succeeding in dividing the national coalition party. In the face of invasion, they would be at one another's throats by noon. But Fouché had yet two more cards to play. Baron Vitrolles, the Bourbons' representative, ex-Minister and head of the so-called provisional government, whom Napoleon had ordered to be shot after his capture in the south, stating: 'He is an intriguer and an agent of Talleyrand's. It was he who was dispatched to the Emperor Alexander, and who opened the gates of Paris to the Allies. This man has been arrested at Toulouse, in the act of conspiring against me; if he had been shot, Lamarque would have done no more than his duty.'⁷ Fouché persuaded Napoleon to allow him to use Vitrolles as a broker in an endeavour to recover the crown jewels. Fouché had used Vitrolles' contacts to communicate with the Allies and the Bourbons. He now released him from the Abbaye prison, and instructed him to mobilize the royalists.

Fouché's second card was Marie-Joseph-Paul-Yves-Roch-Gilbert Motier, Marquis de La Fayette. Fifty-eight years old, he had fought in the War of American Independence, and had been General Washington's friend. He had returned imbued with the enthusiasm for liberty and equality that he had found in the nascent United States, a country that had as yet no national traditions, and whose culture was still in the process of evolution. A country where land was available for all at no cost save enterprise, hard work, and a willingness to brave the wilderness. The aristocratic La Fayette was all for emulating the American spirit in France. But France was still a feudal agricultural society whose poorest elements bore the greatest tax burdens, and were tied to the land that was owned by a privileged minority. Naturally enough, when the people were freed from this oppression they sought revenge on their privileged subjugators. When Tom Paine's notions embodied in *Rights of Man* and *The Age of Reason* reached France with the returning victorious army, La Fayette and others saw themselves in the mould of Washington, leading a new revolution that would be controlled by the enlightened 'upper classes'. During the balmy early months of the Revolution La Fayette, commander of the National Guard, became the darling of the nation. He betrayed the king whom he had sworn to protect, and had him arrested on 5 October 1789. Three years later, disillusioned with the new 'common men' of equality, and the fanatics that attach themselves to any revolution, he deserted the command of his army and went over to the enemy. The Austrians imprisoned him for his part in the arrest and subsequent death of the Austrian princess, Marie-Antoinette, and only the fear of reprisals against the remaining royal children saved him from being executed. In 1797 his release was procured by one General Napoleon Bonaparte, after his victory over the Austrians in Italy. In return, La Fayette refused to help the general when he became Consul and then Emperor. How much of envy was in this refusal by La Fayette, who had become frustrated and embittered by his personal failures, is a matter for conjecture. When the Bourbons returned they treated him with the contempt they felt he deserved, considering him a traitor to their family and his class. Offended, this quasi-republican nobleman aligned himself with the old republicans, and their outdated concepts. Accepting a seat in the Senate on Napoleon's return, he believed that the new constitutional assembly was what he had been trying to achieve all his life.

Fouché took a crowd of republicans to see La Fayette and told him that Napoleon intended to appoint himself dictator; his companions confirmed this rumour which Fouché himself had started that very morning. It was up to La Fayette to save once again the fruits of the Revolution. The old fool fell for it, hook line and sinker. Fouché proposed that he become Minister of War, or command the national army in the new republic. Had not the Allies declared that it was only Napoleon who was their enemy? Did not Article 8 of their Vienna declaration state that it was for the French people to choose their own government? If they could establish a republic before the Allies reached Paris, might not France retain her liberty, equality and civil rights? The great patriot agreed to betray the man who had saved his life and freed him from imprisonment.[8]

At midday on 21 June, the Chambers met under the chairmanship of the comte Lanjuinais. Immediately La Fayette rose and spoke:

'Gentleman, when for the first time for many years I raise my voice that old friends of liberty will still recognize, I feel myself called upon to speak to you of the danger to our country which you alone, at this moment, have the power to avert. Sinister rumours have been bruited abroad; they have unfortunately proved to be true. This is the time for all of us to rally around our ancient standard, the tricolore, the flag and symbol of '89, of liberty, equality and public order; it is that alone which we shall have to defend against pretensions from without and upheavals from within. Gentlemen, allow a veteran of this sacred cause to submit to you certain preliminary proposals whose necessity you will I hope appreciate:

Article 1. The Chamber of Representatives declares the independence of the country threatened.

Article 2. The Chamber declares itself in permanent session. Any attempt to dissolve it is high treason; whoever may be guilty of such an attempt is a traitor to the country and may summarily be judged as such.

Article 3. The army of the line and the National Guard who have fought and who are still fighting to defend the liberty, independence and the territory of France have deserved well of the country.

Article 4. The Minister of the Interior is requested to summon the General Staff and the commanders and senior officers of the National Guard in order to consult about giving them arms and encouraging to the full this citizen guard whose patriotism and zeal, proved over the past twenty-six years, provides a sure guarantee of the liberty, the property, the peace of the capital and the inviolability of the representatives of the nation.

Article 5. The Ministers of War, of External Affairs, of the Police and of the Interior are requested to present themselves to the Assembly immediately.'[9]

La Fayette was again emulating the 'tennis court' assembly of 1789 which had precipitated the Revolution. The declaration was immediately carried. At first glance there was nothing that could be construed as an attack on Napoleon. Rather, it seemed to ensure the liberty of the nation, and even praised the army. It appeared to be aimed at preventing the formation of a provisional government by the upper Houses – which Talleyrand had done in 1814. The clever use of the defence of the tricolore and reference to the enemy 'without and within' (royalists and traitors) veiled the Articles that followed, which were directed against the Emperor. One Chamber alone could not enact legislation without the assent of the other, and the consent of the Emperor. La Fayette had set the scene for a civil war – which was what Fouché wanted. The Chambers were protected by the Paris National Guard, its ranks swelled by returned royalists from the Meaux force, its commanders appointed by Fouché. To oust the Deputies Napoleon would have to use force.

Since his return Napoleon's palace and the faubourgs were crowded by some 14–20,000 volunteers who called themselves *fédérés* after the citizen soldiers of the early Revolution. They were determined to ensure that Paris was not betrayed again. Many had arms, but for obvious reasons Fouché had denied any to the remainder. The Chambers' declaration proposed that they be armed, but they would not be if Fouché had anything to do with it. Since the publication of Napoleon's Bulletin announcing his defeat, they had thronged the palace shouting, '*Vive l'Empereur!*', '*Vive la Liberté!*' and other revolutionary slogans, and yelling for arms with which to defend the capital. Napoleon hoped to incorporate them *en masse* into the National Guard to augment his new field force. Dumbfounded by La Fayette's treacherous move, he was urged by his brother Lucien to use these and his regulars to close the

Chambers and rule by decree. Napoleon refused, declaring: 'I would never lead a *Jacquerie.*' The idea of instigating a civil war was abhorrent to him. Instead he decided to solicit the support of the Chamber of Peers, and use it to influence the lower House in which he had a majority.

On the 21st Marshal Ney had also arrived in Paris, very conscious of his position *vis-à-vis* Napoleon, whose Bulletin and comments appeared to be making him the scapegoat, and the Bourbons against whom he had turned his coat. Napoleon, embarrassed by the failure of his master plan, and ever jealous of his own military reputation (the cavalry had sustained great losses), had from the moment of d'Erlon's repulse complained to all and sundry that Ney had unleashed the cavalry recklessly and too soon.

Ney's first call was upon Fouché with whom he was intimate. From him he obtained two passports in false names; he was already watching his back and intended to run when the Allies were nearing Paris. Fouché, praising Ney's conduct and repeating the rumours, urged him to repair immediately to the Chamber of Peers and defend his honour.

The Peers listened to Carnot reading a true situation report from Rocroi which stated that Marshal Grouchy had beaten the Prussians at Wavre on 19 June and had brought his 30,000 men back into France in good order, and that, with the units of routed troops that had been re-assembled, he was now heading for Paris with 60,000 men (in fact 62,737).[10] As soon as Carnot finished Marshal Ney stood up and in his loud voice declared: 'The news which the Minister has given you is entirely false in every respect. The enemy is victorious at every point. I have witnessed the disaster, for I commanded the army under the Emperor. After the results of those days of disaster, the 16th and 18th, they dare to tell us that we ended by beating the enemy on the 18th, and that there are 60,000 men on the frontier. The statement is false. At the very most Marshal Grouchy has perhaps rallied 20,000 or 25,000 men. When they tell us the Prussian army is destroyed, it is not true. The greater part of that army has not been in action. In six or seven days the enemy will perhaps be in the middle of the capital. *There is no other means of securing the public safety but to make proposals to the enemy at once.*'[11] This outburst by Ney, who felt slighted and resented being unjustly blamed by Napoleon, was the ultimate weapon in Fouché's arsenal. Ney the 'Bravest of the Brave', the French army's hero, had pronounced its doom. Ney silenced any criticism immediately. Raising his hands to protesters, he said: 'Gentlemen, I spoke only in the interests of the country. Do I not know quite well that if Louis comes back I shall be shot!'[12] His speech had a profound effect even on Marshal Davout who remained markedly silent. The Deputy for Baugé in Maine-et-Loire wrote that night to his constituents: 'Ney's outburst has done more harm than losing another battle ... The people of Paris accuse the hero of Krasnoye [Ney] of treason.'[13] The Peers adjourned until the evening.

It was now up to Napoleon. He commanded the capital but had lost the support of both Houses. Commissioners from the Chambers asked him to abdicate in favour of his son. La Fayette had loudly declared that if Napoleon refused to abdicate the

Chambers should depose him. Napoleon was in a dilemma. The enemy was closing on Paris and the time he needed to put together a new force was being wasted by this pompous talking-shop. Who would command this new republican army? La Fayette, who had commanded a small force of less than a corps in 1789? Ney, who had betrayed him in 1814, Louis in 1815, and now him again in the Chamber of Peers? Ney was burnt out, and riddled with guilt; his ambivalence had blurred his judgement. Napoleon now had little choice; Fouché had out-manoeuvred him. If he did nothing, the Chambers would depose him, the *fédérés* might riot and attack the assembly with the army ('treason' was on the peasants' lips), civil war would erupt to the demoralization of the nation. If he tried to remove the Chambers by force, he might succeed, but fighting would still break out in the capital. The republicans would join with the royalists to oppose him. The sight of Paris disintegrating into mob violence would be useful to Fouché and the royalists; the fiction that the army had imposed Napoleon on the people would then appear to be true.

With an eye to posterity, Napoleon was not going to sully his reputation. He was suffering from the stress of having raised an army, planned a campaign, fought two major battles and survived a devastating rout. Now he had to confront the prospect of a civil war, as well as all the Allied forces of Europe. He attempted the same tactic he had used in 1814. He abdicated in favour of his son. This would at least defuse the situation, and give him a breathing-space. Later he was to write:

'I considered for a long time, weighed the pros and cons and, since I foresaw immediately the outcome ... I concluded that I could not resist the coalition from without, the royalists from within, and the crowd of seditious factions that any violation of the legislative body would have created, and finally that moral condemnation which imputes to one, when one has met with misfortunes, all the ills that crowd upon one ... Abdication meant the loss of everything despite all my efforts. I saw it, I said it, but I had no choice. History will judge.'[14]

At the evening session of the Chambers the Peers heard the declaration in silence. Then La Bédoyère moved to the rostrum, and asked why Napoleon II had not yet been proclaimed? There was utter silence. 'Napoleon abdicated only in favour of his son; and unless Napoleon II be proclaimed by the Chamber of Peers, and by that of the representatives, the abdication is null and void. I have heard the voices of those surrounding the throne of the Emperor in prosperity, who withdraw from it now he is in misfortune. There are persons who will not acknowledge Napoleon II because they wish to receive the law from foreigners, to whom they give the name of allies. The abdication of Napoleon is inseparably connected with the succession of his son. If his son is not to be recognized, he ought to draw his sword, surrounded by Frenchmen who have shed their blood for him, and who are still covered with wounds, though he might be abandoned by some base generals who have already betrayed him. The nation owes this to the Emperor. We have abandoned him once; shall we abandon him a second time? We have sworn to defend him even in his misfortunes. If we declare that every Frenchman who quits his standard shall be covered with infamy, shall have his house razed, and his family proscribed, we shall then have no more traitors; no more catastrophes some of whose authors are perhaps within these walls.'[15] The President rose at this deliberate attack on Ney's honour, and the guards physically removed La Bédoyère.

Mud sticks however. No matter how much Napoleon might malign Ney in order to cover up his own errors, which he blatantly had, Ney was a Marshal of France and commander of the left wing of the army. Why had he deserted it in the face of the enemy and returned without orders? His first call had not been to the Minister of War for orders, but to Fouché for false papers. For an army officer to attack his commander-in-chief in the upper House and spread despair and despondency among the troops was treasonous in time of war.

Prince Lucien had already proposed that Napoleon II be proclaimed. Count Cornudet rose and said: 'We are disputing about words. The minutes of the Chamber recognize the abdication of Napoleon. They will also record the claim of Prince Lucien. That precaution will recognize and suffice to guard the rights of Napoleon II, but at present he is out of France. To speak plainly he is a prisoner. Under the circumstances, what does the public safety and national independence require? The establishment of a provisional government, capable of adopting measures for the public safety.'[16]

It was all up now with Napoleon; his bluff had been called. Outside the Chambers, Prince Lucien had brought thousands of *fédérés* and regulars, chanting for Napoleon and death to the traitors. Given this critical situation, Fouché's underlings proposed that the Chambers create a provisional government and disperse. Fouché was elected its President. He gave the post of Commander-in-Chief of the army to Davout who immediately accepted it. Side-stepping his adversary Soult, who was later demoted at Davout's insistence, Davout wrote to Grouchy on the 22nd, telling him that Napoleon had abdicated: '... wishing to remove any pretext for the foreign powers to continue the war ... You can, and indeed you must, send reports of these events to the Allied generals in your vicinity, asking them to suspend all hostilities until they have received the orders of their sovereigns. Write to all prefects to acquaint them of these matters ...'[17] Davout was wasting no time in implementing Fouché's policies. Like La Fayette, Carnot and the other dupes, he had believed Fouché when he said that with Napoleon gone the Allies would allow them to form their own government, under which he, Davout, the 'Iron Marshal', would command the new republican or royalist army.

Fouché insolently ordered Napoleon to leave Paris. Napoleon, fearing his presence might precipitate civil war, left for Malmaison, there to consider his next move. But Fouché had no reason to feel jubilant; he knew that Napoleon could still take back the army whenever he pleased.

Wellington, slowly advancing on Paris, refused, as did Blücher, to enter into any dialogue. The Prussians were bent on revenge. Wellington had other reasons. He had written to King Louis saying that if he wished to become King of France again, he had best pack his bags and follow him. The point taken, Louis of Ghent, as he was

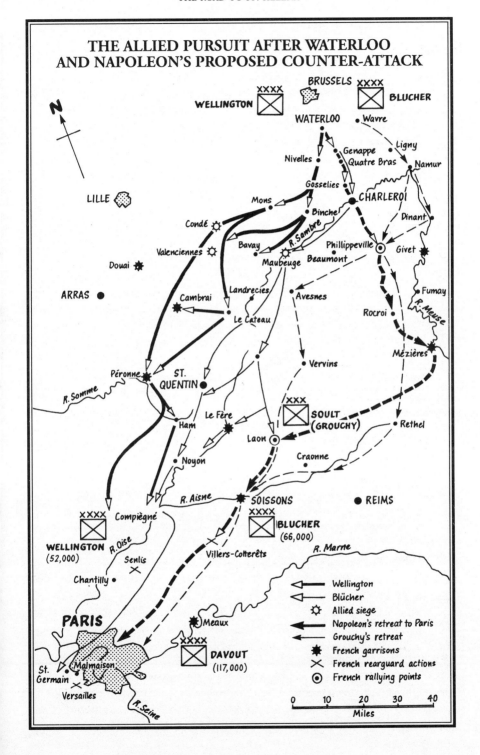

THE ALLIED PURSUIT AFTER WATERLOO
AND NAPOLEON'S PROPOSED COUNTER-ATTACK

now being called, packed his nightcap and the crown jewels and set off in Wellington's wake, entering France at Cateau Cambrésis on 25 June. From there, wasting no time in laying title to France, he issued a declaration (written by Talleyrand) on the 28th:

> 'The Gates of my Kingdom at last lie open before me. I hasten to bring back my misguided subjects to their duty ... My government was liable to commit errors: *perhaps it did commit them* ... My subjects have learnt by cruel experience that the principle of the legitimacy of sovereigns is one of the fundamental bases of social order ... I perceive many of my subjects to have been misled, and some guilty. I promise – I who never promised in vain (as all Europe can witness) to pardon misled Frenchmen, all that has transpired since the day when I quitted Lille ... That treason has summoned foreigners into the heart of France ... I owe it, therefore, to the dignity of my crown, to the interests of my people, and to the repose of Europe, *to except from pardon the instigators and authors of this horrible plot.*'[18]

Louis was serving early notice that punishment would be forthcoming for the 'instigators of the plot', in an endeavour to dupe the people and foreigners that there had been a plot and not a counter-revolution against his ghastly regime. The admission that mistakes might have been made was the nearest he would ever come to acknowledging his maladministration. Fouché, was now occupying the position he had conspired to attain, but he was sitting on a volcano as well he knew. The people were solidly for Napoleon. Unlike 1814, there was no Allied army surrounding a subdued Paris that had been fooled into surrender. Instead the people were still working to produce uniforms, munitions and muskets, recruits were arriving from the provinces, and morale was high. The royalists for obvious reasons were keeping a low profile. The republican element was for a return to the Republic as it had been before the Terror and the Directory had corrupted it. Napoleon's supporters awaited his next move, while loudly proclaiming him and his son. Fouché needed to disarm the people and render Paris defenceless, which would be achieved by removing the army and isolating the opposition, particularly Napoleon.

Fouché emasculated the Deputies by obliging them do that which they were most proficient at – talking. First he set them to formulating a new constitution, creating in the process several sub-committees. Next he discussed with his 'government' what political steps should be taken about the succession – if there were to be one? La Fayette proposed the king's cousin, the social mutant the duc d'Orléans, who had embraced the republic and fought under the tricolore, while believing in the monarchy. The King of Saxony was suggested, probably by Fouché, on the grounds that he would gain support in England, and provide a bulwark against Prussia. Napoleon II was put forward to appease the Napoleonic faction and the army. Fouché declared that these nominees should be put to the Allied sovereigns to determine which of these would be most acceptable. A delegation charged with an affair of this magnitude that would decide the future of France could only be led by the most influential members of the government. La Fayette must lead Messieurs Laforêt, Pontécoulant, d'Argenson and Sébastiani – at a stroke removing the most influential Liberals. Fouché then encouraged the soldiers in the belief that Napoleon II was to succeed Napoleon in order to save France.

News had now reached Paris, and Napoleon, that Wellington's army and Blücher's were advancing in the wake of Grouchy's forces. On 26 June Wellington was at Péronne with 52,000 men, all that was left of his army after Waterloo and the detachments that had been soaked up by the fortresses he had had to invest along the way. Blücher was separated from him by nearly 30 miles, his army (well-nigh 66,000 men) split into three columns at La Fère, Laon and approaching Noyon. Postmaster-General Lavalette had kept himself informed of all enemy movements which he transmitted to Napoleon. The Prussian advance guard was at Gonesse and Stains, the bulk of the army moving towards Senlis on the Soissons road, none of Wellington's army within marching distance. Napoleon saw from his maps that Blücher's Prussians were heading for Versailles, with a view to encircling Paris. He proposed to General Becker, of the provisional government, a move to smash Blücher. He would launch an attack on the Prussians' flank and rearguard, drive them back to the Loire, severing their communications with Wellington, then pounce on Wellington's 52,000 men. A single blow would put all to rights and restore liberty. He ordered Becker to take his plan to Davout and Fouché, and tell that he would be prepared to act in the capacity of a General for the provisional government if need be.

Napoleon was frantic; here was the opportunity that had eluded him in Belgium. Here was a great opportunity to undo and reverse Mont St-Jean. Marshal Davout, his loyal Iron Marshal, had 117,000 men in Paris, and 150,000 men had reported to the departmental depots. Now, here in France, he could avenge Waterloo. The armies of the other Allies had not yet reached French soil. The people and army were solidly with him; he would defeat the Anglo-Allied forces in detail. Certain that his offer to act as a 'general' would not be refused, Napoleon prepared himself and his retinue to leave. Fouché would have none of it. Becker demanded a written reply. Fouché scrawled a reply to Napoleon's secretary: 'I beg you M. le Duc, to use that influence that you have always had on the mind of his Majesty to advise him to leave without delay, seeing that the Prussians are marching on Versailles.'

Napoleon appealed to Davout to give him command of the forces, 'even as a plain General of the government'. To his utter bewilderment Davout refused. If he had agreed Napoleon would have been Napoleon again, and no one could have stopped him. The bleating Liberal leadership had been removed by Fouché, the people and soldiers in Paris were shouting 'Vive l'Empereur!', 'Vive Napoléon deux!'. The decision rested with Davout. He had been appointed Commander and Governor of Paris by Napoleon, and Commander-in-Chief by the Chambers; Fouché could neither arrest him nor impede any decision that he made at this moment.

Davout refused, not to stop further bloodshed, not for France, but because he hoped to command the army under Louis XVIII. Napoleon had twice been overthrown by a clique. Davout had supported him and remained loyal after the last abdication, and paid the consequence – exile and the Bourbons' attempt to have him tried for his life. Davout had urged Napoleon to prorogue the Chambers; he had refused, abdicated, and left Davout and his other supporters to their own devices. Davout had now decided to look after Davout. The man whom Napoleon had counted on as his strongest supporter had apparently deserted him for the promises of Fouché. Napoleon agreed to leave; there was no alternative save capture or civil war. Two naval vessels were off Rochefort, Fouché had said, but he prevaricated about giving the immediate authority and said that he would refer the matter to 'his minister of Marine for the proper authorities to be drafted' and that Napoleon must not embark until a safe conduct had been obtained from the Allies.

Napoleon was not deceived; he knew that Fouché wanted him to fall into enemy hands. He sent his aide General de Flahaut to Fouché and Davout on 28 June. Flahaut explains:

'I had been sent by the Emperor to ask the government that instructions might be given that the commanders of the two frigates at Cherbourg should place them at his disposal. My orders were to say that he would refuse to leave Paris until these instructions were given. I had just announced this decision to the Duke of Otranto, when Marshal Davout, who was standing near the fireplace, intervening quite unnecessarily, said to me: "General, go back to the Emperor, and tell him that he must leave, that his presence is embarrassing to us and will prevent any possible settlement, and that the salvation of the country demands his departure. If he does not go, he will have to be arrested – *indeed I will arrest him myself*."'[19]

Davout knew that so long as Napoleon remained in Paris, Blücher would not grant an armistice unless he were handed over to be executed by the Prussians. Paris and France would fight to the last man to prevent this. He and Fouché would be torn to pieces if they tried it. Fouché's and his salvation depended on a negotiated settlement which could only be arranged if Napoleon had left Paris. To this end Davout was prepared forcibly to remove Napoleon from the capital. Fouché, however, had already arranged for the Prussians to be told that Napoleon was at Malmaison and in a vulnerable position. Let them have the odium of removing Napoleon and the threat he posed. Flahaut returned to Malmaison. Napoleon was deeply affected. 'Well,' he said, with a movement to his throat, 'let him come.'[20] He knew that Davout was quite capable of carrying out his threat. Instead of riding to Paris, calling the provisional government's bluff, taking command of his troops or installing himself in one of the palaces with a guard, Napoleon decided to make a bid for freedom before the 'new government' handed him over as a captive. He left Malmaison at 5 o'clock on the evening of the 29th, bound for Rochefort, and the hoped-for ship to America or England.

To implement the next stage of his scheme, it was important for Fouché that Wellington arrive soon, with Louis in his wake. He had already sent two generals to the Allies on behalf of the provisional government – maintaining the fiction that the people of Paris wanted an armistice and a government of their own choice. He now needed a credible front man with Louis. Fouché knew that no deal was possible with the Prussians who were bent on revenge. Vitrolles would be his liaison with Marshal Macdonald who, trusted by the King, could advise him and Artois as to his progress, and carry letters. After the news of Napoleon's abdication had been circulated, Macdonald had secretly returned to Paris; he was worried about the forces there: 'One of the first proceedings of this new government had been to raise new levies and organize battalions of federates, who soon adopted a bullying, threatening manner towards all who were not in agreement with them – that is to say, the partisans of royal government.'[21] At his house Macdonald assembled a group of royalists who were trying to make up their minds whether or not to attempt a coup:

> '... it brought me an interview with Monsieur Hyde de Neuville, who brought me a note from the duchesse d'Angoulême, then in London, and unlimited powers from the King, with a nomination to a membership in a secret government, which was to regain authority as soon as possible ... We had many supporters in the capital, and it was proposed to risk a royalist movement ... Our party consisted of Marshal Oudinot, of Messieurs de Sémonville, d'André, du Bouchage, and Baron Pasquier ... Baron Pasquier entered while we were discussing the advantages of, and objections to, attempting a rising. He brought Monsieur de Vitrolles with him; both had just come from Fouché. They declared that the movement was unnecessary; that the duc d'Otranto [Fouché] was in the interest of the King; that he had received from him plenary powers later than ours; that our every step was watched, and that we should fail. Baron Pasquier added that in a few days we should have by force things that we might vainly attempt to obtain by other means ... One of us was to be deputed to go to His Majesty, and I was asked to undertake this mission; I agreed.'[22]

Next day Fouché sent for Macdonald:

> 'At the appointed hour I went to the Tuileries, where the temporary government held its sittings ... I found the duc d'Otranto and some colleagues amid a number of generals and others ... They all talked at once, and such nonsense that at last Fouché took me aside and said: "Never mind them; they are a set of fools." One of his colleagues called to me, in a loud voice: "Monsieur le Maréchal, you are going to see the King. Tell him that what we want is independence, the tricolore cockade and –" I did not hear the remainder ... Fouché confirmed all that Pasquier and de Vitrolles had told me on the previous evening ... he was working on behalf of the King. He begged me to assure his Majesty of his devotion and fidelity – to say that if he had played a part in recent events it was only to serve him better. He urged me to impress upon him the advisability of coming quickly ... He ended by asking me to go and see Davout ... who was expecting me, and would give me my passport ... Marshal Davout received me warmly. He told me that the effective force of the army that was going to the other side

of the Loire amounted to 150,000 men and 30,000 horses, with 750 pieces of ordnance; that he would place this imposing force at the King's service if he would leave them the tricolore cockade ... and that His Majesty might then give the army a chief of his own choice, if it did not please him to leave him [Davout] at its head.'[23]

In the meantime Fouché had sent Colonel Macirone, his go-between, with a message to Castlereagh. Macirone was a British subject, born in England of Italian descent, who had become King Joachim Murat's aide during the period 1813 to 1815, when Murat had become allied to Britain – or thought he had.[24] Having this convenient Briton in the capital, Fouché played on his patriotism 'to help end the war'; it is likely that he was a double or even triple agent. Fouché informed Castlereagh of Napoleon's destination and the route thereto. Writing to the Prime Minister on 12 July, Castlereagh, who had only reached France on the 7th, said: '... Jaurcourt and Fouché wish the British squadron to help to arrest Napoleon.'[25] Fouché's agent had already ensured that the information had preceded Napoleon, and had transmitted the message to Captain Maitland aboard *Bellerophon*, patrolling off Rochefort. Maitland wrote in his journal on 30 June: 'Having learnt from a trustworthy source that Bonaparte, coming from Paris, has passed through the town ... with the intention of escaping by the estuary or by way of la Teste ... It would be a good thing to stage a demonstration on shore with at least 8,000 men and to keep a close watch on all American ships.'[26] Any chance that Napoleon might have had of escaping to America was now blocked. Fouché had proffered the ships at Rochefort instead of in the south, knowing that by the time Napoleon arrived there the Royal Navy would have blocked all avenues of escape.

Relations between Wellington and the Prussians had reached an all-time low. Blücher and Gneisenau were incensed that without prior agreement, and against Article 8 of the Vienna agreement, Wellington was unilaterally bringing Louis back, with the despised Talleyrand in his train. The Prussians thought that Britain was trying to pull a fast one as in 1814. This time, come what may, they were determined to wreak vengeance on Paris and to kill Napoleon. At Compiègne, the provisional government's emissaries had been refused an armistice by Wellington (on Fouché's advice) who stated (as Napoleon had told the Chambers he would) 'that the declaration that they were at war with Napoleon not France, had held good as long as hostilities had not commenced. Napoleon had been aided by the French nation, and they must now surrender; his abdication was of no consequence'. Blücher, however, said that he would consider it, if Napoleon were handed over *dead or alive*. Wellington wrote a letter of remonstration against this. He was mindful of Parliament's reproach, and that he had been called 'an assassin's tool' for having signed the infamous document. Gneisenau replied in a series of letters to his liaison officer General Baron Müffling. On 27 June:

'Bonaparte has been declared under outlawry by the Allied powers. *The Duke of Wellington may possibly (from parliamentary considerations) hesitate to fulfil the declaration of the Powers.* Therefore Your Excellency will direct negotiations to the effect that Bonaparte may be surrendered to us, with a view to his execution.'[27]

On 29 June:

'I am directed by the Field Marshal [Blücher] to request Your Excellency to communicate to the Duke of Wellington, that it had been his intention to execute Bonaparte on the spot where the duc d'Enghien was shot. However, *out of deference to the Duke's wishes, he will abstain from this measure ... It appears to me that the English will feel embarrassed by the delivery of Bonaparte to them*; therefore Your Excellency will also direct the negotiations so that he may be delivered up to us.'[28]

Finally, again on 29 June:

'*When the Duke of Wellington declares himself against the execution of Bonaparte, he thinks and acts in the matter as a Briton. Great Briton [sic] is under weightier obligation to no mortal man than to this villain; for by the occurrences whereof he is the author, of her greatness, prosperity, and wealth, have attained their present elevation. The English are masters of the seas, and have no longer to fear any rivalry either in this dominion or the commerce of the world.* It is quite otherwise with us Prussians. We have been impoverished by him. Our nobility will never be able to right itself again ... But so be it! If others will assume a theatrical magnanimity, I shall not set myself against it. *We act thus from esteem for the Duke and English weakness.*'[29]

This last letter was a sop to appease Wellington. Gneisenau and Blücher had not changed their minds, but had decided on a different course of action. They had no scruples in telling Fouché's royalist Commissioner, General de Tromelin, that unless Napoleon were handed over, Prussian vengeance would be wrought in Paris and all over France, wherever their troops had occupation. Tromelin wrote of his meeting:

'Graf von Gneisenau, Army Chief of Staff, received me haughtily ... I found the Prussians more concerned with reaping the benefit of their victory than in making the Bourbon cause triumph. They did not even take the trouble to conceal the lack of interest that it inspired in them. "We are here by right of conquest and it is as victors that we wish to enter Paris," he said to me ... "It does not interest us whether you take back the Bourbon or restore the Republic, for we have not forgotten that three months after restoring Louis XVIII he threatened us about Saxony. We are waging war against Napoleon because no agreement with him is sacred and no firm peace may be expected from him ... After having destroyed him, we no longer care. You may choose any government you like, except that of Bonaparte and his family.'[30]

Artois, however, was only too pleased to authorize this royalist general to relay the information that Napoleon was at Malmaison with a small force. Fouché had deliberately tried to delay Napoleon's departure long enough for him to be captured or killed. That would have satisfied him, the Bourbons, and Castlereagh and Metternich.

Napoleon had departed. Unknown to him, General Exelmans on his own authority had brought a cavalry division of 2,000 men to Malmaison to escort him through Paris and take him to the army so that he might resume command and repulse the enemy. At Vincennes Exelmans was told that he had missed the Emperor's coach which had passed through at 9 o'clock that morning. No one knew where he was heading. The very next day a Prussian cavalry force under the command of Blücher's son- in-law had force-marched around Paris to reach Malmaison, found Napoleon gone and pursued him with vigour, their orders being simply 'dead or alive'. Davout, warned by his cavalry patrols and not wishing to have a hand in the murder of Napoleon, blew the bridge across the Seine.

Marshal Davout was an able commander, perhaps second only to Napoleon in the French Army. If he had wished, he could have taken the war to the Allies long enough for them to agree to negotiate favourable terms for the new government. Instead he was aiding Fouché in surrendering a superior force to two inferior ones that had sustained heavy losses and were short of supplies. Later Wellington wrote to Castlereagh:

'... The French people submitted to Buonaparte; but it would be ridiculous to suppose that the Allies would have been in possession of Paris in a fortnight after one battle fought if the French people in general had not been favourably disposed to the cause which the Allies were *supposed to favour* [their own choice of government] ... the results of the operations of the Allies have been very different from what they would have been if the disposition of the inhabitants of the country had led them to oppose the Allies.'[31]

Why was Davout doing nothing and providing no leadership to the army? Its morale was high. The Austrian main army was moving only slowly towards the French border. The Russians were still distant. When the Austrian corps of General Wärttenberg crossed the Rhine, General Rapp repulsed it with heavy losses at la Suffel on the 28th. In the south, the small force of General Lecourbe, made up of National Guardsmen and second-line troops, fought four successful engagements actions against the vastly superior forces of General Colleredo, at Foussemague, Bourogne, Chévremont and Bavilliers. Not until 11 July, more than a week after Paris had capitulated, did this miniature force sign an armistice. All along the border the enemy was attacked and savaged by the local populace in a fierce guerrilla campaign. At Lyons, Suchet, with a reduced force of 17,000 men, having reinforced Lecourbe, was driving General Frimont's 40,000 Austrians backwards. On 14 June he had taken the war to the enemy and *invaded Savoy*. Marshal Brune, with a minuscule force, had contained General Onasco's 23,000 men, giving ground only after Waterloo and the abdication, and shutting himself up at Toulon where the tricolore flew until 31 July. Wellington had had to tie up troops in investing Condé, Valenciennes, Cambrai and Péronne, leaving him just 52,000 men. For Blücher it had been worse. The Prussians, wreaking havoc and destroying everything in their wake, soon found the locals and the garrisons putting up a firm resistance. He had had to detach

Right: General Henri-Jacques Clarke, duc de Feltre, Napoleon's Minister of War from 1807 to 1814. A massive bribe of gold from England and the promise that he would retain his post, induced him to turn his coat. He rendered Paris undefendable in 1814, and his betrayal of Napoleon's plans to Wellington in 1815 earned him a Marshal's baton from the Bourbons in July of that year. He is seen here with that baton and a bust of his 'benefactor' Louis XVIII.

Right: Napoleon's brother, Joseph, King of Spain. Left to defend Paris, he was bamboozled and outwitted by everyone and threw the game away.

Left: Marshal Marmont, duc d Raguse. Napoleon's oldest friend, his distinguished milita career was brought to nought b his venality. He surrendered hi corps to the Allies, for which Napoleon never forgave him. His title gave a new word to French parlance of the day: *raguser*, to betray.

Below: Clash at Clare, 27 Mar 1814. Marmont and Mortier's troops engaged in a fighting retreat to reach Paris ahead of the Allies.

Right: Marshal Moncey defen the *barrière* of Clichy with the National Guard during the battle for Paris.

Below right: The fight for the strategic heights of Montmartr Napoleon had ordered that the be made impregnable with mo than 600 heavy cannon in earthwork redoubts. Marmont placed 30 guns there, but Clar and Hulin removed the men who should have manned them The heights were finally defended by six field pieces, 60 heavy guns being left in the arsenal.

Above: Napoleon, racing to reach Paris from the unassailed side, is told at Juvisy that the city had fallen four hours earlier, which was untrue. Paris would not be handed over or evacuated for another four hours, and if Napoleon had pressed on he would have been in time to defend the city.

Below: Marshal Ney leads a mutiny of the Marshals at Fontainebleau. They were unwilling to support an attack by Napoleon on Paris, and he was forced to seek terms.

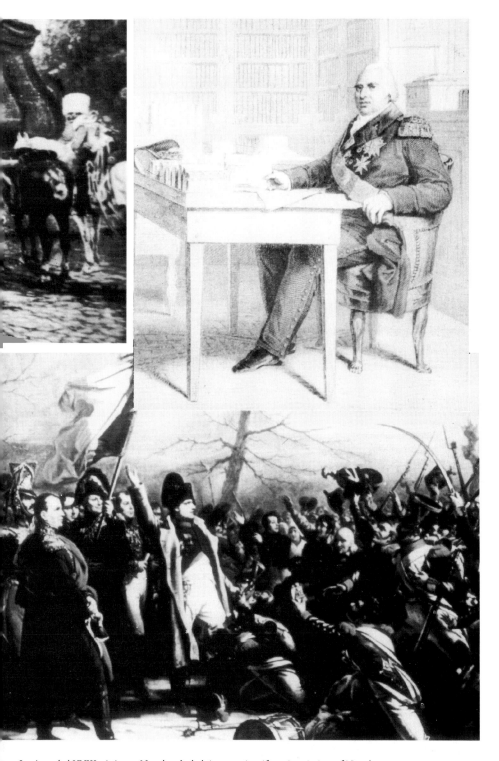

top: Louis, styled XVIII, sitting at Napoleon's desk in a quasi-uniform in mimicry of Napoleon.

above: Napoleon confronts the 5th Regiment of the Line at Gap. They went over to him to a man.

Left: Joseph Fouché, Minister of Police and Bourbon 'mole' in place. Ostensibly working for Napoleon, he was determined to topple him. No mean opponent, at the height of the Terror he had deposed Robespierre and had him guillotined. (Philip Haythornthwaite collection)

Lower left: The comte d'Artois, in the uniform of Colonel-in-Chief of his own regiment.

Right: Napoleon's restoration in March 1815 had the overwhelming support of the entire population. Here the reconstituted Imperial Guard parades at the place du Carrousel to the delight of the populace. (Philip Haythornthwaite collection)

Lower right: The Battle of Ligny, 16 June 1815. General Gneisenau is seen here directing the army to retire on Wavre, a crucial decision to the outcome of the campaign.

Above: French élan and fury could not break the Allied squares. Murat would have supported the cavalry with masses of horse artillery to reduce the squares to human rubble.

Right: An exhausted Napoleon returns to Paris in 1815 to replace his routed army with some of the 350,000 troops still available.

Left: General Charles-Tristan de Montholon. Promoted by the Boubons, he attached himself to Napoleon's household after Waterloo, and was instructed to accompany him to St. Helena and murder him.

Above: Napoleon going on
board the *Bellerophon* at
Rochefort.

Opposite page, top: HMS
Bellerophon in Tor Bay, with
Napoleon on board, 24 July
1815.

Right: The island of Elba,
1814.

Left: Sir Hudson Lowe, the pettish, narrow-minded Governor appointed to supervise Napoleon. Wellington had called him 'a damned old fool', and he did his best to live up to that judgement.

Below: Longwood House, Napoleon's residence on St. Helena (Philip Haythornthwaite collection)

Above: Napoleon lies dead at Longwood on the campaign bed which he preferred. To the right, gesturing, is Montholon, his murderer.

Below: Napoleon having passed into immortality, many fanciful prints were published, especially in France. This one shows Glory, holding her triumphal wreath and joined by an eagle, lamenting Napoleon's passing; the nameless slab under its willow tree marking his grave. Between the trees Napoleon's shade can be seen. (Philip Haythornthwaite collection)

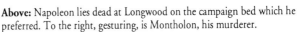

Right: Napoleon's perfectly preserved body in its new coffin, is brought aboard *La Belle Poule,* in effect on to French soil. The prince de Joinville is seen bare-headed beneath the coffin. Through the smoke to the left, the massive volcanic rock of St. Helena is perceived above the tricolore flying at half-mast. The ship's cannon thunder out the salute due to an Emperor.

Above: Napoleon's funeral cortege passes through the place de la Concorde on its way to Les Invalides. (Philip Haythornthwaite collection)

Left: A photograph taken at the time of the Second Empire showing Sergeant Taria, of the Grenadiers of the Imperial Guard (1809-15), in the uniform he wore at the re-interment ceremony.

30,000 men, all of Pirch II's corps, to safeguard his communications and to invest the citadels on the way. Yet Davout and the main field force, gaining in strength daily, did nothing but wait, to the mutinous complaints of its officers such as Vandamme and Exelmans.

Here was the crux of the matter. By isolating Napoleon from the government, creating bureaucratic anarchy in the Chambers, pretending to support first Napoleon, then his son, then the duc d'Orléans, the King of Saxony, and even a republic, Fouché had effectively deprived the country of any leadership during the invasion. By suborning Davout with promises of immunity and perhaps royal favour, the army had been withdrawn to the capital and left inactive.[32] No orders had been given to the fortress commanders save to let them know Napoleon was gone and that they should seek local armistices. Davout, the hero of Hamburg, must have known what that sort of message would convey to a beleaguered commander, outnumbered and with no apparent cause for which to fight. The peasants and the levy *en masse* were neither called out nor given any instructions by him or the government. Fouché had created administrative anarchy, paralysing any resistance, but retaining a massive force around Paris, details of which Davout communicates to the King and Wellington. This immense force could not be ignored or swept aside. To bargain, you must have something to trade. Fouché could offer Paris and France to the Bourbons without further bloodshed, if the King would act quickly.

On 29 June, the representatives of the Government, Marshal Lefebvre, Generals Gazan, Fressinet and Dejean, MM. Arnaud, Jay and Pouget, all proudly wearing their republican tricolore waist sashes, had arrived at Davout's headquarters to congratulate the army. Not only had Davout not been expecting them and had failed to parade the troops, but they arrived to see Fouché's carriages dropping off Baron Vitrolles and Marshal Oudinot. Davout tried to dissociate himself from this treasonous scene by stating that Vitrolles 'could ease the agreements with the Allied armies'; he stammered, became confused and couldn't finish his sentences. The Deputies were angry and started shouting; Fressinet tried to hit Vitrolles; Dejean roared, 'We will never put up with the Bourbons!' Davout tried to calm the situation. There were cries of 'Treason!', and some of the soldiers arrived to watch this incredible scene. Davout ordered them back to their tents – but the damage had been done.[33]

Next day Blücher attempted to attack Paris but was firmly repulsed and withdrew. Davout meanwhile was in trouble with the Government; Carnot called him a traitor, to which Fouché, baiting him, dared him to 'arrest the Marshal'. To justify himself, Davout drew up a declaration, signed by himself, and Generals Pajol, d'Erlon and Vandamme (Ney was not invited to sign) stating: 'The Bourbons present no guarantee to the nation ... History will one day relate what the Bourbons have done to replace themselves on the throne of France; it will also narrate the conduct of the army, of that army essentially national ...[34] Davout had drawn up this document to impress his army commanders and the Chambers of his republican loyalty. They in turn ordered 20,000 copies to be published and distributed. Davout did all he could to stop this, saying that he had been pressurized into signing it. Several paragraphs in the document attacked the Bourbons and obviously finished any chances he might have had of commanding the army under them. On the same day, Blücher again attempted to attack Paris, this time from the rear, deploying a large force of cavalry under Lieutenant-Colonel Sohr which got as far as Versailles. It would appear that they were searching for Napoleon, and acting as the vanguard of an encircling movement. General Exelmans attacked them with his cavalry and a well-placed brigade of infantry and several guns. Davout had asked for an armistice so that the evacuation of Paris might be discussed, but Blücher had decided to attempt this coup. The Prussians, in the last cavalry battle of the era, received a terrible beating. Many of the élite of the Prussian nobility, including the sons of von Yorck, Kalkreuth, Manteuffel and Messerschmidt, were either killed, wounded or taken prisoner. Gneisenau, fearful that the action would escalate and that the army might be utterly defeated – Wellington had not broken the armistice or come to their assistance – called off the engagement. The French Army was still a force to be reckoned with.

Fouché had two secret meetings with Louis and was eventually accorded the recognition he craved and offered the post of Minister of Police. At first the King had declined to meet this man who had lent a hand in the condemnation and execution of his brother, but Wellington had intervened, explaining in polite terms that only Britain was in favour of Louis' restoration. Much British blood and gold had been expended in the process, and only the latter would put him on the throne; without Fouché's aid, it couldn't be done before the Allied monarchs arrived – and they might want someone else. Artois supported Wellington and Louis capitulated. Fouché, supporting Talleyrand on his arm, met the King and placed his hands into his, accepting office from the brother of his previous victim. Chateaubriand commented on the disgust felt by all the ultras at the re-appearance of these two men whose betrayal of Napoleon had twice restored the Bourbons. 'Vice supported by Crime,' was the epitaph he fittingly bestowed upon these conspirators who had betrayed in turn their King, the Revolution, the Directory and the Empire, only to restore a king again, against the wishes of their nation.

Fouché returned to Paris and, keeping his arrangement with Louis to himself, asked the Chambers how long Paris could defend itself? He had asked Marshal Davout to convene a council of war made up of the leading marshals and generals, to answer six questions for the government. Two were purely technical, concerning arms, ammunition and defences. General Valée, commanding the artillery, replied: 'On the right bank work completed. At Montmartre work in progress, 400 cannon in position, in addition to the corps artillery – 600 guns on the heights [as Napoleon had ordered in 1814]. On the left bank some trenches and batteries; 43 guns in position, a large mobile reserve of 132 12-pounders. General Vandamme has in addition 83 guns at his disposal. Munitions available: 200 rounds per field piece, 300 per fixed gun; five mobile parks behind the lines; 2,000,000 cartridges in reserve; daily production in Paris 300,000 assured. Full complement of artillerymen to man the pieces.'[35] This represented an enormous amount of fire power for attack or defence.

The next questions were those Fouché had asked of the Chambers: Could the Allies fight on all fronts simultaneously? No, they had only 110,000 men. In case of a reverse, had Davout sufficient reserves? Could the approaches to Paris be defended, including the left bank? Certainly, although the left bank was not fortified. Fouché knew this, he had had all work on it stopped. The wrangling continued. Masséna declared: '... the city could never be taken if the inhabitants were willing to make it a second Saragossa, but there was not enough unanimity of feeling to dream of a long resistance'. Not perhaps among these ducs and princes, but what of the people? Davout said nothing.

Marshal Davout was capable of taking the war to the enemy; his army was at least comparable to the combined armies of Wellington and Blücher. He had masses of artillery and short lines of communication. His troops had ample food and munitions, and the soldiers were enthusiastic – as were the citizens. If Davout held Paris until the Austrians and Russians arrived, would he commit the army to perhaps thousands of losses for the Bourbons? Why was this not put to the Chambers or to the people?

In the event it was decreed by Fouché that an armistice would be sought and the army would be evacuated from Paris to behind the Loire, to save it and prevent the destruction of Paris. As in 1814, Paris would be occupied and a government would be imposed. On 3 July, a compliant Davout, who throughout 1813–14 had held Hamburg with forces inferior to those he now commanded, took the army out of Paris after having signed a convention. The 18 Articles of this document declared that all public property was to be respected, except that related to War (Article XI). Davout had inserted Article XII: 'Private persons and property shall be equally respected. *The inhabitants, and in general all individuals who shall be in the capital, shall enjoy their rights and liberties without being called to account, either as to the situations which they hold, or may have held, or as to their conduct or political opinions*'. This clause had been inserted to provide a general amnesty against acts of revenge by the Bourbons, their supporters, and the Allied forces. Article XV declared: 'If difficulties arise in the execution of any one of the articles of the present convention, *the interpretation of it shall be made in favour of the French army and of the city of Paris*.'[36] The agreement was signed by representatives of Wellington, Blücher and the French provisional government, who in effect became its guarantors.

No sooner had Davout evacuated Paris than the Allies entered. The members of the Chambers, who had assembled to debate their next move in approaching the Allies, found themselves locked out by armed guards; Fouché having changed the hat of the President of the provisional government, for that of Louis' Minister of Police. They repaired to their speaker's house, but were dispersed from there by the guards. The Allies now occupied Paris, and Louis returned and carried on as if he had never been driven out. This time, however, he had 110,000 foreign soldiers to enforce his will. So ended the brief ascendancy of La Fayette and his talkative patriots who had removed Napoleon and handed the game to Fouché. Carnot was astounded, humiliated and enraged to receive a letter from 'His Most Christian's Majesty's Chief of

Police', informing him that he was now to be exiled internally, and that his movements would be under surveillance. Carnot replied, 'Where am I to be exiled – Traitor!?' Fouché replied, 'Anywhere you like – Simpleton!'

Castlereagh, having arrived at Paris on 8 July, now received instructions from the Prime Minister, Lord Liverpool, in a series of letters and communiqués. The first, written two days after Waterloo, as a lengthy memorandum, outlined British policy and what it expected from Louis in return for having restored him to the throne:

> 'It appears to be quite indispensable that in the event of the restoration of Louis XVIII *a severe example should be made of those commanding officers of garrisons or corps who deserted the King and went over to Buonaparte. Such a proceeding is not only become necessary with a view to the continuance of the power of the House of Bourbon, but likewise for the security of the object for which the Allies have been contending, a safe and lasting peace. The True principle, taken in its full rigour, would be to consider all the officers commanding garrisons or corps as subject to the penalties of High Treason who had gone over to Buonaparte previous to the King leaving French territory; but it might be as well to modify this principle by confining it to those who took that step before the King was known to have quitted Paris, considering the elements for conspiracies and rebellion which must exist in France for some years, there can be no chance of stopping them but by an exemplary punishment on the present occasion of those that went forward to join the standard of Buonaparte.'*[37]

This was music to the ears of Castlereagh and Artois. Liverpool's government, driven into a corner by the Opposition, and having to commit millions of pounds to subsidize a coalition that it didn't now need, wanted its proverbial pound of flesh. Having, as these politicians at home believed, beaten Napoleon in a single battle, and conquered France by military might, it now wanted to use the same policy as used in Scotland after the rebellion of 1745 – terrorize and subdue the people to obedience.

Castlereagh replied that he had communicated this instruction to the King, but before he could implement this policy something must be done about the Prussians and Napoleon.

> 'The immediate difficulty is now to keep Blücher and the Prussians within any bounds towards this town. They have notified to the Duke today that they have laid on the city of Paris a contribution of 110,000,000 Thalers, and equipment for 110,000 men; and they are at this moment mining the Bridge of Jena, with a view of blowing it up.'[38]

This was followed on the 12th by:

> '... we continue to have considerable difficulties with the Prussians, who last night proceeded to arrest some banners [*bannières*, prominent leaders of the Chevaliers de la Foi] in Paris, in order to enforce their demand of contributions ... Jaurcourt and Fouché wish the British squadron to help arrest Buonaparte. *From what has occurred in conversation on the subject, it appears to me that the King of France's Government will not, and appears have not suf-*

*ficient authority to charge themselves with the judging and executing Buona-
parte as a traitor.* If so, and he should fall into our hands, there is no other
course than to confine him as a prisoner ... But if we are to take charge of
him I think it is desirable it should be as a prisoner of the principal powers,
France included, who should each nominate a Commissary to exercise a
joint surveillance.'[39]

Castlereagh, unable to persuade Louis to take the responsibility under the terms of
his own ordnance of 6 March to try to have Napoleon executed, is discussing having
a *Bourbon* Commissioner appointed, even before the Allied monarchs have discussed
the restoration and peace terms. On 14 July the King dissolved the non-existent provisional government and had his own government proclaimed. On the same day
Castlereagh wrote to Liverpool:

'Prince Talleyrand told me yesterday, upon my urging the importance
of adequately indicating the king's authority, and the authority of the laws,
that they meant to be severe when they had the means of acting, but until
they could estimate what was the temper of their new assembly, they could
not judge to what extent or in what manner they could best proceed to
*deliver France from the individuals they consider it indispensably necessary
should be got rid of. In the obvious state of weakness in which the government
stands, it was impossible for me to do more than represent how much the King's
authority must be brought in contempt, so long as the most notorious criminals
were not only at large, but seen abroad as defying the laws.*'[40]

This was unacceptable to Liverpool who replied on the 15th:

'We received this morning your despatches of the 12th instant. Before
entering on other matters, I am desirous of appraising you of our sentiments
respecting Buonaparte. *If you should succeed in getting possession of his person,
and the King of France does not feel sufficiently strong to bring him to justice as
a rebel,* we are ready to take upon ourselves the custody of his person, on the
part of the Allied powers; and indeed, we think it better that he should be
assigned to us than to any other member of the Confederacy ... We incline
at present strongly to the opinion that the best place of custody would be at
a distance from Europe, and that the Cape of Good Hope or St. Helena
would be the proper stations for the purpose.'[41]

Enclosed with this official communication was a private letter, stating that unless
Louis began to make an example of 'these criminals',

'... *the more strongly are we impressed with the opinion of the impossibility
of giving strength* [support] *to this government ... The forbearance manifested
at the present moment can be considered in no other light than weakness, and
NOT mercy; and, though the King may follow the advice which has been given
to him by disbanding his army, I am afraid that very little dependence will be
placed on any army formed out of the same material ... what dangers might not
be apprehended from forty thousand officers unemployed – men of desperate fortunes, and possessing a large proportion of talent and energy of the country! A*

*severe example made of the conspirators who brought back Buonaparte could
alone have any effect in countering these dangers.'*[42]

It will be seen clearly from these letters that in Liverpool's opinion, only a spate of
terror, executions and imprisonment would subdue the republicans and imperialists.
Louis, understandably anxious not to alienate his already hostile subjects, had no
wish to act as the hangman of Europe. Castlereagh, enormously influential, representing Louis' sole sponsor, Britain, whose troops comprised one half of the forces
occupying Paris, was demanding wholesale retribution on behalf of Lord Liverpool.
Britain was the paymaster of Europe, and had yet to declare her own terms. Louis,
the bloodthirsty Artois at his elbow, had little choice. Castlereagh wrote back to Liverpool on 17 July:

> 'At our conference this morning I thought it right to call the attention
> of the Allied ministers to the necessity of urging the Government of Louis
> the XVIII *without further delay, to adopt some measure of vigour against the
> most criminal traitors; there was but one opinion, that the King's authority
> would be brought into utter contempt if some step of this nature was not taken
> without loss of time ...'*

Castlereagh afterwards had an interview with Talleyrand and gave him a memorandum concerning the necessity of punishing the 'traitors':

> '*It is perhaps unlucky that Fouché's office should be at this moment that of
> police, as although the most competent of any to discharge its functions in an
> ordinary sense ... The great service performed by Fouché was in the last fortnight
> of the Provisional government. He had the merit of acting with great personal
> courage and address, opposed successively to the resentment of Buonaparte, of the
> army, and of the assemblies; with a majority against him in the executive gov-
> ernment, he succeeded in saving himself, dissolving them, and bringing in the
> King. It is not that he is not now heartily in the King's cause: I believe he really
> is and must be from interest, but having always played a game of personal popu-
> larity, by covering his friends when they got into a scrape, he has now additional
> motives for endeavouring to screen them, that he may retain some character, or
> perhaps what he values more, influence with his party. Talleyrand assures me
> that he has spoken to him very strongly on this point.*'

Castlereagh went on to discuss other matters: the extension of the Treaty of Chaumont to make:

> '*... a part of the permanent law of Europe, extending the exclusion to the
> family* [Napoleon's] *at large ... If we make a European invasion the inevitable
> and immediate consequence* of Buonaparte's succession or that of any of his
> race, to power in France, I am confident, after the experience they had ...
> that there is not a class in France, not excepting even the army, that they
> will venture to adhere to him at the hazard of being overrun by the armies
> of Europe, of being dismembered, and loaded with contributions ... Except
> Buonaparte the King has no real rival. If he can quiet the alarm of the pro-
> prietors of national lands, break down the parties who are struggling for

office, by using them according to their means of rendering service, and organizing an army comprehending much of the old material, I do not despair of his establishing himself and the succession.'[43]

Fouché did not disappoint the King or Castlereagh; he produced a list of fifty-seven persons to be tried for their part in Napoleon's return – he did not of course include himself. Talleyrand remarked: 'One must do him the justice to recognize that he has omitted none of his friends.' Now, at the British Cabinet's insistence, a regime of horror was unleashed on the French people, which came to be known, from the white cockade worn by its exponents, as the 'White Terror'. Artois, heir to the throne and head of the Chevaliers de la Foi, instigated attacks by bands of royalists on Bonapartist ex-officers and soldiers. Marshal Brune was ordered by the King to come to Paris where he was grabbed by one of these mobs, who had been told to expect him, beaten, shot, stabbed about a hundred times; his body thrown in the river. No one was safe. Retired officers living in isolated farmhouses were attacked by night, taken out and lynched in front of their families. Hundreds of these ex-officers and soldiers were beaten to death in the interests of British policy.

While this was going on all over France, the perpetrators protected by the Bourbon police and Allied bayonets, the Bourbon government moved against the army and many Paris notables. Prodded by Castlereagh, Talleyrand advised the King to replace Fouché; Artois put forward as his replacement an ultra named Decases who found immediate favour, the old king having a predilection for young blond men.

Le Moniteur of 26 July carried the following ministerial announcement:

'All those officers who betrayed the King before March 20th or who attacked France and the government with armed force, as well as those who seized power by violence, will be arrested and brought before competent courts-martial in their respective military districts. To wit: Ney, La Bédoyère, the two brothers Lallemand, Drouet, d'Erlon, Lefebvre-Desnoettes, Ameil, Brayer, Gilly, Mouton-Durvet, Grouchy, Clausel, Laborde, Debelle, Bertrand, Drouot, Cambronne, Lavalette, Rovigo.

'Also the individuals whose names follow, to wit: Soult, Allix, Exelmans, Bassano, Marbot, Félix, Lepelletier, Boulay (de la Meurthe), Méhee, Fressinet, Thiebaudeau, Carnot, Vandamme, Lamarque [General], Lobau, Harel, Piré, Barrre, Arnault, Pommereul, Regnault [de Saint-Jean d'Angly], Arrighi [de Padau], Durbach, Dejean fils, Garrau, Réal, Bouvier, Dumolard, Félix Desportes, Garnier [de Saintes], Mellinet, Hullin, Cloys, Courtin, Forbin-Janson [eldest son], Le Lorgne d'Ideville, will leave Paris within three days and will withdraw into central France to such a place as the Minister of Police shall indicate and shall remain there under surveillance and await there until such times as the Chambers shall determine which of them must leave the kingdom and which shall be brought before the courts.'

This was only the beginning. In vain did Davout and Madame Ney appeal to the Duke of Wellington that this was a breach of Article XII of the Convention. He told them that the Convention was between the Allied armies and the provisional government and had been observed; the Convention could in no way be seen as binding any future French government (although that had been the intention). Wellington's representative had signed it with Louis' agreement. Wellington might have wished to save these men, although he viewed army officers who had broken their oaths to the king as traitors. He could have interceded on their behalf, and Louis would have welcomed it to get him off the hook, but Wellington adhered to his government's policy.

On 19 August, General de la Bédoyère, commander of the first regiment to march to Napoleon's side, and the last to speak up for him and France in the Chamber of Peers, was shot outside Paris on the plain of Grenville. Marshal Ney, who had not fled with his false passports, trusting in the Convention, was shot in the Luxembourg Gardens. General Mouton-Duvernet was executed at Lyons and General Chartran at Lille. Many of the most prominent escaped the country with the help not only of their fellow countrymen but of Allied officers who were disgusted with the business. Generals Belliard, Berton, Cambronne, Debelle, Decaen, the 'honest' Drouot and others were sent to prison or exile by the courts-martial, to the fury of the British Cabinet and Artois' ultras. In the south the terror continued. General Ramel was beaten to death by an ultra mob at Toulouse, and soldiers of the 13th Line who had been disarmed were massacred at Nîmes. It is not known how many men, women and children were killed during this sickening episode; at least 300 were reported,[44] but many relatives were too frightened to make a fuss and were relieved to escape the country. Even the arch-traitor Marmont was sickened and wrote to the King: 'Unjust, deadly and absurd consequences will surely result.' Baron Pasquier echoed these sentiments: 'These examples ... far from producing the desired effect, put a large number of soldiers in a vengeful mood and resulted in a number of conspiracies.'

Before the end of August 1815, Louis' new Chambers had assembled. The age for electors had been reduced from 30 to 21 years, and that of candidates from 40 to 25 years. The Chamber of Deputies was expanded from 262 to 402. With the aid of the Chevaliers de la Foi, Artois packed the Chambers with young ultra supporters.[45] Dubbed by Louis, *Chambres introuvables*, before the opening session they demanded from the King that the new government would not include 'known regicides' which coincided with Castlereagh's wish for Fouché's removal 'so as not to impede the good work'. Talleyrand willing sacrificed his old rival, and Fouché was sent as envoy to Dresden. During his absence a law on regicides was passed which meant that if he returned to France he would be executed. Fouché, having betrayed his country and sacrificed his friends and colleagues to ingratiate himself with the Bourbons, had lasted less than three months – 'Less than the hundred days'. Talleyrand, however, had little to gloat over, or to feel secure about. Having humiliated Artois in 1814 over his recognition as Louis' Lieutenant-General of the Kingdom, he had gravely affronted him at Cambrai in the matter of the King's declaration. He had presenting Louis with the draft in which wanted him to admit that 'he had made mistakes' and ask his people's pardon. Artois had complained that a king should not beg anything from his people, it humiliated royalty. Talleyrand had replied that 'the King has made mistakes, he allowed his affection to mislead him'. Artois retorted, 'Is it to me that you indirectly refer?' 'Yes, since Monsieur has put the question in that way; Monsieur has done harm.'[46]

Now that Monsieur controlled both Chambers and, indirectly, the country, he wanted Talleyrand out. On 22 September 1815 Talleyrand decided to 'retire', the object lesson of Fouché's extinction not lost on him. Later, as 'a sop to his services' and to please Britain, he was made ambassador to London. France was now to suffer years of repression under Artois' control of the government. His party, the ultras, were backed by the Allied army of occupation whose initially 1,000,000 men were all (except Britain's troops) plundering the country to their hearts' content. This force was eventually scaled down to 100,000 men for five years, reduced to three, while France paid massive war reparations. Saarlouis's fortresses and parts of Alsace-Lorraine were taken by Prussia – which France would not forget.

The men of Liverpool's Cabinet, cast in no heroic mould – they were virtual nonentities – took care to conceal from Parliament the role they had played in prostrating the French people under a new Terror, and in announcing the terms of the Second Peace of Paris took care to present Britain as being but one of many signatories. But many British people at home and abroad were horrified at what was going on.

In Paris at this time was one Major-General Robert Wilson, who had fought against Napoleon for twenty years and, uniquely, had taken part in most of the battles of the Napoleonic wars; Eylau, Friedland in 1807, Smolensk, Maloryaroslavets, Vyazima, the Beresina, Lützen, Bautzen, Dresden, Külm, Leipzig, Vallegio. In Portugal he had founded the Loyal Lusitanian Legion which was later incorporated into and served as a model for the British-trained Portuguese army. He had been awarded the Knight Grand Cross of the Red Eagle of Prussia, Knight Grand Cross of the Military Order of Russia, Knight Grand Cross of the Imperial Military Order of Maria-Theresa of Austria, Baron of the Holy Roman Empire, Knight Commander of the Imperial Russian Order of St. George, Knight Commander of the Order of Merit of Saxony, Knight Commander of the Turkish Order of the Crescent, Knight Commander of the Royal Portuguese Military Order of Tower and Sword.

Sir Robert was appalled at what was happening in France. Napoleon's Postmaster-General Lavalette, a civilian who had not conspired against the Bourbons and had only taken office under Napoleon after Louis had fled, was one of the civilians mentioned by Liverpool, and was sentenced to death to appease the British Cabinet. Wilson, with the aid of two other Britons, one an officer in the Guards, the other a civilian, helped Lavalette escape from prison and obtained British passports in false names. Wilson, wearing the full dress uniform of a British general, took him to Mons, thereby saving his life. The Bourbons began a hue and cry to recapture their victim without success. Wilson sent full details of the affair to Lord Grey, imploring him to help put an end to the disgraceful judicial murders. His letter was franked at the British embassy, but the British public were not aware until this incident that *all* mail was being opened by the Bourbon postal authorities, even British official mail. Wilson was arrested and interrogated eight times before being charged. At his first examination the 38-year-old General expressed his indignation that his letter, sent through the British Ambassador, had been opened, and that he had been denied access to his ambassador. On being asked why he had interfered in a matter that had nothing to do with him, he replied: 'To the first part of this question, I reply, that the affair of Lavalette was not foreign to an Englishman. There existed a ratified convention signed by an English general, and ratified by an English government; and the trial of Lavallette was a manifest violation of that convention.' Wilson was then asked why in his letter he had advanced as justification for his involvement, '*Liberty and Humanity*', which the inquisitor equated with republican phrases. Wilson replied:

> 'These two words, "Liberty" and "Humanity", become the proof of my explanation. In fact, the word "Liberty", when rightly understood, expresses respect for the laws and for justice. The laws were outraged by the violation of the treaty, and it is reasonable to regard this as the cause of liberty and humanity. The expressions which I used were caused by the vindictive spirit which I remarked in the persecutions directed against Marshal Ney and M. Lavalette; persecutions which always appeared to me an outrage on the honour and good faith of the English nation, identified with the Convention of Paris.'[47]

Sir Robert was left to his own devices by Liverpool's gang, but the public and Parliament, of whom Wilson was a Member, were outraged that a British general should be put on trial by the French, and that his confidential mail entrusted to the British Ambassador should be tampered with. They poured scorn on the French Government and its King. Liverpool and Castlereagh refused to intervene, but the Tsar protested at a Knight of Russia being held on a charge brought by such means. In this he was supported by the King of Prussia. The French, who were only carrying out the British Government's dirty work, were understandably offended, particularly Louis, who was being insulted in the British press. The French could not understand this because they had asked the British Government whether Wilson should be put on trial in the first place. Louis wanted to know why they were receiving 'brickbats' in the press? which, because of the large English contingent in France, was having wide circulation in France. The French Government insisted through Castlereagh that Liverpool censor the newspapers. Castlereagh suggested that perhaps the newspaper proprietors could be bribed, or threatened that government advertising would be withheld. Liverpool replied:

> 'I can assure you that I am fully sensible of the injurious effect which must result from the general line on present politics taken by our daily newspapers, and particularly by those which are supposed to be Government papers ... rather than to the Opposition of the day: there are no papers over which we have any authority, or even any influence on which we can

depend ... whereas no paper that has any character, and consequently an established sale, will accept money from the government; and indeed their profits are so enormous in all critical times when their support is so necessary, that no pecuniary assistance that the Government would offer would really be worth their acceptance ... they know full well that the public offices will necessarily be obliged, sooner or later, to insert their advertisements in the papers that have the greatest sale, and they hold cheap any menace to deprive them of this advantage ...'[48]

As a consequence of the Cabinet's enforced intervention, in the wake of the Allied monarchs' protests, Wilson spent a mere three months in prison and returned home where he was greeted as a hero. But the resulting publicity prompted Louis to put an end to the murderous regime into which he had been pressured. The Cabinet later took revenge on Wilson. In 1815 new rules were drawn up governing the award of the Order of the Bath to officers who had participated and held commands, however minor, in a specific number of battles. Wilson had not actually held an official command in the great battles for which he had received all these foreign knighthoods and peerages, so was denied a knighthood in England on a technicality. But, scorned and rejected by the ignoble Cabinet of the day, he was the more respected by the public as representing all that was decent in British society.

Napoleon meanwhile had reached Rochefort-sur-Loire on 3 July, to be greeted ecstatically by the people. He was approached by representatives of General Lamarque and others who urged him to take the 15,000-odd troops in the west and join up with the army that was being withdrawn behind the Loire. Napoleon politely refused. He had no intention of returning to lead a civil war, and perhaps be delivered up to the Prussians. Twice in fifteen months he had been betrayed by the men he needed to help him run the country, the army and the other state institutions. Napoleon knew that he was the elect of the people, but it was now up to them to realize who their enemies were.

Napoleon had hoped to get to America, and tried unsuccessfully to arrange a passage on an American ship. To this end, on the 8th, he sailed in one of the two French vessels down-river hoping for a favourable wind, but learning that Fouché had arranged for his arrest by the Allies, and fearing an assassination or kidnap attempt, he decided to surrender to the English – indeed he now knew that Fouché had betrayed his route and that he had no chance of slipping their blockade.

On 15 July he went aboard HMS *Bellerophon* whose Captain Maitland had promised to convey him to England in safety. Napoleon, aware that he owed Britain a debt for his safe passage to Elba and his security while on the island, sent the Prince Regent a letter which was never answered:

'To his Royal Highness the Prince Regent. Exposed to the factions which divide my country, and to the enmity of the powers of Europe, I have terminated my political career, and I come, like Themistocles, to throw myself on the hospitality of the British Nation. I place myself under the safeguard of their laws, and claim the protection of your Royal Highness, the most powerful, the most constant, and the most generous of my enemies.'

On Monday 24 July *Bellerophon* entered the Torbay roads. 'A lovely land! It reminds me of Porto Ferraio on Elba!' remarked Napoleon. No sooner had the anchor dropped than a boat arrived with orders for Maitland from Admiral Viscount Keith. No one was allowed to go ashore. He must wait in the bay for further orders. That day Keith had received a letter from the First Sea Lord, following a meeting of the Cabinet:

> '... I can state for your private information, that in all probability the ex-Emperor will be sent to some foreign colony. In the meantime he will not be allowed to land, or to have any communication whatever with the shore, and we shall not appraise him immediately of his future destination.'[49]

But news of Napoleon's arrival soon swept the country, and thousands of prominent people were converging on Torbay, jostling for a glimpse of the fallen Emperor. The Government and naval authorities were so apprehensive that Napoleon might set foot on British soil that they ordered Maitland's ship to surrounded by naval vessels and several guard boats with orders to fire warning shots if any of the sightseers came too close. On the 30th Admiral Keith informed Napoleon of his fate, but was more concerned with the sightseers, some of whom had come from as for off as Glasgow. He wrote to a relative:

> 'This day we announced his future destination, and I expect Sir H. Bunbury any moment; but this is for yourself only. In France there will be no quiet till he is removed and that villainous army disbanded. I wish he was sent away, for I am plagued to death; the women go near the ship and the guard boats have been desired to fire. Lady Duckworth and a party went with Mrs. Maitland so near as to speak. He came out and took off his hat to Mrs. Maitland. General Browne in full uniform went also too near on board, but was driven away by the guard boats.'[50]

There was of course a sound reason for this paranoid behaviour on the part of the Government and the Royal Navy. In 1815 the laws of Britain were somewhat different from the present time. While Napoleon was aboard *Bellerophon* he was under the jurisdiction of the Admiralty Court, a separate branch the British judiciary that dealt with all matters occurring at sea or in British coastal waters – its powers at the height of Britain's pre-eminence were coequal with those of the other branches of the judiciary; for instance, piracy could only be tried in the Admiralty Court. If Napoleon landed on British soil he would be subject to *the laws of the land*. In 1815 there was no law in Britain that authorized Napoleon's detention. As an ex-head of state, and the recognized sovereign of Elba, he could at worst be treated as a prisoner of war. If his letter to the Prince Regent had been made public it would probably have led to his being granted refuge in England as an exile. This is what the Cabinet feared. The Allied monarchs had agreed to his being placed in the custody of the British and held in a remote colony, where he would be subject not to the laws of

Britain but to those issued by the Colonial Secretary as appertaining to the country in question. Although Wellington had signed the declaration of outlawry in Vienna on behalf of Britain, it had been disavowed by the Cabinet and interpreted in a different form. No man or women in Britain could be imprisoned or executed save by due process of law. If Napoleon, as he well knew, had set foot on British soil, Liverpool would have been powerless to remove him from British jurisdiction while parliament and the courts were in the process of determining his status. Admiral Keith in his lengthy report to the First Sea Lord, registered Napoleon's indignation at being deprived of the benefit of British law:

> '... that as soon as he [Napoleon] was on board the Bellerophon, he was entitled to the protection of the laws of the country; that all Captain Maitland had done was to entrap him; that he was entitled to all the privilege of a *habeas corpus*, but was deprived of the means of obtaining it, and thereby prevented from frustrating the measures now pursued against his rights and liberty ...'[51]

In this Napoleon was correct. Placing himself under the protection of the British flag, gave him the same duties and privileges of a British subject. Not only that; his ship was anchored in British territorial waters, and the law in 1815 in this regard was the same as at the present. Prisoner or not, he was entitled to apply through the captain of the ship for a writ of habeas corpus, which means literally 'present the body', that is to say, the right to be brought before the High Court and to have shown by what lawful right he was being held and by whose lawful authority or warrant. In this instance he should have been able to apply through the captain to the Admiralty Bench of the High Court, but this right was being denied on the orders of the government.

What with officers going ashore, personal letters being sent, such as that from Admiral Keith to his young relative, a gossip with social connections, it was not long before the public were aware of the situation. To their credit, most people were, like Sir Robert Wilson, disgusted by the government's conduct. Very soon influential persons from the Opposition, even HRH the Duke of Sussex, were making their disapproval known. The radical Opposition member, Sir Francis Burdett, who had attacked Castlereagh's conduct in Parliament, now attempted to stop this, as he saw it, breach of faith. He formed an alliance with Anthony Mackentrot, Esquire, a former colonial judge, and Rear-Admiral Sir Alexander Cochrane (who had been accused by the Admiralty of not having engaged a superior French fleet commanded by the Napoleonic Admiral Willaumez under whom one of Napoleon's brothers had served) with a view to getting Napoleon on to British soil. The three, supported by many liberal MPs, demanded the intervention of the Lord Chancellor who was a member of the government and no friend of Castlereagh's. He authorized Lord Ellenborough, the Lord Chief Justice and one of Britain's finest ever legal authorities, to examine the case. Burdett and his colleagues had asked for a writ of *habeas corpus ad testification*, that is to say, to demand that Napoleon be produced in court and held as a material witness on the grounds that he would be able to give expert testimony as to the state of the French Navy at the time in question. In the High Court, Lord Ellenborough, aware of what was being done to deprive Napoleon, a foreigner, of his rights, issued a writ 'Ordering Admiral Viscount Keith to produce the person of Napoleon Buonaparte on November the Tenth, next, to give evidence in the High Court of London.' This was not done lightly, but was the only way that the Liberals and the majority of the public could satisfy themselves that Napoleon would not be exiled, without trial, to some remote corner of the globe.

The law required that the writ be served on the responsible person. The Admiralty informed Lord Ellenborough that this was Admiral Keith, and a constable of the High Court spent the next three days trying to serve it. Keith had been warned by the Admiralty, and at one point had to flee from his house by the backdoor to avoid the constable. He sought refuge aboard one ship after another, and eventually went to ground on the other side of the bay. To Lady Keith, her indignant husband wrote:

> 'What a mercy I left the house before the constable came to it. He followed me to the *Tonnant*: I left that ship and went to the *Eurotas*, he followed; I went out at the opposite side and rowed to sea. Neither of the captains in their ships (so much for wives!) After a time I landed at Cawsand, but my friend followed. I therefore went out to the point and got on board the *Prometheus*, and remained till dark, when I had seen the man land at Cawsand. I should have been had up before the Justice; and Boney under my wing till November next!'[52]

To his relative, Miss Elphinstone:

> 'The crowds of people and their very ill behaviour obliged me to put to sea, with this Reptile to wait the arrival of Sir George Cockburne. Writs of habeas corpus were also sent down to bring his person to the Court of the King's Bench; therefore I am on a cruise, but not going to St. Helena... '[53]

The people of Torbay and the visitors had greeted the High Court constable with excitement. The guard boats could not obstruct them, but Keith's deliberate evasion of a law officer and the knowledge that the navy was taking Napoleon away in breach of the court order had turned the people against anyone in a naval uniform.

Napoleon now resigned himself to the machinations of the faceless British government, not one of whose members had come to give the order to him personally. He lodged an official protest with Admiral Keith:

> 'Milord, I have carefully read the extract of the letter you sent me. I have given you my views in detail. I am not a prisoner of England. I came to this country on the Bellerophon man-of-war, after informing its Captain of the letter which I had sent to the Prince Regent, and obtaining from him an assurance that he had been given instructions to receive me on board and to take my suite to England, if I were to approach him with this object ... From the moment that I came on board the Bellerophon, I considered myself to be under the protection of the laws of your country. I would rather die than go to St. Helena, or be confined in some fortress. I desire to

live in England, a free man, protected by and subject to its laws, and bound by any promises or arrangements which may be desirable ... I assume my Lord, that you and the Under-Secretary of State of your government will make an accurate report of these facts. It is in the honour of the Prince Regent and the protection of the laws of your country that I have put, and still put, my trust ... '[54]

Napoleon knew, as did most of the Opposition, that the navy was breaking the law, on the government's orders. As is usually the case at the successful conclusion of a war, the Opposition was at a political disadvantage, and unable to pursue this matter as thoroughly as they would have liked. Napoleon was now informed that he would be transferred to the *Northumberland*, by force if necessary, and his departure to Plymouth was expedited before a new writ could arrive. On 3 August an embarrassing but true article appeared in *The Times*: 'An Act of Parliament is needed to make the detention of Buonaparte in England legal; another Act is no less necessary to intern him in a colony ...' The Government panicked, and before the expedition was properly fitted out his removal was ordered by Lord Liverpool.

Napoleon's suite was to be reduced from nearly sixty people to fifteen. Among those that were not allowed to go with him were Generals Lallemand and Savary, who were on the Bourbon's hit list. Captain Maitland, who indeed had thought that he was going to disembark Napoleon and his suite in England, was approached on the General's behalf by Napoleon who said that his personal honour was involved. To his credit Maitland wrote to the First Sea Lord: 'I earnestly beg Your Lordship to use your influence to prevent two men who asked and obtained from me the protection of the British Flag from being sent to the scaffold ... '[55] The government had no choice. The Generals were sent to internment in Malta until 1816 when they were released. If, as Maitland stated in his letter, protection of the flag had been granted to them, then certainly it had been granted to Napoleon by the very fact of his having been invited aboard. Maitland's sense of honour saved the lives of the Generals and frightened the government, but did his career no good at all. After Napoleon's departure, he was deprived of his command and was not reinstated until 1818. Napoleon and his small band of followers set sail in *Northumberland* on 7 August, bound for St. Helena, where they arrived on 17 October 1815.

Napoleon had written to the Prince Regent, '... I come, like Themistocles, to throw myself on the hospitality of the British Nation ... But Napoleon was not to be treated like the Athenian. Instead, as predicted by de la Bédoyère, he had already been sentenced by Castlereagh and Liverpool to be chained like Prometheus to a rock, there to be gnawed daily by the memories of his glory and greatness. The rock was St. Helena.

CHAPTER 13

THE ROAD TO GLORY

*'Here I am sitting at a comfortable table loaded with books, with one eye on the typewriter
and the other on Licorice the cat, who has a great fondness for carbon paper, and I am
telling you that the Emperor Napoleon was a most contemptible person. But should I happen to
look out of the window, down upon Seventh Avenue, and should I hear the sound of the heavy
drums and see the little man on his white horse, in his old and much worn green uniform,
then I don't know, but I am afraid that I would leave my books and the kitten and my home
and everything else to follow him wherever he cared to lead. My own grandfather did this
and Heaven knows he was not born to be a hero.'* – Hendrik Willem van Loon (1882–1944)

WE MUST NOW TAKE A LOOK AT THE PEOPLE WHO
accompanied Napoleon when he left Paris for Malmaison. Colonel
(later General) Gaspard Gourgaud, an artillery officer, educated at
the Ecole Polytechnique, had, after several campaigns, been
appointed to Napoleon's staff. In 1813 his assessment of the situation at Dresden
prompted Napoleon to ride to its defence and his consequent victory. He had fought
at Laon and Craonne in 1814, and at Brienne had saved Napoleon's life by a killing
a Cossack. On Napoleon's return he had rallied to him immediately and been
appointed a personal aide. Comte Henri-Gatien Bertrand, an engineer officer who
had been with Napoleon in Italy and Egypt, had risen to become Inspector-General
of Engineers and participated in the campaigns of 1805–7. He had built a bridge
across the Danube during the 1809 campaign. Governor-General of Illyria in
1811–12, he commanded IV Corps in 1813. On the death of Duroc, he was
appointed Grand Marshal of the Palace. With the Emperor in 1814, and on Elba, he
was prepared to bring his family with him to accompany Napoleon to his new exile.
He was without doubt Napoleon's most loyal and faithful servant.

At Malmaison had arrived Emmanuel, comte de Las Cases, a member of the old
aristocracy. Once a midshipman, he had participated in two royalist raids on the
French coast. Afterwards he became a tutor in London where he made many influential contacts, and met the Prince of Wales. He had returned to France under
Napoleon's amnesty. He was a scholar and had published a book on geography. He
had served as a volunteer in the defence of Walcheren in 1809 against the British.
He had been noticed by Napoleon and was made a councillor of state. At the first
restoration Louis had promoted him to captain in the navy. Las Cases, it seems, was
willing to go into exile with Napoleon in the hope of obtaining information with a
view to publication, and may have seen the situation as a gift-horse. It was Las Cases
the scholar, with his knowledge of England and the English, who induced Napoleon
to place his faith in Britain and her laws, much to the vehement opposition of General Lallemand who mistrusted the British.

Colonel Charles Tristan, comte de Montholon (not to be confused with General comte François de Monthion, a divisional general and staff officer at Waterloo), with his wife and children, had also joined Napoleon. Another of the old aristocracy, in his youth he had served as aide to Marshals Augereau, Macdonald and Berthier, and at the age of 26 was made an imperial chamberlain at the time when Napoleon was endeavouring to ingratiate himself with the old nobility to impress his Habsburg wife. In 1812 Montholon had been sent on a mission to Würzburg whence he had asked Napoleon's permission to marry Albine de Vassal, and been refused on the grounds that the 'lady' had been divorced twice, and both husbands were still living. Later Montholon asked permission to marry 'the niece of the President of the Council, Séguir', to which Napoleon consented – only to be informed later that this was none other than Albine de Vassal. Napoleon recalled Montholon and dismissed him in disgrace for his deceit. After Waterloo, Montholon and his wife had reappeared at Court to offer their services to the fallen monarch. Montholon's step-father, some say natural father, was the comte de Sémonville, a *bannière* of the Chevaliers de la Foi, and Gentleman-in-Waiting to Monsieur, Comte d'Artois. It will be recalled that Macdonald had meetings with the comte de Sémonville *after* Napoleon's return from Waterloo; with Macdonald he was one of the royalist conspirators charged with forming a government and staging a coup for the King.

Although he had never taken part in a battle,[1] Montholon later was to boast that he was a general of division and had been promoted to general of brigade in 1811. These claims were false – On 18 March 1815 he had received a general's commission from the Bourbons, at Artois' suggestion. A compulsive gambler, he was under investigation for the misappropriation (theft) of 6,000 francs of his regiment's pay. He was not arrested or court-martialled, but given an eleventh-hour promotion instead. Now, after Waterloo, with his wife and child he turned up at the Elysée dressed in the costume of a Court Chamberlain, offering to assist the fallen Emperor. They went with Napoleon to Malmaison and then to Rochefort. There Montholon, who had been dismissed in disgrace by Napoleon, whose step-father was an intimate of Artois', begged to be allowed to go into exile with Napoleon. Why? Montholon had made no appearance during the Waterloo campaign when Napoleon needed every man he could get; he had not broken his oath to Louis; he had great influence with the Bourbons – indeed had been elevated by them prior to their flight; he had nothing to fear from the restoration and everything to gain. The reason for his promotion and his immunity over the stolen money was because he was Artois' agent and was to be Napoleon's executioner on St. Helena.[2]

At Torbay, Napoleon's household was reduced by the British authorities. As we have seen, Generals Lallemand and Savary were proscribed, and most of the servants were struck off the list, though surely not for financial reasons, because Bathurst had expropriated Napoleon's funds and letters of credit 'to defray expenses'.

Las Cases was allowed to go, and to take his son with him. He had a royalist background and had played little part in the Hundred Days. Colonel Gourgaud, relatively unknown, his name not having appeared as having held a command, was also allowed to go.

Bertrand, the Palace Marshal, likewise had held no command; he had committed no offence and was considered an honourable man, even by Napoleon's enemies. Madame Bertrand, hysterical at the prospect of spending the rest of her life marooned on an island, 1,140 miles off the southern tip of Africa, attempted to throw herself overboard.

Montholon, on the face of it a forsworn royalist, was allowed to go, despite the British Cabinet's insistence that an example be made of those who had gone over to Napoleon. His wife was totally complacent at the prospect of spending her declining years cooped up with the man who had considered her a woman of ill repute and a bad match for her husband. Was this an oversight on Bathurst's part? Not a bit of it. He knew that Montholon was Artois' agent.

Castlereagh had secured a special treaty, signed on 2 August 1815, from the other powers, making Napoleon a prisoner of Europe. It specified that the British were to be his gaolers – in a bid to lend a measure of legality to his detention and deportation, contrary to British law. The preamble stated:

'In the name of the Most Holy and Indivisible Trinity, since Napoleon Buonaparte is now in the custody of the Allied Powers, Their Majesty's have agreed, in accordance with the terms of the Treaty of March 25th, 1815, on the most suitable measures to make impossible any undertaking on his part against the peace of Europe ... Article I. Napoleon Buonaparte is regarded by the Powers, which signed the treaty of March 25th last, as their prisoner. Article 2. His custody is entrusted to the British Government ... Article 3. The Imperial Courts of Austria and Russia and the Royal Court of Prussia will appoint Commissioners who will go to, and reside on the spot ... Article 4. *His Most Christian Majesty* [of France] *shall be invited, in the name of the four Courts above mentioned, also to send a commissioner ... to reside on the spot* ... Article 5. His Majesty the King of the United Kingdom of Great Britain and Ireland shall pledge himself to fulfil the obligations arising out of this agreement.'

Austria's Commissioner was Baron Sturmier; Russia chose Count Balmain; Prussia declined. Castlereagh had insisted that Bourbon France be represented, which enabled Artois to have an agent in place. He chose the aged Marquis de Montchenu who accepted the post 'because it had the advantage of securing him from his creditors'.[3] He was the only Commissioner allowed the singular privilege of being accompanied by an official diplomatic secretary, one M. de Gors, a member of the Chevaliers de la Foi, who had been brought to France in a Royal Naval vessel from Jersey in 1812.[4] Prior to this assignment he had been employed in Artois' household.

Britain's choice of Governor, General Sir Hudson Lowe, was a small-minded pedantic man who could be relied on not to deviate one jot from the letter of his instructions. Bathurst had impressed on this paranoiac the importance of his charge, and that Britain and consequently Lowe were responsible to the crowned heads of

Europe. Lowe had been the Quarter-Master of the Anglo-Allied army in The Netherlands until Wellington arrived. Wellington considered him a fool and had replaced him. But Lowe, as we shall see, had not been selected by the Cabinet for his intellect, but for his obedience to orders that bordered on fanaticism, and because he was a fool. That at any rate was the opinion of Wellington, the Allied Commissioners and Admiral Sir Pulteney Malcom, his naval commander.

The voyage to St. Helena took 67 days. The southern equatorial island appeared from the sea as '... a solitary pillar of basalt, rising sheer out of the ocean and towering 1,200 feet up, showing not a sign of beach or tree'. The island, seized by the Honourable East India Company, as a watering and victualling station *en route* to the Cape, was lent by them to the British Government and was to become the most famous prison in the world – impregnable, and garrisoned by about 3,000 troops with cannon, and four Royal Naval frigates, all to guard one man.

The servants who had been allowed to go with Napoleon were: Franceschi Cipriani, a Corsican who had been with him for many years, nominally major-domo, but, unknown to Montholon and Bathurst, Napoleon's bodyguard, confidant and internal security watch-dog. In private, Napoleon and he always conversed in the Corsican dialect; Louis Marchand, a valet, who had served Napoleon for most of his life; Etienne Saint-Denis, his personal valet, also known as 'Ali'; Abram Noverraz, third valet; Pierron, Napoleon's chef. The Irish-born British naval surgeon, Barry O'Meara, who had made an impression on Napoleon, was offered the post of Imperial Surgeon. O'Meara agreed and so did Bathurst – who thought to acquire a spy in the camp thereby.

The house in which Napoleon was to spend the last years of his life was called 'Longwood'. Five rooms were allocated to him, three to the Montholons, two to the Las Cases and one to Gourgaud. The servants had rooms in adjacent buildings, except Marchand who slept in an attic at Longwood. The Bertrand family occupied a small villa called 'Hutt's Gate' a mile distant.

During the first six months of his exile, his conditions were on the whole admirable. The ex-Emperor was allowed to ride, converse and make friends with many of the inhabitants including the Balcombe family with whom he became intimate. Admiral Sir George Cockburn, who had brought him to the island, was the acting Governor, and treated him well. St. Helena, with an area of 47 square miles, is about one-third the size of the Isle of Wight. Lord Bathurst had drafted a regime that would confine Napoleon within a triangle of about fourteen square miles in the middle of the island. He would not be allowed to ride beyond this area except under close supervision; he must be in sight of the military at all times, and be visited twice a day, in the morning and at night, by the military authorities. If a ship arrived he would be further restricted while it was there. The Governor was empowered to deport anyone, regardless of race, creed or colour, for any reason whatsoever.

The regulations governing Napoleon's sojourn seemed endless.

'No letter that does not come to St. Helena through the Secretary of State must be communicated to 'the General', or his attendants, if it is written by a person not living on the Island must go under cover of the secretary of state ... The whole coast of the Island, and all ships and boats that visit it, are placed under surveillance of the Admiral. He fixes the places which the boats may visit, and the Governor will send a sufficient guard to the points where the Admiral shall consider this precaution necessary. The Admiral will adopt the most vigorous measures to watch over the arrival and departure of every ship, and to prevent all communication with the coast, except such as he will allow. Orders will be issued to prevent, after a certain necessary interval, any foreign or mercantile vessel from going in future to St. Helena. If the General should be seized with a serious illness, the Admiral and Governor will each name a physician who enjoys their confidence, in order to attend the General in common with his own physician: they will give them strict orders to give in every day a report on the state of his health. *In case of his death, the Admiral will give orders to convey his body to England.*[5]

That Napoleon would become a state prisoner for life was only to be expected; he himself had thought so. His charisma, his ability to charm, to win the admiration of friend and foe, civilians and military alike, his potential for wielding enormous power and exerting an emotional hold, not only on his French subjects but those of Italy, Saxony, Poland and the lesser German states, made it impossible for him ever to be released. No greater accolade could have been bestowed on the fallen emperor by the great powers than their acknowledgement of this. But Napoleon had hoped to be held in England, and after several years to be treated more as a guest and hostage, than as a felon. Indeed he himself had imprisoned the Pope in order to impose his will on that unhappy man, and in 1808, by a ruse, he had imprisoned the entire royal family of Bourbon Spain. Even so, Pope and King had been treated by him in accordance with their status. It was the way that Napoleon was being treated by the British Government, and the spiteful Draconian measures that were being imposed that he found outrageous.

At Torbay he had been informed that henceforth he was to be known as 'General Buonaparte', a 'General on the retired list', which quite properly he refused to accept, and which until his death was to be a source of contention between himself and the island's Governor, Sir Hudson Lowe. This matter had been decided by the Cabinet, maliciously to humiliate the fallen man.[6]

Napoleon, it will be remembered, had been anointed Emperor by the Pope whose authority is deemed by nations professing the Catholic faith to be that of viceregent and representative of God on earth. It was given to him, it was asserted, to be the disposer and deposer of Kings. When, in 1814, Talleyrand and others mooted the proposition that Napoleon was not a 'legitimate' Emperor but self-made, the Pope's envoy crushed this notion from the representative of 'His Most Christian Majesty of France', declaring: 'Is it to be supposed that His Holiness the Pope went to Paris to consecrate and crown a man of straw?' It is with this undeniable anointing by the Pope, that all the myths and myriad papers of justification seeking to show that Napoleon was a 'usurper' or had stolen his crown, fall quite properly to the ground. It mattered not one whit whether Napoleon had come from the gutter or from an impoverished Corsican family of lesser noble descent. All the monarchs of Europe, including Britain's, were anointed by an ordained priest – as from God. If the Pope's consecration of Napoleon were invalid, then so were all the others. Every monarch in Europe save Britain's had formulated treaties, sent embassies and curried favour with the Emperor Napoleon. The present princes, dukes and marshals who surrounded the French throne all bore the titles that he had bestowed. He had elevated the Electors of Bavaria, Saxony and Württemberg to Kingdoms whose thrones they now occupied. Talleyrand, traitor and arch-hypocrite, was a prince by Napoleon's decree. Only an Emperor can create kings and princes; if Napoleon had never been Emperor, by what 'legitimate' right was Talleyrand a prince?

When Napoleon received a letter from London addressed to 'General Bonaparte', he remarked, 'Send this to General Bonaparte; the last I heard of him was at the Pyramids and at Mount Tabor.'[7] The frustrated Governor Lowe, who was tied by his orders, asked him whether, if this form of address were unacceptable, he would compromise and adopt an alias. Napoleon agreed and Lowe wrote to London for permission. Lord Bathurst replied: 'On the subject of General Bonaparte's proposition I shall probably not give you any instruction. It appears harsh to refuse it, and there arise much embarrassment in formally accepting it.' Bathurst's embarrassment appeared to stem from the notion that the use of an incognito was a prerogative of monarchs, and not even indirectly could the British Government concede Napoleon that.

So began Napoleon's war with his captors. In his view the denial of his title was a slight on the French nation, a denial of their right to choose their own sovereign, and an attempt to erase the splendid years of his reign. No other monarch had ever achieved his glory and accomplishments. His soldiers had guarded his headquarters at Rome, Cairo, Berlin, Vienna, Warsaw, Madrid, and at the Kremlin in Moscow. What other monarch had ever achieved this?

Having been on the battlefield and in the political arena, Napoleon decided to fight on the field of posterity. Ever with an eye to history, he would use the only weapon available – he would become the martyr on the rock, incarcerated in conditions, which he would amplify, that would shock future generations. The petty-minded members of the British Cabinet would provide the ammunition. He would publish an account of his treatment, his memoirs and observations on a variety of topics to an eager and waiting world. The Colossus that had bestrode the civilized world, now imprisoned on a tiny rock, maltreated by his captors, would be his theme, and perhaps a change of government in Britain, or the weight of public opinion might see his release. He would dictate this *oeuvre* to members of his retinue; if their accounts differed, so much the better. Soon the legend would become even greater than the man, and on this field he would be triumphant.

Since Napoleon's departure from France, Castlereagh had been moving heaven and earth to secure the Second Treaty of Paris. Whereas the first had been agreed in a matter of days, the second took five months to settle. Prussia, having been hoodwinked in the first treaty over the matter of Saxony, was now unilaterally pursuing its own policies. The Prussian army looted almost everywhere it went, despoiled the houses they forcibly occupied, and systematically removed all the art treasures that had been looted from Prussia since 1806, in imitation of the French depredations of that year. Paintings were cut from frames, in some instances sawn in half, and taken back to Prussia with statues, art works and other plunder. To the victor the spoils was the Prussian order of the day. Blücher, determined to blow up the Bridge of Jena, was informed that Talleyrand was coaching to the bridge and intended to place himself on the middle of it to prevent its destruction. Blücher told Louis' Minister that he would delay long enough for Talleyrand to arrive in the middle before lighting the fuze. Only the intervention of Wellington who placed a single British soldier on the bridge prevented Blücher from making good his threat. Blücher held his hand as a personal favour to Wellington, but Louis was obliged publicly to declare the bridge renamed. Count Nesselrode, the Prussian Minister, in reply to Castlereagh's remonstration, declared himself powerless to control the army which, under its generals, he likened to 'Praetorian bands'.

Finally the peace was negotiated. All the art works plundered by the French during the last 25 years were to be handed back (the Prussians had already taken theirs). France lost territory along her border, the fortresses of Philippeville and Marienburg to The Netherlands; Saarlouis, Saarbrücken and their fortresses to Prussia; Landau became a fortress of the lesser German powers. The surrounding region including the River Lauter went to Bavaria. Territory around Geneva and in the Savoy was parcelled out. Seventeen fortresses were garrisoned by the Allies at French expense. France was obliged to pay an indemnity of 700,000,000 francs, and pay for the support of about 900,000 foreign troops in 1815, 150,000 during 1816–17, and 30,000 until 1818. Castlereagh considered this excessive but unavoidable, to appease mainly the Prussians. Britain, having expended nearly a thousand million pounds to defeat Napoleon, declined the retention for the British people – groaning under massive unemployment and runaway inflation – the colonial acquisitions from France that might in small measure have alleviated the financial burden; Castlereagh reasoning that it was, 'essential to the integrity and honour of France being retained'. He did not add that it was to stabilize as much as possible the Bourbon regime that had been forcibly imposed on the French nation. On hearing the terms of the treaty, Napoleon remarked: 'What sort of peace is it that England has signed? ... what just compensations has he [Castlereagh] acquired for his country? The peace he made is the sort of peace he would have made if he had been beaten.' Strangely, Castlereagh and Liverpool reckoned that, given the reign of terror, huge indemnities that would take years to pay, the culling of the French army, and the presence of an army of occupation, the French people would soon have to accept the Bourbons. This would be the reward they long had sought, a weak dynasty, indebted to Britain, that would never be able to compete on land or sea. The only fly in the ointment so far as this roseate outlook was concerned was the existence of Napoleon, prisoner or not. (In early July Castlereagh had written: '... Except Buonaparte the King has no real rival.')

On St. Helena, Governor Lowe was making life increasingly unpleasant for Napoleon. The sweeping powers and authority bestowed on him by his government had gone to his head. Swollen with self-importance, this narrow-minded nonentity was unable or unwilling to discern the calibre of his prisoner – a man who had ruled a greater Empire at its zenith than any monarch since the days of the Romans, and to whom at one time or another all the monarchs of Europe had paid court. An example of his insensitivity, and of the absurdity of the situation, occurred when Lord Loudon, the Governor-General of India, with Lady Loudon, having called at St. Helena *en route*, were being entertained by the sycophantic Governor. Naturally they expressed a desire to meet Napoleon. Lowe wrote the following invitation: 'Should the arrangements of General Bonaparte admit it, Sir Hudson and Lady Lowe would feel gratified in the honour of his company to meet "The Countess".' The Duke of Wellington later told the Earl of Stanhope that he considered him a stupid, suspicious and jealous man, who might have very well let Napoleon go freely about the Island provided that the six or seven landing places were well guarded and that Napoleon showed himself to a British officer every day.'[8]

Much has been written about proposed plans for the escape of Napoleon from St. Helena: that 'it was probable that he might have tried'; that an American was organizing an attempt with 'three hundred men'; that *an attempt with a submarine vessel was intended.*[9] All these unfounded allegations can be found in the files of the Colonial Office, sent by Castlereagh who had them from Bourbon Spain's Commissioner via Artois' agents.

The limited number of landing places on St. Helena had been fortified to withstand attack by a squadron. Napoleon's residence, at the centre of the island, was encircled by sentries and concentric lines of watchers. All mail and baggage was searched, and at the slightest suspicion Lowe could deport anyone. The islanders were under martial law. Four frigates were off-shore, two of them patrolling the island continuously. Britain had a larger and more powerful navy than all the nations of the world combined. Who could attempt to force a landing against such odds, to say nothing of the 60-odd days' passage to Europe? Who would declare open war not only on Britain, but on Prussia, Russia and Austria, the 'Quadruple Alliance'? Would the United States risk war by giving Napoleon sanctuary? Could any of the Latin-American states risk losing their mercantile commerce?

Napoleon's conversations with everyone who had contact with him during the period of his imprisonment indicate that he was hoping for a change of policy on the part of Britain, or for Austria or Russia to intercede for him. He did not contemplate or wish to escape. His reasons, recorded by his amanuenses, were:

'*I should not be six months in America without being murdered by the assassins of the comte d'Artois. Remember Elba – was not my assassination concerted there? But for that brave Corsican, who had accidentally been placed as quartermaster of gendarmerie at Bastia, and who warned me of the departure for Porto Ferraio of the Garde-du-Corps, who afterwards confessed to Drouot, I was a dead man. Besides one must always obey one's destiny, for all that is writ-*

ten above. Only my martyrdom can restore the crown to my dynasty. In America *I shall be murdered* or forgotten. I prefer St. Helena.'[10]

Later he said: 'It is best for my son that I should remain here. If he lives, my martyrdom will restore the crown to him.'

In 1816, however, Bathurst, in response to these unsubstantiated 'threats' of Napoleon's rescue, induced Parliament to pass an Act that would ensure greater security and, in effect, legalize his detention. His movements were further restricted: 'Any British subject who should assist in his escape, or, after his escape, assist him on the high seas, was to be punished with death without benefit of clergy.'[11] His household was to be reduced by four, and expenditure limited to £8,000 per year; no communication to reach him except through Lowe; his perimeter to be more closely guarded. Longwood was fast becoming a prison within a prison: 'We consider it a very essential point, particularly until the iron railings shall arrive, to ascertain, late in the evening and early in the morning, that he is safe.'[12] More ominously, Napoleon – should he die, is not now to be returned to England, but to be buried on the island. Resentful of the indignities being heaped upon him in rapid succession, Napoleon withdrew ever more frequently, refusing to show himself. He refused audiences with Lowe, his officers or anyone the Governor would like him to meet. Lowe wrote: 'To Napoleon Bonaparte. Giving that person notice that the orderly officer *must* see him daily, come what may, and may use any means he sees fit to surmount any obstacle or opposition; that any of Napoleon's suite who may resist the officer in obtaining this access would be at once removed from Longwood and held responsible for any results that might occur; and that if the officer has not seen Napoleon by ten o'clock in the morning he is to enter the hall and force his way to Napoleon's room.'[13]

Napoleon replied in a letter delivered by Montholon, that he would shoot the first person who forced an entry, that he would rather die than live such an ignominious life. Napoleon won. Could Lowe put him on trial if he shot one of the Governor's men? What would the world think of such a situation? He wrote to Bathurst for guidance. Bathurst forbade Lowe to attempt a forced entry. Lowe resorted to hiding men with telescopes around the house. Napoleon, indignant, spent more and more time indoors to avoid the insufferable Lowe. Communication was carried out through intermediaries, he was left to the claustrophobic atmosphere of Longwood with his fellow inmates.

The original area of fourteen square miles in which he was allowed to move about was reduced to a few thousand square feet. Montchenu reported to his government that:

'... if one dog were seen to pass anywhere, at least one sentinel was placed on the spot. The plain of Longwood, where Napoleon lives, is separated from the island by a frightful gully which completely surrounds it and is only crossed by a narrow tongue of land not twenty feet broad, so steep that if 10,000 men were masters of the island 50 could prevent their arriving at Longwood. One can only arrive at Longwood by this pathway, and in spite of these difficulties, the 53rd Regiment, a park of artillery, and a company of the 66th are encamped at the gate – further on, nearer the town, there is another post of 20 men, and the whole enclosure [railings] is guarded day and night, by little detachments in view of each other. At night the chain of sentries is so close that they almost touch each other. Add to this a telegraph station on the top of every hill, by which the Governor receives news of his prisoner in one minute, or two, wherever he may be. It is thus evident that escape is impossible, and even if the Governor were to permit it, the guardianship of the sea would prevent it. For, from the signal stations a vessel can generally be decried at a distance of sixty miles. Whenever one is perceived a signal cannon is fired. Two brigs of war round the island day and night: a frigate is placed at the only two places where it is possible to land.'[14]

No ships except British men-of-war or provisioning ships were allowed to put in under any pretext, or allowed to communicate with the shore.

Sir Hudson Lowe tightened the screw: Unless Napoleon accepts the title of 'General Bonaparte', and allows Lowe's officers to walk in and check up on him night and morning, his movements will be further restricted. Napoleon suspected that the British wanted his life, and referred to Lowe as 'that hired assassin'. His resentment of Lowe's behaviour resulted in a severance of direct communications between the two, and Bertrand, Montholon and Gougaud were used as couriers. Montholon now began a gradual campaign aimed at isolating Napoleon from any influence save his own. He was awaiting instructions from Artois.

After Montchenu had arrived, Montholon, although Napoleon had ordered his entourage to ignore the Bourbon Commissioner, had sought to make contact by offering him a handful of green beans among which were three white ones; on the face of it an innocuous gesture but one that was reported, as was everything, to Lowe. Why did he do this? So far as Lowe was aware, Montholon had no particular interest in agriculture. He reported the matter to Bathurst: '... Whether the haricots blancs and haricot verts bear any reference to the drapeau blanc of the Bourbons, and the habit vert of General Bonaparte himself, and the livery of his servants at Longwood, I am unable to say; but the Marquis de Montchenu, it appears to me, would have acted with propriety if he had declined receiving either, or limited himself to a demand for the white alone.'[15] Bathurst made no reply to this paragraph of Lowe's report.

Lowe's suspicions were well founded but his reasoning was wrong. Montholon was not trying to subvert the Bourbon, but was indicating that he was on the same side. It was necessary for Montchenu to refuse the green beans. The Chevaliers de la Foi, and its political wing, the Société de la Propagation de la Foi, were run, as we know, along Masonic lines whose cells, for security, were unknown to one another. The traditional apparatus of secret signs and rituals had been preserved, but these now derived from Catholic symbology and a fanatical belief in the divine right of kings. The Chevaliers' method of identifying themselves was the offering of something coloured – the hue being one associated with the enemy – among which were three white tokens:[16] during the Revolution and under the Consulship the colour was red, representing the men of blood. When under the Empire Fouché began to penetrate the cells, the colour was changed to green, the colour of Napoleon's livery. The rigmarole stipulated that the recipient say 'I prefer the white', and, in a jocose manner while picking them up one at a time, 'the Father, Son and Holy Ghost [*Saint-Esprit*]', and the giver reply, 'Yes, the father, son and saintly order'. The three white tokens, ostensibly representing the Blessed Trinity, in fact referred to the murdered Louis XVI, his dead son Louis XVII, and the Bourbon descent from Louis IX, canonized as Saint-Louis, whose knightly order in Bourbon France was the Order of the Spirit of Saint-Louis. If all the colours were accepted, as in the case of Montchenu, the ritual was not proceeded with and the '*chevalier*' knew that the recipient was not a contact.

We can assume that Montholon eventually made contact with de Gros. There is written evidence that Montchenu's secretary carried more weight at court than his master. To Montchenu's first report he appended the following note for Artois and Louis:

> 'I am sorry to have to say it, on account of M. de Montchenu, but I am bound to declare that his criticisms on his colleagues are unfounded, and are too much coloured by his own personality. He should have been more just to M. de Balmain [Russian Commissioner], the only one who has taken to heart the common interests of the commission, to which by excess of zeal he has sacrificed his health and repose. M. de Montchenu should not have forgotten that it is to Balmain that the mission owes any degree of interest [influence] that it possesses. But he has never been able to make up his mind to join Balmain in a simple visit to the inhabitants of Longwood. He has chattered a good deal, always blamed what he did not do himself, and has himself never done anything when opportunity offered. He has occupied himself with disputes over precedence; and things have now taken such a turn that the post of Longwood will not be captured without a thousand difficulties.'[17]

This note indicates that de Gros was authorized to report on the conduct of his superior and to provide information. De Gros reports that because of Montchenu's activities Longwood could not be captured 'without a thousand difficulties'. Why should that disturb the Bourbons. Surely the whole idea was that Napoleon be detained there. The answer is that if one had an agent at Longwood and needed clandestine access to him, or vice versa, the ever watchful guards and the strict regulations governing mail presented as much of a barrier to this as to the inmates.

During the first two years of his exile, Napoleon began to dictate his memoirs to Las Cases. The war in Europe was over and Napoleon's captivity was becoming a matter of worldwide interest, his treatment being much discussed in the foreign press. Napoleon exaggerates the bad conditions of his captivity: the rats, which were indeed a menace, assume gigantic proportions; the exiles are half-starved and he has to break up his Imperial plate, to raise money; the climate is making him ill.

Napoleon used his only weapon to the full. Lord Holland and others raised the matter in Parliament, and the British public, for so long indoctrinated with the idea that Napoleon is a bloodthirsty tyrant, personifying all the evils of the revolutionary terror, now began to feel sympathetic towards the vanquished man. Lord Bathurst instructed Lowe to raise the Longwood allowance to £12,000 per year – a one-third increase – and to treat 'General Bonaparte as a distinguished General', – one assumes a one- third increase here as well!

In France the Bourbons were still unpopular; Napoleon's removal, national humiliation, occupation, loss of territory, degradation of the army, all laid at the door of these feudal overlords. Artois' agents, now known as the *Verdets* (greens), who wore the green livery of Monsieur, continued to terrorize Bonapartists, republicans, liberals, and all non-royalists. Police powers were increased, and almost any one could be arrested and detained 'for the good of the state'. But the nationalistic spirit had not been suppressed. On 4 May 1816, sixty ex-veterans, under the nominal leadership of Jean-Paul Didier, assembled around Grenoble, having been told that 'He is coming back, with an army of 600,000 blacks.' With drums beating, they marched Napoleon's old route from Grenoble to Paris. Two hundred peasants soon swelled their ranks, but the Gendarmerie, calling out the local army garrisons, arrested the group. Its leaders went to the guillotine crying, '*Vive l'Empereur!*'. In the ensuing panic, thousands of ex-officers were arrested and imprisoned. The Bourbons were shaken to find that at the merest rumour of 'his return', the peasants were prepared to march. At about the same time the Paris police uncovered another plot to assassinate the royal family. The three leaders were condemned to the death of a parricide, a barbaric procedure abolished at the Revolution. The three men were lead bare-footed to the guillotine, with black hoods over their heads. Each had his right hand cut off by the executioner and was left to suffer a while before being beheaded. No quick death for those who would plot the death of the beloved father, 'His Most Christian Majesty'; mercy was a privilege the Bourbons always expected, but never gave.

In the army conditions were odious, save for the privileged Maison du Roi and the Swiss Guard who were paid at a higher rate and had decent accommodation. In 1818, the Allies, having extracted their indemnity from an impoverished France, departed. No sooner had they gone than resentment surfaced in the army; every *département* reported Bonapartist or republican secret societies in their regiments. At Strasbourg leaflets were found inciting the army to declare for Napoleon II.[18] Napoleon on the rock, was becoming a greater force, a greater threat, to the Bourbons than ever before. Since the second restoration, the Boubons had been engaged in the perpetuation of a 'Black Legend', lucratively encouraging 'literary' authors to publish books condemning Napoleon and blackening his character. There appeared, *De l'état de la France sous la nomination de Napoléon Bonaparte* by Louis-André Pichon. This was followed by the best-known 'black' propaganda, *De Buonaparte et des Bourbons ...* by Chateaubriand. These and many other works sought to depict Napoleon as an insatiable warrior, who disregarded the welfare of his people, muzzled the press, and persecuted such liberals as Benjamin Constant, Friedrich Schoell and Alfred Beauchamps and others. They turned history on its head to give the impression that the Bourbons alone were champions of the 'rights of man'.

The slimiest propaganda, however, came with the publication in 1817 of a book purporting to have been written by Napoleon, *Manuscrit de Sainte-Hélène*, which portrays a man who has total disregard for the lives of his soldiers, for Frenchmen, family – just about everyone. This *canard* was widely circulated, especially in Britain, to the delight of the Bourbons, who knew that Napoleon, thanks to Lowe and Bathurst, was quite unable to refute it. But in London a few months later, was published *Letters from the Cape of Good Hope in reply to Mr. Warden*, dictated by Napoleon, written by Las Cases, and smuggled out by O'Meara. The letters, purporting to be written by an Englishman, were intended to impress Britain and Europe with Napoleon's sufferings. They sought to justify his past actions and portrayed him as Liberty personified, the son and heir of the Revolution, and propagator of the reforms of 1789. They decried the Draconian regime under which he was being held, but, more importantly, invigorated the growing Napoleonic legend. Through the same sources, Napoleon refuted entirely the bogus *Manuscript*, and further to destroy its credibility he later denounced it in his will.

In Europe, all the sovereigns except Louis were busy creating personal Guards in emulation of Napoleon's Imperial Guard. Military theorists, Clausewitz, Jomini and others, were writing about Napoleon's military achievements. All the leading military academies were trying to analyse his campaigns. The legend of Napoleon, was becoming a greater force than the man himself. In France Bonapartism was becoming synonymous with nationalism. The writings dictated to Las Cases expounded his ideas. He was seen as the herald of Italian unity, the originator of a unified Germany. In Holland his removal of the old feudal federalism and creation of a monarchy under his brother was seen by the Dutch as the root of their present modern kingdom. Napoleon had inspired nationalistic aspirations in the Polish people, the Serbs, Roumanians and Greeks, all of whom had been for a short time subject to his laws, and were now eager to throw off their shackles.

The craving for freedom had been invoked by the various monarchs in Europe to induce their subjects to take up arms to repel Napoleon, but after he had been repelled these monarchs, failing signally to realize that what their subjects wanted was freedom from oppression, expected them to return to a meek acceptance of the old order. After Waterloo, the Tsar, feeling himself moved by God, but in fact sensing which way the wind was blowing, persuaded the Allied monarchs to sign a 'Holy Alliance' which pledged its signatories to regulate their conduct in accordance with the Christian faith, in a Christian brotherhood of princes that would support one another against their own subjects in the event of revolution. Other lesser powers were invited to join. This alienated the Turks who saw it as a conspiracy against Islam. The Pope was outraged and would not sign or acknowledge a plan propounded by the Eastern Church which he did not recognize. The United States of America rejected it on the grounds that it was a conspiracy of princes against the rights of the people and the spirit of the age. Napoleon on his rock, wearing the crown of martyrdom, was still reaching out to serve notice on the Bourbons and all autocratic monarchs.

Britain was now suffering from an economic depression. Some 400,000 demobilized servicemen, dockyard workers and military industrial workers were unemployed. Labour became cheap; the burgeoning industrial magnates in the north reduced wages, and the great land owners raised rents. In 1815 the first of the Corn Laws was introduced to restrict the import of cheap corn, so that the land-owning class would be ensured of a minimum return on their investment and be able to maintain their standard of living. Bread prices soared. The Government removed the 10 per cent income tax, paid mainly by the wealthy, which put an even greater burden on the poorer classes. Mass unemployment precipitated riots. On 2 December 1816 at Spa Fields in London, a gathering of some 80,000 people listened to the politician Henry Hunt speaking on parliamentary reform. The people were fed up with the corrupt system wherein the landed gentry controlled Parliament and its members, and a law could be passed to protect their interests at the expense of thousands who were starving. Before the meeting had even begun, people were marching on Westminster London, bent on overawing the politicians – or worse. The Lord Mayor had to call out the army garrison to disperse them. In 1819, at a public meeting in St. Peter's Fields in Manchester, 50–80,000 people gathered to clamour for parliamentary reform and against these corn laws that were depriving them of bread. In scenes reminiscent of France before the Revolution, and under similar circumstances, the magistrates – all local landed gentry – called out the local yeomanry – whose members were mainly employees. The people were charged and sabred by this British cavalry unit; eleven were killed and many hundreds wounded in this appalling affair, called by the press 'The Peterloo Massacre'. The Government, terrified that republicanism and revolution were imminent, hastily passed a mass of repressive legislation – the infamous 'Six Acts': (1) speedy summary trials for 'misdemeanour's; (2) massive penalties for 'Seditious Libel'; (3) imposition of a stamp tax on newspapers – to reduce circulation of radical publications mostly read by the lower classes; (4) curtailing of public meetings, and the number of people allowed to meet in any one place; (5) prohibition of the use of or training with arms, on severe penalty; (6) magistrates to have greater powers of search for 'weapons' – these were not specified but generalized as 'offensive', in effect the re-introduction of the obnoxious 'General Warrant'. Habeas Corpus had been suspended the year before – after Napoleon's application. Liverpool's government was now exiling (transporting to Australia)[19] thousands of potential 'trouble-makers' and unemployed labourers, convicted of serious 'misdemeanours', who would face the death penalty if they returned.

On St. Helena, meanwhile, Montholon had set about the dangerous and difficult task of murdering Napoleon in such a way that his death would not be seen as anything but from natural causes. Montholon – and Artois – were skating on very thin ice. If Napoleon were killed suddenly, the outcry would be such as might very well sweep the Bourbons away, and possibly see them torn to pieces in the process. On St. Helena, Montholon was in like case. Chronic arsenical poisoning was decided upon. Not only would this produce the symptoms of a slow, gradual decline of health, but would coincide with the propaganda that Napoleon had already put out about his ill health caused by the climate. Liverpool and Castlereagh, having financed Artois' organization, probably had an idea, if not prior knowledge, that the Bourbons needed to silence their sole opposition. In fact it would have been utterly naïve of them to think that Artois would not try to rid the Bourbons of Napoleon, trapped as he was, like a fish in a barrel. Artois knew that these British politicians felt about Napoleon as men of the 5th century felt about Attila the Hun; they would shed no tears at his demise. Besides, Liverpool's government was having republican problems of its own and would not grieve at the loss of the man who was becoming the republican symbol.

Montholon proceeded cautiously. He had Las Cases expelled for attempting to smuggle a letter from the island; a stupid idea, probably suggested by Montholon himself. Always the smooth courtier with Napoleon, Montholon prostituted his wife to 'comfort' his great leader. This, together with calculated insults, upset Gourgaud who threatened to call him out. The upshot was that Gourgaud demanded that he take precedence over the Montholons in the household or his honour would not permit him to stay. Napoleon consented, and got him to smuggle out a letter to the Tsar, in response to an inquiry (fabricated by Montholon to swing Napoleon in favour of Gourgaud's leaving).

Next Napoleon's faithful watch-dog Cipriani died of sudden stomach pains, diagnosed as an irritated bowel condition, but consistent with acute arsenical poisoning – a mere servant, so Lowe has no autopsy performed. O'Meara, Napoleon's Irish doctor, was then expelled, on information probably given to Montchenu by Montholon via de Gros, and acted upon in London.

Montholon then set about poisoning the vat containing the wine reserved for Napoleon's use. Arsenic was in common use on the island to kill the rats which, coming from the ships, had bred over the years to a point where they constituted virtually a plague. Montholon would have been able to get it from de Gros. The amount needed to bring about Napoleon's death over a period of years would go into a small envelope.[20] In 1819 Napoleon obtained the services of another doctor, Francesco Antommarchi, an anatomist, sent by Napoleon's uncle, Cardinal Fesch, together with two priests. One of these was elderly and died suddenly of violent stomach pains. The other, a young man whom Napoleon encouraged to learn to ride a horse, was expelled. He had been wearing a servant's green riding-jacket over his soutane, and this was reported to Lowe. Lowe wrote to Bathurst that this might be a plot; the priest to impersonate Napoleon, while he escaped – Lowe did not elaborate as to how or where this could be effected.

Montholon had gradually put himself in good standing with Lowe to whom he was in the habit of 'frankly confessing'. Lowe's predecessor, Admiral Cockburn, had reported Montholon's 'frankness' as early as January 1816. Writing to Bathurst, he said that Montholon, charged with a letter from General Bonaparte complaining that: 'Longwood was the most barren spot on the island, always deluged with rain and swathed in mist', that the exiles were not well provided for as to food and comforts.' Cockburn wrote: '... it was written in a moment of petulance of the General [Bonaparte] ... and that he [Montholon] considered the party to be in point of fact vastly well off and to have everything necessary for them, though anxious that there should be no restrictions as to the General going unattended by an officer wherever he pleased throughout the island.'[21] Here we have proof, as early as the third month of Napoleon's captivity, that Montholon is already revealing Napoleon's true demeanour to his gaolers, and giving the impression that he himself is 'sound'. Gourgaud's journal also reveals his suspicions about Montholon.

Las Cases, Gourgaud and O'Meara all gone. These three were besieged by publishers on their return. Their publications soon increased the public's knowledge of Napoleon: the breadth of topics of his conversation; his wide reading; comprehensive intelligence; humanitarianism; concern for all people ruled by despots. His human defects, uncontrollable temper, tyrannical methods, ambition were played down. The objectionable aspects of his rule were blamed on his enemies and the autocratic regimes that had declared war on him. It should be remembered that in almost none of the wars of the period had Napoleon been the aggressor or the first to declare war. The Napoleonic legend now began to take shape: Napoleon the greatest military captain of all time, peacemaker, statesman, the giant of the age, the martyr of the rock, chained by despotic rulers who feared his gifts to mankind.

On 13 February 1820, Monsieur, comte d'Artois, was presiding over a meeting of his *Petit Bureau* (the inner Cabinet) at his residence, the Pavillon de Marsan. Louis' heir was 63 years old, his ailing brother was 65. The affairs of government had passed increasingly into Artois' hands. He controlled the Chambers, and nightly received reports from the police and his own agents; the Chevaliers were still a force within a force. The meeting was interrupted by shattering news. His son and heir, the duc de Berry, had been stabbed in the side as he was entering the Opera House, and lay dying. In de Berry, who was aged 42, had resided the last hopes of extending this branch of the Bourbon dynasty – his brother d'Angoulême having sired no children. The assassin, a 37-year-old saddler from the royal stables, Louis-Pierre Louvel, had been planning the assassination for four years. Before he was executed Louvel said: 'I cannot avoid believing that if the battle of Mont. St-Jean [Waterloo] was so fatal to France, it was because there were Frenchmen [royalists] at Ghent and Brussels who had sown treason in our army and aided the foreigner.'[22] The imperial flame that still burned bright in the hearts of the French people had extinguished the Bourbons' hopes.

In England ten days later, on 23 February, a republican plot was uncovered. The conspirators, promoted by a certain Arthur Thistlewood who was incensed at the repressive measures being taken against advocates of reform, planned to murder the Ministers of the Crown at a Cabinet dinner, but were betrayed and arrested at a stable in Cato Street near the Edgeware Road. The leaders were hanged for high treason. If the implications of this affair shocked the Government, the news of de Berry's assassination came as a bombshell. Castlereagh, Liverpool and Bathurst were dismayed. Louis was sickly, Artois was in his sixties, and his sole heir was infertile. Bourbon and the Cabinet's hopes now looked to the duchesse de Berry who, it had been announced, was carrying a child. Fears were again raised when in early April several bombs were found hidden in the gardens of the Louvre under the duchess's window. It seemed as if Napoleon's shadow were once again falling across Europe.

It took more than sixty days to get from Britain to St. Helena; on average one boat sailed there every four months. The next ship left for the island on 12 December and in the mail were two letters from Artois, one to Montchenu and the other to de Gros. In accordance with the parliamentary Act that regulated Napoleon's confinement, all foreign mail had to be vetted by Bathurst. Artois' letters would have been opened, copied and resealed with a replica of Artois' seal.[23] One can imagine Monsieur, in his grief and thirst for vengeance, sending the fatal order, probably in cipher, to de Gros to finish it – Now! Quickly! There is no existing proof in writing that the British Government had any hand in Napoleon's murder, but it had known of, approved and financed Artois' *modus operandi* for 25 years, including his several attempts at assassination. When, after Waterloo, Liverpool and Castlereagh's hopes that Louis or the Prussians would have Napoleon executed, had been dashed, they had allowed the terrorist leader to send two of his agents to watch over the 'only obstacle to the Bourbon dynasty', as Castlereagh had put it.

The dispatch ship, HMS *Vernon*, arrived at St. Helena on 23 February 1821, within a year of de Berry's assassination, and the attempted murder of the members of the British Cabinet and de Berry's widow and heir. Almost immediately Napoleon collapsed with severe stomach pains. At that time the treatment for this ailment was the administration of an emetic containing tartar, and this was given to him by his doctor, Antommarchi. A poisoner using arsenic would know that this was what a doctor would do, and in fact it would be a great help to him because the tartar emetic contained salts of antimony which corrodes the stomach lining and inhibits the stomach's natural reflex to eject any substance harmful to it. Within days Napoleon was too weak to eat or drink anything. Towards the end he suspected that he had been poisoned and was suspicious of everyone except loyal Montholon, who was now sleeping on a couch in Napoleon's room.[24] Montholon was soon demanding that a doctor be sent from France – the last thing Napoleon would have wanted, but Napoleon was now delirious. Montholon was alone with Napoleon; Bertrand had asked to remain with him, but Montholon said he would ask him to relieve him if he became exhausted. Antommarchi slept in another room and Louis Marchand, the faithful valet, slept upstairs.

Abstaining from all food and drink, Napoleon rallied sufficiently to be able to make his will: 'I die before my time, murdered by the English oligarchy and its hired assassin. The people of England will avenge me all too soon. The unhappy result of the two invasions of France, when she was so rich in resources, are due to the treason of Marmont, Augereau, Talleyrand and La Fayette. I forgive them. May the posterity of France do the same.'[25] In codicils he left all his money and possessions to his friends and family, mainly his son: 'I urge my son never to forget that he was born a French Prince ... In no way whatsoever is he to fight or harm France.' To Montholon, his Judas, and final betrayer: 'I leave to Count Montholon 2,000,000 francs, as proof of my satisfaction with his filial devotion which he has displayed towards me for six years, and in order to compensate him for the losses which he incurred through his sojourn on St. Helena.' What about Bertrand, universally acknowledged to be Napoleon's most loyal follower, from the sands of Egypt to Elba, Waterloo, and St. Helena? 'I leave 500,000 francs to Count Bertrand.'

No sooner had the will been made than Napoleon was given some wine and a little food – and suffered agonizing convulsions. An emetic was prescribed. At Montholon's pleading a British doctor came to examine Napoleon and decided that his condition was not serious. Napoleon was thirsty. Montholon said that Napoleon would treat himself with a diet, an *orgeat* (syrup) and *soupe à la reine*. The *orgeat*, an Italian, Mediterranean drink, was brewed from barley, with added spice, orange water, and sweet and bitter almonds. Montholon sent the servants all over the island in search of bitter almonds. Napoleon enjoyed his drink, saying that it tasted better with the bitter almonds.[26]

On 3 May Napoleon had two biscuits and an egg yolk, followed by a glass of wine. His condition began to deteriorate again. At 2.30 p.m. Lowe brought an army doctor and a naval surgeon to treat Napoleon, at Montholon's request but against Antommarchi's advice: 'I assure them that it is impossible; they side with Dr Arnott, who proposed a purgative of ten grains of calomel; I cry out against that prescription; the patient is too weak; it will fatigue him for no purpose; but I am alone, they three, and numbers prevail.'[27] Montchenu wrote: 'The discussion was referred to Montholon, who sided with the English doctors, and the medicine was consequently admininistered.'[28]

By itself calomel is harmless, but when combined with the bitter almonds in the *orgeat* which Napoleon had been drinking every day, produces hydrocyanic acid which in turn releases mercurial cyanide from the otherwise inert calomel. The victim loses sight and hearing, the muscles of the body are paralysed and he loses consciousness. If the stomach has been weakened by an emetic it cannot expel the fatal poison, and death occurs within 48 hours.[29]

At 5.50 p.m. on 5 May 1821, Napoleon lost his final battle, betrayed and killed by a man he had thought was his friend. His last words, soon to reverberate around the world and to be treasured in France were: 'France – the Army – Head of the Army – Josephine.'

Napoleon had now passed from the land of the living into legend. He had lost the battle and France at Waterloo, but was to ride triumphant on the field of glory. Memories dimmed the French mind of all the hardships, the conscriptions, the loss of lives incurred in the wars of his reign. The memory of him for France, and the world, was of a small man riding a white horse, wearing an old grey riding-coat, and a tricorn hat, behind whom marched serried ranks of Imperial Guardsmen in tall bearskins, the pride of France and the scourge of Europe's hereditary kings. The people associated the Bourbons with feudalism, brutality, a police state and foreign invasions to take 'him away from them'. France mourned her most famous son, and in England too there was a sense of loss, especially by those who espoused republican principles.

Hudson Lowe, faithful to his orders, had an autopsy performed in the presence of several doctors. The stomach was found to be ulcerated, and cancer was diagnosed, *although none was present*.[30] Lowe ordered one doctor to remove a reference to an enlarged though healthy liver. With as much ceremony as was permitted to 'a General of distinction', Napoleon's body was buried close to Longwood, beneath a willow near a little stream; he had requested that his body to buried near the Seine. Lowe refused permission for the simple headstone to bear the legend 'Napoleon' unless 'Buonaparte' were added Count Bertrand refused to comply and the inscription was left incomplete: 'Here lies ...' – the unknown warrior. So the ex-Emperor of France was laid to rest beneath a blank stone, while with an irony he might have appreciated, the British army's muskets and cannon fired a final salute to their greatest enemy – as prescribed for a 'distinguished General'.

The man on the rock, the conqueror of Moscow, the man who had told his soldiers in Egypt, while pointing to the pyramids, 'Soldiers! Forty centuries look down upon you!' had passed away. Every word spoken in exile, every word recorded by foreign visitors, was avidly collated. A plethora of memoirs appeared. Almost everybody at Longwood wrote or had something 'ghost written'. Napoleon's declaration in his will, 'The people of England will avenge me all too soon,' were prophetic as far as Hudson Lowe was concerned. His pettishness condemned him in the eyes of his fellow countrymen. On returning to England, his rewards were meagre. George IV shook his hand at a Levee; fifty other people were being presented and the king had to ask him his name. He received the colonelcy of a regiment, and four years later was on the military staff of the colonial force in the backwater of Ceylon. Returning on leave, he requested to be made Governor of Ceylon when the incumbent retired. Wellington refused to promise it to him. Lowe then pressed the Duke for a pension; Wellington replied that parliament would not in his opinion grant one, nor 'would Mr. Peel ever consent to propose one in the House of Commons.'[31] In London Lowe was assaulted in the street by the son of Las Cases, but no charges were brought. The seventh edition of O'Meara's book came out, and increased the odium of the common people for Lowe, who was spat at on several occasions – he was by now a 'General on the retired list'. Lowe sought advice from the most prominent legal minds and sued O'Meara and his publisher for 'criminal libel'. For his affidavit he was required to select the most libellous passage in the book. Lowe replied that: 'Truth and falsehood were so artfully blended together in the book, that he found it extremely difficult to deny them in an unqualified manner.'[32] He delayed so long that the court threw out the case, and he had to pay enormous costs. He died without ever having been able to gain the respect of his fellow countrymen.

When he arrived at St. Helena, Napoleon had said: 'If I had shot but two men, Talleyrand and Fouché, I would still be on the throne today.' Fouché's treachery, as we have seen, had availed him nothing. An evil man, who excelled as head of a secret police force with unlimited powers, like all such persons he was neither trusted nor trustworthy. He died, also in exile, a year before Napoleon, unrespected and unmourned.

Talleyrand, the smooth, renegade priest, who saw himself as a kingmaker, and the power broker behind thrones, died in 1838, having spent his last years as French Ambassador to the Court of St James's. Exiled from the Bourbons, not unnaturally he was much admired by the British politicians. Wellington, Napoleon's last adversary in the field, died at Walmer Castle in 1852. He had become Commander-in-Chief of the Army, and Prime Minister. The general public and the government subscribed to the erection of an immense equestrian statue to commemorate his deeds; it was moved around London for many years before the government made up its mind as to where it should be sited. Lord Bathurst died in 1834, having spent sixteen years as Colonial Secretary. There is no monument to him, and little is recorded of his activities save a few lines in a biographical dictionary.

Lord Liverpool did not live to see the bringing in of the parliamentary laws of 1831, which removed for ever the corrupt system that could impose his type of government on the British people, against the wishes of the majority. He was struck down by a stroke in 1827 and died the following year.

Lord Castlereagh, Pitt's disciple and Napoleon's implacable enemy, committed suicide in 1822, having become involved in a squalid court case involving homosexuality; he cut his throat with a penknife. No statesman since the Earl of Strafford had ever been so hated by his own people as he; a hatred so implacable that there was a shout of exultation when his coffin was borne into Westminster Abbey.[33]

Prince Metternich, advocate of the police state and repression of democracy, was driven from office in 1848; he took refuge in England where he died in 1851. Despised by his countrymen and those of France and Italy, he left no enduring monument. Prince Blücher died in 1819, having suffered much mental aberration and grief on the committal of his son Franz to a lunatic asylum. Tsar Alexander II died in 1825, having spent his last years living the life of a monk, plagued by a guilt complex, his mind unbalanced, trying to repent for the role he felt he had played in the murder of his father.

In 1824 Artois at last became King of France as Charles X. The widow of his murdered son, the duc de Berry, gave posthumous birth to a son, and the Bourbon dynasty was deemed safe. Charles' first act was to implement a bill of indemnity, a once and for all payment to the émigrés for the lands they had lost more than thirty years ago. One thousand million francs were to be given to this privileged faction. His subjects, having not yet recovered from the war reparations, now had a burden of almost twice what they had paid to the Allies. Savage laws were introduced in an endeavour to subdue the people to the primitive obedience of the pre-Revolution era; sacrilege, for example, was made punishable by death. By 1830 the French had

had enough of this man of blood, and in July of that year revolution again erupted. Marshal Marmont, in charge of the Paris garrison, drew a defensive position around the Louvre and the Tuileries. The line troops, harangued by the crowds, deserted *en masse*, leaving only the pampered, highly paid Royal Guard and Swiss Guard in position. The Guards fell back around the palace of Saint-Cloud. Charles began to promise the people and the army all the concessions and privileges that he had taken from them during the last six years, but to no avail. Marmont, desperately trying to keep the troops loyal, was arrested by the duc d'Angoulême for being a 'traitor', in that he was discussing politics with the troops. The soldiers of the Royal Guard, believing that d'Angoulême was preparing to march on the Parisians, deserted in large numbers. Yet again, the King's son could not get obedience from his men, just as in 1815. Within hours even the officers of the Guard were deserting. The Swiss Guard, on the initiative of its field officers, had obtained a safe conduct to withdraw *en masse* from the insurgents, and without any notice departed. The Swiss, who had died to a man for his brother, and were universally acknowledged as loyal soldiers, were not prepared to die for this loathsome tyrant. Artois, with but 1,350 men who were deserting by the minute, declared that he would abdicated in favour of his heir, but this was ignored. He was told curtly that if he left quickly he could keep his miserable life. Artois took exile in Scotland at Holyrood House where he had been exiled 35 years before. His presence was an embarrassment to the British Government and he took the hint and left for Prague where he died in agony from cholera in 1836.

In 1832, the duchesse de Berry, widow of the assassinated heir, landed near Marseilles to bring the young duc de Bordeaux into his inheritance, in emulation of Napoleon's return from Elba. No one there was interested. Making her way to the Vendée, she managed to instigate a riot which was quickly quelled. She was imprisoned in Blaye fortress near Bordeaux. Having given birth there to an illegitimate child, the disgraced duchess was released and fled with her children to England. In 1950, the direct descendant of this branch brought an expensive legal action in France, the law of exiles having been removed from the French statute books. This descendant wished to be acknowledged as Prince Jean de Bourbon. After seven years the superior court of France ruled that he had been born in England, of several generations of Englishmen, the son of the heir having accepted citizenship. He was therefore not French, and had no claim to any 'legitimate feudal title, it having lapsed on the descendants having become English'. France's loss was apparently England's gain?

Marmont lived long, and in exile, where he wrote his memoirs to try to vindicate himself. Although Napoleon had written in his will 'May the posterity of France forgive them,' the people of France did not forgive Marmont. Wherever the lonely old man walked in Trieste, the children would point out the man 'who betrayed Napoleon'. Count Montholon lived until 1853. As an executor of Napoleon's will, and fellow exile, he was a hero. He was always short of money; most of the fortune bequeathed by Napoleon and Artois was lost in gambling. Artois and the House of

Bourbon allowed this 'subversive' great favour, and he was the only Bonapartist in France who was allowed to publish his memoirs, although these it should be noted do not correspond with the day-to-day journals of Louis Marchand, Gourgaud or Las Cases.

The Legend of Napoleon, his personification of the ideals of Liberty, Nationhood, a federated Europe, and constitutional monarchy, and the fact of his having raised France to be the mightiest military power since the time of the Romans, had captured the imagination of France and much of Europe. Revolution broke out in Naples, Piedmont, Spain, and the German states, all of whom were seeking republican ideals. Napoleon having broken the power of Spain, revolution broke out in her American colonies, all of which became independent. Poland too sought several times to achieve a national identity. In 1840 Napoleon's nephew, Louis-Napoleon, considered a farcical character by his countrymen, attempted a landing at Boulogne with a small following, including Montholon. The farce ended in the ringleaders being sentenced to life imprisonment. In his defence Louis-Napoleon invoked the spirit of Bonapartism in a speech that proclaimed his uncle's ideals as a political force in France, and that they were the protection of the liberties and the rights of man. His speech was so powerful and aroused such national emotion, that the farce became a *tour de force*. After five years' imprisonment, Louis escaped, which rekindled memories of his uncle's exile. In 1848 a new revolution erupted and he hurried back, to become first Prince President, then Emperor of the French. He participated in the Crimean War, beat the Austrians in Italy, and helped in its unification. Louis, however, was not a military genius like his uncle. In 1870 he fell into the Prussians' trap and became embroiled in a war that devastated France, and brought about his abdication. Even in this crisis, however, the French people clung to Napoleon's legend, declaring: 'It would not have happened if HE had been here.'

France finally became a republic whose military tradition traced its origins and battle honours not to the Bourbons but to Napoleon.

Napoleon's last struggle, for posterity and martyrdom, like the majority of his campaigns, was a resounding victory. The Legend was tenacious. the Napoleon of Legend was not the Napoleon of History. But neither Napoleon was less impressive than the other in consequence. Count Rostopchin, Napoleon's contemporary and enemy of 1812, wrote on hearing of his death: 'Napoleon was in my eyes a great general after his campaign in Italy and Egypt, benefactor of France when he stemmed the French revolution during the Consulate; a despot dangerous for Europe as soon as he made himself emperor; insatiable conqueror until 1812; man drunk with Glory and blinded to fortune as soon as he undertook the conquest of Russia; a genius defeated at Fontainebleau and Waterloo; and at St-Helena, a Jeremiah prophet.'[34] Accurate or not, this was a view certainly held by the majority of his opponents.

However, it is the judgement of one's fellow countrymen that counts at the end of the day. The Bible tells us that a prophet is seldom welcome in his own country. Was Napoleon, the man of blood, the tyrant, the usurper, the Corsican Ogre? A man insatiable for conquest and lustful of glory? Or was he an 'enlightened despot' as described by Voltaire and Rosseau in their contemporary writings, who was attempting to bestow a better way of life on Europe? Was he a man who personified the Revolution, a classless society, with equality under the law, and whose members had a right to qualify for the highest positions in the state, and could obtain them on merit. Not because of caste, creed, or birth or privilege? Or was the answer much more simple?

To the people of France he was Napoleon, their Emperor, created by their will and unbeaten in war. Betrayed in 1814 by Talleyrand's conspiracy aided by Marmont and Augereau and the Senators. Betrayed again in 1815 by Fouché, La Fayette, Davout and the members of the Chambers. Betrayed by his father-in-law the Emperor Francis, and by his wife with another man, and even by Montholon, the man he thought was his friend. But not by the people of France – not by the Nation.

To this end, all the British money, Allied military occupations, atrocities and depredations, could not break the bond between the people and the man who personified their revolution. The bloodshed and the losses expended to gain these civil rights were not to be so easily eradicated. The Bourbons had been driven out twice and restored only by the combined might of Europe. In the end the French people drove them out again. During the years of Napoleon's exile, and the suffering of these free people under a totalitarian regime, Napoleon was not blamed as the author of their suffering and degradation. Napoleon was their hero. He became more than a legend, he became a symbol – the symbol of a sovereign France. He represented to France the right of a free people to decide their own destiny. The lesson was there in the hearts of the French people, and generations of totalitarian governments had yet to learn it: you can kill a man, but not what he represents. You cannot kill an ideal. And Napoleon was the ideal. Had he not said it himself? 'I am France! And France is me!'

THE LAST ROAD

'... my own assessment of myself is based on the extent not of my life but of my glory ...
I count my victories, not my years and, if I accurately compute fortune's favours to me,
my life has been long.' – Alexander the Great, quoted in Curtius,
The History of Alexander, c. AD 41

ALL WAS SOLEMN, DIGNIFIED AND QUIET. THE LAST BOURBON King of France sat on his throne surrounded by his Marshals holding their batons. Princes, dukes and dignitaries from all over the world were gathered around him. The doors of the great vaulted chamber were opened suddenly by two soldiers, immaculate in the uniform of Grenadiers of Napoleon's Imperial Guard. On their bearskin bonnets gleamed the plates depicting the Imperial Eagle grasping a thunderbolt. Each man held a musket and wore on his breast the medal of the Legion of Honour. The Court Chamberlain announced in a voice that echoed through the chamber, 'l'Empereur!' The King of France and those around him stood with bowed heads; behind them a row of tricolores bearing the Imperial Eagle were lowered in salute. Napoleon the First, Emperor of the French, had returned to Paris.

The date was 15 December 1840. That morning the survivors of Napoleon's Old Guard had assembled at first light and their uniforms had been inspected several times. Many still had the uniforms they had worn during the imperial campaigns. Those without a uniform had been outfitted by the comte de Flahaut at his own expense. In the assembled ranks were famous generals: Guyot, Lallemand, Poret de Morvan, Shramm, Petit, Roguet, Barrois and many others. The former General Mouton, comte de Lobau, whose corps had held the Prussians as long as possible at Mont St-Jean, was now a Marshal of France, as was Sébastiani, comte de La Porta. They had been waiting for this moment since 1815.

Napoleon II, the young eaglet, had died, a captive prince in Austria, of tuberculosis on 22 June 1832. Devoted to his father's memory, he had been treated like a leper by his grandfather, the Emperor Francis, and neglected by his mother who had married the comte de Neipperg and borne his brood. Louis-Philippe, son of the duc d'Orléans (who had embraced the Revolution and had been executed) had been chosen by the republicans to replace Charles X and his heirs. Conscious that one cannot undo the past, Louis-Philippe had wished to reconcile his monarchy with Napoleon's memory, and the Revolution. France was no longer to be denied Napoleon, his reign or his glory. Politely but firmly he informed 'Her Britannic Majesty's government, that the prince de Joinville in the French naval vessel *Belle-Poule* was being dispatched to St. Helena to recover the remains of Napoleon I, Emperor of the French, and return them to Les Invalides which would be the permanent resting-place of the late 'Monarch'. His Royal Highness, the King of France and the People of France were sure that this would not inconvenience Her Britannic Majesty's government and that Her Britannic Majesty's government, would assist the emissaries of His Majesty the King of France, if required.'

On 15 October 1840, Count Bertrand, General Gourgaud, the young Las Cases, Louis Marchand, Saint-Denis (Ali), Noverraz, and Pierron, together with Arthur Bertrand, Count Bertrand's son, who was born on the island, and had been presented to Napoleon as, 'the first French citizen to arrive at Longwood without the British Secretary of State's permission'. The group kept a silent vigil all night, around the grave under the stately willow tree. It was the 25th anniversary of Napoleon's arrival on the rock. The French prince and dignitaries were offended and ashamed that Longwood had been turned into a stable; the embarrassment of the British authorities was all too evident.

Next morning the plain slab with its memorial stone marked, 'Here lies ...' was broken open and the mourners were astounded to find that, nineteen years after the Emperor's death, his body had not decomposed at all. It was an emotional shock that visibly affected all present.[1] Marines of the French Navy covered the body with a tricolore flag, and with great reverence took him aboard their ship – on to French territory at last.

Now, on this bitter December morning, the last King of the French sat in silent state under the dome of the Invalides. Awaiting the arrival of Napoleon. In the place Vendôme, his statue had been restored to its black-draped column whose base was surrounded by masses of flowers. The precinct was packed with troops standing to attention while a battery fired a last salute.

People had flocked to Paris from all over France to be here, to see 'him' for the last time. The temper of the enormous crowd was an amalgam of sadness, triumph and joy, overlaid by a sense of appalling loss. But when the cortege moved slowly down the great avenue they roared 'Vive l'Empereur!' and held their heads high as though it were a victory parade – and for them perhaps it was.

Slowly the carriage bearing his coffin came down the Champs-Elysées, to salvo upon salvo of cannon-fire, followed by ex-members of his Imperial Guard. These men, faithful even after death, had come from Poland, The Netherlands, Belgium and from all over France. Troops from the Army and the National Guard, and naval seamen brought up the rear of the cortege. One officer, Loubers, was wearing his uniform of Lieutenant-Colonel of the Grenadiers of Elba. Behind the coffin, as was his right, walked Count Bertrand, Grand Marshal of the Palace, carrying Napoleon's sword upon a pall. Napoleon entered the great chamber of Les Invalides, which during his reign had housed all the trophies of his victories. This was where he was to lie for ever, in Paris, near the Seine, as he had requested in his will. Later, in 1860, his nephew Louis, whom he had often dandled on his knee, would, as Napoleon III, build a magnificent edifice for his tomb, surmounted by the names of his greatest victories. His body was placed under a large slab of Russian stone, commemorating his capture of Moscow. Napoleon had at last returned in triumph, followed by his faithful Old Guard, the French Army and the people of Paris. As his body was lowered through the floor of the vaulted chamber, the Old Guard presented arms with a crash that startled many of the mourners, who thought it was thunder. Outside, a final cannonade bellowed from the courtyard to proclaim to Paris and to France the final victory – he had come home.

THE TREATY OF FONTAINEBLEAU, 1814

Napoleon's abdication in favour of his son, on 4 April 1814, was declared unacceptable by the Allied principals of Austria, Britain and the French provisional government (Talleyrand representing Bourbon and his own interests). The Tsar of Russia, fearful of being attacked by Napoleon's army while trapped in Paris, whose population of 800,000 was mostly hostile, agreed to Napoleon's abdication for himself and his heirs male on terms of Napoleon's choosing – The Treaty of Fontainebleau dated 11 April (although signed on the 12th) 1814.

Napoleon's representatives, Caulaincourt, Ney and Macdonald, conducted the negotiations with the Tsar and Count Nesselrode throughout 8-9 April, and Napoleon did not authorize the handing over of his formal abdication to the Allies until AFTER the treaty had been signed and exchanged. It was a formal treaty between sovereigns and ratified by the signatories. It was officially titled and read as follows:

A TREATY BETWEEN THE ALLIED POWERS AND HIS MAJESTY THE EMPEROR NAPOLEON

ARTICLE I: The Emperor Napoleon renounces for himself, his successors and descendants, as well as for the members of his family, all right of sovereignty and dominion, as well over the French Empire and the Kingdom of Italy, as over any other country.

ARTICLE II: The Island of Elba will form a separate principality to be possessed by the Emperor Napoleon in full sovereignty and property in perpetuity. The Allied powers recognize the style, dignity and title of the Emperor Napoleon as sovereign Emperor of Elba. It is agreed that for the duration of the lifetime of the Emperor Napoleon, the Empress Marie-Louise and the King of Rome, that the style, rank, title and dignity of these sovereigns will be maintained and recognized by the Allied powers. It is further agreed that the relatives of the Emperor Napoleon, will also be recognized in the style, rank and dignity of princes and princesses of his house.

ARTICLE III: The Kingdom of France will provide the Emperor Napoleon two millions of Francs in gold per annum during his lifetime. The Emperor Napoleon agrees by acceptance to relinquish any claims to monies, payments and revenues accrued to him in the Empire of France, Kingdom of Italy, or former territorial possession.

ARTICLE IV: The Duchies of Parma and Placentia (Guastalla) are granted in perpetuity to the Empress Marie-Louise and on her demise to her son the King of Rome and their descendants. The Allied powers agree that the Empress Marie-Louise and her son the King of Rome, shall be provided with passports and an escort to repair to the Emperor Napoleon.

Article V: The Allied powers agree to induce the Barbary pirates and corsairs to respect the flag of Elba and its shipping and to protect them by force if necessary.

ARTICLE VI: [a lengthy article describing the style and title of Napoleon's mother, brothers and sisters, in which it was agreed that a pension to each would be paid annually by the Kingdom of France to the total of 2,500,000 francs.]

ARTICLE VII: It is agreed that the ex-Empress Josephine, shall retain that style and dignity during her lifetime and that the Kingdom of France shall pay an annual pension to the ex-Empress of one million Francs.

ARTICLE VIII: It is agreed that Prince Eugène Beauharnais, Viceroi of Italy, shall be provided with a suitable establishment out of France and a pension of one million Francs per annum.

ARTICLE IX: The Allied powers agree to respect and protect the personal and private property owned by the Emperor Napoleon in his former dominions [i.e., the palace of Laeken in Brussels purchased by him from the Archduke Charles of Austria].

ARTICLE X: The Allied powers and the Kingdom of France guarantee to respect the style, title and dignity bestowed on his officers, military and civil, and the Kingdom of France agrees to continue to pay annually the pensions and annuities awarded to them.

ARTICLE XI. The Kingdom of France agrees to accept and discharge all debts civil and military contracted in its domains by the Emperor Napoleon up to the date of this treaty.

ARTICLE XII: The Emperor Napoleon agrees to return to the representatives of the Kingdom of France the state diamonds, treasury, and bills of exchange in his possession and anything relative unto them.

ARTICLE XIII: The Allied powers agree and accept that the Emperor Napoleon be permitted to take with him to his principality of Elba, one thousand, one hundred soldiers of all arms as his bodyguard and forty pieces of artillery, of his own choosing.

ARTICLE XIV: The Allied powers agree to place at the Emperor Napoleon's disposal a Naval Corvette [20-gun sloop] to convey him to Elba and for the vessel thereafter to remain the property of the Emperor Napoleon.

Signed on behalf of the Allied Powers:
 Prince Metternich [Austria]
 Count Stadion [Austria]
 Count Razumovsky [Russia]
 Count Nesselrode [Russia]
 Count von Hardenberg [Prussia]
Signed on behalf of the Provisional
 Government of France:
 Prince de Benevente [Talleyrand]

Signed on behalf of the Emperor Napoleon:
 Duc de Vincenza [Caulaincourt]
 Prince de la Moskowa [Ney][1]

Castlereagh, who had deliberately remained behind at Dijon, arrived in Paris on 10 April, and berated Talleyrand for agreeing to these provisions. Talleyrand, not wishing to lose his own Napoleonic style and title of Prince, and revert to being Bishop of Autun, explained that this was: '[a] *Pont d'Or* essential to make the army [leaders] pass over in a temper to be made use of'.[2]

In a bitter letter to his Prime Minister, Castlereagh said that he had little choice but to accede to the document on the Tsar's insistence, but had refused to sign it, stating:

'I should have wished to substitute another position in lieu of Elba for the seat of Napoleon's retirement, but none having the quality of security, on which he insisted, seemed disposable, to which equal objections did not occur, and I did not feel that I could encourage the alternative which Caulaincourt assured me Buonaparte [*sic*] repeatedly mentioned, namely, an asylum in England ... I felt I own the utmost repugnance to anything like a Treaty with him after his *déchéance* had been pronounced ... I should have wished, however, if he was humble enough to accept a pension, that it had been an act of grace and not a stipulation [of the treaty].[3]

It was the accepted convention of the period that if the provisions of a treaty were broken and the aggrieved party were unable to receive satisfaction, he was entitled to resume the *status quo ante*, that is the position he held before, the contract in effect having been broken. Similarly, during the period, if a fortress or town were besieged and the besiegers had brought their guns into a position to breach the walls, the governor would be offered the chance to surrender with honour. If he refused the town could be put to the sword and sacked by the soldiers as recompense for the risk and slaughter to which they had been unnecessarily subjected. These ancient conventions and customs of warfare had evolved into an early form of international law. Napoleon had sent General Bresson from Elba to the Vienna Congress to ask that the treaty conditions be honoured. The Bourbons refused and the other Allies were too involved with their own problems to bother. Except Tsar Alexander who asked Castlereagh to insist that Louis honour Russia's signature – but to no avail.

In Paris on 2 April 1814,[4] Napoleon published in *Le Moniteur* a list of the broken terns of the treaty and his right to resume his crown, his conditional abdication, a term of the treaty, having been invalidated. The substance of Napoleon's list was as follows:

(1) The Empress Marie-Louise and her son were not given either passports or an escort to repair to Napoleon.

(2) Napoleon's security and person had been threatened and was threatened by the Bourbons: 'An insurrection was prepared at Orgon [*sic*], on the Emperor's route, in order that an attempt might be made on his life.'[5] That the Sieur Brulart, a confederate of Georges Cadoudal, had been made Governor of Corsica 'in order to make sure of the crime; and in fact, several detached assassins have attempted, in the Isle of Elba, to gain, by murder of the emperor, the base reward which was promised them.'

(3) That the Duchies of Parma and Placentia had not been given as per the treaty to his wife and son due to the actions of Talleyrand, the documentary evidence of which he had found in the foreign office left on the second emigration.

(4) That Eugène Beauharnais had not been given his establishment.

(5) That the stipulated pensions and honours of his ex-civil and military officers had not been met or honoured.

(6) That his personal property, guaranteed under Article IX, had not been honoured and the Bourbons had looted and taken over his houses and possessions, both in France and in Italy.

(7) That his pension and that of his family, amounting to 4,500,000 francs had not been paid – in fact had been refused.

It cannot be argued that the Bourbons did not deliberately break the conditions of the treaty, or that the Austrian Emperor had denied Marie-Louise and her son the freedom to join Napoleon. Under the circumstances Napoleon had every right to seek redress.

Napoleon, adding to this published list, the grievances of the people and the Bourbons' broken promises to them, declared that he had returned without violence and with the will of the people had resumed his station: 'And now, replaced at the head of the nation which has thrice already made choice of him, and which has a fourth time designated by the reception which it has given him in his rapid and triumphant march and arrival, what does Napoleon wish from this nation – by which, and for which, he wishes to reign? What the French people wish – the independence of France, internal peace, peace with all nations, and the execution of the Treaty of Paris, of the 30th May, 1814.' Napoleon then went on to ask what had changed save his replacement for the fleeing Bourbons? and summed-up: 'Nothing has been changed; if, when the French nation only demands to remain at peace with all Europe, an unjust coalition does not compel it to defend, as it did in 1792, its will and its rights, its independence, and the sovereign of its choice.'

THE ROYALIST UNDERGROUND AND THE CHEVALIERS DE LA FOI

Throughout the period of which this book treats, behind the ever unfurling panorama of military might – thunder of charging cavalry, marching men, high hopes, frantic endeavour, lost causes, despair – another war was being waged, more or less ceaselessly, but to deadly effect. The complexities of this sub-war were such as to render it worthy of a book to itself, but the *tour d'horizon* presented here will, it is hoped, give the reader sufficient grasp of the essentials as to better appreciate the web in which the principals in my narrative were so hopelessly entangled.

After the fall of the Bourbon monarchy, those aristocrats that could not accept the principles of *Rights of Man* or the excesses of the later radical republicans, fled from France to become in effect the external opposition to the new regime, exemplified by the *armée des émigrés* whose headquarters were at Coblenz and whose II Corps was commanded by the prince de Condé. From 1793 to 1796 intermittent insurrections in the Vendée, manipulated by royalist nobles, and clergy who were anxious that the executed king's cause be identified with that of the Church, became virtually a guerrilla (and civil) war whose victims outnumbered those of the Revolution.

Both groups of opponents were funded and armed by the comte d'Artois and Britain in the hope that the new regime could be overthrown by force. By 1795, the old revolutionary regimes had been replaced by the Directory. On receiving the news of the death of his nephew Louis (styled XVII) in the Temple prison on 8 June 1795, the comte de Provence proclaimed himself Louis XVIII at Verona on the 24th. From this date there began the intense royalist struggle to regain supremacy. Louis sent agents into France (in support of his 'moles' already in place) to sound out and solicit support from politicians and generals such as Pichegru and Moreau, with a view to a restoration by force of arms.

Louis' brother Charles, comte d'Artois, now known as Monsieur, the hereditary title reserved for a Bourbon king's brother, and in this case his heir, had left France for Britain where he resided first at Holyrood House in Edinburgh and then in the Channel Island of Jersey. Since 1792, with the consent of William Pitt's government, Artois had had a base established in Jersey where the 7,500 *émigré* priests and nobles who had sought refuge there were formed into a resistance movement. Pitt had appointed Captain Philippe d'Auvergne, RN naval commander in Jersey, and had taken care to ensure that his command was absolutely independent of the island's Governor. D'Auvergne, from 1792 titular duke, and from 1802 sovereign Prince of Bouillon, an ancient French dependency, had been lured by Artois with promises of support in regaining his sovereign principality,[1] and was now wearing two hats, one for Britain and one for Bourbon France. Jersey's Governor was ordered to hand over Mont-Orgueil castle to d'Auvergne and his group whose original directive from d'Artois had concerned the formation of armed landing-parties and the supply of arms and funds to the insurgents in the Vendée. Of necessity this group had developed quite independently of those agencies authorized by Louis.

Unknown to anyone save a small clique in the British Cabinet, Artois' group had become the main royalist espionage centre, charged with intelligence gathering, assassinations and the circulation of forged currency. To this end the celebrated writer

François-René de Chateaubriand and his cousin Armand[2] were instrumental with Count Goyon-Vaucoulers in establishing throughout France a network of reliable royalist agents who first used badges and later elaborate verbal codes to identify one another.

At the Cabinet's instigation, the Bank of England and reliable contracted printers produced tons of forged French banknotes,[3] and by September 1795 this bid to destabilize the economy was enjoying great success. The royalists now made an attempt to overthrow the Directory by force, but Paul Barras, with the help of the young General Bonaparte and a certain Captain Murat, put down this, the only serious royalist-led attack on the seat of government, with great loss of life. Meanwhile, an agent of Louis', the comte de Montgaillard, had sent a Swiss editor, publisher and bookseller named Fauche-Borel[4] to General Pichegru, asking for help to restore Louis to the throne, in return for royal favour and one million francs in gold. Fauche-Borel made contact with Pichegru, but before anything could develop Pichegru was recalled to Paris. Fauche-Borel became Louis' chief agent, and remained so until 1814. So there were two separate royalist agencies operating throughout this period: d'Artois' group, and Louis' which he directed from first Verona, then Mittau in Courland, and finally from Hartwell in England.

With the failure of the uniformed *émigré* expedition, landed by the Royal Navy on the Quiberon peninsula in southern Brittany on 27 June 1795 (748 prisoners executed, 428 of them noblemen), and the collapse of the insurrections in the Vendée, by 1800 the west was lost to both Britain and the Bourbons as a potential ulcer to Napoleonic France. Jersey, however, was ideally placed for clandestine landings anywhere along the French coast from Cherbourg to Brest.

The chief of the republican, and then imperial security police was Joseph Fouché. His head of counter-espionage and chief interrogator was Pierre-Marie Desmarest who operated from the notorious Prefecture of Police building in the rue de Jérusalem. Demarest's chief operative and spy-catcher was Inspector-General Pierre-Hugues Veyrat.[5] A Swiss, Veyrat had enrolled a Swiss printer named Charles-Frédéric Perlet as spy and informer.[6] Through his trade, Perlet was acquainted with Fauche-Borel.

In 1797 d'Artois ordered the comte de Montgaillard to infiltrate the opposition. To buy his way in and establish his *bona fides*, Montgaillard informed General Bonaparte of the conspiracy between the royalists and Pichegru, and gave him the name of Louis' agent on whose person the proof would be found – thereby condemning Pichegru and Fauche-Borel, both of whom were considered expendable.[7] Fauche-Borel, however, escaped to England with the help of Director Barras who, it seems, was happy to negotiate with both Britain and the Bourbons, and saw Fauche-Borel as a potential go-between. In 1799 Napoleon overthrew the Directory by a *coup d'état* and dismissed Louis' written request that he imitate General Monk and recall him to the throne. Louis deluded himself to the extent of believing that the French people were only awaiting the chance to return to the awful days of his dead brother's absolutism. In this he was constantly encouraged by like-minded *émigrés*, and by Fauche-Borel who persuaded Louis to appoint him his agent in Paris with a view to suborning prominent Frenchmen capable of effecting this return to the absolutist fold.

One of the leaders of the *Chouannerie* (a band of royalist guerrillas who had operated in Brittany and Normandy, and known as Chouans, a Breton dialect word for 'screech-owl', said to have been applied to them because of the long, fluttering cry with which they signalled to one another at night), Georges Cadoudal, had been offered a commission in the army by Napoleon, after their resistance had ceased, but he declined and escaped to Jersey. There he formulated a plot to assassinate Napoleon with a bomb. D'Artois naturally was in agreement as was William Pitt, who authorized d'Auvergne to provide the half-ton of gunpowder, expenses, and to land Cadoudal on the French coast.[8]

On 24 December 1800, Cadoudal's agent, Saint-Regent, left a wine cart containing the bomb in the rue Saint-Nicaise in Paris, having paid a 13-year-old girl to hold the horse's reins. Napoleon and his family were due to pass on the way to the Opera House. Saint-Regent activated the bomb and fled. Napoleon's coachman, sensing something amiss, whipped up the horses and passed the cart at speed. The bomb exploded, killing the girl and a score of passers-by, and injuring more than two hundred. Cadoudal and his men escaped back to Britain via Jersey.

In June 1802, Louis' chief agent Fauche-Borel was sent back to France, his status with Louis and the British Government suitably enhanced by his rapport with such notables as Pichegru and Barras. He took with him several blank commissions signed and sealed by Louis, giving him *carte blanche* in the way of bribing government officials. On 27 March Napoleon had concluded the Peace of Amiens with Britain, but the British Cabinet, unknown to Parliament, had neither asked the Bourbons to quit England nor closed down d'Artois' underground activities in Jersey.

It should be borne in mind that Fauche-Borel was not an aristocrat. A vain, boastful man, he was more inspired by the flow of British gold than by any loyalty to a Pretender. When he arrived in Paris Napoleon had been installed as First Consul. He took lodgings at No. 6, rue de Tournon, where Perlet, fellow-Swiss and police spy, was staying. No sooner had the two resumed their acquaintanceship than Perlet started to sound off to Fauche-Borel about his disenchantment with the present regime. This ploy soon caused the boastful Fauche-Borel to reveal himself as a royalist agent, and show Perlet the blank commissions. Perlet promptly informed his supe-

rior, Veyrat who, after having Fauche-Borel followed for a fortnight to find out who his contacts were, had him grabbed by two plain-clothes inspectors and brought to the Temple prison[9] where he was kept for eighteen months.

Meanwhile, D'Artois' network continued to plague the First Consul. In August 1802, Captain d'Auvergne, travelling as duc de Bouillon, went to Paris to contact some of his agents, under cover of visiting lawyers with regard to his duchy. He wore his naval uniform as protection against any suggestion of spying. On 27 September he was arrested by Veyrat on Fouché's orders and put in the Temple prison where he met Fauche-Borel, though neither man was aware of the other's role in royalist espionage. D'Auvergne was examined by Desmarest, though without the use of thumbscrews.[10] The British consul intervened and Napoleon ordered his release, but he was told to leave French soil within 24 hours.[11] His deportation caused an uproar in Parliament over the audacity of the French in arresting a British officer in uniform and having a valid passport,[12] but Napoleon was unperturbed. His ambassador informed interested parties in London that Britain herself since the Treaty had used her own Aliens Act to deport twenty Frenchmen who had valid passports, and that if this incident led to the formation of a 'war party' in parliament, he was instructed by the First Consul to give the most detailed reasons why Captain d'Auvergne was deported. The Cabinet was alarmed at the prospect of their clandestine intrigues with the Bourbons becoming public knowledge, and Lord Liverpool spoke in the House in defence of Napoleon, for the first and only time in his career, stating: 'We have an Aliens Law, and we should not suffer any nation to interfere in our execution of it, nor should we complain if other nations do the same.'[13] Writing afterwards to Castlereagh in justification, he said: 'It must be confessed that Captain d'Auvergne was the person who carried on our correspondence during the War with our friends in France, and is charged by the French Government with still giving protection in his island to those who fly from the neighbouring French coast.'[14]

In 1803 Britain resumed war with France and Napoleon ordered Fouché to infiltrate a spy into the Bourbon circles in England to evaluate their effectiveness. Fouché's best agent was one Mehée de la Touche, who not only gained intimate knowledge of Louis' people, whom he assessed as incompetent, but came back to France having tricked Pitt and the Cabinet out off considerable funds. Napoleon made political capital of the incident by publishing de la Touche's account of the proceedings.[15]

In contrast, d'Artois group had by now formed a vast network across southern France. Monsieur, a religious man when he was not ordering executions, used dispossessed and disgruntled priests, of whom he had several thousands at his disposal, to carry his messages and gain intelligence. At about this time his organization which, to confuse Fouché and to survive, had been calling itself by various names, adopted the title Chevaliers de la Foi (Knights of the Faith). Its structure was based on that of the Freemasons, but its rituals and symbology were framed within the Catholic ethos.

D'Artois wished to create a cult based on his martyred brother Louis XVI, the Bourbons' divine right to rule, and their descent from Louis IX (who had been canonized by the Curch), and motivated by the notion of the Spirit of Saint-Louis guiding a Catholic France back to subservience to the King appointed by God. The doctrine, which became known as Ultra-Royalist, held that kingship itself was greater than the man; that it did not matter if Louis XVI had been a good or a bad king, it was his Office appointed by God that was important. The ultras served the throne and God's anointed, rather than the man beneath the crown. A parallel with Catholics' view of the Papacy is readily seen here.

D'Artois' intention of course was that the rewards deriving from this fanatical nonsense would accrue to him as heir to his ageing brother, and in this he was successful. His *Chevaliers* were grouped in cells called *Bannières* under a leader (*Bannièr*), and had to progress through various grades before being eligible to be introduced to the leader of the next cell up. As in the Freemasons, members swore sacred oaths of retribution against traitors or any Chevalier who refused help to another. Unlike the Masons', however, these oaths were for real.

By these means d'Artois attracted thousands of fanatical devotees who acknowledged him as Grandmaster and carried out his orders implicitly, as they has had sworn on their honour to do, and created not only a spy network, but a fanatical personality cult which he would use later as a political party and a state within a state.[16]

In January 1803 d'Artois, with the consent of the British Cabinet,[17] organized a plot to assassinate Napoleon, with the aid of Georges Cadoudal. General Pichegru had escaped from exile and was to be instrumental in influencing his friend General Moreau (whom Napoleon resented for his victory at Hohenlinden in December 1800) to neutralize the army. Inspector-general Veyrat soon got details of the plot through his spies and had arrested the entire group within a fortnight. Napoleon, informed by the confession of one of the group, a M. Querelle, that the intention was to kidnap and kill him, retaliated by sending a regiment of dragoons into neutral Baden to kidnap the Bourbon duc d'Enghien. On 20 March he was found guilty by court-martial and shot, in the moat of the Château Vincennes.

The conspirators had been imprisoned in the notorious Temple prison and were seen by Fauche-Borel who was still languishing there. On 6 April Pichegru was found strangled in his cell – not by a rope or other ligature, but by his own hands, according to Fouché's ludicrous explanation of what was undoubtedly his murder. Fouché had feared that Pichegru might try to purchase his life by giving Napoleon the names of dissidents in his own administration.

On 24 June Cadoudal and eleven others went to the guillotine, which had a salutary effect on Fauche-Borel who, fearful that he too might be executed, offered to turn coat and work as a double agent for the Consular police.[18] This secured his release and he travelled to Berlin and carried out an act of betrayal that cost many royalist lives.[19] In England, Fauche-Borel was welcomed as a hero by Louis. Since his release, Fauche-Borel had corresponded with Perlet, still unaware that he was a police spy and had betrayed him to Veyrat. Perlet informed Fauche-Borel of 'a great secret'; he was working as an agent of the 'Royalist Committee' in Paris, composed of influential people, ministers, marshals and diplomats who, like the late Pichegru and Moreau, were working for the restoration. This of course was music to Louis' ears, but in reality the 'Committee' consisted of Desmarest who hoped to lure Fauche-Borel back and have him executed.[20]

After several months of correspondence, during which time much British gold flowed to the 'Committee', and more importantly, information as to Louis' intentions and operations, Desmarest received indications that the British Cabinet was excited because they believed that Fouché was one of the 'Committee'. Desmarest informed Fouché who, for his own devious reasons, encouraged this belief and Fauche-Borel was asked to bring Louis' instructions back to the 'Committee'. Throughout the correspondence, which continued without a break until 1814, the names of the 'Committee' members were never mentioned for 'security reasons'. Fouché was learning more and more about the royalist operations. Fauche-Borel, not daring to come to Paris, persuaded his nephew, Charles Vitel, an ensign in the British Army, to act as courier. In his walking-stick he carried two blank passports to be signed by Fouché as a sign of good faith.[21] Vitel was betrayed to

Veyrat by Perlet and captured on his arrival. Perlet indicated the concealed passports and Vitel was sentenced as a spy and, on the direct orders of Napoleon, taken to the wall at the barrier of the Grenelle common and executed by firing-squad.[22]

So for most of the period from 1803 to 1814, Louis' intelligence group was being run by two double agents, Perlet and Fauche-Borel, serviced by Fouché's police who were reporting to Napoleon. Some £890,000 in gold (British tax-payers' money) was sent to Paris between 1803 and 1805 to support the work of the 'Committee', only to make its way to Napoleon's imperial treasury – enough to finance an invasion of Britain. In 1808 Fauche-Borel invited Perlet to come to England and discuss the 'Committee' with Louis which, at Fouché's direct order, he did, meeting Louis at Gosfield in Sussex on 22 June. Perlet, unable to refuse to name names, secured Louis' word of honour that he would not reveal them to anyone, gave him some. No record of them has survived, but we can assume that Fouché would have instructed that his own be given as 'insurance'.[23]

The importance that was attached to d'Auvergne's liaison role by the Cabinet can be judged by his rapid promotion. Ostensibly in command of the small Channel Squadron (three frigates) based at Jersey, in 1805 he became Rear-Admiral of the Blue, in 1810 Vice-Admiral of the Blue, in 1813 Vice-Admiral of the White and in 1814 Vice-Admiral of the Red (some seventeen senior officers had to be promoted without portfolio to enable this). Further, he had the rare distinction for a British subject of being allowed by George III the use of his foreign title of Sovereign Prince and Duke of Bouillon, a distinction not granted to the Duke of Wellington, even after Waterloo.

Fauche-Borel, although unaware of the existence of the Chevaliers de la Foi, revealed in a letter to Perlet details of d'Auvergne's *modus operandi* in landing agents on the French coast, and this prompted Fouché to concentrate operations in the area. Chateaubriand, whom d'Artois had ordered to return to France, ingratiated himself with Napoleon and joined his administrative service, as had Louis, comte de Bourmont, one-time Vendéean leader, and now a divisional general in Napoleon's army. Slowly, the Chevaliers de la Foi began to infiltrate all sectors of Napoleon's administration, military and police.

But d'Artois had his failures too, largely because of Fauche-Borel's indiscretions. D'Artois distrusted him, but he was useful in that his braggadocio pleased Louis and tended to diverted Fouché's attention from his own activities. In 1809 Fouché's men were keeping a close watch on the coast opposite Jersey and several local peasants used by the group as couriers and contacts were captured. Veyrat had his own methods of persuading them to 'co-operate'[24] and Chateaubriand's cousin Armand, one of the founders of the Chevaliers de la Foi was lured from Jersey, captured and taken to Paris. Attempts to persuade him to turn his coat were fruitless and he was shot at Grenelle. Fouché's agents managed to infiltrate the Chevaliers to a certain extent, but d'Artois, warned of this, periodically changed the recognition codes, and the police spies were quickly eliminated.

In 1809, Britain attempted the ill-fated Walcheren expedition to seize Antwerp, which failed because of the incompetence of the commanders and because Fouché took control from Paris, Napoleon being absent in Austria. During the operation Fouché opened direct negotiations with Britain, which caused his disgrace in 1810 and exile to Italy. From this point on the Chevaliers grew in strength and at Bordeaux formed a regiment of some 800 men under Mayor Lynch, a member of the organization.

D'Artois' most audacious plot, which nearly succeeded, was the General Malet affair in 1812. Malet had tried to mount a coup in 1807, but it failed and he had been in prison ever since. His wife petitioned Fouché's replacement General Savary, duc de Rovigo, for Malet to be given greater freedom and to be allowed visitors. As Malet's police file had inexplicably 'gone missing', Savary permitted his transfer to a private asylum in which many noted political prisoners were kept at their own expense. There Malet met and conversed with key members of the Chevaliers de la Foi. An agent of d'Artois', Abbé Jean-Baptiste Lafon, convinced Malet that only he could restore Louis.

One night in October 1812, Malet got out of the asylum and went to a pre-arranged hideout where he found a general's uniform, a fake seal bearing an 'L' for Louis instead of the 'N' for Napoleon, detailed instructions, and two accomplices. Even the troops' password 'conspiracy' for that night had been provided. The disgraced Fouché's hand was almost certainly behind the venture. Within hours Malet had announced the death of Napoleon at Moscow, taken command of the 10th Cohort of the National Guard and arrested Savary, Baron Pasquier and Desmarest and locked them up. He had taken control of practically the whole of Paris, and arranged a new venue for the seat of government with the Paris Prefect. Malet's luck ran out when Colonel Douchet, Chief-of-Staff of Intelligence and adjutant of the Paris garrison, recognized him as a subversive and arrested him. Malet and thirteen of his subordinates were tried and shot at Grenelle.

In 1814, when Talleyrand began his negotiations with the Allies, d'Artois ordered the *Chevaliers* in Paris and throughout France to co-operate, and from Italy Fouché ordered his own network of spies in the police force and Parisian society to help d'Artois. When, after the surrender of Paris, Baron Pasquier, Talleyrand's bought turncoat Prefect of Police, ordered Inspector-General of Police Veyrat, who had caught and executed more than 600 royalists in his fifteen years of office, to consider himself under arrest and to leave the city pending further action, d'Artois, who had only just arrived in the city, sent a messenger to awaken Pasquier and tell him that: 'Monsieur, Lieutenant-General of the Kingdom, required Pasquier to cease all proceedings against M. Veyrat.'[25]

After Napoleon's first abdication, d'Artois' agents attempted to murder him *en route* to Elba. On his return, Fouché was d'Artois' principal agent. D'Artois weakened Napoleon's military capability by having Marshal Berthier thrown from his window and killed. After Waterloo, when Napoleon returned to Paris to raise a second army, Fouché ousted Napoleon in almost exactly the same way that he had brought down Robespierre. It is likely that Fouché arranged with Count Montholon to ingratiate himself into the dwindling imperial circle in order to spy on Napoleon, and with a view to his assassination.

D'Artois used both the police force and his agents to terrorize and murder Bonapartist officers and supporters as requested by the British Prime Minister Lord Liverpool. From Marseilles the Inspector-General of Police wrote: 'The rallying cry is to massacre the Bonapartists and pillage their homes.'[26] In Toulon, alone, 800 men and 55 women were imprisoned without charge,[27] and more than 1,000 citizens fled the city.[28] Marshal Brune, who had rallied to Napoleon on his return, was set-up by d'Artois to be murdered by his agents in Avignon.[29]

D'Artois spent the rest of 1815 turning his vast organization into a political party and creating a private police force, whose members were known as *Verdets* after their green coats.[30] He so packed the Chamber with his agents that Louis called it the '*chambre introuvable*.'[31] D'Artois then removed the dangerous Fouché by sending him abroad on a diplomatic mission and using his absolute majority in the Chambers to pass the Law of Regicides which exiled from France on pain of death all those that had voted for the execution of Louis XVI.

In 1816, Admiral Philippe d'Auvergne found his claim to his principality set aside in favour of a cousin of Artois'. In London d'Auvergne threatened to expose the intimate workings of the Chevaliers, but on 18 September he appears, like Berthier, to have committed suicide by jumping from a third-storey window.

Louis XVIII's two principal agents appeared in a civil court on 10 May, indicting each other for criminal slander and libel in 'exposing' each other as Bonapartist police spies. Fauche-Borel, who during his twenty years' service had had intimate meetings with the British Cabinet, and the King of Prussia, won the case, Veyrat's evidence proving that his nephew Charles Vitel had been betrayed by Perlet. But in summing-up the Attorney-General savagely attacked Fauche-Borel for his revelations and for holding Louis XVIII up to public ridicule.

In 1821 Napoleon was murdered on d'Artois' orders, Louis XVIII died in 1824 and d'Artois ascended the throne as Charles X. In August 1829 Fauche-Borel, now pretty well destitute in his native Neuchâtel, tried to blackmail d'Artois' government by hinting that he had embarrassing material to expose. That same month he was thrown from a fourth-storey window of his house – verdict suicide. On 2 March 1830 the Chambers were summoned to hear a speech from the throne in which Charles X stated: 'If guilty intrigues raise for my government obstacles which I do not wish to foresee, I should be able to overcome them in my determination to maintain public order.'[32] As he railed on, his hat fell off his head to be picked up by his cousin Louis-Philippe, duc d'Orléans. Events moved fast, and by the end of July 1830 Louis-Philippe had replaced the odious Charles X as King. With his removal, the Chevaliers were disbanded.

AUTHOR'S NOTE: The above subject matter and indeed all material germaine to the covert operations mentioned in the text will be covered in greater depth in *Treason and Treachery: Covert Political Intrigues in Napoleonic Europe 1789–1821* now in preparation.

NOTES

Prologue: The Road to Juvisy

1. Roncière, p. 250; Norman, pp. 151-2; Houssaye, *1814*, pp. 430-1.
2. Housaye, *1814*, pp. 417-19.
3. Norman, pp. 112, 154; Houssaye, *1814*, pp. 344ff. Houssaye suggests that these weapons and the ammunition were unavailable or defective and that in any case the regular forces had priority over them, but the returns for the period show otherwise. The muskets were available and used to good effect at Waterloo, see MS correspondence, Archives du Service historique de l'Etat-major de l'Armée de France, Château de Vincennes, carton C15/4.

1. The Road to Saxony

1. Oman, p. 121. King George III, who had accepted William Pitt's resignation over Catholic emancipation in Ireland – thereby allowing the 'Peace Party' to gain ascendancy – was thunderstruck, shouting at Lord Malmesbury: 'D'you know what I call this peace? An Experimental Peace! It is nothing else. I am sure you think so, and perhaps you don't give it so good a name! But it was unavoidable. I was abandoned by everybody – allies and all [Parliament].' While Mr Sheridan stated in the House, on behalf of the King: 'This is a peace which all men are glad of, but no man can be proud of.'
2. Orders in Council: 7, 11, 25 November 1807.
3. Napoleon's Decrees: Berlin 1806, Milan 1807, Erfurt 1810.
4. De Pradt, p. 215.
5. Thomas Paine, *The Age of Reason*, vol. ii, p. 20.
6. Hall, vol. II, p. 315.
7. Hales, p. 94.
8. Ibid.
9. Ibid., p. 114.
10. Chandler, *Campaigns* , p. 866.
11. Ibid., p. 867.
12. Ibid., p. 875.
13. Troyat, p. 174. This subject is too complex to treat briefly. Troyat contends that Alexander was mentally disturbed, and that his father, Paul I, suffered from what seemed to be schizophrenia. He states that after the Battle of Dresden, 'The idea was increasingly taking root in his mind that he had been chosen by the Almighty to destroy the spirit of evil incarnated in Napoleon.' These are signs of overlays of religious mania.
14. Shilder, vol. III, p. 142.
15. Nicholson, p. 30.
16. 'Maritime Rights': British phrase describing her freedom of the seas, and which alienated the European nations who contended that neutrality entitled them to freedom from interference on the high seas. Britain took the view that if this principle were admitted no naval blockade would be effective. The insistence on these rights led directly to war with America in 1812. When, before Leipzig, he heard that the Tsar had received two American delegates asking him to mediate on the matter, Castlereagh replied: 'Great Britain may be driven out of a Congress, but not of her maritime rights, and, if the Continental powers know their own interests, they will not hazard this.' (Webster, vol. X, p. 14). In other words, any ally pursuing this matter risked losing Britain's goodwill – and cash.
17. This problem would eventually lead to the Prusso-Austrian War of 1866 and ultimately to the founding of the German Empire in 1870. It was of no small consequence in 1813-15.
18. PRO Adm vol. 568 Nelson to Pitt 12 May 1801; PRO Chatham MS Pitt to Nelson 15 May 1801; Oman, pp. 107-8.
19. Ibid.
20. This treaty was never fully shown to Parliament, an extract only being laid before the House on 5 May 1815, with no references to the Low Countries or the Bourbons at all.

'... It is needless to dwell particularly on the state of the Netherlands. Events have put out of the question the restoration of them to the House of Austria; they are therefore necessarily open to the new arrangements, and evidently can never exist separate and independent.' '... With this view [supposing France to be reduced within its ancient limits] it might be proposed to annex to the United Provinces [Holland], as an additional Barrier, the part of Flanders lying within a military line to be drawn from Antwerp to the Meuse at Maestricht, and Juliers, and the other territories between the Meuse and the Moselle to Prussia.' On the question of Napoleon's replacement: '... the views of the Allies, ought to be directed towards the re-establishment of Monarchy in France, and the restoration of the Bourbon Family on the throne. His Majesty agrees entirely with the Emperor of Russia in thinking that such a settlement is in itself highly desirable for the future both of France and Europe, and that no fair occasion ought to be neglected of promoting it.' The complete treaty as written by Pitt in 1805 can be found in Webster, App. I and PRO FO Russia 65. Compare the above extract with Hansard, vol. XXXI, 178.

21. Nicolson, p. 42.
22. Ibid.
23. Rothenberg, *Great Adversaries*, p. 179.
24. Ibid.
25. Ibid., p. 180
26. General Karl Freiherr von Leiberich, the 'Unhappy Mack' immortalized by Tolstoy in *War and Peace*. He rose to become Quartermaster-General of the Austrian Army. In 1805 Napoleon encircled most of his army so tightly as to induce surrender – which lead to the loss of Vienna and the disaster of Austerlitz. For this he was condemned to death, but the sentence was commuted to life imprisonment by the Emperor. His example was ever before Schwarzenberg's eyes, who well knew that any military disaster would be attributed to him and not to Metternich's policies.
27. Ibid.
28. Griess, p. 132.
29. Ibid.
30. Ibid., pp. 133-4.
31. Pflugk-Harttung, *Befreiungsjahr*, pp. 229-31.
32. Rothenberg, *Great Adversaries*, p. 186.

2. The Road to Leipzig

1. Napoleon, *Correspondance*, vol. XXVI, 20398, pp. 78-9
2. Griess, *Atlas*, p. 55.
3. One of the reasons why the military theorist Jomini left French service and became adviser to the Tsar was that, as Marshal Ney's chief of staff, he had neglected to send returns in on time. After a reminder, Berthier had ordered his arrest.
4. *Correspondance*, vol. XXVI, 20398.
5. The work and contribution of Bacler d'Albe and his staff are often overlooked. His visual representations enabled the astute Emperor to read a strategic situation at a glance. Before his Italian command of 1796, Napoleon himself was in charge of map-making among other planning duties. In his will, Article 27 of his instructions to his executors states: 'When publishing my Italian memoirs use d'Albe for the plans. I had all the battlefields drawn up, and I think he has actually published them. The war ministry will have the plans I made for several battles; I rather think that Jomini has them.' (see de Jonge, p. 104; for detailed study of Napoleon's method of operations and headquarters structure see Vachée).
6. Napoleon, *Correspondance*, vol. XXVI, 21503, p. 151.
7. Bernhardi, vol. III, p. 144.
8. Troyat, p. 173.
9. See Paret, pp. 271-2 whose masterly account covers the tactics of the Prussian Army in detail, including their superior tactical use of light infantry. Scharnhorst shows that even with a smoothbore musket at 100-150 yards good results could be achieved by aiming – a practice not encouraged in other armies, except by rifle-armed troops. To this end he advocated that all Prussian musket stocks be replaced with shaped ones to facilitate this function. Prussian troops were also encouraged to take their time aiming and firing before the bayonet charge.
10. Kerchnawe, pp. 166-7.
11. Friedrich, vol. I, pp. 235-7.
12. Ibid., vol. II, p. 321.
13. Ibid., Vol. II, p. 432.
14. Bernhardi, vol. III, p. 424.
15. Cathcart to Castlereagh, PRO FO Russia No. 65.
16. Rose, vol. I, p. 334.

17. Haythornthwaite, *Source Book*, p. 92.
18. Nicolson, p. 58.
19. Aberdeen to Castlereagh, PRO FO Austria 100, N0. 27 marked 'Most Secret'.

3. The Roads of France

1. On 10 November Lord Aberdeen wrote to Castlereagh informing him that he had agreed [on Britain's behalf] to support Austria in guaranteeing Murat's crown and immunity from British naval attack, in return for joining the alliance: '... As soon as he [Murat] received the last communication addressed to him by Prince Metternich and myself at Prague, he wrote to Napoleon and stated that the affairs of his Kingdom absolutely demanded his presence ... He proposes to declare war [on France] on the instant of his arrival.' (PRO FO Austria No. 102 (No. 32 Most Secret)); and on 19 December: 'You may consider the affair of Murat as settled... it will probably end in Austria agreeing to his having a change of frontier on the Papal territory, just enough to satisfy his vanity and enable him to show something to his people.' (FO Austria No. 102, 61).
2. Nicholson, p. 60.
3. Troyat, pp. 46-57. One of the Generals who wanted the Tsar to return to Poland was Count Peter Alexeyevich Pahlen, the leader of the assassins of Alexander's father Paul I. See also Oman, pp. 110-16, who names General Bennigsen as the executioner. Bennigsen was also strongly demanding a return. See also, Alexander, pp. 112-41 for a detailed analysis of the situation and Alexander's fears concerning these officers.
4. Napoleon's greatest political coup as a young revolutionary general. On 17 October 1797 Austria ceded Belgium (the Austrian Netherlands) to France, and in a secret clause agreed to French occupation of the left bank of the Rhine (part of Holland) and Savoy, and French control of northern Italy was acknowledged. Madame Junot described the conquering hero's return: 'However, great Napoleon's vanity, it must have been well satisfied, for, as I have said, all classes united to welcome him on his return home. The people cried: "Long live General Bonaparte!", "Long live the conqueror of Italy!", "Long live the peace-maker of Campo Formio!"... they [the fetes] pos-sessed the added charm of celebrating the restoration to us of what we had lost.' (d'Abrantes, *Mémoires*, vol. II, pp. 123-34). The symbolic importance of this treaty for Napoleon was recognized by Metternich. The French would not countenance the loss of Belgium which had been won by other revolutionary generals, and Napoleon had made Brussels a second home, having purchased the Palace of Laeken from the Archduke Charles of Austria (see de Jonge, p. 102 for Article 6 of his Will).

5. Aberdeen to Castlereagh: FO Austria 102, No. 27 (Most Secret) and FO Austria, 102 No. 31 (Most Secret): 'Among the conditions, *sine quibus non*, were stated the adoption by Bonaparte of the natural limits of France, meaning generally the Alps, the Rhine, and the Pyrenees ... M. de St. Aignan noted also that England was ready to make great sacrifices in order to obtain peace for Europe. That she did not interfere with the freedom of commerce or with those maritime rights to which France could with justice pretend.' After discussing Britain's maritime rights, Aberdeen added: '... but that, with this understanding, she [Great Britain] had no wish to interfere with the reasonable pretensions of France. I took this opportunity to contradict the assertion which Bonaparte had made to General Merfeldt of the intention of the British Government to limit him to thirty ships of the line, and declared that, so far as I knew, it was prejudice without foundation.'

6. The Prussians, who throughout the period 1812-14 had honoured their British commitment in return for subsidies, leaked information of the treaty to George Jackson, a zealous assistant to Castlereagh's half-brother, Sir Charles Stewart. FO Prussia 64, Jackson to Castlereagh 11 November 1813: '... Upon my questioning the Prussian minister upon the nature of the proposals to be made by M. de St. Aignan, he professed to attach little importance to them ... that it was more an Austrian transaction than any other, and that he supposed Prince Metternich had communicated the whole to Lord Aberdeen ... He then informed me, as a casual intimation, that it was determined to await the result of this overture before they conclude the offensive and defensive

alliance proposed by Lord Castlereagh's late instructions ... I have thought it my duty, Sir, to detail to you this conversation ... ' Castlereagh was shocked by the perfidy of the Allies. Here they were, having pushed Napoleon out of Germany with British financial aid, yet again about to come to terms so that they could divide their spoils, and leaving Britain in the lurch. He immediately sent by special messenger and naval vessel instructions to ALL the commissioners to reject the proposals out of hand.

He wrote to Aberdeen (PRO FO Austria 101, No. 44) ordering him to write to all the ministers: '... of the allied powers who were present at that interview, as may record, your Lordship was NOT to be considered as a party, even unofficially, to the terms in which the memorandum was drawn up, and that this protest may include the sentiments of your Government upon the said minute I enclose the sketch of a note which appears to his Royal Highness's ministers suitable to the question.' Privately he upbraided Aberdeen: 'You know how acutely we feel upon political subjects when our feelings have been long excited by animating events, but that, at all times, a maritime question touches us to the quick. I cannot conceal from you the uneasiness of the government upon the perusal of St. Aignan's minute: and most certainly such a document, if published by the enemy, without any counter-document on our part, would excite unpleasant impressions [riots] in this country.' (Vane, Vol. IX, p. 89).

7. *Correspondance*, No. 23994; see also Rose, pp. 339-46; Nicolson, pp. 59-62.

8. The Cabinet, aware of the need of a diplomat of weight at Allied Headquarters to counter the three monarchs and their ministers, chose Castlereagh. The Prince Regent concurred, adding, 'Chickens are no good when dealing with foxes.' Armed with the most powerful authority ever invested in a British Foreign Secretary, he was sent out poste-haste, and his commission empowered him as he thought fit to make peace or declare war, and put all means at his disposal including an extra £5,000,000 in subsidies [bribes], and more if necessary. See FO Cont. Arch. I, Cabinet Memorandum 26 December 1813.

9. Vane, vol. VII, p. 402. See also Webster, p. 133.

10. Ibid.

11. Castlereagh to Liverpool (PRO FO Cont. 2, No. 3).

12. Vane, vol. IX, p. 212.

13. Ibid.; Webster, pp. 389ff.

14. Castlereagh to Cathcart (Vane, vol. VIII, p. 374).

15. Ibid.: '... Count Münster adverts to a letter of Gneisenau's to the Chancellor Hardenberg, in which he quotes my opinion as countenancing a divided confederacy in Germany, under separate protection of the two great military powers [Austria and Prussia]. I may and probably did speak of *the principle* of both being restored to their former station and authority, as the natural and necessary barriers to secure the North and South of Germany against France ...' However, '*in principle*', translated into German and related second-hand, could understandably be construed as meaning that Britain had 'no principle objection'. At the Vienna Congress Gneisenau's distrust of Britain would stem from this interpretation.

16. Castlereagh to Liverpool (PRO FO Cont. 2, No. 12). It would appear that at this juncture the Tsar was contemplating crowning Bernadotte as King of France for two reasons: it would make him dependent on the Tsar and provide a balance against Austria, and Sweden would then require a new Crown Prince (the King being old and childless). Who better than one from the Russian House or its nominee? Would Sweden refuse? The Tsar was already seeing himself as successor to Napoleon, with an eastern and Baltic Empire.

17. Cabinet Memorandum (PRO FO Cont. Arch. I) '... A subsidy of £5,000,000 is to be under reserve [for your use]. 1. As to sending home the Russian fleet. 2. The acceptance of a proportion [of the debts] in credit bills. 3. The signing of engagements especially as to Holland and the Peninsula as may justify to the British public and the Allies so great an exertion on the part of Great Britain. [Signed] GEORGE P. R.'

18. Chandler, *Campaigns*, pp. 946ff.

19. Napoleon, *Correspondance*, vol. XXVI, No. 20921.

20. Rose, p. 349.

21. Ibid., p. 346.

22. Ritter, p. 110-11.

23. Petre, F. L., pp. 2-3.

24. In pursuance of Pitt's plan, Castlereagh had attempted to have Antwerp seized to create a fortified bridge-head, but friction between the two commanders, the Earl of Chatham and Sir Richard Strachan, brought the project to nought. The then Foreign Secretary, George Canning, lampooned Castlereagh by publishing an epigram:

'The Earl of Chatham with sword drawn,
  Was waiting for Sir Richard Strachan;
Sir Richard, longing to be at 'em,
  Was waiting for the Earl of Chatham.'

This missive, following on Canning's public criticism of Castlereagh's choice of appointees resulted in a duel and a bullet in the leg for Canning. Castlereagh was later made Foreign Secretary.

25. National Archives Paris, Nos. F7 6500-523 contain the complete folio of transcripts and reports by the War Department and Interior Ministry.

26. Artom's book is the best English language treatment of the subject.

27. Duff Cooper's apologia of Talleyrand's career, while giving the reader an insight to this complex character, continually excuses Talleyrand's actions by stating that he always put the good of France before anything else. Many historians have pointed out that this seems to have been the case, but I support Doctor Johnson's dictum that 'Patriotism is the last refuge of a scoundrel.'

28. Duff Cooper, pp. 186ff.

29. Pflugk-Harttung, p. 544.

30. Henderson, p. 216.

31. Ibid., p. 217.

32. Nicolson, p. 76.

33. Von Unger, vol. II, p. 171.

34. Nicolson, p. 76.

35. Steffens, p. 146.

36. Ibid.

37. PRO FO Cont. 2, Troyes, 13 February 1813, Lord Castlereagh's Answers to the Austrian inquiries: '... Whenever a peace, such as Europe may now command from the enemy can be reduced into proper form by the negotiations now in progress, that both in policy and good faith it ought to be seized, if no intervening act of the nation itself shall bring into doubt the competence of Buonaparte to treat and to contract. And I am further of opinion that altho' an armistice in the ordinary sense of the term is wholly inadmissible pending negotiations, yet there may be military sacrifices on the part of the enemy ... as to make it inconsistent for those who would accept the peace, to refuse an armistice so regulated.'

38. PRO FO Cont. 2, Troyes, 12 February 1814, Castlereagh to Liverpool (private): 'The only possible solution to settle the equilibrium of Europe is to place the Bourbons on their legitimate throne. To these ends, I am persuaded that His Imperial Highness the Emperor of Russia will agree, as it will be to his advantage.' PRO FO Cont. 2, 14 February 1814, Castlereagh asks Liverpool for Cabinet backing on this (i.e., 'passes the buck' on paper). PRO FO Cont. 1, No. 4 Bathurst to Castlereagh, 27 February 1814: [Government's answer] '... yet they [the Cabinet] could not conceal their opinion founded upon long experience, and confirmed by the rejection of the terms now proposed, that a restoration of the House of Bourbon, would afford the best prospect of procuring permanent happiness and tranquillity to France itself and the rest of Europe.'

39. Houssaye, *1814*, p. 60.

40. Ibid., p. 61.

41. Pflugk-Harttung, p. 548.

42. Houssaye, *1814*, p. 71.

43. Nicolson, p. 77.

44. Ibid.

45. PRO FO Cont. 2, Castlereagh to Liverpool, Châtillon 18 February 1814 (enclosing copy letter from Lieven to Count Nesselrode): '... I should receive your explanation, from the very embarrassing publicity that has been given here to this document ... it has essentially complicated the business with which I have been charged, and exposed the Prince Regent's name to be very unpleasantly compromised. I cannot, either in justice to his Royal Highness, to you or myself, avoid placing the whole in your hands, convinced that you will do what is most proper upon it. I have felt myself bound, with all deference to Count Lieven, to express my entire disbelief of the accuracy of his conception of the sentiments which he has thus attempted to convey.' See also Vane, Vol. IX, p. 266.

46. Fournier, pp. 363-4, quoting from the Hardenberg diaries.

47. Troyat, p. 179.
48. Houssaye, *1814*, p. 90; Nicolson, p. 81.
49. Woinovich, vol. VIII, p. 234.
50. Castlereagh to Liverpool, PRO FO Cont. 2, No. 12, Châtillon 16 February 1814.
51. Castlereagh to Prince Metternich, PRO FO Cont. 2, Châtillon 18 February 1814.
52. Alexander I, p. 314; Shilder, vol. III, p. 174; regarding Bernadotte, see also Rose, vol. II, p. 369.
53. Castlereagh to Mr. Hamilton, Vane, vol. IX, p. 335; see also PRO FO Cont. 2, 10 March 1814 (Most Secret) Castlereagh to Liverpool.
54. Rose, vol. II, p. 373.
55. Henderson, p. 232.
56. Unger, vol. II, p. 203
57. See Appendix II.
58. Bryant, p. 246. Napoleon's letters to Marie-Louise had been lost until 1934 when they were acquired at enormous cost by the Bibliothèque Nationale at auction in London, a loan having to be raised for the purchase. Many of the French histories, including Houssaye's *1814*, were written in ignorance of Napoleon's thoughts on certain subjects during this crucial period. This fact has sometimes been overlooked, and the letters' contents grafted on to historical assumptions that probably would not have been made if the writers had had access to the material.
59. Norman, p. 70.
60. Ibid., p. 71.
61. Duff Cooper, pp. 34-7.
62. Castlereagh to Liverpool, PRO FO Cont. 3, No. 45, Dijon 307 March; Webster, pp. 173-4.
63. Ibid.
64. Castlereagh to Liverpool, PRO FO Cont. 3, No. 41, Bar-sur-Aube 22 March; see also for a condensed version Webster, pp. 168-71.
65. Britain's involvement in the terrorist activities of the 'Aa' and 'Chevaliers de la Foi' under the aegis of Vice-Amiral Philippe d'Auvergne, titular prince and duc de Bouillon, will be examined in a later chapter, but see British Library Ad. MS 37857, folio 20028 '*Livre des Rapports des differentes Missions remplies par Monsieur de Chateaubriand par ordre du Prince de Bouillon*' which gives a good account of the secret activities of the celebrated writer (and agent) Chateaubriand. The PRO has two volumes marked 'War Office to Bouillon, Lettres d'Anglais Bouillon'. The Treasury papers contain 99 entries of money entrusted to him to finance terrorism. See also Appendix II.

4. The Road to Paris: Betrayal

1. Sutherland, pp. 425-7; Houssaye, *1814*, pp. 196-201; see also: Balleine, pp. 38-132; BL MSS: 37857, f.228 (Instructions to Chateaubriand from the Prince de Bouillon), 38769, ff. 1-8 (Philippe d'Auvergne, Prince de Bouillon, receipts for Secret Service funds), 35 other entries relating to his activities.
2. Sutherland; Houssaye, *1814*.
3. Houssaye, *1814,* p. 200.
4. Nicolson, p. 89. Nicolson states: 'It is not clear why, even before the capitulation of Paris, Castlereagh and Metternich should have permitted and led so public a demonstration. They were not men to be affected with impetuosity.' His book, however, was based on secondary source material, none of which contained any of Castlereagh's ciphered letters to Liverpool; the PRO archives were not available during the Second World War when his book was written.
5. At the beginning of February Napoleon wrote to Marshal Augereau: '... I charge you to march within twelve hours of receiving this letter. If you are still the old Augereau of Castiglione you will obey this order; if your sixty years weigh upon you, hand over the command to the senior of your generals. Our country is in danger; she can be saved only by courage and energy, not by useless delays.' (Houssaye, *1814*, p. 194.) But Augereau was 'dragging his feet'; he neither resigned nor marched until late February, being sure that Napoleon would come to terms, and not wishing to hazard his life for a lost cause.
6. Houssaye, *1814*, p. 265.
7. This was an extraordinary letter to have been sent by a Minister of Police. The Treasury was in credit to the tune of nearly 400,000,000 francs. The arsenals contained more than 20,000 muskets with 2 million rounds, 300 field guns, and 600 cannon of heavy calibre and 200,000 assorted charges. Savary was useless. In his memoirs he tries to excuse his actions, and conceal his complicity with Talleyrand who had frightened

him into becoming an accomplice, probably by offering immunity in the duc d'Enghien affair. Otherwise he would have obeyed Napoleon's order, arrested Talleyrand and nipped the royalist 'fifth column' in the bud. Savary told Postmaster-General Lavalette: 'What is the Emperor thinking of? Do I not have enough royalists to cope with? Does he want to throw the whole Faubourg Saint-Germain on my hands? It's Talleyrand who keeps them from doing foolish things. The Emperor will thank me for not executing this order.' (Lavalette, p. 252.) In these circumstances Fouché would have rounded-up so many royalists as to deter the rest.

8. Archives Nationales, AF IV 16670, AF V3, AF V4; for a faithful account of the atrocities committed by the Allies, the policies of some Allied commanders, and the activities of the partisans see Houssaye, *1814*, pp. 37-48. One band of partisans captured some of the Allied Commissioners including the traitor de Vitrolles whom they took to be Artois (Castlereagh to Liverpool, PRO FO Cont. Arch. 4, No. 50: '... unfortunately the messenger [Vitrolles] mentioned in the dispatch of the 22nd March, after an interview with Monsieur, was taken by armed peasants'. The myth of lack of local resistance started by the Bourbon historians has, by repetition, been accepted outside France.

9. Houssaye, *1814*, pp. 296-310; Norman, pp 91-100; AF V4; Archives de la Guerre 4290-92.

10. Houssaye, *1814*, pp. 329-30.

11. The case that Augereau deliberately betrayed Napoleon and his army is borne out by the facts – and Royalist rewards. It is probable that he had been 'propositioned by a 'Chevalier' on behalf of Artois. Speaking of the events at Bordeaux, Castlereagh hints: '... If Lyons should imitate the example everything may be hoped. I understand that Monsieur has also been well received at Nancy.' (Castlereagh to Liverpool, PRO FO Cont. Arch. 3, No. 45.) Augereau's position was vital, linking Napoleon with Italy and the Armies of Soult and Suchet – it also posed a threat to the rear of the Bohemian army. Augereau then withdrew into the south and there in April, issued a proclamation abusing Napoleon and proclaiming

Louis XVIII. Louis confirmed all his titles and made him a peer in recognition of his services. He was at Caen in 1815 denouncing Napoleon when news of the return arrived. He immediately called his men 'to return to the tricolore', and offered his services. Napoleon's answer was to strike him off the role of Marshals, as did Louis on his second restoration; see Chandler, *Marshals*, London, 1987.

12. Norman, p. 130. Also in Anon. *Memoirs of the Invasion of France*, p. 183.

13. Ibid.; AF V4; Archives de la Guerre, 4290.

14. Personal correspondence between the author and Dr Otto von Habsburg, the last Habsburg Imperial Archduke, son of the last Austrian Emperor.

15. Clarke was a traitor, who changed sides and kept his position under the Bourbons. During the Waterloo campaign he accompanied Louis to Ghent. On their return Louis rewarded Clarke with a Marshal's baton. Pasquier also went over, but concealed his double-dealing, and handed in his notice to Napoleon after the Allies had entered Paris. Within a year of the restoration he was a duke and a very rich man. General Hulin took office under the Bourbons from day one, and suggested the formation of an élite National Guard of royalists to protect the provisional government. Savary's memoirs read as though he were a mere observer during this fateful month, and it seems strange that the Bourbons did not have them suppressed; even more strange that they did not have him executed for his part in the execution of their relative the duc d'Enghien. Certainly he was not as big a fool as he makes out, nor was he Talleyrand's unwitting tool.

16. Houssaye, *1814*, p. 343.

17. Ibid., p. 340.

18. Ibid., p. 342.

19. Ibid., pp. 335ff.

20. Savary, vol. III, pp. 227-8.

21. Bryant, p. 237.

22. Ibid., pp. 238-9.

23. Ibid.

24. This was the sole route by which Joseph would have been able to correspond with his brother-in-law, without committing an act of treason that could be traced back to him. Napoleon allowed the Crown Princess of Sweden immunity – she was family after

all; Napoleon was Godfather to the Bernadotte's son Oscar, named after Napoleon's
favourite poet, Ossian. Bernadotte obviously told Joseph that he hoped to take the
French throne with the Tsar's backing, and
that there would be a place for him. I would
speculate that Bernadotte told him to
remove the Empress and her son, and only
use token resistance to the Tsar before capitulating. Lord Castlereagh, writing to Prime
Minister Liverpool from Dijon on 4 April,
relating the events of the last week of March
said: 'We have a secret intimation from
Nesselrode [Russian Secretary of State]
through Schwarzenberg that the Prince
Royal's intrigue with Joseph is understood
and that Talleyrand and others in authority
will counteract it. This is fortunate, as I find
that Charles Jean (evidently in expectation
of a crisis) has gone to Headquarters. The
plan was an intermediate system ostensibly
to favour the return of the Bourbons at the
head of which Bernadotte expected to
appear as dictator for a limited time, Joseph
looking through his influence to some suitable settlement.' (PRO FO Cont. Arch. 4,
No. 50.) In this political can of worms, we
can also see the Russian minister, betraying
for gain, the Tsar's secret plans to Austria
and Britain. Castlereagh mentioned that
'the Tsar did not even trust his own minister' – res ipsa loquitur.
25. Houssaye, 1814, pp. 368-9.
26. Napoleon, Correspondance, No. 21210
(Napoleon from Rheims).
27. Peyre; Houssaye, 1814, pp. 395-9; Troyat,
p. 184; Norman, p. 138.
28. Orlov, pp. 116-7; Houssaye, 1814; Norman.
29. PRO FO Cont. Arch. 4, No. 50,
Castlereagh to Liverpool.
30. Houssaye, 1814, pp. 393-5.
31. Du Casse, vol. X, pp. 23-4.
32. Houssaye, 1814, p. 410.
33. Ibid., p. 402.
34. AF IV 1659; Norman, p. 142.
35. Houssaye, 1814, p. 411. Under their constitution the Paris National Guards could not
be ordered to fight outside the
environs of Paris without their consent.
36. Weil, vol. IV, p. 206-7.
37. Norman, p. 164.
38. Ibid.
39. Norman, p. 170; de Montagnac, pp. 122-3.

40. PRO FO Cont. Arch. IV 4, No. 50
Castlereagh to Liverpool, Dijon, 4 April;
Webster, p. 174.

5. The Road to Fontainebleau

1. Chandler, Marshals, pp. 255ff.
2. AF IV 1670 No. 236.
3. Belliard, vol. I, pp. 171-9.
4. Ibid. Belliard had been misinformed by
Marmont, probably deliberately so – no
convention prohibiting the return of him
and his men had been entered into. Belliard's men were at Juvisy at 11 p.m.. The
terms of capitulation had not yet been
signed. Nesselrode and Orlov had made it
clear that they could not stop Marmont's
men leaving by the road to Fontainebleau,
through the southern part of Paris, which
they could not invest. They left, unob-
structed, on the Marshal's orders.
5. Ibid.
6. Caulaincourt, vol. III, pp. 55-9.
7. Almost one year later, in much more haz-
ardous circumstances, Napoleon would
march from the Mediterranean with 1,000
men of his Imperial Guard and recapture
not only Paris but the whole of France.
8. For Napoleon's plan of attack on Paris and
his orders, see: Correspondance, C 21554;
Archives de la Guerre C/2 No. 187; AF IV
1670 plaque 2.
9. PRO FO Cont. Arch. 4, No. 50 Castlereagh
to Liverpool.
10. Talleyrand, vol. II, pp. 164-5.
11. Ibid. Napoleon had always been the legitimate monarch of France since his coronation. He could not usurp what did not exist.
He had been appointed by plebiscite, and
anointed by the Pope as Emperor. This title
had been accepted by all the European
monarchs save Britain's. In her case, if she
applied this principle of legitimacy to herself, then Bonnie Prince Charles was the
legitimate monarch in 1746 and his
younger brother Cardinal York was now the
'legitimate' king instead of George III. The
act of succession, promulgated by the will of
the people of Britain, would not have been
able to remove this 'legitimate' right. Louis
XVI had been removed from power by the
Legislative Assembly in 1792. A republic
had been declared for almost a year before
he was executed for encouraging a counter-
revolution, of which his correspondence

showed he was guilty. Twenty-three years and several governments had succeeded that event. No less an authority than Macaulay, who considered Napoleon a tyrant, upheld his legitimate title as Emperor of the French. The Bourbons had through time lost legitimate claim. Macaulay wrote: 'If Bonaparte was a usurper so was Hugh Capet [the Bourbons' founder], and so was Pepin; yet there is, probably, no votary of legitimacy who would think it right to depose the Bourbons in favour of a pretender who might be able to make out, by the clearest evidence, his descent from the long-haired kings of the Merovingian race. If power, which originates in proceedings inconsistent with the laws, can never become lawful, Louis XVI had no more right to the French throne than Marat or Santerre [revolutionary leaders]. If power, unlawful in its origin, may by lapse of time become lawful, what length of time is necessary?' (Macaulay, p. 72).

12. Talleyrand, vol. II, pp. 164-5.
13. Masson, vol. IX, p. 432.
14. Balleine, pp. 115ff.
15. Choix de rapports, vol. XX, p. 491.
16. Weil, vol. IV, p. 264.
17. Houssaye, *1814*, p. 472; Norman, pp. 216-17.
18. Ibid., Norman.
19. Chandler, *Campaigns*, p. 1001.
20. Norman, pp. 224ff; Houssaye, *1814*, pp. 482ff; Mackenzie, pp. 18-21.
21. Napoleon, *Correspondance*, C21555; AF IV No. 906.
22. Macdonald, p. 279.
23. Ibid.
24. Rochechouart, p. 337.
25. Macdonald, p. 279.
26. Bryant, pp. 256-7.
27. RO FO Cont. Arch. IV 4, No. 54 Castlereagh to Liverpool 19 April; Hansard, vol. XXX, p. 736.
28. Kelly, pp. 8-9. This book contains masses of primary source material culled from documents of all the participants involved. It is not a history, but a collection of documents.
29. Nicolson, p. 82.

6. The Road to Saint-Ouen
1. Nicolson, p. 107.
2. Troyat, p. 199.
3. Ibid., p. 200; Nicolson, pp. 108-9.

4. Ibid.
5. Sutherland, pp. 393, 397. Sutherland mentions a connection with the Malet plot, the mysterious Abbé Lafon whom he names as a member of either the 'Aa' or the 'Chevaliers de la Foi'. Funded and armed by Britain, they were the more dangerous in that they were controlled by the heir to the throne. The ultras provided the 'political' or respectable front. See Appendix II.
6. To see how Artois used this organization after Waterloo to create 'The White Terror' and to gain political power in the Chambers see Bertier, *French Politics*, pp. 342-56.
7. Elting, pp. 629ff.
8. Ibid., p. 631.
9. Ibid., p. 635.
10. Hales, pp. 88-90.
11. In 1795, Artois tried to take advantage of the rebellions in the Vendée and Chouan by providing arms, funds and aristocratic leadership. His propaganda made it seem as though the peasants' Catholic beliefs were allied to the concept of monarchy. After the failure of the *émigré* landing on the Quiberon peninsula, he returned to Britain and concentrated on covert operations. See Appendix II.
12. Brett-James, p. 1; Horricks, p. 180.
13. Police reports, AF V5 1178. The parallel of French attitudes to the 'March traitors' in the Paris of 1814, with those of the Germans in 1918 is too obvious to be ignored. The German Army, unbeaten in the field, blamed the 'November traitors' in Berlin, and the consequences contributed directly to the military support given to Hitler during his rise to power.
14. The Duchess of Angoulême was the sole surviving child of Louis XVI and Marie-Antoinette. She had been isolated with her brother, the presumptive Louis XVII, in the notorious Temple prison. They had both been made to work in a degrading fashion and been subjected to both mental and physical abuse. Her brother had died there, and she had been sold to the Allies by the corrupt republican officials, so her hatred of the Revolution and its heir had a sound personal basis.
15. Horricks, p. 180.
16. Ibid., p. 184.
17. It is said that Oliver Cromwell told Parliament that 'The soldiers are the heart and

conscience of the people.' This statement has sometimes been misunderstood. He meant of course that the army represents the people it protects, and will rarely take up arms against them if its heart and conscience are in accord with theirs. In 1813-15, the French army was closer to its civilian roots than at any time since the Revolution. The police reports showed that nearly 80 per cent of the population supported Napoleon and didn't want the Bourbons.

18. Police reports. Artois, who had enjoyed his English Sundays, pressurized the Director of Police (the title had now been changed) to sign an ordinance prohibiting all work and trade on Sundays and religious festivals. A further (illegal) decree was issued, without reference to the Chambers, enforcing respect for the *Corpus Christi* processions.

19. Madelin, vol. 16, p. 245.

20. Fisher, vol. IX, p. 570.

21. Guedalla, p. 252; Kelly, p. 153.

22. It was during this inspection in 1814 that Wellington considered that the Waterloo position would be ideal for the defence of Brussels, and he said as much in a letter to Lord Bathurst, attached to his memorandum of suggestions for the refortifying of the strategic towns. On 22 June 1815, Lord Bathurst, addressing the House of Lords, said: 'The position of Waterloo was one well known to Lord Wellington; in the summer of last year his Grace went there on his way to Paris, and on that occasion he took a military view of it. He then declared, that if ever it should be his fortune to defend Brussels, Waterloo would be the best position he could occupy.'; Kelly, ibid.; Hansard.

23. Colonel Campbell was assigned by Castlereagh to accompany Napoleon to Elba and remain there with him to protect him. Napoleon had requested asylum in England, but Castlereagh did not want him there for fear that he become a popular celebrity. Castlereagh could not dismiss this official appeal, known to the Tsar, without ensuring Napoleon's safety to and on Elba. Campbell's only authority and instructions were contained in a single letter from Castlereagh. Campbell, besides being informed of the clauses dealing with Napoleon's safety route, was to show 'every proper respect and attention to Napoleon, to whose secure asylum in that island it is the wish of His Royal Highness the Prince Regent to afford every facility and protection'. Further, it gave Campbell sweeping powers: '... to call upon any of His Majesty's officers by land or sea', and he was to stay on Elba indefinitely if Napoleon ... should consider the presence of a British officer can be of use in protecting the island or his person against insult and attack.' With this letter, signed by the Foreign Secretary, Captain Ussher was instructed by Campbell to give Napoleon – as a ruling sovereign – a salute of 21 guns on embarking. Napoleon, as can be seen, was not a prisoner; he was not exiled, and Campbell was not his gaoler. See Mackenzie, pp. 38-47.

24. Metternich mistrusted Talleyrand, and conducted his correspondence with Louis through the comte Blacas. In January 1815, Metternich even suggested that the Austrian army eject Murat, in return for France agreeing to some minor adjustments in northern Italy. Castlereagh acted as Metternich's go-between on his way back to England in February 1815. Nicolson, pp. 192-3.

25. Castlereagh to Wellington, Downing Street, 7 August 1814 (Vane, vol. X, p.76); PRO FO France 99, 27 July, 7 August; Webster, pp. 189-93.

26. PRO FO Cont. Arch. 7, No. 1. Castlereagh to Liverpool Geneva, 3 September 1814; Webster, Ibid.

7. The Road to Vienna

1. Nicolson, p. 142.

2. Ibid., pp. 140-8. Nicolson would have us believe that Metternich and Castlereagh were so naive and inept that they conceded the moral point. It was nothing of the sort. As has been seen, Metternich and Castlereagh had to engineer Talleyrand's acceptance into the council to bring French weight into their resistance to the Tsar's plans.

3. Troyat, p. 212.

4. Ibid., p. 213.

5. Ibid., et. seq.

6. Nicolson, p. 170.

7. Ibid.

8. PRO FO Cont. Arch. 7, No. 9 Castlereagh to Liverpool Vienna 14 October 1814; Webster, p. 206.

9. PRO FO Cont. Arch. 7, No. 12 Castlereagh to Liverpool Vienna 24 October 1814; Webster, pp. 212-15.

10. Jeremy Bentham (1742–1832), English writer on jurisprudence and ethics, Founder of University College London. Bentham held that 'actions were right and good when they promote the happiness of the greatest number'. He had a worldwide reputation, and was highly respected in London circles. See: Life by Bowring in the Collected Works, London, 1838-43

11. PRO FO Cont. Arch. 7, No. 9; quoted in full in Webster, pp. 206-10.

12. Ibid.

13. Ibid.

14. Ibid.

15. PRO FO Cont. Arch. 7, No. 9 Castlereagh to Liverpool.

16. PRO FO Cont. Arch. 7, No. 14 Castlereagh to Liverpool Vienna 25 October 1814; Webster, pp. 216-7.

17. Wellesley, *Supplementary*, Castlereagh to Wellington, Vienna 25 October 1814, vol. IX, p. 372; Webster, pp. 217-19. This last paragraph of Castlereagh's must rate as the greatest understatement of the century. In this matter Talleyrand was right. In emulation of Napoleon, who had shown the way, Prussia wished to lead a German confederation, and have its Empire, 'its place in the sun'.

18. Metternich, vol. II, p. 570.

19. Troyat, pp. 213-15; Nicolson, pp. 168-77; Gulick, vol. IX, pp. 649-52; PRO FO Cont. Arch. 8, No. 16 Castlereagh to Liverpool Vienna 11 November 1814; Webster, pp. 229-33.

20. PRO FO Cont. Arch. 8, No. 16.

21. PRO FO Cont. Arch. 8, No. 15 Castlereagh to Liverpool Vienna 15 November 1814.

22. Wellesley, *Supplementary*, vol. IX p. 382, copy Liverpool to Castlereagh 28 October 1814; Webster, p. 219-21.

23. Ibid.

24. Wellesley, *Supplementary*, vol IX, p. 401; Webster, pp. 221-2.

25. PRO FO Cont. Arch. 8, No. 16 Castlereagh to Liverpool 11 November 1814; Webster, p. 231.

26. Wellesley, *Supplementary*, vol. IX, p. 421; Webster, pp. 228-9.

27. Fisher, pp. 565-6.

28. Mackenzie, pp. 147-215. Mackenzie deals in depth with all the police reports, Austrian and French, concerning the matter.

29. Ibid.

30. Wellesley, *Supplementary*, vol. IX, p. 503, Wellington to Liverpool: 'I concur very much in opinion with the King, that the chances of disturbance, particularly in this country, are very much increased by leaving Murat on the throne of Naples.' He also advised Liverpool that if Britain were required to evict Murat, he estimated the force should comprise: '10,000 infantry from Spain, 12,000 infantry from Portugal, 20,000 of all arms from Great Britain; and 10,000 of all arms from Sicily; with 60 pieces of field artillery and a battering-train from Great Britain. This force, with 40,000 men [French], which might be sent from the southern ports of France, by sea, into the Roman states, would be more than sufficient to ensure the object almost without striking a blow ...'

31. PRO FO Cont. Arch. 6, No. 3 Bathurst to Castlereagh 27 November 1814; Webster, p. 247-8.

32. Hansard; Nicolson, pp. 185-9.

33. Ibid.

34. Wellesley, *Supplementary*, vol. IX, p. 438.

35. PRO FO Cont. Arch. 8, No. 27 Castlereagh to Liverpool Vienna 7 December 1814; Webster, pp. 255-7.

36. Ibid.

37. PRO FO Cont. Arch. 8, No. 27.

38. Nicolson, pp. 176-8.

39. PRO FO Cont. Arch. 10, No. 44 Castlereagh to Liverpool Vienna 1 January 1815.

40. PRO FO Cont. Arch. 10, No. 45 Castlereagh to Liverpool Vienna 1 January 1815.

41. Ibid.

42. Nicolson, p. 178.

43. Reilly, pp. 247-57. Prior to Castlereagh's letters indicating that Britain was heading towards a European conflict, Britain had offered only to negotiate peace with America on the principle of *uti possidetis* (one is entitled to keep what one has acquired). Given the circumstances this stance was changed dramatically to *status quo ante bellum*, that is to say 'as it was prior to the war'. Bathurst in a secret letter to the Governor-General of Canada, Lieutenant-Gen-

eral Sir George Prevost, indicated that Canada would have greater security by the acquisition of 'Fort Niagara, and the restoration of Detroit and the whole Michigan County ...', and '... on that part of our frontier which extends towards Lake Champlain, the occupation of which would materially tend to the security of the Province'. (PRO CO/43/23, 3 June 1814.

44. Moscow State Archives, APX A OCA 1274, Prince Lieven to HIM the Emperor, London 3 December 1814; Nicolson, p. 203.

45. PRO FO Cont. Arch. 10, No. 50 Castlereagh to Liverpool 8 January 1815.

46. Ibid.

47. Castlereagh, unaware of the 'leak', was trying to keep face by appearing to give ground in accordance with the Cabinet's wishes, rather than his own 'good judgement': PRO FO Cont. Arch 10, No. 52 Castlereagh to Liverpool 11 January 1814. See attached Circular to the Plenipotentiaries of the Conference, dated for the next day, the 12th. The Circular is a veritable *cri de coeur* ending: '... it will only remain for His Royal Highness most anxiously to hope, that none of those dangers to the liberties of Europe may ever be realized, which might justly be apprehended from the reunion of a powerful Polish Monarchy with the still more powerful Empire of Russia, if at any time hereafter the military force of both should be directed by an ambitious and warlike Prince.' This putting on record, if you like, to the other delegates was counter-productive, if with all this heart-felt opposition, Britain was agreeing to the situation, they were not going to oppose him either.

48. PRO FO Cont. Arch. 10, No. 52 Castlereagh to Liverpool.

49. PRO FO Cont. Arch. 10, No. 57 Castlereagh to Liverpool 22 January 1815.

50. PRO FO Cont. Arch. 10, No. 63 Castlereagh to Liverpool 29 January 1815.

51. Ibid.

52. PRO FO Cont. Arch. 10, No. 66 Castlereagh to Liverpool 6 February 1815.

53. Henderson, pp. 264-5.

8. The Road to Grenoble

1. Bryant, pp. 272-4.

2. Mackenzie, pp. 134-200. The reader is recommended to this book in which Dr Mackenzie, using archive material, presents one of the best pictures of Napoleon on Elba. The intrigues by the Bourbons to kill or remove him are covered in detail, as are his clandestine communications with his supporters and family. Mackenzie also names Artois' spy on Elba as Alessandro Forli.

3. Baron Hager, Chief of the Austrian secret police, whose service had taken on more than 3,000 auxiliaries during the Congress, had intercepted a letter from Mariotti in Livorno to Baron Dalberg, one of Talleyrand's *coup d'état* clique who was with him at Congress, in which he speaks of 'not much chance of carrying off Napoleon ... the extraordinary precautions which he has taken against all strangers, especially those who arrive from France and Livorno, the continual change of domicile'. (Mackenzie, p. 163.) Mariotti also speaks of a plan to capture Napoleon aboard his ship, and take him to a prison isle off Toulon.

4. Mackenzie, pp. 121, 144.

5. Ibid., pp. 188-9. Napoleon's intelligence sources were formidable. He spoke candidly to Campbell about Mariotti's plot. He had placed his safety in British hands, but he was well aware that Castlereagh had no liking for him. What if he withdrew Campbell and the man-of-war after the Congress ended. He would then be at the mercy of the French and Spanish Bourbon fleets. If Louis succeeded in returning Ferdinand to Naples, he would be surrounded on all sides, by hostile Bourbons out for revenge.

6. Ibid. Napoleon's answer really does dismiss this slur on his reputation. He did not have suicidal tendencies. This rumour started among servants at Fontainebleau, no doubt a good story for the influx of English tourists – long denied the continent, and taken up by Caulaincourt in his memoirs long after Napoleon's death.

7. Longford, pp. 378-9.

8. Ibid., p. 198.

9. Ibid., p. 149. Mackenzie tells of two packets that were intercepted between Napoleon and Murat. In one instance a brawl was staged to divert attention, while the valise of the second officer of the *Inconstant* was stolen. It contained two pieces of paper, both blank, one bearing Napoleon's signature, the other that of Bertrand, Grand Marshal of the Palace.

10. Wellesley, *Supplementary*, vol. IX, p. 540; Nicolson, p. 181.
11. Ibid., vol IX, pp. 573–8; Webster, pp. 307-9.
12. Nicolson, pp. 187–8.
13. Ibid.
14. Ibid.
15. Mackenzie, pp. 195–7. It is obvious that the garrison was in on this ruse, and Napoleon indirectly. This rumour which was put about by Artois during the campaign of 1815, was very damaging coming from a dependent ally. Britain at Congress and at each capital, had tried to get the colonial powers to outlaw the slave trade. Louis had said that he would try to achieve this within five years, but the slave owners saw this as a British ploy to cause them financial ruin and destroy competition. Napoleon gave further credence to this rumour with a decree outlawing slavery as soon as he returned. Britain's allies, incidentally, were not so co-operative. Spain replied that when they had 're-stocked as many slaves as the British have, then they would consider it'. In the end Britain had to pay Spain £800,000 and Portugal £400,000 to ban the trade.
16. Brett-James, pp. 3–4.
17. Mackenzie, p. 245.
18. Archives Nationale; Manceron, *Napoleon*, pp. 61–3 (quoted in full). There is much truth in this proclamation which prophetically summed-up well the national feeling. By 1840 all the remaining survivors of the *Grande Armée* would be so honoured by the nation.
19. The Council of the *Champ de Mars* was the general assembly of the Franks under Clovis. In AD 752 Pepin restored it under the name *Champ de Mai*. This assembly had voted to give Pepin the crown of France. It was used frequently by Charlemagne the Great who had restored the western Empire. Under the feudal system and the rise of the Capets and their Bourbon descendants, the people's assembly had been abolished by feudal absolutism. Napoleon, a great student of French history, now reverted to an ancient pre-Bourbon French institution that allowed the nation to name its monarch. Macauley wrote: 'The name of the field of May could not, therefore, but have a pleasing sound to a man who was the enemy of feudal privileges, and the competitor of the third race [Bourbon], who had held his crown by a title similar to that of Pepin the Great's, and who had extended his authority over dominions as vast as those of Charlemagne.' (Macauley, p. 94).
20. Manceron, *Napoleon*, pp. 53–4.
21. History has tended to treat Napoleon's return as a mere adventure. The military aspects are covered, but it is portrayed not as a revolution – which it certainly was – but as a military coup. It suited the later French historians, writing from 1815 to 1830, living under the Bourbons, to propagate the idea that the people supported the king and only the army supported Napoleon. This was not the case. British historians of the period followed the French line. For an extremely unbiased analysis Professor Pieter Geyl's *Napoleon For and Against*, London, 1949, is recommended. Professor Geyl discusses at great length the bias for and against Napoleon, by all the famous French historians. In 1940 Professor Geyl wrote an article about Napoleon which provoked a great deal of amusement. The Nazis assumed that he was in fact referring to Hitler and put him in Buchenwald concentration camp until the end of the war. Geyl says that he hates a comparison between the two, as being between the sublime and the ridiculous.
22. Manceron, *Napoleon*, pp. 30-1.
23. Horricks, p. 197. I entirely agree with this author's sentiments. Ney sums up in this paragraph what he truly felt, and who could blame him?
24. Fouché, vol. II, pp. 262-3; Manceron, *Napoleon*, pp. 92-104; for official confirmation see PRO FO Cont. Arch. 17 (Private and Secret) Castlereagh to Clancarty 15 April 1815: speaking of the royalists still active in Paris: '... some of them as Fouché are in situations of great trust ... the most essential services might be rendered by them to the general cause'.
25. Manceron, *Napoleon*, p. 156.

9. The Roads to Paris and Grenoble
1. Archives Nationales.
2. In dealing with the reactions of the Allies at Vienna to the news of Napoleon's escape and subsequent campaign, most historians

quote from Metternich's *Mémoires*, but these were written years later. At the time of the sovereigns' meeting no one knew where Napoleon was. Most assumed that he would head for Naples or elsewhere in Italy. Metternich says that he informed Talleyrand that it would be France and that he had interrupted his troops' withdrawal from France, '... carrying to the several army corps, who were retiring, the order to halt. In this way war was decided on in less than an hour.' (Nicolson, pp. 227-8.) But in fact the Austrian forces had been withdrawn months earlier, and were now variously deployed on the disputed Polish border, around Budapest, and in northern Italy. At this point the Allied sovereigns had agreed only to implement the provisions of the Treaty of Chaumont if necessary. After Napoleon had landed in France, Talleyrand thought, as did the Duke of Wellington and others, that the Bourbon forces would soon capture him and his 'thousand men'.

3. Kelly, p. 1.
4. Wellesley, *Supplementary*, vol. IX, p. 590, Castlereagh to Wellington (No. 3), 12 March 1815.
5. Wellesley, *Supplementary*, vol. XI, p. 592, Castlereagh to Wellington (No. 4), 12 March 1815.
6. Webster, p. 310 fn.
7. Ibid.
8. Nicolson, pp. 187-8.
9. PRO FO Cont. 14, Wellington to Castlereagh (private), Vienna 12 March 1815; Wellesley, *Supplementary*, vol. XII, p. 267; Webster, p. 312.
10. This ciphered paragraph is omitted in Wellesley, *Supplementary*, vol. XII, p. 267, but appears in full in Webster.
11. PRO FO Cont. 14, Wellington to Castlereagh, Vienna 25 March 1815; Wellesley, *Supplementary*, vol. XII, p. 278; Webster, p. 316.
12. PRO FO Cont. 14, Castlereagh to Wellington (private), London 26 March 1815; Wellesley, *Supplementary*, vol. IX, p. 623; Webster, pp. 317-18.
13. Godechot, p. 87.
14. Ibid., pp 81-106.
15. Alison, App. The government raised £5,000,000 for foreign subsidies. Wellington received £703,566 14s. 5d. in gold from Rothschilds for operational funds. After the

campaign he received a receipt for the return of £168! See also Longford, p. 395; Chandler, *Hundred Days*, pp. 176-7.
16. Kelly, pp. 12-14.
17. Ibid., p. 15.
18. Ibid., pp. 22-5 quotes the act verbatim.
19. Ibid., p. 7.
20. Hansard, Series 1, vol. XXXV, pp. 334-60; parliamentary debates, loc. cit.
21. Ibid.
22. Ibid.
23. Webster, p. 319 fn.
24. Longford, p. 394.
25. Vane, vol. X, p. 301; Webster, pp. 319-20.
26. Ibid.
27. Vane, vol. X, p. 305, Castlereagh to Clancarty, St. James's Square, 12 April 1815; Webster, pp. 322-4.
28. PRO FO Cont. 17, Clancarty to Castlereagh (No. 17) 17 April 1815; Webster, p. 324
29. PRO FO Cont. 17, Clancarty to Castlereagh (private and secret) 17 April 1815; Webster, op. cit. pp. 325-6.
30. Ibid.
31. Wellesley, *Supplementary*, vol. IX, p. 583, note 39, Liverpool to Wellington.
32. State Papers, vol. II, p. 301, ed. Foreign Office Library; also quoted in Webster, pp. 331-2.
33. PRO FO Cont. 18 (No. 41) Clancarty to Castlereagh, Vienna 13 May 1815; Webster, pp. 332-4.
34. Ibid.
35. Vane, vol. IX, p. 353; Webster, p. 335.
36. Ibid. For the Tsar's activities during this crucial period see Troyat, pp. 221-6.
37. Troyat, p. 221. According to Metternich's *Mémoires* the Tsar threw the document into the fire and announced that all was forgotten, and the time for diplomatic trickery was past. That was his version, but, as has already been shown, Alexander loathed Metternich.
38. Alexander wrote to his brother Constantine: '... that he could no longer trust the Austrians, or Bavarians and Britain. That he would be guided by events. That he would not hazard his army at the expense of the Austrians and British, to replace their Bourbon puppet. It would suite Austria to weaken Russia and then turn on us in the Polish Kingdom ...' Russian State Archives, vol. XIX, p. 275.

39. Such was the speed and eclipse of the 1815 campaign, that the feelings of betrayal and mistrust rife among the Allies from January to July 1815 have been forgotten. This was convenient for the participants and the contemporary historians of the period, writing soon after. It was 'politic' to overlook it.

40. Lamartine, *Restauration*, vol. III, p. 339.

41. Stenger, p. 333.

42. Ibid., p. 214.

43. Houssaye, *1815*, pp. 32-3.

44. For obvious reasons I have named Artois as the man who arranged for Berthier's murder. In June 1815, there was no certainty that Napoleon would not repeat his successes of 1813-14 against the coalition forces. Berthier, insulted and dishonoured by the Bourbons, had decided, like Ney, to rejoin Napoleon, whose constant companion and right-hand man he had been for twenty years.

Artois, who had ordered the murder of many hundreds of Bonapartists and several times had tried to have Napoleon assassinated, would not have hesitated in having Berthier removed. Just as Ney before Waterloo had been under observation by Artois' agents for signs of disloyalty, so also would Berthier have been after leaving Louis at Ghent.

Although terrorist organizations rarely keep incriminating records, when they operate under the aegis of governments references are sometimes made to past deeds. The story that Berthier had died accidentally originated with the Bamberg correspondent of the *Journal of Cologne*, 10 June 1815: '... it was from his children's apartment that he threw himself out of the window. His little boy, who caught his leg to save him, narrowly escaped being dragged out with him.' This lie, paid for by Artois' gold, was later carried by all European newspapers, but it is known that Madame Berthier and her children were at Grosbois when the news of his death arrived.

Conclusive proof that it was murder and not suicide exists, and was known as early as four weeks after Waterloo. When Artois had regained power, his protégé, Elie Decazes, an advocate, was made the new chief of police and was charged with the prosecution of Bonapartists during the 'White Terror'. A secret agent of Fouché's and of Britain,

Colonel Francis Macirone, a naturalized British subject of Italian descent, was being 'fitted up' by the Bourbons for liquidation. He knew too much about the death of Berthier and of arrangements being made to kill King Joachim Murat. Macirone was released by the direct intervention of the Duke of Wellington on whose service he had been engaged when seized. Macirone wrote of his interrogation: 'He [Decazes] began with asking me whether I was acquainted with the circumstances of the death of Berthier, Prince of Neufchâtel [*sic*]. I answered I had heard that he had not met his death by accident, as had been reported, but that I was ignorant by whose order he had been *put to death. On my appearing to be acquainted with the facts of Berthier's having been murdered*, M. Menars [second interrogator] expected that I should be able to furnish him with particulars of his death ... he added that the death of the personage [King Murat] and the murder of Berthier were most particularly connected.' (Macirone, pp. 143-4.)

Decazes called it murder and so did his deputy. Maciron's file is in the Archives Nationale (AF7 6773). Decazes wrote in it: '*He* [Macirone] *knows from Fouché of the two murders, but I think he is ignorant of the names of the Chevaliers concerned.*' As the 'Chevaliers' refer to Artois' men, I think the evidence is conclusive. (See Appendix II.)

10. The Road to the North

1. Stenger, pp. 142-3. Some 10,000,000 francs in cash, 3,000,000 in silver plate and snuff boxes, 15,000,000 and the Napoleonic crown diamonds in the Tuileries cellars. Artois had grabbed most of this for himself. The new finance minister Baron Louis persuade him to hand over less than a third to the State, perhaps forgetting that one of the Bourbon family's mottoes was: '*L'état c'est Moi*'.

2. Arch. Nat. AF IVv 1936; Stenger, pp. 279-81.

3. Ibid., p. 143, quoting de Vaulabelle: 'A traffic in places, titles, and decorations was carried on at this time on the largest scale ... the place was assessed in accordance with what it produced. Every title of nobility, too had its market-price. The order of the Legion of Honour was listed at 250-300

francs ... One need only refer to the Moniteur of 1814 to learn that during the months of August, September, October, November and December to learn that there were more patents of nobility and more titles of count and baron granted than during the previous two centuries of the monarchy. In the same period, more Crosses of the Legion of Honour were distributed than Napoleon had given in twelve years.'

4. Archives du Service historique de l'état-major de l'armée, cartons C14/1-20, General d'Erlon to Marshal le prince d'Eckmühl [Davout] 2 Mai 1815: '... Two days ago, a soldier from the 19th regiment of the line, while storing his cartridges, found some whose composition consisted of iron filings instead of powder; since this regiment received its cartridges from the magazine at Lille, I immediately ordered a scrupulous verification of the existing munitions in that magazine. That verification took place yesterday morning, and I was informed that all the munitions had been found to be of good quality. Yesterday evening, when they were distributing cartridges to a company of light infantry from the 42nd regiment of the line which I had placed with the cavalry at Tourcoing, they noted while opening the packages, that each one was composed of five cartridges of good quality and five others without a ball and for the most part filled with bran, ashes or clay ... This gives me grave suspicions about Colonel Levavasseur (parvenue), director of Artillery in Lille, who, if he is not guilty of treason, is at least of very great negligence; consequently, I have ordered the commandant of the military police to keep a close watch on him, and the artillery commander of my army corps to appoint on the spot a superior officer of artillery to provisionally carry on the duties of director in Lille, and to make sure of all the magazines in the stronghold ...'

5. AF IV 1936, Davout to Napoleon; Houssaye, *1815*, p. 5.

6. Carnot's report to the Chamber of Peers of 13 June, reproduced in *le Moniteur*, 15 June 1815.

7. AF 7 3774, correspondence of the prefects; Napoleon, *Correspondance*, No. 22047.

8. Houssaye, *1815*, p. 21, gives an accurate break-down of the last Imperial army in his notes, quoting the archive sources, pp. 310-12.

9. Ibid., p. 21; AF iv 1936, Davout to Napoleon 11 June; Carnot's report to Chamber of Peers; Davout's report of 23 June to the government commission.

10. Napoleon, *Correspondance*, No. 21755, Napoleon to Davout 23 March.

11. The career of Davout, probably the most able of the marshals, and certainly one of the most loyal, is covered in Gallagher. See also Chandler, *Marshals*, pp. 92ff.

12. Stenger, pp. 325-6.

13. Ibid., p. 299.

14. Ibid.

15. *Le Moniteur*, 19 April 1815, letter from Marshal Masséna:
    'The duc d'Angoulême who had already taken three regiments away from me, also wanted those that were at Toulon, and told me through M. de Rivire [Prefect] that it was his intention to put the harbour into the hands of the English, who would in return furnish the king of France with money. In this difficult situation I determined, after putting Antibes into a state of siege [under martial law] so as to remove it from the authority of the prefect of the Var, to repair to Toulon, in order to preserve that town and its shipping for Your Majesty.'

16. Chandler, *Marshals*, pp. 323-4. Napoleon was referring to the Bourbon flag and cockade 'le Blanc'. Mortier was unable to take part in the campaign because of an attack of sciatica, which may or may not have been a 'diplomatic illness'. His journal is produced as evidence of his loyalty to Napoleon, but it was written much later. He was soon reinstated by the Bourbons, however, while Ney, Brune and others were executed.

17. See: Horricks; and Atteridge. For personality clashes before and at Quatre-Bras see Hamilton-Williams, 'Ney at Quatre-Bras, a New Appraisal' in *Waterloo Committee Journal*, vol. IX, No. 1, April 1987.

18. Stenger, p. 294 quotes a letter from de Jarcourt's memoirs. Talleyrand's deputy recounts the incident at Vienna to Talleyrand as an example of what a good royalist Soult had become.

19. AF IV 1936, proclamation of Minister of

War Soult, 8 March; see also *le Moniteur* 8
March 1814; also quoted in Stenger, p. 308.
20. Ibid.
21. Hayman, p. 223. Although quoting the
same sources given above, this author seems
to have missed Soult's proclamation and
ministerial orders. The Hundred Days is
but briefly covered and seems to exclude
more than it reveals. For background on
Soult see Chandler, *Marshals*, pp. 456-78.
After Waterloo, Soult, as Chief of Staff,
should have rallied the troops and organized
a rearguard; instead he handed command to
Marshal Grouchy and fled, abandoning the
army and the nation. He later claimed that
he had only accepted an appointment under
Napoleon because as a soldier it was his
duty to defend France from the invader. His
actions, however, belied his words. In his
Mémoires Justicatives (pp. 9-10) written to
excuse his conduct to the Bourbons and
refute the charge of treason, he pleads: 'I am
accused of having provoked, by various
unjust and untimely measures, the discontent of the officers of the army. First: by
neglecting them in favour of officers who
are Chouans, Vendéeans or émigrés. The
court well knows that the places and favours
granted on both hands were granted by its
own orders. None knows better than I how
many French officers have not received the
pensions and places they well deserved. I
have constantly worked with the comte de
Bruges [Artois' aide] and have profited by
his intelligence. He knew my work and my
thoughts. My association with him and his
reputation should have been enough to preserve me from the reproach of "treason".
This from the man who had prosecuted
Count Exelmans for 'treason' and 'breaking
his oath' in offering his services to King
Murat.

On several occasions after Waterloo Soult
is captured by royalist bands of the 'White
Terror', but manages to escape, whereas
Marshal Brune and scores of other officers
are killed out of hand by this organized mob
of royalist witch-hunters. Marshal Ney,
General de la Bédoyère and Postmaster
Lavalette are being tried for treason and exe-
cuted, while Soult, ex-Royalist Minister of
War, Peer of the Realm, and Napoleon's
Chief of Staff, bears a charmed life. He is
even given parole by one royalist prefect and

allowed to pass into exile unmolested, by
order of Artois. No doubt, as Soult says in
his memoirs, 'He knew my work'.

Where did Soult seek asylum? At Hard-
enburg, on Prussian soil, with the approval
of the Prussian government. Not only did
they not shoot him for his part at Waterloo,
or send him back to Louis in chains, but
their police reports on him were entirely
favourable. The Bourbons allowed him to
return in 1819, and he was even granted an
audience with Louis.
22. For background on these generals see:
Chandler, *Dictionary* and *Marshals*; Haythornthwaite, *Source Book*; Horricks.
23. Napoleon designated the units of his field
army from the name of the *département* or
military district in which they were based.
He also dignified small formations with
army designations to confuse enemy intelligence sources. The reader may wonder why
Marshal Brune was given a mere 5,500 men
while General Rapp had 23,500? This will
be made clear later.
24. Gourgaud, pp. 28-9, which also lists the
fortresses.
25. Ibid.; Houssaye, *1815*, p. 21; AF IV 1936,
Davout to Napoleon 11 June. See also:
Carnot's report; Davout's report; Napoleon,
Correspondance, No. 21755, Napoleon to
Davout 23 March.
26. PRO FO Cont. 14 (private) Wellington to
Castlereagh Vienna 12 March; Webster, p.
312. This report is quoted in Wellesley, vol.
XII, p. 267, but the ciphered paragraph
about the Tsar is omitted. It appears in full
in Webster.
27. Chandler, *Waterloo*, p. 78.
28. Marshal Brune would have been well
equipped to hold the coastal strip until
Marshal Suchet reinforced him. There
would have been nothing to prevent Suchet
using the alpine pass to arrive in the rear of
the enemy, trapping him between the Alps,
the sea and Marshal Brune. Much has been
written about the 'law of numbers' – that an
Austrian army of 210,000 men would have
steam-rollered a force of 10-50,000 men,
but one should remember that this was not
the era of attritional warfare with thousands
upon thousands of men repeatedly advancing over the fallen bodies of their comrades.
The Allied commanders would never have
tolerated the losses inherent in such *modus*

operandi, not in 1814 or in 1815. Given that the number of men able to advance at any one time was limited by the width of the front, a narrow frontage rendered a huge force a logistical liability and not an asset.

29. As the defile between Basle and the Alps was only 2½ miles wide at the most, not more than 42,000 men could have deployed for attack in the conventional formations of the day. See Kennedy, p. 88 for explanation of frontages.

30. Napoleon sent many disguised officers into Belgium to acquire intelligence. The British and Hanoverians were not very familiar with the United Netherlands' new uniforms whose colours were very similar to those of the French troops, nor could they distinguish between a French-speaking Belgian and a Frenchman. See Mercer, who gives several incidences of suspected spying; also Gourgaud, pp. 29-30; and Vacheé, pp. 33-76. Espionage was an accepted practice. Napoleon, for example, wrote to Berthier on 19 July 1813, ordering him to send four wounded officers who could speak German to convalesce at Toplitz and Carlesbad; they were to be 'exceedingly clever men, to act as spies, and report everything that occurs'.

31. See Becke, *Appreciation*.

32. AF; Wellesley, vol. X, pp. 439-81 for countless references to deserters coming forward and volunteering information so misleading as to have been deliberate.

33. Chandler, *Waterloo*, p 75. For more information on Napoleon's 'manoeuvre of the central position' and all other tactics and strategy, see Chandler, *Dictionary*, and *Campaigns*. Chandler's analysis of Napoleon's techniques, based as it was on original primary sources, is the foundation of most modern interpretations.

34. Ibid., p. 75.

35. For more information on the *Grande Armée* and the role, composition and history of the Imperial Guard see Lachouque, *Anatomy*, and Elting.

36. Chandler, *Waterloo*.

11. The Road to Mont St-Jean

1. Fortescue, p. 20 fn. Fortescue's book was culled from vol. X. of his *History of the British Army*.

2. See Hamilton-Williams, *New Perspectives* for an in-depth analysis of the battle.

3. Wellesley, *Despatches*, vol. XII, p. 358, Wellington to Lord Stewart, Brussels, 8 May 1815.

4. Fortescue, p.24.

5. Hamilton-Williams, op. cit., chap. 3 *et seq.*; Fortescue, op. cit., pp. 23-40.

6. Wellesley, *Despatches*, vol. XII, p. 291.

7. Hamilton-Williams, op. cit., pp. 133-4. The role of British infantry was in the ascendancy at this time. The cavalry lacked training and experience as a consequence of the government's reluctance to release them for service abroad.

8. Hansard, vol. XXXI, pp. 223, 265, 653; George III, Statutes caps. 76, 77.

9. Hamilton-Williams, op. cit., p. 191.

10. Von Ollech, p. 14.

11. Ibid.

12. Von Ollech, p. 212.

13. PRO FO France No. 116. Wellington also wrote to Sir Charles Stuart at Ghent, defending this decision on the grounds that both he and Blücher had very raw troops, and could not advance into France and invest the fortresses without their numbers being depleted unless the Russians and Austrians co-operated.

14. Hamilton-Williams, op. cit., chap. 5, pp. 108-9ff.; but compare: Houssaye, *1815*, p. 21; AF iv 1936, Davout to Napoleon 11 June; Carnot's report 13 June; Davout's 23 June; Napoleon, *Correspondance*, No. 21755 Napoleon to Davout 23 March; Wellesley, *Despatches*, vol. XII, pp. 394-409. In his memorandum to the Allied commanders Wellington gives a complete breakdown of the French Army to the last horse ('The Gendarmerie have supplied 4,250 horses'). He states that he has received this intelligence from a reliable source. Davout and Carnot's reports are identical with Wellington's memorandum, and this identical information culled from various sources and reaching Wellington via London so rapidly means that someone on the council of ministers had access. That someone was Fouché according to his memoirs, pp. 290-1, and this is confirmed by Castlereagh, PRO FO CXCVII, 16 May 1815.

15. Unger, vol. II, p. 272.

16. Hamilton-Williams, op. cit., pp. 144-6.

17. See Hamilton-Williams 'Ney and Quatre-Bras'.

18. Soult's conduct in this regard has been dis-

missed by some authors as being due to inexperience, but a close scrutiny of orders and registers issued by him in his capacity as an independent commander and as Minister of War show this to be absurd. Deliberate or not, this was the only campaign in which Soult departed from the standard procedure, and where his order registers are incomplete.

19. General Karl von Steinmetz (1786-1877) was fighting throughout the period 1813 to 1815. His brilliant rearguard action at Charleroi and his role at Waterloo raised his reputation in the army. He was held in such awe by the army that neither Bismarck nor the Crown Prince would reprimand him. For more details about his career see Ascoli.
20. Hamilton-Williams, *Waterloo*, pp. 172-3.
21. Ibid., pp. 176-7.
22. Hamilton-Williams, *Waterloo*, pp. 178-9.
23. Napoleon, *Correspondance*, No. 22,058, Napoleon to Marshal Ney, Charleroi, 16 June 1815.
24. Hamilton-Williams, *Waterloo*, p. 188.
25. Ibid., p. 191.
26. Ibid., p. 210.
27. Ibid., p. 237, fn. 2.
28. Ibid.
29. Ibid., pp. 228-9.
30. Ibid., p. 224.
31. Ibid.
32. Napoleon, *Correspondance*, No. 22,061, reproduced in *le Moniteur*, 21 June 1815.
33. Wellesley, *Despatches*, pp. 478-84, Wellington to the Earl of Bathurst, Waterloo, 19 June.

12. The Road to St, Helena: Betrayal

1. Fouché, pp. 279-80, writes gleefully: 'Carnot, seeing that he persevered, told him, "It is in your power to have Fouché shot, but, tomorrow at the same hour, your power will have departed ... there is no time to dissemble; the men of the revolution will only suffer you to reign as long as they have security that you will respect their liberties. If you cause Fouché to be put to death by martial law, Fouché whom they consider as their strongest guarantee ... If Fouché be really guilty, you must obtain convincing proofs of it, expose him subsequently to the nation, and put him on trial according to form."'
2. Ibid., p. 283, he adds: 'Situated as I was, it was incumbent on me to neglect nothing to

preserve favour of the public opinion: I also possessed my vehicles of popularity, in my circulars and ant-royalist reports. I had just established throughout France, lieutenants of police, who were devoted to me alone; I got possession of the Journals [17 newspapers in the capital] and thus became master of public opinion. But I soon had on my hands an affair of quite different importance; the unseasonable insurrection of la Vendée ... It was incumbent on me to have the royalists on my side, but not to have them meddle with our affairs ... I easily persuaded some idiots of the royalist party, whose opinions I modelled after my own fashion, that this war of some few fanatics was unseasonable [badly timed]: that the measures which it would suggest would reproduce the reign of terror, and occasion the revolutionary party [republicans] to be let loose; it was absolutely necessary to obtain an order from the king, to cause this rabble to lay down its arms.'

3. Ibid., p. 290. There is no reason to doubt this gloating statement, and it certainly explains how Wellington was able to produce a paper identical with that of the Minister of War (Davout) in the limited time span.
4. Ibid., pp. 291-300. Fouché states that Wellington's delay in concentrating on the 16th was due to his waiting for this information. This was probably Fouché's non-military interpretation after the event, and he obviously believed it. But the delay was caused by Wellington's advance intelligence being blocked by General Dörnberg, of which Fouché had no knowledge. The statement does confirm conclusively the statements in Castlereagh and Foreign Office papers that Fouché was the Allies' 'mole'.
5. Ibid., pp. 292-5.
6. Ibid.
7. Ibid., pp. 272-3.
8. The great French historian Frédéric Masson wrote that La Fayette's agreeing to help mount a *coup d'état* was: '... a revolt against lawful authority, an outrage on the country, the most foolish and dastardly aggression against the only man who can still save the nation, the work of a man who, in the annals of his wretched life, has registered three memorable dates: 5 October 1789,

when he betrayed his King, 20 August 1792, when he deserted to the enemy, and 21 June 1815, when he overthrew Napoleon - his benefactor.' (quoted in Lachouque, *Last Days*, p. 67.).

9. *Le Moniteur*, 22 June 1815, verbatim.

10. Arch. du Service C14/20, Returns for 23-26 June; see also Bowden, pp. 331-38.

11. Atteridge, p. 331.

12. Ibid.

13. Lachouque, p. 84. Lachouque's work is somewhat partisan, but his quotations are highly accurate; see AV 1935 i 123.

14. Ibid., p. 72, quoting from La Cases, St. Helena 3 April 1816.

15. Kelly., p. 117

16. Ibid.

17. Lachouque, pp. 86-7.

18. Kelly, pp. 186-7, verbatim and *in extenso*.

19. Kerry, pp. 132-6. Flahaut had fought throughout the Napoleonic wars. He was extremely loyal to Napoleon, and his letters, honest and without bias, are a valuable source. He was an illegitimate son of Talleyrand's – whom he loathed. He had a long love affair with Hortense Beauharnais, ex-queen and Napoleon's step-daughter; their illegitimate son later became the duc de Morney. Flahaut later married the daughter of Amiral Viscount Keith. His correspondence is in the hands of his descendants in England, the family of the Marquis of Lansdowne. He was chosen by Napoleon III to join the commission to edit the massive collection of Napoleon's correspondence.

20. Ibid.

21. Macdonald, vol. III, pp. 328-30.

22. Ibid., pp. 331-2.

23. Ibid.

24. Macirone, pp. 157-200ff., app; Fouché, pp. 312-13.

25. PRO FO Cont. 21 (No. 5) 12 July 1815 Castlereagh to Liverpool; Webster, p. 342 (the brackets in Webster denote written in cipher on the original as was this message).

26. Bowood Papers, pp. 145-6, Lord Melville [First Sea Lord] to Admiral Keith, Private and Secret, 27 June 1815: 'My Lord, reports have reached His Majesty's Government from various quarters that, in the event of adverse fortune, it was the intention of Bonaparte to escape to America ... if he should wait till a frigate or sloop of war

can be fitted out for him, you may perhaps receive information of such preparation ... and intercept her.'; see also Lachouque, p.151.

27. Von Müffling, pp. 272-75; PRO FO France, No. 117, Stuart to Castlereagh 27 June: that Gneisenau had declared that '... The Duke of Wellington was held back by parliamentary considerations and by the wish to prolong the life of the villain whose career had extended England's power.' Letters written after Waterloo show clearly the mistrust and grudge that the Prussian officer corps had for Castlereagh's government, Wellington and Britain, thanks to Britain's reneging on her promises in 1814.

28. Ibid.

29. Ibid.

30. Lachouque, p. 142.

31. Wellesley, *Despatches*, vol. XII, p. 596, Wellington to Castlereagh.

32. Chandler, *Marshals*, pp. 106-10.

33. Lachouque, p. 152.

34. Kelly, p. 189.

35. Arch. du Service C/14-20; Lachouque, p. 164.

36. Kelly, pp. 193-4, *in extenso*.

37. PRO State papers, vol. II, p. 373 (Most Secret) Liverpool to Castlereagh 30 June 1815; Wellesley, *Supplementary*, vol. X, p. 630 (abbreviated); Webster, pp. 339-41 (*in extenso*).

38. Vane, vol. X, p. 419 Castlereagh to Liverpool 8 July 1815.

39. Ibid., p. 420 Castlereagh to Liverpool 12 July 1815.

40. PRO FO Cont. 21, No. 8 Castlereagh to Liverpool 14 July 1815.

41. Vane, vol. X, p. 430 Castlereagh to Liverpool 15 July 1815.

42. Ibid., p. 431.

43. PRO FO Cont. 21, No. 13 Castlereagh to Liverpool 17 July 1815.

44. Chandler, *Waterloo*, p. 199.

45. De Sauvigny, pp. 342–3.

46. Duff Cooper, pp. 270–1.

47. Kelly, pp. 245–59, interrogations and trial given verbatim *in extenso*; see also Glover who covers the life of Wilson but this episode is abridged.

48. Vane, vol. XI, p. 16 Liverpool to Castlereagh 15 September 1815.

49. Bowood Papers (MS letters of Admiral Keith) p. 154: First Sea Lord (Viscount

Melville) to Keith (Private) Admiralty 24
July 1815.

50. Ibid., p. 162: Keith to Miss Elphinstone 30
July 1815.

51. Ibid., pp. 171–3: Keith to Melville 7 August
1815.

52. Ibid., Keith to Lady Keith *Tonnant* 5
August 1815. Mackenrot wrote to the
Empress Marie-Louise on 31 August 1815,
explaining what the trio had tried to do.
Marie-Louise handed the letter to Prince
Metternich who sent it to Castlereagh; he
had Mackenrot charged with 'criminal
fraud' but the jury to the chagrin of the
judge acquitted him. He was re-arrested,
brought before the Board of Lunacy (whose
members were government appointees) and
committed to the 'Bedlam' hospital for the
criminally insane until 1821, when
Napoleon died.

53. Ibid., Keith to Miss Elphinstone off the
Eddystone 5 August 1815.

54. Lachouque, pp. 276–7.

55. Ibid., p. 275.

13. The Road to Glory

1. Chandler, *Dictionary*, pp. 285-6; Palmer, p.
184. For Commission see Arch. Serv. Hist.
C/14, March 1815, first restoration folio.

2. Larochejaquelein, pp. 504-35; Macdonald,
p. 329. For evidence of Napoleon's murder
see Forshufvud, *Enquête* and *Who Killed
Napoleon?*; Forshufvud and Weider; Weider
and Hapgood, pp. 134-228; Warren, in
Nature magazine, No. 192, 1961, pp. 103-
5.

3. Rosebery, p. 217.

4. Ibid., p. 219; BL Add. MS 37867.

5. Kelly, pp. 265-6, Bathurst's provisional list
of instructions (verbatim), War Office, 30
July 1815.

6. Rosebery, pp. 130-40. Of a plethora of
works on Napoleon at St. Helena, I find
Rosebery's the least biased and most factual,
but, having been Under-Secretary of State
for Home Affairs, Foreign Secretary and
Prime Minister, he had access to State
papers denied or unknown to other historians. Of Liverpool's attitude to Napoleon's
surrender he says: 'The option as it presented itself apparently to Lord Liverpool at
that time was, that Napoleon might be
handed over to Louis XVIII, as being
beyond the pale of humanity and to be

treated as vermin.' (*Napoleon*, pp. 102-3.)
From State papers he quotes Liverpool writing to Castlereagh: 'We wish that the King
of France would hang or shoot Buonaparte,
as the best termination of the Business.' (p.
103.) Rosebery was rebuked for his apparent criticism of the government of the day
by Professor Holland Rose (*Life*, vol. II, p.
484, fn.).

7. Ibid., p. 131.

8. Rose, vol. II, p. 506.

9. PRO Colonial Office, St. Helena, No. 4,
reports from Bourbon Spanish Ambassador
in Washington to Madrid, copy sent to
London. This concoction was the work of
the notable Hyde de Neuville who spent fifteen years as Artois' secret agent, *Mémoires*,
vol. II, pp. 79-99: 'On the 27th of this
month through an incident which seems
almost miraculous ... I obtained irrefutable
proof – such as would convince a court of
law – of a plot woven by some [French-
American] refugees ... As a Minister of
France I at once requested an audience of
the Federal authorities ... I am sending to
New Orleans; and the Spanish Minster, to
whom I have given information of this
plot.' (pp. 95-6.) This report is about the
'third hand' account of a supposed landing
by 300 men dressed in British uniforms
from a boat commanded by an ex-French
officer named Fournier. This, he admits,
was 'only a rumour' supplied by a French
Bourbon Commissioner. Letters Nos. 5 and
6 likewise talk about *émigrés* using a submarine vessel originating from Rio Janiero. See
PRO St. Helena files; Rosebery, pp. 165-6.
These fabricated reports, at best wishful
thinking, certainly appear to have arrived
together at a convenient time for Bathurst,
enabling him to push through a Bill legaliz-
ing Napoleon's detention and empowering
him to adopt Draconian measures for his
treatment.

10. Rosebery, p. 169.

11. Ibid., p. 188.

12. Ibid., p. 189.

13. Ibid., p. 162.

14. Ibid., pp. 159-61.

15. PRO St. Helena, No. 5, Hudson Lowe to
Bathurst; Rosebery, p. 121 (verbatim);
Rose, vol. II, p.510.

16. BL Add. MS 34992, d'Auvergne; BL Add.
MS 38769, Armand de Chateaubriand to

Guyon St. Loyal, 12 February 1795: 'You will offer M. de Ferté three of your best blanc [wine] and also ask if he would prefer some of the rouge. Only if he rejects the rouge, saying he only favours the blanc, will you then pass them to him in trinity. He will reply with the esprit [spirit].' There are many more examples, using flowers, *assignats* (bank notes), etc. See also Appendix II.

17. Rosebery, pp. 219-20 (verbatim).

18. Porch, p. 11. Dr Porch's book, a unique analysis of the French Army from the time of Napoleon I to that of Napoleon III, has a wealth of detail concerning the continual conspiracies and royalist secret societies rife within the army.

19. The British Government had long used the punishment of transportation to the colonies as a profitable enterprise: at a stroke ridding itself of the expense of housing felons, and exporting cheap labour for a price. With the loss of America, convicted persons were sent to Australia, a total of 21,834 being deported during the 21 years from 1793 to 1815. During the nine years from 1816 to 1825, 78,400 men and women were transported (PRO Privy Council Papers 1/67- 92, 1816-1844, letters and petitions from convicts and families, etc.). Fears of 'radical' revolution resulted in the formation of the Metropolitan Police. Unrest in the wake of the Corn Laws prompted the suspension of Habeas Corpus, and the notorious 'Six Acts' gave the agricultural squirearchy, most of whom were magistrates, swingeing powers. Then, as now, a magistrate's court had no jury, and a local malcontent hauled up on the pretext of being 'suspected of theft' could be found guilty 'on probability' and sentenced to transportation without any right of appeal. To this day at Dorchester in Dorset, the small cattle bridge bears a notice: 'Anyone found damaging this bridge, in any manner, will be liable for Transportation for Life. 1820.' (Damage would include the writing of political slogans!)

20. Weider and Hapgood, p. 150. Weider has compared the daily journals of the people around Napoleon at his death. Sten Forshufvud's comments on each, and his detailed forensic explanations are indisputable. For the scientific evidence which shows beyond doubt that Napoleon had been poisoned by arsenic see Forshufvud and Weider. The author accepts unreservedly the findings of these books. Having spent ten years in researching the period and the comte d'Artois' *modus operandi*, the hallmark is clear. Artois was ready to eliminate anyone without compunction, and his state of mind after the death of his son and the attempted assassination of his son's widow and the child she was carrying can be imagined.

21. PRO FO St. Helena, No. 1, Admiral Cockburn to Bathurst, 12 January 1816; Rose, vol. II, p. 502.

22. Weider and Hapgood, p. 162.

23. PRO HD/17 1742-1792: Papers concerning Secret Office of GPO; memorandum concerning its activities. This clandestine government operation to examine all foreign and internal mail of prominent officials and personages continued until the 'Mazzini affair' of 1844. Lord Palmerston closed the operation in 1847. In reply to the chief of the department concerned, William Bode, who wrote asking 'What shall I do with all my brass dies?' (the seals of foreign princelings, etc., accumulated since 1732) Palmerston wrote: 'Melt them down.'

24. Weider and Hapgood, pp. 191-227.

25. Ibid., p. 36.

26. Ibid., p. 211.

27. Ibid., p. 217.

28. Ibid.

29. Ibid., p. 218.

30. PRO FO St. Helena, No. 18, Hudson Lowe to Bathurst, 5 May 1821, medical reports appended.

31. Rosebery, p. 127.

32. Ibid., pp. 127-8.

33. *Chamber's Biographical Dictionary*, p. 252.

34. Godechot, pp. 395-424.

Epilogue: The Last Road

1. Arsenic had long been used by medical practitioners and scientists to preserve specimens. The arsenic administered to Napoleon over a period of years had been absorbed into the tissues, and thus preserved his body. Had it been otherwise, or if he had died of cancer, nineteen years in the soil of St. Helena would have resulted in decomposition.

Appendix I. The Treaty of Fontainebleau, 1814

1. Hansard, vol. XXX, p. 376. Castlereagh however omitted certain passages to Parliament. See Webster, pp. 175-6 and footnotes; Nicolson, pp. 90-5. For the original text see: Napoleon, *Correspondance*, No. 22789.
2. PRO FO Cont. 4, No. 45, Castlereagh to Liverpool, Paris 13 April 1814; Vane, vol. IX, p. 472.
3. Ibid.
4. *Le Moniteur*, 21 April 1815; Kelly, pp. 3-7.
5. Yet again Napoleon's intelligence was correct. One sees from this statement that he was quite aware that Artois had arranged the murder attempts at Orgon and on Elba, which charge is reiterated in his Will.

Appendix II. The Royalist Underground and the Chevaliers de la Foi

1. Balleine, p. 41.
2. BL Add. MS 37857, Chateaubriand's instructions from the prince de Bouillon 1794; BL Add. MS 38769, Armand Chateaubriand to de Gouyon de St. Loyal, 1795.
3. Eighteen British printers turned out one million assignats (French banknotes) per day, bales of which were sent to France by d'Auvergne to destabilize the economy. See Balleine, pp. 73-4; BL Add. MS 37863, d'Auvergne to Dundas, 1795. D'Auvergne mentions one delivery of several hundred: 'Two million assignats were landed yesterday night on the coast of Brittany.'
4. Fauche-Borel, vol. I, pp. 24-6.
5. ANF F7 6241, Police dossier on Veyrat.
6. ANF F7 6468, Police Dossier on Perlet.
7. When writing his biography of Montgaillard, the author Lacroix was obviously unaware of his role as informant to first the republican and then the imperial police, and that the police had a dossier on him together with his letters. See ANF F7 6431 for his dossier which includes his letter betraying General Pichegru to 'General Buonaparte'. But the proof that he had carried out this work, and later had written abusive pamphlets against Louis XVIII, on d'Artois' orders, to show his loyalty to Napoleon's regime, is clearly shown by his shaking hands with the restored King and his brother in Paris in 1814, with the remark: 'Your Majesty has too much sense of humour not to have misunderstood me.' (Lenotre, p. 210).
8. BL Add. MS 38769, 11 September 1800, d'Auvergne to the Treasury, receipts for bills for the Secret Service: 'One half-ton of powder for M. Cadoudal.'
9. Fauche-Borel was taken to the Temple prison on 7 July 1802 (the register shows 18 Messidor, Year X).
10. This 'mild' torture was allowed by the Revolutionary and Napoleonic administration to assist interrogation. Dreadful though it might seem to us, it was trivial compared to that employed under the previous Bourbon legal system, when any common suspect could be put to the 'ordinary' examination, which consisted of four wooden wedges being hammered into the poor wretch's ankles and knees, one at a time, while he was being questioned by the clerk of the court. If this failed (usually because of the victim losing consciousness!), the 'extraordinary' could be applied, which repeated the process, the wedges being applied again in the holes already made. This torture was not allowed to be used on the nobility or the clergy. Similarly, the guillotine was seen by many Britons as an instrument of terror, which patently it was not. It had been designed to kill as swiftly and 'humanely' as possible. Until the Revolution, the Bourbons' death penalty involved the condemned being broken on the wheel: first tied to an iron frame shaped like a St. Andrew's cross, and every bone in his body broken by blows of an iron rod, and then left to expire. (See Manceron, *Men of Liberty*, pp. 412-22.).
11. Anon. *The Paris Imprisonment*, pp. 4ff.
12. Ibid.
13. Liverpool's letter, quoted in Balleine, pp. 101-2.
14. Ibid.
15. See *Alliance des Jacobins*.
16. Bertier de Sauvigny, *Un type d'ultra-royaliste*. Professor Bertier de Sauvigny presents the most informed account of the Chevaliers and ultras, from an insider's viewpoint, but his book was based on his ancestor's papers. Not having had access to the d'Auvergne and Chateaubriand papers in the British Museum Library, he assumed that his ancestor had started the organization some time between 1807 and 1810. See also Suther-

land, pp. 425ff.

17. Sutherland, p. 363. Dr. Sutherland points out that when discussing projects for Napoleon's assassination, the British Cabinet rarely objected on the grounds of moral principles, but merely on the impracticability of various plans.

18. ANF F7 63194, Fauche-Borel's police file. Desmarest had written on it: '26 Prairal year XII (June 15 1804) – Wants to be employed as a spy'.

19. Ibid. Letter to Desmarest informing him of Louis' speech. Fauche-Borel had 10,000 copies the size of a playing-card printed in Berlin and sold them. He sent some to friends and prominent people in France, condemning them in the process. Desmarest confiscated as many as possible. Their origin was traced to Fauche-Borel by a letter enclosed with one, and this letter can be seen in the police file.

20. Lenotre, pp. 105-7.

21. Ibid, pp. 141ff. for an account of Ensign Charles Vitel's mission and subsequent interrogation and death .

22. ANF F7 63194 for Vitel's police dossier.

23. Lenotre, pp. 190-2.

24. Veyrat usually had one or two of his victim's relations arrested and threatened to have them shot unless he complied. This use of hostages was approved of and used by Napoleon, see Balleine, pp. 117-18.

25. Pasquier, vol. II, pp. 388-9.

26. ANF F7 3786, Bulletin de Police 19 October 1815.

27. Ibid., 27 and 30 August 1815.

28. Ibid.

29. ANF F7 9248, comprising two bound registers of the judicial inquiry instigated by Madame Brune in 1819. See also Resnick, pp. 18-19. Resnick's study on the Bourbon Terror is the best to-date, but he had no knowledge of the British State Papers cited in the narrative or of the d'Auvergne Papers in the British Library, and the Société Jersiase Manuscripts.

30. For an example of the way d'Artois used his Verdets see the murder of General Ramel in Resnick, pp. 31-2.

31. Bertier, *French Politics*, vol. IX, pp. 344-9.

BIBLIOGRAPHY

MANUSCRIPT SOURCES

France

ARCHIVES NATIONALES
[AF] IV 906, 990B, 1047, 1100, 1147, 1186,
1588, 1670, 1688
AF3; AF4; AF 5; AF7 (Consulate, Imperial
Security and general police files)
AF19
AF VI (minutes, acts and decrees)
R1408-10, K555/8 (affairs of comte d'Artois)
314 AP (Archives Privées) General Baron Gour-
gaud's papers

ARCHIVES DE LA GUERRE
C/2, 184, 185, 186, 187
C/15 1-6, C/16 1-23, C/17 192-3
C/7 185
ARCHIVES DEPARTMENTALES DE LA MARNE

M-28, M-43, M-233, M-201-19, 574/21

ARCHIVES DES AFFAIRES ETRANGERES (QUAI
D'ORSAY)
FR.1805 (reports of de Gros and Montchenu,
with various
correspondence germane to the exhumation of
the Emperors' remains)
Fonds Bourbon: vols. 88, 623-47
BIBLIOTHEQUE NATIONALE
Fonds français 6645 (Napoleon's captivity)
BIBLIOTHEQUE DE L'ARSENAL
MSS 395-8, 4546 (documents and letters of the
comte d'Artois)

Great Britain
THE ROYAL ARCHIVES

Papers of: King George III; King George IV
(Prince Regent);
HRH The Duke of Cambridge; HRH The
Duke of Sussex; HRH The Duke of York
PUBLIC RECORD OFFICE
Audit Office Papers
AO 1/2121 (declared accounts, Secret Service,
1779-1801)

AO 3/949 (various accounts, Secret Service
1779-1837)
Foreign Office
FO 7 Austria
FO 29 (The Army in Germany)
FO 33 (Hanseatic towns (Hamburg))
FO 37 (Kingdom Of Holland and The United
Netherlands)
FO 63 (Portugal)
FO 64 (Prussia)
FO 65 (Russia)
FO 67 (Sardinia)
FO 70 (Sicily and Naples)
FO 72 (Spain)
FO 73 (Sweden)
FO 74, series 1 (Switzerland)
FO 83 (Great Britain)
FO 92 (Continent (Treaties))
FO 93 (Protocol and Treaties)
FO 94 (Ratification of Treaties)
FO 97 (Supplements, general correspondence)
FO 120 (Embassy and Consular Archives (Aus-
trian correspondence))
FO 139 (Continent, correspondence)
FO HD 1-3 1791-1827, (Receipts, affidavits,
etc., relating to expenditure of 'the secret
[service] vote abroad')
FO HD 17 (Papers concerning Secret Office of
the GPO)

HOME OFFICE
HO 1/1-3 (Correspondence with *émigrés*)
HO 5/1-3 (Correspondence with groups 1794-8
Criminal)
HO 10/1-15 (Convicts transported to New
South Wales and Tasmania 1788-1821
(sexes, general muster, embarkation))
HO 13/9-35 (Correspondence and Warrants)
HO 16/1-4 (Returns of convicted prisoners)
HO 40/1-16 (Disturbances (internal), Luddite
riots, military reports, misc. correspondence
relative to the disturbances, including Peter-
loo)
HO 42/24-202 (George III letters and papers)
HO 50/6-15 (Commander-in-Chief (Military),
1797-1822 correspondence)
HO 50/17-39 (Militia)

333

HO 50/40-56 (Volunteers)
HO 50/57-462 (Internal defence, county correspondence)
HO 64/1/2 (Rewards, Pardons and Secret Service correspondence)
HO 69 The Bouillon Papers (Vice-Admiral Philippe d'Auvergne, prince de Bouillon)
HO 98/30-37 (Channel Islands correspondence)

PRIVY COUNCIL PAPERS
PC 1/37 (depositions of Irish officers captured at Fishguard)

WAR OFFICE
WO 1 In-letters:
WO 1/388-92 (French royalists, 1793-1800)
WO 1/663 (Correspondence, 1795-9)
WO 1/746 (Correspondence with Foreign Office, 1796-7)
WO 2 Out-letters

ADMIRALTY
Adm 52 (Masters' logs)
Secretary, In-letters: vols. 5-18, 121-59, 407-31, 534-76, 608-11, 817, 4353-61 (Secret)
Secretary, Out-papers: vols. 143-66 (Orders and instructions)

TREASURY
Ty 1 Treasury Board Papers
Ty 29 Minute Books
Ty Warrant Books

WALES
28 190 Treason Papers relating to the French Invasion

PRIVATE PAPERS
Bathurst Papers (NB. Those relating to Napoleon are reproduced by the Historical Manuscript Commission: 'Report on the manuscripts of the Earl Bathurst preserved at Cirencester Park.' HMSO,1923)
Chatham MS Papers 30/8
Dropmore papers (MS J. B. Fortescue, Hist. MS Commission)
Granville MS Papers 30/29
MS 1801 Journal of Vice-Admiral Nelson
Lord Castlereagh's Correspondence
Dublin Castle MS Papers

BRITISH (MUSEUM) LIBRARY
Aberdeen Papers (43073-43079)

D'Auvergne Papers (35200, 34992, 7988-9, 15945, 19346, 37857-868, 37860, 38769)
Armand Chateaubriand Papers (37857, 38769)
François Chateaubriand Papers (35653)
Drake Papers (46822, 46825, 46828-9, 46831-6)
Liverpool Papers (38248-261, 38325-326)
Grenville Papers (418-420 58)
Puisaye Papers (8074, C III)
Siborne Papers (34703-8)
Vansittart Papers (31230-231, 31236)
Wellesley Papers (37286-37288, 37292-294, 37310-37415)
Windham Papers (37844-846, 37859-863, 37875-876, 37903)

Russia

STATE ARCHIVES MOSCOW
State Papers vol. XXIX (Tsar Alexander I and the Vienna Congress) 122 vols. 1953–71

Italy

ARCHIVO SEGRETO VATICANO
Vat/Nap/1827 (Rapporti del Ministro di Polizia Napoletano ed altri documenti officiali (sulla morte del Murat a Pizzo) Police reports for Naples and Rome, 1815

Austria

KRIEGSARCHIV WEIN:
Feldakten (1813), Hofkriegsrat (1814), Militärischer Nachlässe Kaiser Franz I, B/473, Nachlässe Mack B/573, Radetsky A/1
Landeshauptstadt Wein – Diplomatic

Germany
NIEDERSCHERSISCHES HAUPTSTAATSARCHIV HANNOVER
Baring MS
Dornberg MS
Guelphic MS
Notizen MS
Wynecken MS
General Commando MS
Ak. Hann. 38D, 18, 22, 99-137, 188, 200, 230-47, 297
Ak. Hann. 41. XXI. Nr. 150-6
Ak. Hann. 48A. 100-30
BRAUNSWISCHWEIGISCHES LANDESMUSEUM HANNOVER
Lübeck MS

The Netherlands

THE ROYAL ARCHIVES
Papers of King William I
Papers of King William II (Prince of Orange, 1815)

PUBLISHED BOOKS

Abrantes, Laure Duchesse d'. *Mémoires*. Paris, 1831

Acton, Harold. *The Bourbons of Naples*. London, 1956

Aerts, W. *Waterloo: opérations de l'armée Prussienne du Bas-Rhin*. Brussels, 1908

Albemarle, Lord. *Fifty Years of my Life*. London, 1876

Alexander, Tsar. *Politics and Diplomacy*. St. Petersburg, 1892

Alison, Sir A. *History of Europe*. ((From the Revolution to the Restoration of the Bourbons) 14 vols., Edinburgh, 1860

Ambrosio, A. d'. *La campagne de Murat en 1815*. Paris, 1899

Anon (an officer of field rank). *Memoirs of the Invasion of France by the Allied Armies, and of the Last Six Months of the Reign of Napoleon, etc*. London, 1834

Anon. *Campagne des Autrichiens contre Murat en 1815. Précédée d'un coup d'oeil sur les négociations secrètes qui eurent lieu à Naples depuis la Paix de Paris*. 2 vols., Brussels, 1821

Anon. *The Paris Imprisonment. The Case of Philippe d'Auvergne, Duke of Bouillon, a Captain in His Majesty's Navy*. London, 1803

Antommarchi, F. Derniers Moments de Napoléon, 2 vols., London, 1825

Artom, Guido. *Napoleon is dead in Russia*. London, 1970

Ascoli, David. *A Day of Battle*. London, 1989

Atteridge, A. H. *Marshal Murat King of Naples*. London, 1911

— *Marshal Ney: The Bravest of the Brave*. London, 1912

Avout, Vicomte A. d'. *L'Infanterie de la Garde à Waterloo*. Paris, 1905

Bailleu, P. (ed.). *Briefwechsel Königs von Pruessen Willhelm III und der Königin Luise mit Kaiser Alexander I*. Leipzig, 1900

Bainville, Jacques. *Napoleon*. London, 1938

Balleine, Revd. G. R. *The Tragedy of Philippe d'Auvergne*. London, 1973

Balmain, comte de. 'Les prisonniers de Saite-Hélène' in *Revue Bleue*, 8 May – 12 June 1897; Abr. English tr. Napoleon in Captivity, London, 1927

Bas, F. de, and T'Serclas, de Wormerson, J. de. *La Campagne de 1815 aux Pays-Bas d'après les rapports officiels néerlandais*. 1908

Batty, R. *An Historical Sketch of the Campaign of 1815*. London, 1820

Baudus, *Etudes sur Napoléon par le Lieutenant-colonel de Baudus*. 2 vols., Paris, n.d.

Beach, V. W. *Charles X: His Life and Times*. University of Colorado Press, 1971

Beamish, N. L. *A History of the King's German Legion, 1807-16*. 2 vols., London, 1837

Beauharnais, Eugène de. *Mémoires et correspondance politique et militaire du prince Eugène, annotés et mis en ordre par A. du Casse*. 10 vols., Lévy, Paris, 1858–60

Beauvais, General (ed.). *Napoléon: les princes, les ministres et les généraux français et étrangers, etc., etc*. 7 vols., Paris, 1819-20

Béchu, Marcel. *Murat: Chevalier, Maréchal de France, Prince et Roi*. Paris, 1934

Becke, Captain A. F. *Napoleon and Waterloo*. 2 vols., London, 1914

— 'Waterloo: An Appreciation of the Situation from the point of view of a French Staff Officer, on June 1st, 1815' in *United Services Magazine*, vol. XXXXVI, No. 541, 1908

Belliard, comte. *Mémoires*. 3 vols., Paris, 1842

Bernardy, Françoise de. *Son of Talleyrand: The Life of Comte Charles de Flahaut, 1785–1870*, tr. Lucy Norton. London, 1956

Bernhardi, V. *Denkwürdigkeiten von Toll*. 5 vols., Leipzig, n. d.

Berthier, General L. A. *The French Expedition to Syria*. London, 1799

— *Registre d'ordres du Maréchal Berthier pendant la campagne de 1813*. 2 vols., Paris, 1900

Bertier de Sauvigny, Professor Guillaume de. *The Bourbon Restoration*, tr. Lynn Case, Philadelphia, 1966

— *French Politics, 1814-47. The New Cambridge Modern History*, vol. IX, London 1988.

— *Un type d'ultra-royaliste: le comte Ferdinand de Bertier (1782-1864) et l'énigme de la Congrégation*. Paris, 1948

Berton, Maréchal de Camp, J. B. *Observations militaires et critiques sur le précis des batailles de Fleurus et de Waterloo.* Utrecht, 1819

Bertrand, comte Henri Gratien. *Cahiers de Saite-Hélène, Jurnal, 1817–17. Janvier–Mai, 1821.* Manuscrit déchiffré et annoté par Paul Fleuriot de Langle, 3 vols., Paris, 1949–59

Biot, Colonel. *Souvenirs ... du Colonel Biot, aide-de-camp du Général Pajol.* Paris, 1901

Bodart, Gaston. *Militaer-Historisches Kreigs-Lexikon 1618-1905.* Vienna, 1908

Bogdanovitch, M. *A History of the reign of Alexander I and of his Times.* 6 vols., St. Petersburg, 1869-71

Boulger, D. *The Belgians at Waterloo.* London, 1901

Bosch-Kemper, de. *Staatkundige geschiendenis van Nederland, 1795–1814.* Amsterdam, 1867

Bowden, S. *Armies at Waterloo.* Texas, 1983

Boylan, Henry. *Theobald Wolfe Tone.* Dublin, 1981

Brett-James, A. *Europe against Napoleon.* London, 1970

— *The Hundred Days.* London, 1964

Brotonne, L. (ed.). *Lettres inéditées de Napoléon I.* Paris, 1898

Brunn, Geoffrey. *Europe and the French Imperium, 1799-1814.* London, 1939

Cadoudal, G. de. *Georges Cadoucal et la Chouannerie.* Paris, 1887

Cantile, Lieutenant-General Sir N. *A History of the Army Medical Department.* London, 1974

Casse, Albert du. *Le général Vandamme et sa correspondance.* 2 vols., Paris, 1870

Caulaincourt, A-A. marquis de, duc de Vicence. *Mémoires.* 3 vols., Paris, 1933

Chair, S. de (ed.). *Napoleon's Memoirs.* London, 1948

Chandler, David G. *The Campaigns of Napoleon.* 5th edn., London, 1978

— *Dictionary of the Napoleonic Wars.* Arms & Armour Press, London, 1979

— *Napoleon's Marshals.* London, 1987

— *Waterloo: The Hundred Days.* London, 1980

Charras, J. B. *Histoire de la Campagne de 1815.* Brussels, 1857

Chesney, Lieutenant-Colonel Charles. *A study of the Campaign of 1815.* London, 1868

Chritchley, T. A. *A History of the Police in England and Wales.* London, 1979

Clausewitz, Carl von. *Hinterlassene Werke über Krieg und Kriesfuehrueng, der Feldzug von 1815 in Frankreich.* Berlin, 1862

— *Nachrichten über Preussen in seiner grossen Katastrophe.* Berlin, 1839

Coignet, Captain Jean-Roche, *Notebooks.* London, 1928

Cole, Hubert. *The Betrayers: Joachim and Caroline Murat.* London, 1972

Colleta, Pietro. *Opere Inedite o Rare.* 2 vols., Naples, 1861

— *Storia della campagna d'Italia del 1815.* Turin, 1847

Colomb, E. von. *Blücher in Briefen aus den Feldzuegen.* Stuttgart, 1876

Constant Rebeque, Baron de. *Mémoires sur les cent jours.* Paris, 1820

Costello, E. *Adventures of a Soldier.* London, 1852

Costin, W. C. and Watson, J. S. *The Law and Working of the Constitution: Documents, 1660–1914.* vol. II, London, 1964

Dalton, Charles. *The Waterloo Rollcall.* London, 1904

Dante Alighieri. *La Campagne Murattiana della Indepensenza d'Italia.* Rome, 1911

Davies, Catherine. *Eleven Years' Residence in the Family of Murat, King of Naples.* London, 1841

Davout, Marshal N. *Correspondance inédité 1790–1815.* Ed. by marquise de Blocqueville, 4 vols., Paris, 1885

De Lancey, Lady. *A Week at Waterloo,* ed. Major B. R. Ward, London, 1906

Delderfield, R. F. *Imperial Sunset.* London, 1968

Desmarest, Pierre-Marie. *Quinze ans de haute police sous le Consulat et l'Empire.* Paris, 1828, repr. 1900

Dito, Oreste. *La Campagna Murattiana dell' independenza d'Italia; con un' appendice sulla morte del Murat a Pizzo.* Rome, 1911

Drouet, Jean-Baptiste, comte d'Erlon. *Vie Militaire,* Paris, 1844

Duff Cooper, Alfred. *Talleyrand.* London, 1932

Dumaine, J. *Napoléon à Waterloo....* Paris, 1866

Dumas, Général comte de. *Souvenirs 1770–1836.* Ed. by his son, 3 vols., Paris, 1839

Duthilt, Capitaine. *Mémoires.* Lille, 1909

Elliot, Marianne. *Partners in Revolution: The United Irishmen and France.* Yale University Press, 1982

Elmer, A. *L'Agent secret de Napoléon, Charles-Louis Schulmeister: d'après les archives secrètes de la maison d'Autriche.* Paris, 1932

336

Elting, John R. *Swords Around A Throne*. London, 1989

Emsley, C. *Policing and its Context, 1750–1870*. London, 1983

Espitalier, Albert. *Napoleon and King Murat*. London, 1912

Fauche-Borel, Louis. *Mémoires de Fauche-Borel*. 4 vols., Paris, 1828

Fisher, H. A. L. *The First Restoration 1814-1815*. Cambridge Modern History. vol. IX, 1906

— *Studies in Napoleonic Statesmanship: Germany*. Oxford, 1903

Fitzpatrick, W. J. *Secret Service Under Pitt*. London, 1892

Foord, Archibald S. *His Majesty's Opposition, 1714-1830*. Oxford University Press, 1964

Forshufvud, Sten. *Napoléon a-t-il été Empoisonné? Une Enquête Judiciare*. Paris, 1962

— *Who Killed Napoleon?* London, 1962

Forshufvud, Sten, and Weider, Ben. *Assassination at St. Helena*. Vancouver, 1978

Fortescue, Sir John. *The Campaign of Waterloo*. London, 1987

Fouché, J. *Memoirs of Joseph Fouché, Duke of Otranto*. 2 vols., London, 1892

Fournier, August. *Der Kongress von Châtillon*. Leipzig and Vienna, 1900

Foy, General M. S. *A History of the Peninsula under Napoleon*. London, 1829

François, Captain Charles. *From Valmy to Waterloo*. London, 1906

Frazer, E. *The War Drama of the Eagles*. London, 1912

Friedrich, Rudolf. *Geschichte des Herbstfeldzuges, 1813*. 9 vols., Berlin, 1903-9

Gallagher, J. G. *The Iron Marshal*. Illinois, 1976

Gallatin, Count (ed.). *The Diary of James Gallatin*. New York, 1920

Gamot, M. (Officier de la Légion d'honneur et ancien préfet). *Refutation: En ce qui concerne le Maréchal Ney, de l'ouvrage ayant pour titre; 'Campagne de 1815, ou Relation des opérations militaires qui ont eu lieu pendant les cent jours, par le Général Gourgaud, écrite Sainte-Hélène'*. Paris, 1818 (suppressed by Napoleon III)

Garnier, Jean-Paul. *Murat, roi de Naples*. Paris, 1959

Gates, Dr D. *The Spanish Ulcer: a History of the Peninsular War*. London, 1986

Geyl, Pieter. *Napoleon: For and Against*. London, 1949

Gilmour, Sir Ian. *Riots, Risings and Revolution*. London, 1992

Girot, J. (ed.). *Vie Militaire du Général Foy*. Paris, 1900

Glover, M. *A Very Slippery Fellow: The Life of Sir Robert Wilson*. Oxford University Press, 1977

Godechot, Jacques. *Napoléon: le Mémorial des Siècles*. Paris, 1969

Godechot, Jacques, *et alii*. *The Napoleonic Era in Europe*. New York, 1971

Gomm, W. M. *Letters and Journals of Field Marshal Sir William M. Gomm*. London, 1881

Gore, J. (ed.). *The Creevey Papers*. London, 1963

Gourgaud, General. *The Campaign of 1815*. London, 1818

— *Sainte-Hélène: Journal inédit de 1815 à 1818*, 2 vols., Paris, 1889

Griess, Thomas E. (ed.). *The Wars of Napoleon*. West Point Military History Series, New Jersey, 1985

— *Atlas for the Wars of Napoleon*. West Point Military Series, New Jersey, 1986

Griewank, K. *Leben Thaten und Charakter des Fuersten Blücher von Walstadt, ein Buch für Deutschlands Volk und Heer*. Leipzig, 1836

Griffith, P. *Forward into Battle*. Swindon, 1990

— *Military thought in the French Army, 1815-1851*. Manchester University Press, 1989

Gronow, Captain. *The Reminiscences and Recollections of Captain Gronow, being Anecdotes of the Camp, the Court and the Clubs, and Society, to the close of the last war with France*. 1862, reprinted London, 1900

Grouchy, Emmanuel, Marquis de. *Mémoires du Maréchal de Grouchy*. 5 vols., Paris, 1873–4

— *Observations sur la relation de la campagne de 1815, publiée par le général, et réfutation de quelques unes des assertions d'autres écrites relatives à la bataille de Waterloo*. Philadelphia, 1818

Guedalla, Philip. *The Duke*. London, 1931

— *The Hundred Days*. London, 1934

Gulick, Professor E. V. *The Final Coalition and the Congress of Vienna, 1813-15*. New Cambridge Modern History. London, 1981

Guy, J. (ed.). *The Road to Waterloo*. London, 1990

Hales, E. E. Y. *Napoleon and the Pope*. London, 1962

Hall, Angus (ed.). *Memoirs of Prince Talleyrand*. 5 vols., London, 1892

Hall, Sir John. *General Pichegru's Treason*. London, 1915

Hamel, E. *Histoire des deux conspirations du général Malet*. Paris, 1873

Hamilton-Williams, David. 'Captain William Siborne' in *Journal of the Society for Historical Research*, vol. LXVI, No. 266, 1985

— 'Ney and Quatre-Bras: A New Appraisal' in *The Bulletin*, The Military Historical Society, vol. XXXIX, 1987

— Waterloo: *New Perspectives –The Great Battle Reappraised*. Arms and Armour Press, London, 1993

Handel. M. I. (ed.). *Clausewitz and Modern Strategy*. New Jersey, 1986

Haswell, C. J. D. *The First Respectable Spy: The Life and Times of Colquhoun Grant, Wellington's Head of Intelligence*. London, 1969

Hayman, Peter. *Soult: Napoleon's Maligned Marshal*. London, 1990

Haythornthwaite, Philip J. *The French Revolutionary Wars, 1789–1802*. Dorset, 1981

— *The Napoleonic Source Book*. Arms and Armour Press, London, 1990

— *Napoleon's Campaigns in Italy*, London, 1993

— *Napoleon's Military Machine*. Tunbridge Wells, 1988

— *Nelson's Navy*. London, 1993

— *Wellington's Military Machine*. Tunbridge Wells, 1989

Heijn, Dr Vico Vels, Waterloo: *Glorie zonder helden*. Amsterdam, 1990

Henderson, Ernest. *Blücher and the Uprising against Napoleon*. London, 1911

Herold, J. C. *The Battle of Waterloo*. London, 1967

— *Bonaparte in Egypt*. London, 1963

Hill, G. *The War of the Vendée*. London, 1930

Hittle, Colonel J. D. *The Military Staff, its History and Developments*. Harrisburg, PA, 1952

Horricks, R. *In Flight with the Eagle*. Tunbridge Wells, 1988

— *Marshal Ney – The Romance and the Real.*Tunbridge Wells, 1982

Horsetzky, General A. von. *Historical Review of the Chief Campaigns in Europe 1792*. Vienna, 1909

Houssaye, Henri. *1814*. Paris, 1888; London, 1914.

— *1815*. 3 vols., Paris, 1903; London, 1914

Howarth, T. E. B. *The Life of Louis-Philippe, Citizen King*. London, 1961

Hughes, Major-General B. P. *Firepower*. London, 1974

— *Open Fire!* London, 1983

Hyde de Neuville, J. G. *Mémoires*, tr. F. Jackson, 2 vols., London, 1914

James, Lieutenant-Colonel W. H. *The Campaign of 1815 Chiefly in Flanders*. London, 1908

Johnston, R. M. *The Napoleonic Empire in Southern Italy*. London, 1904

Jomini, Baron de. *The Political and Military History of the Campaign of Waterloo*, tr. S. V. Benet, New York, 1862

Jones, Commander E. H. *The Last Invasion of Britain*. University of Wales Press, 1950 .

Jonge, Alex de (tr.). *Napoleon's last Will and Testament*. New York and London, 1977

Kelly, Christopher. *The Memorable Battle of Waterloo, etc*. London, 1817

Kennedy, Sir James Shaw. *Notes on the Battle of Waterloo*. London, 1865

Kerchnawe, Hugo and Kerchnawe, Alois. *Feldmarschall Karl Fuerst zu Schwarzenberg der Fuehrer der Verbuendeten in den Befreiungskriegen*. Vienna, 1913

Kerry, Earl of. *The First Napoleon: some unpublished documents from the Bowood Papers*. London, 1925

Kielmannsegger, Gräfin von. *Memorien ... über Napoleon I*. Dresden, 1927

Kiernan, T. J. *Transportation from Ireland to Sidney, 1791–1816*. London, 1954

Knoop, General W. J. *Beschouwingen over Siborne's geschiedenis van den oorlog van 1815 en wederlegging van de, in dat werk voorkomende beschuldingingen tegen het Nedelandsche leger*. Amsterdam, 1846

Lachouque, Henri. *The Anatomy of Glory: Napoleon and his Guard: a Study in Leadership*, tr. Ann S. K. Browne, London, 1978

— *The Last Days of Napoleon's Empire*. 1966

— *Waterloo*. Paris, 1972

Lacroix, Clément de. *Souvenirs du comte Montgaillard*. Paris, 1895

Lamartine, Alphonse-Marie-Louis de Prat de. *Histoire de l'Ambassade dans le grand-duché de Varsovie en 1812*. Paris, 1815

— *Histoire de la Restauration*. 8 vols., Paris, 1851–2

Larochejaquelein, Marchioness de. *Mémoires*. Edinburgh, 1816

Larrey, Baron D. J. *Mémoires de Chirugie militaire et campagnes*. Paris, 1817

Las Cases, E. P. D., comte de. *Mémorial de*

Sainte-Hélène. Journal de la vie privé et des conversations de l'Empereur Napoléon à Sainte-Hélène. 4 vols., London and Paris, 1823

Lavalette, Antoine-Marie, comte de. Mémoires. Paris, 1831

Lavasseur, O. Souvenirs militaires d'Octave Lavasseur, officer d'artillerie, aide-de-camp du Maréchal Néy, 1802-15. Paris, 1914

Lavery, Brian. Nelson's Navy: The Ships, Men and Organisation 1793–1815, London, 1989

Lecestre, L. (ed.). Lettres inéditées de Napoléon I (1799-1815). Paris, 1897

Leeke, W. History of Lord Seaton's Regiment at the Battle of Waterloo. London, 1866

Lejeune, Baron. Memoirs. London, 1897

Lenotre, G. Two Royalist Spies. London, 1924

Lettow-Vorbeck, Otto von. Napoleons Untergang 1815. Berlin, 1904 Longford, Lady Elizabeth. Wellington: The Years of the Sword. London, 1969

Ludwig, Emil. Napoleon. London, 1927

Macapine, Ida, and Hunter, Richard. George III and the Mad-Business. London 1993

Macaulay, Thomas Babington. Napoleon and the Restoration of the Bourbons. London, 1831; 1977

Macdonald, J. E. J. A. Souvenirs du Maréchal Macdonald. Paris, Macirone, Francis. Interesting Facts relating to the fall and death of Joachim Murat, etc. London, 1817

Mackenzie, Norman. The Escape from Elba. Oxford University Press, 1982

Madelin, Louis. Histoire du Consulat et de l'Empire. 16 vols., Paris

Manceron, Claude. Austerlitz. London, 1966

— Men of Liberty. London, 1977

— Napoleon Recaptures Paris. London, 1968

Marchand, comte Louis. Mémoires de Marchand, Premier Valet de Chambre et Executeur Testamentaire de l'Empereur, Publiés d'après le manuscrit original par Jean Bourguignon. 2 vols., Paris, 1952–75

Martineau, M., and Litto, M. (eds.). Correspondence de Stendhal. Paris, 1962-8

Masson, Frédéric. Napoléon et sa famille. 13 vols., Paris, 1900-19

Mauduit, Capitaine H. de. Les Derniers Jours de la Grande Armée. Paris, 1847

Maurice, Colonel F. 'Von Ziethen's Defence on the 15th June', in The United Services Magazine, No. 743, October 1890

Maxwell, Sir Herbert. The Life of Wellington:

The Restoration of the Martial Power of Great Britain. London, 1899

May, Sir Thomas Erskine. Constitutional History of England. 3 vols., London, 1889

Mercer, Captain. Journal of the Waterloo Campaign. London, 1870

Metternich, Prince Richard (ed.). Memoirs of Prince Metternich 1773-1815. London, 1881

Metternich-Winneburg, Graf von, and Klinkowstrom, A. Oesterreichs Theilnahme an den Befreiungskriegen. Vienna, 1887

Montagnac, Comte de. Mémoires. Paris, 1861

Montchenu, Claude Marie, marquis de. La Caprivité de Sainte-Hélène d'après les Rapports inédits du marquis de Montchenu. Ed. Georges Firmin-Didot, Paris, 1894

Montgaillard, Jean-Gabriel, comte de. Souvenirs du comte de Montgaillard, agent de la diplomatie secrète pendant la révolution, l'empire, et la restauration. Paris, 1895

Montholon, Albéne H. comtesse de. Souvenirs de Sainte-Hélène. Ed. Comte Fleury, Paris, 1901

Montholon, C. J. marquis de. Récits de la captivité de l'Empereur Napoléon à Sainte-Hélène. 2 vols., Paris, 1847

Montor, Alex-François Artuad de. Histoire du Pape Pie VII. Paris, 1837

Moore, Thomas. The Life and death of Lord Edward Fitzgerald. 2 vols., London, 1832

Müffling, Baron von. Passages From My Life. 2nd edn., London, 1853

Napoleon, Emperor. La Correspondance de Napoléon. 32 vols., Paris, 1858-70

— Mémoires pour servir à l'histoire de France en 1815. Paris, 1820

Ney, Maréchal M. Documents inédits sur la campagne de 1815. Paris, 1840

— Military Studies., tr. H. G. Gaunter, London, 1833

Nicholson, Harold. The Congress of Vienna. London, 1948

Noel-Williams, H. The Women Bonapartes: The Mother and Three Sisters of Napoleon I. 2 vols., London, 1908

Norman, Barbara. Napoleon and Talleyrand. London, 1977

Nostitz, Captain A. von. Tagebuch des Generals der Kavallerie Grafen von Nostitz. Berlin, 1884–5

Odeleben, Otto Baron von. A Circumstantial Narrative of the Campaign in Saxony in the year 1813. London, 1820

Ollech, C. von. *Geschichte des Feldzueges von 1815 nach archivalischen Quellen*. Berlin, 1876

Oman, Carola. *Britain Against Napoleon*. London, 1942

O'Meara, Barry E. *Napoleon in Exile*. London, 1822

Orlov, Count Mikhail. *Memoirs*. St. Petersburg, 1862

Paget, Sir Julian. *Hougoumont*. London, 1992

Paine, Thomas. *The Age of Reason*. 2 vols., Paris, 1795

— *The Rights of Man: being an Answer to Mr. Burke's attack on the French Revolution*. Dublin, 1791–2

Pakenham, Thomas. *The Year of Liberty: The Story of the Irish Rebellion of 1798*. london, 1970

Palmer, Alan. *An Encyclopedia of Napoleon's Europe*. London, 1984

Paret, Peter. *Yorck and the Era of Prussian Reform*. Princeton University Press, 1966

Parkinson, R. *Clausewitz*. London, 1977

— *The Fox of the North*. New York, 1976

Pasquier, E. D., duc. *Histoire de mon temps. Mémoires*. Ed. d'Audiffret-Pasquier, 6 vols., Paris, 1893–4; Eng. tr. London, 1893–4

Petre, Sir Charles. *Wellington*. London, 1956

Petre, F. Lorraine. *Napoleon At Bay, 1814*. London, 1914

— *Napoleon's Last Campaign in Germany, 1813*. London, 1912

Petrie, Sir Charles. *The Jacobite Movement*. London, 1932

Peyre, Alexander. *Précis de la Mission*. Paris, 1814

Pflugk-Harttung, Julius von. *Das Befreiungsjahr, 1813*. Berlin, 1913

— *Vorgeschicte der Schlacht bei La Belle Alliance*. Berlin, 1903

Regrault, Commandant Jean Charles. *La Campagne de 1815: mobilisation et concentration*. Paris, 1935

— *The Wars of Liberation 1813–14*. Cambridge Modern History, 1907

Pignatelli-Strongoli, Francesco. *Memorie intorno alla storico del regno di Napoli dall'anno 1805 al 1815*. Naples, 1820

Pollio, General A. *Waterloo*. Paris, 1908

Porch, Dr Douglas. *Army and Revolution: France 1815-1848*. London, 1974

Pradt, l'Abbé de. *Histoire de l'ambassade dans le grand-duché de Varsovie en 1812*. Paris, 1815

Reilly, Robin. *The British at the Gates*. New York, 1974

Resnick, D. P. *The White Terror and the Political Reaction*. Harvard University Press, 1966

Richardson, E. *Long-Forgotten Days*. London, 1928

Ritter, G. *Staatskunst und Kriegshandwerk*. Munich, 1954

Robertson, Sir Charles Grant. *England under the Hanoverians*. London, 1911

Robertson, D. *Journal of Sergeant D. Robertson, late 92nd Foot*. Perth, 1842

Robespierre, *Charlotte Robespierre's Memoirs of her two Brothers*. Paris, 1910.

Robinson, Major-General C. W. *Wellington's Campaigns from the Peninsula to Waterloo, 1808-1815*. London, 1907

Robinson, L. G. (ed.). *Princess Lieven's letters to her brother, General A. Benckendorff, during her residence in London, 1812–34*. London, 1902

Rochechouart, comte Louis-Victor. *Mémoires*. Paris, 1870

Roncière, Charles de la (ed.). *The Letters of Napoleon to Marie-Louise*. London. 1935

Ropes, John Codman. *The Campaign of Waterloo*. London, 1984

Rose, J. Holland. *Life of Napoleon*. 2 vols., London, 1902

— *The Detention of Napoleon at Saint Helena*. London, 1902

— and Broadley, A. M. *Dumouriez and the Defence of England against Napoleon*. London, 1908

Rosebery, Archibald Philip, 5th Earl of. *Napoleon: The Last Phase*. London, Nelson, 1922

Ross, Michael. *Banners of the King: the War in the Vendée*. London, 1975

Rothenberg, Professor Gunther E. *The Art of Warfare in the Age of Napoleon*. London, 1978

— *The Military Border in Croatia, 1740-1881*. Chicago University Press, 1966

— *Napoleon's Great Adversaries: the Archduke Charles and the Austrian Army, 1792-1814*. London, 1982

Rousell, Camille (ed.). *Recollections of Marshal Macdonald*. London, 1892

Roylance-Kent, C. B. *The English Radicals*. London, 1899

Rumigny, Comte de. (ADC to Gérard and Louis-Philippe). *Souvenirs du Général comte de Rumigny*. Paris, 1901

Sabine, Major-General (ed.). *The Letters of Colonel Sir Augustus Frazer, etc.* London, 1859

Santini, M. *An appeal to the British Nation on the treatment experienced by Napoleon Bonaparte in the island of St Helena.* London, 1817

Savary, A. J-M. R., duc de Rovigo. *Mémoires sur l'empire.* 8 vols., Paris, 1828 *et seq.*

Scheer, J. *Leben des Feldmarschalls Grafen N.von Gneisenau.* 3 vols., Leipzig, 1862-3

Scheltens, Colonel. *Les Mémoires d'un Grognard Belge (1804–1848).* Brussels, 1880

Schom, Alan. *One Hundred Days: Napoleon's Road to Waterloo.* London, 1992

— *Trafalgar: Countdown to Battle, 1803–1805.* London, 1992

Selliers de Moraanville, A. de. *De l'occupation des positions dans la défensive.* Brussels, 1894

Shilder, N. K. *Imperator Aleksandr I.* 4 vols., St. Petersburg, 1897

Siborne, H. T. *The Waterloo Letters.* London, 1891

Siborne, W. *The Waterloo Campaign.* London, 1844

Smith, G. C. *The Life of John Colburne, Field Marshal Lord Seaton.* London, 1903

Soloviov, S. *Emperor Alexander I, Politics and Diplomacy.* St. Petersburg, 1877

Soult, Marshal. *Mémoires Justificatives.* Paris, 1815

Stead, P. J. *The Police of Paris.* London, 1957

Steffens, Henry. *Adventures on the road to Paris, 1813-14.* London, 1861

Stenger, Gilbert. *The Return of Louis XVIII,* tr. R. Stawell, London, 1909

Stuhr, Professor P. F. *Die Drei Letzten Feldzüge gegen Napoleon.* Lemgo, 1833.

Sutherland, D. M. G. *France 1789-1815: Revolution and Counter-revolution.* London,1985

Taylor, Professor A. J. P. *The Habsburg Monarchy 1809-1918.* London, 1948

Thorpe, F. N. (ed.). 'The Journal of Henri Niemann of the 6th Prussian Black Hussars' in *The English Historical Review,* vol. III, July 1888

Tranie, Jean. *Waterloo, la Fin d'Un Monde.* Limoges, 1985

Tratchevski, A. 'Diplomatic relations of Russia with France in the time of Napoleon I', in *Archives of the Imperial Russian Historical Society.* 5 vols., St Petersburg, 1890-3

Truenfeld, B. von. *Die Tage von Ligny und Belle-Alliance.* Hanover, 1880

Troyat, Henri. *Alexander of Russia.* London, 1982

Tsouras, P. G. *Warriors' Words.* Arms & Armour Press, 1992

Unger, General W. von. *Blücher.* 2 vols., Berlin, 1907

Vachée, Colonel A. *Napoleon at Work,* tr. G. F. Lees, London, 1914

Vane, W. W. (ed.). *Castlereagh Correspondence.* 12 vols., London, 1851

Vassal, Albine-Hélène, Comtesse de Montholon. *Souvenirs de Saint-Hélène.* Paris, 1901

Vitrolles, E. F. A. d'Arnaud de. *Mémoires et relations politques.* 2 vols., Paris, 1841

Ward, S. P. G. *Wellington's Headquarters.* Oxford University Press, 1957

Webster, Professor Charles K. *British Diplomacy, 1813-1815.* London, 1939

— *The Foreign Policy of Castlereagh, 1815–1822.* London, 1958

Weider, Ben, and Hapgood, David. *The Murder of Napoleon.* London, 1982

Weil, Maurice Henri. *La Campagne de 1814.* 5 vols., Paris, 1914

Weinar, M. *The French Exiles, 1789–1815.* London, 1960

Wellesley, Arthur. *Despatches* (ed. J. G. Gurwood). London, 1834–8

— *Supplementary Despatches* (ed. 2nd Duke of Wellington). London, 1858–72

Williams, Alan. *The Police of Paris, 1718-1789.* Louisiana State University Press, 1979

Williams, Gwyn A. *Artisans and Sans-Culottes.* London, 1989

Williamson, A. *Thomas Paine.* London, 1973

Woinovich, Emil von, and Veltze, Alois (eds.). *1813-1815 Oesterreich in den Befreiungskreigen.* Kreigsarchiv: Oesterrreich-Ungarn. 10 vols., Vienna, 1911–14

Wolfe Tone, W. T. (ed.). *The Life of Theobald Wolfe Tone, written by himself and continued by his Son.* 2 vols., Washington, 1826

Woronoff, D. *The Thermidorean Regime and the Directory 1794-1799.* London, 1984

Wuppermann, General. *De vorming van het Nedelandese leger aan de omwenteling van 1813 en het aandeel van dat leger aan de veldtocht van 1815.* The Hague, 1900

Choix de rapports, opinions, et discours prononcés à la Tribune Nationale depuis 1789.

Hansard Parliamentary Debates. vols.I–XXXI (from 1801), London

The Security Service. HMSO, 1993

The Parliamentary Register or the History of the proceedings and the debates of the House of Commons of Ireland. 17 vols., Dublin, 1782–1801.

Report from The Committee of Secrecy of Lords and Commons, relating to seditious societies, & reported by Mr. Secretary Dundas, 15th March 1799. London, 1799

Report of the Secret Committees of the Lords and Commons with an Address of both Houses with an appendix, 1798. Dublin, 1798

La Revue Hebdomadaire, No. 168, 10 August 1895 (General Baron Delort's account of Waterloo)

Journal of the Waterloo Committee. vol. 9. No. 1., pp. 10–24, April 1987

Alliance des Jacobins de France avec le ministre anglais, suivi de stratagèmes de Frère Drake, sa correspondance, ses plans de campagne. Paris, Year XII (1803–4). Published by order of the Emperor.

INDEX

Y